PATHFINDERS

GAIL SHEEHY'S
#1
BESTSELLER
PATHFINDERS

"Miss Sheehy's work stands squarely in the American tradition of Thoreau, Emerson, Dale Carnegie and Norman Vincent Peale. . . . Miss Sheehy and her predecessors extol the admirable traits of grit, pluck, willingness to take individual initiative and accept individual responsibility."
—*The New York Times Book Review*

"A wonderful, intelligent, and (in the best sense) inspiring book about people who have come through crises into the elusive state of 'well-being.'"
—*Newsday*

Bantam Books by Gail Sheehy

PASSAGES
PATHFINDERS
SPIRIT OF SURVIVAL

QUANTITY PURCHASES

PATHFINDERS
Gail Sheehy

BANTAM BOOKS
TORONTO • NEW YORK • LONDON • SYDNEY • AUCKLAND

For Maura, and her times

PATHFINDERS
A Bantam Book / *published in association with
William Morrow & Co., Inc.*

PRINTING HISTORY
*Portions of this book originally appeared in
Ladies' Home Journal in slightly different form.
Portions of the material in this book originally appeared
in another form in Esquire, Life, New York magazine,
New York Daily News, The New York Times, and Redbook.
William Morrow edition published October 1981
A Literary Guild Selection
Serialized in Book Digest and People Weekly magazine
Bantam edition / December 1982
4 printings through September 1985*

Grateful acknowledgment is made by the author for use of the following:
From *Collected Poems* by Conrad Aiken. Copyright 1953, © 1970 by Conrad
Aiken; renewed 1981 by Mary Aiken. Reprinted by permission of Oxford
University Press, Inc.
From *The Poetry of Robert Frost* edited by Edward Connery Lathem. Copy-
right 1916, © 1969 by Holt, Rinehart and Winston. Copyright 1942, 1944
by Robert Frost. Copyright © 1970 by Lesley Frost Ballantine. Reprinted by
permission of Holt, Rinehart and Winston, Publishers, and by Jonathan Cape
Limited, London.
Copyright 1951 by Richard Rodgers & Oscar Hammerstein. Williamson Music,
Inc., owner of publication and allied rights throughout the Western Hemi-
sphere and Japan.
International Copyright Secured
ALL RIGHTS RESERVED
Used by permission
"When You Are Old" from *Collected Poems of William Butler Yeats* by per-
mission of Macmillan, New York, 1956, and M. B. Yeats, Anne Yeats and
Macmillan London Limited
Excerpts abridged from pages 14, 80, 85–86, 122, 123 and 303 in *In Search
of Identity* by Anwar el-Sadat. Copyright © 1977, 1978 by The Village of
Mit Abul-Kum. English translation copyright © 1977, 1978 by Harper &
Row, Publishers, Inc. Reprinted by permission of the publisher.

CONTENTS

PART I: WHICH WAY AT THE CROSSROADS?

1. HUNTING THE SECRETS OF WELL-BEING 2
    *Secrets of Well-being—The Ten Hallmarks of Well-being
    —The Vital Statistics of Well-being—The Heredity of
    Life Satisfaction—Optimism-Negativism Dial—Personal
    Tempo—A Brief Review—Seeking Out High-Satisfaction
    People*

2. EARLY CANDIDATES 30
    *The Corporate Life Cycle—The First Test—A Hell of a
    Guy—The Second Test—"I'm Entitled" Candidates—The
    Third Test*

3. HOW DOES ONE BECOME A PATHFINDER? 59
    *Finding One's Way Through a Passage—Pulling Through
    a Life Accident*

4. ANATOMY OF A PASSAGE 69
    *An Ordinary Man—No Place to Run—Anticipation Phase
    —Separation and Incubation Phase—Expansion Phase—
    Incorporation Phase*

PART II: WHAT TO TAKE INTO THE WOODS

5. WILLINGNESS TO RISK 96
    Men and Magicthink—Why Playing It Safe Is Dangerous

—Women of Well-being—Women and the Happyface—
Between Two Selves—The Best Armor—Falling Up—Fail
a Little—One Risk Leads to Another—The Master Quality—The Creative Connection—When to Stay, When to
Go?

6. THE RIGHT TIMING 130
Good as Goals—Anticipating Needs—The Postponing
Generation—Success or Children?—Society's Timing—
Laid-back Men—Intensity versus Balance—The New
Integrator—Alternative to Me-ism—Rolling with the
Punches

7. CAPACITY FOR LOVING 178
Loving and Identity—Time for Love—When the Feeling
is Not Mutual—First Love at Forty-two—Digging Out—
First Love: Oneself—Loving and Laughing

8. FRIENDSHIP, KINSHIP, SUPPORT SYSTEMS 206
The Many Shadings of Friendship—Man-to-Man Friendships—Friendships Woman to Woman—Friendship on
the Last Frontier—Reciprocal Passages—Polestars and
Survivor Guides

9. BEST OF MALE AND FEMALE STRENGTHS 234
The Sexual Diamond Revisited—The Nurturant Man—
The Comeback—The Archetypal Female Myth—A Woman of Courage—Julia's Compromise—Tapping Our Natural Resources—The New Conventional Couple

10. A CERTAIN AGE 277
Women and the Comeback Decade—Men in Midlife—
Myths of Middle Age—The Walking Dead—The Sec-
ondary Saboteur—The Single-Track Compulsive—Last-
Chance Leap—Not Too Late to Transfer—Passionate
Sideline—Teaming Up—His Happiness, Her Happiness
—The Sexual Shell Game—I Am Who I Am—Admitting
the Unknownable—Do You Sincerely Want to Be Eighty-
five?—What Really Matters—Who Goes the Distance?

11. PURPOSE 325
Work as Purpose— Children as Purpose—Finding Purpose
at the Local Level—A Blue-Collar "General"—A New
Battle of Bunker Hill—The Purpose of Purpose

12. FAITH 356
     *A Down-to-Earth Comeback to Faith—A Reanimation
     Through Religion—Ma Belle, a Moving Church—New
     Territory for the Religious Caretaker—Is Happiness Un-
     limited Narcissism?*

PART III: DARK HOURS

13. COPING AND MOURNING 385
     *Protective Strategies—Cinderella with a Second Act—
     Would You Know a Healthy Defense If You Saw One?
     —Desperate Measures—The Mourning Process—Pathfind-
     er Steps to Full Recovery—A Personal Memoir of De-
     tachment*

14. THE LIGHT BEYOND MOURNING 410

PART IV: TRAVELING THE HIGH ROAD

15. WITHDRAWAL AND COMEBACK 434
     *Cycles of Revitalization—Where Have We Been?—Where
     Are We Going?—Youth, Health, Vigor!—Pilgrims of the
     Sixties—Back to the Old-Time Religion—Return with a
     Difference—The Role of Transcendent Pathfinders*

16. AN ACT OF COURAGE 464
     *Private Courage, Public Courage—Sitting on an Accident
     Waiting to Happen—Mr. Bridenbaugh Goes to Wash-
     ington—Separating, Reconnecting—Playing the Part of
     "Techno-Twits"—Deciding for the Promethean Path—
     When the Personal Path Sets a National Direction*

17. VIEW FROM THE TOP OF THE MOUNTAIN 492
     *Pathleaders as Failures—Pathleaders in Withdrawal and
     Comeback—The Great Refusal—Stand-up Women of the
     19th Century—Where Women Pathleaders Go Wrong,
     and Right—The Saga of Sadat—Transmitting Personal
     Powers of Rebirth*

     AFTERWORD 528

     ACKNOWLEDGMENTS 534

     APPENDICES

        I: Life History Questionnaire 540

II: The Well-being Scale   562

III: Statistical Analysis of Life Line Chart   570

IV: People Who Suggested Pathfinder Candidates   571

NOTES AND SOURCES   580

BIBLIOGRAPHY   598

INDEX   606

Part I

WHICH WAY
AT THE
CROSSROADS?

Two roads diverged in a yellow wood,
And sorry I could not travel both
And be one traveler, long I stood
And looked down one as far as I could
To where it bent in the undergrowth;

Then took the other, as just as fair,
And having perhaps the better claim,
Because it was grassy and wanted wear;
Though as for that the passing there
Had worn them really about the same,

And both that morning equally lay
In leaves no step had trodden black.
Oh, I kept the first for another day!
Yet knowing how way leads on to way,
I doubted if I should ever come back.

I shall be telling this with a sigh
Somewhere ages and ages hence:
Two roads diverged in a wood, and I—
I took the one less traveled by,
And that has made all the difference.
—ROBERT FROST, "The Road Not Taken"

1.

HUNTING THE
SECRETS OF
WELL-BEING

All of us have stood at a point where two roads diverged and doubted our wisdom to choose. Many of us have chosen by refusing to risk moving at all; others have made a choice by default or been unaware even that they stood at a crossroads. But some among us have recognized that crossroads and seen in it the path to another beginning, an opportunity to make themselves more. What can such people teach us about the process of finding and choosing paths to expansion in our lives, about avoiding the ruts into which most lives eventually fall, the meagerness of lives spent on a safe and narrow track, the blind alleys, the bitterness and breakdown of nerve that overcome people who hit the bumps completely unaware?

Our personalities do not stop developing at the end of adolescence. Each time we move from one stage of our lives to the next we face a transition, what some have called a "psychosocial crisis" and I have termed a "passage." To know that such passages occur throughout our lives, however, does not give us any clues about how to navigate them, how to move forward rather than backward in growth. As I traveled around the country after I finished *Passages*,[1] I heard the same question in one variation after another:

"Help! I'm stuck between the twenties and the thirties—how do I avoid the old traps?"

"Maybe I am in a midlife crisis. You can talk all you want about what causes it. When is someone going to tell me what to do about it?"

"I'm a non-person because I'm in my fifties. Aren't there any more passages left for me?"

It was good old American pragmatism: *Okay, here's a new problem. Now, what's the solution?* I determined to continue the work on which I had embarked. But how? Few data existed, except for other life-cycle theories that also track the tasks and obstacles common to different stages of adult life. Biographies of the celebrated and sainted were not particularly applicable, nor were the autobiographies of glamorous neurotics who by and large proclaim the attractions of narcissism. Some promising longitudinal[2] and cross-cultural studies were under way. And the whole climate surrounding social science investigations was beginning to warm to the idea of probing the characteristics of the well person instead of remaining preoccupied with the unwell, maladaptive, and clinical populations. Still, there was nothing yet about ordinary people engaged in the normal struggles of life, nothing to explain why certain of them navigate a critical passage in an expanding, self-renewing way, while so many others slip backward, blame others, go to sleep, attempt frantic escapes.

Given the pressures to conform in the American Midwest, it was a particular challenge to begin there my search for people who dare the less-traveled road. Before long, I found a Milwaukee woman who had spent the first half of her life pleasing others in predictable ways, but after raising her young family, to everyone's amazement, she summoned the resources to stretch herself and break ground for others. She had gone down into the swamps of depression twice and would sink again even after we met, before completing the full transition from immobilized wife to ordained minister. Delia Barnes* became the subject of the pilot interview for

---

* Except in the cases of public figures, biographees throughout this book were given the option of being identified by their real names or by pseudonyms (fictitious names). In several cases, when the biographee would have been easily identifiable, at least within a community, he or she elected to permit the use of his or her real name. In cases in which a pseudonym has been used, other proper nouns, such as names of secondary people, places,

this book. I started with her in the heartland of Wisconsin and worked my way west, south, and east, stopping every so often to check back with Delia as she began her journey along a less-traveled path.

After bearing her third daughter, Delia Barnes began to sleep twelve hours a day. In her torpor she tried without success to recall the wiry, energetic, highly responsible woman she had been for twenty-eight years. Thyroid pills were prescribed. Still she was unable to sit down in a chair without floating off to sleep. She gave up on trying to conceive the son she wanted to give her husband as an heir for his contracting business.

It was suggested that she and her husband consult a psychiatrist together. "I want to keep people happy," she told the doctor, "so I never confront them. Pleasing people is a big thing in my life."

What the psychiatrist said then had never occurred to her: "You've been trying too long to please everyone else. You've got to start now doing something for yourself."

Her husband stomped out of the psychiatrist's office and refused to speak of the matter again.

Should she succumb to the clichés common to women in her circle, sit back and wait for her skin to shrivel, her breasts to wither, and the lighted tinder in her heart to go out? Truth was, she had never felt fire in her loins. She pretended. She pleased.

It is at such a crossroads that so many people freeze, fearing to drop masks they have discovered to work or identities that suit other people's expectations. There is a locking of feeling, a giving up on the attempt to reconcile conflicting needs, until a comforting sort of capsule firms up around them, making it possible to tread water, avoid the risk of changing, and kill time—although the time they are killing is their own.

Delia's first depression was vague, characteristic of the transition from the twenties to the thirties when the choices we have made early in our lives first begin to pinch. It grew

---

and institutions, have been changed to ensure privacy. In every other respect, the facts of the life story, conversations, and quoted statements are unchanged from transcribed interviews. Delia Barnes is a pseudonym.

worse before it got better. Alarmed, her husband said he would "allow" her to go horseback riding or take some courses. And so, with no specific goal beyond occupying her mind, she began working on an advanced degree in education. That was the only field she knew. Her parents would be pleased.

Sole child of a mail carrier who had not had the luxury of exceeding eighth grade, Delia had been given every affordable lesson and told again and again that if she tried hard enough, she could succeed at anything in life. With her parents' constant support, she excelled in school. They had a uniform all cut out for her, beginning in second grade. She should be a schoolteacher, play the organ, and be a fine, upstanding neighbor lady: a sum of the "might haves" her mother and father saw as the destiny they had been denied. Their daughter was too good for the likes of the local boys, they believed, and probably would have to perform a faultless spinsterhood. Delia went along with their dream in every respect except for taking a husband, but he turned out to be a husband with money so it was all right.

But now, at 30, suffocating inside that uniform, Delia could not stop the words before they flew out of her mouth: "I hate education!" She stopped teaching. Ten years after the usual time for pulling up roots, Delia cut the girlhood knot to her parents and now faced the expanse of adulthood. The more compelled she felt to "do something," the more anxious she became. Confounded by being unable to please her husband with a son, knowing better than to try to please her parents in a role she hated, Delia had no idea how to go about finding an identity of her own.

Her social initiative slumped into the drowsiness of deep depression. For six months she was all but inert. Delia went to her local pastor, who gave her instruction and introduced an entirely new possibility. She could do God's work. It was the perfect compromise! She could have permission to do something for herself if she offered up her efforts to a higher purpose—pleasing God.

She was not conscious of her thought process until much later, of course. But once having defined the conflict inside, even superficially, she asked to be admitted for study to the local seminary; and when the seminary tried to deny her permission, she was ready to dig in her heels.

"There is no place in the church for women," she was told, "as far as advancement goes."

"I want to go anyway," Delia said.

The blood came up strong in her body as she won her first confrontation and plunged into courses. Having forgotten completely her failed regimen for conception, she conceived. Rejoicing in the birth of a son, at 32, she cut back on her studies to be with him until he was three. By the time she was ready to resume a full load at a new seminary, there was real motivation: one denomination within her religion had decided to ordain women.

The tired old woman of 28 who had needed twelve hours of sleep a day could now, at the age of 37, survive on half that amount. Every day was a thrill. The world opened up to her through her fellow students—young people, Vietnam vets. They did not see her as old. They took sensitivity training together. She felt alive and tingling, happy every night to put all four children to bed and even to put on her own pajamas and snuggle up with her husband until he fell asleep, then to crawl out and tiptoe into the living room to study through the dead hours.

There was an unexpected reward. In those four years from 37 to 41, while learning to serve the Lord, her body came alive for the first time to its sex. Had her future parishioners known, they would surely have put the business of their souls in other hands.

"I should have sent you to the seminary fifteen years ago," her husband teased. But from almost everyone else in the community, aside from her fellow seminarians, she became estranged.

"Everybody else was against what I was doing," she told me, "probably because I was striking out into new territory. I wasn't too confident. But I told people, 'I'm trying something new and I don't know if I'll make it or not. But I have the right to try.'"

For the first time, at 39, she had a dream. Believing that men and women should learn to work together in the world, it was her goal to be a pastor side by side with a male pastor, to do worship services together and preach together and show the congregation that men and women can contribute as equals. To ensure that she would be well enough prepared, she earned not one but two master's degrees.

Several months before Delia was to be ordained, she and her husband attended their old church. She thought it would be nice to reconnect with the minister who had pointed her down this path before she became ordained as a minister herself. The old pastor ascended to the pulpit with the heavy silver cross swinging gravely against his long black cassock. Looking out over all her friends and neighbors, this man of God put Delia Barnes to the test.

"The work of the Devil can be cleverly disguised, even in our congregation," he prophesied in high theological tones. "The Devil often comes in the form of a woman." All eyes turned to stare at Delia.

Heads began to turn away when Delia shopped in the neighborhood stores. One mother hid her child's eyes from "the lady who went against God's commandments."

A cloud of depression began to float back over Delia's days, but she dealt with it more effectively this time. She hung a sign in her study that said *Smile, God loves you,* and she filled the holes of insomnia by writing vitriolic letters, which she burned in the morning.

"It's funny," she was able to say much later, "how something that was meant to stop you ends up doing exactly the opposite. When I hear, 'You can't do it,' that's just about the time I'm sure going to do it."

"One of these days we'll show that minister," Delia's husband vowed. All at once, now that it pitted his pride against insult from another man, her husband appeared to be involved in Delia's struggle.

But a week or so later, Delia's husband came home after his usual twelve-hour day and did not turn on the television or pick up the paper or open a beer. Instead, he demanded, "You're not really going to go through with this, are you?"

The gasp caught in her throat. For four years full-time and eight years part-time she had been preparing for "this." Clearly, there was only One who could give her permission to take the last step.

The day she knelt to receive the crimson stole of God's authority, she felt affirmation from an unexpected quarter. Twenty-five men circled around and placed their hands on her bowed head. Their hands were gentle. Most were pastors who had come in violation of their parishes' rules excluding women from the ministry.

In her first year as a minister she played it safe, working with a counseling service. The second year she felt ready to risk rejection by becoming a preacher in a church. She found a small congregation and a pastor who agreed to try it.

"I don't know when I'll let you preach," he said that September. "It may not be until Easter."

She gave her premiere sermon in December. The church overflowed with friends and reporters and freak seekers who had come to record the first time a woman had ever preached in that city. Delia Barnes had written out the sermon a month in advance and memorized every comma, but while she was giving the prepared sermon, her mind set off obstinately in another direction:

This moment of triumph is not just for me, it's gone beyond competing against the men who make the rules of this religion. I'm not up here like some bright and shining star while all the rest of the women still grovel at the foot of the Christmas tree; we are all in this together!

That marked the beginning of another level of perception about her purpose in life. She began helping other women to enter the ministry. The congregation of her small church embraced the Reverend Delia Barnes wholeheartedly, shouting, "Hi, pastor!" on the street and showering her and her husband with invitations to dinner.

But her senior pastor began to grow critical, then irrational. His own acceptance by the congregation was suffering by comparison.

"I didn't really mean 'assistant pastor,'" he mumbled, referring to the original description of her job. "What I meant was a parish assistant, sort of a helper. You can do pastoral things when I want you to, but remember, you're not really a pastor."

It was during this time that Delia Barnes and I first talked. A tall, handsome woman with a soft voice, demurely dressed in a jumper with a bow-tied blouse, she seemed agreeably authoritative without being threatening. On the whole, she embraced the complexities of her new life with evident enthusiasm. The immediate problems with her superior were growing worse, however, and in them were troubling echoes of an old handicap.

"Any difficulty I encounter now," she related, "is because I cannot please my boss and still keep my integrity. He's telling me there is something wrong with me."

What did he think was wrong?

"He tells me I'm aggressive. I don't give up. When I don't get what I want the first time, I keep at it. So I question myself."

It was the archetypal female response: *What's wrong with me?*

Intellectually, Delia Barnes knew that these same qualities in a man would be cause for praise. She knew they described her fairly. She also knew that no one can be honest with others after turning falsely against oneself. But emotionally, the costs of social isolation were piling up. She had no natural support group. To tell her problems to any member of the congregation would not be appropriate, and although there were now many women in the ministry, none was in her denomination. She could form no tie with other women closer than that of big sister. And so she faced the next crossroads, once again, alone.

"My boss wants me to change, to go back to being the submissive little girl. And I want to please him," she said. "But I don't want to change backward! It's tearing me apart."

Could the central theme of her life be the conflict between wanting to please others and needing to be true to herself? I asked.

"I wouldn't doubt it," she mused. "Maybe even pleasing God, with this call to the ministry, was what enabled me to take the risk of making a lot of people angry."

The dilemma she faced was real. The city had only three churches of her branch of this particular Christian denomination. The other two had refused women as ministers. If she wanted to be a pastor, she had to risk changing one way or the other. She could continue trying to please her superior by forfeiting the chance for growth in authority and pleasure in her work. Or she could change denominations—and leave her religious family altogether.

"I know what that pain is," she admitted quietly. "And I don't want to go through it."

Here was a woman who had been able to excel as long as her parents were supporting her, who flourished as long as

her pastor was supporting her, but who now faced the task
of surmounting the need for approval.

"I still want to keep people happy," she said as we parted,
"but I'm beginning to understand you can't always do that."

Some months later, the problem led to confrontation. The
bishop wrote Delia Barnes a letter acknowledging the difficulties the senior pastor was having with his own congregation. But because she was the assistant, the bishop concluded,
it was Delia who should resign.

This time she did not bottle up her outrage, or try to dissi-
pate it by writing it out. This time she addressed the conflict
directly. She would go, but not before she risked setting off
an avalanche of disapproval, from the bishop down through
the church council and the entire congregation. She made
the bishop's letter public within the church.

The congregation was aghast, but they all took a look at
the letter. Furious church members drew up one petition after another to keep her. Even council members cast their
righteousness on her side. But the pastor would not leave.
And the bishop remained unyielding.

She held her ground to the end. The loyalty of her congregation and the pride of her husband remained constant. And
when she left, one-third of the church members resigned
with her. Her newly emboldened nature had not been com-
promised, nor did she have to limp away, believing what her
rivals would have her believe: that she was no good. Yet the
fact remained that she had taken the risk of standing her
ground and suffered a shattering loss. Other members could
join different churches, but Delia was out of a job and distanced by the scandal from all her parishioners. It was April,
but for her the spring brought no joy.

For the third time depression swamped her. It was impossible to smile. She felt as if something had died inside. It
had; several of her identities, in fact—the spinster schoolteacher dreamed up by her parents, the wife who waited to
be told what to do, the ordained minister who feared the
pain of confrontation more than submission. Each of these
personas had served its purpose, but she had outlived them.
For the time being, Delia Barnes was lost.

She chose to volunteer at the state hospital for the insane
and severely retarded. Clanging through four locked doors to
a bin of the living damned, she worked each day in a ward

filled with people whom no one else cares about or remembers until they are found dead in their beds. Her patients had their own revenge: they did not remember caretakers like Delia from one day to the next, if they noticed them at all.

Angry, bitter, dreaming at night that she had the pastor down on the ground and was pushing his face into the mud, Delia found the hospital a therapeutic environment. Fantasies of rage cost her nothing. And after four months, the great sadness she carried around inside began to lighten. She learned to love her patients as they shuffled about the ward mumbling their litanies of grievance. They made her troubles seem petty, her depression an indulgence. She also found an extended family among the other volunteers. They had all chosen to work in a mental hospital because, like Delia, they were in transit in their own lives. It was natural to offer each other strength and support.

"I think I died and went to heaven." That was how Delia Barnes described the nine months of dying time before the next stage of her life began. She knew it would come. She was unlike many people who deny the need to face a crossroads and later regret roads not taken. That obsession with the past serves to keep them imprisoned in it.

In January of 1977, Delia was offered an unusual position open only to an ordained minister. A statewide social agency, run by her religious denomination, would send her around as a guest preacher and family-life educator to all forty churches in the area. She was ready. Delia Barnes began working in a teaching pair with a man who was a minister and family-life educator. They dovetailed beautifully. Their reputation spread; Delia and her partner are now invited to address seminars for a hundred pastors at a time.

It is not the same as working side by side with a male pastor in one church, but at this point Delia is delighted with the compromise. She and her colleague are models of a harmonious pastoral team before their peers.

"My dream is not achieved yet," she told me in our last interview. She was 47. "I'll never adjust downward. I may never get there before I die, but what comforts me is that somebody else will."

After two years of working in an atmosphere of acceptance, she says, "I'm very, very happy. When you met me,

I had partially caved in but I was satisfied to continue. I hate to think I was willing to give up like that. I've come to realize it's a marvelous thing that has happened to me; it made me take the chance of standing up, and the pain was only temporary. I'm content." She had just been asked to become chaplain to the city's police association. And she had embarked on her doctorate in theology. Delia Barnes sees the partial attainment of her dream as a happy and satisfying outcome. What is more, she is secure, not solely in her bond to parents or mate, to children, peers, or employers, but now also in her tie to the culture. It transcends labels. She truly can say, "I feel at last a firm sense of my identity."

In following Delia's saga, I was fascinated by the *process* by which she accumulated confidence and control, and ultimately real courage. She had to become a rebel in order to live out the most traditional kind of moral and ethical existence. Having risked taking a less-traveled route, she had navigated back into the mainstream, but now knowing exactly where she wanted to go—and why the trip would be worthwhile. That knowledge would continue to pull her, like a favorable tide, toward what might be called a state of well-being.

Many other life stories of men as well as women, at all ages and stages, serve to illustrate variations on the same process as the book progresses. Undoubtedly, we would all like to be people of high well-being. Such people radiate enthusiasm for life. They attract others. Their personalities can be infectious; being with such a person makes one feel magnified. But although we know how they make us feel, we don't know how to feel like they do.

What are their secrets?

Secrets of Well-being

Like the dance of brilliant reflections on a clear pond, well-being is a shimmer that accumulates from many important life choices made over the years by a mind that is not often muddied by pretense or ignorance and a heart that is open enough to sense people in their depths and to intuit the meaning of most situations. It would be enlightening, I thought, to compare the experiences of people who feel exceptionally good about themselves and to explore the qualities of mind and heart they call upon at important crossroads. This was the task that excited me.

But first, the elusive concept of well-being itself would have to be more precisely defined. It is more than happiness. In its narrow sense, as Freud[3] defined it, happiness generally conveys relief from pent-up frustration or deprivation of pleasure. Although the need may have reached great intensity, its satisfaction is most often instantaneous. By definition, then, happiness is only fleeting.

Well-being registers deep in our unconscious. It is an accumulated attitude, a sustained background tone of equanimity behind the more intense contrasts of daily events, behind even periods of unhappiness.

I developed a Life History Questionnaire to probe the self-perceptions, values, goals, coping styles, and experiences at each stage of life of adults between the ages of 18 and 80. Within the questionnaire was a complex instrument for measuring well-being; it would identify the people who find the keenest contentment in the many dimensions of a full life.*

The twenty-five items on the well-being scale asked both directly and indirectly how satisfied a person had been during the previous several months with work, love, children, success, finances, and health. People were queried, too, about how pleased they were with their personal growth and development, their spiritual life and sex life, their friends and social life. They were asked how their spouse's or lover's life was going, how they felt about their own physical attractiveness and fitness and about the degree to which they were making a contribution to others. The questionnaire measured the balance they believed they had forged among job, family, leisure activities, and home responsibilities, as well as how satisfied they were with life as a whole. The level of boredom and the degree of control and responsibility a person felt over his or her life rounded out the scale.

The final score on the well-being scale was based not only on how pleased people reported themselves to be within each of these spheres, but also how they compared with all the

* See Appendix I for details.

other respondents in their peer group. Each group was divided by quadrants into four levels of life satisfaction, from highest to lowest.

This pencil-and-paper part of my work shared some of the handicaps common to all personality research. It can never be as exact as, say, testing for hereditary components in people's heights or the width of their shoulder blades, measurements that are quantitative and tests that are easily replicated. But the pool of people the questionnaire would select out for personal interviews—people who appeared to know something about navigating through life successfully—would offer a rich catch indeed.

Casting lines into many different ponds during 1978 and 1979, I gathered Life History Questionnaires from groups of congressmen, corporate chiefs, corporate wives, entrepreneurs, professional managers, lawyers, a group of exclusively women lawyers, a group of women brokers and bankers, homemakers, professional athletes, union representatives and officers, automotive workers, municipal employees, white-collar employees, semiskilled and technical workers, women returning to school for professional degrees, and working people attending community colleges.

In addition, I arranged to turn twelve of the invitations to lecture into cooperative research workshops. Each sponsoring organization circulated the Life History Questionnaires to attendees in advance of the program, enabling me to analyze the results and discuss them in my presentation. This method afforded a fine selection of prospective candidates to interview while I was at the meeting. The group as a whole usually responded to the results in a general workshop.

By the spring of 1978 I was ready to cast the widest net of all, by publishing the Life History Questionnaire in two mass-circulation magazines, *Redbook* and *Esquire*.[4] These two national surveys were a rich source of subjects from every age and economic group.

The research process took three years and yielded sixty thousand questionnaires. Although that does not constitute a statistician's random sample, it greatly enlarges the data pool on which life-cycle theories have drawn up to now. A computer team tabulated the data at New York University under the supervision of Dr. Phillip Shaver, associate professor of social psychology. With the aid of Dr. Carin Rubenstein, then a doctoral candidate in psychology, I conducted hundreds of telephone interviews to narrow the selection to candidates I could visit in person.

Then I made an odyssey that crossed thirty-eight states, four Canadian provinces, three European countries, and many more occupational, racial, ethnic, and social-class boundaries. Most surveys skim over this step. In my view, subjective understanding of a human being can come only from face-to-face experience.*

What first emerged from the surveys and interviews was an outline of that enviable creature, the person who enjoys optimum well-being. (Because the well-being scale will be referred to throughout the book, you may be curious about how you would rate. Appendix I contains a reproduction of the Life History Questionnaire, with a simplified well-being scale on which you can score yourself.) The person of optimum well-being is best characterized by the ten statements of self-description that follow—clues with which to begin mapping a path toward our now brilliant beginnings.

The Ten Hallmarks of Well-being

1. "My life has meaning and direction."

This is the characteristic that correlates most closely with optimum life satisfaction. People of high well-being find meaning in an involvement with something beyond themselves: a work, an idea, other people, a social objective.

If such a commitment gives their lives meaning, it appears to be their long-range vision of the future that gives high-satisfaction people direction. That power can be cultivated.

Now, should you take this to mean there are people who actually go around saying, "Hi, there. I have meaning and direction in my life"? You probably would cross the street to avoid someone like that. These statements were never actually spoken; they simply are the best way I have of dramatizing dry data. The first five characteristics discussed

---

* I did not tell the people I chose to interview that I was looking for people of high well-being or anything about the nature of the book I was researching, except that it would be a further exploration of adult development.

here rank in order of the strength with which they correlate with high overall well-being.

For instance, Delia Barnes described herself as feeling a "oneness" and being "happy and alive and tingling." Also, she had begun at 47 to anticipate a future goal toward which she would strive in her work: "I may never get there before I die, but what comforts me is that somebody else will." Her personal concerns had expanded to include concern for the future direction of the human family.

When we consider the strengths Delia cultivated, we find an almost perfect match with other primary characteristics of high-satisfaction people.

2. "I have experienced one or more important transitions in my adult years, and I have handled these transitions in an unusual, personal, or creative way."

People of high well-being are not insulated from difficult passages. On the contrary, they are the *most* likely to report having confronted at least one important passage or transition and having made a major change in their outlook, values, personal affiliations, or career. This contradicts the widespread assumption that a consistent life with no great changes or surprises is the most rewarding. Far from it.

Coming up with creative solutions to common life crises registered clearly in every sample as characteristic of adults who enjoy optimum satisfaction. Not that these people tend toward having exotic life-styles. They are, simply, a little more courageous in facing reality and a lot more resourceful in thinking up ways to extend their capacities than people who wait for life's events to happen to them by chance or who sit around and complain about them.

People of low satisfaction often become obsessed or depressed about roads not taken in the past. Toward the future these people may adopt a "this or nothing" attitude and as a result feel cheated if they do not get what they want. Unable to make satisfactory compromises with their weaknesses or desires or to dare to take other avenues, they may become soured, believing that life is unfair to them, that they have been singled out for an injustice, or that they are simply no good. Instead of turning their energies toward handling the transition at hand, or anticipating the future, they often become relentlessly negative and mired in the past. They look backward for scapegoats or flaws in themselves to blame for their current trap or dilemma.

And these are usually there to find.

It was surprising to learn that frequent introspection is not correlated closely with high satisfaction. The happiest people do plan ahead, but they seem to take time for critical self-reflection only when approaching a tough transition or after making one. Otherwise (except for creative people) they do not spend much time contemplating their inner thoughts and feelings.

3. "I rarely feel cheated or disappointed by life."

How they respond to failure is another of the signal differences between high- and low-satisfaction people. As might be expected, the most contented people are less likely to report having failed in the first place. In actuality, some of them probably would be seen by others as having taken a fall, but they have recast the experience in their minds, erased the outcome from the error column, and come to see it as a plus.

The important thing is that roughly half of all the high-satisfaction people *have indeed failed* "at a major personal or professional endeavor." What is different about them is their response:

Having failed, almost every one of them found it a useful experience and say they are better off for it.*

Exactly the opposite is the case with low-satisfaction people, who usually describe their failures as destructive experiences. Obstacles in general are seen as evidence of their own inadequacies or of the selective injustice with which they are treated by life.

Even when Delia Barnes was baited by her minister, ostracized by her neighbors, and betrayed by her bishop, she was able to believe in her worth—which was undergoing repeated shocks of repudiation—and although she had to battle back from depression three times, she sustained that belief. "I've come to realize it's a marvelous thing that happened to me" was her adjusted view, ". . . and the pain was only temporary."

* All but two to three people in the uppermost quadrant of life satisfaction in every sample saw their failures as constructive.

4. "I have already attained several of the long-term goals that are important to me."

The same three long-range goals held up across the board as most important to Americans at all satisfaction levels: a comfortable life, family security, and a sense of accomplishment.

People in every group agreed on the three things most worth striving for, but more than half the high-satisfaction people in every sample said they already had attained a comfortable life, family security, and a sense of accomplishment. They had also achieved mature love, true friendship, freedom to make independent choices, self-respect, and an exciting life. No wonder they're content!

Success is not everything to those who apparently know the secrets of well-being, however. Not by a long shot. One of the most striking differences between high- and low-satisfaction people is this: the most satisfied people are the *least* willing to jeopardize their family lives or sacrifice a love relationship for professional success. The most miserable people are the ones readiest to move to another part of the country, to allow a marriage or love affair to break up, or, if divorced, to move away from their children, all in pursuit of their career. It must be added, though, that the people with the most gratifying lives tend to be older, and much of their furious running is already behind them.

5. "I am pleased with my personal growth and development."

When it came to the personal characteristics most highly prized by all, men and women throughout the surveys aspired to the same three:

Being honest, loving, and responsible.

Again, the people who are well pleased with their lives are likely to say that these qualities already describe them. And the optimally satisfied reflect some additional qualities:

The happiest women are also ambitious, courageous, knowledgeable, open to new experiences, and playful, and they have a sense of humor.

The most-satisfied men are also comfortable with intimacy, courageous, open to new experiences, physically fit, and able to lead effectively.

That says something significant about sex roles and the penalties of stereotyping. The optimally situated adult has incorporated the characteristic most closely associated with his or her sexual opposite—being comfortable with intimacy in the case of the men; being ambitious in the case of the women.

Delia Barnes spent most of the parenting years adhering to a traditionally restricted sex role: her husband was the initiating one, with a tight career container for his identity and a plunger to keep down his emotions; she was the nurturing one, who derived whatever identity she had from others and who tried to provide an heir to carry on her husband's dream. Having worked her way slowly through conflict, Delia much later allowed herself to have ambitions (albeit mitigated by their being in the service of God). As a result, she assumed the freedom to make independent choices, tested her own dream, found it possible to forge a new kind of friendship with a man—working with her co-pastor—and now enjoys courage, thrice renewed, to face the unknown.

6. "I am in love; my partner and I love mutually."

Whether married, divorced, cohabiting, or commuting to be with a lover in Beirut, people of high well-being usually love mutually. They are rarely involved in relationships in which one exploits for services and the other depends for security, or in which one loves and the other consents to be loved. (Ordinarily, when the weight of affection and commitment lists to one side, it is the woman who loves more and the man who feels more uncomfortable about it.)

People of high satisfaction not only spend more time than average people with the person they love; they want even more time to spend. An impressive number described finding a new tolerance and companionship with their mates as one of the signal experiences of their middle adult years. Many also reported reaching a new level of sexual pleasure sometime in their thirties, forties, or fifties. Low-satisfaction people rarely mention these experiences.

Are there class differences in love? Yes; the self-presentation of the blue-collar people suggested that love was a little too high in the hierarchy of values even to reach for until they had taken care of the business of family security and attaining self-respect through their work. Work was more important as a source of happiness to the working-class group than anything as undependable as "mature love." It is worth noting that one-third of those in my blue-collar sample are divorced, many of them single mothers trying to put the pieces back together after an early marriage that failed.*

How important is the erotic side of one's love life to overall satisfaction? Among one group of young, highly successful professional women I surveyed, there was a ripple of amused acknowledgment when the greatest contributor to their satisfaction with life was revealed—and it wasn't career promotions. The more contented these women were with the quality of their sex lives, the happier they were with their entire existence.

Yet while satisfaction with one's intimate life was very important, the broad range of erotic or epicurean pleasures did not contribute much to well-being for the usual respondent in my surveys. "A life full of sensual pleasure" went to the bottom of the list of lifetime values every time. For all our openly displayed pornography and the sexual buzz in the air, most Americans are still closer to their puritanical past than they know. Another study of life happiness found that most people thought *everyone else* had more sexual partners and adventures of the flesh than they did.[5] In fact, the number of sexual partners a person had was totally unrelated to his or her happiness.

7. "I have many friends."

Very few relationships offer loyalty, forgiveness, and reciprocal human nourishment. Full-time wives used to, and certain long-term husbands. Beyond that—and many Americans are beyond either today—people are pretty much limited to religion, therapy, and friends.

The numbers say it eloquently in this instance. Optimally satisfied people have more friends. Along with finding it easier to love than most other people, they probably are more lovable. In fact, they enjoy roughly twice as many friends as the average person in my surveys. When the chips are down,

---

* The National Women's Political Caucus reported in March 1981 that 90 percent of all single-parent families are headed by women, and more than one-third earn incomes below the poverty line, even with public assistance.

they have more people they can count on for understanding and support.

Women find it easier to build friendships—by which is meant genuine, deep, loyal, noncompetitive relationships—with other women than men do with other men. Friendships among men are rather rare, except, significantly, among the high-well-being men. A desirable life is also strongly linked to the willingness to reveal intimate thoughts and feelings—something else that comes more easily to women.

A somewhat less intimate aspect of friendship shows up as important to high-satisfaction people. A majority of them have had a mentor, often more than one. In this regard, men have the advantage.

8. "I am a cheerful person."

That optimism is evident everywhere in the outlook of the most contented is to be expected. What is intriguing is that people of high well-being seldom mention chronic depression as one of the hallmarks of a whole stage of adult life. (Delia Barnes is an exception in this respect.) For low-well-being people, "being seriously depressed and discontented" shows up significantly among the 22- to 28-year-olds and continues to be one of the three feelings most characteristic of every life stage. Twenty to thirty years later, the distance between those of high and low well-being is so vast that mere life experiences fail to explain the gulf. Some of it may be biochemical in origin—more about that later.

Being cheerful not only makes it more pleasant to live with oneself; a person with a positive outlook is more likely to attract friendship and love, which promise in turn the richer intimacy and emotional supports that characterize overall life satisfaction.

People who allow themselves to become soured on life often set in motion a self-reinforcing cycle. Their anger or self-pity becomes so off-putting that it deprives them of the friends and help they otherwise would deserve and that might restore their buoyancy.

9. "I am not thin-skinned or sensitive to criticism."

The people of highest well-being apparently have learned to distinguish between their ongoing intrinsic worth and their fluctuating extrinsic value. This is demonstrated by their reaction to criticism as well as to failure.

A person of high well-being does not perceive an attack on his or her work or ideas as a reflection on his or her innate value as a person. As a result, he neither reacts with uncontrolled anger or defensiveness nor absorbs the blow in some vital organ, only to have it erupt later in physical symptoms. Even when satisfied people agree with the criticism, it does not wash out their sense of self.

10. "I have no major fears."

It is common for young people (those under 28) to worry about "not advancing fast enough" and to fear that "others will find out I'm not as good as they think." But the least-satisfied adults also worry as early as their mid-twenties that "time is running out."

How does that compare with the experience of those who exhibit the most satisfaction? They are more likely than anyone else to say, "I feel secure enough to stop running and struggling, to relax and open myself to new feelings."

High-well-being people seldom describe themselves as feeling "locked in," and they register awareness of time running out only when they reach their late forties. What is even more extraordinary, they report no major fear at any stage of adult life.

Common fears among the unhappiest people are of feeling lonely, messing up their personal lives, being locked in by their work; and, among those over 45, of no longer being attractive, being abandoned, or being overtaken by illness.

In every group the most satisfied are also more likely to be religious. Most were raised in strong religious traditions, although by midlife they frequently had discarded dogma and repudiated religious conformity in favor of forging their own relationship to the Divine.

The Vital Statistics of Well-being

Are there other factors common to the highest-well-being people besides those ten self-descriptive statements? Is well-being an accident of birth? Hardly, but there are some other qualities that correlate.

Broadly speaking, older is more contented than younger, married is happier than unmarried, and professionals are more satisfied with their lives than blue-collar workers. Birth order is not a factor. Even being born pretty or handsome has little material effect on a person's overall well-being in adulthood.

Despite government statistics that imply the satisfaction of Americans is tied exclusively to their economic status, my own research and other contemporary studies indicate that income is less closely correlated with overall well-being than age, the capacity to love and be loved, and the enjoyment of one's work.[6]*

Age: A clear message in the results of my research was that the people who enjoy highest well-being in life are likely to be the older ones. It is young people who are most alone, bored, restless, and easily tripped up by their fears. This dovetails with recent studies that show the most troubled age group to be late adolescents, followed by young married couples with small children.[8]

Occupation: The most-satisfied people are the most highly

---

* The watershed family income level among people who were well satisfied with their lives across all my samples, except the blue-collar families, fell somewhere between $20,000 and $30,000, in 1978–79 dollars. To keep up with inflation from October '79 to February '81, those numbers would have to be increased by 12.4 percent (or more, to compensate for higher tax brackets), bringing the 1981 income level to between $22,500 and $33,750.

Compare these figures with Department of Commerce statistics showing that the *average* American man earns $23,000 and the average woman $12,000, and it becomes apparent that most families need two paychecks to put them comfortably within the high-well-being range. Even then, families with two incomes earn on the average, nationally, slightly *less* than families in which the wife does not work, obviously now more a choice of the upper-middle class.

Among blue-collar workers, in my surveys, gradations in family income between $15,000 and $25,000 (again, in 1978–79 dollars; currently the range would be closer to $17,000 to $28,000) did not have a decisive impact on the degree of satisfaction with life. But earning less than $15,000 (now $17,000) did correlate negatively, and anything near the poverty level almost always meant low satisfaction. Of every ten black Americans, three live at or below the poverty level.[7]

educated; typically, they are in business or the professions. If not in the upper reaches of corporate management, they are likely to be running their own smaller businesses or to be self-employed within one of the medical, legal, financial, or artistic professions. A disproportionate percentage of younger men who scored high in life satisfaction are self-employed.

The average blue-collar person in my surveys registered a significantly lower level of satisfaction with life as a whole than did any of the professionals. There were notable exceptions, however: typically those in administrative positions, often union representatives or full-time officers who had professional or management status within their work environment. For the most satisfied of the blue-collar workers, self-respect was more important than material comfort. Their sense of well-being was tied primarily to job satisfaction and the degree of personal growth they felt they had attained. There was evidence that being included at a decision-making level in their work place had a more important effect on morale than wages or hours.

The most dispirited of the men typically worked in white-collar jobs or were stuck in middle management. The lowest-satisfaction women were in secretarial positions or were housewives.

Marital status: Married people are as a whole happier— and live longer—than those who are single. This is especially true of men. That finding has been confirmed by all the major investigations into adult well-being.

Divorced women with small children and aging men who have never married are the most-dissatisfied people. The reasons may be more pragmatic than psychological. Most divorced women have to work (71 percent) and care for children (84 percent) without economic, psychological, or moral support from their former husbands.

Distinctions must be made. Being divorced is not necessarily a permanent state. Small children do grow up. The amputee who survives the surgery of divorce is pushed toward self-examination and into initiating actions she might never have dared while complacently attached to a "stronger one." No small number of my highest-well-being respondents *had* been divorced, although usually not recently. Even if they had not remarried, they were happier in general than those who had never married.

Class background: This turned out to have little bearing on satisfaction with adult life (a peculiarly American phenomenon, no doubt). There is only the slightest tendency for high-well-being people to have upper-middle-class parents. Most of the people who are optimally satisfied with their adult lives were born into lower-middle- or lower-class homes. By the time I interviewed them, most were comfortably middle-class or better. But their attitude toward life appeared to be linked less to income status than, among other things, to the pitch between their youthful expectations and what they had achieved as adults.

That certainly does not imply that children of the near-poor have the same advantages as children of the elite. It does make the point that the highly motivated young in a mass meritocracy can slip through the eye of the needle and come out supremely happy, enjoying full social acceptance despite their class background.

The Heredity of Life Satisfaction

How greatly does heredity influence our eventual level of life satisfaction?

A continuing conundrum is whether—and which—personality traits and characteristics are determined, or at least influenced, by nature. Behavioral scientists ponder. They have it! Study and compare identical twins raised separately. If they have the same attribute, it must be inherited. Unfortunately, it isn't that simple. Each study concludes that both heredity and environment play a role and that personality is the area of human functioning that is most strongly affected by the environment.[9]

What is innate? Folklore has always viewed artistic talent as inherited. The studies of twins bear this out; even when only one of the separated twins had been trained in, say, music, the other twin, although untrained, still scored high in musical aptitude. Twins may have the same high-pitched giggle or a similar stutter. There is some evidence that the intensity of sexual drive is genetically linked.

The one trait that appears to be strongly consistent from childhood throughout adult life is social style. That is to say, as many mothers discover, some babies are just born more gregarious and seem to reach out to others for reinforcement, whereas other babies tend toward shyness and seem better able to amuse themselves. The gregarious child is likely to grow into an outgoing adult, which may mean being anything from pleasantly sociable to painfully exhibitionistic. The quieter child probably will be described in adult life as "a private person," one who mulls over things before expressing strong emotions.

Other longitudinal studies of personality are in agreement with the twins studies that a person's character may be most fixed in this domain of introversion-extroversion.[10] If one twin was generally optimistic and lively, or somber and muted, the other was usually described in similar terms. But there is still considerable room to maneuver. All the studies point out that we are born with a potential *range* of sociability. Depending then upon how much encouragement we receive from our parents, our teachers, and our peers, that potential may be fully realized or not. Which brings us back to environment.

The other two aspects of personality in which heredity appears to play an important part are a person's "basic mood" and energy level.[11]

Optimism-Negativism Dial

If, as my data suggest, people destined for optimum life satisfaction set out, at least by the end of their teens, with a basic mood tilting toward the cheerful and optimistic, and those destined for chronic discontent enter their twenties with a tilt toward the depressive and negativistic, the additional evidence that basic mood and sociability are relatively stable personality characteristics leads to intriguing speculations.

It may be that we all have something like an optimism-negativism dial inside, and that each person starts out with a basic setting—some of us with a background hum of euphoria, some with a chronic minus charge. Others display a more neutral setting, and still others (notably manic-depressives) seem cursed with a widely oscillating needle.

To some extent, that setting may have biochemical origins. Science already has located a region in the brain and a biochemical process that make us feel good, naturally. The "internal opiates," or endorphins, as these newly discovered peptides within the body are called, are released spontaneously and seem to produce a mild, relaxed euphoria. The endorphins also have been artificially stimulated by researchers to block pain. It appears now that the potency of these natural substances in the body is greater than that of the synthetic opiates such as morphine.[12]

I discussed the subject with Dr. Jonas Salk, who agreed that each person seems to carry a basic optimism-negativism setting and speculated that in the future we may be able to induce the endorphins, by natural means, to help stimulate a state of well-being. After all, Dr. Salk said, mystics since the beginning of time, as well as creative people, have been releasing such chemical reactions within themselves through meditative states and various other methods of altering consciousness.

People who feel mildly depressed all the time may be able to be educated to "turn up" their optimism dial naturally—and, as a result, to approach the future in a basically cheerful, constructive mood. But optimism and negativism are mood poles at either end of a very broad spectrum. Even if we do set out with a tilt one way or the other, there is a great deal we can do to raise our optimism level. That is in some measure the enterprise of this book.

Personal Tempo

One other self-description given by many of the highest-satisfaction people was "I am an unusually energetic person." That may be one of the factors contributing to their optimism. The mere knowledge that one has the vitality to get a great deal accomplished is cheering. And for those who express their energy in physical ways, the "feel-good" effect of a sustained period of exercise is medically recognized. Exercise stimulates production of the endorphins. Moreover, regular energetic exercise is a way of immunizing oneself against some of the energy killers of middle and later age.

When we discover unusually high energy among people who are very happy with their lives, remember, we are not talking only about young people, or about baseball players or jazz dancers or anybody else with energy to burn. We are referring to people who are mostly over 30 and many who are much older than that. The fact that they feel so vital could be the result of their having made many of the right choices and having emphasized the right personality characteristics. By setting out with optimism, anticipating the future, finding meaning and direction in their lives, and pursuing these cheerfully, rarely slowing down over disappointments and not allowing themselves to be set back by others' criticism, these people establish a forward momentum that most probably steps up their personal tempo. One might say that nothing breeds energy like attacking life energetically.

Yet if personal tempo is to some degree innate, it, like our basic mood and social style, is not an absolute but a range. By learning to make prudent choices, each of us can extend our range to its outermost limits.

A Brief Review

One of the most striking similarities among blue-collar, white-collar, and professional groups included in my research is that the five self-descriptions most closely linked to well-being were identical in all. Their importance even ranked in the same order:

1. My life has meaning and direction.
2. I have experienced one or more important transitions in my adult years, and I have handled these transitions in an unusual, personal, or creative way.
3. I rarely feel cheated or disappointed by life.
4. I have already attained several of the long-term goals that are important to me.
5. I am pleased with my personal growth and development.

The other five major self-descriptions characterizing high well-being are:

6. I am in love; my partner and I love mutually.
7. I have many friends.
8. I am a cheerful person.
9. I am not thin-skinned or sensitive to criticism.
10. I have no major fears.

Seeking Out High-Satisfaction People

In addition to discovering candidates for high well-being through the Life History Questionnaire, I also wrote to five hundred people from all over the country who were in close touch with their communities and asked each to recommend one person from among his or her acquaintances who seemed to be navigating through life's predictable turns and surprise twists with uncommon success. I was looking for people who might be considered models for living—but no saints, please! I appealed to these five hundred not to divulge the purpose of my search. People who thought they were being chosen as exemplary might try to hide important complexities.

As I hoped, these pivotal Americans reflected a diversity of community values and standards in their interpretations of the sort of person I was looking for. Some of the early candidates seemed to have everything, but a warning bell kept ringing in the back of my mind. They may have been the envy of their peers and have scored high on the well-being scale, but in person something important seemed to be missing. The scale might measure only fleeting happiness for some people. I needed to know what factors go into *sustaining* well-being.

To find people who had an enduring sense of being at home in their own skin and who were open to the future, I realized I would have to weed out those who were headed for a fall.

The first stop was a famous convention hotel.

2.

EARLY
CANDIDATES

It was a ritual of corporate life: close to a thousand members
of middle and top management from different tribes within
one industry gathered together for a gala. Rich multinational
companies enjoy such opportunities to behave like sovereign
nations, to parade their corporate jets and the cream of their
troops before other rich multinational companies, hoping the
best men will defect. At the same time, young comets of the
industry attempt to impress the VIP's of competitive firms,
hoping to rocket through to top management.

One such rising star was recommended to me as a model
among corporation men, a man we'll call Herb Cashian.* An
apparent winner on the well-being scale, he was very clear
about his life's meaning and direction, appeared indefatigably cheerful and energetic, showed no fears, bore no failures,
seemed unfazed by criticism. Nice family, too—four children,
no divorce; in fact, a wife who was an asset. Moreover,
several pivotal members of the industry who recommended
him assayed that he was a "fast tracker."

The language of any culture contains the greatest number
of synonyms for the issues of profoundest importance to its
members. A dozen terms exist within the corporate culture
for the person who looks as if he will be an accelerated
success. They range from *high flier* to *wunderkind* to *tiger* to
the most imagistic—*water walker*. The vocabulary reflects the

* The names of persons and companies in this chapter have been
changed and their professions altered to a near equivalent.

thinking of many within the corporate culture that the best and quickest way to reach the state of high well-being is to be tough-minded, task-oriented, hard-driving, and able to set aside personal or emotional considerations in the interest of one's own advancement. To be a man like Herbert Cashian.

It is Friday afternoon, and the dominant tribes are arriving with the flourish of Aïda, the dust of elephants. They must land on an airstrip sunk in densely wooded hills hospitable to no sort of farming, not even to cattle or goats. This airstrip receives only private planes and corporate jets that disgorge guests for the Greenbrier, one of two lavish resort hotels that function as alternate Camps David for America's permanent government. The top brass cushioned in company jets buzzing around above the ubiquitous fog generally are willing to sacrifice a certain air-safety margin in exchange for service, since the fact that this is one of the most economically depressed pockets in the nation guarantees a plentiful and submissive serving class.

"There it is!" An operative of the firm we'll rename Swenck and Swenck points at the sky. You can always tell his company's flagship plane, he says, by the number of stars in the semicircle on its tail. The founding father of the company likes landing in foreign countries where the populace gasps, "Who's the *six*-star general?" Word is passed that Swenck and Swenck's Grumman American Gulfstream is the most luxurious model of corporate jet—only two hundred of them in the world. Arrayed along one side of this tiny airfield are easily fifty Gulfstreams already arrived for the week-long fun and fracas—one-quarter of the multinational air force, right here, noses to tails, linked in a web of wealth and power. It is the sort of display that seldom fails to get a good middle manager's blood racing.

Herb Cashian and his wife, Judith, are already working the hotel lobby when I arrive. I see only a lot of blazers and plaid pants in postcard colors, but the Cashians have the players sorted out. "The white badges are the clients, blues are the agencies, yellows are the guests," Judith Cashian informs me. "The blues pursue the whites. That's the game."

If this is supposed to be a week of recreation, why does Herb Cashian jot down notes after every conversation with the thoroughness of a kitchen spy scraping other people's brain plates? Why is Judith wearing full eye makeup to go jogging at six the next morning, with a name badge clasped to her sweat suit?

It seems the "girls" are given daytime badges with stars on them and nighttime badges with little rhinestones. To go badgeless is very bad form. Not to remember a name is the number-one faux pas at such a corporate gathering, Judith tells me, which is why people protect one another by wearing their badges religiously, even over sweat suits. Besides, badge color is all she has to go by when determining which cluster of people to "invade."

To the uneducated eye, the whole thing looks about as jolly as canvassing one's neighborhood for contributions to an Arab terrorist defense fund.

"It's all done in a very pleasant setting," Herb explains, "but it's a serious game." His road map calls for becoming president of a division by the time he is 40. Herb is now 39. He is a man in a hurry.

One would never know the Cashians are in their late thirties. Both on the small side, wiry, with bright questions all over their faces, they appear almost to be frozen in their twenties. They work as a team, playing off each other with the peak form of two tumblers on a trampoline. Through the other wives, who tend toward doughiness in the legs and diffuse movements, Judith moves expertly. "I always say *we* work for Highgate, or *we* work for Teagarten-Jones." Both Judith and Herb were born into blue-collar families. At the annual Greenbrier rites she has to pinch herself. "It's almost unreal, how far we've come."

At dinner, although they now work for Spitzer, they are seated at the prestigious Swenck and Swenck table. This cannot be coincidence. Wherever Herb and Judith are, they are "present to a purpose." They believe in "strategic seating." Judith is next to R. W. Petershouse, president of the highest-profit division. Herb is next to another officer of the company. "Feelers" are being put out all over the place. This business is very incestuous, the Cashians tell me. Many of last year's faces are with different companies this year, having moved one step up or laterally for the promise of promotion.

Half the men here are vice-presidents; 15 percent are

presidents or chairmen of the board; another 15 percent are straight middle management. In any large company, most executives over 50 remain stuck in middle management or are given a diluted status in their own little pot labeled "vice-president"—with the lid clapped on. "Topped off," they call it. That must be why the seasoned game birds at this table are feeling out the red-meated ones in their late thirties and early forties—men like Herbert Cashian—and reaching right past the middle-aged middle managers within their own companies who sit in a glaze, as if fricasseed.

I watch R. W. Petershouse play the part of crusty corporate president. He is enjoying himself. It is natural for others at the table to see Petershouse as exactly what they would like to be in another fifteen years or so. In fact, he too was recommended to me as a model of optimum life satisfaction, an older model, age 55.

The Corporate Life Cycle

Ten years from now R. W. Petershouse will probably will himself to die.

That is what he told me when the mask was off, in a private interview. Ten years from now he faces the guillotine of mandatory retirement. It can't be done legally anymore, but there are ways. His greatest satisfaction in life at this stage is feeling he has power over people—"in the best sense"—meaning he can persuade, con, cause people to come back to him spouting ideas he has planted.

When that power is taken away, what else is there?

"I never took time to be a romantic adventurer," Petershouse explained. "We all got married too soon. But I'm probably too egotistical to make any love relationship work anyway. I'm paid to be that way, so I must be."

The life pattern he cut out for himself in his twenties was the cookie-cutter pattern chosen by most businessmen of his generation. The surpassing goal was to attain career success and a comfortable life, toward which aims a man should take a wife and begin a family at the start of the game. Postponing marriage and parenthood in the interest of prolonging self-development was not a consideration, as it is among young men today. When the professional managers gathered at the Greenbrier were asked, in my questionnaire, to do a cost-benefit analysis of their chosen life pattern, they rated much the same as Petershouse. They saw the benefits as having been motivated to provide, being young with their children, and enjoying early career success. "Loss of freedom as a youth" and "grown away from marriage partner," together with "routinized sex life" and "limited funds," were the most commonly cited costs. Or, as one man put it succinctly, "No freedom, no money, no flexibility."

The corporate life cycle superimposes its own stages over the stages of individual growth and development. What is good for the corporation, of course, is not necessarily conducive to individual well-being.

In the corporate *learner stage* the individual is busy qualifying to join the professional tribe. Depending on the energy, loyalty, and leadership ability a person demonstrates, and the willingness to jump whenever the company says "move," he or she is promoted to a junior membership status usually sometime in the late twenties or early thirties.

The *doer stage* that follows brings increasing responsibility and the excitement and danger of being "under the gun." As those in the ranks of middle management come closer to the bottleneck leading to command positions, competition intensifies, uncertainty mounts. Making one's mark consumes one's energies. Much depends on the coattails to which one is attached—and that person's fate. Political skills assume major importance.

Most doers, as the men of this group who answered my questionnaire admitted, enjoy being pressured and challenged. They seldom pay attention to the drains on their personal life. It is not until the doers are past 40, or more likely after the last child has grown and gone, that they total the cost in human relations. When 780 chief executives of this country's 1,300 largest corporations were interviewed in a joint survey by the *Wall Street Journal* and the Gallup Organization, 80 percent of the top dogs acknowledged that their family lives had suffered because of their careers. Six of every ten said they believe a business executive must make personal sacrifices to succeed.[1] Presumably, most rationalize those sacrifices by rewarding the next generation of doers for doing the same thing, thereby perpetuating the cycle.

Maturity in the corporate life cycle is reached at the *diplo-*

mat stage. The person admitted to top management becomes at that point part of the institution, an ambassador at large, his destiny virtually indistinguishable from the company's. There is little if any difference between work and play when one is on top. All social relations are freighted with business meaning. For the happy CEO's, work is pleasure. Yet job pressures only increase at the top, say two-thirds of the 780 chief executives queried, prompting them to work sixty- to seventy-hour weeks, travel six to ten days a month, give up many weekends, and watch their health deteriorate. It is worth it, however, to know, every day, through title, salary, and the obeisance of employees, that one is top dog—and therefore that one must be a good person. Almost all the chief executives I interviewed believe their work makes a contribution to society.

Those who reach chronological maturity in corporate life but are not admitted to senior management, and therefore are blocked from advancing to the diplomat stage, often drift into a holding pattern—or enter the ranks of the walking dead.

Petershouse had consciously narrowed his focus to be certain of moving up through the bottleneck to top management. "I realized in my forties," he told me, "after spending years in corporate life trying to be the personality kid, life's too short for that. Being 'nice' to people is not what you're paid for in senior management. So I became basically antisocial. I don't have any true friends." His pale blue eyes filmed over with that gelid impersonality with which people learn to defend the decisions that have diminished them. Only when we talked of the one romantic fling of his forties did he fumble for words and show flickers of sadness and passion. "I'm too old now for romantic liaisons; it's too much trouble," he added. "My satisfaction in life now is making people think and act as I want them to. At the top," he said, "all you're paid for is two or three decisions a year. So I spend the rest of the time plotting the novels I'll write when they retire me." If the novels don't work, he plans to lie down and let his life run out.

Is this the scenario for Herb Cashian? Or have he and his wife thought up an innovative path to avoid the traps of the corporate life cycle?

Their twenties were classical. Herb started out in the

qualifying rounds of the corporate game as a field salesman, on the road three-quarters of the time. The company was trying him out in different territories; he was trying to prove he was ready to move up to the first rungs of management. This effort took almost all his energies during the "Trying Twenties," a stage of adult development in which the individual establishes a provisional identity and builds the capacity for intimacy—or doesn't. The learner stage of corporate life doesn't leave much time for intimacy.

The strain on the Cashians' marriage was greatest during their twenties. They lived in what they called "company ghettos." Company policy discouraged friendship even within the enclave, based on the theory that a man cannot supervise other men once they become personal friends. "My husband was so interested in his career," Judith recalls, "he devoted every moment to getting ahead. He hardly knew me or the children. By the time I turned twenty-eight, I believed I would never, *ever* be anything but pregnant."

At 28 Herb saw the first cut coming: the company was comparing its sales force with the graduates of M.B.A. programs and deciding who would be brought in to staff the home office. In the manic attempt to show off well, Herb set up an office in his basement.

At that point Judith was leaving her fourth pregnancy and entering her first depression. During the learner stage of corporate life the wife's connection to the firm is virtually nonexistent. The company has no use for her yet. While her husband is out proving himself, her function is pretty much limited, as Judith says, to "keeping the children quiet." And moving.

The Cashians moved four times for Herb's career during their twenties. "Where's Oshkosh?" Judith had to look up the place in the atlas. Sometimes she had only a weekend to find a house. Each time they resettled, Judith planted a flowering bush. They never lived anywhere long enough for her to see the bush flower.

She tried to see the bright side. "All that moving broke our dependence on our parents. Herbie and I learned to depend on each other because there was no one else."

Impatient with being obedient to the "shoulds," as most of us are in our twenties, we find that a new vitality springs from within as we approach 30. It is common for men and women alike to speak of feeling too narrow and restricted. The pinch comes from the choices of our twenties, choices that, no matter how appropriate they were to the previous stage, must be altered, let out, sometimes even ripped up, in order to make room for expansion of our possibilities and a broader, more certain identity. Because it often seems a patchwork of inconsistencies, I have called this passage "Catch-30."

Herb's experience in the Catch-30 passage was expansion. Promoted to the home office, he moved his family to New York. A year or so later, he took the time-honored step up to a bigger job in a smaller company. "It was the point in my life when I realized I was cut out to be a chief. I had the ability and opportunity. My road map then called for becoming president of a division by the time I was forty." He felt good about himself. He had a goal that meant something to him, a clear direction. "And I think I continued to grow," he says. "From a personal viewpoint"—here I expected him to express some concern for the toll on his young family—"the move was good because it took me only ten minutes to get back and forth to work."

Judith's Catch-30 passage was a failed attempt to expand. "When my last child went to school, I could see it was the beginning of the end—and I was only in my early thirties!" She decided she wanted to become a lawyer. Not having had a textbook in her hands since college, she took the LSAT's and did very well. New York University accepted her. It was "walk-on-air" time, right up to two weeks before the term began, and then—

Fallback. Mrs. Herbert Cashian could not risk making herself something on the outside that she had no inner image to support. "I couldn't possibly be a lawyer, not a woman with four children," she told herself, and withdrew her application. Her husband was becoming very nervous, she noticed. She signed up for an accounting course instead. She would learn how to back up her husband with business skills.

But Herb moved the family again, this time to a town we'll call Pleasantville in New England, to an even smaller pond where he could assume a much bigger job.

"If a woman has no career of her own but becomes very involved in the community, and then they move her, she walks into the new town as a nobody," Judith learned. "Who knows that she's handled money, learned organization, maybe even run programs on the scale of a city department? I was that nobody, and it's terrible.'"

But once the man is in the doer stage, the company does have work for the wife. By "handling" people for her husband and interpreting the psychology of situations, she gives him an advantage in dealing with his subordinates, bosses, and competitors. She is also tacitly expected to provide much of his motivation to do better, while accepting the fact that the company has foreclosed her own life choices.

Judith saw her first bush flower in Pleasantville. She blossomed there herself, given eight full years in the same place to put down roots and send out her own new shoots. "And I was a success!" She shivered with delight at the recollection. "For the first time!" She had been elected to the school board and was planning to run for state office. She was actually *becoming* a politician.

Her husband said he felt he'd hit a plateau. He was 37. He'd had an offer back in Atlanta where they had begun, and he was going to take it.

Tears welled up and turned her nights sodden, leaked over into her days and into the middle of impersonal conversations, drove her into the watery silence of the YWCA pool in the hope of swimming them off—*wrenched out of where I feel good about myself . . . give up what I've worked for . . . go back to being nobody*—but the feelings she couldn't admit kept boiling up. The tears filled her goggles, blurred everything, as if the only way to contain this red-hot ingot of emotion was to take it inside herself and try to drown it.

"I didn't know it was anger," she told me at the Greenbrier a year and a half after the move. "Finally, a friend told me I was having a 'grief reaction' and got me to a mental health center. For the first time I realized I had a choice. I could go, or not go!"*

---

* A national survey by Catalyst (funded by Exxon) of the top 1,300 corporations and two-career couples found that 90 percent of wives and husbands thought companies should help, when one is relocated, in finding the other a new job. Only 4 percent of the corporations had a policy of assisting spouses of relocated employees. Despite survey findings suggesting that the major reason for

When Judith did decide to recommit to being her husband's partner, she felt like "an intelligent woman making an adult choice—freely." She believed that if she had wanted to, she could have stayed in Pleasantville alone. But she chose not to. "Making a free choice to go has strengthened our marriage tremendously," she assured me.

I asked if her husband was aware of the magnitude of this transition for her.

"Oh, for sure."

But any resemblance to a midlife passage in the foregoing is coincidental, from Herb Cashian's perspective. He rejects any notion of transitions: "Thinking about that stuff just slows people down. I haven't noticed any milestones." The simple fact, he explained when we met at the Greenbrier, was that the company had been going through some problems and he was concerned that he was not progressing as he should. Sitting at dinner, in his element, he looked compact, silvery, utterly assured.

"Had you begun to feel at all stagnant?" I inquired.

"No, it wasn't a passage or anything. There was nothing significant about my age—I could have been forty-three or thirty-seven—I just happened to be thirty-seven. And a recruiter came along."

I recalled the deadline he had set for becoming president of a division by the age of 40.

"Yes, but I carry my age pretty well. I look half a dozen years younger than I am. Only weigh fifteen pounds more than when I graduated from college." He tugged his vest smooth and shuffled the numbers of life a little: "I'm a long way from middle age," he said.

Since Herb's chief coping mechanism seemed to be denial of any facts that were unpleasant or emotionally charged, I asked how he had reacted at 30 when Judith became interested in law school.

"No problem. Judy just couldn't get accepted, as I recall. She did go on to study accounting. Unfortunately, she didn't finish the last few courses to get the associate's degree she wanted."

---

employees' refusal to relocate is career requirements of a spouse, the corporations continue to insist that two-career couples resist moving for economic reasons.

"When you were considering making another career move, did you discuss the fact that it would prevent her from finishing up?"

"That was not an impediment."

"Do you think Judith took it hard?"

"She's like a lot of women—she's not that easy to move."

"Do you remember Judith going on a crying jag over this last move?"

"I can't recall. I think we went to a family therapist. But I think that was because of the kids."

"Were you aware of her making a choice between staying in Pleasantville to complete a career cycle of her own and recommitting to the marriage and moving back to Atlanta with you?"

"As far as I'm concerned, she's always wanted to be with me."

The edges were all very sharp, the way Herb saw the track. That was why he was out in front of the pack. He then offered his own philosophy of how those destined for satisfying lives are naturally selected. "People are somewhat like flowers or trees. You can pull them up and transplant them. There's a period of getting used to the new ground. But there's no doubt in my mind that the children are fuller human beings for having had the experience of living in many different places. My wife is a good example of the old parochial style. That's not the world today."

The company paid for the family therapist. The two youngest Cashian boys were pulverizing each other; that is how angry they were at first about the move to Atlanta. One boy demanded to go back to Pleasantville to rejoin his championship swim team. The Cashian girl gave up music: she had been about to make first-chair trombone. Judith was barely functional and for the whole first year continued to live in Pleasantville—in her mind. She gave people their old phone number, which tended to discourage new friendships. She did not have the proper attitude about company conventions and wearing a badge on her sweat suit.

The people who had recommended the couple as models of well-being, of course, knew nothing of this dark side. Safe to say, no professional colleague would want to know.

"Companies are too sophisticated to formalize the wife's

contribution; it would open up a hornet's nest," Judith came to understand, "so they pay you off in bennies instead."

"Bennies" means fringe benefits and conveys an element of addiction, as to a drug—the best moving and storage company, a week at the Greenbrier, family therapy. The therapy was added only in recent years when too many employees began turning down promotions that required a move. Judith had watched one family move, fail to "adapt," and move back; the man's career was finished when he was 33. Another friend's husband had a nervous breakdown. "For some people, moving has to be close to death," she concluded. Knowing the score by now, Judith had to find an innovative way to stay with the game without going nuts.

At the darkest point in the tunnel, she had turned around. *All right! If we have to be here anyway, we're going to squeeze everything that's good out of this city.* They had done the museums and restaurants, pulled closer as a family, recharged the children until they shone in school. *Never mind!* she told herself about the perforations in her own career line. She would read all the management books and study Herb's trade magazines until she knew as much about her husband's business as he did. She gave him ideas—ideas that sailed! Sometimes she thought she was just a frustrated product manager. But that was all right too. Just wait another five years, that was her plan, until the kids were gone and she could get an M.B.A. Then she wanted to be in charge of something.

"I'm not afraid to talk back anymore," she declared. "I want to be a boss."

I tried to get Herb to anticipate future changes:

"In another four or five years, all your children will have left home. You'll be forty-five or so. How do you think your outlook will change at that stage?"

He hadn't given it any thought. "I guess I'll have more leisure, time my wife and I can spend together, opportunities to travel, or whatever."

"Do you worry that Judith might have a problem if she doesn't have some other purpose in life by then?"

"If she's interested in having some kind of position, she could do that when she's in her forties."

"If you were interviewing her, what position would you have in mind?"

"Something in accounting, or, like, administrative assistant."

"Is that what Judith wants to do?"

"I don't know. I've encouraged her to do whatever it is that's going to make her feel more fulfilled. I'm all for it. However, her prime responsibility over the next few years is to get the family well settled."

"Do you think she'll be a little behind, entering the job market at forty-five?"

"Definitely."

"How would you recommend she counteract that?"

"She won't be able to make up for that. It's a race. There's no way."

"Herb, where are *you* in your life at this point?"

Without hesitation: "I'm on the track; in fact, I'm a little ahead of myself! It was worth it to change companies," he told me that week at the Greenbrier in 1978. "This is going to be the last change."

"The end of the story," Judith bubbled as we said goodbye, "is that we are all very happy where we are. We have adjusted well. The children have tons of friends. Our sex life is better. I think we all learned something from that last, tough transition."

There was one loose end: a feeler put out to Herb that week would necessitate another move, if he accepted.

"I'm hoping that Herbie won't take a new job, because this time *he'll* realize the move would tear up the children and be too hard on me."

The Cashians looked the very picture of the working team as they left the gala that weekend. No wonder they had been recommended as models of life satisfaction within the corporate world—their strategy was an appealing one. Herb did not make passages or transitions. He did not change and did not believe in the need to change. That philosophy seemed to work a sort of magic that froze his youthful good looks in place and provided the accelerating force that put him ahead of his peers, even ahead of himself, on the fast track.

Judith Cashian had the right idea for expanding her identity at the Catch-30 passage, but she did not have the confidence—or bargaining power—to go through with it. Headed off at the pass each time she made a brief charge at becoming something more in her own right, she resolved her midlife passage with an altruistic surrender. She would transfer all her ambition and personal goals to her husband. She would count on him to carry out the campaign for self-respect and to develop the strengths in which she believed herself to be handicapped by her sex.

There was only one question left hanging: How long would it work for them?

Bulletin. Same time, one year later. Reached Judith Cashian in Stamford. Moved again. Herb's new job: president of Swenck and Swenck. R. W. Petershouse? Out. Herb was at the Greenbrier gala alone this year. Judith was home waiting to go to court. The Cashians' 14-year-old son had just stolen a car.

"I don't know what I'm doing," Judith whispered into the telephone. It was a devastated voice.

Anger? Her most defiant act had been to get a frizzy permanent before the move. Herb calls it her "liberal pinko hair."

Friendships? "The older I get," Judith said, "the less I want to make the effort. After so many ruptures you become self-protective."

A flowering bush? "We bought a new house. It has no shrubbery. I'm just as glad."

Had she considered, this time, letting Herb move alone and staying put until the children finished their school year?

"Oh, no. That would have been terrible. He just couldn't get along alone, not *now*."

She sounded oddly wrapped up in this new image of husbandly weakness. Her voice was transformed.

"Herbie was fired from his old job last September—don't say anything. A new team came in and wanted their own players. He fell apart at the seams. Men are so fragile, don't you think?" she crooned conspiratorially. The tinge of triumph was as clear in her voice as a claw under soft fur. "Herbie needs me now more than he ever did. We're both aware of it."

How did such a dramatic turnaround take place?

"Simple. I withdrew my support. I wouldn't look at him when he came home. I never asked him how he felt about being fired or how he liked his new job. He began crying at the office. I could see what was happening. As I've become stronger, he's become more dependent."

Did she still want to be a boss? I asked.

"Oh, sure. I could fill Herbie's shoes tomorrow; I could be president of a company easily. But I'll never reach my potential. So I'll help him instead. He's politically naive." And then her voice became chillingly defiant.

"Withdrawing my support from my husband gave me real *power*. It may not be a nice word," Judith Cashian said coldly, "but now that I have it, I intend to keep it."

Starved so long for any independent sense of self-worth, she still did not recognize her anger. The voice on the other end of the phone conjured up the image of a caged animal, thought to be domesticated. When the time comes for it to trample the sleeping husband or children, people will say, "Pity, she didn't know her own strength."

It takes courage to confront inner changes. Like moving from one part of the country to another, it is temporarily disorienting to shift the walls of that outer structure we build around our lives, and to move from one stage of adulthood to another. But no one can stay in one place indefinitely. Some of the people suggested by their peers as models of happiness were simply better than most at denying inner change, denying the progression of stages, denying their commonality with millions of others who also progress and retreat, who doubt and weep and reach again in the unending struggle toward those startling plateaus when, for a time, we know who we are and what our days mean.

The First Test

Getting to know the early candidates in person helped to combine the many objective clues to life satisfaction already provided by the surveys and to crystallize from them what seemed most nearly essential to *sustaining* well-being. Consequently, in sifting through candidates for those who could serve as models, I settled on the first criterion:

The person must have confronted a crossroads, chosen a path, and emerged from the completed passage with renewed strength and expanded potential.

By that standard, the Cashians were becoming increasingly handicapped in the pursuit of well-being. Herbert Cashian refused to have passages, and Judith couldn't complete them. When a transition was forced on Herb as a result of his first failure, he fell apart. Up to then he had relied on the defense of neurotic denial: refusing to connect actions or events with the feelings they produced in himself or others. That defense had severely inhibited his own growth.

As a result, Herb Cashian is becoming less with time: more driven, narrower in vision, with a diminishing capacity to change or grow, to anticipate the future correctly, or to learn from failure. He fell back on his wife when he failed, covering his own feelings of fear and inadequacy rather than examining them and putting them into a realistic perspective. He continues even in midlife to swallow whole the values of the corporate culture as his purpose and safety, and he makes no attempt to distinguish his worth as a person from whatever status is conferred by the company. Herb appears to have learned no lesson from his first failure, except that he must run harder and faster and more ruthlessly in order to stay ahead of the others. Indeed, his future seems land-mined. Small explosions can be heard already. When he got wind that Petershouse wanted to head another business for Swenck and Swenck, Herb gambled on the older man's failure and joined the company. Petershouse's business was a disaster, Herb captured the older man's presidency, and now Petershouse is out looking for a job. But if Petershouse could be blown out of the water that easily, so can his replacement.

It is almost inevitable that by the time an executive has made enough rounds on the playing board to reach 45, he or she probably will have been fired at least once or moved out to make room for someone else's team. It is therefore imperative, if one is to continue to flourish, to develop more than a single source of identity and self-worth. To be entirely dependent on job status as proof of *who I am* puts the full responsibility for well-being in the hands of institutions. But institutions are not set up for the purpose of seeing to it that every individual gets an equitable allotment of life satisfaction.

Meanwhile, Herb Cashian has a son who is beginning to express his rage in embarrassing delinquency. His wife, having tried to resolve her own midlife crisis by an altruistic surrender, was betrayed. She will take her revenge by trying to *become* him.

At the age of 40, Herb Cashian's entire sense of self-worth hangs by a rope from the company ship that happens, at the moment, to be pulling him. He has forfeited almost all control over his destiny by pretending there are no inner sea changes, which leaves him a prisoner of events.

True models of "well-being" became easier to sort out from the successful counterfeits once I had worked with more professional organizations in cooperative research. Whether I was dropping in on the annual spring rites of corporate managers, or starting with the sweeper at the Ford Dearborn plant and working up to the company president, or addressing a thousand members of the American Bar Association in the mirrored gilt of the Waldorf-Astoria's Starlight Room, I could look out into the audience of people who had answered my questionnaire and almost read their thoughts. They were often more guarded with their co-workers, who might describe them as "a hell of a guy," "daring as he is different," "probably the most happy fella among us." Such a man was endorsed by several fellow CPA's in his professional society after his questionnaire revealed a high score on the well-being scale.

A Hell of a Guy

John Florio did not look particularly remarkable. Short and slight with raven hair, he wore enormous wavily thick glasses that projected his light blue eyes out of his face like those of an exotic bird.

"You should see him go up in his antique Army fighter—the guy flies a single-seat biplane with goggles and a leather cap, everything but a silk scarf. . . ." "He's broken records for flying around the world. . . ." "Let him tell you about his, uh, rather exotic private life. . . ."

It was clear that John Florio led one of the more colorful off-hours lives of any sober CPA in the whole state society. Indeed, his colleagues seemed to take vicarious pleasure in presenting him as evidence that they weren't just a bunch of stiffs.

Florio had arrived by his late forties at a position of respectability in one of the more prestigious accounting firms in Cleveland. He did the boutique work—corporate tax plans, partnerships, new business setups, and cradle-to-grave accounting for a few faithful clients. The silver-framed pictures he kept on his desk established the quality of his private possessions: a beautiful full-time wife he had married because she seemed "highly acceptable," two children groomed at fine prep schools, a timber-and-stucco house in affluent Beachwood, a new Austin-Healey—the latter being his first insurrectionary act against the proper WASP core culture of which he had wanted so badly to be a part. Here was a man, you see, admittedly a "slow learner," who, having served the objectives of the first half of his life, described himself—when he looked back at the man he was at 40—as dull, typically out of condition, nobody unusual. What is more, "I didn't like myself."

To be the daring innovator who finds a different or better way, the scrappy competitor who compensates for his less than giant intellect by sheer staying power—this was the image Florio had secretly nursed, until the day the skies all but parted and for the first time he saw his path clearly.

The cruelest blow of his boyhood had come the day a doctor told John, who had been cursed with a lazy eye from birth, that his dream of becoming a pilot was hopeless. No amount of lying, cheating, or faking records had worked to get him past the Air Force physical either. To make up for this rejection he had pumped a jackhammer at night to get through business school and worked his way up to officer's rank in the American Institute of CPA's. At home he made model airplanes, which to tell the truth was a pretty wimpy compensation. One day in his 37th year he chartered a plane for the hell of it to take him to an out-of-town probate hearing. The pilot encouraged him to take lessons. Florio explained about his bad eye. Then the pilot gave him an amazing piece of information: "Hey, as a civilian, with good glasses, you can get a waiver for bad eyes."

So close was this to being granted a second life that John Florio went right out and bought an airplane and started to take lessons as though there were no tomorrow. He had earned an instrument instructor's rating before he reached 40.

"It gave me a whole new perspective," he remembered. "Suddenly there were no limits on the places I could go, dreams I could make come true—it was astonishing how good I felt."

He upgraded to a six-seat Cessna 210 and flew the whole family plus dog to Europe for a trade meeting. The next adventure was flying in and out of Communist countries and enjoying the awed reception—not too many private planes land in places like Prague. But the peak experience of his life was yet to come.

Entering true middle age (45 to 60) in search of "another challenge, something new, incredible," this meticulous preparer of corporate tax plans departed from type entirely by flying clear around the world in a small plane and breaking a record on top of it. What a hero he must have been to the 18-year-old son he took along, and to the other middle-aged men from the firm who came out to the airfield with a bottle of champagne for his triumphal return.

What a guy, this Florio . . . flying through thunderheads, making an instrument landing in Sri Lanka . . . really in shape, too, made it in twelve days on three and a half hours' sleep at night . . . the guy's forty-seven years old, for God's sake!

What they didn't know yet was how Florio's rapidly expanded physical identity had encouraged him to stretch in other ways. He had met a "breath of fresh air," titian-haired and 22 and adorably devoted to becoming a karma yogi. Jhana, as she had renamed herself, was quite an innovative piece of work for a man of probity nearing the half-century mark. They met while he was handling the accounting for her father's meager estate. Florio was not prepared for her to drop into his office several months later.

"She hugged me. It really flattered me. I didn't realize this is just something they do," he recalled, "they" meaning young women today.

Jhana asked to have dinner with him that night and told him what was on her mind. It wasn't quite what he had expected from one devoted to "discovering what lies behind life's facade," but not to quibble—so he let her take him to bed.

"She helped me."

After all, he told himself, there had been only one brief transgression in twenty-three years of marriage. He began to feel good about providing stability for Jhana; she had just lost her father, she was going through a rough transition. She needed him almost any night of the week. (His wife monopolized the weekends with family trips to their country camp.) In time, Jhana decided she wanted a baby. She made it her business to rent a carriage house very near the Florios' home. John was by now up to his ears in a double life, loving it, fearing it a little, but too fascinated with himself to do anything but let it happen to him.

And so he became a second father. He felt bad about being away at the camp the weekend Jhana had the baby. Later, he tried to make up for it by giving in to her wish to show off the baby at some of their favorite places. One mild summer day they put the top down on his sporty white Austin-Healey and rode around town with Jhana's titian hair flying, big as life. Florio's wife heard about it, of course. At least she did not connect the baby.

"I just didn't look down the road far enough," Florio said in our first interview. He was still wistfully ambivalent.

"Do you think at some level you wanted to get caught?" I asked.

"Sure." He said he had considered leaving his wife but rejected the idea. She was too much a part of the veneer of respectability he needed to support his other activities, which in the context of a pin-striped accounting firm could be seen only as "flaky."

While Florio was caught up in his double life, someone else flew off with his world's record for circumnavigation. He stewed for a month and decided to recapture it. But this time his son refused to go. In fact, the young man's hero worship of his father had deteriorated to something closer to contempt—why, Florio did not really want to know.

At four in the morning, a few days into the year he would turn 50, John Florio took off solo, with nothing but a life raft, mosquito head net, a couple of gallons of water, and *The World According to Garp*. In no time he was piercing cloud banks like a charmed arrow, driven by ninety-mile-an-hour tail winds. Through the inky heavens he glided, wakeful and exhilarated, over continents and across the South Pacific on three legs and thirty minutes' sleep. Truly, here was a man on top of the world.

His wife and son, surrounded by fans, were waiting at the airport when his wheels touched down to establish a new world's record. It was a moment to savor—but suddenly he spotted Jhana in the crowd, holding the baby. A ripple of dread went through him as he saw the evil looks pass between the two women. Then the television cameras and the swell of celebrity distracted him. It was not until that night that his wife confronted him.

"He's *your* baby, isn't he?"

Florio went limp. He simply, passively, acknowledged it was true.

His wife grew livid. He let her believe what she seemed to want to believe: that he was waiting for Jhana to find someone her own age who would marry her and help raise the baby.

"I couldn't bring myself to say the truth," Florio told me. "I felt like I was in love for the first time, with Jhana, and I wanted to keep the arrangement going, but I also wanted to keep up the facade of home and a stable marriage with my wife, too."

With many a tearful scene, Florio managed to hold up both ends of the emotional seesaw until the child was nearly two.

When I visited John, Jhana, and the baby for a second interview, I was surprised to find he still occupied a passive center position between the two women. He was surprised himself that his wife still put up with him. But as long as neither woman risked putting the weight of demand on her side, he could maintain this delicate balance, keep up the appearance of stability, and be constantly buoyed by the evidence that two beautiful women wanted him badly enough to put up with each other's existence. Florio was becoming something of a scandal around town, but with that came another kind of trophy from his peers. Not many guys 49 years old . . .

So his secret fantasies of being daring, innovative, and different had all come true. The sticky side was evident only offstage—in the scene that morning, for instance, when John dropped by Jhana's house for a second breakfast on his way to work. The baby's moon face rolled up apprehensively as John began to make the motions of leaving. His pudgy arms began flying around—Jhana said this happened every time— until they were beating the air convulsively. The little body heaved at the restraints of his high chair.

"Does he think he's going with me?" Florio asked.

"Yes."

But Jhana knew better. John never touched the baby. He never talked to it. When he referred to the baby at all it was not by name. A wall of guilt kept him from acknowledging the baby to be real.

Months passed. Very early one morning I had a call from John Florio. He was in town on business but had not slept all night. His whole life was suddenly falling apart; he needed someone to talk to.

The man I saw that day was not a high flier; he was a wreck. About all he could do was stand on his head, but that was no good either, because every second of it reminded him that Jhana had taught him yogic postures. Jhana had called the night before to say a young man was moving in. "She was very nice about it. He's only thirty-five, single, much more into her basic philosophy—he's probably perfect for her." At that moment I thought John Florio would weep. His face crumpled. He told me his son had discovered a picture of his other family some time ago and would never get over the trauma. His wife, now bitter, wanted a divorce right away.

"I just couldn't bring myself to terminate this other life we'd had for twenty-three years," he half whispered, haltingly. "I think now I should have. I know I'd be a different person . . . would have changed . . ."

He agreed that he had behaved like a bystander at a collision waiting to happen. He said it was because he feared losing the stability of his marriage.

"Now that stability's gone," he whimpered. "Both of them are gone. . . ."

The Second Test

The descent of Florio highlighted another aspect of well-being that bore careful scrutiny as I got closer to the candidates. Did they show sensitivity to the needs of family, friends, and colleagues at *their* stage in life—even when those needs might not synchronize with their own? A person hell-bent on blazing the best trail to his or her own well-being, who fails to take into account the pain inflicted upon others, almost certainly will run into trouble farther down the road. Rare are the people so clearly superior that they compel selfless devotion from others. The rest of us are on dangerous ground once we see others as merely bit players in our own life story. Everyone else has a story too, and in it his or her needs are paramount.

Although he was willing to take risks of a physical nature, John Florio sped along encapsulated in his own Walter Mitty fantasy without taking responsibility for how the bodies would fall. Operating without a code of ethics for personal relationships, he lacked the will to follow through on the second family he had allowed to start. Even as some of his colleagues were envying him for being a swinger, Florio himself was riddled with insecurities about preserving his "respectable" image as a good gray public accountant with a proper marriage.

The daring pursuit of his own passage into middle age with no thought to the consequences of his acts for those closest to him resulted in harm to his wife, his mistress, his illegitimate son, and his first son. In the end, having lacked the courage to choose one path over the other, he lost both women. And having relied exclusively on his wife and mistress as his confidantes, he was left with no sources of friendship. The very crisis of respectability Florio so feared, he was left to face utterly alone.

His story crystallized another fundamental criterion for finding people who are building long-term life satisfaction:

He or she should have done a minimum of human damage and not have left behind a trail of injured family members, friends, or colleagues. (If divorced, the person should be

working toward an amicable network of past and present family attachments.)

"I'm Entitled" Candidates

As my search for candidates for well-being took me around the country, I began to pick up tracks on fresh paths cut through the first half of life by young men and women of the post-counterculture. They are still under 30. Given the uncertainty of youth, they could be counted on to have strong ideas about how to build a model life, uninhibited by some of the hang-ups of previous generations.

The objectives among sons of the most upwardly mobile fathers turned out to have changed the most acutely. In examining the results of the survey published in *Esquire* and following that up with personal interviews, I learned:

The new young men do not want to work hard.

They demand more time for "personal growth" than for any other purpose in life.

They dream of achieving the perfectly balanced life in which there is time for love and leisure and children and personal expression and playing lots of tennis.

Their new happiness formula is expressed in a startling shift of values. Highest on the list of personal qualities these young men consider important is "being loving." Dismissed to the bottom of the list of qualities they care to cultivate are "being ambitious" and "being able to lead effectively."

Not that their zeal for becoming the post-ideological man of many forms—this protean man—should interfere with the old business. A comfortable life they take as a given. The inalienable right of every American, they tend to believe, is to work less and be more self-fulfilled while enjoying a consistency of comfort that never dips below Holiday Inn level.

In the postwar era, of course, most Americans came to take for granted that their nation's resources were unlimited and their children's material progress was assured. We became inflated with expectations. Now we are in the midst of a national transition. Just before this transition began, our resources had become pinched and expensive, our productivity had slowed to near zero, our willingness to take entrepreneurial risks had become tied up by the multiplication of bureaucratic Lilliputians. Our nation had broken down into hundreds of bloated parts, each of which resisted shrinking its expectations, each member of which believed he or she was entitled.

We were stuck in the Age of Entitlement.

Consider David. Product of a suburban New York overachieving affluent background and four years out of college, David is a journalist for a major newspaper. Among the fifty bright young men under 30 I interviewed,* all of whom either had high scores on the Life History Questionnaire or were recommended by their peers, David was closest to fitting the model of modern laid-back well-being.

By the standards of the old success David had already reached the top—well, not the *top* top, but he had done as well as somebody his age could expect. And so what? Now it was time to do something else, switch channels, look for the new success, move to Martha's Vineyard. Blond with pinkish ears, his skin golden except for one or two recalcitrant adolescent pimples, David was a likable fellow. He had never been a hippie. On the contrary, he dressed like young gentry: creamy suspenders slung over a mocha shirt, silk tie, slender ankles each clasped in a seamless sheath of Italian leather and propped on the coffee table of his office lounge.

"Conflicted—is that the word?" he pondered, lying back on the velvet couch. He explained that his generation, adolescents during the 1960's when the flower children were extolling the virtues of personal anarchy, absorbed a whole new layer of values.

"It's as much a part of our consciousness as the overachieving drive of our fathers, built in from birth," he said. "We've got both. The two strains have run together and produced a lot of very conflicted people."

"And you?" I asked him.

"I ask myself, 'What am I doing this for? Why aren't I just living on Martha's Vineyard and working as little as possible?' The principal difference between my contemporaries and our parents' generation is they believed what they were doing was full of purpose and virtue," he observed. "I don't think we kid ourselves. We have more of a sense of how limited and almost purposeless what we are doing probably is."

* Half were from the *Esquire* survey.

What does a television baby do when he is bored? Switches channels, changes images, interrupts the trite linear flow. David talked about repairing to the Vineyard "to pursue a life-style that is separate but equally redeeming in its social purpose," as he put it. He hastened to add that he would not sit up there and drink all day.

"You've got to do something of redeeming value, I suppose," he said.

"What might that be?" I asked.

"Well, playing tennis."

He wasn't kidding.

When two thousand young men were asked to spell out their greatest concerns for the future, they expressed two major fears in equal weight—and absolute contradiction: fear of not having enough money, and fear of being locked in by the constant pursuit of money. To purchase freedom at the sacrifice of a comfortable life is virtually unthinkable. If only they could have their cake and eat it on Martha's Vineyard . . .

This is the modern inflation equation. One may be encouraged by the new emphasis on balance and sensitivity over blind ambition and role-boundedness, but many young Americans seem also to be hanging on to an old promise their society cannot now keep. They are presenting the final due bill from the Age of Entitlement—but that age is already entering the history books.

In the course of my quest for people who exemplify life satisfaction, I stopped by a Trappist monastery in Snowmass, near Aspen in Colorado. The Trappists for fifteen hundred years have been dedicated to a life of labor, prayer, and silence—the antithesis of "me decade" self-fulfillment. Most of the religious men at the monastery near Aspen had been through est training and other self-help therapies. It did not bother these trendy monks that I was not now, nor had I ever been, a Catholic, or even that I was divorced. But when I told them I was looking for people "who show virtuosity in handling change at the turning points of life," a stricken look crossed the faces I could see.

"*Virtuosity*," the abbot stammered, "is a very difficult word for us."

I explained that by virtuosity I meant creativity, in the sense of the creative task of existence.

The abbot was visibly relieved. "Oh," he said, "I was

afraid you meant goodness." In contemporary America, even monks have trouble with the concept of selflessness.

It was no problem to find candidates engrossed in a complete overhaul of their life-styles and psyches in order to achieve the goal of improved personal development. A few were so filled with themselves that it was a feat of endurance to sit through the interview. I listened to one man for four hours, a 57-year-old who was so excited about his postdivorce self he couldn't stop talking about it.

"Yes, I'm devoted to Number One. That's correct. I have nothing to lose at this stage, except maybe money. So I don't give a damn *what* I do as long as it pleases me or gives me strokes."

Paul can run marathons, stand on his head, curl his body like a cobra. He invited me to his yoga class to see. He has conceived of a mechanism that will prevent elevators from trapping thousands of helpless citizens during earthquakes, and he keeps telling the state safety commission about it (but in the end he'll probably have to hop from building to building to free them all himself). He admits to being something of a superman, but that's because he has discovered the secret of never growing old. It is: to live backward, to pursue every path back to the primal feelings and the guiltless stroking that Mommy gave Baby whenever Baby fell down and went boom. His age does not stop him from being playful. He can sit on the floor, and before you know it, he's talking out his problems with Bambi the deer. He can stand in front of a mirror and guide the imagery until his own idealized self steps out and he is able to caress his own cheek and hear from himself what a superb and sexy fellow he is, and—it's okay! The therapy guide says it's a way of "really validating" yourself.

He was a Dagwood sandwich of every processed shortcut to self-love that California's human potential packagers have concocted. The interview was a talkathon devoted to the cause of himself. He spoke in a drone, like a redded-out deejay on a radio left on in the next room. *C'mon, you people out there, we're up to 1,246 strokes for our boy and we're shooting for a goal of ten thousand, twenty thousand, a lifetime supply! And that means a lot of strokes, guys, because he's never going to die!*

The famous psychiatrist who had recommended Paul thought he was one of the most highly evolved adult males in America.

The Third Test

These encounters raised another area of subjective concern in making the final selection of models of adult development. Does the individual's development exclude the society's well-being? In these enlightened times, should the society be expected to enhance one's personal evolution but exempt the person from the old notion of leaving society a little better than he found it?

One of the items on the Life History Questionnaire specifically asked, "Are you devoted to some purpose or cause outside yourself and larger than yourself?"

The majority of respondents said no.

Further investigation indicated that not only had the sacred temple become "me," but that some people were proud to admit it. Respondents were asked in a follow-up question, "Would you *like* to be devoted to some cause outside yourself but feel your idealism is frustrated by society; you can't afford idealism yet; you are too busy?" Instead of copping one of the acceptable pleas, several people went out of their way to explain:

"My own cause is most important. . . ." "I can't find one to enhance my own state of being. . . ." "My cause is expanding myself. . . ." "I don't *feel* outside myself. . . ." "Belief in any cause demands a commitment of effort to the self. . . ." "*My* cause is consuming." The preferred explanation given by lowest-satisfaction people was that they had been frustrated by a cause. Translated, that probably means the cause was not solving problems for *them*.

Striking by contrast was the experience of their opposite numbers. Consistently, the highest-satisfaction people *do* have a cause or purpose beyond themselves.

Given the contemporary cultural tilt, "purpose" is the one element you or I might not have predicted as crucial to life satisfaction. Yet the results were dramatic: The greater the well-being person reflected, the more likely he or she was to have an outside purpose. The distinction is so considerable that it makes the current pop philosophy of looking out for Number One sound like a national suicide pact.

Having no purpose beyond finding his own ideal work-pleasure balance was the reason David's vision was off. Not that I don't suspect a lot of that laid-back business is talk, a stylistic second cousin to "cool" and just as susceptible to one good poke in the eye or two weeks without a paycheck. Nevertheless, there are much older men, like Paul, the seeker of "strokes," who are busy making of themselves as retreads what David yearns to be: a simple sensory-intake center. My research leads to me predict that people who take this path will build not toward well-being but toward emptiness.

These early research experiences alerted me to add a third criterion:

The person should not be involved exclusively in "doing my own thing" or solely in "caring for others," but should be seeking a balance between individual growth and a purpose outside himself or herself.

Now, lest you think I incorporated an empirical study of the Boy Scout code, be assured that purpose comes in many different forms, from shepherding a child through difficulties to becoming involved in a community project to acting as a guide or mentor to others. Going to the wall for a cause is only one form of purpose, and it is quite extreme in the demands it makes on other important aspects of life. There must be a balance. What all these variations on purpose have in common is the extending of devotion to something apart from oneself.

After many lengthy personal interviews had pointed up holes in my preliminary pencil-and-paper data, then, I was able to add three tests for identifying those who are likely to *sustain* well-being:

Has the person completed a passage and emerged stronger?

Has the person shown concern for his or her intimates?

Does the person have a commitment to a purpose beyond his or her own pleasure and advancement?

I felt ready to use these three criteria to search for people whose lives were complex models for lives truly worth living.

These are the people I would come to call pathfinders.

3.

HOW DOES ONE BECOME A PATHFINDER?

After the first year of research, I began to sense instinctively when I was in the presence of a pathfinder. Each radiated optimism, humor, energy, even across a telephone wire. It was as if they had enough batteries to generate the life force for two. One caught a spark and almost immediately knew—this is one!

People who demonstrated the characteristics of well-being on the questionnaire, however, did not always qualify as pathfinders. What were the distinctions?

People who enjoy high well-being may not have been tested yet. What they take as the natural condition could be perpetuated by fortunate circumstances or particularly supportive people around them, allowing them to remain, amiably, at a relatively simple stage of development.

Pathfinders have already met a test.

By successfully navigating through a passage or emerging victorious from a life accident, they know what strengths they can count on when under fire.

People of high well-being may have been born that way. If they have been blessed with all the advantages of mood (cheerful), social style (gregariousness), and personal tempo (high energy), they may have a natural insulation against many of the events that might upset a more anxious or naturally pessimistic person. But no one is immune consistently or in all cases.

Pathfinders are not born but made.

They demonstrate important qualities—quite apart from basic mood, social style, and energy level—that are shaped by life experience and enable them to attempt further development leaps or to withstand a life accident.

People who register in the upper brackets of well-being today may derive their sense of well-being from temporarily wearing a social or occupational uniform of high status. If they lose that status, they may or may not have the strength or self-esteem to maintain themselves through the next transition.

Pathfinders are just as concerned with their inner achievements as they are with their outer attainments.

How well they do in developing strength of character, deepening ties to their intimates, doing something worthwhile in their culture, and finding a disposition toward the Divine or toward death—these are achievements that can only be self-measured. No one else may notice.

We are all engaged in the process of finding paths through the maze of life. How does one become a pathfinder? When do people have the best chance of making such a breakthrough?

Repeated to a striking degree in the histories of the most-satisfied adults was a history of a troubled period during late childhood or adolescence, when many rated themselves as very unhappy. Some hit close to rock bottom. In interviews these people filled in stories of rejection or of emotional, if not actual, abandonment. A significant number were forced prematurely to take on adult roles to compensate for a weak, failed, alcoholic, sickly, or absent parent.

And yet, the incipient pathfinders pulled forward, sometimes inch by inch, sometimes by breaking away altogether. They did not fall back on the behavior of an earlier stage.

Their difficult periods rarely lasted longer than five years, but for children, who cannot control the good things that happen to them or do much to prevent the bad, it is hard to imagine that times ahead can be different.

"Why didn't somebody tell me it was going to get better?" asked a woman whose well-being fell precipitously between the ages of 16 and 21 but who broke through to the blue sky of optimum satisfaction by 30. Her mother had died when she was 14, thrusting her into the somber role of surrogate mother for her seven brothers and sisters. Their needs overshadowed her girlhood like a seven-year eclipse, until her father remarried. "At the time I felt, 'There is no way out of this.' Now I'm thirty-two and I realize that life is full of those valleys and mountains."

Anyone who overcomes a difficult childhood is likely to acquire that key characteristic—a concentration of optimism—and quite possibly an orientation toward the present and future rather than an emphasis on the past. Although an unhappy period during childhood is not something to be wished on anyone, those who struggle through it evidently do develop important personality skills and proceed into adulthood with a reference point in reality that may enhance their later happiness.

Even when pathfinders had an absent or severely flawed parent—and many of them did—somewhere they found a person who became a transformative figure for them. It might have been a strong brother or bold grandmother, a teacher or a coach. Instead of allowing a less than ideal set of parents to set them back permanently, the potential pathfinders usually gravitated toward another figure who did have purpose and direction and who offered something healing, cohering, possibly even inspiring. It is this capacity to draw from the environment what they need—even when it is not at all readily available—that recurs in the stories of pathfinders.

Fortunately, or unfortunately, most of us do not have excessively unhappy childhoods. Some people doubtless do become pathfinders through that route, but for the majority there are two other important catalysts:

We are most likely to become pathfinders during one of the predictable crises in our own adult lives, or as a result of an unexpected life accident that acts as a springboard for a developmental leap.

Finding One's Way Through a Passage

As we approach each new stage of adulthood, changes begin to register, deep down, in our gut-level perceptions of who we are in relation to others, how much time we have ahead or have already used up, what dreams we have left out, what portion of risk or security we now feel in our lives, and how alive or stagnant all this makes us feel. It was this kind of continuing and often predictable change in the inner realm that concerned me in *Passages*. People who are ready to engage a normal life passage are not afraid to confront some of the old questions from this new and unfamiliar perspective:

In what ways are my goals, values, and aspirations being invigorated or violated by my present life patterns?

How many parts of my personality can I bring into play, and what am I leaving out?

How do I feel about my way of living in the world, and why am I doing it all?

If we pause and examine the fit between our inner and outer realities in this way, we may be startled to discover that the identity that felt so right at a previous stage is now restrictive, or that we are ready to let go of it, to try to stretch.

As we move through the stages of adult development, we find ourselves alternating between periods of relative stability and the more disquieting transitions or passages. To review the major ones:

Pulling Up Roots (18–22)

The first passage to adult life is Pulling Up Roots, when we begin to separate our own individuality from our parents' and to leave the security of home. This most commonly happens between the ages of 18 and 22.

The Trying Twenties (23–27)

In the more stable stage that follows, we try on life's uniforms and possible partners, engrossed in the attempt to establish a provisional identity, busy cultivating the capacity for intimacy, and determined to prove ourselves unique.

Catch-30 (28–33)

Then comes the passage I have called Catch-30, which usually occurs sometime between 28 and 33, when the first sense of stagnation and discontent ordinarily sets in—pushing us to reappraise relationships, reassess our earlier decisions about career and family, and either reorder our commitments or intensify them. The early-thirties stage, from 33 to 35, I have termed Rooting and Extending.

Deadline Decade (35–45)

Sometime in the ten years after they reach 35, both men and women confront an often harrowing passage when mortality first becomes real and time suddenly begins to press in. As we examine the gaps between our youthful illusions and where we actually are, we may experience the same confusion and fears we thought we had left far behind in adolescence. Such inner turmoil has become well known as the midlife crisis and is often concentrated between the ages of 38 and 43. My studies indicated that for women the turmoil may begin as early as 35.

For those who face this major passage and make peace with themselves, the mid-forties can bring a strengthened sense of self and a refreshed sense of purpose, ushering in a stage of renewal in the fifties that can be the gateway to life's most confident and satisfying years.

In a later chapter, "A Certain Age," stages not included in *Passages* will be described. They are:

The Comeback Decade (46–55)

For both the men and the women in my studies, the years leading up to the half-century mark represent something of a danger zone. Their perspectives on the balance between work and play, on time spent and time left to live, on their physical self-image, on what they want from love and what they need for health—all are changing radically. There is also an important shift in their place among the generations as they move into the custodial role with their growing children, their aging parents, and their communities. As former roles and once-dominant concerns are outgrown, some of the earlier sources of pleasure become stale. Coping strategies that worked in prior stages no longer seem as effective. All these symptoms are natural to entry into the next major transition—the passage to middle age, which eventually affords new delights, concerns, and coping strategies that are exclusive to that stage of life in which many find renewal. The most commonly reported experiences were these:

People in this stage felt secure enough to stop running or struggling; found it easier to relax; were not so concerned about what others thought of them; were no longer so competitive or compulsive. They were also more acutely aware that time was beginning to run out; that their friends were beginning to look old; and they had begun actively to monitor their own health.

Men as they move into the fifties generally become more interested in and attuned to their affiliations with people and begin to find some aesthetic enjoyment in their environment—something they may seldom have noticed before. Women, by contrast, generally become more aggressive and managerial. The issue of accomplishment becomes paramount for women in the middle years. The degree to which they have prepared for this reality and are ready to expand or to pick up deferred interests in the world—occupational, social, or intellectual—becomes an important factor in determining how smoothly the transition through menopause is made.

Comebacks—second lives—are becoming so prevalent among today's young middle-aged that many of my biographees described moving, in this decade, from the depths of stagnation up to the peak of excitement about their existence.

The Freestyle Fifties

The major task of this period is to arrive at the place where one can say, "I am who I am."

For men and women who rally and come through the danger zone more certain of themselves, the fifties usher in the happiest period of their lives. They find greater tolerance and acceptance with their love partners than ever before and take the greatest delight in their companionship. The women are freer in expressing their true emotions and can stop trying so hard to please. Men can express the need to be caressed and can admit what it is they really think, emerging from behind the dozens of small hypocrisies they must perform every day.

A signal pleasure of this period is giving permission to oneself to do not only the things one should, but also the things one likes to do.

The Selective Sixties

It is often assumed that old people are pretty much all alike. On the contrary, older people's personalities are far more distinctive than they were in their twenties or thirties.

People in their sixties who maintain excitement about life commonly feel a detachment from many concerns that used to matter a great deal to them. At the same time they feel an even greater intensity about those things they do consider important. Becoming selective in the sixties means separating out what is truly important about one's life, one's loves, one's work, one's friends—knowing what matters!

Aging is a commutable sentence, yet we are our own harshest judges. Although there is no fixed number at which we stop being middle-aged and become "old," people generally anticipate that old age will arrive sooner rather than later; only at the last moment do they give themselves an extension. It is not uncommon to cut off some activity in the fifties by arbitrarily deciding that one is "too old for that now," only to turn around and resume it in the sixties. An important task of the sixties is to decide: *How long do I want to live?*

The Thoughtful Seventies

The healthiest and happiest septuagenarians, in my studies and others, have two overriding similarities. First, they have made themselves independent; that is, they have prepared themselves in advance to fill their days with varied and engaging activities that do not depend on anyone else but that do involve them with their communities. Second, they still plan ahead—for five years at least. Those who are least content in their seventies have no involvement in their communities or in work and have gradually disengaged from people, stopped visiting friends, and withdrawn to small quarters from which they view the world as threatening.

The seventies are the ideal stage for exploring the life of the mind, for studying history, religion, philosophy, and for thinking about the meaning of one's existence. Older people are uniquely strong in their ability to think in abstract concepts. Their visual imagination often becomes freer as well.

The Proud-to-Be Eighties

The pride of survivorship is a source of pleasure, together with a self-perpetuating battlefield grit. The proud-to-be-eighty-year-old has seen many falls, but like a tough old general, he or she is still planning ahead for life and is more wily and efficient than ever in devising stratagems for eluding death.

Detached contemplation is a natural and satisfying occupation at this stage. The task is to resist a retreat into self-absorption. The best defense is to continue to risk by remaining ready to experiment and eager to learn something new.

Another important task of the eighties and thereafter is to strike the right balance between giving and taking aid and comfort. The older person who still gives thought and service to weaker ones naturally feels better about himself or herself than the person who is comfortable only in the role of invalid. But older people who have become handicapped make a new transition—and gain a new victory over the ego—when they can begin to permit others also to feel good, by allowing *some* things to be done for them.

The approach of the final passage transforms the grains in the hourglass to the dust of gold and cinnamon—precious enough to be spent well and to be savored in the smallest ways.

Pulling Through a Life Accident

There is another kind of life crisis that dramatically influences the kind of people we turn out to be. What I have called a *life accident*, unlike a normal passage, by definition cannot be predicted or prevented. The unexpected death of a person we love, our own physical setbacks, abandonment by a mate, being fired, suffering severe financial reverses—all such events demand we do the work of change and acceptance with no preparation at all.

Most people do not negotiate either predictable passages, especially the later ones, or life accidents successfully. Out of a failure of nerve or imagination, people get stuck in ruts and traps and often resist making the effort to extricate themselves. Since change so commonly appears harder or more frightening than staying put, people tend to resign themselves, to blame their rut on someone else, or to find a comfortable rationalization.

Becoming a pathfinder requires small acts of courage. But that does not reduce pathfinding to being receptive to the new; we all know champions of the latest fashionable idea who are consistent only in their shallowness. No, one has the best chance to become a pathfinder as the result of doing the sometimes tedious, sometimes terrifying work of making a normal life passage and fully completing it. Or by refusing to go under in the onslaught of a life accident and emerging victorious, finding in the process a catalyst to growth.

People with the best chance of sustaining well-being, then, are those willing to let go of it.

Pathfinders are not paragons, however. The concept of "pathfinder" is not intended to describe a singular and superior state of being to which the rest of us would hopelessly aspire. Rather, the concern of this book is with the *process* of pathfinding. For illustration, we will look into selected lives and into particular times in those lives when the person actively and successfully found a path through a normal life passage or through an unexpected life accident.

Some of the people whose lives are described felt held back or washed up for years at a time. The ways in which these people exhibited courage and imagination should suggest similar important victories of your own—a moment of risk in childhood, or of looking back after a failure and saying, "That wasn't so bad."

This is not a book about extraordinary or glamorous people or herculean efforts. There are unknown people and famous people, there are people who have made a lot of money and little money; but the struggles they have faced are those common to all of us.

How, then, do people grow into pathfinders? What can they teach us about the process of becoming pathfinders ourselves? What qualities do such people have in common? The most important fact about all the qualities of personality that fortify pathfinders in seeking and risking uncommon solutions to common life crises is this: none is innate. We can strengthen each of these qualities by our own efforts.

Insofar as we are prepared to accept our humanness and

struggle with it, we are *all* incipient pathfinders. That does not mean being perfect or singularly free from sadness. Distinctive as we are one from another, the sounding brass echoes those common notes described by British author H. G. Wells:

> Every one of these hundreds of millions of human beings is in some form seeking happiness. . . . Not one is altogether noble nor altogether trustworthy nor altogether consistent; and not one is altogether vile. Not a single one but has at some time wept.

4.

ANATOMY
OF A
PASSAGE

I learned at least this by my experiments. That if one advances confidently in the direction of his dreams, and endeavors to live the life which he has imagined, he will meet with a success unexpected in common hours. He will put something behind and will pass an invisible boundary.
—HENRY DAVID THOREAU

Pathfinders are raised with a set of expectations and social instructions common to their generation, but somewhere along the line, like almost everyone else, most of them run up against changes in the social contract that nobody warned them were coming.

Who would have thought in 1970 to tell a ten-year-old boy that by the time he finished college, most bets would be off on the traditional American expectation that his standard of living would surpass his father's? Did anyone warn the women who are today over 40 that for most of them being Mom would not be enough for a lifetime? What happens when people invest a good part of their lives in a contract that society rewrites?

Consider many men who were young during the 1930's and early 1940's. They carried the Great Depression in them like vestigial nerve damage; it predisposed them to be dependent on institutions. What it meant to be a man also was narrowly defined; it had nothing to do with the "personal growth" and "balanced life" that excite young men today. Being a man meant doing your duty to your country, getting a good job, marrying young, and becoming a father; it meant learning to keep up your guard with all the other men in the lifelong competition to win. Most of those men set their course by the assumptions of their generation: Go to work for a big corporation; if a man is loyal, works hard, and performs well, he will be rewarded and live comfortably ever after.

But for many of those men, there was the devastating shock of *not* being justly rewarded.

Bill Johnston's* middle years contained elements that touch almost every man at that stage. The cost of efforts to live up to the "strong" male image—grounded as it is in a young man's physical powers and aggressive drives—is too great to sustain forever. Sooner or later, psychologically or physically, something blows. Many men who refuse to confront this issue exhibit pathological reactions that are now commonly recognized. They deny their age and stage, or they attempt to escape through sexual delinquencies that eventually may make life more restricting, or they coexist with chronic anxiety, depression, or diffuse rage.[1]

But Bill Johnston's middle years also contained elements that touch everyone, of every age. He can teach us as much as any person can about the change that is inherent in every act of pathfinding. What follows is a step-by-step description of how one man broke out of his dependencies and turned a too-common life script around before he died from it.

An Ordinary Man

The Idaho sky was a shawl of uncombed wool stretched loosely across the frozen land. Glad of the alcohol smoking in his bloodstream, Bill Johnston stood, sunk to the hips, in a remarkable archaeology of snow. Ninety-two inches of it had effectively buried the city of Boise over the past two months and had nailed down the human prospect between a sunless sky and a frozen slab of earth.

Inside the house, his wife would be expertly wooing the

* A pseudonym.

children to their math books. Whatever else existed beyond that and a lost circular driveway demanding to be shoveled did not immediately spring to mind.

*Might as well be a gravedigger in Buffalo.**

He laughed, but there was little mirth in his memories of a snowbound boyhood in abominable north Buffalo. The country was shuddering through the Depression. A winter's day like this would have found his father inside, gathering the dust of shame for lack of work, while young Bill would have been outside helping his mother hang up other people's half-frozen sheets. How he hated Buffalo, hated his father for allowing his mother's fingers to bleed until they left delicate red flowerets in the snow.

He broke his mother's heart himself, leaving as he did . . . *no one else left*. He could hear the family chorus still. But he didn't belong there! Truly Buffalo was a cryonic city—families remained for generations preserved under ice; but he—how to say it?—he always knew he had something special. If he just kept moving along, he would find out what it was. . . .

"Hello, Mom, I've joined the Navy."

"Oh, Billie, ye've ruined yer loife."

A brogue like that stays with you. Yet Bill could not bring back his father's voice, once full of lower-class Limey bluff. It was as if his father had stopped in mid-sentence at the start of the Depression and had never gotten around to finishing.

And so Billie ran.

A wicked winter's day, just like this one it was, when Bill Johnston, high-school dropout, copy boy for the *Courier-Express*, frequenter of the Palace Burlesque, desperate to make a change in his life, decided to skip town on a troop train to Chicago. Eighteen years old.

"Imagine that!" he blurted to himself, hip-deep in the snow packed around the accumulated possessions of his 38 years. "That was half my life ago."

Rose, oh, please, God, let me catch one more show of Rose LaRose.

Sneaking into the balcony of the Palace where Rose

* Thoughts expressed as interior monologues in the biographies in this book were those the respondents told me they had thought.

played, when there was nobody there to see a good Christian boy kneading his fantasies into lilies in the gloom, had always ranked high among the experiences of his boyhood. Rose was not only beautiful; Rose was sacred. The last glimpse he had prayed for was on the day he ran away to the Navy. He staggered in, scared and beery, hoping to have in the presence of Rose a holy send-off. Rose was not there.

In the Philippines he played war games with the world's biggest slingshots, catching and catapulting fighter planes off the deck of a carrier until it was time to go home. But on his way home he was told to sail back; there was a real war game for him this time, called the Inchon invasion.

After a year the Navy sent Johnston stateside to an old island base where World War II lingered in the jukebox of a big USO club. He was happy. One night he saw a vision in a white buttoned-up blouse and ballerina skirt. Pinned beneath her snowy neck and auburn hair was a tiny red flower. He was transported. She assumed he was a nice middle-class boy with prospects, and he let her. Haunted by this young woman who was all the things he was not—she had been to college, she belonged to a sorority, she personified beauty and purity but also intelligence and position—he told his mates he had met the woman he would marry.

"Wait for me, I'll catch up!" he wrote from Hawaii. April waited and became Mrs. Johnston early in 1952. Johnston promised the Navy he would start college and finish high school simultaneously, if only they would let him out early. They gave him a month's break.

"Typical of me," he thought aloud. "Always in a hurry."

He began to shovel furiously. Stabbing at the ice and spearing loaves of the snow beneath, he hurled them with his whole hulk to one side. The task of freeing at least one lane assumed great importance in his mind. He worked hard, trying to catch up. By and by, stopping to get his breath, he saw that the palisades of snow behind him had toppled into the clear lane and put him right back where he started.

A cruel question casually tripped across his mind: *Why did you do all this to yourself?* Odd, it was the first time in 38 years the question had come up. *Why did you get married so young and have three children and take on all these responsibilities?*

●　　●　　●

Their first son had been premature, and so had Bill's first job. Even before finishing college he started selling for the company. Immediately after graduation he left his wife with two tiny babies and marched off to company headquarters for a summer of management training. It wasn't all that different from being in the military. Right on schedule, at 29, he was promoted to assistant supervisor and sent to Portland, Oregon. He found it too elitist a town for his taste. But at 30 he felt a surge of impatience. On a fishing trip in the wilderness of Montana the pioneer spirit came upon him. In such an outpost, he discovered, a young man could jump the line.

"We're moving to Montana," Bill Johnston announced to his wife. "I'll be made district manager there."

That was the way it was done. It never occurred to him to question the order of priorities: the company and his advancement within it came first—above family, above friendships, above himself.

At 35 he was offered the position of general agent in the Boise office.

"We're moving to Idaho."

Twelve years with the same company and he was close to having his own agency—close, but no cigar. No big city yet. Other agents out of his company graduating class were beginning to get major cities while he was still getting the cow towns. Why? Most of them came from middle-class backgrounds, he told himself, but he was too much an American to be consoled by a class analysis.

Suppose, it suddenly occurred to him in that snow-buried driveway, *suppose that you gave them all your guts and loyalty, and up the road, when it was too late to turn back, they didn't pay off?* A wrinkle of dread began to form in Bill Johnston's soul.

"Okay." He shrugged it off. "That's the way life is."

He went inside and emptied the brandy bottle, and the next day he came home in time for several drinks and wine with dinner, and before he knew what he was doing to himself, Bill Johnston was inside a mild boozy haze that for the next seven years would pass for his normal condition. It insulated him from something he did not want to understand.

Between his 38th and 43rd years, Bill avoided depressing questions by taking up tennis and skiing. He did not learn to play; rather, he *became* a tennis player and he *became* a skier, thereby ascending to social rungs known when he was a boy only to the rich.

Boise turned out to be every bit as inbred and elitist as Portland had been. Both he and April were shaky at the start; class had been irrelevant in Montana. They had forgotten there were people who made whole careers out of maintaining marginal social differentiations. His wife became active in the Junior League. He joined all the better clubs and made political conquests of them. By the time he was 40, he and April had been accepted in every role that at that stage mattered to Bill Johnston. He saw himself as singularly fortunate in having such a beautiful and agreeable wife and children who gave him no trouble (except for the son who refused to go to Vietnam). About his own person there remained a ginger-haired agility and in his eyes no conceit. He wanted, above all, to please.

When the company began to get into funny business, for instance, it did not occur to him to criticize. There must be something wrong with him. After all, insurance companies industry-wide were healthy with 8 and 10 percent earnings at the close of the 1960's. The beautiful pension plans his company wrote, its conservative investments, disappeared almost overnight. No explanation. Word simply went out to every agent: "Move the new product"—a mutual fund. Clients were to be hustled into doubling their front-end load and paying a new commission to take back their old policy, prettily trimmed with this additional speculative investment.

"It will be exciting," Bill Johnston told himself. But as the company grew, a big central bureaucracy usurped freedom from the agents in the field. There were more rules, reports, time studies. Bill's annual physical showed that his blood pressure was going up.

All over the land the Vietnam War was amputating sons from their fathers. The Johnstons were no exception. Bill's son turned 18 in 1969 and registered as a conscientious objector. The same week, his wife made Bill the victim of a 40th-birthday party.

Surprise!

Two of the guests got drunk and fell to haranguing a West Point graduate about the war until matters deteriorated into a contest between Bill and his son.

At one level they were fighting about the father's old class fears: *What will the neighbors think about a boy who goes C.O.?*

There are times to take a stand, his son replied with infuriating restraint.

"But I have the letter from the doctor!" the father countered. "You're 4-F. You can't see."

That wasn't the point, his son said. He wanted people to know how he felt.

Mrs. Johnston stepped into stereotype as the mother-protector. If Bill's usual role with the children was that of drill instructor, this battle on his 40th birthday drove him into the posture of a Patton.

"Goddamn it, life's tough out there. If I did it, why can't he?"

But at a deeper level Bill felt a crazy surge of jealousy. He envied his son the freedom to break out, just when he himself was beginning to feel the trap closing . . . *Run, son, run for your dad.*

April tried to calm him down with the old mouth-to-ego resuscitation. Life wasn't so tough anymore. Didn't they have a beautiful house in the nicest part of town? And he was making a nice salary—

"No man needs only a decent salary," Bill Johnston blurted out. "A man has to be going for something." For him, the dream all along had been to become an agency manager—one of ninety-two men in the field who ran their own agencies.

Hadn't they given him his own agency this very year? April coddled him. Yes, but he was still stuck in a second-class agency in a cow town, he brooded.

"Every time I make a touchdown," Bill Johnston said softly, "they move the goalposts."

His son suggested he try meditation. The young man had picked that up from counseling sessions on what to do about the war, he said, and found it helpful.

"Vietnam," exploded the father, "is not going to be won by meditation!"

What he was really talking about was the battle for self-respect in his own life. April brought him a sedating brandy, and he slid on its amber chute away from things he was not ready to face: that maybe he wasn't as good as he had thought he was, that he was not moving fast enough, that his health was beginning to go.

Once the emotionalism of the birthday party faded away, a comfortable smugness settled in, and Bill and April Johnston, doing by now all the things they thought middle-class people should do, congratulated themselves on being the perfect family.

No Place to Run

Two more years went away. Before dawn one morning Bill awoke with the sensation that a chain saw was hacking through branches of his brain. Secretly he had taken up meditation, but his hangover had not worn off and the phone was already ringing. A call from the new district vice-president mousetrapped him.

"Hey, Willie, I got something for ya. You got any guts?"

"What do you mean?"

"How'd you like to take over Portland? The manager's been fired."

Number one in a first-class town. Big Whopper where he had begun his climb to the top. An office spread over the bay. Another chance to run away. It would cure his malaise for certain. The axing of his predecessor gave Johnston some pause, but he put that down to the flashy new hiring policy the company had introduced. "We're going to throw mud on the wall" was how the v.p.'s in the home office put it, "and just keep what hangs on." Johnston did not ask too many questions.

The measure of his desperation registered in the amount of consideration he gave his wife on this move. April had grown and thrived in Boise like a runner plant in a garden.

"I'm taking over the Portland agency."

Being a good corporate wife, April took her sentence silently. She withdrew into a dark and cool place inside herself, like the bulbs one stores in the cellar never knowing if they will winter over.

The minute they got to Portland, Bill Johnston knew he had made a mistake. The company had cut the pie in half—two general agents in Portland, not one. He had half the authority he had expected. Later the company reneged on a clause in his contract under which Johnston was entitled to an additional $11,000. No explanation. A man hired for the purpose simply called one day and announced, "Bill, that expense rider we had in your contract—we're dropping those."

Johnston phoned the home office and asked to talk to an old friend who was now a vice-president.

"Hey, old buddy," Bill said, "the company's going to hell. What's happening?"

"Well, Bill, that's the way it is." Old Buddy had obviously gotten the new religion fast. "We've taken the same stand with others, and no problems. It's a buy-it-or-get-out proposition."

Johnston flew east just for the pleasure of throwing his resignation down on Old Buddy's desk. When he got there, his friend had the soft soap ready. "We want to keep you, Bill. Let's see if we can't work this thing out."

Bill found himself opening up in a way he had not planned. "I don't know how else I can tell you this, but it's the way I've always felt. I've always believed I had something special. I didn't know what it was, how I would find it. I thought if I just kept moving along, you know, I would find out what it was. . . ."

"Mnnn, yes. Well, your own agency, in Portland, after all . . ." They pumped him up and sent him back to Portland taut as a helium balloon. He had considerable drinking to do to mute his instincts and dim the fact that he was approaching an age—43 now—when the younger guys coming up, those greedy little snots he was training himself, were being groomed to knock him over.

Four months after the contract humiliation, Johnston's blood pressure climbed out of sight: 160 over 115. Depression, clinical.

At some level he knew already that he was at the end of the road emotionally. He saw a new G.P. who said, "If you keep this up, you'll have a heart attack by the time you're fifty-five."

Right on the old statistical schedule!

The collapse of all desire was stunning. The choicest part of life was reduced overnight to a chore, within a fortnight to an improbability.

He went back to the doctor to ask if the hypertension medication could be causing his, uh, sexual embarrassments.

No, it definitely wasn't the medication, the medical establishment defended itself, leaving Johnston to draw the conclusion that on twenty-five years of rambunctious sex life the clock had suddenly, capriciously, stopped.

A year after the return to Portland, Bill sat alone in his lavish office, the very reproduction of a 19th-century gentleman capitalist's. He said to himself, "This is what you always wanted, Bill. Are you happy with your success?"

I'm so goddamned unhappy I don't know what to do.

He turned to meditation in earnest. Stress began to seep out of scalding places inside, and feelings floated up to the surface that he had never allowed himself before. "It occurred to me finally to ask myself, 'What am I running away from? What am I running to?'" He could not decide which. He had an answer for neither.

Examination of the most fruitful passages made by people who emerge as pathfinders indicates that the process consists of four important phases. Some of what takes place is conscious, some is unconscious, although much should be recognizable just below the level of our articulated awareness. Seldom does anyone proceed in a neat progression through the phases. People usually weave back and forth, or begin in the middle, or skip a phase and perhaps return to it many years later, but it is necessary to *complete* all four legs of a passage. Only then is it worth the trip. Laying it all out, through Bill Johnston's story, should provide a map of one person's successful navigation.

Anticipation Phase

The first stage, *anticipation*, involves preparing to meet transitions rather than becoming lost in day-to-day details or vague procrastinations. People who are unusually well prepared as they approach a normal life passage are those who have collected the skills, maintained the confidence, and filed away the images—including images of themselves as well as positive models among others—for enthusiastically pursuing what is possible at the next stage.

Anticipation shapes one's vision of the future. Some of the most-satisfied adults in my studies have trained themselves to anticipate as far as ten years ahead, and that gives their lives direction. But their view is not so rigid that if things do not work out as hoped they are devastated or embittered.

Yet many people who became pathfinders plodded through most of the first half of their lives just trying to keep up, never mind anticipating the next stage and preparing for it. Such a man was Bill Johnston. He went through 40 years seldom enjoying anything like well-being and not quite even knowing what he was missing.

For Bill, the anticipation phase had been a brief and accidental by-product of the meditation he used to reduce his blood pressure. It had started a year before his decision to leave the company. But it wasn't until he sat in his new office and confronted himself with "What am I running away from? What am I running to?" that he realized he had been operating not from the wrong answers but with the wrong questions. At that point, having completed the Anticipation Phase, he was free to move on.

"The friends I know who have been through a divorce have described the same state of mind," he said, "the sense of failure, of guilt, the fear of the future, of being alone—it was all there. I was leaving the big fraternity."

Developmentally, Bill was entering the *separation phase* of a major passage. Both he and the company had necessary tortures to perform.

The stately Banff Springs Hotel had been the scene of some of the happiest times; the forced hilarity of a company holiday always brought together old friends and their wives, and everyone drank hard and embellished stories that kept the meaning of fraternity alive. There would be something final, ceremonial, about divorcing himself from the corporation in that setting.

For the first leg of the trip Bill kept to himself in his sleeping compartment, having brought his own Scotch and cigars. The train sped along the Fraser River Valley, and as it climbed into the uncivilized grasses, higher and higher through the detached and solitary trees, a kind of reckless euphoria overtook him.

In the dining car the ostracism was as brittle as the shell of an egg. The word was already out: *Bill Johnston is a gentleman and a nice guy, but he is no longer a team player.*

"Where's April?" one or two old friends dutifully asked.

He made up a lie. The truth was, April feared that Bill was going to his own funeral. She had tried to talk him out of it, but somehow he couldn't bring her into the whole picture. He felt ashamed, a failure. He knew something was wrong with the corporation, but that was upstaged by his own self-doubts: *Where did I go wrong?* He found himself fantasizing about stewardesses with water beds. But he had forgotten how to play. His children had beards.

Bill ate without moving his eyes from the train window. Leering behind him, he knew, was the face of total defeat. From the soaring climb through the mountains the terrain fell to flat, and it grew dark. Back in his compartment he smoked and drank until the now-sluggish hilarity outside had been soaked up nearly to inaudibility. His ears ballooned as if filled with cotton wadding. He tingled everywhere. His blood pressure would not stop climbing. He felt as though someone had plugged an electric cord into his spine.

In the soiled washroom mirror he caught a glimpse of himself. He looked sicker than he felt—looked, in fact, like a half-asleep bartender who had just been shot in the gut with a .45.

They arrived at seven on a Sunday morning in sunshine inappropriately dazzling. The hotel lobby swirled with faces of men he had known from other places and loved and worked and laughed with; many still smiled. Soon they would smell his blood in the waters.

Bill Johnston waited in the lobby for the lead shark from the home office, a man wholly unencumbered by empathy. Flipping idly through old newspapers while he waited, Bill kept turning to the obituaries. One caught his eye: Rose LaRose.

He began to cry. The sound of her music rang a requiem in his ears. In a pool full of sharks, some looking his way even now for the right moment to dart in and lop off one of his fins, here he was bawling over a burlesque stripper who had kicked off.

Oh, Rose, you were sacred!

Someone was shaking his arm. It was Old Buddy from the East, the one man to whom Johnston had confided that he was quitting.

"Lie to them," Old Buddy whispered.

Startled, Bill answered too loudly. "That's what triggered this whole thought process. They lied to me."

"Give yourself six to eight months to find something else first. Then tell them."

"I would be running away again," Bill insisted. "If you're honest with people, they'll accept you."

"They'll fire your ass on the spot."

Bill knew that what he was about to do did not have the practical beauty of, say, a rigged balance sheet. But there was something less rational and more important here, a crazy bid to retrieve a clear idea of himself.

When the lead shark did appear, he tried to brush Bill Johnston off. "I've got to talk to you," Bill pressed. "Right now." They stepped out onto a veranda and ordered coffee.

"I want to do this the right way," Bill said. "My health is suffering and I've got to leave. I'd like to stay and take care of the agency until the end of the year. Then I will quietly resign next January."

Bill went home a "terminated employee" but feeling energetic and eager enough to put out the scent of availability. He let his secretary at the agency announce the out-of-town calls: they were obviously job offers. He needed that indiscriminate flattery, just as one rawly divorced seeks it by dating or sleeping around. An old-style San Francisco agency was really hot for his body, he joked. One day his secretary announced that San Francisco was calling again.

"William, I've got bad news for you." It was his latest corporate suitor. "We really wanted to hire you, but I'm afraid you can't pass the physical."

With impressive fraud Bill finished the conversation, phoned his doctor to say he was coming over, fought the dizziness and pounding while he found his car, and sped off.

How nice it would be, he thought while crossing a bridge, to drive north into the woods and get out and run, run so hard his blood would leap, burst through its walls, flood free and warm. . . . *Please, God, let me have a heart attack, right here, right now*, he thought, *then all my problems would be solved*.

He fantasized about lying on the hospital bed, the grainy, impersonal sheets, the whispers and tears. His wife, who had lost interest, would know that notice should have been taken. His sons would appreciate. His old corporate fraternity brothers would stop by with shame in their faces and mumble, "What you did, Bill, took a lot of balls." It would be a corporation man's purple heart.

"Damn," the doctor said when Bill did arrive, "I'm gonna put you right in the hospital. Your head's about to blow off."

"No."

The doctor addressed him as if talking to one mentally disturbed. "Now, Mr. Johnston, your blood pressure is one-eighty over one-twenty—"

"No way."

He was up against his own death by dull formula, and a defiance sprang up inside him. He snatched his body from the edge and propelled it toward the door, calling back to the doctor what seemed at that moment the overpoweringly clear and present danger:

"I haven't been laid yet by a Jewish Scorpio stewardess with a water bed!"

Someone suggested a well-known cardiologist. He took Johnston's pressure and looked at the pills he had been taking since the last episode. "You're light-headed, depressed, you've got a headache half the time, and you can't get a hard-on, right?"

"Then it *is* the medication!"

"Hell," the cardiologist said, "I'd rather live with high blood pressure. Or work on bringing it down."

Johnston rushed home to tell April they were going to take a week's holiday. They had almost taken his sex; he was not going to let them take anything else.

The couple scarcely left their hotel. It was after that holiday that Bill Johnston began to engage as a full-time player in this game they called his life.

His three Scotches before dinner began to taste like gasoline. He switched to bourbon, vodka, registered nothing but gasoline. Could he be turning into a gasoholic? In meditation it became clear what his body was telling him. He did not want to drink anymore.

His three-month holdover with the company would run out in January. He had lunch in November with a very old friend to talk about what the hell he was going to do. He was 44 now, and everyone had told him that if you don't get out by 45 . . .

"My whole life was set up to make me dependent on institutions." The words spilled out. "I went from dependence on the institutionalized church to the Navy to the institution of marriage to dependence on the corporation and then on doctors. Now all the support lines are gone. I'm going to be out there all by myself. It's crazy, but I feel a thrill."

His old friend was a strict religionist; he implied the real trouble was that Bill did not go to church enough.

At three that morning Bill bolted upright in bed.

"My God, go into sales!" was his answer. "That's where I can run my own life." He had sold for the company at the very beginning and been good at it. It was so obvious, so right.

Separation and Incubation Phase

Change always involves loss. Part of the experience of the separation phase is, of necessity, some degree of anxiety and depression. Mixed with frightening and mournful moods is often an innocent, springing joy: a lightening, a washing away of the caked mud of compromise. The alternation of those moods is what gives this phase its bittersweet quality, like the swing of moods in early adolescence.

In this acute and often painful phase, we separate from a former stage and give up aspects of an old self so that an expanded personal identity can take its place. Outgrown social roles and "shoulds," along with old fears and handicapping defenses, need to be reexamined in the light of new possibilities for strengthening and integrating our personalities in the stage to come.

When the separation and incubation processes begin, we are likely to find that we have new perspectives on the time already lived and the time left to live, on our own position in relation to others, and on the degree of aliveness or stagnation we feel. To accomplish the separation requires letting go of some former supports and earlier certainties. That may introduce a moment of panic, at which point we all want to retreat to the known. The time has come for releasing our conscious hold on the problem.

A period of incubation is critical. If we turn our attention from the immediate and obvious problem and allow time for reverie—that state of relaxed awareness that some people find in walking on the beach or driving in the country, that others find in tinkering with their cars or meditating or playing a musical instrument—images can float up from the unconscious, uncensored by the ego. We may see ourselves freshly as we have behaved in previous stages. It is possible to link repressed aspects of ourselves into new combinations appropriate to the future. These are the raw materials from which creative solutions to commonplace transitions are made.

A classical description of the separation phase appeared on one Life History Questionnaire: "While making up my mind, I was depressed. During the transition, I was anxious. After it—exhilarated!"

Bill Johnston tried to describe the contradictory feelings to his old friend before he severed his ties. As with most divorces, it took him fully two years to get through the separation phase. Going in, he had felt as if he were taking a train to nowhere.

The individual who is separating from aspects of an old self must endure some loss of belonging while a new and different path is being explored. It may be temporary and end with rapprochement. But a pathfinder must also be prepared to face ostracism from his or her reference group. The whole notion of friendship may be redefined by the experience, as later happened to Bill Johnston. By the time those who are most sorely threatened by the pathfinder's changed course are ready to accept it, the pathfinder may no longer care about their friendship.

Bill sought advice from other men who had left sales management and gone into sales. Everyone thought he would make it. Much as he was tempted to start his own insurance business, Bill knew by now to heed those inner cues commonly called "instincts" or "hunches" or "intuition." He knew he was not yet emotionally ready to break out on his own.

"It's like knowing the right time to have a baby," he explained to April.

So he cast his lot with three proved million-dollar producers. They invited him to join in forming a small firm as insurance consultants for an investment company. He was flattered. The hell with it. He had $30,000 in savings; the family could live on that while the business got off the ground.

Practical matters: one son in college, two more children at home. Even if three out of three decided on a full four years of school, Johnston could come up with the tuition if they all went to the state university, as he had. Having pretty much followed a pay-as-you-go philosophy, there was no rope of debts or heavy mortgage around his neck. He and April were pleasantly surprised to find that dropping from a salary of $31,000 in 1973 to $15,000 in his first year out meant giving up little that really mattered.

There was only one trauma. For as long as he could remember the company car came as automatically as flowers in the spring. He had never had to buy an automobile for himself. Driving to the grocery store on breaking-out day, Johnston was stricken with the thought, *Jesus, how the hell am I ever going to afford a car of my own?*

April, after twenty-five years in the phantom job of corporate wife, was "fired" not with a letter but as if she had never existed. Frustration is the mother of risk. It pushed April back to school.

The head man among Bill's new partners conducted prayers at the end of every sales meeting. Bill went out all fired up and peddled $2 million worth of life insurance. At the end of his first year he had sold 60 percent of the goods. The partners gave him 25 percent of the profits. You might call his partners the Nickel-and-Dime Brothers—everyone runs into them somewhere along the line. It subsequently became evident that their praying leader was a crook.

Later, looking through the retrospectoscope, Bill would insist that jumping first from the giant corporation into the small firm, even if it taught him only how *not* to run a business, was the right move, a necessary way station. He still felt the tingling. The blood pressure problems were diminished but undefeated. At the damnedest times a melancholy would come over him as he thought of the big fraternity.

"The world hasn't come to an end," April would say. "Feeling sorry for yourself isn't going to help you. We're gonna make it." The one thing she refused to indulge was his self-pity. He learned to shut himself in his office before he began to cry. He felt, as he describes it, as if he were carrying a heavy wet ball around in the well of his abdomen. He recognized that much of it was a sludge of "shoulds" he had accumulated over the first half of his life.

"Okay," he said to himself one afternoon. "For forty-five years I've had all this stuff pumped into me. I'm going to spend all the years I have left cleaning it out."

He declared his body a reclamation project.

Over that year and a half in the misfit union with the consultants, he cut off all the medicines and chemicals that had been going into his body. He started running. The intrusion of oxygen on the smoke-filled cave of his lungs took the fun out of cigars. He began phasing them out too. He even went through est. He quickly cut that dependency and decided the manipulation of young people was "reprehensible," but he had picked up insights on his trip.

Expansion Phase

Stretching, plunging into new territory, being "in the flux," a person in the *expansion phase* often experiences heightened sensation. Time itself expands. Our senses are enlivened, our insights quicken, our focus often becomes more selective. Having dared to get our feet wet in a different stream, we may be swept along in a fast current of events and sometimes feel dangerously out of control. But the likely undercurrent, at this phase, directs us toward the future with feelings of certainty and joy. "Somehow, things will work out."

The expansion phase is a demanding one, but if the choice is made for life and for following our true convictions, our energy level is intensified. New possibilities present themselves for personal and moral development and for progress toward reconciling some of the recurring conflicts of maturation (for instance, dependency versus autonomy, risk versus security, pleasing others versus self-validation, personal status versus social responsibility).

At the conscious level, expansion takes place as we *try out* new ways of responding to people and events: this time, for example, trying not to overreact, or forcing ourselves to confront the problem directly, or daring truly to *listen* to the other person and granting him or her the same emotional credibility we insist upon for ourselves.

At the unconscious level, dreams and reflections may later recall this period in full and vivid images. We may see ourselves as hero or heroine in our own life story. Protecting or in some way recording these images establishes a new baseline of inner strength.

Well, I got through that crisis. I guess I won't die from the next one.

The expansion phase was a long one for Bill Johnston; his lack of anticipation did exact its toll. If he had known that his metamorphosis, from the time he began meditation at 40 until his physical plant was back at optimum functioning, would take seven years, he might have been discouraged. It was not clear to him that he was breaking away from most of the support systems he had built up and believed in all his life. Later, he would see that alcohol was part of that grid. The corporation was part of it, and so were the friends he had chosen, the expectations he had had of his children. One by one those props had wobbled and fallen away. But each small step he took alone, sloughing off old uniforms, gave him another boost of strength to reach for control of his own life.

Which he did one rainy day in his 45th year, simply by picking up his office furniture and moving it across the bay to start all over again in his own insurance business.

He had no money, no clients, no prospects. What could he do differently from everyone else? He watched April struggling to learn how to hold the reins of her own life. He took up classical guitar while she went to assertiveness training. It occurred to him that his own industry conspired to keep women such as April cripples. The husband, the attorney, and the insurance agent stuffed the pillow of her sunset years and presented it to "the little woman" all sewn up. She was assumed to be too soft-headed to have anything to say about it. Johnston hit on the idea of contingency planning for wives; he began designing workshops to bring them into the estate-planning process from the start.

April came home from one of her seminars with an idea passed on by a young married couple. Once a year the couple went away together to talk about what they could do for the coming year to enrich their marriage. Two weeks before the Johnston's anniversary, they independently jotted down ideas. On a long escape weekend to Vancouver Island they compared lists and made love and agreed they no longer wanted to hold each other to account for what they had promised when they married. That is to say, they were not responsible for each other's happiness, and they no longer had to present themselves only as a couple. Their individual needs for friends and refreshment acknowledged, they came home happy as truants from a beach party.

As we now know, with age men and women begin to manifest the sexually opposite sides of their natures, aspects that have usually been suppressed or ignored. Bill Johnston had reined in both his aggressive and his tender sides, afraid of each for different reasons. He hid his aggressive tendencies for fear they would make enemies for him within the company. Once Bill had taken the risk of becoming an independent operator, however, he began to feel more comfortable with letting out hostile competitiveness and channeling it into building his new business. Releasing aggressiveness in turn seemed to give him the confidence to show his more tender, caring side. Now that the lid had been pried off his bottled-up emotions, all sorts of surprising things began to happen.

A shadow of the number 50 fell across his path, and Johnston became obsessed with the fact that he had never sown his wild oats. The sexual itch moved down from his head until it made his skin jump like the flanks of a horse never free of flies. He grew a strawberry beard, a statement of virility. His dreams were filled with images from the major discovery of his Navy days: Japanese girls who wore angora sweaters and loafers and looked just like American girls except that they said yes.

He and April talked about the problem on their next Annual Marriage Revival Weekend. They decided that it would be a shame to go through this entire physical existence having surrendered to only one passion. But if either one had the opportunity, they agreed, the other didn't want to know about it.

Two interesting things happened in the wake of that decision. Johnston began to see that he had always flirted easily and indiscriminately and that it made his wife feel insecure. It was irresponsible to present himself as if he meant, *Let's get something going;* he began to anticipate his impact on people and became pretty good at guiding it. So it was when he least expected it that a woman he knew walked into his office and casually suggested they take sexual refreshment together.

Running the blood again, that is how it felt—swift and strong and refreshing of absolutely everything. The second surprise was that once the brief affair had released him from his obsession with sex, he tumbled back into romantic love for his wife. It was his first and last affair.

April had finished school and gone to work at a local college as a peer counselor for other women like herself who were trying to piece their lives back together. She had all new friends, very different from the people she and Bill had sought out when they were moving up through the city's social hierarchy. Bill observed the profound effect she had on other people. She listened. They loved her.

"I'm thrilled with what you've done with your life," he told her. "You are more beautiful than you've ever been." Her hair, he saw, was the same fiery auburn; her cheeks glistened like apples in the sun. The small breasts that had always embarrassed her became the tea roses of his sweetest desire. She still had a nearly perfect body.

Christmas, a year later: they were riding horseback in the mountains when out of the blue April felt a numbness in her fingertips. It inched up her hand and arm and down her side, and by the time they arrived home, her right side was virtually paralyzed. She was 47 and looked 35 when the third diagnosis confirmed multiple sclerosis.

Her phantom job as a corporate wife terminated, her mothering duties done, her husband's trauma resolved, his attitude totally supportive of her need to become self-sufficient—the monstrous unfairness of it!—now that everything was ready and it was her turn, she wasn't going to get it.

"How could my body do this to me!" she railed. "I've always taken great care of myself."

Some things you just cannot anticipate. Bill Johnston had always taken it for granted that he would be the first to go. Once the shock and anger subsided, they agreed they were strong enough to deal with her illness. Bill knows he never could have done so before. Blessedly, the disease went into remission and flared only occasionally.

Not long thereafter, they cut formal ties to their church. Already challenged by their youngest son, who said it was hypocritical to go to church just out of habit, they had gone to hear Bill's staunchly religious friend preach a lay sermon.

"It's time to pick your friends on whether they are for abortion or against it" was the message.

Deep down, the Johnstons were probably against abortion, but they could not in conscience inflict their personal views on others. The issue focused their growing frustration with the monolithic decrees of an organized church. After a period of exploration, Johnston tried to explain his thoughts in a letter to his friend:

"I feel creative for the first time. I don't know how to describe it other than to say that I feel part of whatever God is. There is a great deal of strength and beauty in my universe, and no fear about the other side of death. Every single thing I'm going through now is a preparation. A rehearsal. I am not a reborn Christian. I am a reborn human being. And while I don't have formal religion in my life any longer, my spiritual life is many times richer."

A five-page letter of hostile condemnation came back. It hurt Johnston deeply. The few men he counted as friends had turned out to be merely business "associates" or recreational sparring partners or, in this case, a bigot. April came through with the healing insight on the subject of friendships.

"If you're going to grow, you're going to leave some people behind."

Incorporation Phase

After the hurly-burly of expansion comes a resting, dormant phase during which we attempt to process what has changed and integrate the meaning of those changes into our philosophy of life. It is important to allow this time for the mind to absorb and clear and for our batteries to be recharged. There is every reason to recognize and take pleasure in our new personality strengths.

"I feel gigantic!" says the man who broke out at 45.

Between his 45th and 50th years, all the important curves

of Bill Johnston's existence changed direction dramatically. His blood pressure came down to a consistent 140 over 80. He hasn't needed a doctor in half a decade or taken so much as an aspirin.

His income climbed slowly at first, from a low of $12,000 in his first solo year to $21,000 in the second and $30,000 in the third, at which point he took a mortgage on the house or he would have gone under. The business began to take off in his fourth year, and in his fifth he will gross $70,000.

The workshops are booming. Gone beyond business, beyond a way of putting his bottled-up aggression to work, they have become for him almost a calling. He used to sell life insurance mainly to make the rich safer. The idea of preparing women for widowhood, of seeing people nod and identify in the audience when he challenges them to reject helplessness and take charge of their lives—that is truly a thrill.

Bill Johnston is now in the *incorporation phase*. In his contingency-planning workshops he has the opportunity to tell his story over and over again, in disguise. He edits it, works out the unfinished emotional business of it, gradually incorporates it, and turns his insights into a gift to others, who in turn help to endorse his new philosophy of life. He is also enjoying generativity—that voluntary obligation to strangers that marks successful development in middle age.

Referrals through churches and colleges are sending Johnston all over the West to present his workshops. He has begun to train widows in major cities to take over the job themselves. Instead of living out his days as a duplicate of ninety-two other employee-managers, he is now a sole proprietor in a position to clone himself. He plans to write a book, perhaps to franchise his workshops. There is no end. It is a circle.

Although he has no real men friends at present, he is delighted with the more than half a dozen peer friendships he has developed with women. Some vindication of his values came with a story in the *Wall Street Journal*. None of the big clients down whose throats the mutual funds were stuffed still hold policies with his old company, and at least one agency manager was caught playing it fast and loose.

This year, on their Annual Marriage Revival Weekend, the Johnstons anticipated talking not only about how to improve but about how to simplify. The youngest child is leaving for college. Moving into the post-parenting stage, they both find that the simpler things are, the more beautiful their life together becomes.

Just before they were to leave for that weekend, April's usually dormant nerve disorder flared up in her leg. Bill took over doing the dishes and gently stretched out the evening so that it would seem natural when they didn't leave. Turning over in his hands objects rich with the nicks of their twenty-eight years together, he choked up. *I can't imagine someday being here without her. I want to live the rest of my life with her.*

April's condition stabilized but would continue to be uncertain. What was important was their life together, as long as it could last.

Bill has no more heroes. But he does take inspiration from the philosophers he now reads avidly. And here, in sum, is what he has come to think about his 50 years on this earth:

"I can't describe the joy I feel that I have survived a transition that was in some ways shattering. I'm convinced that I had to go through all the pain and loss and mistakes of it to come out the other side more whole. Every once in a while now I get this powerful sense of well-being. I have no idea where it comes from. Everything isn't perfect. But I feel for the first time that I'm in control. I've lost weight and grown tougher and more resilient. My life has expanded beyond what I ever imagined possible. I'm on the threshold and I feel gigantic!

"But I know there is no arrival point. You just keep going around the mountain as far as you can in this life and then, in death, as in every ending, there will be a new beginning. Sometimes I feel pessimistic about how far we've come as a species. It makes me anticipate death with some excitement. You see, I've begun to feel that I have an old soul. And I'd like to do as much as I can with it in the time I have left on earth so that maybe, this time, I can graduate."

SUMMARY OF THE PHASES OF A PASSAGE

To approach a passage with some confidence that we can guide our way through it calls for an openness of mind—what we have called the period of *anticipation*.

Once receptive, we are ready for the *separation and incubation* phase. Separating from the restrictions of a former self, from an old role and set of rules that may have served ideally in the former stage but will not transfer intact to the next one without inhibiting further development, does not mean our identity will be lost. We are changing, and change means transforming old patterns of thinking and acting. We are about to engage in the untidy but exhilarating process of reassembling our identity. With effort, that identity will be a broader one, composed of some mysterious new personality parts fitted back together with our more sustaining aspects. But some of the old self—its outgrown "shoulds" and immature defenses, its former supports and earlier certainties—must be let go.

The *expansion* phase of a passage is the time for deliberately intervening in our own life script. We might ask ourselves at this point: What can be done, here and now, to change a constricting situation into one allowing for expansion? What am I contributing to the situation that is constructive? What am I doing that is destructive? Am I really helpless in an impossible situation, or have I learned helplessness?

The natural resolution of a fully realized passage is the *incorporation* phase, a resting. We need time to absorb what has changed and to integrate it into a new way of thinking about ourselves in the world.

Part II

WHAT TO TAKE INTO THE WOODS

To exist is to change; to change is to mature; to mature is to create oneself endlessly.

—HENRI BERGSON

The early part of my research, and of this book, pinpointed the characteristics that radiate from people of high well-being and identified three basic criteria for predicting those who will sustain that enviable condition. Now that we have a silhouette of what we are after, we are ready to look more deeply into what makes a pathfinder.

As I came to know such people, and to examine the nearly two hundred models of successfully navigated adult lives they represented, I began to discern something of the essence of pathfinding. It comes down to certain aspects of mind and heart that seem to animate the state of well-being. These particular qualities are cross-validated by historical biographies as well. And, as it turns out, the same qualities that permit change are those that are strengthened by the *process* of pathfinding. Each of the next eight chapters looks closely at one of the qualities of pathfinders.

The first, the most essential, is a *willingness to risk*.

5.
WILLINGNESS
TO
RISK

One of the first things I discovered about pathfinders is that they are willing to risk change. They do not expect to cruise through life in a sports car along a well-marked superhighway. Confronted with an obstacle or an accident along the way, they try a detour that usually turns out to be constructive. Faced with something even more treacherous—a normal passage unaccompanied by any high drama to explain the discomfort they feel—they take the risk of inner change.

Certain life crises, either managed or accidental, are inevitable. And all major life changes are potentially stressful. Beginning with the eruption of birth, proceeding by well-documented stages through childhood, there is a pattern: stable periods alternate with the passages in between, all through adulthood.[1] Even a major life change that is anticipated and generally thought desirable—standing on the threshold of a bittersweet good-bye to childhood—changing from teenager into "young adult," from single to married, from Indian to chief—demands letting go of a familiar, protective identity, and that is always a risk. For a while we are left exposed and vulnerable, forced to live with ourselves in a state of uncertainty. But it is from that very urgency and stress that we gather the grit to go through the change, the heightened awareness that offers hope it will be worthwhile, and the appetite for living that is whetted anew.

Yet even when we know rationally that the alternative to change is malaise, stagnation, a rut, a trap, a grind, most of us fight it. When the roads diverged in Bill Johnston's life, one leading to almost certain death and the other to unknown territory, he was tempted to choose the first for its sheer familiarity—so ominous can be the threat of change. Besides, there are secondary gains in what might be called the *exhibition heart attack*. It speaks eloquently for the effort and sacrifice that a hardworking man may feel for his family or superiors do not appreciate. The damaged heart is testimony to the fact that he didn't whine, didn't give up. Any weakness or failure that might have been attributed to him has been transferred to a value-free bodily organ: it was the heart that quit. He went to the wall a man. Somatization—the translation of emotional ills a person is afraid to express to one of the body's organs—is one sure signal of the need to risk change. Another common sign is unusual weight gain (or loss) for no organic reason. Such a person often feels as if sunk in aspic, unable to move without shaking everything up, or describes feeling "all pumped up," as if afraid to change for fear of puncturing the balloon. We humans are infuriatingly creative at finding ways to avoid risking change.

It is when all hope of change has been abandoned that one's spirit may break. For when we dare not hope for change, we lose even the desire for it. We submit to tedium, and our lives eventually become muffled with apathy. As the philosopher Descartes wrote, desire awakens only to things that are thought possible.[2]

What evidence do we have that a willingness to risk change is healthier than a commitment to continuity throughout adult life?

In my own studies, the people enjoying highest well-being were the most likely to describe having undergone a major change in their outlook, values, personal affiliations, or career. They had experienced one or more important transitions during their adult years and were justifiably pleased at having handled those transitions in an innovative way.

When social scientists in the Human Development Program at the University of California, San Francisco, launched in 1970 a study of transitions among adults in four different life stages, their major expectation was that those men and women who showed strong continuity in their values and goals as they moved through life, especially in the spheres of work and love, would be the most content. The researchers also anticipated that these consistent people would be the "best adapted" by mental health measurements. Both hypotheses were exploded.

"The sense of well-being," Marjorie Fiske reported ten years later, "was far more likely to be associated with the sense of past and future change in goals and behavior patterns than with continuity."[3]

What penalties are paid for an *un*willingness to risk? And how do pathfinders get around the fear of risk that all of us naturally feel?

Men and Magicthink

People who stay on the well-traveled road, play it safe, take no individual risk or exploratory routes in their careers, usually do so for the promise of security. They often subscribe to an implied social contract, as stated to me by a Harvard Business School graduate: "If you work hard and try long enough, you will be rewarded"—but there is only one signatory to that contract. It is a variation on what psychologists call the "just world" theory—that people get what they deserve. The notion that the world is not just, that many events happen arbitrarily and without cause, is too threatening a concept to apply to oneself. Hence, middle-class *magicthink*.

So seductive is the magicthink, which promises that institutions will reward merit fairly, the brightest men and women frequently ignore a simple mathematical reality: for the vast majority, the outcome is not the top of the pyramid. If there are five hundred presidents of the Fortune 500 companies, there must be five thousand vice-presidents; for every individual who runs a large store, chairs a department, supervises a section of a vast bureaucracy, there are scores of underlings hanging by their knuckles at his feet, waiting for him to fall. Even those who do make it to the top, or close to it, face other common pitfalls. Companies are bought, sold, taken over, merged, and otherwise mongrelized, often leaving the people who think they run them stunned to discover they are board-game pieces who certainly can be moved and who are always replaceable. When a new senior executive arrives, he often brings along his own trusted number two, if not a whole second team. Nor are companies above reducing their pension load by firing senior personnel before they can cash in.

By the time this sobering arithmetic cuts through their magical thinking, many people are already too dependent on the institutional "parent" even to contemplate a risk. Five years after he had topped off in middle management, one businessman could admit with good-humored chagrin how fiercely he had rationalized staying with the company. He saw his status within the firm as the only measure of his worth in the community; to slip in financial status, even temporarily, would make people think he was no good.

"I heard a voice inside me arguing, 'I need it, I want it, I gotta have it.' Then, for the first four years into my forties, I cursed myself: 'Where are your damn guts? When are you going to take a chance again?' You become a prisoner. Either you have to realize you've sold yourself and accept it, or get out." At what seemed the last moment he could still feel like a man, he got out.

Too often people observe that other people experience little deaths of security but think of themselves as somehow immune. That was apparent in several of the management and professional groups I studied. Most people tell themselves they will cross that bridge if they come to it, but in the meantime they ignore the need to explore alternate avenues to self-esteem *before* the bridge blows up in their faces. Then, often around the age of 50 and the passage I call the Half-Century Reckoning, they conclude they have been cheated by life. This is the exact reverse of the pathfinding pattern.

It is not that men are oblivious. Faced with evidence that they will not make it to the slot for which they aimed, they feel anger and dread. But the signal for a need to change *themselves* is often mistranslated. Men characteristically respond to a painful emotion by attributing its cause to another person or an external event. Once having located the problem somewhere outside himself, a man can then blame or attack this "enemy." Possibly he can line up allies to help him.

When blows to the ego are potentially crippling, a man

may be able to retain his inner sense of control and potency *only* by blaming someone or something else for his problem. And in games of high power, this technique can be diabolically effective. Fear plus hate is directed outward in attacks on a third party. The Ayatollah Khomeini, for example, deflected attention away from his own and his country's grave internal problems by making Jimmy Carter a "Satan."

But the person who routinely ignores the uncomfortable emotions that signal the need to change himself is a person refusing to risk the next step of development. The longer he ascribes his discomfort to other people and events, the more painful the crunch when he can no longer escape it.

"It's your fault, your weakness, your problem, not mine" represents the defense mechanism called projection. It is, simply, scapegoating. Energy that might have gone into the true risk—confronting confusion and fears within—is spent instead on making others, particularly those less powerful, appear foolish or wrong or deserving of punishment.

Sometimes the only thing that can penetrate magicthink or neutralize projection is a bad shock—being passed over, pushed out, or having an exhibition heart attack. Yet more and more people today are making some preemptive change within their professional spheres to ready themselves for another orbit.

Why Playing It Safe Is Dangerous

The relative merits of preemptive change versus playing for security showed up dramatically in a cooperative research project I conducted with Harvard Business School graduates of the Class of '49. A stunningly successful group, dubbed by *Fortune* magazine "The Class the Dollar Fell On,"[4] it includes the executive officers of Xerox, Elizabeth Arden, Johnson & Johnson, and Resorts International. All the men in the class were trained to believe that unless they became number one, they had not quite made the grade. By the time of the study they were 53 years old. The central distinction between those who emerged at the top of the well-being scale and those at the bottom was this:

The happiest were presidents.

The unhappiest were vice-presidents.

Despite the fact that everyone in the Class of '49 had done exceptionally well in comparison to any other group of American men of their vintage, those who had not quite made it to the top seemed to be soured on life. They insisted upon comparing themselves with their most illustrious peers. They suffered from a vivid sense of number-two-ness, tossing back and forth between the feeling of betrayal and the fear that they were truly second-rate. This ego wound appeared to be the source of a spreading discontent that eventually stained most other aspects of their lives: their marriages, their relationships with their children, their health. Yet of all the businessmen I interviewed, the unhappy number twos were the most resistant to change!

To shake down the data and probe for more subtle insights, I interviewed at length twenty of these businessmen in their mid-fifties. The composite dialogue that follows should put some flesh on the profile of men at both ends of the well-being scale. Mr. Low represents the unhappiest men; Mr. High speaks for those who were most content.

MR. HIGH: I'm the president of my own company. It's small (smaller than the corporation that Mr. Low works for, certainly), but it's all mine.

MR. LOW: I'm the vice-president of a rather large corporation. I *was* in line for one of the top jobs—it looked like clear sailing—until somebody else took over the ship and brought on a new crew. My chances for making it to the top in the future are not great. I'm probably locked in. Time's running out.

MR. HIGH: I thank my lucky stars I got out when I did. I left the corporate rat race when I was in my forties.

Not all the high-satisfaction businessmen followed this pattern. *But more than half did generate a new dream and took a risk in midlife.* One man left the corporation at 45 to go into politics and became mayor of his city at 50. Two others were run over by tenders and mergers and, rather than fold their tents, set out in their forties to start their own businesses. Another high-well-being man is a late recoveree from Father's Footsteps Disease: having run the family store as an obligation to his father, he did not feel free to expand professionally or psychologically until the older man died. He has since expanded the business eight times.

By contrast, two-thirds of the unhappiest men said they would love to change what they do—but they don't.

MR. LOW: I just can't justify the income loss. But to tell you the truth, I'm afraid of risking a failure. At the same time, I fear lack of recognition where I am. It's a double bind.

I asked the businessmen if they had already experienced a major failure in their professional or personal lives and was startled to learn that the highest-satisfaction men were just as likely as the lowest to have had a flop. I asked if it had been a useful experience or a destructive one.

MR. HIGH: No one's immune. But there is one big difference. For me (and all but two of the men in my group) the failure was useful. I learned from it.
MR. LOW: My failure destroyed something in me.

For a couple of the least-happy men there was a problem with no apparent solution, such as cancer. But for most, the setback was no different from setbacks suffered by the most-satisfied men. The following was a common story among the latter:

MR. HIGH: I was given a tough deal when the company re-shuffled things. I should have resisted, but I didn't. I stayed on a few more years and wrestled with myself. I told no one. Part of the agony, you see, was beginning to realize that you are becoming *owned*. It's a dying process. Anything is better—even risking failure. So I quit and started my own business. But you have to be prepared for toughing it out through the transitional period, because even if you were the one to quit everybody in town believes you were dumped.

Low-satisfaction men placed the greatest emphasis on success; therefore, they often misperceived how much success they actually had attained relative to others. The disappointment in their career dream appears to be the source of the spreading infection of discontent that measurably and adversely affects their marriages and their health. And, in fact, most of the low-satisfaction men indicated that their health was getting worse.

MR. LOW: I seem to tire so easily. I often feel irritable or angry, sometimes sad and depressed. So it won't come as any surprise to hear that I sometimes feel I've lost my interest in sex.

Yet deprivation in love, sex, and health does not cause them nearly the same distress as that which stems from the feeling of being second-rate in job status.

The conclusion I drew from this study was that even among men for whom a superior education has opened many doors, well-being is not easily sustained without a continuing willingness to risk change.

Women of Well-being

Those women who consistently score at the very top of the well-being scale have suffered just as many hardships and losses as their most miserable contemporaries report; they describe the same disappointments in husbands and children, the same losses of jobs, homes, money, dreams.

The critical difference is this:

Women of high well-being usually have confronted a difficulty, rocked the boat, picked themselves up, and taken the painful steps necessary to free themselves from what they finally perceived as a trap, self-made or imposed. This is the source of a good part of the euphoria of a prominent number among the happiest women. They gain a great boost in self-esteem from having taken the risk and having sprung themselves from the trap.

"I'm Lila Morgan and I'm forty-five and next year I'll graduate from college" was the effervescent self-presentation of one high-well-being woman I called, but it was her next sentence that made it ring true. "I started this new life after staying home for ten years so my husband wouldn't feel inferior. If I die tomorrow, I've had a ball. The confidence I have now is in myself. Before, I was an eggshell."

The common denominator among the least-happy women was that, one way or another, they all felt trapped. They might be trapped in a high-powered career or a dead-end job or in a bad marriage. More than half were homemakers or clerical or secretarial workers, which squares with the findings of many studies that a married woman with no outside work or with a low-prestige job is more likely than anybody else to be depressed. Although they were the least satisfied with their occupations, like the vice-presidents from Harvard these same women were the least confident about making any change. Two-thirds confessed that they wished they could make a major change in the kind of work they do or the career they pursue, yet the great majority said they did not think they should change, or said they did not believe they could change because they lacked training.

Women and the Happyface

Little in the average woman's life encourages within her a willingness to risk. It is, therefore, the pathfinding quality that women find the most difficult to cultivate—so difficult, in fact, that they have cleverly devised an unconscious mechanism that makes it possible for them not even to notice the need.

The biggest handicap women have in recognizing a need to change is their tendency to handle "unacceptable" ideas or impulses by holding them inside, where they try to dilute them, neutralize them, take the sting out of them, turn them into something more pleasing. Judith Cashian, the corporate wife we met in Chapter Two, for example, had built up so much anger over the repeated forfeiture of her own development to her husband's career that she could no longer keep the lid on the bottled-up feelings beneath. Tears literally filled her goggles as she swam. Uncontrollable weeping is one way the unconscious attempts to neutralize unacceptable emotions.

When anger, sadness, anxiety, or boredom reaches a level that signals the need to move on to the next stage of development, the "bad" emotion is likely to be thrust down into the unconscious. This is the defense known as repression.

It has its benefits. Adopting a happyface temporarily to

carry one through a dark or fearful episode, such as Anna's first confrontation with the King of Siam, is a way of radiating optimism and friendliness. It may defuse a hostile situation and even dispel fear so that one has the courage to pursue the risk: "For when I fool the people I meet/I fool myself as well." At times, repression preserves sanity. Consider the behavior of the two American female hostages in Iran who, whenever they appeared in Iranian propaganda films, were always smiling, hyperanimated, enthusiastic over how much sleep they were getting or weight they were losing.

But repression always has its costs. Women in particular go to incredible lengths to cosmetize the worst kinds of deficiencies in their existence. Prolonging the fraud that painful ideas or frightening impulses simply do not exist eventually becomes a habit of repression, and if the pretense is kept up long enough, people begin to believe it themselves. Nothing in reality is changed or improved. In fact, things may be getting considerably worse, but one will never know it so long as the repression is maintained.

Like all defenses, the happyface is self-protective and probably derives in part from the typically female pattern of self-blame. The quality of personality on which a majority of all the women surveyed place the highest value is responsibility; fully three-quarters of them believe themselves to be "totally" or at least "very" responsible for the way their lives are turning out, even when their lives are not turning out at all well. Moreover, the written descriptions of how they handle crises and transitions given by the most troubled women indicate that they are all too ready to assume personal responsibility for the husband who cannot hold a job, the child who is not getting along in school, the alcoholic father, the ill-tempered employer, the dissolute brother who is always asking for money. And when their friends become disloyal or their bosses do not give them promotions, they think it must be because of something *they* have done.

The paradox is that the same low-well-being women seldom take responsibility—or credit—for the good things.

Some low-satisfaction women derive their only distinct identity from absorbing the blame for all the inadequacies in their lives and the shortcomings of those around them— being a martyr in a hopeless situation. Because they have no independent source of self-esteem, the disabilities of others become their primary reason for being.

But it is the average wife and mother, programmed by society to feel responsible for the well-being of those around her, who provides the best clue to why women in general are so fiercely defensive of the happyface. Any speck of discontent on the surface of her own or her family's life is seen as a reflection of a woman's own inadequacy. It must be wiped away. Like waxy buildup, if discontent accumulates, it is her fault—she is a bad emotional housekeeper. And so, because women insist upon shouldering so much responsibility for the way things are turning out in the domestic realm, they must convince themselves that it's all turning out for the best.

Traditionally, women have had trouble claiming their successes as the direct result of their own abilities. Studies suggest that when women of low self-esteem do succeed, they usually deprive themselves of feeling good or gaining confidence by attributing even small triumphs to something external: "I was just lucky" or "The task was easy, anyone could have done it."[5] Perversely, when the same women fail, they commonly resist using the same external factors to explain it.

They seldom say, "It was just bad luck" or "The timing was off" or "It was a no-win situation for anyone," which is what pathfinding women and men characteristically tell themselves. Instead, most women explain failure by finding fault within: it was their own lack of ability, their stupidity, carelessness, inherent worthlessness. This is a central element in the fact that women suffer more from depression than men.[6]

Many women therefore think success to be beyond their control, not to be stable, not likely to be repeated in the future. No matter how bright and naturally talented a woman may be, this kind of thinking is a severe handicap. One of the few studies to measure the importance of noncognitive characteristics of success was Christopher Jencks's.[7] As reported in his book Who Gets Ahead?, the sense of "internal control"—or how much an individual believes success can be determined by his or her personal initiative rather than by external events—does indeed affect success.

The link between a sense of internal control and the willingness to risk and to plan ahead for change is a strong one. Studies apart from my own have established that little planning goes with a weakened sense of inner control; and, conversely, having some plans for the future strengthens the person's assurance that he or she can have a positive impact on future events—in particular, on making the next transition.[8]

Unlike men, who tend to project their own inadequacies outside themselves, women tend to take on more than their share. "I've gone through my life blaming myself for almost anything that harmed me," admits the aging woman in Lillian Hellman's novel *Maybe*. There is a desperate vanity behind it, she realizes in the end, "to think so much depends on you."[9]

To keep the plunger down over repressed feelings, to put on a happyface, requires hyper-alertness and therefore energy. Even when sleeping, one remains in a state of "held arousal"—the body is on alert, but the mind will not let it act—which accounts for why the repressed person feels tired all the time.

More light was shed on the happyface syndrome when the Life History Questionnaire was published in *Redbook* and drew revelations from thousands of women, most of whom said they led "ordinary lives" and handled critical turning points in the "usual ways." (If I had to put a single label on this group, I would call them "The New Conventionals." Two-thirds of them were married and showed a strong preference for work outside the home, although a sizable group presented themselves as the storybook happy housewife who loves her home and children, period, and was not looking any further than that.)

Their choices of primary goals revealed a strong yearning for enclosures—a sanctuary of love, a secure home, a serene self. For the entire sample, the most important goals were mature love (41 percent), family security (40 percent), and inner harmony (34 percent). The goal that remains the most consistently important throughout their lives, for every age and income group, is: to reach inner harmony. When asked directly how much satisfaction they found in different dimensions of their lives, the overwhelming majority of women in this study presented themselves as blissfully happy on almost every count, except for wishing that they got a little more exercise. But when asked indirectly about their emotional life, a startling number—almost 60 percent—revealed symptoms of chronic depression.

The longer angry or self-deprecatory feelings are allowed to accumulate, unacknowledged, in the unconscious, the more explosive the crisis when the lid finally blows off—just as is the case for men. By that time, one's perception of reality may have become pathologically distorted.

A subtle version of repression is practiced by the woman who cannot risk separating from her tormentor. A grim 1980 statistic reveals how common a trap this is: one out of five Americans is personally aware of spouse or child abuse so serious that authorities had to be called in to investigate.[10]

A Montana woman described her particular trap:

"The first six years of my marriage my husband was an alcoholic. He used that as the excuse for beating me. He would apologize later, but he didn't have to; I always forgave him first. I began to have blackouts for no reason." To bury the evidence of such extreme unhappiness calls for the most extreme defenses: her blackouts were an intense form of repression. Most of her conscious life was passed in that form of depression known as learned helplessness. "During those nineteen years I did everything my husband said. I tried so hard to please. I did lose two children through beatings—miscarriages.

"As I got older, I got stronger; I didn't stand up for myself until the end. The children were the ones who said, 'Mother, take the chance!'"

The ultimate risk in attempting escape from a trap is that one will die from it. But there are living deaths, too. That thought stayed with the woman when she found newspaper clippings left on her pillow about husbands who had killed their wives. Her husband warned her directly that if she tried to leave, people in her office would have to be "taken off" too.

One night she faced her husband at last with the words "I'm going to leave." She waited for him to tear at her in a terminal rage—but he did not. He broke. It was the last thing she expected. That too she survived. She did not go back.

She moved into a trailer and met a man at Parents Without Partners, and before the year was out her life had changed from a nightmare into a trailer-park love story. Wisely, she waited to marry the man until she had learned to like herself. Today, five years later, she feels almost new-born. Even the physical evidence is striking.

"I'm forty-three now but most people think I'm under thirty. I have no wrinkles and my body is like it was when I was in my twenties. And I'm a grandmother! It's so wonderful being in your forties. I seem to be more my own woman. I'm looking forward to being fifty."

As the poet said, "Happiness is just a thing of contrasts and comparisons."

Between Two Selves

Obviously, to face reality can be frightening. It makes the necessity for change more real. And change involves the deepest sort of self-doubt. While struggling through change, the pathfinder is between two shells: his or her former identity is at least partially cracked, and a raw and fragile new carapace is trying to form in the chilly air of uncertainty.

Even if we do not seek change, our hold on our identity is tenuous. The identity crisis originally linked by Erik Erikson to adolescence turns out to recur throughout adult life. When asked in the Life History Questionnaire to choose the one or two most important changes in perspective that characterized each stage of their adult lives, both men and women emphasized, for their late teens and early twenties, *feeling a firm sense of my own identity*. The surprise was that this same attitude signaled for many people the successful passage into their thirties. For those in their forties it was the mark of midlife. For those passing 50 it represented yet another kind of consolidation. At each stage most people asserted that now, at last, they felt "a firm sense of my own identity."

The most striking difference between men and women to emerge in my surveys was the greater difficulty women experienced in forging their own identity. The women in every sample—whether they were between 18 and 20, or between 29 and 35, or between 36 and 45, or even between 46 and 55—described the same developmental dilemma: *How do I stop trying so hard to please others and begin to validate myself?*

This may be the central task of adult development for

women. Although women report at every stage believing they have overcome it, the same task pops up again as primary in the next stage. Their attempts at self-validation do not seem to stick. The only reason it becomes a secondary issue for most women after the age of 55 is that by then their primary attention turns to monitoring their health. It appears to take the average woman no less than a lifetime to outgrow her training to be a pleasing little girl.

Low-satisfaction men share with the average woman the same primary experience: how to stop trying so hard to please others and begin to validate oneself. Bill Johnston, in status-conscious Boise, wanted above all to please. When his company began to play fast and loose with professional ethics, for instance, it did not occur to him to criticize. Retrieving a clear idea of himself was inextricably bound up with breaking a lifelong habit of needing to please. And once he did, Johnston was able to rise from a low-satisfaction man to a high-well-being pathfinder.

Black Americans—even those who enter the middle class, even those of relatively high well-being—struggle with this dilemma of self-validation all their lives.

Here is a striking contrast. High-satisfaction white men, no matter what their age or stage, never even mention the problem. A white boy with promise is programmed to develop his uniqueness and to use his powers to make others follow him, not to make others like him. Given that context, it is natural that as a grown man he does not see any issue in self-validation versus pleasing others. It might even be said that women, low-satisfaction men, and blacks are as different from high-satisfaction white men as fat people are from thin people. If you have never been fat, how to get thin is never an issue.

Even for men of moderate well-being, however, the grasp on identity is not consistent and sure. It is for this reason that the prospect of change is so frightening. At some level they sense that they risk not only losing status or material possessions. They risk, for a time at least, losing the self.

It would be beyond mortal scope to keep everyone else calm and completely happy while we are making an important change in ourselves. People (most especially our mates and children) have a vested interest in our past roles. Picture, for example, the equanimity with which a wife would receive the news that her husband has decided to give up his job at the bank and fly to Tahiti to paint naked women.

In describing their decision to risk a major change in their lives, many pathfinders said, "I had no choice; it was the only thing I could do." They said so quite matter-of-factly, although objectively there must have been a choice.

In some ways it is easier to risk being a pathfinder if there *is* a major loss or obstacle to overcome. The premature widow with small children to support is more likely to risk breaking into an innovative career than the adequately supported wife.

In the absence of a precipitating event, some people must render the devil they know considerably worse than the devil they don't know in order to present themselves with the rationale for taking the risk of getting out. "I was unable to move because of my fear of how a divorce would hurt my children," said a woman pathfinder who ended a thirteen-year marriage to an alcoholic. "But then I somehow convinced myself, probably irrationally, that if I stayed in the marriage, I would not survive for more than another two years—I would go crazy or I would get cancer. And so I presented myself with a situation in which I had to divorce in order for my children to have a mother. I had no choice."

For the pathfinder, it may be that an inner gulf is crossed, and a new degree of inner strength felt, before important outer bridges are burned. It is that silent leap of self-mastery, and the sense of having reached a new equilibrium, that makes a pathfinder certain there is no way of going back.

It is important to know that one inevitably feels some sadness over parts of the old self being left behind during a passage, as well as some apprehension over the new sense of self that has yet to take shape. Most of us felt that way during the adolescent passage. Even the healthiest among us will again feel a certain dread each time another major transition is attempted. To put it simply:

Change always involves loss—and consequently some degree of anxiety and depression.

The Best Armor

What do people use to protect themselves when they risk change, or when change or uncertainty is forced upon them? Pathfinders, in all groups, turn most often to the same four coping devices:

Work more.

Depend on friends.

See the humor in the situation.

Pray.

It was more common for men in my studies to turn to work and noncareer women to prayer. But high-well-being people of both sexes were able, with remarkable consistency, to rely on their friends and associates for help and to see the humor in tough situations.

People of low well-being describe an entirely different set of responses when they hit a rough passage or have to live through a period of uncertainty. These were the four most common responses across all groups:

Drink more, eat more, take drugs—indulge.

Pretend the problem does not exist.

Develop physical symptoms.

Escape into fantasy.

In every sample the low-well-being people *did* suffer many more stress symptoms than anyone else in their group. At some level they know what they are doing to themselves, and they know that the techniques of pretending, physical symptomizing, and artificial escape do not work.

Obviously, when a serious failure or loss is faced, the coping devices used by pathfinders during normal transitions are not sufficient. (The stronger defenses used against major life accidents are discussed in Part III of this book.) But in fact, it is often in the course of dealing with failure that a person is transformed into a pathfinder. Roughly half of all the pathfinders admit to having "failed at a major personal or professional endeavor," but almost every one of them had the same response. They found it a useful experience and say they are better off because of it.

Their resiliency in failure does not mean immunity. Pathfinders feel the blows—often severely. It is just that they do not go down for the count, or retire in fear from the fray. Knowing that one has survived a failure adds to the armor needed during times of risk, transition, and uncertainty ahead.

Resiliency in failure and the ability to take criticism are not qualities with which one is born; they are acquired strengths. By definition, however, one cannot acquire expertise without experience. Let us look now at a man who learned how to roll with the punches early, and how that strengthened him later in life. He was recommended to me by one of the two hundred pivotal Americans whom I asked to suggest a pathfinder candidate from their communities.

Falling Up

A Depression kid, he had to quit high school in Brooklyn at 16 to drive a truck for his father. He limped through night school, but his father was hard as stone on him, as he was, being embittered by circumstance, on everyone who worked for him. He was convinced that his son, a man we shall call Stan Kristol,* would be a bum.

Stan tried college but made abominable grades. After that early failure, Stan figured he wasn't good for much more than working as a common laborer in the steel mills of Gary, Indiana. He moved on to shoveling mud in South Carolina as an enlisted man. One day he looked up and shuddered; this might be the rest of his life. At that moment something came alive in him, something that later became determination.

"When the war was over, I applied to a lot of schools, but they all asked if I'd been to college. My transcript would finish me off every time. Then I read that Hunter College was going to open up to veterans. So I marched myself down to the all-girls' school and bluffed my way in by saying I'd never been to college."

Three months later he was found out. He felt guilty, he remembers, but he was also aware of bringing to his studies a motivation that was vastly improved over that of four years before, when he had flunked irredeemably.

"I had no choice—unless I wanted to live out my days as bitter about life as my father had been."

* A pseudonym.

Hunter threw him out, but the gamble had been worthwhile because they placed him elsewhere. He managed to work his way through a degree in economics.

"I was independently poor for a long time."

Economics professors were not in great demand at the time, especially those who thought Joe McCarthy and his loyalty oath were for the birds and the worms. But Stan Kristol joined the trust department of a bank and fell into a career at which he was superb: researching companies. Everything was not heaven—as Stan moved up, he came under the umbrella of a boss who was a malevolent lout—but reaching the age of 37, Stan was considered one of the bright young men on the street. He and his wife, Janice, bought a showcase of an 18th-century home in southern Connecticut and began scouring the countryside for antiques until they had the house restored to its full former glory. Stan's ego was in roughly the same condition.

One day he blew up at his boss. "You're sick," he had the satisfaction of saying, and picked up his coat and walked out. He had made enough money in the stock market to cash in and start his own business. Exhilarated, he took the risk.

"There were a lot of people whose money I'd managed over the years, so I just took all those accounts and went to Westport and became an investment adviser. After a year I opened my own firm. I was going to do things I didn't think anybody on Wall Street had the capability to do."

He was right.

"Nine months later I was in the tank."

He had a negative net worth of a third of a million dollars. A slip from the bank demanded delivery of $50,000 the next morning.

"I thought of jumping out the fourteenth-floor john window. I didn't think I'd land very well. It didn't seem any way to solve a problem, certainly not for my wife and kids." So he talked to the senior bank officer, who agreed to postpone the demand and to let him invest the little money he had left. He got a job as a researcher for a brokerage house—strictly on commission, no status—but he ignored the comedown and concentrated on one thing: paying off that debt.

"Sometimes it looked like a mountain I could never take. But then I'd remind myself, 'Hey, schmuck, you did it once;

you're going to do it again.' Having been a boy failure made it much easier."

Fail a Little

Everyone in the autumn of childhood conjures up an image of his idealized self, the person he would like to be. That ideal usually casts our virtues and desires in a mold so pure and nearly perfect that only life behind a museum case could protect it. The dream of adolescence is always a little beyond our power to realize.

The earlier that first, idealized ego case is cracked and a person discovers he does not die from it, the sooner he can allow more self-compassion and humor inside his container and begin to accept that his identity will build, show blemishes, suffer injuries, repair itself, and be renewed again and again—if he lets it. Therefore, the best thing that can happen to most people may be to fail a little—early.

The ability to cut one's losses and to shift to a present and future orientation distinguishes the approach of pathfinders. That involves learning how to detach an outside evaluation of one's immediate products or decisions from the inner evaluation of one's self and one's value over time. The goal is to be able to respond to criticism by saying, *This is the best I could do under the circumstances; there are naturally some things wrong with it, but basically I think it's pretty good.* Better still is the ability to objectify, to stand outside the product or decision and criticize it first oneself: *Here are the shortcomings I see in it, and these are the reasons I did it that way.*

Most dissatisfied people see a failed project as further evidence of their own inadequacies: *If what I did is bad, I must be no good.* Even more punishing is the habit of believing that a failure is the result of intrinsic and unchangeable qualities in oneself. A person with this habit of self-blame, so common among low-well-being people, is likely to see a flubbed assignment as proof that "I just don't know how to get along with people" or "I'm just not smart enough." He or she is unable to detect the factors that made it hard to execute this particular assignment. The antidote would be to begin to string together a series of successes, no matter how minor, to prove that he or she indeed does have some worth. But the low-satisfaction person characteristically does not think that way. The conclusion is a self-fulfilling prophecy: *I always bring failure on myself; therefore, nothing I do will make any difference.*

The opposite extreme—placing all the blame for the failure elsewhere—is equally destructive. The scapegoater cannot learn from criticism or failure. Nor does projecting the cause of his failure on someone or something else remove it from his mind. Both those who blame others and those who blame themselves are equally obsessed with the past, equally convinced that they have been cheated by life. All are examples of risk-allergic thinking.

Stan Kristol took his first failure, in college, as evidence that he was fit only for common labor. But when it hit him one day in the Army that only *he* could make the difference between a lifetime of shoveling mud and learning to be a success at something, he took a risk. By bluffing his way into another college, he started the wheel of chance turning again and created new possibilities. His wife passed along an insight. Before Stan lost his business, he secretly had believed his successes might all have been sheer luck. "It was only putting his career back together again and making it a second time around," Janice said, "that proved to him that *he* was making his success."

Pathfinders also fail, and pathfinders suffer life accidents as frequently as anyone else, but they see themselves neither as failure-prone nor as singled out for disaster at the hands of fate of others. That view represents a victory over self-preoccupation.

One Risk Leads to Another

The greater demon for him, Stan Kristol discovered, was not failure but boredom.

"A lot of people seem to think life 'crises' are caused by specific things. I don't think that's the way it happens. It's not that rational. Most people live on a day-to-day basis, and when the days get lousy, and you don't know why, it isn't necessarily because you didn't achieve a goal. I know the major change in my life came because of boredom. I was on top of the world. No way I would ever have expected the achievements I'd made—they went way beyond my goals."

After four years as a researcher, his debt repaid, Stan was tapped by one of the top brokerage firms on the New York Stock Exchange to start a research department. By his mid-forties, he was a partner.

"I was sitting on top of my field. I had created a department that was a moneymaking machine. It was strange to say to yourself, 'I got it all; why ain't I happy?'"

It took him two years, between 45 and 47, to identify the cause of his malaise. It was not the kids and it was not his wife. In fact, he got such a kick out of taking them all skiing for the first time he even broke down and put on a pair of the clumsy boards himself. The first day he crashed like an idiot into rocks. "I'll never do this goddamned thing again!" he cursed, his first attempt to cure the staleness also having failed. But when the family trundled off to Vermont to try it again and again without him, he was caught up by their spirit. Soon, he found that he was shuffling around his work schedule so that he could spend a week or so every month skiing in Utah. That went on for two winters. It amazed him.

"The need to get away and ski was the symptom. Gradually, I realized the real disease. It wasn't failure—it was boredom."

He took the arduous ski instructor's test. "It was a gag—and I passed!" Stan Kristol, from Brooklyn, the street kid; the most physical thing he had ever done was to power-mow his five-acre lawn as a 40-year-old semiretiree in southern Connecticut—and look at him now!

The next hurdle, after diagnosing his ennui, was to identify what was *not* holding him back and to let go of that—which is difficult when more than one person is involved.

"Let's move to Utah."

"But the kids are just going into high school—" Janice protested.

"Kids have a hundred years; we have maybe thirty." He added a chaser of black humor. "Besides, no matter what you do with kids they turn out rotten."

"But the house, the Queen Anne chests we just bought . . ."

It was certainly true that they were not going to find in Utah a manor house with tiny-paned windows of hand-blown colonial glass. But Janice Kristol could see that her husband was excited again. That was pure gold. Once she set her mind to taking the risk of change with him, she led the way.

"We'll have an auction. We'll go over every piece of furniture we've loved and have it assessed; we'll watch it being appreciated by people who bid for it; and then we'll say good-bye to it—and be rid of it."

As the leave-taking from their old life proceeded, Stan had another part of himself to give up. "I had all these 'children' I'd brought into the business—seventy-five of them, working for me in the only profit center in the firm." Letting his ego relax a moment, he realized that of course they were all talented and would get along quite well without him.

Letting go of the house, piece by piece, and of the authority conferred by Stan's job, took a full year.

"It gave us time to finish things," Janice realized. "Near the end I was still sad about leaving Connecticut but excited about going west and seeing what would happen next. I felt no real loss."

Stan told me later, "What we learned is that if you're going to reconstruct a new way of life, you can't hang on to the old skin."

A new life in the Golden West began with going backward a bit. "I was going to be a full-time singing ski instructor with sixteen-year-old girls idolizing me. Four months a year I'd be on a big ego trip, and the other eight months I'd be a bum." (That would show his father, who had never given him credit for anything anyway.)

Often, the developmental paths we follow are zigzags: we drop back in order to live out some aspect of the past that was out of reach at the time. In the flush of that exhilaration—"I never dreamed I could do this"—we may feel enough optimism to risk something more taxing.

A close friend of Stan's, another ski instructor, went blind. From ego-tripping on deferred boyhood pleasures, Stan plunged into an effort to start programs all over the country to teach the blind to ski. He ran into resistance everywhere. He could not get ten cents from the foundations or from the Fortune 500, which only made him more passionate. So he made films and traveled around the country himself, with his friend, training instructors to teach the blind. The program caught on.

"First time in my life I'd ever had a cause," he admitted,

somewhat prickly at the word *cause*, which still held for him connotations of gap-toothed kids rattling canisters for some children's fund that of course went into the best ninety-nine-cent Muscatel for the old man. Stan had always abhorred committees. But without seeing the connection, he had replaced with this crusade the purpose he had felt in guiding young people in his old job.

"I just thought that teaching blind people to ski was something worth doing," Stan said by way of brushing it off, "but the impact—and the reward—were immediate. There was a hell of a lot of good all the way around."

By the time I caught up with the Kristols, they had been settled in a booming western ski town for years. In fact, when the inevitable shoot-out shaped up between home-owners and developers, Stan Kristol headed the big-city boys off at the pass by running for and becoming the town's first mayor.

Stan Kristol, from Brooklyn, the street kid, and look at him now—mayor of Alta Pass!

His hazel eyes were hooded with reddened lids from the windburn of mountain life. He looked lived-in, like a man who had learned how to get a few laughs out of himself. "That's true," he agreed. "After I went broke, I stopped taking myself so seriously." Janice had so well acclimated herself to the change that she appeared younger than she did in the pictures of her on her Connecticut lawn; her eyes were indelibly blue, her skin a rosy tan, and the forearms under her ski warm-up suit were elastic with strength.

I asked Stan Kristol if his failures in life had turned out to be constructive.

"Oh, sure. When I went belly up with my own business and had to start all over again, I had every confidence I was going to do it because I had done it once before. You don't have the psychological hang-ups because you've failed and come out of it at least once. If I lost everything tomorrow, I'd know I could do it all over again the third time."

He sounded not only convincing but almost eager to try.

In their next transformation, the Kristols may move on to semiretirement with a double base—one foot in a raw ski town and the other in a desert town where they can play tennis the other half of the year. Stan had decided by our last conversation to leave the Alta-Vail-Aspen axis.

"I don't want to get stuck being an Aspen type," he quipped. "They're into obligatory freedom."

He wasn't about to settle in some Sun City either, where all one sees are five hundred retired General Motors executives with nothing to talk about but their lousy stockbrokers. At this stage, for the Kristols, keeping risk alive means chucking any material things that might tie them down. It tickles them to think they will probably end up in a closet—but with a beautiful piece of outdoors for their real home. As Stan Kristol tells his wife:

"The most important thing is to stay excited."

Stan Kristol managed to avoid a common mistake many people make when they correct their course after a risk has ended in failure. When one is raw, vulnerable, just plain scared, it is natural to maneuver toward whatever seems most secure. The problem is that treading water is safe, harmless, and controllable, but eventually one is pulled under by a sluggish weight of days that are sealed in sameness.

The Master Quality

A willingness to risk is the master quality for pathfinding. Because it is the linchpin, I have taken it up first, despite the fact that it is the most difficult quality to cultivate and requires the greatest strength.

It would be convenient if there were bromides for instant strength, and splendid if they could be reduced to self-help formulas. Unfortunately, strength is built layer by layer. Each layer is inevitably composed, at least in part, of wounds, failures, losses. Even greater strength is required to ensure the scar tissue does not grow so hard over our psyche that the carapace becomes too brittle to stretch. The other qualities common to pathfinders, described in the rest of this section of the book, are what fortify them to take intelligent risks and to make innovative changes. People who become pathfinders layer these strengths from every other dimension of life until they have a core that is resilient and enduring.

Philosophy has been far ahead of psychology in describing the benefits of accepting the risks inherent in changing ourselves.

The original paradisaical state depicted in the Bible was

one in which the sense of self was absolutely unchanging. That remains always a pull. Who among us has not felt "a passion for the safe and the permanent, along with a knowledge of the futility of such longing?"[11] Philosophy has gradually surrendered this wish for sameness of self. in 1690 Locke coined the term *self-consciousness*, only to have the notion of one true self, certain of its identity, attacked fifty years later by Hume. Hume found it impossible to "catch" a self and pin it down, asserting that we are instead a "bundle of different perceptions, which are in perpetual flux and movement." Yet until the 19th century, the quest was for certainty and universal conditions. Then came a burst of motion and speed: breakthroughs in communications and transport blurred time units and visual images, powerfully altering man's perceptions of himself and his relationship to the Divine.[12]

Philosophically, the 19th century belonged to Hegel. He proposed that once we leave the original state of innocence and become conscious of self and of history, we are *in* the flux whether we like it or not. Better that one's limbs should be torn asunder by risking the turmoil of remaining in the flux, he exhorted, than to stand still and drift eventually into a leaden and lifeless calm. Although we never can return to the state of natural paradise, it is possible through growth and development, according to Hegel's scheme, to move through the flux and eventually to reach a transcendent end state. This is the point of self-knowledge and self-acceptance at which one can feel again "at home," no longer "homesick"—in other words, where alienation is overcome.

But the real business of living, and of philosophy, Hegel insisted, is that middle corridor where the individual is in a constant *state of transition, in process, in a pattern of self-formation*.

The emphasis in the first half of this century shifted with the work of Freud to a rigid definition of the human capacity to change. Freud theorized that the shaping of major elements of personality was a fait accompli by the age of five; at the most, adults did not develop beyond the age of 20. The eternal self—that collection of roles we present to the outside world—became the preoccupation of behaviorists in the 1950's. Then suddenly they were confronted with affluent young Americans who began to rage against the roles they were expected to play—"gung-ho soldier," "little woman," "organization man"—role assignments that restricted them and that denied them opportunities for expressing other dimensions of the self. Emboldened by the social revolutions of the Sixties, a critical mass of people were willing to risk becoming freer.

Human institutions prepare people for continuity, not for change. Marriage, the family and its child-rearing practices, schools, churches, government, the legal system—all reflect the basic human wish to ensure predictability and stability. Even in the face of evidence to the contrary, all those institutions assume that relationships are permanent. In an effort to disallow the maddening impermanence of human feelings, institutions impose penalties on those who depart from the status quo. But social norms change, laws change, institutions change, and as hard as a society may try to prevent it, people do change.

Institutions that have a vested interest in the status quo take a long time to reflect or even to acknowledge the changes people are making. I offer one of thousands of instances:

Every year the Department of Labor's Bureau of Labor Statistics issues urban family budgets to portray three relative standards of living, which the Bureau describes as "lower, intermediate, and higher." As its report reads: "These budgets are for a precisely defined urban family of four: a 38-year-old husband employed full-time, a non-working wife, a boy of 13, and a girl of 8. After about 15 years of married life, the family is settled in the community, and the husband is an experienced worker."[13]

That hypothetical family (working husband, wife at home with two children) represents no more than 6.5 percent of married couples in the United States[14] and an even smaller percentage of the total population. When I queried the Bureau, I was told it is "thinking" of making minor modifications. Enthusiasm did not ripple through the telephone wires, however; to change would invalidate its comparisons to earlier years, because the statisticians cannot revise the older figures.

As usual, people are ahead of their institutions. They are *living* the reality of divorce, single-parent households, two-paycheck families, displaced homemakers, alimony-poor and unemployed fathers. Young people who are now forming households scarcely have time for the old brick-and-board bookcase and Danish Modern ice bucket. They are more likely to advertise for a roommate, to rent "living space" and "take-out" furniture systems, than to build anything so quaint as a nuclear family.

The new protean men and women must sense that they are working with a different human prospect. The will to power and expectation of unlimited progress have run into finite limits that were unimaginable to Americans only a generation ago. We have moved into a period in the West that may require for sheer survival an individual who is capable of shifting in the blink of an eye between a collection of many selves—between striver and sharer; idealist and pragmatist; between the assertive spouse and the compliant one; between the law-abiding citizen and, when attacked, the counteraggressor.

Sharing fears of an uncertain future in an economically unstable and militarily perishable world, we seem increasingly to demand that daily life be reliable, safe, certified, risk-proof. "Our greatest moral problem today is cowardice," asserts the Reverend William Sloane Coffin, Jr. "Common integrity now passes for courage."[15] In the rest of this century we probably will see continued attempts to return to a state of childlike, paradisiacal certainty by embracing various airtight religious packages, whether it means curling up safe and sound in one's own living room to be stroked by a TV evangelist or following a cult figure off to some island of the mind, hoping to gain protection in exchange for a total surrender of free will. Many people find that their faith is what *allows* them to risk, among them millions of fundamentalist Christians. But there is no risk in the ready-made, superficial emotional experience sometimes proffered by religious entrepreneurs today.

It is startling to realize that many of us would rather risk even death than change, and that we stand ready to employ our faculties overtime to avoid acknowledging those changes taking place right under our noses.

The very process of pathfinding, however, helps people who risk to become fluent with change—capable of engaging future transitions with more ease, freedom, and readiness. Delia Barnes, the woman who struggled out of the torpor of self-doubt and attempted the less-traveled path to becoming an ordained minister, risked loss and disapproval, and she did so more than once. Each time it was easier to risk because she had done so before. People who choose the less-traveled path often lose their way among new darknesses and dangers but eventually break through, or come back, most of them richer in spirit and stronger in will than they were when they set out. What they find is not an alternate life-style but a different way of looking at the whole enterprise of living.

The Creative Connection

Creativity could be described as letting go of certainties.

To risk change requires letting go of a protective identity. Could the processes be similar?

The experts have not formed any major theories on what effect creativeness might have on healthy adult development; large-scale studies are virtually nonexistent.

"We are generally afraid to become that which we can glimpse in our most perfect moments, under conditions of greatest courage," observed psychologist Abraham Maslow.[16] He then asked what kind of individuals might be arrogant enough to *dare* to reach for their highest possibilities. People who invent or create, he answered, because they *must* have what he called "the arrogance of creativity."

There is fairly wide acceptance among researchers of the idea that the creative process consists of four phases: preparation; incubation (and a state of relaxed receptivity); immersion and illumination; and, finally, revision.[17]

Swedish film director Ingmar Bergman gave a striking description of this invisible process, which operates while he sits in a chair and appears to be doing nothing but looking out the window.

"I make all my decisions on intuition," said the 62-year-old director. "I throw a spear into the darkness. That is intuition. Then I must send an army into the darkness to find the spear. That is intellect."[18]

In *preparation* for any sort of creative work, people store up their most vivid impressions. The second stage, *incubation*, requires a release of one's conscious hold on the problem: let go, step back, detach from it—without any specific expectations.

"You start by thinking about irrelevancies," as award-winning furniture designer George Nelson described it to me. "I turn over my conscious mind, slip in the clutch, and let my mind idle. This may go on for some time, but when the breakthrough comes, it takes no more than a split second. Suddenly you are connecting the unconnectable. There must be the most incredible switching mechanism that scans all the memory paths."

Theories of creative imagination generally hold that images are stored in the unconscious mind; that over time they form streams of images; and that these can be juxtaposed to picture in the mind's eye something a person has never seen or experienced. But if we are to have access to these unconscious images, we must be in a state of relaxed receptivity. Once the intellect becomes involved, or the emotions, our ego rushes in to censor or inhibit the formation of new images, or makes certain that they combine in known, stereotypical ways.

Cultivating a state of receptivity as in the incubation stage is a practice used throughout history not only by creative people but also, in meditation, by Eastern mystics. Prayer itself is often most illuminating when approached as an act of reverie, rather than with specific expectations.

Immersion in one's subject matter, after having made oneself fully porous, is the stage during which solution or inspiration spontaneously occurs. Often the illumination comes at an unexpected moment—"It suddenly came to me . . ."—a moment buoyant with feelings of certainty and joy.

Letting go of certainties, reframing the central question, spotting the wrong questions, using errors and failure—all these steps are fundamental in seeking the creative solution. The same techniques would seem ideally suited to moving our development forward, particularly when we feel caught in a situation where change has appeared impossible. When we reframe the problem, it is possible to shake free of the symptoms and to loosen inflexible positions others around us may have taken up.

It is always a good idea to "sleep on it."

"Our return to green chaos, the deep forest refuge of the unconscious, is a nightly gift, which psychiatrists tell us is essential to preserving our sanity and is also inherent in any process of creation," says essayist Edward Hoagland.[19]

Over and over again, people in the arts describe learning a valuable lesson about obstacles. The greater the creative problem, the greater the prod to go beyond conventional solutions and break through to a more imaginative solution. Even when one's back is against the wall, an obstacle may be converted into an opportunity. Playwright Edward Albee admits with amusement, "The things I cannot do anything about—that a director insists upon—I incorporate into the play and claim were my ideas."

Can people who are not by genetic gift or training artists learn to adapt the creative process to approaching risks in their lives? My work has convinced me that a person can accept the basic script handed to her or him at birth and play it out, passively, safely, or bitterly. Or a person can intervene consciously in the process of inner expansion from one stage to another—the most creative process of all. The difference is between "I do" and "I am aware of what I do."

There is a clear parallel between the phases of a completed major life passage and the phases of the creative process. This is schematized in the chart on page 127.

Knowing that designer Milton Glaser would have some insights relating to the pathfinder's use of innovation, I asked him, "What is the tension for designers between being truly innovative and operating within the confines of an audience's understanding so that the new idea isn't rejected?"

"That raises a heartbreaking question," Milton Glaser said. "Professionalism really means eliminating risk. Once you become good at something, everyone wants you to repeat it over and over again. But the more you eliminate risk, the closer you come to eliminating the act of creative intervention."

Reopening oneself to risk, keeping that willingness to experiment alive, turns out to be as important in life as it is in art.

When to Stay, When to Go?

It is not always time for a change. All pathfinders go through long periods when they are not actively changing, when they are building a family or laying the foundation for a career, putting down roots or simply enjoying doing what they have learned to do well, or when their energies are absorbed by seeing someone they love through a bad time.

Often it is not time for a change even when change looks like the easy way out. Pulling up stakes to move to another part of the country, for example, may be no more than a temporary evasion of problems that could not be solved back home unless preceded by the hard work of self-examination. When we are in our twenties and our work commonly holds no greater meaning—we have no commitment to the product, are not being paid very well, and feel frustrated much of the time—the best course often is to stay.

PHASES OF THE CREATIVE PROCESS	PHASES OF A SUCCESSFUL PASSAGE
Preparation	**Anticipation**
Gathering impressions and images	Imagining oneself in the next stage of life
Incubation	**Separation and Incubation**
Letting go of certainties	Letting go of an outlived identity
Immersion and Illumination	**Expansion**
Creative intervention—risk	Deliberate intervention in the life conflict—risk
Revision	**Incorporation**
Conscious structuring and editing of creative material	Reflection on and integration of one's new aspects
Dormancy—a creative pause for the replenishment of self	Dormancy—for rest, reward, and play to offset stress of change

If we wait and gain competence or a financial base, or perhaps find a mentor, we will be better prepared to gain by a change when an opportunity that is clearly better presents itself. Nor is feeling oneself in a trap necessarily a sure signal that change is called for. In collecting the biographies of hundreds of women, I have noticed a strong similarity in the way many of them speak of their twenties. If they had children, particularly if they had more than two, they usually described themselves as having felt trapped to some degree. That does not mean they should have chucked it all and headed for Hollywood to try for a bit part on a sitcom. Even if they had been offered the chance to do something more exciting during those years, most of them would not have taken it. Despite the frustrations natural to young parenthood, it was not a period when outer change was appropriate.

We never should see alteration of circumstances as the only possible change. At times our circumstances must or should be accepted. But we can move mountains, so to speak, by risking a change in our inner landscape. Instead of giving up too soon on a situation that is not ideal or on a person who is not living up to our wishes, we might better change our perspective into a patient, constructive, supportive frame of mind that can help to salvage the situation. In the end, this approach may establish bonds of trust and loyalty that are to be cherished.

There are other instances when, even though it might be the most natural time to make our own passage, someone we love simultaneously suffers a setback in fortunes or health. Most of us would agree that the greater courage is shown in not abandoning someone who is ill or dying. If there are young children involved, breaking up a marriage merely for a my-mate-doesn't-make-me-tingle divorce would show not a willingness to risk but a readiness to indulge oneself in escape.

Although most of the pathfinders in this book took action that resulted in some outer change of situation, the process always began with an *inner change* in their basic approach. The kind of risk-taking under examination here, for the most part, is the willingness to give up our self-limiting behavior patterns, the spunk to risk changing our role or our work when in an unnecessary backwater, or to shift emphasis within our professional tribe as our values mature. In the private realm, willingness to risk may mean the guts to give the "other" in an important man-woman or parent-child relationship the same license to change and grow as we have demanded for ourselves. And on a more philosophical level, willingness to risk can be the spirit that allows us to challenge our own private beliefs and values and the daring to include others whose beliefs are different.

No one can tell you when to change. The many biographies in this book are the closest I can come to offering specific instances in which people, presented with a normal passage or an unpredictable life accident, have found ways to change and become in the process what I would call pathfinders. It may not be necessary that you change immediately or extremely. The only error is to rule out the possibility that at some point you may need to change, and that with enough acquired qualities and enough backup support you may become the pathfinder who can do it.

If we anticipate taking the risks of personal change and do not become defensive or angry or fearful about the process, we can guide change and allow ourselves to be animated by it. We can even, ourselves, become agents of change who anticipate and shape events on a larger scale.

But before that is possible, we need to nurture another quality that distinguishes the pathfinder—a feel for *the right timing*.

6.

THE RIGHT TIMING

And what I pity in you is something human,
The old incurable untimeliness,
Only begetter of all ills that are.

—ROBERT FROST

The willingness to risk and the courage to change can still lead down a blind alley—for lack of foresight. To the degree that we learn to anticipate the future, we increase our control over the direction of our lives. As we know, the primary source of well-being is the conviction that one's life has meaning and direction. To arrive at that conviction—to weave the delicate web of love, work, family, purpose, and pleasure that might support a fully engaged life—depends to a considerable degree on the right timing. And to get the timing right demands that we train our powers to predict the future.

The rich think in decades. Poor people think about Tuesday all day Tuesday. They cannot afford to take time out of Tuesday in order to prevent a setback next week or next month. The idea of giving up a day's wages to wait hours in a public clinic for a prenatal examination, for instance, on the chance it might prevent a defect in a child who will not be real for months and who probably was not planned for in the first place—it's all abstraction. Dinner on the table Tues-

130

day night is real. Carfare to go to work on Wednesday is real. It might be said that anticipation is one of the truest measures of social class.

A world apart are children of the upper-middle class, encouraged from the beginning to look ahead, set goals, plan their futures well in advance. Many will become executives, trained to management by objective; or doctors, lawyers, professors who through years of graduate education will learn to defer rewards while working hard to earn credentials. Often they have grown up around people who made investments that were not expected to pay off for years. Before the psychology of inflation took hold in the 1970's, trust funds and tax shelters and five- and ten-year plans were normal artifacts of upper-middle-class life. Middle-class people anticipate automatically in many ways they do not realize: just to have "a dream"[1]—a vision of one's future possibilities—is a form of anticipation.

Pathfinders, although most often from middle-class backgrounds, do stand out from others in being more likely to begin adulthood with a clear dream. And they seldom give up dreaming of new possibilities for extending themselves in the world. Depending on their age, some see themselves as being still on the way to achieving their original dream. Some have attained their original dream and have replaced it intentionally with another. And a good many, aware that they might be approaching a dead end in pursuit of the first dream, have searched for and found a new one. Although many pathfinders have become so in the course of an accident to their careers, it is important to remember that most pathfinders usually do not race toward one goal until they run into a brick wall and then try to pick up the pieces. They are adept at anticipation—imagining future bends in the road and preparing to shift gears in advance.

If anyone should be aware of the need to plan for the future, it is professional athletes. The handwriting is on the wall for them from the start. When the strength and agility of early youth drop away, the athlete will need to have prepared another path. For most athletes this time comes in the early thirties, when more than half of life is still ahead. The more prepayments of time and thought that have been made on that alternate sense of self, the greater are the dividends of confidence and excitement waiting to be cashed in at the start of the transition.

But the professionals who manage them and the fans who fawn over them elevate professional athletes to the bogus immortality of infant gods. It is almost as if, by indulging them like pampered children, we find it easier to deny the passing of time in our own lives. In fact, many athletes who retire when they are still relatively young stumble through emptiness, anger, divorce, and sometimes years of degradation, trying to recover that intensity of focus. The love and money lavished on celebrity athletes hardly teach deferred gratification.

"I used to ask myself what I was going to do when it was over," Bernie Parent,* former hockey star of the Philadelphia Flyers, admitted to the press after he retired in 1978 and slipped into depression and heavy drinking. "It was scary every time I thought about it, so I would play another game and forget about it."[2]

Since the principal reason for fear is surprise, much of the vague menace surrounding the prospect of change is *minimized* by projecting ourselves into the future. Parent lived for a dangerously long time in the present. "In hockey, you live by what you do on the ice, not what you are as a human being," he discovered in retrospect. "I was so self-oriented, things were hell for me and my family."

So it was with mixed feelings that I attended an Old Timers Game at Shea Stadium hosted by the New York Mets. I wondered why people came to see this menagerie of old baseball players being carted around the field in stock circus tradition—the crippled one, the sightless one, the great DiMaggio standing up all the way because his back now makes sitting an ordeal, and big, bad Don Larsen, who pitched the only perfect game in a World Series, back in '56, now a paunchy rancher, who busted through the gate like a has-been cowboy.

Why did they come back? Was it for those few seconds of hesitation after the announcer built up to each of their names, those terrifying few instants of dead memory time before the fans remember and break into cheers, or don't remember and slide into vacuous applause? The game itself

---

* Real names are used in all references to sports figures.

is always a clown act. Since there is no team, there is no teamwork. The players exchange positions and goof up double plays, and before you know it the stadium organ segues in daytime-TV style, and out onto the field come the custodians to rake up after the dog-and-pony act before the real, big-league, game begins.

At the party that followed the game, I asked Don Larsen how he had made the transition from athlete to civilian. He said, "I really didn't. I just lived from day to day."

One of the former major-league players at the party had anticipated his future, and it had made all the difference. Frank Torre wore the look of a prosperous and enthusiastic businessman. He was 47. While playing ball for the Philadelphia Phillies, Torre took a full-time off-season job with the Pepsi-Cola Company. He wanted to learn how to be a first-rate salesman so that he would have something to look forward to when the shouting was over.

"I didn't live in the dream that it was never going to end," Torre said. "I knew I was an average player. It was obvious why the girls were coming so easy. You could have green hair on your chest, but so long as you're wearing a major-league club's shirt, you're a celebrity." Dark and handsome, Torre drew on his cigar and smiled in self-amusement. "I used to go to great pains to seduce women who *weren't* impressed with that, so my sex life didn't change when I became a civilian."

Too often professionals push beyond their naturally gifted years until they become common laborers. The fun goes out of the sport and the body becomes rebellious, ushering in a long, dread period known, if not admitted, to be the beginning of the end. Torre, however, had promised himself he would stop playing when it no longer was fun to put on the uniform. That happened when he was 31. By then, the thrill of selling equaled for him the thrill of hitting a home run. What is more, he had demonstrated to himself that he was good at something else. That self-knowledge provided the boost of confidence he needed to open a sporting-goods store, which became successful, and to marry and start a large family. Later, after joining a conglomerate, he advanced to international sales director.

"Now I play tennis for fun and have a new life with my five children."

Looking around the party depressed Frank Torre. There were résumés in his drawer from men in that room. A few were sincere, he said, but most former ballplayers who came to him for a job did not really want to work; they came hoping for some magic that would restore the glory.

"I still see too many athletes not preparing for their future life." Torre shook his head. "Baseball is just a *part* of it all."

Later that evening I watched Frank Torre get next to one of the Mets' most promising young stars, Lee Mazzilli. Only 23 then and aglow with youth and stamina, the kid assumed a sassy Travolta pelvic tilt while the old-time catcher took him to task: he was losing sight of the future, letting his eyes wander to girls and custom-made clothes and blow-dryers, and now, flirting with television producers!

The kid said he didn't need plans for the future. He hadn't even reached his peak. He liked the idea of playing in a soap. He wanted to be a superstar.

The old-timer looked at this beautiful young man, possibly gifted with the kind of natural talent that is passed out once or twice every generation of ballplayers, and he wanted to shake him into the future. He tried to make him understand that if vanity lured him away from discipline, the parade would pass him by, and once he was dropped back to the minors, he would be just another pretty face. All through the heated lecture, Frank Torre's hands punched the air and his breath came in bursts. All the while his pupil stood there posing, implacable, moving nothing, and his face said, *I'm only standing here because you're the manager's brother; otherwise, I'd tell you you're a silly old man.*

A sense of future time, counselors find, is the most difficult thing to teach young unwed mothers. "Their concept is now; there is no concept of future, or planning," says Mary Ann Shiner, therapist at the Thomas J. Riley High School for Pregnant Students in Los Angeles.

Their longest future usually is a month, from welfare check to welfare check. Linguist Daniel Fader points out that poverty-level inner-city adolescents usually talk in the present: "Yesterday, I be goin' to the store. Today I be goin' to the store." The present is all they have. With nothing much to count on in the future and nothing particular to cherish from the past, they live and talk in the now.

Man's elevated state among primates is caused in part by the long delays in response our nervous system makes possible, delays that allow time for past experience to educate our response to immediate events.[3] One of the great advantages of higher education is the further training of secondary reactions—that is, the ability to extend one's response time and to delay gratification at will. Scientists have demonstrated that people who score high in this aspect of intelligence do more long-range planning and are less influenced by temporary fluctuations in their environment.[4] This training, like any other, has its down side. Out of the ranks of these superrational thinkers, some voices will pipe up years later, bemoaning the fact that "I should have followed my instincts!"

Whenever I joined a discussion group of contemporary college women, they began with the assumption that everything was going to be different for their generation. They were naturally impatient and pragmatic: all they wanted was the secret formula.

"Women just ahead of us talk about holding a terrific job, and marrying a guy with a terrific job, and having a baby between making dinner and going to the health club," as one student at Washington University in St. Louis summed it up. "How *do* you put together a life when you want it all?"

Back I went to Manhattan to talk to some of those women "just ahead," the New Young Tigresses who are traveling with finesse toward impressive titles and salaries along career paths formerly open only to men.

Good As Goals

ZZhhnnn, ZZhhnnn, Azzhhnn—round and round go the six treadmills jammed into the space of three phone booths while six panting professional women warm up in the corridor outside. The health club is so saturated with these women that a card in the window of the treadmill room warns, *Ten-minute limit between the hours of 12 and 2 and 5 and 7*—which are the only times they can break away from Goldbrick, Silverstein, and O'Shawnessy; for God's sake, hurry up in there! *Zzhhnnn, azzhhnnn*—all the machines are occupied by men, smoke coming out of the tops of their heads; BTU's are vanishing into the atmosphere with the same useless magnificence as desert art—unharnessed, irrelevant. Never mind! The young women waiting have come out of the top professional schools, trained to take their places in the post-industrial society where the premium is on producing information, where physical work is of course obsolete, but where competition demands that they be able to *keep pace.*

"Nothing like a middle-aged man at the office who tells everybody you can't cut it, to make you dig in your heels," says the business-school graduate we shall call Meredith.* "And before you know it, they've turned you into a hard charger."

Exasperated at having her exquisitely timed schedule thrown off, even slightly, by a dumb health club, Meredith simply went out and bought her own secret $500 home running machine—"secret" because, having one of the better minds of her generation, Meredith is keenly aware of the public-relations problem inherent in letting people know how nearly she has the world by the tail.

It's . . . embarrassing: 26 years old and counting among her blessings a solid brass business-school degree, a $35,000 job with a consulting firm, loads of friends, dozens of promising young men calling her, membership at a private club where she takes the men *she* calls dancing, plus being able to give dinner parties for sixteen several times a month—and all of it timed to perfection. Having some extra money from your parents helps, it really does, she admits. But the bottom line, the "net-net" as they say in business circles, is that she has it all—*all*—under control.

And the minute she gets married, Meredith is convinced, she blows it all.

Like other young professional women competing for advancement at the same rate as young professional men, she knows she has to work at least one-third harder. It is not fair; it just is. High-aspiring women routinely put in seventy-five-hour weeks, whereas their male counterparts may average closer to fifty-five. But before the clock starts running and play actually begins, aspirations tend to run to the preposterous.

* A pseudonym.

"Right up until I graduated from business school," Meredith admitted with a laughing roll of her amber eyes, "I was sure I was going to have ten kids, run a hundred-million-dollar company, and take all the tennis tournaments."

It did not take her long to recognize she might be overreaching a bit. Even after scaling down her goals, she had to learn so many tricks simply to stay on track. How to dress unprovocatively, for instance: always being upholstered in pebbly tweeds or demure in choir-girl collars; and how important it was not to wear one's long blond hair loose to the shoulders. Meredith's solution was to jog to work with her hair flying, to arrive well before anyone else, then to disappear into the rest room and pin up her hair in a bun. It sounds picayune, but a woman is always being compared with the "norm," which is a six-foot male in a three-piece suit. She must learn how to be likable but not appealing, firm but not threatening. Meredith wore minimal makeup but smiled vigorously to compensate for the pallor. She established good eye contact and spoke with a little hitch of a drawl, even to the point now and then of dropping a "y'all." It is not easy to be smart as a whip and an ambitious young woman M.B.A. One must work out a strategy with compulsive attention to such details.

Even then, with all her goal-setting and minute-by-minute planning—such as leaving the office at 6:30 P.M. and dashing out to the Brasserie to fill two kettles with cassoulet for her dinner party, knowing her cleaning woman would have fluffed the pillows and the college girl she hires part-time to do errands would have picked up the endive, and the next morning taking care to run only half time on her secret home treadmill because she cannot afford to work up a real sweat on a non-hair-washing day—even then, the best-laid plans . . .

For instance, Meredith had a bandage around her ankle; why?

Saturday afternoon she had stopped by the office to pick up a report. Her department head spotted her. "Say, Meredith, would you do some tables for me on the circulation plan?"

Of course she would. This is part of her life plan: "to run as hard as I can to get ahead of the game now, accumulate a terrific amount of expertise—cram three years of experience into a year and a half—so that at my peak for attracting the best mate, I can get married and step off the treadmill and coast for a couple of years while I start a family. By then I'll have made myself so valuable that everyone will want me when I'm ready to come back." She could regain her spot on the treadmill without having lost a beat.

The hidden problem is that acceleration tends to be viewed within a large company with as much suspicion as three-hour lunches. It throws off the corporate tempo. Managers view it as "disruptive," and fellow employees look upon it as personally subversive.

That Saturday Meredith's closest-ranking colleague also dropped into the office. Finding her there, he erupted in an extraordinary fit of paranoia. "You know, Meredith, turning out all these memos and doing all these cost-benefit analyses—you just make me look bad. Why are you doing this to *me?*"

But don't you understand? she wanted to say. *I'm on a different life schedule. I've got to do time-and-a-half now so that I can coast later.* But that would only intimidate him further. So she slipped into the rest room and had a little cry. These outbursts of tears were becoming more frequent all the time, the only hint behind the superrational exterior that for Meredith, as for most women, the quality of her relationships with people affected her at least as much as the quality of her accomplishments. She dampened her eyes with cold water and returned to the office.

To placate her colleague she bluffed: "The truth is, Dan, I'm really not that smart. I had to come in today just to finish yesterday's tables." (The real truth was that probably nobody in her field could do a better cost-benefit analysis than Meredith. Two different bosses of hers confirmed that to me.)

On that Saturday afternoon, Meredith worked until 6:30 P.M., then called her date to arrange to meet him directly at the theater. Thinking ahead, she always wore running shoes on Saturdays so that she could get around faster. She flew out of the office and downtown thirty blocks, intending to flash in and out of her apartment to shower, change clothes, and then make a beeline to Broadway before the 7:30 curtain when—crunch! She ran into a pothole and sprained her ankle and spent the evening in the Bellevue emergency room.

So every day's plan is not the best timing coefficient. And if Meredith had stopped to think about it, she might have taken a hint from that pothole.

"Any professional woman I know who's twenty-five or twenty-six or twenty-seven," Meredith told me at the time, "if she's riding high in her career and she's also interested in men—that woman carries around a huge wad of anxiety. She knows that if she makes a personal commitment to a guy, she's going to have to slow down. These women either have to fall behind at work, or cut back their aspirations, or give up having any time to themselves at all. If they try to continue in a high-powered career and add all the family commitments on top, they'll probably crack at some point." Therefore, in addition to setting long- and short-term goals and attempting to streamline all the details of existence, Meredith was trying to systematize her selection of the right husband. She divided the world into Easygoing Supportives and Hard Chargers.

The first type is sensitive and warm. He likes hearing about a career woman's problems and is always available for advice or to lighten things up. The only trouble with the Easygoing Supportive is that it truly stings him when she doesn't want to accompany him on a fishing trip all weekend. And he is horrified if she says she doesn't want to take five years off to have children. He can't imagine that she could find anything more rewarding, because basically *he* couldn't think of anything more rewarding, if only it were within his powers.

The Hard Charger never makes an ambitious woman feel guilty, because he's always "held up" at the office an hour later than she is. He is entertained by listening to her talk for a few moments about her work, "but don't bore me with the details," because he is too self-absorbed in being the *real* business dynamo. Prediction: an absentee father and generally poor prospect for family life.

No wonder most young professional women do not want to get serious until they have come up with a *strategic plan*. One cannot dally forever, of course. As Meredith analyzed it, she was still attractive and sought after at 26, but after 27 and 28 she saw diminishing returns. When one factors in the dwindling universe of eligible men, 28 worked out by her calculations to be probably the peak age for picking one's best prospect. And then . . . hold on for the ride!

People who set goals get there faster—a simple empirical fact. But is that all there is to the right timing?

Obviously, to set up every act as a goal is exhausting. Trained to think in terms of management by objective, some of the New Young Tigresses think even of marriage as an MBO. Work is their fun, and biting off a new hunk of the world through work can certainly be exhilarating. But there is little chance for a gasp of spontaneous delight at the sunset.

One day at lunch, her capable shoulders hidden beneath a smocked dress suitable for a latency child, Meredith made an ominous prediction. She knows young professional women at virtually every major corporation in New York City, and she has consulted with all of them on this matter of timing. Most are so busy working seventy-five-hour weeks to prove themselves that they say they don't have time to look ahead. But even Meredith, synchronizing the parts of her life with the precision of a Swiss clockmaker—even Meredith fears that this insistence on fulfilling all their roles perfectly is going to lead to trouble for herself and her friends—around age 30.

"We're all racing," she confided, "and underneath, we know we're heading off the edge of a cliff."

Yet if they wait too long to start a family, biology will have its cosmic joke at their expense. It is a matter for the most careful cost-benefit analysis.

"Oh, that's terrible, isn't it, doing a cost-benefit analysis of my single state?" She backed away in learned bashfulness from the application of this bloodless business tool to her personal life. Then the assured smile slowly returned. "I can't hide it; that's the way I'm trained to think."

The most obvious task in giving a life direction is to set external goals:

Where do I want to be, when? And what do I have to do to get there?

Answering machines with portable beepers, programmable pocket calculators, home computers, microwave ovens, even running machines in the bedroom, may help us make better use of our time, but a mechanistic mind set is no substitute for a philosophy of life. The most difficult and subtle aspect of getting the timing right is this:

To anticipate what one is going to *need* five years from now.

Anticipating Needs

Absentee fatherhood is a fact of Capitol Hill life. When I interviewed the sixteen youngest legislators who were retiring from Congress in 1978, almost all of them spoke about that problem. By then, most were standing on the outer rim of their flown children's lives, desperately alert to their regrets.

The son of a Lebanese pack peddler, Jim Abourezk* had gotten himself booted out of school at 16. He had no idea at all of what he wanted to do when he married at 22, and he didn't begin college until he was 26 and didn't finish law school until he was 35. Between those bursts of discipline, he ran a casino and leaped from speedboats and got into fist-fights—pulling almost any kind of stunt that would attract attention.

"It took me an awfully long time to grow up," he told me. "It's probably still happening." Even his successful run for the United States Senate at 40, he admits, was largely a matter of proving that he could do something very few others could: get elected as a Democrat in Republican South Dakota. His talent for showboating endeared Abourezk to the Washington press, who went out of their way to protect him. Once, when Phil Jones of CBS was asking questions that were too good, Abourezk smiled into the videotape camera and said, "Fuck you, Phil. Let's see you use that on the evening news."

Abourezk needed a few pals in the press corps, because one can never make close friends in Congress. "It's a nut-cutting place," he said. The man's face fell into quiet lines of thought when he was asked to enumerate the greatest moments of his Senate career.

"Let's see, the times I floor-managed legislation for Phil Hart when he got sick. The all-night filibuster we staged on natural-gas deregulation . . ." He was silent for a moment.

---

* Real names are used in all references to political figures.

"That's about it. Three or four highs in six years. Ain't enough to stay around for, is it?"

For Jim Abourezk, the hard truths of absentee fatherhood did not hit until his oldest son, Charlie, was already 22. The senator was out speaking in South Dakota and had invited Charlie, whom he hadn't seen for months, to join him at the Howard Johnson's motel after the speech. Charlie stood in the motel-room doorway while the staff swarmed over his father with scheduling questions and the hangers-on fawned over him and the phone kept telling him how loved he was, until it was midnight, and Charlie said, with nothing in his voice, "I'll see ya."

"That's when it finally dawned on me what a horrible thing . . ." Abourezk left the self-reproachful statement incomplete. Of course, it was not only his six years in the Senate that interfered with forging close relationships with his children. The generally unstructured, goal-free pattern of his life before entering politics had been a drain on family relations as well as on finances.

"I kept telling my kids I pissed away half my life, you shouldn't do that." Naturally they followed not what their father said but what he did, and not one of the four children had set foot in a college to that day. One was tending bar, another was a telephone lineman.

Preparing to retire after one term, the senator's disappointment was palpable as he considered some of the results of having pursued the unanticipated life. "I used to want to mold my kids; I'm over that now," he said. "To be honest with you, I don't give a damn what they do."

A year later, Abourezk had turned to private law practice in Washington; one of his clients was the new Islamic Republic of Iran. As he assessed his present status, his remarks ran along these lines:

"Specializing in the problems of the rich is just a way to make a living. I don't give a shit about law. I essentially do what I please. And that's the way I'll keep it."

He flies small planes for escape.

Gary Myers, congressman from Pennsylvania, entered politics at 35, the same age as Jim Abourezk. Five years later, Gary Myers had arrived at a new personal philosophy: "I see the next six or eight years as ones in which I don't want the major orientation of my life to be a job. I've come to a stage where the number of hours required to do this job are just not compatible with having an active family life."

Forty and out?

Yes, 40. Gary Myers is a conscientious, humorless, big-knuckled, blue-collar, family sort of a guy—a night-school kid, not a law-school man. He never was a natural member of the Washington club. I watched him one night, following his announcement that he would leave Congress after his second term. He was enjoying what he now treasured most: being a father.

The dusk was sweet with matted curls of moist grass under the ten-speed bikes of the spectators. Two dozen parents sat in the bleachers cheering the McLean Little League team. Congressman Gary Myers and his wife, Elaine, were among them. Moments later, their 12-year-old daughter Michele walked to first. Suddenly she was stealing second, and her father watched her long legs running, running out their girlhood with merciless swiftness.

"In no time they pass out of your life," he murmured. His wife didn't have to remind him of it; she had to console him.

It was another, earlier occasion that had provided the moment of crystallization for Congressman Myers. Watching his daughter run up the steps to enter junior high, he realized all at once that one more campaign would put her in high school, and one more after that would put her out. The next slide was blank, and there was the surprise: the glimpse of that emptiness stung him, the father, more than anyone else in the family.

It took him back to his first political campaign. He was working as a turn foreman at the Armco Steel Hot Mill in Butler, Pennsylvania—hardly a likely challenger for a Democratic incumbent with twenty years of government-subsidized supporters. Often, Myers slammed most of his forty hours at the steel mill into weekends. Every other waking hour he and his wife were out campaigning; of sleeping hours there were virtually none. His eyes looked like those of a night bomber pilot's. That first campaign was something for which they never could pay back their two kids. Then the personal debt grew, and eventually, like all debts in Washington, it swelled into abstraction.

At the crossroads into midlife, Gary Myers took the less-traveled path. To savor those sweet years of his children, he apparently went backward, back to the Armco plant and the tedious security of producing steel. He took a 45 percent cut from his congressional salary and became a supervising engineer, a lower-management job. Two and a half years later, I checked in to see how Gary Myers was doing.

"When I look at the projections surrounding my decision, they were pretty accurate," he said. "Had I let my life be consumed in a job, I would have missed all the activities the kids were getting interested in—a marching band, soccer, dramatics, skiing. Children might still do these activities on their own, but there's more motivation if parents are able to participate."

Given his commitment to reviving the kinship network of their western Pennsylvania family, Myers will not accept a transfer from the company, which he realizes probably puts a cap on his pipeline into higher management.

"Sometimes, on the job, I wonder where I'll be when I'm fifty . . ." His voice trails off, then returns with a quiet confidence. "But my work situation is stable, so I can meet other objectives outside the job."

The right timing for Gary Myers involved anticipating his needs at another stage of life. Jim Abourezk, by contrast, played it day by day. But the unanticipated life, for all its short bursts of excitement, did not add up to sustained meaning in either his work or his family relationships.

Do not assume, however, because Myers put family first and Abourezk did not, that becoming a pathfinder is a clearcut matter of favoring relationships over career. There is no way of knowing yet whether Myers chose rightly or wrongly. Ten years from now, it could occur to Myers that if he had given up baseball with the kids and snuggly Sundays at home with his family, he might have built more meaning into the last third of his life. As a more senior member of Congress, he might have broadened his paternal instincts by speaking up for his constituents or helping to "father" important legislation.

No one can make all the right decisions. One can, however, improve the ability to make the best decisions. Learning to anticipate our future needs is one of the most valuable tools in timing those decisions soundly. It is a tool we will need when we are older—the right timing on retirement, for example. It also is a crucial tool for those in the

Frantic Forties, when people's time perspective usually becomes distorted. Fearful of time running out and resistant to identifying themselves with the next stage—middle age—inhabitants of the Frantic Forties are handicapped in accurately predicting what they will really need as 50- or 60-year-olds. Certain that at any moment they will be over the hill, they are likely to dash out with a "last-chance" attitude and do something foolish.

Of all the ages, however, the tool of timing probably has the most profound impact on youth. The early part of adult life is full of firsts; yet which should *come* first? The order in which we make the major commitments of life to a considerable degree determines our life pattern and when and whether we will become pathfinders. The rest of this chapter will focus on younger people; the second half of life will be treated at length in a later chapter.

The Postponing Generation

The response of many of today's young men and women to the pressure to make decisions about the future is—not to. The most notable characteristic of the post-counterculture generation is that both men and women are postponing the major commitments of life. Faced with decisions usually made in the Trying Twenties—*Should I marry? Should I have children? Should I commit to this career path or that one?*—the preferred decision among a large segment of educated young Americans is no decision at all. Put it off. Keep all the options open.

The baby-boom generation, now between 20 and 35 years old, has by sheer weight of numbers drawn the focus of the nation to its own tastes and concerns at every stage of their lives. We can now expect to be drawn into the problems of young adulthood: how to find a job, buy a home, raise a young family, and balance personal commitments with career. What is unique about this group—45 million of whom will turn 30 in the next decade—is that the economic and social realities have flipped upside down since their childhood expectations were formed. Few can afford to buy today the houses they grew up in; two children now come at the price of four; and the dual careers demand that the balancing act be done with one hand behind one's back. As a result, some of the decisions they are postponing will become "no's" by abstention. The pattern for this society in the last quarter of the century is one of people making fewer commitments of any kind.

About 25 percent of baby-boom couples will not have children at all, and another 25 percent will have only one, according to demographers' estimates.[5] Postponement of marriage was the change highlighted as the most significant in a study of the family life cycle with an eighty-year perspective conducted for the Bureau of the Census by Paul C. Glick.[6] A significantly larger proportion of women who were of the usual marriageable age in the 1960's and 1970's are now heading toward middle age *never* having been married—an estimated 6 or 7 percent.

The educated new young man in my studies is decidedly a postponer.[7] The centerpiece of his game plan is to remain unattached, at least until he is 30, and to keep his career line tentative. Here, in particular, he is breaking new ground. The great majority of his father's generation chose as their life pattern to launch all three aspects—career, marriage, and family—in their early twenties.

Don't lock me in! is the motto of the new freewheelers. As one of them says, "I fear getting trapped in this life indefinitely. If I thought I was going to be doing this for the next forty years, I'd probably shoot myself."

Postponement makes sense on paper. While the pacesetter male claims his highest priority is being loving, his female counterpart is out there burning up the achievement track with her born-yesterday ambition. Maybe she will have a child, maybe she won't. Suppose he does manage to "prioritize" and "trade off" with a professional woman and they actually find the time to produce a child together, but then she gets an offer in Abu Dhabi, or he does. What is their order of priorities? Does his career, her career, or placating the baby's nurse come first? Since a married man no longer can be sure of calling the shots, postponing marriage creates less conflict all around.

But it is not only the cutting edge of the young who are postponing. The majority of women are still marrying and bearing children, but they are doing so in an economy in which a two-paycheck marriage is almost a necessity, and in a social climate in which most women realize that by the time they reach midlife, wifedom and motherhood will not be enough. Those who still approach marriage as the be-all and end-all are postponing the work of anticipating their future needs, which probably means anticipating a need to work.

Young men in my surveys have yet to reconcile two equal but contradictory fears: "I'm worried about not having enough money" and "I'm afraid of chasing money until I find myself fifty years old and locked into a job I hate."

Over the parade of achievements being marched out by the pacesetting young women of today there occasionally passes a different cloud of apprehension: "I might end up at fifty without a child, feeling I'd outsmarted myself."

Each of these groups is struggling to get the timing right, and many of their adaptations could bring a refreshing flexibility to the old life patterns. But evidence of high well-being in a young person is not automatically synonymous with pathfinding. Until these younger generations move into their middle years, we cannot know if their experiments will work out.

Success or Children?

Surprises were in store when I conducted a workshop with more than one hundred successful young women in finance. They were trailblazers in an area that was formerly the exclusive preserve of men. Their work demanded foresight, and they had it in abundance. These women planned ahead in their careers an average of 9.6 years!

Most of these bright women had always put a premium on achievement. Their average age was 32 years old, half were unmarried, and 60 percent were childless. They described themselves as "professional" or "managerial" women, and their salaries were mostly in the $30,000 to $40,000 range. There was a bracing aura of exhilaration and energy about this group, stimulated in part by successful risk-taking. The ability of these women to plan ahead set them apart from others who were waiting for life to happen to them or who were adhering to some arbitrary time schedule. These women initiated action. One pleasure buoyed up all the professional

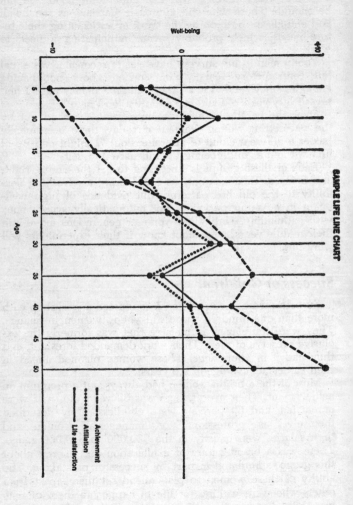

Well-being

SAMPLE LIFE LINE CHART

Age

- - - - - - Achievement
·············· Affiliation
———— Life satisfaction

women I interviewed, even when, because of their lack of a past on which to draw and their paucity of role models, they were confused about the timing of their careers: the sheer excitement of managing the enterprise of their own lives.

The financial women were exceptionally hardworking, successful, and bright. But when we did a little exercise together, they were as startled as I was by hints that some important needs might be getting lost in all this rigorously learned goal-setting. (The reader may want to do this exercise too, using the materials and instructions given here. A sample Life Line Chart appears on page 148.)

The women were asked to draw their Life Line Chart. Given graph paper and marking pens, they were instructed to make an age line across the bottom of the paper from birth to their present age, dividing it into five-year segments. The vertical line on the left side of the graph ranged from a midpoint of zero, to plus 10 at the top and minus 10 at the bottom. The midpoint (a line was drawn across the center of the chart as a reference point) signified moderation, quiescence, not much happening one way or the other.

On this chart the women were first asked to graph with a broken line the ups and downs in their achievements. Typical up periods were marked by winning an award or being graduated from a tough school or landing a prestigious job. Typical low periods coincided with failing to get into a good school, being passed over for a promotion, or experiencing a period when other priorities or problems prevented working toward outside achievement. If memory wavered, one could identify the most memorable points and then connect the points. The horizontal midline reflected the periods when achievement was flat.

With a dotted line, the women next drew the ups and downs in their personal relationships—as they perceived them at the time. This was called the affiliation line. Typical up periods were times when relations with parents were close and harmonious, when one was in love or had a lively circle of friends, or when a marriage was bringing joy; the down periods coincided with the reverse.

The last line, drawn unbroken, represented a person's perception of her overall life satisfaction at each age and stage: how generally cheerful or gloomy she felt during that period.

Then came the interesting part. Which other line did that

long solid line more closely follow? Did it run roughly parallel to the person's achievement line, or did it stay closer to
the affiliation line? (If the solid line was lower than both the
other lines, the person was doing *something* wrong—depriving herself of satisfaction in both love and work.)

A statistical analysis of the 106 charts from this group was
startling. The achievement line was consistently high for these
professional women. But it was their affiliation line that ran
closer by a significant degree to their overall life satisfaction
line. Although most of their efforts were being directed
toward achievement,* their zest for life was much more profoundly affected by their relationships with people.

The results made one woman think differently about the
management of her own life: "Unless you step back and look
at what you're giving up to be a high achiever, a malaise
might come over you from years of neglecting needs you denied you were dragging around."

Some of the women in the workshop seemed to have
learned to trade stereotypical emotional female thinking for
stereotypical analytic male thinking. Like Meredith, these
new young professionals are often in a hurry. Egocentric, almost defiantly non-intuitive, they may fear that to use their
ability to register the emotions of others might distract them
from their goals. In the effort to "pass," they tend to reject
spontaneous behavior in favor of following rules to the letter,
thereby reducing their chances of making a blunder. These
leanings are understandable: formerly powerless groups always find it safest at first to mimic the dominant group. It is
also tempting to adopt the tools professional planners teach
at the business schools as the new religion and to translate
them into strategies for achieving the right timing and a superior balance sheet in life. But to undervalue the grasp of
complex emotional interrelationships and the human commitments that have always come easily to women, in my
opinion, can result in suppression of some of the most vital
strengths in the human armamentarium.

A sad glimpse of the price of admission to certain male
preserves came from one of the workshop participants who
described walking down the corridors of her financial institution: "All of the men's offices make a proud display of

* See Appendix III for statistical results.

pictures of their wives and kids. The women's offices show no trace of the personal. They don't dare call attention to that part of their lives."

Interestingly, most of the twenty-nine women enjoying highest well-being among the financial group did have children.* But for the rest of the young pacesetter women, children did not even appear among the top five on their list of dimensions from which they derived the greatest joy in life. After satisfaction with sex, they thrived on love, money, personal growth, and their spouse's or lover's happiness. Then work. And only then children. It is this that emerges a few years down the road as the clinker in the New Young Tigress's game plan.

"All my friends around the same age are obsessed by the same subject—children," I was told by a single, 35-year-old television correspondent. "We always end our discussions with the same conclusion. It would be impossible to stop now and have one. And it would be impossible not to."

Other women I interviewed had planned the ideal time for their first conception with the same precision they brought to slotting in free-lance projects or deciding how much work to take home for the weekend in their briefcases. This whole childbearing business was just another matter of efficient work flow. How confounding it was to find themselves not pregnant after a summer, six months—a whole year and still not pregnant! One managerial husband could not conceal his exasperation when his ordinarily splendidly organized managerial wife shrugged and said, "I guess we'll just have to keep at it."

"I'm not interested in inputs," he declared, "only outputs!"

It might be nice to know that if one scaled down one's work load, a child could be produced between the ages of

---

* The refreshing thing about this optimal group was that no one pattern prevailed. Instead, the three most-satisfied professional women represented diverse life patterns. One was a "never-married" money manager who spent most of her time alone and did not intend to marry or have children. One was a "deferred nurturer" who had waited until she became a vice-president in her thirties to have two babies. And finally, there was a super "integrator," a chairwoman of the board who had been mother and stepmother to no fewer than a dozen children.

31½ and 32⅝, but nature simply does not cut it that fine. And fertility does decline in the thirties.

Even when the problem of bearing is surmounted, there are problems of rearing peculiar to the occupation of parenting. Parenting shows no *product* at the end of the work week. It is only the process, in the early years a process of cutting a narrow trail of civility through the jungles of infant lusts and savage sandbox rivalries, a process that might tax human endurance to its limits yet produce no more than a few days of order before the undergrowth chokes the trail back to the aboriginal.

A bizarre development within the ranks of this first wave of new women is what might be called *baby givebacks*. A tiny, transcontinental baby-adoption market has sprung up for upper-middle-class white professional couples who have found that they cannot cope with a child on top of two careers and a marriage. Some are giving back their offspring to carefully chosen counterparts who are eager for a child and who promise to provide the same kind of home.

Erik Erikson's[8] suggestion is that, in place of having one's own children, the urge to procreativity among the new generation can be satisfied by active efforts to improve the condition of every child *chosen* to be born.

For a black woman to forgo having children for her career simply is not an option, I was told by a 35-year-old black attorney with one son. Yet she feels little support for her dual role from other professional women who have remained childless, and secretly, she fears that parenting will limit her potential success.

Carlotta Miles* has another point of view. Coming out of a black professional family herself, she never suffered the handicap of equivalent white social patterning that presents marriage, career, and motherhood as *choices*. It therefore never occurred to her, as she marched through medical school while twice pregnant and had her third child without missing a beat between internship and residency, to consider doing anything else. She is still married and a happy, successful, if not publicly recognized, Washington psychiatrist.

A historical perspective was offered in the book *Three Hundred Eminent Personalities*,[9] based on an academic

* Real name.

study of the subjects of biographies written since 1962. Although the eminent married men studied usually did have children, almost 60 percent of the women were childless. And only seven of the eighty-two women had sustained a lasting marriage and children, as well as a distinguished career.

Most of those fortunate seven had husbands who shared their values and were not competitive with them. There was no time in their lives when either spouse had had to sacrifice a career for the sake of the other. The husband accepted the wife fully as a working person but was not made to feel inferior to her. "[These] strong, able women seem to marry men who are kindly, lovable, and loving and who are often cultured and intelligent but are less driving and ambitious than are their wives . . ." observed the authors. There also was help in the house to care for the children.

Elizabeth Arden, Indira Gandhi, Golda Meir, and Helena Rubinstein were among those studied who regretfully separated from their husbands because their family life and career could not be reconciled.

A contemporary journalistic study of seventy-five successful women[10] revealed that those who are most content and have the most-balanced lives were not driven by the competitive rule of "gotta get to number one," not compelled to repeat the conquest again and again. The happiest of these women had anticipated the slot to which they thought they could aspire without knocking the balance out of the rest of their lives—and had aimed for that goal, reached it, and now felt content about it.

We might see the story of Meredith, whom we met at the start of the chapter, as an early warning for the professional women of today and tomorrow—and their numbers will be legion.

More than *one* college woman in *four* is planning a career in business, engineering, law, or medicine, according to the UCLA Education Association's Joint Study of 1981.[11] This represents a more than 400 percent increase since 1966. (During the same period, the percentage of men pursuing these four careers has risen very little.) With equal educational backgrounds and equal aspirations, many women will

learn to look at life in the same way that hard-driving young
professional men always have.

Yet career paths in most professions were long ago established to reflect the male life cycle. Despite years of
lobbying by the women's movement, little has changed to accommodate the woman who wants to use her creativity both
maternally and externally. A junior faculty woman in line for
tenure at a prestigious university, for example, follows a pattern almost identical to a man's, except that the woman
usually gives up having children.

"The eight-year track to tenure—when most faculty members are between age twenty-six and thirty-four—was invented
by men who had wives," charged Ursula Goodenough, now
professor of biology at Washington University, during a Harvard 1977 alumnae colloquium on the life cycle.[12] "Women
would never set up an institution that made prime time of
those years." Those years coincide, of course, with some of
the optimum years for childbearing and child-rearing. But
the route to tenure demands that one get the grants to do the
research to rush into publication using the scut work of underlings to accrue credits to one's own name, which rates
bigger grants, more underlings, and ultimately the crown.
Women who do not share this disregard for other purposes in
life, such as establishing a strong family, remain somewhere
in the tenure warp between perpetually "promising" and prematurely "over the hill."

Society's Timing

Today's younger women—those under 35 in my surveys—
are as confident as today's young men that they will fulfill
their career dream. Of the fifty thousand M.B.A.'s coming
onto the market each year, the professional schools now are
graduating classes of between one-quarter and one-third
women, almost all of them gushing into the pipeline at the
middle-management level where currently only 2 percent of
the jobs are held by women. No wonder they feel confident!

But these bright young women may not be entirely aware
of the challenge they represent to society's timing. Individually they may be doing everything right. But collectively

they are shaking up the roles, the reward system, the very values of the corporate culture—all at one time.

Corporate America is beginning to grapple with the problem of women moving up career ladders alongside men, wanting to be judged on their abilities rather than on their appearance, but often unable to escape age-old sexual cues and stereotypes. Their very presence in upper corporate corridors is unsettling to many older men, who tend to get their social and work roles confused when confronted with young high-performance professional women. These women can be threatening to the executive secretary who is used to seeing her relationship to her boss in a "monogamous" light. And the sense of rivalry often felt by the corporate wife, whether or not well founded, can be virulent enough to do in one of the two women.

Yet, the fact remains that American industry is going coed. And whenever another of the nation's institutions loses its all-male exclusivity, there is certain to be some shock, some excitement, some sabotage, and a good deal of silly gossip. Behind it all, however, is a real issue and one that is already producing casualties in the executive suite.

The issue is corporate incest.

The fact of men traveling with women associates is the greatest problem females in the work force present, declared the president of E. F. Hutton, the large securities firm, at a 1980 conference on women in the work force. "We don't quite know how to cope with the objections on the part of some of the men's wives," admitted George Ball. "We have to learn to overcome it, but now we sidestep it."

The issue is both unique to the Eighties in America and as old as incest within the family, around which taboos had to be created and codes of behavior learned to prevent the deterioration of civilization. Those behavior codes are by now so internalized that a father and preteen daughter, who might share the same motel room without giving it a thought, several months later will split up into separate rooms. No one has to say a word. They simply know.

Just as tribal cultures have totems and taboos that dictate how each member will act toward fellow members and outsiders, so does a corporation's culture influence employees' actions toward customers, competitors, and one another. Indeed, so firmly are certain values entrenched in a company's behavior that responses to sudden change are almost predictable.

As the famous Bendix duo—Mary Cunningham and William Agee*—found out.

Given her profile—the strict Catholic upbringing, the singular devotion to work, the absence of private life or real friends, the ambition fueled by altruism and sublimated desires—Mary Cunningham fits ideally the stereotype of life at the top of corporate America, which is most often, whether lived by a man or a woman, lived in a straitjacket. The mold cut out for the chief executive officer of a Fortune 500 company—a position her Harvard Business School dean predicted Mary will achieve within ten years—calls for being married to the corporation. Rigid custom also keeps almost all male CEO's married to their first wives, although the relationship may afford little more intimacy than attendance at a rubber-chicken dinner. Both marriages are necessary.

As much of America knows, Mary Cunningham, then 29, was forced to resign from her vice-presidency at the Bendix Corporation when her quick promotions touched off rumors of a romance with chairman and CEO William Agee. A blitz of press coverage in the autumn of 1980 elevated the incident to a national issue.

While hiding out at the La Costa health spa to rest and think, Mary spent hours walking on the California beach. In our conversations that week, she swung from being in cool control to casting about imperiously for villains. If she had to do it over, I asked her, would she have taken the promotions to vice-president at Bendix?

"Somebody has to trailblaze. If all the Bill Agees and Mary Cunninghams are afraid to take promotions for fear people aren't going to be ready for them, then how are we ever going to reach the point where people are rewarded with what they deserve?"

Should she have moved up so fast? I added.

"We have to ask ourselves," said the New Young Tigress, "must we wait for a 29-year-old man to be made a vice-president before it's okay for a woman to do it? Or can a woman be the role model and the first one to break a record?"

* Real names.

What she represents is seditious. The meaning of Mary Cunningham is that the inevitable echelons of male executives in corporate America may not be inevitable any longer. Women, even young women, are beginning to intrude, to disrupt the network, and—most insubordinate of all—they are moving ahead on sheer merit. To be sure, they will start fires. All it takes to start the fires of envy is a woman too bright and a man too progressive, surrounded in an organization by more ordinary mortals.

Yet some have called Cunningham's an "isolated case." One test of an isolated case is whether or not it grips the public's interest. The Cunningham story aroused so many people because it symbolized a frightening new equation between men and women: the women wanting parity and the men beginning to fear they deserve it. It is not a problem confined to male executives wrestling with how to handle meritorious women who threaten their traditional domain and dominance, but a problem being thrashed out in squad cars between male policemen and the new female "quota cops" assigned to them as partners; between outraged, hard-working men and their wives who want to go to union meetings instead of making dinner. The easy attack of sexual innuendo deployed to stall Mary Cunningham in mid-ascent will become less and less effective. Eventually, the sheer force of numbers of high-performance women will make ambushes on their private lives appear ridiculous, if not irrelevant.

Ten years from now, predicts Mary Cunningham's former dean, this controversy will seem rather "quaint."

. . What lessons can be drawn from the Cunningham case?

Her strategic plan was to jump on the fast track, concentrate her energies exclusively on career advancement, and find a mentor who could take her to the top. She had all the willingness in the world to take risks. What was missing from her plan were several other crucial qualities—the right timing, the capacity for loving, and friendships or support networks.

If you intend to be a wunderkind and to break speed records, you must *understand the timing of your society*. The pacesetter, the wunderkind, the one who is "first" to do anything, shakes up norms. To do so without backlash you must be enormously skillful in anticipating your impact on others.

You must teach people how to think about you, how to treat you, what not to be afraid of. Emerging women of achievement who are most successful make a constant effort to forecast the effect they might have on others: the preconceptions that will be brought to meetings, the guilty rivalries they may stir in their female peers, the rational and irrational fears men may have of being made to feel diminished by a woman who is more than they are used to handling.

Mary Cunningham threatened corporate timetables and age and gender norms simultaneously. She made some of her male peers feel inadequate. Others were vitriolic at her "unfair" rise. She interrupted the "monogamous" relationship between boss and secretary by moving into an office adjoining the chairman's. And any corporate wife would have felt pale by comparison to Mary's performance as the ideal "office wife." On top of that, she and Bill Agee were shaking up the whole institution from bottom to top with a massive divestiture program. People had no idea when their jobs might be taken away.

Under these conditions, Bill Agee did Mary Cunningham no favor by inviting her into an embrace of hubris. They flew so high and so fast above everyone else, they were almost asking to be shot down sooner or later.

Unfortunately, Mary Cunningham's business-school training did not include seminars on how to build bridges and form friendship networks within the company or without. Many of her male classmates from Harvard seethed with rage as they recalled her classroom strategies. According to them, she seized every opportunity to ask a question of an instructor and made a point of drawing her professor aside after class for a few additional comments. These "sins" of sycophancy in an equivalent male would have been no less aggravating—only more familiar. Miss Cunningham made few friends at Harvard Business School. Nor did she make many friends within the corporation. When I spoke with her in her small, unadorned apartment outside Southfield, Michigan, Mary Cunningham admitted to having no friends except for her boss-mentor. She lived a monastic, if not monstrously unbalanced, existence. But, she told me, there had been no room for love in her early strategic plan. That plan called for, in her twenties, finding her weaknesses and developing her "instrument"; her thirties would be for amassing credentials and maximizing her financial independence; her forties for jockeying for real power—then on to a world contribution. Mary later recognized that she had been using her work in part to deny her other needs. After her fall, and the anger, depression, and self-examination it forced, she began to yearn for balance in her life. Early in 1981 she accepted a vice-presidency at Joseph Seagram and Sons, where the level of responsibility matched that of her previous position. But now, with the storm of Catch-30 passage clearing, Mary Cunningham is thinking about adding marriage to her life plan.

Laid-back Men

The irony is that while the bright young women are being indoctrinated into Old-Boy timing, the pacesetting men of our society recently have begun to question, *Why should I work that hard? What else am I missing in life?*

The organization-man mold into which we have been pouring men for years has always had its monstrous aspects. It cuts off most emotional circulation for fifty to seventy hours a week. It compresses well-rounded 25-year-olds into projectiles with tunnel vision. It rewards cold-bloodedness in competing with peers and sycophantic skills in dealing with bosses. It teaches ready-made group rationalizations for manipulating the consumer and makes the current rules of the game more fashionable than old-fashioned ethical or humane behavior. The organization man was well known to most of the Sixties radicals. He was the father they never saw.

The new young men surveyed would like to work no more than six hours a day. With the extra time they would double the hours they spend alone. If they had two, they wanted four; three, they wanted six—as much time as they possibly could cadge to work on "personal growth." Fifty or sixty hours a week buttoned into the executive uniform did not fit the male pacesetter's order of priorities.

These and other observations on the pacesetters among young American men are based on two thousand completed Life History Questionnaires and sixty personal interviews. Most of the men were between 18 and 28 and were beneficiaries of lavish educations: 72 percent had a bachelor's degree and half as many had at least one graduate degree. Most were being or had been groomed for traditional three-piece-suit professions—business, law, medicine—or creative careers as artists, designers, or writers.

These were men with choices. If they did what was necessary, most of them had a shot at being winners in American life—by the old standards. But many of them questioned the old standards. The great majority had a different outlook on work from that of their fathers.

Fully one-quarter of the two thousand men were self-employed. They seemed to be willing to go small in order to be in control and make their own hours. Their ideal was the sort of cake-and-eat-it-too capitalism that would allow them to put their own values into the product, take four-day weekends when the powder was good for skiing, and be president of the company as well. This part of their new dream was already showing positive results. The young men who ran their own businesses were well represented among those enjoying high well-being.

But who were these men who said they were *not* ambitious, did not care to lead, wanted more time to spend on themselves, wanted to be more loving, yet did not particularly want the responsibility of taking care of a family? They were not the dropouts of half a generation before. Their idea of well-being appeared to be having the ability to shift personae at will, from hotshot to laid-back, from lover to loner, from high earner to guiltless dependent, from idealist to pragmatist, from virile to vulnerable.

Consider a man I shall call Mark,* a gifted public official who is the housing czar of a major city. Mark had to schedule our interview at seven in the morning because he is always tied up at the office by seven-thirty. Bending like an eager beaver over the questionnaire, he admitted, "I was always good at tasks; that's how I got where I am." His skin was unlined, his hands ringless. Except for one interlude of living with a woman, his personal life had been pretty much catch-as-catch-can, although he now insisted that the most important thing in life is to find a loving relationship.

He would like to spend, he said, *eight hours* a day working on this being-loving business. How it actually goes is that

---

* A pseudonym.

he has spent twelve hours a day for most of the past sixteen years working on working.

He claimed that his is the worst job in city government. "But that is what makes a job truly worth doing," he said in the next breath, "when it extracts from you every last ounce of energy." At 36, Mark was not even in the right generation to be talking laid-back. Yet he sat there over coffee insisting that he was not a workaholic, absolutely not.

"I *look* like a workaholic," Mark allowed, "but I would be very happy for very long stretches of time not to work at all."

Don't laugh; he had already rehearsed it. When he was 31, he got bored with his job as a congressional staff member and quit. For six months, while turning down comfortable positions with law firms and corporations, he didn't lift a finger to look for work, and he loved it: "Loved the freedom, loved sleeping until ten every morning, loved going out to the beach."

He was living with a professional woman at the time. She would already be at work by the time he woke up. "I felt no guilt. I'd look out the window; which direction to take for my walk was a major decision. They were leisurely, nonentity-type days." No kidding. He would come home from the park and make lunch and unplug the phone and then—eat your heart out—then came the best part of the day. Summoning vivid images of all the bureaucratic stiffs stuck in their cubbies, he would lie back on pillows still hollowed with his head print, and he would take a two-hour nap!

By then it would be time for his lady friend to come home and deliberate over their plans for dinner and the movies. Sometimes he would pay for the evening, sometimes she would—the way it is with professionals who keep company these days. But she paid the rent on the apartment, and that was the key. His fall from the state of bliss came when he tired of the crumminess of her apartment, found a better one, and the new rent began to rip into his savings.

Not to complain. He'd had a sublime six months. He scarcely missed influencing events. He could pick up the metropolitan section of the paper and read with delicious negligence about breaking scandals and public outcries, because somebody else's hindquarters were burning for a change. Mark discovered the therapeutic effect of genuine indifference. Going cold turkey was . . . cleansing.

"I can do that," he said, "throw myself into extremes."

And so we see a new pattern appearing—the alternating of extremes. Intense work and striving for accomplishment, tempered by a period of unstructured time for one partner while the other carries the ball. Women have traditionally enjoyed the option of interrupting their careers. Now the wunderkind male can avail himself, too.

Not all men with dreams of high achievement follow the wunderkind pattern. The classical wunderkind not only takes bigger risks; he creates them—as long as they have the potential for being a winning showcase for him. The line between work and private life is hazy from the start for him. Work is not only his pleasure; work is usually his bulwark against feeling helpless and insecure. The danger is this: in the process of subordinating everything else to the drive to enter the winner's circle—in the expectation that then insecurity will vanish and one will be loved and admired and never again humiliated or made to feel dependent—the gulf of loneliness grows wider and wider. And when the wunderkind's grand expectations are shot down, there is no one else to care.

Having tried out a variation on the orthodox wunderkind life-style, and liked it, Mark had a reformist dream: "to have the option to live a nonworking life. I wouldn't do it forever, but I'd like to exercise the option from time to time." He looked forward to taking a more extended breather when and if the mayor who appointed him lost the next election. "I'd like a year, two years, when I would have no professional responsibilities," Mark fantasized.

Two years later, still the overworked housing administrator, Mark did have an appealing and capable woman in his life. He spelled her, while she took a moratorium on political life and tried a private-sector job. If the chips fall right, she may be able to do the same for him. This is one of the contemporary pairs who will attempt a new kind of timing: alternating as breadwinners.

As I got to know the young men I interviewed, I noticed something odd. Their posture was laid-back, but beneath the surface there was an edge. These pacesetters talk of a life suffused with the soft glow of nonstructured time and unlimited personal space, of loosely arranged but loving relationships, of the body as temple and the mind as instrument for their personal expressions. But beneath the rhetoric was the rigid success ethic instilled by their parents. These postponers seemed to be leaning against a velvet-sheathed sword. And underneath that edge, there was something else: a refusal to choose, to commit, to give up any pleasure for the pursuit of meaning and direction that might be more lasting.

Although the lowest-well-being young professional men did not usually see themselves as loners, the sad echo throughout their self-descriptions was an impaired capacity to form friendships or to love. Some of them had prolonged ties to their parents, if not by living in the same house with them, then by remaining at least partially financially dependent. So bound were they emotionally that even if they tried, they could not achieve intimacy with anyone else.

Perhaps the new young men with all their laid-back talk about postponing commitments in search of the balanced life will make better decisions when their moment does come. On the plus side, being older then, they should know better what they want and a good deal more about how to get it. But they will also bring to late commitments the handicap of habituated selfishness.

Intensity versus Balance

We would all like to achieve a balance among time for cultivating our talents or skills and directing them into satisfying, useful work in the world . . . and time for building a love partnership on the basis of many evidences of mutual trust and caring . . . and time to give ourselves to (not just support) our families and children . . . and time to shoulder our share of responsibility for protecting the fragile social contract . . . and time alone. But to achieve such a balance, or anything close to it, takes many years.

In the first half of life the tension is between intensity and balance. How much intensity should one pour into learning and competing for personal advancement? At what cost of time for love, nurturing, and social participation? And of course, vice versa: What must be sacrificed in order to develop dimensions of identity not dependent on success at one's primary vocation, whether that is being a mogul or a mommy?

Achieving *excellence* in some endeavor requires ignoring balance during at least one phase of life. For a person who is graced with uncommon athletic ability or artistic talent, or with obvious nurturant gifts or pure brain power, and who wishes to develop that endowment to its limit, a fierce and singular focus is generally demanded in the early years of adulthood.

If the person is going to be more than just good, he or she eats, sleeps, and dreams one goal. Nancy Swider was a national team speed skater who set a record in 1976. Four years later, at the age of 23, her motivation had reached a new level of intensity. "I've known for years how I wanted to feel," she said. "I've seen it in other people. It's a look of total purpose. Just once in my life, I want to live at the absolute edge of my potential." Similarly, if one wants to excel in business, science, or the professions, the disciplined intensity required approaches an obsession.

"How do you win a Nobel Prize?" a friend of *New York Times* editor Jack Rosenthal[13] once asked a colleague at Stanford who had just won one. The professor drew a line on a cafeteria napkin, divided it into three equal segments—zero to 90, 91 to 99, 99 to 100—and marked an x next to each. "You have to be willing to put equal effort into all three x's," he said, "and then be damned lucky."

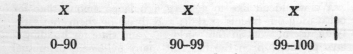

X	X	X
0–90	90–99	99–100

Most people do not have the problem of being born with a major talent or a stratospheric IQ. Their aspirations are far more manageable than trying out for the Olympics or becoming president of General Motors. But even for the less than extraordinary, balance in the first part of life is difficult. Analyst Carl Jung[14] cautioned people away from seeking a "roundedness" of personality before the age of 35. In the first half of life, a narrower focus is quite in order.

Consider the woman who tried in the past to have it all in her twenties. Often she made a good pretense of being Superwoman but secretly felt herself being pulled apart. She was trying to juggle three acts at once before she had developed much proficiency in any of them. Too often, before she was much past 30, one of the balls dropped.

After the divorce (more common than giving up her child, her work, or her sanity), she was likely to spend her early thirties practicing single parenthood, often not daring to remarry until her career was consolidated for fear the competing priorities would overwhelm her again. Some women were ready to remarry by their middle or late thirties—*if* they happened to find on the shelf a man in midlife secure enough to see a successful, independent, emotionally balanced, sexually experienced—and slightly shopworn— woman as preferable to a cupcake.

But for all the difficulties, and for all the casualties, the women in their forties and fifties who came out at the top of my well-being scale were mostly women who had made commitments to marriage, career, and motherhood, all before the end of their twenties. They did not postpone. Usually, theirs were serial commitments; sometimes they waited to have children until they passed 30. If there was a trade-off, it was that for the most part the highest-well-being women were not extraordinary successes in a professional sense. Few of them had gained much public recognition. Probably they had resisted devoting to their work the kind of time and absorption required to make a bigger mark. A further exploration of this dilemma for women, as it may be played out in the second half of life, appears in Chapter Nine, "Best of Male and Female Strengths."

By contrast, the lowest-satisfaction women in this generation group had followed the more traditional path of postponing outside work until their families were fully established.

What is encouraging is the emergence of new patterns aided in large measure by the changes that have taken place in society.

Distinctions, however, between the various age segments of women must be drawn very finely. Those only a few years apart, having been shaped by rapidly changing social attitudes during the 1960's and '70's, may be miles apart in the way they approach the world. Those of a new consciousness, who were launched into the first years of adulthood during that period of history and who are now nearing their mid-thirties, I call *point women*. Like point men at the front of a military patrol, they took the first fire drawn by the women's movement. Those who fought to be taken seriously as full and equal citizens had little with which to defend themselves but an inflexible ideology. Sometimes cursing and copulating like true soldiers, they united against men as the common enemy. They sustained some casualties. Many of these women were at least temporarily alienated from normal human needs that were feared at the time to be signs of weakness. And many of them are now trying to integrate what they had to leave out.

The integrator's pattern as it used to be defined meant women who tried to combine it all in their twenties—to integrate marriage, career, and motherhood. The new integrators often have the equivalent of two lives: one they pursued before the culture caught up with the women's movement, and one after. A fair number ended the marriage of their twenties in divorce. Some have remarried, some not; but many of them, rather than drive themselves to desperation trying to do it all on the same schedule as a man, are today tailoring their own timetables.

The New Integrator

If anyone looked the part of the delicately featured, glossy-haired, slightly overbred college coed who would make some corporate executive the perfect wife, it was Rebecca Fried.* But she resisted by prolonging her education in every possible way. Immediately after college and the wedding to a well-to-do young man, she went with him to Thailand to live in a slum on two dollars a day. It was 1968, and to be in the Peace Corps was to her the apotheosis of the romantic life. Danger and urgency were all around, yet she felt amazingly potent: build that school, put in that water system. She made impassioned speeches at village meetings, she got things done, she improved people's lives

* A pseudonym.

dramatically. After three years the couple came back and her husband entered a program in nuclear physics. What to do? "I don't want this to end." Why not graduate work? Yes! At Stanford. That would be four more years for her Ph.D. In Art History, of course.

"The Ph.D. was really a way of putting off having children," she later understood. "I wanted to have a solid career under my feet. It was like putting boards down over the abyss."

The abyss was something she had grown up with in the suburbs of Indianapolis, with a depressed mother who never quite functioned after her "nervous breakdown" when Rebecca was six. The three children had had to be split up and farmed out when her mother was first taken away. Rebecca spent a wretched six months, believing that her life would be fragmented like that forever. Her father came to their rescue, brought the youngsters back under his roof, and became himself an integrator—coming home from his job to the work of cooking dinner and reading to the children; juggling it all just as working mothers have always done. Rebecca was intelligent enough to discount her mother's pattern as possibly unique. It was the other mothers, the ones you could not help overhearing in a suburban development where the houses are linked like a long paper cutout: the tantrums carried across the summer nights, after the husbands came home; the shrill, doomed voices saying, "This day has been awful, you don't understand . . ."

Don't end up like those women. That was the guiding principle Rebecca brought with her from her childhood.

Early in her stint at Stanford, the women's movement took off. Suddenly the idea was abroad that women could go to business and law schools too, and graduate and get things done in the world. The idea whose time had come was just a few years too late for Rebecca, it seemed. Her husband and his family had already picked her out to produce perfect children and flawless dinner parties and to lead fund drives for museums. After enough association with the exquisitely sensitive types who moldered away in the arts library buried in Byzantine architecture, she began to forget what she had done in the Peace Corps.

Rebecca was starting to think of herself as one of the world's fragile resources. She would be unexcelled at training young eyes to appreciate the motifs of Jewish synagogue art in Chagall but not too competent in life. She would need a scholarship to life. People would have to understand that she couldn't possibly take care of herself, not on an assistant professor's salary of $12,000 a year. (That little fact was a well-kept secret until people were almost finished with graduate school: Oh, incidentally, there are no tenured positions available—too many graduates.) She was not sufficiently dedicated to leap at the prospect of spoon-feeding the lives of the Impressionists to dummies in some second-rate school in Kansas where there was a chance for tenure. That was one of the problems with going to a top school; you were always looking for another Stanford.

In the stacks one foggy day, at 27, Rebecca began to feel a little flaky. Imagine the progress she might have made in the Malay Peninsula in the nine hours one routinely spent sitting around the fine-arts library reading all alone—by God, she could have laid in part of a sewer system!

On her way home she squinted through the steaming fog at the business school. *That's where the jerks go,* she thought to herself out of Sixties habit. All the way home she tried to think about how to hold back motherhood a little longer. Bursting through the door with a wonderful idea, Rebecca blurted to her husband, "What I really want to do is go to the business school!" He slowly put down his book on quantum mechanics and came over and placed his hands on her shoulders.

"Becky, that's not you."

The next few months were hard. She still functioned, but inside, she felt as if she were squirming around, blocked, helpless, sorry for herself; nobody *else* realized how much she needed a scholarship to life, and all her colleagues in the arts department thought it was vile of her to consider "selling out" by going to business school. Rebecca had no models and no support—she was a point woman.

"That's how I happened to have two lives," Rebecca Fried explained. "There were two cultures—and I crossed over the firing line when I was thirty."

It came to divorce. Her husband would never forgive her for having the kind of intelligence that was better equipped than his to cope with the practical world. She could never accept his emotional weaknesses. They agreed to part. She found herself thinking, *Okay, where is the next person who's going to take care of me?*

She knew she had crossed some sort of line when she took the chairman of the fine-arts department to lunch and announced, "Guess what? I'm going to the horrible business school." A bridge burned. She had not even been accepted.

The next battle was to pass her orals in the midst of a psychological blackmail campaign by her estranged husband. That caused her to think out a very useful coping strategy for getting through a crisis.

All right, kid, you have two weeks until the oral exam, she told herself. *You can keep cramming. Or you can call it off and have yourself a good emotional crisis. Just make up your mind. And then be single-minded.*

It made her happy, once she had set a goal that way. It gave some assurance that the future would be better. She passed the orals, settled the divorce, and started business school. That was enough for a while. She didn't want any more big changes.

But a strange turnaround occurred while she was dating a law student. Was the real reason she found him compellingly attractive that he was caught up in working for the government, interviewing people about Watergate, involved and doing things? She questioned herself.

One day she found herself saying, "I don't have to marry him. I'll just *be* him."

And to be sure, once Rebecca had been graduated and had gone to work for a prestigious financial consulting firm, she made a startling discovery: "It's not that hard to do what men do. Basically, it's overrated. What I do now for a living, after all, is sit around and tell men who are business executives where they're being illogical."

One day during her militant period, in the midst of a singles game with her tennis pro, the other woman asked, "Would you like a blind date?"

Rebecca went out with Larry that night, and they saw each other the next day and every day thereafter for the next five years. Both having midwestern backgrounds and sharing the same mythology, each having enormous respect for the other, they could not have been closer if they were clones.

He asked her to marry him after the first three weeks. She already felt he was "family."

Mature love . . . the relief of it was almost staggering. "All of a sudden that whole part of my life around which there had been so much anxiety was solved. It's made a big difference in my life."

They agreed to a basic treaty. He was a demographer but wanted to write someday. She talked about "leveraging your vision" by attaining a position with enough power to allow for making a moral or social contribution. But under their treaty one did not pull out and go for "fulfillment," leaving the other to do the heavy lifting. They worked hard for three years to pay off their graduate-school debts and then began to talk about having a child. She was 33.

"I'm excited about getting to know our children," Rebecca told her husband. "I want to meet them as people."

They found a house that would embrace all their fantasies. Rebecca imagined it as a bulwark against the world, and only when they were settled inside did she begin to cry. At last, almost three decades after the fact, the tears came that belonged to a child of six who had had to be mother to her little brother of three.

Why did they take our mother away? She must be going to die. Otherwise, why would they be getting rid of us? Why do my brother and I have to go and live with these people we hate? Why can't our sister come with us? Who will remember her insulin shots? This house is too big. These guard people or whatever they're called are too old. Listen! Is that my little brother crying? Walking down the big dark scary hallway all alone to the bathroom? "Wait—I'm coming! I'll protect you!"

· She had not allowed herself to dwell on these memories. Not until now, not until she felt safe.

Nearly two years elapsed. The nursery was painted. And Rebecca still was not pregnant. Another dilemma for the modern integrator: her postponed children may well not respect her timetable after all. But the waiting did give Rebecca time to think, to anticipate her feelings about children and their demands of her. Gradually, almost all ambivalence had dropped away. One evening, shortly before Rebecca turned 35, I sat in her living room and we talked.

She still looked soft and poised, with teeth as uniformly perfect as Chiclets and a naturally shining ponytail, but she was strong. She could foresee what she would need in the future. And she knew a good deal about how the world worked.

"The easy part is deciding to cash in on my own career value—to put this asset to work at a high return—in order to get enough time to be there for my children," she said. "I haven't quite sorted out yet whether it's better to stay in a high-powered field and work part-time because the money's so good, or to take a nine-to-five corporate job."

At present, she was being billed out by her firm at $1,000 a day. That meant every day was like taking a final exam.

"I think the only thing that frightens me," she went on, "is that children would make unlimited claims on me—legitimately. And I would feel an unlimited desire to make their lives good. I know I can't do that and have a high-pressure career, too."

Her natural support system consisted of the men at work who had wives with careers and were juggling a child between them. These mid-thirties men would corner her at lunch and wax poetic about what it's like to go in at five-thirty in the morning to pick up this amazing wiggling joyful miniature human being. When she had to work into the evening with one of them to write a report for a client, it would have to be at the man's house—his wife was on a business trip—and they would sit at the kitchen table while he fed and burped the baby. The most startling thing, to her, was to hear them say, "I never read books anymore."

"It's really hard for me to imagine not reading," she admitted. Because she has a grasp of future stages, she was able to add, "But it's not going to be a disaster. I'll read again."

The biggest change in her life, she was aware, would be to move off center stage. "My life will become very sensitive to other people's needs."

Did that make her apprehensive?

She thought quite a long time.

"I would have to answer to myself at the age of forty-five if I weren't one of the people on the lists," she replied.

The lists?

"Lists for government service, for foundation appointments, for, let's say, an undersecretary position in the Cabinet."

This contemporary vision of a young professional woman took my breath away for a moment. Imagine being able to look ten years ahead and conceive of putting oneself in line for a possible Cabinet appointment. The women in my circle, most of them as smart as Rebecca and as diligent too, would not have thought at her age beyond waiting to be asked—if they had thought of it at all.

But if she were shooting for that level of recognition, she could not lapse for the next ten years into a nine-to-five job while raising two children, I said. Wouldn't she have to join commissions and give speeches and go to learned conferences?

"I think you're right; I'll have to make those choices," Rebecca said with equanimity. "I'll probably choose the children. I'm going to be exhausted a lot. I'm gonna be sort of on the survival edge, just coping, but that's the choice. I'd rather do that well than do it badly and have acclaim."

Having grown from a conception of herself as the "fragile nurturant resource" who needed a scholarship to life, to deciding she would "be" a man rather than marry him, to the point of integrating her new independence with the security of a mutually supporting love, Rebecca had redrawn her future several times, each time more broadly. If she is to continue to be a pathfinder, she will not castigate herself for failing to have it all by an arbitrary deadline of 45.

A man would not have her problem. Life is not fair, at least not yet. But that does not mean a woman must shoot herself in the foot to prove the point. And, in fact, before I left her home, Rebecca was beginning to talk about extending her schedule. After all, the first shuttle into space had had to be postponed three years.

"Maybe being on the lists can wait until your fifties," she mused. "It seems to me a goal worth putting out there. . . ."

All of the new integrators are not women. But unlike most of the laid-back young men, the new integrators among men do not put their primary energies into the attainment of mellowness. Their lives, even at this early point, while busy and sometimes exhausting, appear to have meaning and direction.

Alternative to Me-ism

Meet Alan Prater,* a young man who appears to have resolved successfully a major part of the conflict of values besetting his generation. At 28 he is amazed to say that he has just gotten his cake and the means to eat it too. He also turned out to be one of the happiest young men of all I surveyed. But he did not get there by being laid-back or by staying single or even by starting from a swell childhood. He grew up middle-class in Shreveport, Louisiana. His father and mother separated when he was an adolescent, leaving the boy desolate and tied by guilt to his mother, who transferred to him her entire self-abnegating belief in upward mobility through a man. He was her only son.

Then, too, there were the expectations of Prater's wife. When she asked Prater to marry her, she thought she was asking for the hand of an attorney. He was in his first year of law school at Washington and Lee University. She was eleven hundred miles away in Shreveport. "I'm ready to get on with it," she said, "or break away."

It didn't fit his plans. True to his generation, he had intended to postpone marriage, but he said he'd call her back. He thought about it for half a day and made his first true commitment—to marry her.

There was Prater at 23, halfway through a fine legal finishing school, having graduated with honors from a southern college so self-consciously upper-class that besides wearing Top-Siders and khakis, the young gentlemen wore their Lacoste shirts *underneath*, as undershirts. He was being supported by a new wife who thought him a successful attorney-to-be. But his heart was not in being an attorney, and, naturally, the grades were not there either.

"I thought it was best to withdraw a couple of steps," Prater says, "to see if there wasn't something else I wanted to do and, if not, go back to law school with renewed vigor." And so he took an eighteen-month leave. The courage to take one step backward eventually paid off by allowing Prater to triple his options.

* Real name.

After a year and a half in a holding-pattern job, Prater decided to become, of all things, a cop. He joined the Roanoke, Virginia, police force. He was its first Phi Beta Kappa officer. He had been with the force for almost two years when he filled out my Life History Questionnaire. What I could not tell from his answers was that Prater had filled out the survey at one A.M. after a hard day's work because he could not sleep that night. He was at an important decision-making point in his life.

The great dilemma for Alan Prater, nearing his late twenties, was: *Did I make the wrong choice? Should I go back to law school?* It was not the frustrating nature of the job. In fact, he found police work enormously satisfying and did not want to give it up: it was something he believed in. If he went back to law school, he might eventually make much more money, but he would be locked into the old achievement syndrome. If he stayed with police work, he feared he would never have enough money.

"The terrible thing was," he said, "I had an either-or choice."

Luck played a part in what happened to Alan Prater next, but he also had the determination to push his luck. He stumbled on a section in the city personnel handbook about an educational leave-of-absence program. If a public employee could persuade the city fathers that the city would benefit by advancing his or her education, they might send that employee to graduate school on half pay in exchange for three years of service afterward. Only one person could have a crack at it each year. Prater seized the opportunity and promoted himself back to law school on half pay without sacrificing his dream of social contribution. He graduated the next spring.

A policeman with a law degree is a new creature. As a result, Prater will not have to pretend to be satisfied with being a high-paid trial attorney. His new dream calls for integrating his interests in active crime-fighting work and in the more intellectual rigor of law—as well as "wanting to find a way to contribute." He hopes to become a prosecutor.

One does not often get that kind of outcome without being willing to work like the devil, to live with uncertainty, and to sacrifice in the present in order to achieve future goals. Prater's commitment in an age of self-indulgence is special.

On balance, Prater has resolved only some of the conflicts of his generation. There is another question now pressing for which he has no comfortable answer, the question of children.

Frankly, the Praters don't want the responsibility, the sacrifice. They have made the decision to postpone having children. "Right now, neither of us wants to have to give anything up to stay home and raise a child," Alan protests. Their life clock will run splendidly without kids; they are adamant about that.

"Do you have any friends in their mid-thirties or older who are still without children by choice?" I asked.

"Yes, several couples."

"Have you looked at them with an eye toward how it might feel *then* if you remain childless?"

"No, because we know we're not going to be anything like them anyway," the answer came shooting back. "We're different people, and our relationship is going to be totally different from theirs."

The classic response of people in their twenties: *We're unique! No other generation has anything to tell us!* The posture is familiar and even to a large degree protective. If people in their twenties could not close off certain choices while pumping their energy and hope into others, they would probably stall at the first crossroads.

In fact, a rather surprising finding surfaced when all the young men of high well-being from different groups were compared. The married ones who were fathers were the happiest, and they also reported that more than anything else—more than work, more than success, more than the love of a mate or sex or money or any of the rest of it—it was children who brought them satisfaction. Like Rebecca Fried, these men were not consuming all of themselves in a mad pursuit up the ladder; they were saving an important part of themselves for their families.

Rolling with the Punches

Timing is setting goals.
Timing is anticipating future needs.
And timing is also something more.

Remember Meredith, who jogged from the office and sprained her ankle in a pothole? A first-rate anticipator and a world-class goal-setter, right? At 28, in perfect timing with her strategic plan, she found herself a Hard Charger. Radiating at her wedding an almost manic energy, she was quite obviously engrossed in *getting married*. The husband figure was hazy, an archetypal young banker. "She's a little scared of him," her mother said. "She likes him because he's so cool when he makes those big oil deals."

Six months later, Meredith's husband was offered a splendid opportunity in Australia.

All Meredith's "systems" suddenly were on the blink. She went about looking dazed. But eventually she said:

"Maybe I'll do a venture . . ."

The more she thought about it, the more she began to see the obstacle as opportunity. By then it was clear to her that working for a consulting firm or an investment banking house required so great a commitment of hours that a parallel commitment to a family was virtually impossible. Looking at the corporate route, she decided, "By the time you have a little space to breathe, you're so exhausted and so close to sixty you can't enjoy it—it's too late." The best way to balance it all, she concluded, was to be self-employed.

Here is what else timing is: Timing is realizing that the best choice does not always turn out to be the right one, and having the ability to accept that. Much of the bitterness among low-well-being people derives from their dwelling on a rational choice that turned out to be wrong. *If only I hadn't gotten pregnant then . . . If only I'd taken that job instead of this one.* They fail to realize that time is a line that continually branches, presenting more choices.

The truth is that one is rarely caught in an absolute dead end as the result of choosing one road over another or, through the capriciousness of life, having a road chosen for one. A pathfinder is a person who continues looking ahead, who keeps anticipating future possibilities, and when the road clears again sees the opening, and risks taking it. Timing, in the end, is also flexibility.

In the winter of 1981, Meredith started her own business. Now all she has to do is run back and forth to manage it from half a globe away. No doubt she will. Youth and energy will carry her a long way. I would only hope that the redemptive value of growing older might relax her enough so that every time she crosses the International Date Line she doesn't cry, "But where's my day! I lost a day!"

7.
CAPACITY
FOR
LOVING

The only gift is a portion of thyself.
—RALPH WALDO EMERSON

Poets, novelists, and playwrights have used up a great many forest products trying to put into words what it is about love that allows us to hear a little singing beneath the thunder of the darkest days. Otherwise quite disagreeable or formerly "difficult" people can be seen to soften around the edges when they let themselves love, and be loved. To do so we must learn to let down our guard, smooth some of our edges, let out some of the rope on "mine" and "me." Particularly for the pathfinder, who is always striving to master his or her environment and to become something more, it is vitally important that a hand is there to hold the other end of the rope. Most pathfinders carry a little secret: they are not entirely alone. Someone else takes their dreams and illusions, their good and bad times, their triumphs and defeats, almost as seriously as they themselves do.

An eminent anthropologist told me something personal and touching about how he lost strength on all counts when he was suddenly cut loose by divorce from the moorings of love and family.

"I no longer had an inclination to work hard. I didn't have

a family to work for anymore. To work for just myself wasn't enough."

He traveled to a lovely European city to attend a professional conference some months after the formal separation from his family. As he lay awake in the luxurious hotel room, as if he had come loose in the world, neither his mind nor his heart could bring forth any orientation.

At last he said to himself, "I am away from nowhere."

People were asked in the Life History Questionnaire about their closest relationship. Was their love returned? Did they love more than their partner, or less? Or did they love mutually? People of high well-being, overwhelmingly, had relationships in which love was mutual. So, I later discovered, did pathfinders. What does "mutual love" mean, exactly?

I interviewed a man who ranked among the highest-well-being members of his prestigious professional association. He met me at his hotel-room door with an almost puppyish enthusiasm. Behind him stood the cool, dry, self-collected figure of his European wife. Exquisitely dressed in Italian silk, she had a deeply private smile of confidence that contrasted markedly with her husband's eagerness to be liked. They had been married almost twenty-five years.

Maria Teresa* smiled graciously but hung back and sat on the opposite side of the room. She had not returned her questionnaire, she said, because she was afraid of shocking me with how different she was from her husband. That led me to ask whether he would be entirely comfortable discussing his convictions in her presence.

Both Maria Teresa and her husband smiled. They had no secrets, they assured me, and even though they disagreed about certain fundamental things, they harbored no animosity toward each other.

He had joined a charismatic church four years before. He had had no religious exposure for the first half of his life, so his sudden, fervent embrace of the miraculous work of God took his wife totally by surprise. His personality had changed dramatically. "I used to be anxious, a workaholic, extremely self-centered, and an impossible husband. Now I *know* the

* A pseudonym.

importance of sensitive communication between a husband and wife."

As he was describing the force of his commitment to sharing his faith with others, including his clients, he stopped to say, "That really turns my wife off," and he urged Maria Teresa to express her reservations. She calmly stated her disapproval of proselytizing. She even joked about why, early on, she had stopped accompanying her husband to worship. "When I go to church, which is seldom, I want a church, not a country club."

But when I turned to ask Maria Teresa directly what effect her husband's religious awakening had on her, and on their marriage, she spoke from a very different sensibility.

"My husband can do everything. That's why I married him. And he is very loving. But until about three years ago I suffered, because I knew how much good he had in him, though it was not coming out to other people. He didn't know how to allow others to get close to him, to see the real man. Now, it's coming through . . . and . . . it's beautiful!"

It was not so much her words as what happened to her as she spoke them. Her eyes filled suddenly with glistening, glad tears. They spilled onto her cheeks like pure spring water. Even though she disagreed with her husband on many aspects of his new faith, his exuberance in being able to release that part of himself gave *her* utter, uncontaminated joy. It was as if beneath the treacherous currents of self-love ran a wellspring of clear intensity—the feelings of pure gladness or sadness in watching someone else live. This, to me, symbolized the meaning of mutual love.

Loving and Identity

A sense of confidence about who we are is essential to developing this most fragile and imprecise form of creativity—the capacity for loving mutually. As we become more independent, the capacity for loving seems to expand. People often believe quite the opposite: that if a mate is not dependent, he or she might leave. Yet it may be the strong sense of their individual differentness that allows a man and woman to accept the emotional risks of intimacy.

"We can love them precisely because they are different,

because they surprise us by adding something that we can never find within ourselves, and because they *need* as well as give," elaborates psychologist David L. Gutmann.[1]

Most torch songs lament the one whose love is unrequited, but the burden of being overloved is just as heavy, according to those who suffer from it. In roughly half the marriages surveyed in my studies, one partner, usually the wife, loved more than the other. Yet it was the husband, burdened with dependent love, who felt uncomfortable and guilty. Very few of the happiest men fell into that category.

"Mutual" love among the happiest couples does not mean that one derives his or her identity from the other, or that if she starts glockenspiel lessons he does the same, or that they always travel together or have friends only in common. The most-satisfied couples have the confidence in themselves and the trust in each other to have a life separate from the marriage, although rarely a sexual one.

Nor does mutuality of loving mean that two people always want the same things at the same time. That is wishful thinking in a culture that now permits four score years of vigorous living. Any two healthy people change from stage to stage and find themselves sometimes out of sync. As their primary needs are met, they want things from life and from each other that go beyond their early romantic ideals. Replaced goals, reconsidered values, and the achievement of personal insights, although often welcome, also change a couple's original contract. There is no future in repeating, "But you said—!"

Subsequent studies have affirmed my observation in *Passages* that the most striking differences between people are not between those at different stages but between men and women at the same stage. How, then, do two people sustain mutual love within a marriage for thirty years? Or even for more than the average seven years between one passage and the next?

"You have to be willing to support your partner in what he or she wants to do, even though it's not what you want for yourself" is the straightforward answer from a pathfinder of 55. He has been both ahead and disastrously behind in the race for economic well-being, but his marriage has endured and grown richer. "Ginny* and I are so many opposites," he said when I sat down to lunch with them. "She's a health-diet nut, and I'm a junk-food devotee. I want to die from white bread." They laughed easily, as they have learned to laugh over differences far more profound. "It takes awhile to learn not only to *let* a person be where they are," Ginny said, "but to *enjoy* their differentness."

Time for Love

While a sense of confidence about who you are is essential to developing the capacity for loving mutually, no less important is simply taking the time to love. The lowest-well-being men of all ages admitted to having difficulty with close personal relationships. It was an effort for many of them to make connections with people. Looking back, some of them regretted not having given more time to "this human thing." They rated themselves generally low on personal growth. Years of emotional scrimping had cost them dearly.

"If there were only a few years in our lives that we could be together—you know, people are never *together* . . ." It was Gary Worby's wishful remark that set him and his wife to the task of strengthening their capacity for loving.

Turning 30, the Worbys† felt themselves losing the texture of full human relationships between the ties of high-speed career tracks. For many people at that stage, unless they redirect themselves or at last rattle a few gates before recommitting to their original career paths, a sense of stagnation in work often creeps into homelife. If left unchecked, that ennui can begin to weaken the whole foundation of middle adulthood.

"A lot of it had to do with getting to the point in our marriage where we were ready to start a marriage," admitted Trisha Worby, a woman as open as her broad, blond, Polish face.

In Chicago they had the childless marriage a young liberated couple should, but they wondered in private, *Why are all these people having babies?* Intellectually they subscribed to the concepts of equal paychecks, parity housework, no-

* A pseudonym.
† Real names.

fault marriage. Yet it seemed, in the choice-tipsy climate of city life, with commitment out of style and inconvenience a ground for divorce, that they had lost a certain grasp of definitions. What, really, was a marriage "partner"? What did people mean by "a sense of place"?

"Both my husband and I loved our work," Trisha Worby told me, "but we needed to take time out from doing everything we thought we 'should.'"

She posed a rhetorical question to her husband: "We've been using our wings, but where are our roots?" Their roots, in the suburbs, had long since been paved over by the cement glacier of superhighways.

They refused to succumb to the Catch-30 trap. Galvanizing all their grit and imagination, the Worbys found a way they could afford a moratorium. They bought an old van, fixed it up, resigned from their comfortable professional jobs, and began a year of thundering up and down the country. For the first time, their world had no walls, no phone, no fixed vanishing point. They fell in love with the natural world. It drew them up and out to the wildest edge of the continent, and before they stopped, they were in a fishing village in the Northwest, population 2,055. In order not to be crowded, they set up housekeeping twelve miles outside town.

"But you're leaving such wonderful jobs," warned their baffled friends back home. "You'll lose your places on your professional ladders. Buzzards will fly in your windows."

All buzzard talk, Trisha and Gary scoffed. Yes, they were scared, until they learned how to pull laundry on a sled and to "go coaling" for free fuel on the beaches with their neighbors—until they made the quick, solid friendships natural to a rural environment.

Following their own instincts in work, Gary set up a studio to make Tiffany-style lamps and stained-glass windows—not your everyday fishing village handicrafts. He was able to talk enough people into commissioning these intriguing artifacts to earn $10,000 the first year. Trisha became a public-health nurse for the state. With six villages under her care and much of the authority of a doctor, she could set up immunization programs and women's clinics and teach self-help to her heart's content, at a salary of $25,000 a year.

Having made a splendid resolution to their Catch-30 passage, the Worbys decided to put down roots. Living without water while they worked with a carpenter to build their own home, they learned to appreciate a sharpened distinction between necessity and convenience. A compost toilet is a necessity. Water is a convenience. To hike twelve miles into town—by herself—to play the flute in a chamber-music group once a week is, for Trisha, a necessity. But to love mutually, interdependently, fiercely—this became essential.

"Your relationship becomes much more precious and intimate when you commit to doing something like this together," Trisha found. "You can't run away, you can't say so easily, 'I don't like the way you look' or 'You don't talk groovy so I'm shutting you out.' You need each other. We made ourselves"—she paused thoughtfully—"cherished."

The last time I talked to Trisha Worby, it was her 32nd birthday and she was on cloud nine. She had just found out that her pregnancy test was positive. Driving home, she had had to stop the truck to marvel at a mother deer nudging its fawn. Trisha felt the wonder of her own highly estrogenic body, the slight tenderness already in her large breasts—this pregnancy was going to be a breeze!

"I remember having no idea in my twenties why people were having babies." Amusement skipped through her voice. "I'm just at another place now. Gary and I have a nucleus—we've been together in every sense these last three years, and we'll let that carry us in whatever we do from here."

When they were still living by the ideological canons of their generation, the Worbys believed the husband should work half-time and the wife half-time, and that he should change the diapers four times a day, and so on. "Sometimes I don't know what kept us together." Trisha can laugh about it now. "We found out life isn't like that. There's no such thing as half-time or even equal time. Our marriage works like pistons in a truck—the intense periods for each of us don't go up and down at the same time; they alternate."

She will stop work when the baby comes. For how long? "I think I'll just know," she says confidently.

Despite her enthusiasm for her work, there is not a hint of resentment in her approach to this next change. As her husband said gently, "Trisha, hard as I know it will be for you to quit your job for a while, I want you to realize that unless

I had given up a full-time job for a while, we couldn't have built this house."

For these two, pathfinding meant intuiting the need to pay attention to their marriage and at the same time to put some risk back in their work.

What if the Worbys had not gone away? Does one have to move halfway across the country to learn how to risk, or to become more loving and open to being loved? I would answer no, with an extenuating explanation.

One does not automatically become a cuddly bear by moving one's habitat to the west coast. And even small fishing villages have their share of crabs and snoops and people who are scared to risk stepping on their own shadow. What was universally important in the way the Worbys went about engaging a major passage was their willingness to detach from an old, even comfortable, structure. Knowing only that they wanted to be something more to each other, they were not ready to make permanent alterations in their family or professional lives—until they had experimented. After anticipating their passage, they initiated the second phase—separation and incubation—by holding a moratorium with the van trip.

A moratorium is a deliberate delay of future commitments. Although it requires living with uncertainty, it often spares the person in passage from taking a blind leap that he or she may later look back upon as evidence of "my bad judgment."

"The breaking of our pattern, stepping out of it—that was the critical thing," Trisha has realized. "It helped us see other doors."

The amount of mileage one puts on during a moratorium is not the point. It is a condition of mind permitted by temporarily suspending some of the old cues and role confinements. The conditions of incubation could be created as easily by walking on a beach regularly, or driving around the countryside on weekends, or by adopting a relaxing hobby that provides a natural time and place to be alone. The Worbys themselves may return to the city in a few years to bone up with new degrees and seek other opportunities, but for the time being they love being in the capsule of their own forming family.

Taking the time out to be together taught them to sense something that can be gained only by close observation: to know what effect a given circumstance will probably have on one's partner. Suppose criticism rolls off Trisha Worby's back, but Gary is hypersensitive. Knowing that he will feel hurt after hearing a braggart put down the way he has built their house, she will not say, "Why can't you laugh it off the way I would? What's the matter with you?" She will be sympathetic to a sensitivity she does not share. Any one of a hundred such invisible fibers might now reverberate within one person if stroked by circumstance in the other. This is quite different from the old togetherness concept, which too often caused people to presume, "If you really loved me, you'd know what I want." The Worbys also have friends and activities of their own and work that is autonomous, the combination of which not only refreshes a marriage but reinforces the independent strengths of both partners.

Trisha Worby did score among the highest-well-being women of her age group. It is too early to know how the Worbys' story will proceed, but in amplifying this pathfinder quality at least—the capacity for loving—both Trisha and Gary have been uncommonly creative. Still young, they have already accumulated the empathy and commitment that make of any good marriage a sanctuary.

It should do no harm to remind ourselves of several other characteristics of pathfinders that quite likely contribute to their success in loving mutually:

They do not automatically allow work to take precedence over the people with whom they share their lives.

They are comfortable in revealing their innermost thoughts and feelings to their mates, as well as to close friends.

They spend more time with a spouse or lover—three to four hours a day—than the average person in my surveys. And they would like to have even more time to spend.

Women pathfinders, in particular, must have discovered somewhere along the way that loving and pleasing are not quite the same thing. In fact, the evidence is that women are better able to love once they free themselves from the tyranny of trying so hard to please. Rather than looking to one man as the sole assurance of their worth, women pathfinders develop multiple sources of identity.

Those women who enjoy high well-being in their forties and fifties most often arrive at that stage with busy careers *and* flourishing family lives. Their choice of the integrator's path has generally allowed them to develop more mastery in social and professional skills earlier, which enabled them to build confidence, which fortified them to take risks, which permitted them to change and grow instead of playing it safe or putting on a happyface over a crippling inner timidity.

In the process, most of these women have accumulated courage, knowledge, humor, and a certain élan that allows them to greet new experiences enthusiastically. With all those qualities *and* the capacity for loving, when a pathfinder woman offers the gift of "a portion of thyself," she must be easy to love.

Some of the older men in my studies who had not been happy with their love lives in earlier years had begun making a priority of intimate vacations with their wives. It was these men in their fifties who often described having found a whole new dimension with their mates: a clearer understanding, a reinvigorated love, and a new level of sexual pleasure and satisfaction (not the least of which, with the kids gone, was staying in bed in the morning with the door open).

As the inhibitions of youth and former social mores fall away, the young middle-aged seem more eager than at any time in their lives for sexual experimentation. In fact, the mid-forties are a peak age for extramarital affairs, but most of the high-well-being people of this age remain attached to the same mate. An impressive number of the highest-well-being men and women described reaching a new level of sexual pleasure in their late thirties or early forties, and after 45 finding a new tolerance and companionship with their mates.

When the Feeling Is Not Mutual

It is almost axiomatic that when a marriage is good, it is very, very good, and when it is bad, it is horrid. A bad marriage can poison the well until even the best qualities of both partners become contaminated.

There are many marriages between the extremes of very good and horrid, of course. Partnerships based on a love that later fizzles out or marriages of convenience are many, and they can either go sour or become sources of strength. As many of us know, from having experienced a relationship that moved from infatuation through heartbreak and on to trust and affection, some of the best friendships can be with former loves. But when a partnership does become toxic, people begin doing to each other what they would never dream of doing to anybody else—behavior matched only by the cruelty some adolescents can show to their parents.

In a recent film called *Every Man for Himself*, French filmmaker Jean-Luc Godard presents a violent depiction of our incapacity for loving. Using stop-start photography whenever a contemporary man and woman come together out of the desert of desensitized city life, Godard renders an image of the spasms to which we have become reduced when we reach out, desperate for the human touch we have denied ourselves in the name of personal freedom and self-development. The visual cubism, and its comment on contemporary human connections, seemed to be a filmic version of Picasso's *Les Demoiselles d'Avignon*. That painting, which stood Paris on its ear in 1907, seemed to predict the affliction that would characterize the second half of the 20th century—fragmentation.

Pathfinders, too, often have to extricate themselves from personal relationships that become chronically destructive. But most of them do so only after considerable self-examination (this is one of the times when pathfinders *do* tend to be introspective), and then in a spirit more positive than defiant or vengeful.

A good number of the high-well-being women in my studies have been divorced—roughly 30 percent. By the time most divorced women pathfinders are in their forties, however, they are likely to be in love, and mutually so. By 50, like the high-well-being women who have remained married all along, they too generally enjoy more tolerance for their mates than ever before in their lives.

First Love at Forty-two

The woman we shall call Cate O'Neil* married in a hurricane in a full-length lace gown—to please her mother. There was a note of subversion even then in the raincoat and baseball cap she wore to the church and in the tears that she shed copiously to the end of the ceremony. Her thoughts were unthinkable: *This is it. Imprisonment. I don't even know if I want to be married.*

Her premonitions were realized in eighteen years of going up and down on the same loveless escalator. "Nobody would let you off. They would look at you as if you were crazy if you suggested you might want off. This was what women of my generation were programmed to do."

Particularly within her social milieu—white-gloved Catholic with money, sealed throughout childhood in all-girls' schools where children were trained like laboratory animals to acts of repetition and self-control guaranteed to lead to a "better good"—Cate O'Neil came to betrothal age with the basic female social programming well internalized:

"My rules were, you stuck it out, managed everything well, and tried to please."

There was, however, her aberrational side—that risk-loving girl who was once given to jumping out of windows and scrapping with bullies and coming home with wild schemes. "Marvelous," her father used to say, encouraging her to go after what she wanted the way a boy would.

"Not on your life." Her mother usually elbowed in and restrained young Cate from any act of precocity, passing on the old teachings of mothers to daughters. A girl must not go after what she wants directly but must *wait* for it (and rig the game behind the scenes every chance she got). "I could always manipulate," Cate learned.

Certain unfeminine slips Cate just couldn't help: making top grades in math and physics, fighting when she saw something unfair ("discipline problem," the nuns labeled her), and being first with the right answer ("abrasive personality"). Why couldn't she be like her sister, who never won any honors but was always so nice that everyone liked her?

Cate made a bittersweet discovery in her junior year of college when she ran for class president and lost. The reason was clear: coming up first with the right answer was very useful, but nobody loved you for it. She learned from that failure to deflect envy by spreading the credit around.

Cate let Mother move in before graduation and begin merchandising her. He had to be Catholic and have a college degree and go to Mass on Sundays; otherwise she had free choice of a husband. Cate contemplated the man who fit best and figured, "Okay, I can create his life. All he needs is social confidence and perfect children with blue blazers and white knee socks and he'll be very successful. I can pull it all together behind the picture frame."

She did not marry before committing the last and boldest subversive act of her young years: persuading her father to send her to Yale Law School. Cate O'Neil was bright enough to know that was the kind of credential a woman would need if she ever wanted to get back into the world.

But these early evidences of her strengths in at least two pathfinding qualities—the willingness to risk and the ability to anticipate—were soon obscured when she subscribed to the approved social program. Having slipped out of the mold for three aberrant years at Yale, Cate was back in place— *snap!*—with a baby to prove it, before she had completed so much as a year on her first job.

"My husband was adamant that I stay home. I was excited about motherhood myself. I decided I'd have them all at once, and *then* go back. It was also the perfect excuse for putting everything off, right?"

Cate O'Neil produced five sons. Somewhere along the way between numbers two and three, with herself nearing 30, she took up certain nondomestic activities that fell under the heading "keeping my hand in."

Not to worry, she tried to reassure her husband. Nothing was changing. She would continue in full service of their otherwise admirably mainstream, socially impeccable, exurban Philadelphia family life and see to it that they all skied and sailed and belonged to the right clubs.

She would simply pursue a double life.

In the secret interstices Cate practiced as a country lawyer and social crusader. It became a game, called "getting away with work." The logistics of dispatching her husband to his brokerage business and finding someone willing to watch five kids while she slipped out to the law library to do research for several hours appealed to her problem-solving aptitudes. Given her high energy, the double-life solution worked quite well. Even when she pulled a mainspring ligament, Cate structured a way to get maximum efficiency from the fifteen minutes a day she was able to be on her feet. She swept through their fourteen-room house like a demented dust-woman.

"Then I'd go right back to being the same smiling soul who managed everything and was the envy of all her friends—but not too threatening because I was careful to admire the things that *they* could do."

This double life turned out later to be a crucial form of anticipation. "It kept me in touch with what real people were thinking, not just a rarefied minority of country-clubbers," she can see today, "and it kept alive the confidence that one could deal with the real world in a businesslike way." The woman who opts instead for early motherhood and deferred achievement—and does not keep her hand in—often is shocked at the erosion of confidence when she does reenter. Although a degree from Yale Law School was a sterling-silver credential that few have the brains and opportunity to attain, the important clue to pathfinder behavior was Cate's determination to complete her education before she dropped out and to "keep her hand in" during the years of deferred outside achievement. It doesn't have to be Yale, but it helps to have something stored in life's safe-deposit box for later use.

But despite her credentials, Cate did not stretch at 30, nor did she change much over the next ten years for that matter. She did what traditional women have always done: she endured creatively. Repressing any emotions of her own that are usually thought inappropriate in a woman, especially anger, she took hour-by-hour readings of her husband's emotional state. At the first bristling of his abusiveness, she acted to appease him.

The sticky moments came at parties. Cate made certain to sit with the wives, and when they dropped the first cube of sugar-coated hostility—"I just don't know how you do so many things, Cate"—she used the strategy she had learned for disarming envy: "It's easy: I don't do any of them well. I couldn't put on a feast like you did tonight in a million years." But just let one of the husbands mention the exciting debate she had started at the town meeting and out it jumped—her other life—and soon at least some of the men would be in her corner talking politics.

"You don't think that stuff supports us, do you?" her husband would cut in. "That's just Cate's playwork."

When they got home, he would take the car keys away

from her for a week. In truth, she did not approve of herself either, sneaking around like this to work, think, study, and test her own beliefs.

"I thought I had bad needs."

Just don't rattle any doors until you've passed forty, she told herself. After that, according to the script she had been taught, "you would slow down, lose your sex drive, stop feeling competitive, and be satisfied by your children and a home with no dust and acceptance by society."

The actual course between her forties and fifties kicked over all those worn guideposts. As is often the case with the women in my recent studies, that decade took her from the pits up to the peak. It turned out to be her Comeback Decade.

Jazzing through the moguls behind her youngest son on one of the ski weekends that allowed her antic side to show, Cate scudded across a rock, jackknifed, and broke.

"Don't move," the doctor decreed, "and you can lead a limited life."

Her husband brought her flowers in the hospital and said, "We'll have a wonderful time together, now that everything is settled."

"What's settled?"

"That you won't have to go out anymore, or practice law, or any of that."

Nor was her mother able to conceal a certain delight. Perhaps at last, with maverick Cate broken, good Cate would conform. Mother brought her needlepoint.

"I'm defeatable—me!" Cate O'Neil was appalled. "Up to that point I had been able to defer, to tell myself, 'When the children are older, I'll do all I really want to do.' In the very back of my mind I had always thought, 'Someday I'll walk out.' Now here I was—forty, with talents totally unexpressed—and I was paralyzed."

"How soon can I ski again?" she pushed the doctor.

"Mrs. O'Neil, you'll be lucky if you ever walk again."

Day-to-day psychological battering in a bad marriage can become so normal that one can no longer conceive of what it might feel like to stop banging one's head against the wall. That is why nonmutual, destructive love can so badly disable even a pathfinder. Common blows are humiliation, possessiveness, and the undermining of confidence. A sort of punchiness may perpetuate the illusion that the weaker partner, the truly insecure one (in this case, the husband), is somehow the strong one who cannot be challenged. Cate's situation no longer aroused a fighting response. By habit, she continued to put a happyface on the marriage for the world to see and to collect most of the conflict inside, where she concentrated on neutralizing it. She never stopped to question the old wives' tale seldom articulated but traditionally accepted by women:

"Anything wrong with the marriage was *my* fault. I was responsible for everyone's mental health." When her husband escalated to physical abuse, she thought, *I must have aggravated him, he's not very stable after all.* . . . When he went on a jag of hating himself, she stepped up her efforts to perform as his psychiatric geisha.

Cate's father died while she was in a body cast. When she recovered from her grief, it was a surprise to her to feel somehow lighter.

When we resist making an important passage by our own initiative, it may be forced upon us by a life accident. But although life accidents can be the spur to change for the better, the handicap is that they give us no time to anticipate.

It took two severe life accidents—her father's untimely death and her own paralysis—to shatter temporarily Cate O'Neil's protective illusions about the future. She had a bad marriage, that was plain. Rare is the person who is dealt the perfect hand and can play out his or her ideal self. Given the hand Cate was dealt, how could the least damage be done to all the people involved?

"I might even have stayed in," she admits, "except for wanting those boys to be all they could be."

Digging Out

Her doctor shut her inside a leg brace, and she existed as a cripple for six months, until July of 1970. That was the bottom of the pit. To remain in an incapacitated role for the rest of her life—no! She would not, could not; she left no lead unexplored until she found a woman orthopedist who also had five children. This doctor would have to understand.

"Throw away the brace; start swimming!" the new doctor advised.

With that boost, Cate outwitted her brace and crutches. She shoved a law book under the accelerator—her leg movements were still difficult to control—and taught herself to drive to a pool where she could wriggle around every day like a tadpole. As her body began to reanimate, her spirit came back.

While she was still the club foot of her crowd, there was one among the O'Neils' acquaintances who made a practice of waiting for her. Kenneth Ross found Cate's outrageousness a tonic. A public figure who ran many businesses and enjoyed risk himself, he told Cate she was so much more interesting than other women. He asked her to do some tax planning for him. She thrived on talking to him about the world. He became not her lover—that was too far outside the rules—but her gentle and adored confidant.

One Sunday morning in the summer of '72, most of their sailing crowd was leaning heavily on the second Bloody Mary when Kenneth leaned over and whispered to the cripple, "Let's grab the kids and go play tennis." Ten hours later they were back to pick up their respective spouses, having spent a sun-kissed day clumsily batting tennis balls and attempting volleyball and sailing, and having fallen ridiculously, illogically, in love.

"The first time—at forty-two!"

No, Cate told herself, it was too late, too irrational. It did not add up, she told Kenneth, and repeatedly broke off their unconsummated romance. It didn't matter that Kenneth was as miserable as she in the beds they had made; people were supposed to be like that in middle age, she told him. Those were the rules she had been taught.

One day Kenneth Ross said, "Listen, if Bobby Orr smashes his knee, he gets it fixed and goes back to playing hockey." Kenneth took Cate to Boston to see Bobby Orr's doctor. Her break was too bad to reset, the athlete's doctor said, "but I've never seen a limp on anybody who skis—you have to use both legs." She left with a prescription for 150-meter skis and Spademan bindings, giddy beyond imagining.

Two years of incapacity officially ended that day, in 1972,

when Cate was fitted for a new pair of ski boots. There followed over the next two years a series of moves preparatory to a jailbreak, not one of which Cate acknowledged at the conscious level.

Having taken over the practice of a lawyer friend who had suddenly died, Cate began commuting into Philadelphia—only temporarily, she said. The lawyer's contacts could be helpful to her husband, she told him, and he agreed. The next year she bought a junk heap and registered it in her own name: the getaway car. "Looking back, obviously I was setting myself up to earn my own living and leave. But to admit that to myself—with a husband who would grab the keys and throw a tantrum when he found out that his toy was going to meet a client at ten in the morning? No, I kept on doing what I'd always done: giving in for peace."

It took the cruelty of unconcern about one of their children for Cate O'Neil to dig in her heels and fight back. The youngest boy smashed his skull and face in an auto accident in October of '74. His father never spoke with the doctor. Alone, Cate had to make the harrowing decision of whether to let surgeons burrow into the boy's brain.

Shouldn't her husband take some responsibility for others? she asked herself. And for making the marriage at least tolerable? She decided to stop trying. When he launched into two-day harangues, she kept a suddenly effortless distance. He took to calling her a cock-chaser in front of the boys. All five sons were between 15 and 20 and in the blaze of adolescence: their own fantasies of cuckoldry were inflamed. The two older boys became convinced that Mother was being stolen away by another man. Her husband threatened to liquidate his business and leave town.

"Try supporting five kids all by yourself," he sneered.

From that day in October when she first let the conflict begin rumbling to the surface, it came to Cate that a certain insanity ran through it all. While she juggled a miserable double life for the sake of rules that were supposed to raise her sons to the "better good," her actions were teaching them something else: *Forfeit your values whenever you run into resistance.* She looked at her five young men, talented and aggressive every one, but also possessing the sensitivity to make the world a little better. She thought, *I want them to be all they can be.*

The decisive operation on her youngest son was set for New Year's Day. The day before, Cate told the surgeon, "I'm not leaving him in the hospital tonight," and talked the boy's way out by promising to alternate hot and cold packs on his head all night. But that night, New Year's Eve, her husband demanded to have all her attention.

"Mom, Mom, Dad's screaming and yelling; he wants you to go to a party with him!" The other boys tried to persuade her that they could look after the youngest; she should do what Dad said—to keep family peace. It was the last time she gave in.

The boy recuperated beautifully. The day Cate brought him home, a thought hit her hard as she entered the house. *I won't do it anymore!* It was the first time she had faced the conflict head-on.

She could leave, but she could not take the boys with her unless she was willing to subject them to a vicious custody battle. And how could she leave her husband to his own psychological resources? "That was the hardest thing for me—feeling responsible for his mental health."

She sought counsel from a priest. "The greatest commandment is 'Love others as I have loved you,'" she began. "Should I take that literally, or is that a calling to sainthood?" The priest said he could not answer her question. "It's unknowable." She turned in desperation from the Bible to a novel, and there, on page 74 of Arthur Hailey's *The Moneychangers*, she found a clue. A man with a wife in a mental institution is wrestling with how he can leave her. He asks the psychiatrist what to do. "Those last few paces each of us walks alone," the psychiatrist says. "Few people are qualified for sainthood." (Later, although she would laugh at the source of the insight, she was amazed at how much love she had available to give to others once she was relieved of nursing a single self-pitying husband.)

Hoping to find him a substitute therapist, she suggested that she and her husband see a psychiatrist together. Six or seven times during the interview, the psychiatrist interrupted Cate to insist, "Mrs. O'Neil, I didn't ask you how your husband feels or your children feel or how your cleaning woman feels. I'm asking how *you* feel!"

For once in her life, she had absolutely nothing to say.

First Love: Oneself

The focus in this biography is on mutual love—the ravages of its total absence, the splendid emollient effect of its presence even when it develops quite late in life, and the need to know and love oneself before it is possible to engage in mutual love with someone else. But although the capacity for loving is highlighted in Cate's tale, her story also illustrates the four phases involved in completing a passage: anticipation, separation and incubation, expansion, and incorporation.

Looking back, Cate O'Neil can see that taking her first full-time job filling in for a lawyer and buying a car in her own name were "subconscious beginning steps toward independence." The expansion phase, in her case, began well before she had the courage to initiate the separation phase. But all the while that Cate was preparing to back out of a marriage in which she had felt imprisoned for many years, she denied what she was doing: "I don't think I faced up to it." The repressive defenses common to traditional women worked for her right up to the day of decision that spring. Three days later she was gone.

Cate O'Neil did not go into the incubation phase until she rented a tumbledown weekend house on the Maryland shore that was large enough to accommodate all the boys. She could manage to be with them near the sea without their father. Whenever she did not have to be at the law office, she stayed overnight there and crawled into one basement room and the next day walked on the beach for hours. She had to be alone to allow time for a process that was not natural to her—introspection.

A human spirit in need of repair often cries out for solitude in natural surroundings. Highly disciplined and rational from childhood on, Cate found a rich bed of her mind that had been entirely neglected. The colors and wild treasures there were uncovered only when she was exposed to sea, wind, waves, the wonderful chaos of nature.

To walk in the teeth of the wind and to know the stinging clarity of the survivor was strangely beautiful. Those six months were lonely, but Cate sensed that the work of reading her own thoughts was too important to escape in a flurry of professional activity.

"It's like peeling an onion," she explained later. "Each layer had to be taken off before I could peel the next one." Tears sprang up, and pain, but there was the amazement too of uncovering selves and parts of selves she had not noticed in years under the layering of accommodations. When she was alone at the shore house, she retreated for safety into the small basement and kept it padlocked.

Friends were certain Cate O'Neil was having "a nervous breakdown." The two older boys thought of her as "bad Mom," a broken stove. Her husband avenged his sense of rejection by bringing a nasty alienation-of-affections suit against her and Kenneth Ross. Everyone was busy analyzing her, including a 26-year-old family therapist sent by her husband to find out what was the matter with her.

"Mrs. O'Neil, do you think you're menopausal?"

"Look, lady, when the day comes that I have time to sit still, if I have a hot flash I promise to call you right away."

The truth of it was that Cate felt at 44 indecently fertile. She was still in love with Kenneth Ross. But having forced her code upon him, he remained in his marriage. She was completely cut off. It was nonetheless a robust aloneness.

"It came to me very quickly that I was a good person with a lot to offer, that my responsibility was not solely to my husband and children but also to the world around me."

If her father had still been alive, Cate knew she never would have hurt him by disrupting the facade of her "good" life. Though it did not occur to her then, Kenneth Ross had picked up where her father left off in childhood and had endorsed the plucky spirit arrested inside her. He loved her for what she loved in herself.

"I peeled all the way down, and then I began to come back."

While wandering on the beach she stumbled upon another discovery. "When you sail, you have to adapt to the waves. You can't predict winds or storms; it's a constant adaptation. And life is like that. Those waves aren't problems, they are opportunities. There's a difference."

The alienation-of-affections suit gave her husband the advantage if there was a custody battle. He used it to threaten her once again to come back to him.

"I could not go back. I had no other choice. I had to take the chance that the children would find me." She took the gamble that since the children were mostly ready to strike their own first tentative bargains with life, they might be strong enough to withstand a temporary break. She moved into the house on the shore. She prayed that all five boys would come to live with her, but she knew she might lose one, and maybe two.

About October, a year after pushing off into a channel full of squalls, Cate O'Neil began to notice some mildly pleasant days popping up between the bleak and gray days. The storm had passed.

"Let's meet in the arcade and talk about your million-dollar body."

"My what?"

That was the price tag her husband had put on her in his lawsuit against them, Kenneth Ross told Cate, so it seemed only fair that they should discuss the appraisal. He was divorced by now. She was close. They met and laughed, and Cate felt the sexual pull she had never allowed before the separation. From then on they could not stay away from each other. Private detectives shadowed them. Incorrigible as grass springing up between paving stones, they squeezed their love into whatever cracks could be found. Into an elevator with the Stop button pushed. Into a broom closet in a downtown hotel where they couldn't tell if they were swooning from love or from janitor's salts.

Had Cate's mother gone around the bend? She invited Cate, with Kenneth, to have dinner in full view at her club. Astonishing.

"To put it in a nutshell, Cate," Mother pronounced after the dinner, "I put the *Good Housekeeping* seal of approval on the whole thing."

As Cate's mother became more spontaneous, Cate's rebelliousness wore thin, and she began to find threads of empathy beneath it. "I didn't like my mother until after I was forty-five. Now I think she's a super lady."

When Kenneth invited Mother for dinner at his apartment and did all the cooking to demonstrate that he and Cate had "gotten beyond roles," Mother hissed to Cate, "Get up and help him—he could have loads of women who would love to make dinner for him!"

Still merchandising me at forty-four. Cate chuckled.

It was not until three years later, in the incorporation phase of her passage, that Cate would begin to put the pieces together and celebrate some of her hard-won strengths.

Why did all the old coping devices that had worked for Cate O'Neil before fall apart in her forties?

If Cate had not suffered the ski accident, not let the unresolved issues and emotions come to the surface, her underlying conflict would have required more and more hysterical defenses, perhaps resulting in real character deterioration. Or Cate might have been moved to examine her life later in middle age, as evidences of mortality accumulated while her emotional connections became more hyphenated.

As it was, a life accident accelerated the process. Cate's usual strategies for coping—running on high energy, keeping everything pleasant and organized above while everything unpleasant remained repressed below—were undermined by a suddenly shrunken sense of time and a robbery of the most basic assumption: that one can stand on one's own two feet.

Her near-paralysis acted as a negative pole against which to set up a positive field and risk moving toward it. Cate could not begin coming back, however, until she was ready to face conflict, make a painful detachment, risk irreplaceable losses, and ultimately engage in a compromise. Cate O'Neil made a pathfinding turn in the classical female pattern of creative endurance when she recognized the unsalvageability of her marriage and the distortions it was producing in her relationships with her children and in the values for which she thought she stood. She acted on that insight and endured the pain of detaching herself temporarily from those beloved sons.

The chance Cate took of losing her children's love is probably the most terrible risk a woman can face. But if she had remained in a chronically destructive marriage, and given up her integrity and self-respect to make peace, she would more certainly have lost the love of her children and prevented them from emerging whole. Three years after the separation, which became a divorce, she can weigh the outcome. She sees it, on balance, as good.

"It was a risk, but this mother was not going to go away that easily." She fought for her two youngest boys, both diagnosed a dyslectic, won them over, and got them into special schools, despite their father's insistence that she was wasting her time. In the spring of 1979, both made the honor roll. Cate's income now allows her to pay school tuition for both.

"The younger three have really found me," she totes up. "The second one is still, appropriately, at the age of twenty-one, rebelling. The oldest one is lost to me."

Stunned at first that such a thing could happen, she now accepts that being a mother does not mean you will automatically feel fondly toward all your kids forever. "As children grow older, there is some responsibility on *their* part to listen and empathize. My oldest son cannot. At twenty-three, he still sees me exclusively in the social role of 'Mom.' That's not a relationship. I care about him, but the person he is right now, I don't like."

The honesty of that last statement shocks people. But if Cate had not by now developed an immunity to the inevitable social disapproval of expressing herself honestly, she would be in constant conflict.

"I've learned that some people will like me and some people won't," she can say with healthy equanimity, "and that's okay. I'm no longer in the business of pleasing everybody."

A striking change.

Nevertheless, it often takes years for others to accept such a change, because it disrupts the role or picture they have come to expect the person to conform to indefinitely. Cate's view that her children "would have to find me" was both poignant and realistic. Today, her sons see their father more clearly. The younger ones are concerned that his continuing volatile behavior gives him trouble functioning, she says. Three of the sons would like to become lawyers like Cate.

Loving and Laughing

The love of Cate and Kenneth outlasted the postpone-
ments, the separations, the giggly infatuation period, the ugly
legal settlement. It is a love of an altogether different order
from anything Cate knew for her first 42 years—and it gives
every other surface of her life a shimmer.

Which is not to say these two people have escaped entirely
the a-synchrony between the developmental lines of men and
women. After so many years of being grounded, Cate is now
soaring in her work. "I'm very much in demand as a lawyer.
Kenneth has already made his mark. He's ready to gear
down, but he recognizes that I'm still gearing up." Having
built his businesses and found good people to manage them,
Kenneth is moving beyond compulsive attention to work.
"After all," Cate recognizes, "this should be the richest
period of his life."

So they created an ingenious modus vivendi together, one
that would allow them to be on the water, where Kenneth
could sail whenever he pleased, but still close enough to
City Hall for Cate, so that she could work a long day and
have four or five hours left to spend with her love. They
moved into a houseboat in Philadelphia harbor. Snuggled in
for their first winter, they found it delightful to pare down to
nature. Cate's sons loved the boat. It turned out to be a cozy
if somewhat primitive place to entertain friends for dinner.
What with the head door banging open and dishes flying
across the cabin, it tended to discourage visitors from staying too long. And the more time Cate and Kenneth had alone
together, the more they wanted.

Their approach to play is as good a demonstration as any
of the way these two have worked out their mutual love.
Each races a small skiff alone. They come together on a bigger boat, which he skippers while she navigates and uses
tactics.

In life and work, too, Cate has developed new and more
effective tactics.

Anger had reached dangerous concentrations in Cate's
unconscious during the latter part of her marriage. That is
often the case for a person who feels trapped but denies real-

ity in order not to face it. By releasing her anger, recognizing it, gaining insight into it, and studying its effects, both positive and negative, Cate was able to take control over most of her anger, recognizing it, gaining insight into it, and studying its effects, mature and attractive defense—humor—after first brushing it up, trying it out, and learning to slip it into her act whenever it was least expected.

"Now, walking into City Hall, I take off my hat and put it on backward and say, 'Cate, you're entering Never-Never Land, so be sure to laugh when you meet the March Hare.'" For example:

Forty men, representatives of the finest Philadelphia banks, plus architects and builders, gather in a boardroom—with Cate. She is about to negotiate a $20-million loan for a hospital. During the pre-meeting politicking her stomach does a flip. She leaves the room to talk to herself.

"Cate, what in God's name do you think you're doing here?" It is her shaky ego speaking. "You don't know enough about construction loan contracts."

A beat, and her imagination brings up the image of a cripple in a brace. She talks back to herself: "How would you feel if you *couldn't* go in there and do it?"

Moments later, Cate O'Neil is sitting at the opposite end of the boardroom table from the vice-president of the key bank. "Don, most of the agreement I can take," she begins, "but I'm going to advise the hospital not to tolerate any penalty for prepayment."

"Cate"—the vice-president exudes paternalism—"before the banks get into bed with you, you have to do certain things."

"You mean," Cate says with wide-eyed mock innocence, "with *all* the banks?"

It brought the house down, of course. The vice-president blanched, the hospital got the loan without the penalty, and Cate took home another notch of confidence that she could get along with "the boys."

"If you never risk, you never grow," she hears herself coaching her sons. They see her in her law practice, "continually putting myself in positions I have no business being in."

Cate looks ten years ahead with goals and gusto. She sees "total expansion"—launching her sons and loving Kenneth and (granted a touch of the Messiah complex) helping to make the world better. In a decade she could afford financially to go on the bench, and, believing that she has the temperament and ability to be a judge, she would like to have the chance. When she was first emerging from her transition, Cate took on the role of Survivor Guide through her *pro bono* work with "other women who were getting the shaft." She would say, "You can't afford to pay me, but I need some experience, so let's go!" By now, freed from personalizing the problem, she is able to act as a third-party mediator in divorce cases.

"I think women are like that," she says bluntly. "We have a social orientation. We don't simply look at the divorce client and say, 'How much is this one worth?' We're more inclined to say, 'Gee, this lady is really trying to get her act together; what can I do to help?'" She adds vehemently, "I will never lose that."

A reexamination of her beliefs in light of her personal renewal has enhanced her faith. "I am more religious now than I ever was," she muses. "I've gotten beyond the rebellion stage. Basically, I'm a Catholic—I just won't let them kick me out. But I'm becoming ecumenical. I know now what is important to me: it is the imitation of Christ in everyday life. My personal relationship with God is much more precious to me than any institution or church."

The slowest growth for Cate was in learning to manage the business of her life. The simple fact of having to earn a living was new, not to mention restructuring her professional and financial foundations so that she could build on them. Kenneth was of enormous help. In 1972, beginning at the bottom of her profession, her income ran between $10,000 and $12,000. Now, juggling as many as forty cases at once, she is billing $70,000 to $80,000 a year.

Having taken care of business, Cate is currently committed to increasing her social participation. She offers her services at no cost in complicated brain-death cases. And now that her expertise in divorce law is well known, the court has appointed her as a "master" to find the facts in contested proceedings.

"The days aren't long enough," says the lady who once could not wait for the day to end.

Each morning now, clambering off the boat and up the gangway in the variable calm and chop of the days, watching the gulls arrive for a day's work, then strolling through a sylvan park and into the new market being hosed down while its fresh pastries are heating up, she marvels at how dramatically the crowd changes in the space of less than a mile. She enjoys the singles, the newly marrieds in resuscitated row houses, the young fathers ferrying sons to school on the backs of their bikes, the hurrying businessmen; and there, at the epicenter, the lawyers and pols stalking up the steps of City Hall for another day of sport at one another's throats. She races to join them.

"To see the city coming alive, all its parts coming together—I never imagined how exciting it could be." Cate O'Neil might just as well be talking about the process she herself has weathered, finding all her parts and fitting them together for a comeback.

"I'll be fifty in June," Cate said the last time we spoke. "It's hardly a sunset. I've flown. I love every day, my work, my lover, my friends, my clients, and, I guess most important, I finally love myself!"

As seldom as we contemplate ourselves objectively, even less often do we try to comprehend love. In order to become free from an exclusive focus on single instances of unfair human behavior—the volatile husband, the runaway wife, the man or woman who runs down the former spouse to live up to agreements—it is imperative to reach out to others. What new kinds of mutually beneficial alliances can we achieve? How can we convert an acquaintance into a friend? A friend into a confidant? A child of divorce into a partner for helping to civilize daily life?

When the links of romantic love are suspended or broken, those are the ties that sustain. Perhaps pathfinders intuitively sense this, because for all their openness to mutual love they are not confined to that channel for sharing affection. Characteristically, most of them cultivate a flourishing circle of friendship and kinship links.

8.

FRIENDSHIP, KINSHIP, SUPPORT SYSTEMS

Not wanting to ruin my weekend, Donna* didn't tell me until Sunday afternoon. We caught the last chair lift up the mountain.

We had met in kindergarten and thrown clay in each other's faces and become, for all time, best friends. Being together again had brought back a collage of our girlhood adventures—rowing all over Long Island Sound and spinning fantasies out of ancient newspapers found in abandoned houseboats, fleeing feral dogs on deserted islands, almost taking a tramp steamer to Spain—but the unusual thing was that the friendship in recent years had branched out to bear friendships between our children and our men. In fact, Donna's marriage was a source of vicarious delight for many who knew her. This was the marriage that had lasted. This was the one couple who would never be old, slow, or down. Unfailingly vivacious, Donna and Leo seemed always to be surfing or hiking or roller-skating their way through another idyllic family holiday with their miraculously unspoiled children.

"You and I will be forty this November," she said on the ride up.

"I know; let's give ourselves a present." I felt a surge of

* A pseudonym.

our old mischief. "Let's always do something adventurous. Once a year. You and I. Let's make it a pact."

"Done."

She told me later that was a gift of the future. I was somebody who would always want to do things with her.

Our skis chattered over the ice until we came to the first stop. The sun was low. The cold clamped around us. Shadows cut purple ruts into the frozen mountain. Our silhouettes on the snow were sharp and definite.

"Leo and I are separating."

It came out clear as a smoke ring and as impossible for me to take in. I asked her to repeat.

"He's in love with someone else."

Another puff of smoke.

"He says I'm too up all the time."

One by one, the unconnected pieces of information smoked out of her mouth and hit the cold air and crystallized, flying up into the twilight as separate slivers of doom.

"She's thirty. He smokes pot with her . . .

"Seventeen years. The children—aren't they wonderful children . . . ?

"Everything I thought was there, isn't . . .

"I must be a terrible person . . .

"He says he knows now he never loved me. . . ."

She was trying to give me all the information as quickly and clearly as possible in the hope that I could make some sense of it. She couldn't, she said.

This was how it looked to me: the person closest to her in the world had asked her to swallow a torch that had incinerated her tenderest parts. It was scorching timber now, the foundation on which rested any idea at all of herself. Any moment there might be a shudder, a great implosion, and my dearest friend would cave in.

I told her the things she was. I tried to put some of the bricks back, one by one. "You're one of the most valuable people God ever made. I love you. I'm with you. If I can ever get these bloody skis turned around, I just want to hold you."

She later described how it looked to her: "There was nobody else on the mountain. It added to the feeling of isolation I'd had for a year. There we were, sharp outlines in all that white snow—but now it was two, instead of just one.

I felt so close to you. When someone has rejected you so badly, you can't help thinking, 'I must be a worthless person.' But you said it wasn't true. And because you'd known me so long, I could believe you."

The Many Shadings of Friendship

If the risk of change and loss is essential to the process of pathfinding, friends are the haven in the wilderness—even more so when a person is struggling for bearings in the face of a life accident. It simply is too hard to imagine confronting a normal passage or a major setback all alone. We need to know, from past experience, that we'll get a little help from our friends. By listening, by caring, by playing you back to yourself, friends ratify your better instincts and endorse your unique worth. Friends validate you.

On the other hand, friendship is time-consuming; friends are expected to do things for each other. Friendship is emotionally demanding; a friend can become dependent, or let you down. Personality theorists such as Abraham Maslow and Carl Rogers indicate that "mature" people do not need friends.[1]

That strikes me as plausible only if "mature" means beyond passages and impervious to life's accidents. For the rest of us, friends are essential. *This is how it feels; is there something wrong with me?* one can ask a friend, having confided secrets, fears, shame. A friend can let you speak when you must. A friend can tell you that you are not the only one.

People of high well-being in my studies, contrary to the assertions of Maslow and Rogers, enjoyed twice as many close friends as the average person's three or four. And the evidence was that these friends provided one of their front-line defenses during rough periods.

Not that the value of friends is confined to the bad times. Regular personal reporting to friends helps us keep our perspective. A young woman ship's engineer on the Great Lakes described a friendship with a co-worker:

"Whenever we're off at the same time, we go out to dinner. We laugh over nothing, or just window-shop. I use her as a sounding board—'What would your reaction be if I were to say such and such to you?'—about work and also personal problems. I'll tell her about my boyfriend sounding depressed, and she'll tell me about hers. I always feel exhilarated after I've spent an afternoon with my friend."

Even in the absence of need, so many more are the opportunities friendship gives pathfinders for embracing the differentness of others and extending the range of songs within themselves.

Strong friendships have many different shadings and move easily among them. Sometimes one is the parent and the other the confused kid. Sometimes a friend plays brother or sister, with that same fierce loyalty. When one is a basket case, the other acts as therapist. And sometimes two friends are two teenagers again, sitting around the locker room talking about scoring, or gabbing about boys and clothes. A few months after our Sunday on the ski slope, I taught Donna a jazz-dancing routine. In no time we were kicking our legs and bumping our behinds. Our daughters crept in with a camera to snap a shot of their moms as oblivious kids.

Some friendships have only one color, but a vivid one. They encourage the clown or the charmer or the tutor in you with a full canvas on which to experiment briefly. These may turn out to be sketches for changes in one's own life.

Good friends know when you need help simply by the sound of your voice. The day Donna called me to say her husband planned to decide that weekend whether to stay or to go, it did not take a doctor to know she should not sit around waiting to bleed to death. I flew to her city the next morning and brought her back with her children to use our friendship as an emergency room.

The first thing my teenage daughter said to Donna was "You're going to have to tell me something pretty fierce about Leo before I'll believe anything bad about him." Her loyalty did not come or go cheaply. Donna appreciated that. It reminded us of the uncompromising honesty of friendships between adolescents. To adults they often seem hypercritical, yet that candor is crucial to finding out who they are; it is infinitely easier to be sincere before one develops masks. The job of adolescent friends is not to be nice to each other, but to be real to each other.

We spent that whole weekend sitting around the dining-room table in robes and slippers. At the nadir of her self-recriminations, Donna blurted out, "Oh, God, Gail, how could I ever have told you I wouldn't be friends with you if you didn't stop wearing undershirts! You see, I really am terrible!"

"Hey, there's a statute of limitations on evidence. We were thirteen then."

Everyone laughed. "The weekend was pure therapy," my friend said when she left. "It was all I could handle."

One of the most notable differences between the happy and the miserable people I studied was the degree to which their marriage partners were good friends. Fully 95 percent of all the married people of high well-being said they turned to their spouses for support during rough periods. They themselves also found it easier than most to reveal their thoughts and to sense the feelings of others. Among the low-well-being people who are married, fewer than 70 percent could turn to a spouse and expect support.

Even when there is a supportive partner, other friends are important. They do not carry the same emotional freight as a spouse, nor are they handicapped with the sexual possessiveness of a romantic relationship. One doesn't go crazy because a friend is seen cozying up to someone else at a party. Friends are easily shared. They are not expected to bring the world to you. There is no particular tension about pleasing. And unless one borrows a lot of money from a friend, there is no reason one has to be dominant and the other dependent. The effect of these distinctions may be to make friendship one of life's greatest relaxations.

A real friend allows you, supports you, and suspends judgment when you do something stupid or wrong. But for all that to develop, a friendship needs time to season, to be proved enduring, to establish unswerving loyalty. Good times together must be stored away against the gloomy days. One cannot suddenly call an acquaintance and say, "I think I'm going through a passage; will you be my friend?"

Man-to-Man Friendships

Men's friendships with other men tend to be instrumental rather than emotional. They bounce ideas back and forth, compare strategies for moving up or making money, share mechanical know-how. The emphasis is on "how to" rather than "How do you feel?" Men also make indispensable colleagues and mentors for one another. Without asking a single question about the demons a man is struggling with—after losing his job, let us say—another man can make a profound gift of friendship by using his position to have a pal hired. Taking a friend out to a hockey game can pry him away from his personal problems for a while, even if it cannot solve them.

In most of the practical aspects of pathfinding—how-to, expertise, contacts that would help a person in the throes of change—men are in a far better position to help each other through friendship than women are. But trading confidences in an atmosphere of trust and honesty is pure gold—and for many men rarer. Commonly, men look to their wives as their sole confidantes. A few men acquire women friends for that purpose. It is seldom that other men can be trusted with admissions of naiveté, failure, fears, or even with the disclosure of a man's bluntest ambitions.

"I never had any real male friends," said one pathfinder in his forties. "Men in this society are trained to compete. I'm fine as long as I control the situation, but the other guy wants to do the same thing. I'm trying to prove him wrong, and he's trying to prove me wrong." Harvard Business School psychologist Harry Levinson warns of the pressure of middle-aged managers to deny any feelings and restrict close relationships: "Commitment to executive career goals . . . inhibits close, affectionate relationships. One cannot allow himself to get close to those with whom he competes or about whom he must make decisions, or are likely to make decisions about him."[2]

In fact, the men in my studies generally did have fewer close friends than the women. They adapt less easily to the loss of a mate and seem able to satisfy their need for intimacy only by remarrying—which they do far more rapidly than do widowed women. A classic study of widows, by contrast, showed that the women made a much more flexible shift from intimacy with a husband to friendships within their own sex. The man with no male friends is particularly poignant during a divorce. The one person to whom he was able to show his pain has now turned away—and turned into another adversary.

Friendships Woman to Woman

Women's efforts at pathfinding have not always been aided by friendships with other women. For the first time on a massive scale, in the 1970's women began to form cooperative and noncompetitive relationships with other women. That may be the single most revolutionary change wrought by the women's movement. As long as women believed they could get by only if men took care of them, and the laws and customs were arranged accordingly, the competition for high-status males made long-lasting friendships among young women undependable. Besides, their time, love, and loyalty were supposed to be devoted to the men in their lives. "Men have always been afraid women could get along without them," Margaret Mead once told me.

As it turns out, women's friendships are easier than men's to cultivate, in large part because for women there is no stigma attached to admitting powerlessness. I never cease to marvel at how naturally and frequently one woman sits down next to another, a total stranger, on a plane or in a Laundromat, and before you know it, they're comparing notes on how to maneuver with men, work, and children. Women have little hesitation about admitting self-doubts to each other. And there is little shame—at least in America in this shank of the century—in revealing one's suffering.

The bond between young mothers goes a long way toward alleviating the social isolation of being at home with small children. Another mother is somebody to meet in the park, somebody to ask, "Do you think we'll be pregnant forever?" As women grow older, they again gravitate toward intense relationships with other women, in preparation for the later years of the life cycle when male companionship will be scarce.

One formerly sedentary widow told me enthusiastically about the calisthenics class she and three or four others had set up in the neighborhood. "I hate to do the stretchies; they hurt like the devil. That's why you need friends. I don't have the courage to do back arches alone. I'd feel ridiculous." After one winter she was walking upright again and stretched out to feeling ten years younger.

Women can talk to other women in shorthand; they don't need the big windup. They possess highly touted powers of empathy—being able to sense what another feels—because they must. They have to know which way to jump; it is only dominant people who can afford to be insensitive. The wealth of confidences they exchange with each other, therefore, amounts to strategies for survival.

KINSHIP

In other parts of the world, kinship ties with family often remain close and strong throughout adult life. One-third of French university students, for example, live with their parents, and according to surveys a majority of them think, act, and even vote just like Mère and Père. Even after French students marry and produce their own children and nest, they are not expected to fly very far. French society is organized around *la famille*. The warmth and humor as well as the frustration of that condition are beautifully captured in the film *Cousin, Cousine*. Two cousins, both in their mid-thirties, both married to unfaithful mates, are thrown together at one family gathering after another. They strike up a romance. Soon, they cannot be pulled apart. They are shameless. The cousins make love on the other side of the living-room wall right straight through the family Christmas, but the family grins and bears it—just as long as they don't get divorced!

This is a far cry from the peripatetic life in the United States, where 44.4 percent of those in their early twenties move every year. A 20-year-old American can expect to move about ten more times in life, having already relocated with his or her family on the average of three times as a child. Among those living in developed countries, only Australians and Canadians come close to this level of national mobility.[8]

Kinship *within* the new American household has been drastically shrinking. Over the past decade the ranks of the unattached have nearly doubled; one in five home or apartment dwellers across the nation today is a person living alone. Add the trend toward postponing marriage while establishing a career to the continuing rise in the divorce rate and decrease in childbearing, and the result is the prediction that by the end of the century as many as one in every three American households will be occupied by a solitary person or by people who are related by neither blood nor marriage.[4]

Technology has shrunk our world to a global village in which satellites bring us the British at a royal wedding, or the sobbing villagers of an Italian hill town pulverized by earthquake, even a satellite's spin around Saturn. Streamlined high rises with automatic elevators dispense with the need for chatty operators. The corner computer comes across with a $20 bill before the last bar closes and gives you none of the guff of a daytime teller.

But who is there to *talk* to, to hug when you're happy, to commiserate with when you're sad, to spend Sundays with for the next ten years? A mate, perhaps, but that doesn't always last.

Running into an old friend who had dropped out of sight when a lover she adored moved in, I asked how the relationship had turned out.

"Oh," she said with a cavalier flick of the hand, "just another one-decade stand."

Now that most Americans live in complex urban environments where the business of *physical* survival is taken care of largely by pushing buttons or telephoning toll-free numbers, and where classic kinship ties are weakened into anachronisms, more than ever we need friends for *emotional* survival.

"In fact, you don't know it until you go through a period when you really do need them," my friend Donna reflected later. "You give and give, and you don't understand what you're doing at all. When you suddenly need someone, and they're *there*, it's a miracle! It changed forever how I value my friends."

Friendship on the Last Frontier

Of all the pathfinders who emphasized friends as vital, none was more passionate than those living in rugged or out-of-the-way places. Such friendships had more of the quality of kinship. Although the people were not related by blood, their ties were reinforced by rituals and by mutual survival needs. A likely place to observe this phenomenon, I guessed, would be Alaska—America's last frontier.

"Alaska is Israel for the WASP's," one of my guides quipped.

Yet all kinds go there. They go for the same reasons that state is flaked with the bones of stampeders who rushed the Klondike for gold, and with the icicled sweat of pipeline boomers who went to tap its dark purple underbelly of oil. There is no past there, no social-class divisions to speak of; little attention is paid to physical attractiveness, and the artificial differences between men and women quickly fall away. Everyone looks the same in the ubiquitous parka and big fur boots. Or frozen to death. The business of survival must be shared.

In Anchorage I watched a stocky blond woman jump out of a hospital meat wagon to slide her stretcher under a filthy man in front of the Montana Bar. The survival ethic cuts both ways. While men learn to share the load and respect the friendship of women, women must learn to bluff violence.

"You son of a bitch, you get outta my cab or I'll blow your head off!"

The petite young cabbie whirled around and stared at her fare. It was late and they were outside town. He wanted action. She faked a gun under her parka. He got out. By the time she picked me up back in town, the lady cabbie was as calm and polite as you please. One begins to get the picture that Alaska does not suffer dependent women gladly. But almost any other handicap is allowed. People can go there with a past life as a loser, a lowlife, even from high society, and pretty much erase the slate and quickly make friends.

"You know you can depend on people here, because everyone has to," one man told me. "It isn't just that they'll dig you out if your car is stuck. You can tell them things like 'I'm hurting inside.'"

A solid second chance does not mean that most of the former losers flourish. They don't; they fail there too, because it was not place that pulled them down. Anchorage is full of people demanding free acreage, who talk about going out into the bush to break land and cut moose, who talk about it sitting in their centrally heated condominiums in a big city and drinking beer.

I caught a small bush plane to western Alaska on a gamble. Based on a questionnaire that scored high in well-being and a phone call with its author, Diane Carpenter,* maybe, just maybe, there was a pathfinder to be found on the last outpost of land before the Bering Sea.

The region's history is tracked all over with resourceful individualists, I told myself as the plane banked out over Anchorage and the cold splendor of the Alaska range loomed up. The icy arm of a fjord thrust deep into the land mass below. And then—curtains—a total cloud cover. My fellow passengers were a characteristic lot: three young social reformers relocated from California, an Eskimo escorting his wife home from the hospital, and the son of a Sicilian immigrant who saw *Call of the Wild* three times one Saturday afternoon as a boy in Bayonne and never got over it. Today he is a high roller in the bidding for cable-television franchises.

An hour and a half later we began our descent through high, thick clouds. A layer of light was quickly devoured by a blanket of fog that blurred everything right to the ground. We drifted down through snow, started icing, and suddenly dropped onto a gravel strip at two hundred feet visibility.

"You should see what it's like in bad weather," my seat partner said. He, like the others, was disembarking here, at Aniak.

"Where are you headed?" he inquired.

"Bethel."

"Bethel! That's the end of the world, the wasteland, the pits!"

"How long were you there?" I asked, thinking it must have been months, and without his family.

"Two nights. That's all it takes."

But two nights later I had met the most amazing collection of women—hearty, strong, resourceful, full of humor, some of them married, some not, all making good money—among them a city manager, a homesteader, a black model from Manhattan, a pipeline fitter putting away wads of dough, a former porno queen with a mink farm. My hunch had panned out after all. When I found the Carpenters, probably the liveliest and most loved people in town, I found a woman and a man flourishing as few people nearing 50 do.

They had married more than thirty years before—she was

* Real name.

18—and had started out conventionally in Louisville, Kentucky. He became a dentist, and she, a dynamo of far ampler frame than the southern feminine ideal, felt herself, after the first two children, sinking into the petty conformity of middle-class wifery. The women she knew did not themselves produce much. They seemed always to be in training as exquisitely discriminating critics of the creative work produced by others.

After a couple of experimental visits, Diane and Bob Carpenter decided in their mid-twenties to give Alaska a try. They spent the next two years as a teacher and a dentist, respectively, based in Bethel and sponsored by the Public Health Service, flying up and down the Kuskokwim River to villages in the bush. Everyone would be gathered for the big event, the once-a-year day when Dr. Bob, the flying dentist, came to town with his entire practice fitted into a Cessna Skywagon 180.

The event consisted of one light bulb dangling from the ceiling of the trading post, Diane operating the portable generator, one kid in the portable chair, and a hundred others sitting around on cartons to watch: "Oooh, big roots, lotsa blood!"

They felt useful. They had two more children. By the time the Carpenters were 28 and 32, they reacted much the same as did Trisha and Gary Worby to that stagnant patch common to the Catch-30 passage. It prompted them to take a year or two off and leave town to go upriver and homestead.

"We wanted to give the kids the opportunity to see what it's like to exist on their own," Diane reflected, "and to see what kinds of values we ourselves would develop away from other influences."

They built their own home and operated a light-generating plant and opened a trading post. Beyond the trading of furs, they soon became the local dispensary, learning on the job how to treat frostbite and gunshot wounds. Their home became a favorite stopover for friends on their way from Bethel to Anchorage. They learned the bartering ethos from their native neighbors, who began swapping family baths at the Carpenters' for things like flying lessons.

The competitiveness they had been raised with died away. A group spirit developed both within the family and without.

The children absorbed the fatalism of the natives and the indigenous value system: "People exist for each other."

Everyone in Bethel predicted that the Carpenters would be back before the first snowfall. Diane said, "I think the reason we made it that first winter was, we weren't going to give them the satisfaction. And after we'd survived that long upriver, we realized we had never seen such poverty. Since we did know how to play the bureaucracy and the natives didn't, we thought we could be of some help."

They stayed ten years.

Their bodies, no less than their mental state, were profoundly shaped by sharing a rugged existence with friends who constituted a close extended family. Diane's natural fleshiness evolved, layer by layer, into straps of great muscular strength. Her calves were as solid as petrified wood—and thank God they were, for her neighbors' sake, the day the fuel tanker ran aground three miles upriver. Bob was away on a field trip. Diane was seven months pregnant. In unspeakable cold with the area fresh out of fuel and no other barge able to get through the ice perhaps for days, people became terribly frightened. A dangerous passivity seeped out of their fatalism. Diane whipped up a rescue party and led them to the disabled tanker, whereupon she demonstrated that a 750-pound oil barrel could be rolled along the riverbank. Her rescue party pulled together. They saved the town from freezing to death.

After that, the boundaries between individuals became almost nonexistent. Blurred by the common efforts that had drawn out whatever strengths each person had to offer, then blended by the osmosis of emotions, gradually, imperceptibly, the defenses among them were nearly disarmed altogether.

The whole Carpenter family felt ready for something different after seven years. The girls decided they wanted a baby in the house. And so at 35 Diane gave birth to her fifth child, a son. So strong were the Carpenters' kinship ties with their neighbors that Diane had hot and cold running baby-sitters and found the new child an effortless delight.

After ten years of homesteading, the family decided to return to the "big town." They moved back to Bethel. Diane was 39. The dwellings in Bethel are mostly Quonset huts, sheds on sleds, or little brown boxes perched on skies. Since permanent frost for many feet down renders indoor plumbing impossible, the waste is collected in "honey buckets" and set on the front porch. Bethel, "Garden Spot by the Sea" as the inhabitants lovingly call it, has one tree. It is memorialized with a sign by the side of the road: *You Are Now Entering Bethel National Forest.*

A cloud descended on Diane. She could not remember ever having been depressed before. "I began to feel life had passed me by. I didn't fit in anywhere." Her pre-pioneering identity had been tied to teaching and learning. In a formal sense she was dismally rusty. Hundreds of acts of mutual survivorship with their neighbors had revealed to her and to Bob and their children the real stuff of which they were made, but the experience had produced no professional accreditations and nothing so civilized as a career résumé. She felt a stab of inadequacy for that aspect of herself she had tied off in order to stretch in other ways. Not knowing what she wanted to do, Diane took a government job as administrative director of social services. "For one really bad year, I just sort of rattled around."

The next Christmas her husband built her a very special gift: a tiny, round, peak-roofed bonnet of a dwelling out back—an escape house. Her children's gift was a week for Mom in solitary; they brought her meals, tended the family house, and allowed no one to enter her hut. For seven whole days Diane simply "not did." When she came out, she knew she wanted to go back to school.

"Back to the womb, that was part of it," she can see, "but I also needed to find out what was going on in the world. Getting an M.A. legitimized it, but I can't justify it in economic terms. What was most important to me was to be learning something new."

Bob Carpenter offered to take over care of the children while Diane moved in with a relative in Anchorage and attended the university there, coming home several days a month. "I knew Bob would take care of everything, and I could immerse myself in the work. I felt freed."

The successful resolution of her middle passage, and Bob's, gave the couple a sense of refreshment as they plunged into their forties and political and social activity at all levels. In a few years their home in Bethel became the hub of efforts on the part of western Alaska to keep its autonomy while continuing to receive government aid for schools and social programs. Once again, the Carpenters became central to a thriving kinship network.

"I think for people to be really close," Diane realized, "they have to depend on each other." In survival conditions that are usually found only in combat or physically violent environments, one *knows* one can depend on one's friends. "You're never alone here, in terms of a support system. And when you know people in a number of different roles—as neighbors, at work, as parents, in community organizations, and socially—it's impossible to keep up the kinds of masks you can manage in other places." She added, "But you must be resourceful enough to make your own amusements."

Any Alaskan town attracts more than its fair share of misfits, morons, lushes, and psychopaths. During the frozen half of the year, people are shut up in a few rooms and limited for entertainment pretty much to chopping moose meat or kicking over the honey bucket. There's no telling who might shoot up a spouse or go helling around in a snowmobile until he gets a leg stuck in the track and has to sit there in the seventy-below cold trying to decide whether to let his limb freeze or to chop it off. If he's lucky, one of the sober ones will drag him into a bar, where it's customary to pile up the drunks on the floor and step over them on the way home.

That is why one needs the imagination to create entertainments out of pure fantasy. Diane Carpenter's abilities in this regard were still the talk of Bethel when I arrived, six months after her brainstorm: a three-day festival in Mexico.

Diane commandeered the huge two-room gym in town and threw up butcher paper all around the walls and over the windows and set her friends to painting murals depicting an ocean, a Mexican village, the whole *mise en scène*. She had sand trucked in to make a beach beside the swimming pool. Another end of one room was bowered with mattresses from the armory so that people could sleep whenever they wanted to—after all, this was going to be a three-day festival with something going on every minute. The rules were that no one who left could get back in; they were all supposed to be away from Bethel for the long weekend—the fantasy had to be preserved. It caught on.

A hundred Bethelites arrived in swimsuits and sunglasses. They watched bullfights and listened to mariachi bands and passed the salt for Margaritas, and by the third day everyone was very, very mellow.

"We decided we were all doing so well at keeping our bodies fit, we would take them into the steam bath and pamper them," recalled one of the participants. "We were all chatting in a slow, lulled way when we heard Diane thundering down the hallway: 'Get ready for the Mazola Oil Orgy!'"

The door opened and ten gallons of warm oil oozed into their cocoon. Bodies floated about, bumping up against one another like raisins in a candy syrup before it has solidified. Howls of laughter seeped out of the gym over the next hours (while the orgiasts were hopelessly trying to wash the oil out of each other's hair) until word of the Mazola Oil Orgy spread all over town. One woman's husband met her at the exit door and demanded, "Tell me what happened in there!" She tried to explain the joke. Of course, one had to have been there. The answer the wife settled on became the official word, thereby perpetuating the amusement for months more.

"Sam, I can't talk about it," she said. "There are just too many people involved."

The following fall, when I walked into the town luncheonette with Diane Carpenter, the whole place cheered. She had just been elected to the city council.

Mutual love is, of course, another of the secrets of Diane's path to well-being. The Carpenters' love for each other has been amplified by the building of a true, working friendship. Diane brings guts and garrulousness to their friendship. Bob Carpenter's dynamism has the impact of a four-wheel drive: it knocks you over. Underneath it are the sweetness, the ear for nuance, the even disposition, and the generosity of spirit that tame their relationship. Diane now teaches at both the college and local levels; sometimes she and Bob teach together.

Beating a path back to pioneer life may have been crucial to the Carpenters' development as pathfinders. In the rigid social stratification of a southern city, Diane would have been cruelly handicapped by the very physical characteristics that have become sources of warmth and strength, drawing people to her in the cold Alaskan expanse. Her personality, too, could have been wasted on social rivalries in a setting where a forthright woman would be a misfit. Instead, she has become a richly loved member of her community and a woman of continually expanding resources.

It must be said that the Carpenters' journey back to a rugged existence in search of undefiled values has limited their children. Only one of the five has been able to stick it out in any kind of city, and that had to be within Alaska. As Diane's eldest daughter explained, the lack of training in competitiveness and individual goal-setting left the children without defenses they would need to get along in college and certainly to make their way in the lower forty-eight. The value system instilled in them, that "people exist for each other," was, sadly, an anachronism. One, at most two, of the five children will be able to take hold outside rural Alaska. The others have never "been outside" and probably never will be.

The rinsing of our souls may well require escape into wilderness from time to time, and it may be what preserves our sanity enough to preserve the world. Yet the cities are the future, that is clear. No important social theory since the 19th century has been predicated on rural life. It is the extent to which reasonable relations can be arranged among competing social, racial, and religious groups pressed together in the cities—think of the pathological sensitivity of Belfast, Beirut, Jerusalem—that will determine whether we keep peace in the world.

One does not have to go to Alaska to make real friends, but the Carpenters' story does serve as a reminder of what friends meant when the environment was harsher and daily life held more surprises and accidents.

Awakening in the Carpenters' house on the morning of my departure, I pulled the curtain and gasped to see the sky run forever. The stingy sun, having not yet climbed that icy wall, threw a dust of gold up and over the rim of the globe. The thermometer read twenty-one degrees; it was early October. Already the land was powdered with termination dust, as they call the first snow. The trumpet swans had fled. As I walked down to the river there were more signs: the punch of feet through first ice, the crystallized honey buckets in front yards, and suddenly a glistening trail in the sky. A jet trail? No, too voluptuous. A kite? No, too long. A mile or more long, the white V-formation swirling across the sky had to be guided by evolutionary destiny. I stood in awe.

"It's the snow geese." Diane Carpenter spoke up behind me.

The final sign: the last of the warm-blooded birds were migrating. Winter plunders in here, with no prelude. But the snow goose reminds one that life goes on, the seasons will come around again, and here on the tundra people will continue existing for one another because they have no other choice.

Reciprocal Passages

Important friendships can develop between a grown child and a parent, or even earlier. A television producer described touchingly how she turns to her 16-year-old daughter to talk over the dilemmas of the mother's passage into middle age. Although she also has a son and a husband, the producer knows there is one person in the world who has studied every crevice of her personality.

Even more common today are real friendships between single parents and their children. One out of every six children now lives with one parent. In five out of every six instances that parent is the mother.[5] It is almost inevitable that the single parent and the child undergo at least one of their major passages simultaneously. The mother may be breaking through to a comeback at 38 while her son is facing the terrors of inadequacy at 13; the daughter may be in her triumphant twenties and about to be married while her mother is faltering for the first time as she faces menopause. One of the most joyous expressions of kinship can take place at such junctures. The two can engage in a reciprocal passage, each helping the other to find a new path and taking strength from the interchange.

James Conti, Jr., and James Conti, Sr.,* fit this pattern. Jim Jr. always remembered his father taking him by the hand into his diner—it was the "in" place in an Italian working-class town in New England. The young man's earliest memories were of nuzzling the warm breasts of waitresses.

* Pseudonyms.

Because that had been his introduction to the restaurant business, he had a sentimental attachment to it. But by the time Jim Jr. came to manhood, he was almost neurotically afraid of being sucked into the family business and having his own drive sapped, as his father had.

"My father was the first in the family to marry, the first to have kids; he was a real go-getter," as the son saw it in his boyhood. "But he was always the intermediary in family quarrels, the soft touch. His own brother took merciless advantage of him—and he settled for second best." The father's nickname was "Mild Jim." The son made sure he was "Wild Jim."

Mild Jim scrimped to send his boy away to prep school, which paved the way for him to be the first Conti to graduate from college. Jim Jr. went on to law school and for ten years he was away from home piling up diplomas and degrees. He wanted to be away from it all—from the narrow neighborhood pugnaciousness, and the politics, and the family's exploitation of his father, from the drink-to-get-drunk and "Let's go find some pigs who are into sex" approach to life among his contemporaries who were middle-aged at 25.

Only later and with painful gratitude did Jim Jr. realize that his father had wanted him to get away. "He prepared the escape route and *steered* me away." But by then the son had repudiated many of the values as well as the religion of his kin.

Approaching his 30th year—and the passage that prods us to reexamine our origins and to reconsider walls we might have erected too hastily, before our own identity felt secure—Jim Jr. began to have second thoughts about his family. He felt a longing to go home and try to find the man who was his father.

But by the time he got there, he discovered his parents, now in their mid-fifties, gone to pasture.

"The shades were drawn; my mother would be in bed all day, depressed, sick without being able to understand why. My father would come home and fall asleep in front of the TV at night. My youngest sister was out all the time with her greaser boyfriends. And my grandmother, having buried her husband and two of her sons, had moved in and was getting stronger by the moment. My father was in danger of being run over by everyone in the family."

After a while, Wild Jim confronted his father:

"A lot of money has run through your hands, and what have you got for it, Pop? Most of the people who work for you have summer homes, but not you."

"I'm a diner man," the father said.

"If you have a fault, it's that you haven't wanted enough. And you give the rest away!"

Jim Jr. tried to talk his father into selling the family diner and starting over with a restaurant in another town. He was getting the short end of the stick from his brother, and their business was beginning to fade as the town changed character.

"I'm not moving. I belong with my people."

"Your people are gone from this town, Pop! They've been replaced by people from other places who hate your guts because they think you've made it!"

The father remained obdurate: he had to take care of family business.

"Pop, your business mind is so fouled up with family disruptions; how can you ever run a successful restaurant?"

It was a bad blowout. The father turned away, silent.

"I didn't think he'd ever come to grips with what he's all about, how much he could do, not even with how good he is," Jim recalled. He left town thinking their rupture might be permanent. But his words had sunk in. When Jim Jr. dropped back into town several months later, he saw his father beginning to make a major passage.

"He had decided himself. He was going to sell the diner. It was brave, brave to the point of standing up to the whole family. But he needed a backup."

Always before in a showdown, the strong uncle had won. This time Jim Jr. sat down with his father and planned the move the way an invasion is planned. "My father's greatest fear was my mother. I acted as his sounding board. One day my father came home and told the rest of the family, 'I've sold the diner. I've dissolved the partnership with my brother. I'm going into business with our son.' Well, my sister cried. My mother went bananas. But he stuck." Jim Jr. added proudly, "My father's creed is to be a 'go-through guy.'"

Did he think his father would have made the transition without him?

"No, I don't," Jim Jr. said with certainty. "But I'll tell you one thing. This crisis has produced his best qualities."

The father and son chose a town that represented the same hard-core working-class style that Jim Jr. had so vigorously rejected. "That's why it intrigued me so much—it represented the opposite of everything I'd learned." But, of course, it also represented everything he knew, felt, believed. It was another confrontation—during the young man's own passage—with his origins.

The two men borrowed better than a million dollars to buy and refurbish the new restaurant. During the first year of their partnership, while the most was at stake and they were pressing the hardest, things of course were touch and go. Deep down, Wild Jim felt an irrational terror that he might be punished for having incited his father to give up a comfortable if not entirely satisfying life, only to lead him into debt or disaster. But a year and a half after the Contis began operating the new restaurant, the sale of the original diner was completed. They immediately swung into action to start two more establishments.

"I love working with my father now," Jim Jr. says after three years. "You end up with a uniquely intense relationship. We have no secrets, Pop and I."

In coming back to join forces with his father, the two of them going through transitions together, there was a reciprocal effect on Jim Jr. He honored the effort the older man had shown in helping him to escape as a boy and better himself. Jim Conti, Jr., as a man, could take pride in living up to his father's abiding value in life. He, too, was now a "go-through guy."

SUPPORT SYSTEMS

The effect of the group on the individual was ignored in earlier philosophical constructs. Each presented man as a singular being in relation to God, to nature, or to mankind as a whole, but not as part of a group that affected his hopes and opinions—including his opinion of himself—all the time.

One of the dominant refrains in accounts of suffering brought to psychotherapists is that of isolation.[6] The mushrooming of group therapy and of all sorts of informal support groups, pressure groups, and special-interest groups represents a significant philosophical shift. People no longer view their problems as exclusively their own affair. So aware are many of the need for allies to confront the causes of their difficulties that they can scarcely imagine how one could become healthy entirely on one's own.

Certain ironies arise from this shift. The more therapeutic attention that is drawn to a difficulty represented by a group—whether it be suicide, alcoholism, or homosexuality—the greater the increase in the number of those who adopt the "problem." Another irony: people generally assemble to express a common frustration, not to transcend it. They can focus many of their problems with the help of the group, but most therapeutic support systems probably should be temporary. That would be salutary both for the individual and for the political system, for if a support system becomes a permanent crutch, the person being supported probably has become a cripple. Friendships made within such a group may develop lives of their own, of course, and often outlast the group's original function.

Networking is a more recent concept that extends the range of group supports. Private men's clubs have traditionally functioned as bastions of exclusivity within which to identify the "right" people, to forge bonds that will consummate a deal, open a door, shoehorn one's son into the proper prep school. The collective alumni of certain colleges and graduate schools have traditionally made up the larger Old Boys' Network.

What is newer is the New Girls' Network. The first woman investment adviser to buy a seat on the New York Stock Exchange for her own firm told me why she thought it was worthwhile to join that expensive club: "I always make it a point to find out how really successful people got their start and made their breaks. Invariably, there's a whole system of contacts, old school ties, and family relationships among the people who make big money and do big things." Toward that end, as well as to relieve the deadly isolation so often felt by women entering male-dominated fields, professional women in recent years have been building networks on their own. Many of the functions are precisely those of the Old Boys' Network—making contacts, exchanging information, taking care of their own. But something else took place in the small women's network group to which I belong.

When it started several years ago, the idea was to bring together once a month women who work eight days a week at their successful corporate or creative careers, but who also have husbands, children, dogs, and plants—or wanted them— and were interested in comparing strategies for how to handle it all. It started out in a very practical vein. But even as we thrived on discussing "What works?" we were forming bonds that turned out to be far more important than how to pack the perfect briefcase. After several months the first broken wing was announced.

"Molly is in the hospital with breast cancer," said the note. "Call her or see her if you can." Next, our youngest member, who was having a pregnancy for all of us, sent word of a stillbirth. And so we became much more than a self-help professional group. We became a network of friends.

Professional care-givers are another link in the support system that keeps most successful women on an even keel. The dirty little secret is that every one of the professional women pathfinders I interviewed has another woman backing her up at home.

By the time Ella Council* appeared at my door to apply for the job of housekeeper, I had all but given up.

"Miss Council, you look like a lovely person," I said right off the bat. "Let's save each other a lot of grief. Let's not pretend this is a time in America when either one of us can feel comfortable about a black woman working in a white woman's home."

"I like your smile," Miss Council said.

Over the past ten years I have watched Ella Council tame the temperamental players and master the hundreds of eccentric moving parts that make up a home. She is the extended mother to my child, the urban guerrilla who can always find cheap meat or charm the super to turn up the heat, the Jewish mother who leaves me homemade chicken soup for a weekend alone with my typewriter.

It can be said that without her, my career would have tied me up in knots of guilt and undone laundry long before this. But there is much more between us. No matter how early my

* Real name.

flight, Ella Council is always there to make sure I get up in time and find a cab to the airport to make the interview in Milwaukee or Munich. She hasn't let me miss a plane yet.

"Come back with a good story, Ms. Sheehy," she always says, waving me off. It is an old Irish custom and it means a great deal to me: in Ireland you have not really left until the woman of the house comes to the end of her garden path and waves you off.

It goes both ways. Ella tells me she is dignified by my work. I let her know I am liberated by hers. She can tell me to keep my temper down, my spirits up, my stomach in, my sleeve out of the soup—and I listen. When she calls me in shock to say her sister has just passed away, I can talk her back from that point of surrender where the next of kin line up to take a number for their own final summons. She could do the same for me. And would.

In this decade, government estimates project that 45 percent of all children under ten will have mothers who work. Will those children ever know the swoon upon coming in the door to the smell of spice cookies baking? The purr of a persistent vacuum cleaner? The feel of familiar hands on a feverish forehead? Why does the desperate need for surrogates in the home have to be the dirty little secret that it is?

No woman who leaves her most precious charges in the care of another is altogether free of guilt. And no black American woman who works in the home of a white woman can forget entirely the shameful antecedents of slavery. In the absence of new and more equitable forms for two women sharing responsibilities for the same household, silence and misconceptions lead instead to many unnecessary abuses. Many professional women say about their housekeepers, "Oh, May and I are like family." May does not sit down and eat with them, of course; nor does May say much about what is bothering her, usually because she is afraid that she cannot articulate it or because she does not want to hurt people's feelings.

"Household workers are very good at lying—to survive," explains Carolyn Reed, the head of the National Committee on Household Employment, "until one day they do the disappearing act." Anyone who has been through this knows it happens only on a morning when the youngest breaks the juice bottle, the dog is in heat, and you have a luncheon speech to make in Boca Raton. The only other defense comfortable for most household workers is what Mrs. Reed calls, disapprovingly, "the dumb act." The theme running through all the complaints Mrs. Reed hears is that the professional women who hire household workers almost never define their jobs clearly. They forget to pay on time and seldom think about other benefits. A fair offer by a woman who earns $45,000 a year in New York, has two teenage children, and wants a household technician to do the cleaning, cooking, and laundry five days a week, insists Mrs. Reed, would be $200 a week.

It is going to cost to bury the Superwoman myth. Certainly the millions of working mothers whose incomes are a fraction of that $45,000 cannot provide a decent living for the women they employ ($15 for a day's work leaves a full-time, year-round household worker with a gross income of $3,750). Tax deductions for general household workers would go a long way toward fortifying this vital support system.* But serious consideration must be given to more realistic support systems: on-site employer child-care facilities, cooperative alliances with friends, perhaps profit-sharing arrangements with care-taking relatives.

Polestars and Survivor Guides

Most pathfinders describe at least one strong model who influenced them during childhood. Those who had an absent or undependable parent usually gravitated toward another figure who exerted a forward pull and offered some guiding principles, who helped them to make a leap of growth instead of falling into a developmental ditch.

A term that might encompass the many variations on the sort of person who serves this important function is *polestar*. The polestar is a conspicuous guide—but not a parent—often described by pathfinders as having had a major impact on the roads they have dared to take.

More evidence that the surpassing influence in childhood is the people one is close to, and that these early relation-

---

* Only 4 percent of all divorced American women can afford to hire someone to help with housework.[7]

ships outweigh even the influence of social and economic factors, comes from the twenty-five-year longitudinal Grant Study of Harvard men. George Vaillant, in his insightful book based on the study, concluded, "It is not the isolated traumas of childhood that shape our future, but the quality of sustained relationships with important people.[8]

People take from polestars whatever they need. Polestars themselves come in various levels of intensity; the role may be played by a teacher, a coach, a doctor; or by a sibling, an uncle, a grandparent; or by a friend, a lover, all the way up to a full-fledged mentor. A mentor is a trusted friend and counselor, usually from ten to twenty years older, who endorses the apprentice's dream and helps in a critical way to guide him or her toward realizing it.

It is a fact that the majority of pathfinders have enjoyed the guidance of one or more mentors in adulthood. One can speculate that a good childhood experience in following a polestar might set up a disposition that attracts, and is attracted by, such people later in life. But whereas a child or very young person may be heavily dependent on a polestar, the mentor-apprentice relationship is an adult one. It is dynamic: the apprentice rewards his or her mentor by growing increasingly able, by reflecting the mentor's own qualities; and ultimately, although the moment is bittersweet, the apprentice must break with the mentor to become fully established. The relationship is also reciprocal: while the apprentice gains competence and insights, the mentor acts almost as an instrument of God, continuing the "creation" of the individual, and gains an unusual sense of singularity and importance.

Since women traditionally have not had a dream that involved their work, not surprisingly, very few women other than young career women report having had mentors. Those few who do most often cite their therapist.[9] (Interestingly, 89 percent of psychiatrists are men, but 80 percent of psychiatric patients are women.)[10]

Sometimes imagination is all one has to go on. During the 1950's, not a period notable in our national life for female models of achievement, a girl had to turn to books, movies, fan magazines, and her own fantasies.

Enchanted by a biography of Pavlova, for example, I performed a toe solo until my toes bled and left on stage the stain of my baptism as a Serious Dancer. The ballerina dream had to be abandoned, however, when I saw *The Red Shoes* at 15 and realized the awful choice to be made after you had tortured your body at the barre for ten years to become a prima ballerina: either give it all up to keep the man you love, or rededicate yourself to career and wind up crushed under a moving train.

It was not apparent to me until many years later who my childhood polestar had been, but it must have been she who planted the solution to my adolescent dilemma. A book searcher recently dug up the Beverly Gray Mysteries[11] series for me. A fictional heroine with "a knack for adventure," Beverly was drawn to Manhattan to begin a career as a reporter for the *Tribune*. When the time came for my emancipation, I made a beeline to Manhattan to try for a job as a reporter for the *Herald-Tribune!* Beverly's job had flung her around the globe on fascinating assignments; my career eventually led to investigative adventures from Anchorage to Cairo. The crucial point on which Beverly had reassured me was this:

> Beverly knew nothing would supplant her urge to write. That was a part of her. But writing was something that would not interfere with married life . . . at least not as much as acting or dancing. No matter where she went Beverly could take her ambition and working materials with her.

Eureka! Throw out the toe shoes! I did not have to choose between love and death after all. My polestar had guided me toward another destination. I could be a writer instead.

For an incipient pathfinder who is struggling through a rough transition that requires separating from something on which he or she has become dependent—alcohol, drugs, neurotic defenses, a destructive marriage, or an outlived ideology—it is enormously beneficial to turn around and in some way guide or educate others in the same fix. I call this temporary role that of the *survivor guide*.

We saw one example of the survivor guide in Cate O'Neil's *pro bono* work as a lawyer for women caught up in difficult divorces. Her efforts undoubtedly helped others who did not have her educational advantages. But the benefit was reciprocal. Cate was eventually able to neutralize conflicts about her own divorce, not inside, through repressing them, but outside, through advising others who might otherwise have made some of the mistakes she did.

By offering oneself as a coach, one can talk constantly about the problem—and the need to talk compulsively about it far outlasts the actual dropping of the behavior. By doing so the survivor guide gathers reinforcement against falling back into the problem, and self-esteem from the fact of having worked most of the way out of it. The point at which the survivor guide mutters "Oh, no, I can't stand to go over this again" probably marks the entry to the completion of his or her passage.

By fortifying us in the continuing need to seek new openings in our paths and to rebound from setbacks, friendships and kinship and support systems are important aids to the pathfinding process. But they also offer the incipient pathfinder the opportunity to become something more—an all-weather friend, a person who sees the strongest kinship ties all the way through, and a polestar or survivor guide. These are roles that the pathfinder becomes ideally suited to playing for others, thereby perpetuating the roundelay of full human friendship.

9.
BEST OF
MALE AND
FEMALE STRENGTHS

Sex roles that may have been played according to the book by very young men and women at pains to be good "providers" and good "nurturers" can—and inevitably do—become far more relaxed once the long parental emergency is over. But, as it turns out, more than roles are involved in the startling exchange that I described in *Passages* as the Sexual Diamond. Almost everyone experiences some degree of exchange in gender strengths as they grow older. But pathfinders make a great gain of it.

The Sexual Diamond Revisited

From behaviors that are wide apart in the twenties and thirties, men and women first come together in the forties and fifties, as each gender begins exhibiting characteristics that used to be more or less exclusive to the other. Each becomes something of what the other used to be—the woman more independent and strong-minded, the man more emotionally responsive and interested in human attachments. (See the visualization of this important exchange in the drawing opposite.)

Evidence that these changes in middle life are developmental, not circumstantial, that they can result in personal growth, and that they occur in predictable sequence across widely disparate cultures is now available from the studies of Professor David L. Gutmann* at Northwestern University, as reported in 1980.[2]

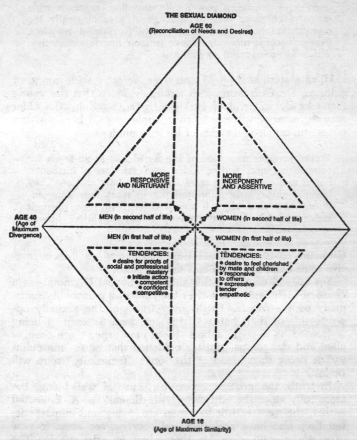

THE SEXUAL DIAMOND
AGE 60
(Reconciliation of Needs and Desires)

AGE 40
(Age of Maximum Divergence)

MORE RESPONSIVE AND NURTURANT

MORE INDEPNDENT AND ASSERTIVE

MEN (in second half of life)

WOMEN (in second half of life)

MEN (in first half of life)

WOMEN (in first half of life)

TENDENCIES:
• desire for proofs of social and professional mastery
• initiate action
• competent
• confident
• competitive

TENDENCIES:
• desire to feel cherished by mate and children
• responsive to others
• expressive
• tender
• empathetic

AGE 18
(Age of Maximum Similarity)

* Professor Gutmann's cross-cultural studies[1] have been conducted with urban American men, with the Navajo of Arizona, the Maya of Mexico, the Druze of the Middle East. His interviewees were divided between younger (ages 35 to 49) and older (age 50 and beyond).

We find that, by contrast to younger men, older men are more interested in giving and receiving love than in conquering or acquiring power. We also find, across a wide range of cultures, that women age in psychologically the reverse direction. Even in normally patriarchal societies, women become more aggressive in later life, less affiliative, and more managerial or political.

Having studied men 45 and over, across a wide range of cultures, Dr. Gutmann offers strong evidence that the young man's heady snoutful of ambition is tempered by the older man's greater sensitivity to the people around him and the tastes and smells and sights of his surroundings.

Where younger men look at the world . . . as an arena for competition and action, older men take some incidental bonus and aesthetic pleasure from their daily routine. They become particularly interested not in what they can produce, but in that which is produced for them: food, pleasant sights and sounds, and uncomplicated, supportive human association.

Gutmann concludes, "Over time and across sex lines a massive trans-cultural shift seems to take place."

Yet instead of seeing this shift—the Sexual Diamond—as a chase of high excitement after their missing personality parts, many people freeze. To discover traces of the sexually opposite side of their natures frightens them. Instead of being welcomed as new potentials, these new aspects are seen as alien and dangerous, sinister evidence that one's "masculinity" is being threatened or that one's "femininity" soon will be lost.

In truth, the greater a person's sense of well-being, the more fully he or she embraces both dimensions. As indicated earlier, the most satisfied women are loving and empathetic, but they also have ambition and courage, are open to new experiences, and consider themselves knowledgeable. The most satisfied men, too, are courageous and open to new experiences. They enjoy being physically fit and are able to lead others effectively. But they also, uncommonly, find themselves comfortable with intimacy.

It is significant that the people of highest well-being have incorporated the primary characteristic of their sexual opposite—in the case of men, being comfortable with intimate relationships; among the women, admitting ambition. This acceptance of opposite-sex-linked strengths was borne out in the biographies of pathfinders again and again, although sometimes not until the second half of their lives.

In the earlier part of our lives the hold of archetypal sexual myths is particularly strong. Potential pathfinders and ordinary mortals alike, all bear the engraving of these ancient myths on their fantasies. The archetypal male fantasy is adventurous and animated, although often it ends catastrophically. A man sets out in high excitement, full of pride and combativeness, surging with sexual energy. Compelled to test the limits of his powers, he takes risks, reaches higher and faster, soars in anticipation of ascending above the heights—when suddenly he falls to destruction, despairing of his original dream.

Every time a man captures the imagination of the world by scaling Annapurna or the World Trade Center, the archetypal male fantasy is reinforced. After flying a balloon across the Atlantic Ocean, Maxie Anderson admitted that the compulsion to test his powers knew no surcease: "All of a sudden, what I guess you'd call my impossible dream came back to haunt me. I couldn't analyze it, but I kept thinking there was some test I hadn't passed."[3] The next time out he weathered ominous storms and subzero temperatures to make the first balloon flight across the United States—with his son—exulting in extremes of emotion: "We cycled from the heights of elation to the depths of depression."[4] The third time, he and his son dropped to near-disaster over the Himalayas.

Test pilots play out the male myth to perfection. In writer Tom Wolfe's telling phrase, they are always going for *the outer envelope.*[5]

What makes it so exciting is never quite knowing if this vision is one of beauty and ultimate freedom or hallucination born of man's hubris that lures him to destruction. Hubris, in the modern sense, may be described as the refusal to accept limits, the impetus to reach out continually, to go beyond mortality.[6]

One man who lived through the fantasy of soaring toward ultimate power described the trip to me most vividly. He had

been caught up in solving a major crisis in his state, catapult-
ed by publicity up and over the heads of ordinary mortals
and set on the outer rim of ambition. At the time he was a
recent entrant to middle age and freshly divorced. The psychic sensations of that year were intense:

"I felt myself going over the curve. I was drunk with it.
Everything became one montage—the daily newspaper head-
lines about what I was doing, the beautiful women's bodies I
left in bed, the mornings of tough negotiations, the TV lights
waiting to explode in my face when I came out—it all remains overlapped in my mind in one great montage. I
couldn't have had any life beyond the pursuit of that glitter-
ing something that turns you on completely. No woman
could possibly compete—the state was the Woman in my life.
I was obsessed with her, wooing her day and night, awed by
her, sparring with her. This must be a singularly male reaction. I'm sure a woman in that position would be much more
involved with the realities of the problem rather than the
fantasies of power. I had to stop myself when I started going
around the curve. I knew if I kept going that way, eventually I'd be destroyed—if I didn't burn myself up with desire
first."

This man did not run for office, as was rumored he would.
He went back to being a businessman and earning large fees
for his firm. Grateful to the Furies who had guided him
through an astonishing sexual passage, he no longer needed
to find the unattainable woman to prove again he could conquer her. It became possible for him to discern in a woman
near his age the first truly companionable partner in his life.
They married. And from that stable base, having broken the
crazy momentum of riding the chariot of the sun, he was
able a couple of years later to come back to public life in a
part-time, caretaker capacity.

Solitary, disciplined effort to master a skill or to conquer a
technical or political problem is a characteristic strength expected of men. Such experience allows men to be "objective,"
"cool," and "rational" when hard decisions must be made. It
also permits them to be "detached," "desensitized," and "arrogant" when they are discussing limited nuclear war and
other scenarios for taking most of the human race down with
them. They have been taught from an early age to shut off
their feelings, so their connections to other people often are

weak, as are the bridges between the emotional and intellectual hemispheres of their own minds. The region of feelings is a dark and frightening territory, and many men do not know the language spoken there.

The closest thing in Greek mythology to the fantasy pattern common among American men is the story of Phaethon,[7] which moves from high expectations and energy to sudden destruction.

Like any red-blooded adolescent out to prove himself, Phaethon demanded to drive the family chariot. In this case, the vehicle happened to be the chariot of the sun. Knowing that to grant his son's request would be to give him the gift of death, Helios tried to dissuade the boastful young man from this mad demonstration. But Phaethon had demanded proof for all eyes that he was indeed a descendant of the god of the sun, and the father had sworn an irrevocable oath to grant whatever proof his son wished. So the father set aside his grief in favor of upholding the rules and handed over the reins. Plunging through space, quickly overpowered by steeds unused to his hand, the young man careened toward earth, out of control, and began to scorch the soil and dry up rivers. He would have destroyed the universe if Zeus had not struck him down with a thunderbolt.

Women's lives have a very different texture. The surface is thickly woven with connections—love and friendship links, umbilical cords, family rituals, often a hypersensitivity to their own and others' feelings—and these form a web of loyalties to human ties that most women put before rules or abstract principles. For this reason, women are often accused of "fuzzy thinking," "sentimentality," "emotionalism."

Seeking and risking in the world therefore are cast as the natural male prerogatives, whereas nurturing and enduring intimate relationships are assumed to be the female assignments.

But pathfinders break through these destructive confinements. By allowing themselves to become more than the narrow stereotype of "man" or "woman" they turn the Sexual Diamond into the jewel that makes middle life sparkle.

Two pathfinders who illustrate this phenomenon were pushed by circumstance to take on the strengths of their sexual opposite early in the game. For both, the process began in earnest in their mid-thirties. One was an athlete who gave up mastery of a sport to spend time with his family, only to have his wife walk out on them—a jolt that forced him to search for mastery of the much more treacherous territory of human relations. The other was a woman widowed at 33 who went on to raise a household of children while simultaneously pursuing a career in finance that eventually brought her exceptional success. These two lives show us what is possible—two more illustrations of what goes into the making of a pathfinder.

The Nurturant Man

Consider Al Oerter:* discus thrower, four-time Olympic gold medal winner, full-time father, retired engineer, and a man of 44 with a brand-new dream to go with the second half of his life. How did he avoid the fall of Phaethon? It was not because he was spared accidents of life that might have shattered others.

As a young man, Al nurtured the classic male fantasy, and in the most literal terms: he was going for perfection of motion. He would break through to the farthest galaxies of physical strength. He would be the best in the world.

When he was about 28 and going for his fourth gold medal, he predicted that he probably had one more Olympics in him. "But once an athlete reaches thirty-seven or thirty-eight, it's all over. It's impossible to increase strength levels."

To his own callous prophecy of sudden fall Oerter paid no attention. Like most other young men, he severed himself from Al Oerter, older man. Any leveling off in the climb of his own strength or the pitch of all-out athletic ambition was unthinkable. Overreaching, for Al Oerter, had become conditioned reflex.

His sport, the throwing of the discus, put him into a sweet slow spin, the scapula rotating first and then one bundle of muscles after another sweeping into the momentum . . . the weight and speed filling his body until he was taking the whole world with him, until his being was the *fulcrum* . . . movement itself!

* Real name.

And yet he departed from stereotype as early as the age of 32. The heat was on to commit to the next Olympics, to break his own record, to shoot higher. Every night before he went to sleep he heard the infectious voices of sportswriters, coaches, fellow competitors. Eat, sleep, train, go to work—he had little time for anything else, certainly not for dawdling at the beach with his two children: that dissipated energy. And when he lay with his wife, he wondered if she knew that he was usually thinking about the next throw.

One voice he could not hear—it came as a revelation to admit he had no long-term goals of his own.

"The most important thing, as far as I could make out, was that my girls were growing," the athlete recounted. "They were eight and six and their questions were changing from 'Why is water wet?' to 'Why did the President say that?' If I missed those next years I wouldn't be able to feel good about their leaving when the time came. To realize—ten years later—I'd been following everyone else's priorities and not my own, son of a bitch! What a terrible waste of time that couldn't be recaptured!"

He left sports in 1968. Finished. No throwing, no further strength training, no sort of athletics at all, not even running, which he found intolerably dull. He luxuriated in being able, wherever they were, to stay as long as the family liked.

He did not try to kid himself about not missing sports. The feeling was not so intense that he brooded, but he did miss the buzz that competition put in the body, and the daily discipline of working toward a goal of excellence. He became a home-renovation nut, which did not quite make it. His job was no place to look for intrinsic satisfaction. He had become a computer engineer to please his father; it was bread and butter, nothing more. In dozens of other ways he tried but could not quite fill the need for the old intensity that came from amateur sports—until his wife, a Sunday painter, hit a streak of originality.

"Terrific. Those wildlifes are really good! Let's take them around to the art shows." He was thrilled; she seemed to love what she was doing. His wife went in a matter of months from *What do I want to do with my life?* to being a working artist who brought in several thousand dollars in a weekend. Since she had turned out to be the sensitive artist in the family, Al happily adopted the role of "bull worker"—framer, hauler, driver, accountant.

"I couldn't have been happier. That became my consolation. The business began booming, my daughters were learning how to handle the public, it became a whole family enterprise, and everybody was doing very well," says Al as he remembers that period. "All of a sudden it became threatening to my wife. She developed an allergic reaction to competing. A positive thing turned negative overnight. She stopped painting. Just flat-out stopped. I don't know why to this day."

For six months Al tried to "get inside her head." But it was impossible for a man who thrived on competition to understand the unconscious terror that can overtake a woman once people start counting on her to repeat her success. Since many women attribute their successes exclusively to luck, not to any lasting attribute within them, there is little to look forward to except letting people down when the lucky streak runs out.

His wife, Al thinks, was done a disservice by the local NOW chapter. The women's movement was at its doctrinaire peak in 1974, and the diagnosis Mrs. Oerter brought home was that her environment was depressing her, undercutting the very independence her artistic talent would provide if she went into the world on her own.

"They pumped her up to the point where she believed she could handle anything that life could throw at her. This proved not to be the case—even the art shows, which were a family affair, could not be handled by a single person," Al remembers. Their marriage ended, with each sharing custody of their two daughters, who were to live with Al full-time. Although apart, they both attended to the needs of the children, but it was a difficult time for Mrs. Oerter.

So it was that at 37, left to pick up the pieces of a destroyed marriage, Al Oerter went into the full-time second job of raising daughters, then ages 11 and 13. The simple mechanics of it stymied him at first—how to cook and thread a bobbin, and where to hang those funny blue things that sweeten the toilet. If it was not shaped like a discus, he fumbled it. But those things were soon learned. It was being deaf and blind in the region of intimacy that almost threw him.

"The emotional strength required was what I found strange, and very demanding. I had never really known what 'emotional strength' meant. One daughter comes home and she's on the outs with her girl friends. The other one's been jilted. What language were they speaking? If you're there from the beginning when your children come home from school and spill their guts, perhaps it's easier to handle. We just had to start from scratch and learn a new level of communication. I didn't take over a traditional mother role. Everything was shared. It was the three of us in the kitchen bumping hips and preparing meals and cleaning up, together." His voice changed from mild amazement almost to reverence. "It was wonderful."

After two years of pouring his creative energies into bringing his brood over the brink of adolescence, Al Oerter saw ahead—to his utter astonishment—what promised to be the toughest transition of his adult life: losing his children.

He was 39. Was it too late for a comeback?

"What for?" people said. "You're gonna make a fool of yourself." "You haven't lost an Olympic competition." "Gotta go out a winner."

The confidence and the corpus are running against anyone after the mid-thirties; that is simple fact. But by the time Al approached the sport again at 39, with the dramatically different perspective of a man *in* midlife, the callous view of the young athlete had changed altogether. He was stagnating. He needed a goal. What could ignite him more than an attempt to surpass himself?

In 1976, after an eight-year hiatus, he started training again, looking toward a place on the 1980 Olympics team. Al Oerter was now giving sportswriters a different story:

"I realize now that strength levels may be able to be increased up to age fifty. That's an eye opener. The last time I trained and competed, I started at fifteen and went to thirty-two. This time, I've started at forty and I'll continue for another thirty or forty years. No one's done anything like this. That's why it's exciting for me."

The Comeback

It is brittle cold in the unfinished cellar. The sounds are of benign self-mutilation. His head flops out of sight behind the mountain of his chest; Al Oerter lies flat on the lifting bench. Up comes a steel bar, bent like a fishing pole, with six tricycle-wheel-sized iron weights on either end. His biceps rouge with blood. His diaphragm humps. Then he throws on another weight, stretches out, thrusts up his arms again, and this time lowers 450 pounds over his chest.

"Beautiful," breathes John Boos, formerly Mr. World, in whose home gym Al Oerter works out. Since Al has just finished throwing a discus for an hour, it takes a certain fierceness of determination to lift the next load.

"Je-*sus*," he grunts, as the bar lists dangerously and grazes his chest before his friend guides five hundred pounds of weights back onto the rack.

"You did good on that one, Al. Now get some blood into the area," John says. "You just tore a lot of ligament."

The first day back in training Al had started lifting his own body weight. Nothing pulled. The second day things began to go. Pulling only a leg muscle meant a good session. But there were a hundred other muscles to go, and he ripped all of them. He kept pushing it, sooner and faster than he should, counting on the two or three days it took for muscle repair as a young man. At the next session it would feel as if someone had smacked him in the back of the leg with a two-by-four: ruptured calf muscle. He hadn't given the pull time to heal.

"That's the difference with age," he admits. "Repair now takes two or three weeks." He does not have that kind of time. "Not when you have to push a little bit harder today than you did yesterday."

In the middle of the training session a small voice calls downstairs; it is John Boos's four-year-old reporting on his younger brother. "Dad, Eric's hided the trouble, but it's still there."

Having thus offered to cooperate with the authorities, the boy is admitted to the training session. Al discards one dumbbell and cups his friend's son in his palm and pumps him up and down toward the ceiling, "One, two, three, how many reps would you like?" The boy jumps off and comes back with a storybook. Would the 285-pound man read it to him? Al hoists the boy up onto his back. The book looks the size of a postage stamp between the athlete's bulging arms.

He is patient, almost delicate in his handling of the child. The little boy touches the puttied places on Al's face where alien skin covers old sports wounds. The athlete's blue eyes dance. He tickles the little boy.

"I'm starting to burn down," Al says. Leaving the boy on his back, he sits at a pulley like an oarsman to work his rear deltoids and trapezius. These form the strap of muscles across the upper back that puts the plunge into his throws. The passion comes from somewhere else. And that has changed, too. It is more rounded, not so pointed toward a specific goal.

"What happens if you fail?" people were beginning to ask him.

"How can you fail at something you thoroughly enjoy?" he would reply. "If I were going through a four-year effort just looking for the day I might make the Olympic team, and I missed by a quarter of an inch, the whole experience would be worthless. But you've had fourteen hundred other wonderful days along the way." Al lies facedown on the floor. His trainer walks up his back. The vertebrae crack gratefully.

Moments later, having arrived at his small home down the street, the athlete pulls a turkey out of the oven and starts the tea steeping and plunges up to his elbows in breakfast dishwater. His is a rounded life.

By January 1980 he had put in three and a half years of training. Diet, weight, strength levels, everything was falling into place. If he kept going this way, sustaining this long, unbroken line of ascending effort . . . "it will be difficult, but wow! It's possible!"

To be pointed toward peaking in June of that year—and participating in the Moscow Olympics—was essential as a stimulus. The only way to increase the power of a muscle is to multiply the stimuli, to dispatch so many impulses down the nerve at so rapid a rate that the muscle has no time to relax. The nerves act like hundreds of trails of gunpowder down which travel waves of electrochemical heat. The hotter the competition, the stronger the stimulus. The muscles bunch, tear, pull tighter, contract, burn like hell—explode into action. It is that unremitting state of muscle contraction, day after day, year after year, that builds up the firing power of an athlete like Al Oerter.

"What do you think of the idea of boycotting the Moscow Olympics?"

Al had just finished a high-energy session. He looked at the NBC sportscaster uncomprehendingly.

"Boycott?" That long, beautiful line was going to be broken? Anger exploded in his gut. Disbelief.

"No way! I'm going to throw."

Two days later Al Oerter was venting his spleen on the PBS television show "The MacNeil/Lehrer Report." "Let's go over there and show some strength and national character, show them American athletes can win—" Suddenly the camera switched to Red Smith. The crusty sports columnist for whom Al had great respect pointed out how cleverly Hitler had exploited the same American sentiments in the 1936 Berlin Olympics and scored a propaganda triumph.

The next close-up of Al Oerter showed a man doing something on television that is almost never seen—he was listening.

Here I am shooting my mouth off, he began to think. *What kind of national character am I showing?*

A week later he was ready to change his mind in public. Testifying before the Senate Foreign Relations Committee, Al said, "We can't just go to Moscow as if nothing has happened, as if Afghanistan had never been invaded. It's not right." This public appearance pinned down for Al certain new thoughts about responsibility to the community that had been sliding around in his mind. But it was when he read letters from all over the country—only one in hundreds opposed his view—and when former Czech or Hungarian citizens poured out their hearts to him about having to leave their homelands after Soviet invasions for the same reasons Al was citing, that his entire perspective began to change. "I began to feel there are a lot of people who really understand me—that's an amazing feeling."

That can be one of the rewards for pathfinding toward a social purpose: a sense of alienation overcome. *People see my point, I am not alone.* That feeling may also put the individ-

ual on the path toward the self-acceptance most of us yearn
for and may help to realign an individual's outer posture
with his or her inner convictions.

As Al's concern expanded in the next year beyond his particular interest group, he began moving into a new role that
would inspire him to change careers and eventually begin to
connect him to his culture at a deeper level—as something of
an ombudsman for the family of man.

But all that had to wait for the preparatory phases of his
major passage. First, the painful separation from his dream:
"I guess it took a full two months for it to sink in. The goal
had been withdrawn. I was convinced I would not go to the
Soviet Union and compete. So I began to withdraw energy
from my training sessions. They were a labor. Strangely, during that period I had some of the best throws of my life."

When he went to Oregon to compete for a place on the
three-man Olympic discus-throwing team, it was after several
months of diminishing effort. A protective instinct was at
work, he was convinced, holding him back from another, existential disappointment, since the team would never go
anywhere. He placed fourth.

That summer Al set off on a grueling competition tour—in
and out of twelve cities in sixteen days—carried from town to
town and displayed and put back in the caravan, like a
caged animal. He saw it as a death march.

"That tour was a purging thing," he told me later. "It kind
of washed the whole previous year out of my system."

With the incubation phase of his passage out of the way,
Al was ready to resume a relaxed training schedule for international events in 1981. But more important, he was ready to
accept that Al Oerter had seen his last Olympics. Evidence
that he had completed a period of mourning for his loss
came with his decision to commit a new burst of creative energy to the next undertaking. He was tired of a technical
career. His instincts told him, "One of these days the technology is going to overrun me, and I'm trying to get out of the
way." (It was an interesting psychological transference from
his fears of being physically overrun, but also a realistic form
of the self-protectiveness common to the middle years.) He
quit his job.

"What I'm really interested in is protecting the sports environment," he decided. The National Training Center concept

seemed nonsense to him. Because the Center was wholly dependent on private contributions in a tight economy, training opportunities were curtailed for many young athletes; in addition, if an athlete was not chosen for a two-week session in Colorado Springs, he or she was out of luck. Al Oerter got an idea.

"Why not set up training centers locally, as self-supporting profit centers, and gear them not only to athletes but to families and all the people in the community who have been hurt with the curtailing of school athletic budgets?" Next, Al was proposing to banks and sporting-goods manufacturers that they stake him to put up a prototype, to demonstrate the financial potential of the concept. There was lively interest. The more he thought about the idea of whole family memberships in the training center, even corporate memberships, so that businessmen and high-school jocks and senior citizens could train alongside committed athletes in the same superior facility, each motivating the other, the stronger his enthusiasm became. Yes, he wanted to provide for the physical needs of the American community.

"I know I'm on the right track," he told me.

I asked if that track—civic commitment—had been developing in him in his forties.

"It's always been there," Al said, "but it was pretty much all invested within the family." His second daughter had just begun her freshman year at college. "I miss them tremendously. All of a sudden, it was just myself rattling around in the kitchen, nobody to bump into, and it hit me. But something replaced that feeling when I saw her developing in her first year, really out on her own and independent with new friends and new thoughts. Her life was changing so much for the good that I thought, 'How could you be so selfish just to want her with you? Wasn't this a wonderful thing for her to experience?' I will still miss them both, but that feeling will be overtaken by the positive directions in their lives. By then," Al Oerter promised, "I'll be on to something different."

And when I called him in 1980, he was.

Al's reaction to the emptying nest exactly parallels the reaction of many mothers. Margaret Mead called it "post-menopausal zest." Perhaps nowadays it should be renamed "post parenting zest."

With a new horizon opening up in Al's work has come a new freedom to love and be loved by a woman.

"She's a long-jumper." Al describes his new companion as something of a revelation. She has a drive equal to his to excel in a sport; she is the first woman he has known with a compatible physical energy, yet he feels none of the conflict he always expected such a woman would arouse.

"Perhaps it's my ego . . ." he ventured.

"Perhaps it's because you're not in the same kind of competitive period in your life that you were in earlier," I offered.

"Exactly. I don't want to use the word *mellow*"—yet even as he said the word, a pleased look rippled across his face—"but I'm certainly a lot calmer about the whole thing than I was in my twenties."

Al's newest daydreams are about having another family. Three or four or five years down the road . . . when he is close to fifty . . . why not? "In all honesty, I'm starting to look at babies and say, 'Aw, jeez.'"

With Al Oerter as a model, there should be little doubt that a man is capable of incorporating the tender side of his nature with no loss of virility. Learning the language of feelings in order to communicate with his daughters filled out a dimension of joy in his life that earlier was confined to the good feeling of having fulfilled his family responsibilities. Having tasted one of the more passive pleasures—watching his daughters become citizens of the world—Al perhaps was better equipped to enjoy the physical feats of his new love, rather than being compelled to surpass her—and everyone else. Having made a comeback in every other area of life, it is only fitting that Al Oerter should be contemplating starting a family all over again in his fifties.

The Archetypal Female Myth

Can a woman develop qualities of ambition, forcefulness, clear thinking—the whole parcel of qualities usually thought of as "male"—and still be loving and lovable? Not if she submits to the archetypal female myth. The story should be familiar:

She sets out with high expectations of finding meaning in human attachments. She feels helpless when alone but thrilled when she finds a man who will take care of her. Sooner or later she runs into disappointment and loss. Having little confidence in herself, she either endures her loss passively, or uses hysterical defenses (denial, repression) or escapism (alcohol, drugs, heavy fantasizing). Her looks go, her fertility goes, but not her sexual desire—although it grows more difficult to find satisfaction with an aging male partner. She feels superfluous. In the attempt to bind her straying husband and emancipated children to her, she may turn loose on them the mounting aggressiveness common among women in the middle years and become a virago. Sometimes she makes the best of her lot and persuades herself she is content. And sometimes she ends up a castoff: lonely, timid, anxious, and—to most of those in the mainstream of life—invisible.

Intriguingly, this story line for women and the Phaethon story line for men turn up quite consistently in studies of the fantasy patterns among today's women and men. The studies are based on reactions to an ambiguous picture that shows a man and a woman, each on a trapeze, flying with their arms extended, either toward each other or apart. Asked to tell a story based on the drawing, women spin tales of timidity, anxiety, dependence, that culminate in suffering, doubt, and loss. Ultimately, however, the deprivation is accepted, and the woman presents herself as content. The stories told by men move in the opposite direction, beginning with great physical and emotional excitement and often pride. But the man's soaring strength is cut down prematurely, and he collapses into failure or despair.

Ten separate studies have shown little variation in these story patterns, reports Dr. Robert May, director of the mental health clinic at Amherst College, in his recent book *Sex and Fantasy*.[8] What is more, these male and female fantasy patterns begin to emerge sometime between the ages of six and nine. Only one group of women has offered stories that transcend the stereotypical melodramas in which the woman is dependent on the man, suffers familiar anxieties, and finds it thrilling when at the last moment he saves her. The sagas told by people in this group revolved around pride, self-confidence, and personal achievement. This fantasy pattern was confined to politically active feminists. Similarly, in the feminists' stories elicited by New York University psychologist Carolyn Saarni, the woman was usually depicted as the more accomplished one and the man in a supporting role. If there was any anxiety, it concerned the possibility of male envy, leading the woman to compartmentalize her professional and emotional lives. If she took her performing partner as a lover, a wounded male ego might break up the act!

"It's interesting that the only positive fantasy pattern comes from feminists," Dr. May commented to me. "Their stories parallel those of the men's with one crucial difference: there is no catastrophic end. The women depict instead a rather steady growth of achievement and self-confidence. In some, there are intimations around the edges that something might go wrong. They often leave off endings. Things are going well and probably will continue to do so, but their stories don't exactly say."

In all ten of the studies in which men responded to the trapeze picture, the male fantasies started with excitement, success, or fame and wound up in injury, death, or catastrophe, or they ended in a humdrum way when the man lost his strength. I asked Dr. May about men who had taken this test. Were they all young, all healthy, nonpatients?

"The studies were originally developed on Harvard and Radcliffe students, whether you want to call them healthy or not," he said with a chuckle. "But one of the limitations is that with men, none have been tested beyond college age."

That made a difference. It made sense to me that men in their late teens and early twenties would idealize themselves in tales of overreaching ambition (except when the prevailing style is laid-back). Young men are loath to compromise about anything, and they do not have to compromise in their fantasies. To end their stories destructively gives them heroic proportions. Young and believing themselves immortal, they can simply split off the second half of the story. Their common concern is now—flying to the sun, boom or bust. They can worry about bust later.

"Unfortunately," added Dr. May, "that's what happened to a lot of them at age forty-five. They went bust. And it came as a total surprise."

The new myth for the achieving woman is not Superwoman. Pursuing that myth leads to exhaustion or failure.

Nor is the new myth woman as victim, the stereotype with which this section began. Much closer to the model for today's healthy, loving, and achieving woman is the classical myth of Demeter and her daughter Persephone.

The goddess of the earth and harvest was coveted by both Poseidon and Zeus. She loved another, however, and spurned the king of the gods. Deceiving Demeter, Zeus left her with child. The child became the joy of Demeter's life.

One day her daughter ran through the fields to pick an unusually pretty narcissus. The earth opened, and Hades dragged her down into the kingdom of the underworld. Demeter heard only her daughter's strangled cry for help. "Then," says the Homeric hymn, "bitter sorrow seized her heart. . . . Over her shoulders she threw a sombre veil and flew like a bird over land and sea, seeking here, seeking there."[9]

When she discovered that Zeus had awarded their child, in spite, to his brother Hades, Demeter descended from Olympus in rage and disgust with the Establishment. Inconsolable, she prepared to use her powers to confront Zeus, refusing to permit the earth to bear fruit unless she saw her daughter again. All the supplications of the other gods failed to shake her resolve. Ultimately, realizing that if earth could not produce he would receive no further fringe benefits, Zeus capitulated. He commanded Hades to return the young Persephone.

"My daughter!" Demeter cried when Persephone came back. But her joy was cut short when the girl admitted to having tasted the pomegranate seeds by which Hades rendered their union indissoluble. Demeter seemed destined to suffer again.

But no. She exacted a compromise from Zeus. Persephone would live for a third of the year with her husband and return to her mother for the other two-thirds. Demeter set aside her anger and made the soil fertile again. And so it came about that each year when Demeter enters mourning for her beloved child, the earth shudders and loses it leaves and enters winter. But when the child rises in radiance out of the shadows, her mother garlands the earth in the flowers of spring.

Demeter is a very modern figure. She represents the basic single mother head-of-household who makes it on her own, incurring the envy of powerful males for doing so without them. Zeus, the punitive father, cannot bear being rejected. He conspires to take from Demeter the one thing she most loves and who serves to replace him in her affections: her daughter.

The story contains many of the elements of the female stereotype: idealized expectations of happiness tied to personal relationships, interrupted by disappointment and loss, followed by wandering in sadness and inconsolability. But Demeter does not stop there and passively accept her shriveled fate, putting a happyface on it. She meets reality. Marshaling all her powers, she challenges the unfairness of the Establishment and holds fast, until it is understood that she is resolute. Ultimately, she makes a compromise. This is not taken, as it might be by a young man, as evidence of failure or a destroyed ego. Demeter sets aside her anger in a less than perfect resolution, knowing that perfection is never possible. In so doing, she comes back from despair to a working balance between sadness and love, deprivation and beneficence. She teaches the kings of earth her agricultural mysteries while enduring the winters. And when her daughter is borne back in the sweet-scented spring, she exults.

Any woman, to be a pathfinder, must go beyond creative endurance. Only several women in the world, of course, have anything approaching the powers of the goddess Demeter—Margaret Thatcher, Indira Gandhi, and, earlier, Golda Meir—whereas many men both decent and dubious hold the power of partial world destruction in their hands. But there are also battles for hearts and minds, for fairness and enlightenment, and in those arenas, given the perspective of history, women are incorporating male strengths at a remarkable rate.

Pathfinders like Delia Barnes, the woman expelled as pastor of a church as a scapegoat for a man, remind us that Demeter's pattern is alive and in practice in the contemporary world. "When you met me, I had partially caved in but was satisfied to continue," Delia Barnes told me after several setbacks. "I hate to think I was willing to give up like that. I've come to realize it's a marvelous thing that happened to me; it made me take the chance of standing up, and the pain was only temporary. I'm content." Like Demeter, Delia suffered a shattering loss and came loose in the world, descending into despair as an attendant in a madhouse, but she did not give up. When the chance to come back presented itself, Delia used all the powers at her disposal to effect a compromise that would preserve her hard-won parity with male pastors. And just as Demeter rejoiced over her partial success, Delia Barnes accepted the partial attainment of her dream as a source of joy.

The capacity for compromise among women has been criticized in recent years: why should a woman have to settle? Although there is validity to the criticism, the ability to accept partial success as a reason for contentment—after exhausting one's best efforts—can be an enormous advantage. What might drive a man around the bend can often be seen by a woman in a realistic light as the best that could be done, and not half bad.

Moreover, on the highest levels, the ability to compromise is crucial. The most powerful and resilient men also learn this approach to life.

"I live in a world of compromise," Lee Iacocca admitted in an interview with me shortly before he was sacked as president of Ford Motor Company and landed on his feet as head of Chrysler. "They always talk about the rugged individualist who just says, 'I'm the boss, I'm going to order it.' Well, whoever that is, in government or in business, usually ends up getting his head knocked off. The higher up you go in an organization, the more you compromise."

Sometimes the full dream can be reconstructed, even after a disaster. Let us now look at a mirror image of the same pathfinder quality demonstrated by Al Oerter—the incorporation of the best male and female strengths—this time in a woman.

A Woman of Courage

When I conducted a workshop with more than one hundred of the most successful women in the financial world, I found that many enjoyed high well-being, but one, above all, emerged on paper as almost larger than life. She was not present, but everyone recognized her from the profile she had sent and spoke of her with admiration, if not wonder. How many human beings could manage to be mother and stepmother to twelve children while continuously keeping up a career, then leave corporate life at the age of 54 to start a securities business that two years later was earning her a personal income of over $100,000?

Julia Walsh* was her name, I was told. I feared she might be one of those people who make you say to yourself, *Oh, God, where did I go wrong?* Yet there certainly was no clue in her modest background that she would become a pathfinder. She reminds us again that pathfinders are made, not born.

Father: a laborer.
Mother: a clerk.
Julia as a child: "Very ordinary." "Never out of Ohio before eighteen."
Nor had she found a path free of traps.
Joined the Foreign Service at 22.
Posted to Germany at 23.
Ranking female officer in Munich at 24.
Expelled from Foreign Service at 25.
Offense: becoming a married woman.
Judging by the bare facts of her first 33 years, there was every reason to expect that this "subject" would fall into the archetypal female pattern. But:
Widowed at 33; husband killed two days before Christmas in freak military accident.
Left with four children, one eleven months old.

In her own eyes she was always a big galoot. A long and loosely bolted piece of work, hipless but broad of shoulder and of smile, she was what mothers diplomatically call a "slow starter socially." Though not particularly adventurous as a girl, she did harbor a longing to take flight at the first possible moment: overseas, to see what the world was like. She dreamed of the day she would be an ambassador.

She had never been party popular, so when she found herself as a pioneer woman Foreign Service officer among ninety thousand men stationed in Germany—and suddenly *very* popular—her thoughts turned for the first time to romance. She married a military man. She was so fond of him, and so well indoctrinated in sexual stereotype, that she never thought to

* Real name.

question the automatic expulsion from the Foreign Service. She looked upon it as she looked upon being an Irish Catholic or five foot ten. It just *was*. Her husband had been attracted to the dashing lady diplomat and harbored some guilt at depriving her of that dream. He approved, therefore, of her working as a paid professional for the State Department while he served two years in Turkey; then back to Washington, D.C., and housewife status.

They hoped to have two children and produced four. One day, the young son of a family who owned a brokerage business offered Julia Walsh a job; he said he could see she had a real feel for the business. She was working on a master's degree at the time.

"What do you think?" she asked her husband, who had served with General Patton.

"Oh, doll," she remembers his words, "you'll learn a hell of a lot more on the battlefield than you ever will at the war college."

"They're not going to pay me anything," she told him.

"I'll support you through it for six months. Let's see what happens. It's probably the best investment we'll ever make."

So it was.

The company gave her a desk and a phone: be a broker. Even that was daring. In those days women in the brokerage business were as scarce as men wearing gold chains. Six months later she became a registered broker. With her husband's support she paid a housekeeper and dressed the part of a successful professional woman for eighteen months—with never a whimper out of him—before coming home with her first $1,000 commission.

"Oh, doll, that's great." But he had news, too. He was being transferred to Fort Leavenworth, Kansas. She left her job on the Friday before Christmas. She drove across country with the four children to join him on Christmas Eve. Midway, she was informed that her husband had been killed.

Everyone who knew her remarked at how well Julia Walsh handled it all. She gave every appearance of "breezing right through" the shocking funeral. In the somewhat manic aftermath, she set up a whole new *modus vivendi*. It hung on decisions made under pressure:

If she had wanted to invest her major effort in becoming more successful, more visible, and earning more money, it would have been logical to take one of the several entry-level jobs in New York. That would have meant commuting and sixty-hour weeks and housekeepers whose faces changed before she could learn their names. She had sons of eight, seven, two and a half, and eleven months of age.

Decisions: "The emotional energy to be a real parent to those boys involved my being able to come home with a little bit left." She would stay in Washington. Her old firm had offered to take her back.

Inspiration: She invited her husband's mother to come and live with them.

"Let's make a deal." She approached the longtime widow enthusiastically. "This is a commission business. The only way I can make any money is to give a lot of time and emotional stamina to it. I'll give you twenty percent of everything I make after taxes if you'll be my housekeeper."

Joy came into the older woman's face at the prospect of giving these fatherless little boys the kind of life she had not been able to give her own son.

But, no, it was not to be a gift, Julia insisted. "You'll be in *business* with me." The older woman did not comprehend. "You'll be my partner. If I make it, you make it."

The older woman flushed. She had value.

From that point on, she read to the boys, dressed them to the nines, ran the house, and followed every exploit of its breadwinner with great relish and pride. "You can't hire that—somebody to sit up all night with a child," Julia acknowledged.

It was like having a wife.

Three months after her husband's death, Julia Walsh enrolled in the Wharton School of Business, the first woman in the school: one hundred men in the class, and Julia with empty seats on both sides. Almost no one spoke to her. "John, I'm going home," she told one friend at Wharton. "I'm not in very good shape."

"Goddamn it, Julia, you're here and you're going to stick it out." He rallied his friends. So it was that a group of young bucks from Texas and California, men who today run companies like Texas Instruments and Teledyne, adopted the widow lady into their network and took her to lunch and tipped her to all their favorite stocks.

"We'll go for broke." She rallied her mother-in-law. "Our

net worth is forty thousand dollars, insurance money and all. Let's keep ten thousand for the kids and emergencies and play thirty thousand on the stock market."

Where did she find the guts for all this? First, she had kept her hand in. "I never would have had the courage to go into business if I hadn't had eighteen months of practice while my husband was still alive, supporting me in every way." Second, she had seen a highly speculative investment pay off once before, when she had had to work eighteen months before earning her first commission. This time, as a widow, it was no hands: no husband there to catch her financially or pick her up emotionally if she fell flat on her face.

She did not.

In one year she had tripled her equity. It was 1959 and Julia Walsh was 34, full of beans and flying with ambition. She found a beautiful Federal brick house on a solid gold triangle of inner-city Washington land and picked it up for cash. Two weeks later she was made a partner of her firm.

The market took off, and so did Julia and her "partner." The first year she could give her mother-in-law only pickup money, but by the third year the grandmother was making $20,000 and Julia put her on a savings program. Eventually, they hired a cleaning woman so that the older woman would not have to do the heavy work. Whenever a business trip or a lecture called Julia out of town, the woman at home knew she would get a piece of the action. And when Julia came home, they went on shopping sprees together.

"It was one of the smartest things I ever did," Julia said.

One Saturday morning, a year and a half after being widowed, the dynamo broker awoke in her splendid new family home and a few moments afterward fell back on the pillows. All at once it was too much trouble to make connections between things. *Tired, yes, Mommy must rest.*

Her four-year-old son brought her breakfast in bed. A pale arm, splotched with freckles but with no trace of sun—there had been no time for summer—lifted sluggishly from under the sheet. It flapped in the direction of the coffeepot. Suddenly, the pot went over and the steaming brown liquid spattered everywhere, boiling the mother's body and leaving blisters the doctor called third-degree burns. The doctor wanted to put her in the hospital.

"I can't leave this house with four little boys." That was the last thing Julia Walsh said before going to sleep for seven days.

She was fed intravenously. The family was terrified. She turned a fishy gray. The young boy filled with horror at the thing he had done. What he did not know was that he probably had saved his mother's life.

"I've never talked much about that period," Julia told me. "It was very difficult. I always worked too hard and tried to do too much."

That has not changed. After putting in a snappy day at the office, she had taken me home to dinner with her children, apologized that there were no fresh flowers, stayed up half the night talking, and well before seven the next morning the house already reverberated with her.

"Baby, are you up and at 'em already?" she prodded her youngest. Then down the stairs to arrange fresh strawberries and leave an individual filter coffee and newspaper beside the place meant for her guest. "I'm off to the hairdresser—I forgot," she called, "because tonight I leave at six for my first annual board meeting in New York." A flash of a smile. Glimpse of a blue suit. Gone.

There were pictures in the guest room. The woman in them was square-jawed with widely spaced vivid blue eyes and a turned-up nose, a good-kid Irish face, a natural boy's buddy. She looked at home in the outdoors, riding in convertibles, walking on the beach, whacking a tennis ball—or standing beside the President of the United States, shoulder to shoulder.

"Biggest mistake in my life," she had told me about that picture: in it, she was refusing the job of assistant secretary of commerce. With all those children to educate, she did not think in 1967 she could afford it.

I had to make another trip to Washington to persuade Julia Walsh to sit down and be introspective, which is something she seldom does—and in that she is like many other pathfinders. I said I would like to know where the other major transition points were, what she brought to them, what weaknesses had to be overcome, and what creative turns and innovative paths she had tried that had made her life so rich. She started by describing how the delayed shock of her husband's death had hit her.

"I put up this big front that I had the whole thing under control. I hadn't done any mourning for my husband. So when it all caught up with me, I collapsed. Everything went."

Her coping style had been the same since she was a girl. "When you get hit, you just go faster" was her family's credo. "I was also blessed with high energy." That developed into a style that is more common among men. When the heat is on, they work harder and deny the pain. "It's maybe a good defense but partially not," she says.

When at last she did collapse, emotions bubbled to the surface and had to be favored, like blisters, for fear they would be rubbed raw. Prematurely, her thick black Celtic hair turned gray.

"The really tough thing I had to learn after I started back in the rat race was the conserving of emotional energy. Anger is a very tiring experience."

Much of the anger at having her husband taken from her became converted into an accelerated career push. "I was really awfully ambitious in those years." Julia Walsh grinned without apology. Those were the first seven years after the loss of her husband. There was no lack of incentive, what with six people to support. Except for her colleagues from business school, who always took her out for dinner when they came through town, she did not have time for friendships.

"And my relationships with men were really surface."

But mentors she had in abundance. As her particular tap into the business became a profit-gusher, the chairman of her firm became increasingly paternal. His son and rival had his own plans for Julia. At the age of 39, when she began sinking into a mid-life slump the market also went slack. It was 1962. The son packed her off to Harvard, pulling the right strings to have her admitted to the advanced management program.

"I went in with all kinds of fear and trepidation," she admits today, "playing the dumb female role all the way. The first month was really tough. Then I sat through thirteen weeks with one hundred sixty guys who were supposed to be the top men coming up in the world—and they had more problems than I did!" Her laugh is fresh, unstressed. Then, seriously, "That year was the major turning point in my life. Philosophically, everything changed and began for the first time to fall into place."

She realized she had tied herself up with "women can't do's" because when she came in, there were no women in the financial field: "couldn't" sell stock to older men; "couldn't" be adventurous for fear of being thought "unstable"; could only do a circumspect business with widows and older ladies. Well, good-bye to all that. She would be as dynamic as Julia Walsh had it in her to be.

It had never crossed her mind to remarry. *Forever I have made my pledge* was the demented legacy of some religious lesson she had learned too well, too long ago. But no! She was bored silly with being single! To be sure, she had been through five or six nice beaux, Sunday dinners, treats for the kids; but being stuffy about such things, when a beau wanted to move on to an affair, Julia moved off.

In the course of that Harvard year she shifted from strict conformist to—almost—playgirl. She had men flying in from various time zones for dinner or breakfast, a different escort for each weekend. She became less defended. She was 40 years old and pretty terrific—why work so hard at proving it?

The same turnaround took place in her image of herself within her firm. Because they had taken her back as a widow, and because they had not held being a woman against her, she had felt beholden. Gradually, imperceptibly, from being a go-getter on her way, she had slipped into the role of good daughter in the "family" triangle. Wasn't it her responsibility to provide the mediating influence between father and son? Harvard turned that thinking upside down. Those guys were lucky to have her!

Julia Walsh returned to Washington a changed woman and in the market for a new sort of merger. "I am a person who should be married," she realized. "I like the tradition, I like children. Marriage is, in a sense, a protective device." Her mother-in-law was beginning to lose pace with the household; that added incentive. Julia had provided a lovely apartment and generous pension as part of the older woman's retirement plan.

"You can't do these things alone," Julia Walsh told me. "If

she were still here, I'd have called her up and said, 'I'm bringing Gail home for dinner. Will you order flowers?'"

Her "wife" was retiring. She needed a husband.

Seven faces flecked with candlelight, seven voices leap-frogging in the excitement of trying to tell *their* story about Julia—and only part of the family had been able to come to dinner this night, in 1978. The full complement was twelve children—four of hers, seven of his, one of theirs—because when Julia Walsh made her second marriage, she made it a permanent institution.

"I was pretty much determined I wanted to be married in the Church," she recounted at the dinner table. "That's a tough one for a gal forty years old of my size. You don't find many attractive men between forty and forty-five on the shelf. So I married a man with seven children—think about that!" She laughed heartily.

"We were desperate for another mother," one of Julia's stepdaughters chimed in. (Their mother had lingered in a long illness before her death.) She proceeded to tell what it was like when Julia, a 40-year-old woman whose entire life had been spent in the company of men, met her first daughter: the girl was 15. Tom Walsh had arranged for the two to have a weekend alone together, at the beach, to get acquainted.

Panic pinched the face of the trial stepmother as seen through the eyes of the trial stepchild. It was dead of winter at the beach. Not a thing to do. Stasis. Julia raced out to buy the girl every teen magazine in the drugstore. The girl hated teen magazines. Desperate to do something, Julia hit on "How about a Toni home permanent?" When Tom Walsh came back on Sunday to pick up his daughter, he blurted the obvious:

"My God, what did you do to her?"

In the midst of the laughter around the table, Julia inserted, "I don't even remember that! It was just so easy, the merger. Tom and I are very good friends. He's a lovely human being. The children wanted it too. You couldn't put that kind of group together with anything but a commitment to a permanent institution."

The notion *If this doesn't work out, we'll quit* had never

been permitted in the thinking of either Julia or Tom. They made a Catholic marriage, for keeps.

"If you were down in the dumps and needing support," added another stepdaughter, "you only had to walk in this house. Julia would make you *wonderful*. We grew up with a role model who made us realize we could achieve almost anything. I was twenty when I started in the brokerage business at—"

"And her son was sixteen when he chauffeured her to the White House," chimed in another child. "She got him dressed up in my father's raincoat and a chauffeur's hat, driving the Lincoln. He hops around to open the door right in front of the South Lawn entrance and she sings out, 'Okay, now go home and do your homework and pick me up at ten-thirty.' My mom is an incredible woman. She's so alive!"

"But sometimes you had to make an appointment to see her!" This voice belonged to the "difficult child" in the assimilation process, as she was known by both families. Ten years old when her father told her he was giving them a new mother, she was still at the stage where social conformity is of core importance. "I thought, 'Great, no more store-bought cookies.' Well, wrong-o!"

Somebody else's mother would be driving her somewhere and remark, "Oh, I saw your mother on TV last week." The girl's expectant "Oh, yes?" would be answered with "Of course, I'm just a mother. I'll never be on TV." At which point the girl would shrink beneath the seat, moaning to herself, "Why can't Julia be just a mother, too?"

It took about six years for this stepchild to surmount her suffering and to be able to recognize Julia as a different but admirable person in her own right. "From then on, I blossomed."

The decade of her forties was Julia's consolidation. She gave up being the free spirit. "The merged household was, for me, the epitome of having done it all." It was not until her late forties that the wanderlust began seeping back. *Why had she stayed twenty years with the same firm?* More puzzling than the question itself was the fact that she had never thought to ask it before. Most of the best analysts had left, all of them men.

"I'm convinced that I would not have hung in had I been a man." For the first time she set out a strategy for how to handle her life over the next years. Having learned the art of anticipation late, she made out not one, but two five-year plans—"alternates," she called them.

A case study at Harvard had pointed up a business reality: she could stay on forever as the loyal mediator, but there was no room for her in top management between the senior and junior partners of a family-owned firm. The other route was to spring out on her own.

She debated: there were strong "family" ties to the firm. And God knows, one had a lot to lose by leaving a safe and profitable existence to start over as an entrepreneur at 54. Still . . . she was restless. Her older boys wanted to try the business. And after all, working as hard as she was, why should Julia Walsh be a high-profit center for someone else, instead of preserving a business and its profits for her own children? The bottom line was:

"I wanted a chance to see what I could do."

She took the plunge in 1977. Setting herself up as one of the new breed of professional financial-planning consultants, she put on one son from each of the merged families as president and vice-president and took a woman partner. With middle-income people desperate for safety from inflation, the time was ripe for her approach.

"Everything I've done over the last twenty years is coming together now," Julia Walsh told me as we sat in her Washington office, across the street from her old firm. "It's almost eerie. All the causes I've worked for are paying off, all the contacts I've made. I belong now within a world formerly reserved only for men." She was clearing off a desk symbolic of the meeting of both sides of her nature: soft silk flowers stood to one side of the cool green electronic monitor on which she checks puts and calls.

"Call you-know-who, and tell her I bought her a thousand shares of Occie," she says breezily to the secretary on the way out. Having made it a point to take on about thirty successful women with high incomes as personal investment clients, she found they all shared a common attitude: saving on taxes means you're cheating the government. "They never expected to make money in the first place, so they don't think in terms of how to conserve it," Julia decided. She set about to teach them some of the facts of financial life.

"We've done terrific things together. We've gone to Europe, sent kids to Harvard, bought antiques, financed scholarships, taken care of sick mothers. . . ."

Clearly, Julia Walsh was having the time of her life at that stage, being chairman of the board in her own family enterprise and reaching out to play financial mother to a new brood of professional women.

"I'm so convinced by now that if you don't take risks, nothing big is going to happen," she said. "Maybe nothing big will happen anyhow, but if you hadn't tried it, there would be no chance."

In February 1981 I called Julia for an update. She had suffered a "transient episode" in her physical health and a transient collapse of the market in the fall of '79. The minor stroke at the age of 54 had shaken her illusion of being physically infallible. To be at the same time on the block, with all her assets exposed in a new business, led to the first period of fearfulness in her life. But as soon as the market came back, she pushed herself to the edge and began taking risks again. Broadening the business well beyond stocks and bonds with a more profitable mix of managed accounts, she has increased revenues 500 percent since 1978, when I first met her. Her personal income now comes close to $750,000.

Five years or so from now, Julia Walsh hopes to phase herself out of the business her sons will inherit. And then . . . it's never too late to resurrect her original dream. She looks off into the distance, like a lady Gulley Jimson.

"I was thinking about ambassador to Ireland. . . ."

Julia's Compromise

Julia Walsh is bigger than life, but in another sense she is every woman writ large. We have all known women left by divorce or abandoned to fend for their children and marveled at their pluck and perspicacity. Some manage to pull it off even in New York City. I watched one woman, Virginia Dajani,* support four children in a subsidized artists' housing project, while keeping her sense of humor and teaching the children how to "audition" for scholarships to the best prep schools. I saw my former assistant, Peggy Barber,* calmly build a lucrative manuscript-typing business in a one-room

* Real names.

apartment on West Broadway, while her four pugnacious kids took part-time jobs and bloody well learned to pick up "the room."

Julia Walsh is not important because of how big she made it, but because of how well she did it.

That bears breaking down. First, there were the givens:

Courage: that was proved after her husband's sudden death. But variants of courage—the willingness to risk and openness to new experience—were in evidence in Julia Walsh's girlhood. She was dealt a handicap as a child, but by overcompensating for her bigness, she took herself out of the romantic competition for boys and learned early how to be a "buddy." Later in life, that experience made her easily acceptable as "one of the boys" in any team effort. Straightforward rather than sensual, utterly without ambiguity, she was not threatening to men or women as she moved up.

Religious stability was another given. The values she had been taught, along with her moral and sexual code, remained solid and relatively unchanged. There was no time lost over the question "Will this marriage work?" Finally, she was born with exceptionally high energy: at 55 she could still work until two in the morning after flying in from a business trip.

Ambition was a released quality, not a given; it came to the surface only because she had the courage to allow it to and because she picked up the skills to support it—"otherwise I wouldn't have had the courage." Objective thinking was something she learned at business school, then applied to the personal realm: *What do I need to make my life work?* At one point she needed to make a deal with her mother-in-law; at another, to make a "protective" second marriage. Inner control was self-taught—ruling out anger, for example, when she realized that excess emotionalism drains energy. Anticipation she learned as well.

Yet for all the traditionally "male" strengths she incorporated, she did not lose her female ones.

It would be a mistake to suggest that Julia Walsh had everything that matters, all the way along. The fact was that through no desire of her own, she had no husband to think about for the seven basic career-building years between 33 and 40. She was "spread too thin to have an emotional life. I isolated myself from normal social relationships," she acknowledges. There was no time for friendships, no deep human connections at all beyond those with her children and her mother-in-law. "The biggest cost was not being able to deal emotionally with the idea of marrying again," she told me.

Her real secret, to my mind, was accumulating a large enough family through her second marriage to provide her own children with a built-in support group—a family as institution. The price was a superficializing of emotional relationships.

"The girls laugh now about the transition period when we became one family," she said, when there was time to take a retrospective look, "but there were some pretty rough times there, too. I kept all the relationships surface." She responded to any inquiry from a child in a rational, problem-solving way, never skidding onto the thin ice of emotional problems that might have been hidden below. She was aware that she could not duplicate at home the constant attention to detail that went into her business life. The children did not get the same attention to details of feeling.

A mother can be lucky, but she always knows when she is winging it. At any point, something that was not nailed down could have caused the whole wobbly scaffolding of Julia's family life to take a dangerous list. Certainly, women can have careers and families at the same time. But one can not in conscience support the prevailing myth that a woman can, during the intensive career-building years, strive for excellence, recognition, becoming president, and combine that with excellence as a wife and mother—unless she is exceptionally lucky. Two crucial elements that add to luck are age—older is easier—and an item that highly accomplished women often boil down to three words: The Right Man. But for most women, only two out of three can be done well: high-powered career and motherhood, high-powered career and husband, or husband and children.

There is always some price. Julia Walsh's compromise turned out well. "The fact that I never had any serious health or psychological problems with any of the children was the greatest blessing of all," she says. But she admits to being afraid, still, of touching greater emotional depths, especially in herself. Toting up all her successful investments in life along with the debits, including the recent stroke, Julia

Walsh is filled with a sense of her good fortune in having achieved partial victories.

She no longer pretends to be Superwoman or waits for the bottom to fall out, as it did following her first husband's death. She has learned to go to the beach for three days at a time and collapse voluntarily.

Tapping Our Natural Resources

The latent strengths upon which both Julia Walsh and Al Oerter called when in trouble were there to be tapped: that is the lesson. Putting those additional qualities to work brought pleasure and new possibilities into their lives, while at the same time rendering them more valuable, lovable, and resourceful to their families and to others. Al and Julia should be valuable to us as well, not because we are going to become Olympic athletes or fabulously successful financial analysts, but because their lives point the way to discovering unmined natural resources in ourselves that can enrich our personalities and become new storehouses of strength on which all those around us can draw.

THE NEW CONVENTIONALS

The conventional combination used to be a locked-in man—one who made solid commitments in his twenties but without much self-examination—and a care-giver wife who lived for human relations and tacitly agreed, in exchange for full support, to realize any personal ambitions through her husband and children. Today, given inexorably rising inflation, the option to be other than a two-paycheck family is open only to the privileged—and women's liberation has probably gotten to many of them. People are redefining their family roles as best they can around the necessity for or desire of the majority of women to work. The backlash is most clearly seen among those blue-collar men whose only power base is at home and who feel that base is being threatened. The new pattern seems to be: wife goes back to school, husband grows jealous and resentful, couple separates, and perhaps—once she settles down in a job—they reconcile for the sake of personal stability.

Whenever I surveyed groups of American women who might be characterized as being among the new conventionals, ambition was pretty much masked, or suppressed, or rationalized away altogether. What came through loud and clear was their success shyness. Asked what value they placed on "recognition" as a long-range goal, the great majority of conventional women in every age group pushed it close to the bottom of the list of sixteen goals. Intrigued by this response, I followed up with telephone interviews to find out what they thought about people who were visibly successful.

First, their definition: "Recognition is having people recognize you from some achievement when you walk down the street." Or "Recognition is getting your name in the paper."

Conventional woman said they were impressed by such people, felt sorry for them, loved to read about them, but would not want to be them. Why? "I wouldn't be comfortable." "It would be frightening." "They are in a different world." "They have no private life." "They get so busy with themselves, they don't have time for others." "They forget their humble beginnings."

Deeper probing brought out fears of upsetting the applecart at home—where these conventional women felt most secure and comfortable—by pursuing a parallel commitment outside:

"My husband is more important [than my being recognized], and so is being a good friend or a good person," said Gretchen Smith,* a 30-year-old housewife from Mound, Minnesota.

"Since my marriage and being a mother," explained Lucy Castle,* a homemaker from Longmont, Colorado, "my husband always says, 'Hold your head up and be proud of who you are.'"

For reinforcement of their worth, these women commonly turned to the same tight circle:

"The people around me who love me are sufficient," said Kay Allin,* a 26-year-old mother in Kirkwood, Missouri. "It would be nice to be recognized," said another homemaker who echoed many others, "but I never worked for it. It's

* Real names.

more important that my husband and children recognize the little things I do for them."

Even those who had ventured into a career were reluctant to seek recognition beyond a limited safety zone. Connie Heike,* a housewife-artist from Marine on St. Croix, Minnesota, voiced the attitude of many: "I have a little recognition in my area as an artist, and I have no need to go higher. I do seek a teensy bit of recognition, but I don't want to be Picasso."

In talks with conventional women who shy away from recognition, I got the impression that "recognition" implied to them such effort to reach, and such discipline to maintain, that it would almost inevitably disrupt the peace they work so hard for in family life and the inner harmony they consider their foremost personal value. They try to draw a sufficient sense of esteem from the immediate circle of those they love.

Women who shy away from success are often really allergic to competition: they want people to like them more than they want to win. Competition throws them because they focus on preserving relationships rather than on playing by the "rules," meaning those unwritten codes of behavior expected by various institutions of anyone who wants to succeed.†

If a noncompetitive role as a care-giver to others is a woman's *choice*, there is reason to anticipate that it will be a sound one. As a 30-year-old homemaker from Boston thoughtfully observed, "At twenty, I would have liked recognition, but by now I find that my values are more internalized. I am really content with having a family and

---

* Real name.
† Citing recent studies in which sex differences in performance levels showed up only for competitive tasks, Georgia Sassen (former director of field studies at Hampshire College in Amherst, Massachusetts) argues that the climate of competition arouses anxiety, not the fear of success as Matina Horner proposed in the late 1960s. She concludes that women find it difficult to commit themselves to competitive success because of their interpretation of social situations. They focus on preserving relationships rather than the rules and view moral dilemmas in terms of responsibilities rather than rights.[10]

being a mother. The important thing is to do what's right for you."

If neither partner found any obstacles to picking up the strengths of his or her sexual opposite, the life of a couple would be infinitely easier and more nearly accident-proof. Too often, however, one member of a couple is ready to try on some of the best of the other's characteristics, but the mate is too threatened to allow it. What happens then?

In the story of the couple that follows, we see how, in the wife, one pathfinder strength fortifies another—how the willingness to risk permits her the capacity to change, how courage and openness to new experience aid her in anticipating the future, planning it, learning to time it right. But we also see a man who is afraid to change, unwilling to accept new possibilities presented to him, too down on himself to learn, or to lead, or to open himself to anything like a chance for intimacy. It is a commonplace story among middle American marriages today. The point of it is that even an uncooperative mate can be compensated for, as long as the potential pathfinder is ready to adopt the strengths of both genders.

The New Conventional Couple

Joe Novak* is one of the people who does the everyday work of the world. He grew up in the projects in a tight white working-class enclave outside Detroit. He spent his boyhood hanging around in gangs, which later hooked into going down to the docks to do a day's work for a day's pay: adventurous, dangerous, hard physical work, drinking and helling around, and sticking together in a tribe of men. He was also class president. It looked to others as though he had a lot of promise. And he did have the chance to go to the state university on an athletic scholarship.

"You never finished." His own boy throws it back in his face today.

The guys from the docks used to heckle him as he passed by, wearing a shirt and tie and carrying books: "Hey, project rat!" He never studied. He blamed the college kids for mak-

* Pseudonym.

ing him feel stupid. He tried to blame his girl friend, Irene,* but she was the one who was always pushing him to go back to the dorm and write his papers. He dropped out after the first semester.

Then came the ridicule from his old college mates; they looked the other way as they passed Joe Novak, dressed in his blue work shirt and oafish steel-toed safety shoes, banging spikes into rail ties along the same route he used to walk to college.

"You could have had tutors." His own son never lets him forget.

Joe has to admit: "I could have hacked it. But I took the easy way out."

Irene Novak, the girl five years his junior who became his wife, read *Passages* in 1976. "I could identify with the people's problems," she told me, "but not with their solutions. They have options." She believed a woman belongs in the house. Irene was the only one in her family to graduate from high school. Her parents were thrilled. And when she took a job as a secretary with the phone company, they said that was tops, their girl had made it, there was no place further to go. She moved from there into her husband's house and sat at his dinner table while he enlightened the family on the mischief in the land wrought by educated white libs who were trying to take everything away from people of their kind.

At 30, like most of his buddies, Joe took a civil-service job for the security. He liked being a fire fighter and spending most of his time during and after work with the guys. Irene had more babies. He had more whiskeys. By the time his buddies were 35 or so, four or five of them had keeled over from too much booze, and Irene began to drop ultimata about his drinking. She also put their youngest son into the Head Start program, where she did a little volunteer work. As chance would have it, a job came up for her.

"So Irene took this Mickey Mouse job, like a Head Start mother," Joe recounted. "It started out real small. But now she's moving up. She went back to school and got all this, what do you call it? Psychology? She's like a supervisor now."

* Pseudonym.

When she started at the community college, Irene would alibi, "I need it for the job." She knew her husband was afraid of what education would do to her.

"What the hell are you goin' down there for?" he would holler.

But it did not bother her that much because suddenly she was on the bandwagon with hundreds of thousands of blue-collar wives who started back to school in the 1970s[11] for some explicitly utilitarian purpose: to learn accounting or to finish credits for their high-school diplomas so that they could bring in the second paycheck. Many had been convinced from girlhood that they were probably never meant to succeed in school. But once idealistic educators got their hooks into the minds of such women and began stretching them, exposing them to the pure nectar of knowledge uncut with any putrid agent of everyday commerce, there was no telling! Irene's supervisor, for example, turned her on to a course on human development. She came home bubbling over with excitement and information.

"What's all this *yoomin* stuff?" Joe said. He was pretty good at shamming, having had experience being on the other end. He goaded his daughter into the act.

"Whaddya think, you're a professor, Ma?"

Irene moved home to her mother's until her husband would agree to go on the wagon. He was bloated up to 330 pounds.

"Okay! I'll give up drinking." He rallied. He went out for football again, dropped to 190, and got into great condition. "I was running as good as the twenty-one-year-olds. Here I was thirty-seven. I got my kids into the league. Irene came down to watch us work out. Hey, we won the championship! Proved I could still hack it."

When his hair began graying at 38, giving him what he thought was a feeble, middle-aged appearance, Joe's wife brought home a bottle of tint for him. He touched up the gray. He talked a lot about what he called his first long-range ideas.

"Something's gonna come along," he told the family. "A business of my own, maybe." He sent away for brochures on chimney sweeping and rug cleaning. Time passed. Nothing happened. His son asked why.

"If I'd had a savings account, I'd have taken a shot," Joe

Novak would say. Or "If I get a windfall, I'll do it." His chances of getting a windfall, he knew, were the chances of a flamingo floating by the docks on an iceberg.

The arguments over Irene's progress at school and work grew uglier. "It had dawned on me that I had some control over my own destiny," she told me. "I had never looked ahead of myself my whole life—that's why I've stayed in the same place. I've never put a goal down and worked toward it."

Irene was 35. She took no personal credit for her job advancements. And when she was offered the job of her supervisor with a staff of forty people under her and a budget of $200,000, she refused it.

"That's the kind of job they give the Jewish girls with the pieces of paper from the University of Chicago," her husband said. He was right, Irene agreed; she did not have the formal academic credentials, she could never succeed. Like most women, she could not take credit for her own successes; all that had led up to the offer must have been accident or luck.

In private, Joe Novak had quite a different perspective. "Her job was never meant to get this big." He admitted another secret: "When I gave up drinking, it was in the back of my mind I might sneak back to school myself. Kept quiet about it. Hey, I'm readin' the newspaper and here she's readin' all these books. Everything seems to be pushing for the woman, know what I mean? Probably it's a jealous thing on my part."

Confronting Irene personally, he would shout: "What are you trying to prove?"

Once, she tried not being defensive. "I'm going to school because I want to," she replied evenly. "Because there's so much I'd like to learn. You could go too, you know."

That was all. No argument. Things began to work better after that. Either Joe was reconsidering the situation, Irene thought, or he was beginning to realize that his old bullying methods of control were no longer effective.

"I wish to heck I'd gotten into the books before," Joe Novak began to lament. "All the guys on the job are jumping into books and the younger guys are coming out of better schools; it's tough for me to keep up." In fact, everyone he worked with was beginning to move to supervisory levels.

Joe had made no attempt to move up. It meant taking an exam. "Now with the minorities coming on—some of 'em Puerto Ricans who can't even speak English, but they get in on lower marks 'cause the government said they had to—I don't know, I'm just not up to taking an exam right now."

"What are you so afraid of?" Irene asked him.

Making a fool of himself.

He could not admit it to his wife, of course. And he was not sure whether he preferred her scorn for his desperate vanities or the insufferable pity she sometimes showed—as if she were his caseworker.

In the fall before his 40th birthday, Joe's union offered him the nomination for president. He turned it down. "Why—why let one more opportunity slip away?" Irene demanded.

"Deep down, honestly?" Joe told me in a near-whisper. "I was afraid I'd win. I'm probably right now afraid to take the chance."

Irene knew the reason without his telling her. "He feels like a loser." Their communication became more strained than ever. They were going in separate directions.

Irene: "I'm seriously thinking of going for a bachelor's degree in social work. It would be the first time I'd really set a goal for myself. I guess once I get to be fifty it would be a helluva lot harder. So this is it. The next decade. Do or die."

Joe: "This winter was really bad for me. Up in my room, kinda depressed, watching TV. You get picky with the kids, you take a look at yourself, and what do you see? I'm just a nobody. You know you're still alive, but I'm just goin' through the motions."

Joe Novak points up the crucial link between the right timing and the willingness to risk. The first retreat from risk—when he feared competing with college boys and "took the easy way out"—became the pattern of his life. During the drinking years, he could imbibe instant machismo, mask all his self-doubts, and at the end of the evening slip back into being a little boy, so "wild" he would have to be walked home by his friends and put to bed by his wife. But the drinking became the catchall to explain everything. As Irene says, "We'd never faced our problems before he gave up drinking, so we had no practice for dealing with them afterward. I don't see where we've ever helped each other through any of our stages."

Although Joe's impressive victory over alcoholism boosted him toward what might have been a comeback in midlife, he could not set goals because he could not face any test, take any risk (aside from athletics), that might manifest to others the self-image he carried around inside himself: that he was a loser. Having missed fifteen years or so of adult development under the disguise of coping through drinking, Joe had never outgrown his short-term vision of the future or his boyish style of magical thinking that opportunities or windfalls would find him.

They do not find you. The chance for renewal in midlife is one to be seized—if not anticipated and planned. For Joe the rub was that his wife did not fear to do that.

Irene Novak demonstrates that a conventional woman, given no vision growing up, can without question learn to extend her concept of future possibilities and build the confidence to set goals. The next step for Irene will be to learn to claim her own successes.

Not that we should give up on Joe Novak. He may have been down for the count, but he may yet prove he can anticipate—through his son.

"I have him in private school now. It's overdoing it financially, but when he tells me I can't afford it, I throw this up to him: 'See these kids you're going to school with now? Their fathers are stockbrokers and things. They make good money—and they did that by goin' to good schools!' "

Trying to get this message through to his boy provides Joe Novak his greatest meaning in life. The lure of drinking beckons him in another direction—toward dead time. At 40 he sees his future with an accuracy of perspective tied to his own life pattern:

"Things are going smooth, but underneath they really aren't."

In sharp contrast, Irene Novak, from inside the same homely row house crouched in the same neighborhood where vision was so cruelly foreshortened by both their childhoods, Irene sees a very different future:

"*Things* aren't necessarily better, but I *feel* better all the time as I get older."

10.

A
CERTAIN
AGE

Everyone knows that the best part of life is when you belong to the Pepsi generation. When you're a footloose teenager with a transistor plugged into your ear and have time to sit home and style your hair all day. When you're so cool you can stop in the middle of the ski slope and light up a Salem for your new bride. When you're home with a teething baby watching the television commercials idolize you as the couple just meant for that special low-low-fare weekend of sizzling and snorkeling in Jamaica. What comes later is better left unsaid. After all, middle age is when everything turns gray, leaves home, is harder to see, or you've already seen it. Right?

Wrong. If people in the Comeback Decade (Americans between the ages of 45 and 54) got into a game of Monopoly with people of the Entry Decade (those between 25 and 34), it would be the oldies who got Boardwalk and Park Place and all the other valuable holdings—to reflect the share of property they actually own in this country—while the young ones would be lucky to get Marvin Gardens. And every time the gray-haired ones passed "Go," they would collect an extra $5,000 to reflect the elevation of their annual income over that of the young competitors.*

* Census Bureau figures for 1979 show the average income for the twelve million working men between 25 and 34 to be $17,967;

Since Mom is 47 and Dad 50 when the last kid goes down Atlantic Avenue to play his own game,[1] older people usually get to spend much of this money on themselves. And if these middle-aged geezers decide they don't like the rules, why, they can simply rewrite them. They run Congress, after all, and dominate all the rest of the ruling bodies of the globe.

Middle-aged men get to play and cry. Middle-aged women get to tell their mothers off and leave notes for their husbands: *Put in oven at 350° for 30 minutes—I'm off to the airport*. It is, in fact, the middle-aged who have the tennis elbows and the year-round tanning line from that fling in Jamaica or the deck of their weekend place.

True, they are seldom chosen by those who create TV commercials to represent the peak of life. For at least fifteen years—between being burst in upon as a young housewife to be ridiculed for having dull, gray, lifeless laundry; to being assumed, by 60, to be terrified that your smile will come out in the spareribs if you have failed to squeeze on the Polygrip—there is a grace period when advertisers pretty much pretend you don't exist. Blessed reprieve!

Most people assume that being middle-aged in America is akin to contracting a mild case of leprosy. It only gets worse. And old age—isn't that supposed to begin at 65?—is one long trial of chronic health problems, having him home for lunch, listening to her nag, while the two of you subsist on sexual memories and a can of dog food now and then.

Since one of the qualities we take as a given into the woods of any passage is our age, I was curious: according to the prevailing mythology, to be younger is to be better; therefore, we should expect to find young people in the majority of those who reflect high well-being and of those who are pathfinders.

But no. Consistently, in every sample, whether men or women, the people of highest well-being were most likely to

---

the eight million middle-aged men between 45 and 54 were earning an average of $23,002. Women have to be left out of our game, however. Whatever her age—from 25 to 70—the average American woman working full-time the year round never breaks the national income barrier of $12,000, give or take a few dollars on either side. Women appear to form a permanently underpaid underclass.

be the older ones. When you stop to think about it, two of the five chief self-descriptions of people of high well-being are almost by definition associated with being older: "I have experienced one or more important transitions in my adult years, and I have handled these transitions in an unusual, personal, or creative way." And "I have already attained several of the long-term goals that are important to me." Most high-well-being people were already enjoying the universally sought long-term values of a comfortable life, family security, and a sense of accomplishment. More than half of them had also attained mature love, true friendship, the freedom to make independent choices, self-respect, and an exciting life.

And when I interviewed people of high well-being to identify the pathfinders, the weight again was with the older ones. The results were corroborated by workshops and by further personal interviews. In fact, the one finding that registered more consistently and emphatically than any other in the course of my research was this:

Older is better.

Women and the Comeback Decade

The women who go off the charts in happiness are middle-aged; just past menopause; friends with, but unconfined by, their now-grown children; and feeling a firm sense of their own identity for the first time. In general, being older correlates with being less bored, less lonely, more in control of one's inner needs and outer environment, and more likely to report no major fears. Much happier than they expected themselves to be are women in the Frantic Forties. They present their lives as relatively free of serious problems, except for marital strains, and are less likely to be depressed than their counterparts who are ten to twenty years younger. The majority of 35- to 45-year-old women in my studies expressed surprise and delight at having reached a new level of sexual pleasure and at having shed some of their fears of personal confrontation. On the whole, they feel much better about themselves than they did when they were younger.*

* The National Science Foundation awarded a $200,000 grant for a study to be completed in 1981 of women between the ages of

This is a very different view from the myopic picture of the life cycle drawn by many of the younger women. Under 30 themselves when they filled out my questionnaire, they generally expect the first half of life to bring more and better of everything, at no risk, no cost. They are still at the stage of trying on different life uniforms and possible partners with the slapdash enthusiasm of a Saturday shopping spree. The prospect of turning 30 holds spooks. As a teacher about to cross the line described it in our interview, "I picture thirty as the end of a giant game of Statues. You get to play around, try all sorts of poses, and then somebody shouts—*Freeze!*" Looking beyond the mid-thirties, the younger women predict that the "woes" of middle age will cut into their happiness soon—and severely.

In fact, most of the women who were between 46 and 55 when surveyed did seem to be passing through something of a danger zone. Indications of it riddled their questionnaires. Coping strategies that had worked fine for them in earlier stages did not seem to hold up against the volatile dips in optimism and blips of depression that characterized their late forties. Just as men are almost invariably premature in sentencing themselves to sexual incapacitation, so are women brutally premature in disqualifying themselves as attractive to men, simply because they are no longer young. Also, certain harsh losses such as a parent's illness or death are real and new at that time. And this is the decade of the menopause.

The greater influence on how smoothly one maneuvers into middle age is one's sense of accomplishment. That emerges as the number-one long-range goal for women between 46 and 55—although "accomplishment" seldom even appeared among the sought-after values of these same women at an earlier age. Few middle-aged women of today were prepared, professionally or emotionally, for the reality that paid employment becomes central to the self-esteem of the middle years. The shift in body chemistry is a casual matter

---

35 and 55, in Brookline, Massachusetts; preliminary findings were identical to my own: the women reported a marked increase in self-esteem in their maturing years. Those who scored highest in well-being were women in high-prestige jobs who also were married and had children.[2]

compared with the sense of having the rug pulled out from under your identity as your mothering role becomes distant and custodial and your sex role becomes ambiguous.

The decade between 46 and 55 is not likely to proceed smoothly at first for the deferred achievers either—women who started out with a career but who postponed or interrupted it for many years. These are the women labeled "independents" in a satellite study by Florine B. Livson, based on longitudinal data from the Oakland Growth Study.[3] It was clear as early as adolescence that these girls were independent, when tests sorted them out as "doers" with intellectual interests and an achievement orientation. But they "suppressed their competence" during long years of marriage, most of them becoming conscientious wives and mothers. Entering mid-life, these women commonly reported their energy level going down, their weight going up, and their spirits—especially as the youngest child prepared to leave home—sinking into despondency. The investigator sounded surprised to note: "By age forty, the independents are depressed, irritable, conflicted. They seem out of touch with their intellectual interests and creative potential. They seem unable for a time to connect with a workable identity."

Of course they are out of touch! Most cannot move smoothly into a satisfying identity until they find work with some substance. It takes many deferred achievers a while to swallow the idea of themselves as receptionists or salespeople or clerk-typists. That was not how they saw themselves when they were taking calculus back in college.

And yet they rally. The independents studied by Livson leaped forward. She observed, "It is disengagement from the mothering role by fifty that stimulates these women to revive their more assertive, goal-oriented skills." Many also parlay their puny reentry jobs into responsible positions. Then there occurs a dramatic clearing of their intellectual focus and a general freeing of their emotional life.

And so, despite the danger zone, a mobilization usually begins in the late forties that registers with rising exhilaration as women move into their fifties. They drop happyface masks. They break the seal on repressed anger. They overcome habits of trying to be perfect and of needing to make everyone love them. They often shed the terror of living without a man that may have trapped them in a crippling

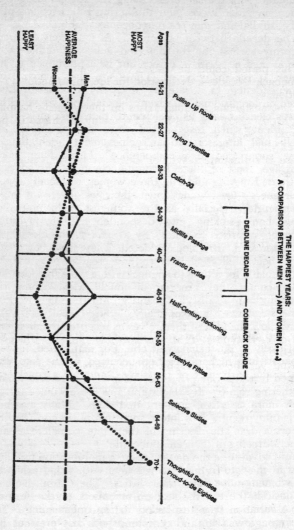

THE HAPPIEST YEARS:
A COMPARISON BETWEEN MEN (———) AND WOMEN (·····)

marriage. Many women, during this decade of the mid-forties to mid-fifties, find the sustained courage to extricate themselves from the web of a thousand familiar ways that ordinarily keep people bound up in lives of desperate repetition.

This period could be called, in the deepest sense, the Comeback Decade—a declaration for life, an intentional reanimation.

Life satisfaction gradually rises on the women's happiness graphs through the mid-fifties, reaching a dramatic point around 57, when it takes off and soars. For the first time, between the mid-fifties and 65, the issue of trying too hard to please is surmounted. Women begin at last to value themselves.

Men in Midlife

A sweep of the results on all the men studied showed a pattern that is more volatile than the women's. Not only do men's up and down periods occur more frequently, but they are usually out of sync with the life cycle of the women. Still, it is easier to be a pathfinder as an older man than as a younger man.

Right around the Half-Century Reckoning—the early fifties—the men whom I studied, whatever external position they had attained, whatever their class or income level, were most likely to hit their lowest ebb. For many men, however, a takeoff into high satisfaction occurred in the late fifties, rose in the early part of the sixties, and for a considerable number leveled off beyond that on a high plateau.

Yet men, like women, fear that getting older means that things will get worse. This complicates the pathfinding process in the early middle years. Since our perceptions of the future are skewed, the path ahead is not seen clearly. A background buzz of apprehension all through mid-life commonly registers in the conviction that just over the next rise, it is all going to be downhill.

Consider the twelve hundred members of the American Bar Association who responded to my questionnaire. Their average age was 46, and compared with any previous stage in their lives, they were enjoying the peak of satisfaction. But just over the other side of 47—as perceived by the men who were still on the younger side—they anticipated heading straight down the chute.

The facts of life disagreed. Those lawyers who floated to the top of the well-being scale were almost all *older* than 47. And those who had passed the age-55 barrier and were living the next stage, rather than anticipating it, were loving it. The most-contented age group of all was made up of the attorneys over 65.

It was illuminating to separate the lawyers into discussion groups by decades. Men in each age group were asked to describe where they were and where they thought they were going. Their responses, summarized below, are characteristic of professional men in general.

Ages 37 to 45

- Not enough time for anything but work
- Obsessed with money and material success
- Feel this is my last chance to "pull away from the pack"
- Worry about becoming trapped, about others finding out I'm not as good as they thought I was, about messing up my personal life
- Uncertain about my objectives; ambivalent about my values
- Envy the spirituality of others

Ages 46 to 55

- Feel I finally "have it all together"
- Secure enough to stop running or struggling
- Easier to relax, open myself to new feelings, take vacations
- Not so concerned about what others think of me
- More willing to help others; not so competitive and compulsive
- Feel that time is running out
- Suddenly notice my friends are looking old
- Aware of monitoring my own health

Ages 56 to 65

- Delighted to see vigor of life is continuing
- Pay more attention to my body and am in *better* physical condition than five years ago

- Sex is still important
- Feel a new tolerance for and companionship with my mate
- More focus on the spiritual dimension
- Vacations are essential
- Less concerned with money, more concerned with comfort
- Extremely confident of my ability and find it easier to win, with more friends in high places

Not all men emerge euphoric in their late fifties, of course. There was one prophetic characteristic in the self-descriptions of virtually all the most-satisfied men: the dream with which they had started out was broader. The low-well-being men began with no clear dream or described it exclusively in materialistic terms: "unlimited material success" or "wanting to become very rich," but they were vague about how. The high-well-being men, by contrast, wanted more than just career success. "To succeed with children" and "to enjoy a stable family" were among their early goals. Some added a third dimension: "to make a contribution to the world," "to help society," "to lead a happy and fruitful life," or, as one man modestly summed up, "to gain the respect of the world, to become well known, and also rich."

Here is the payoff on those two different paths:

The men who have attained the highest overall life satisfaction *are* broader. They have expanded well beyond the narrow career treadmill that confined them during their thirties. By their fifties they are involved in art, music, gardening, dancing lessons, gourmet cooking. Community service often supplies them with a new source of self-esteem and leadership. They laugh more and find aesthetic enjoyment in their environment—something they seldom noticed before. The surprise and delight of their fifties is an opening up of their artistic, expressive, and intuitive side—the "feminine" aspect that earlier had to be repressed in the service of ambition.

Not that their corporeal side was neglected. The most happy late-middle-aged fellows were backpacking in the mountains, playing strenuous sports, shooting rapids with their kids. Some turned their physical activities into teaching stints, thereby enjoying a little generativity and making a buck at the same time. All I can say to mute their wonderfulness is that some tended to be a little smug—they have it so good, they are not as clear about anticipating future needs and difficulties as they should be.

But even those enviable men who exhibited the highest well-being in all my surveys did not begin to feel they finally "had it all together" until they were between the ages of 36 and 45. Within the general sample of sixty thousand, the *average* man did not begin to feel secure enough to stop running and struggling until ten years after that, when he was in his late forties or early fifties.

My findings are echoed in the conclusions of other contemporary studies by, among others, Lowenthal; Campbell; and Freedman and Shaver.[4] For instance, more than a thousand people whose mental health has been measured since the early 1950s by the Midtown Manhattan Longitudinal Study[5] afforded researchers evidence that "both the average man and the average woman beyond the age of 40 are objectively and subjectively healthier than ever before in the history of this Republic." The researchers, Dr. Leo Srole and Anita Kassen Fischer of Columbia University's Center for Geriatrics, also discovered that women's impairment rates had been as much as three times higher than men's for people socialized back in the 1950s, but dropped in the last decade to near-parity. This dramatic upturn in women's mental outlook they attributed to the broader social opportunities and enhanced status of women in the 1960s and 1970s, when the younger people were in their formative years. The study also found city dwellers enjoying mental health superior to rural people's—another presumption challenged.

Myths of Middle Age

Things do not automatically get better as we get older, of course. But the doctors and psychoanalysts and social scientists who have represented aging as synonymous with loss have drawn their conclusions from a severely limited group: from women who came to them with their anger disguised as depression; from men who brought psychosomatic complaints to cover their fears of impotence; from people in mental hospitals and on relief rolls, in hospitals and homes for the aged. The people to whom the experts had easy access *were* more likely to have suffered losses.

A similar problem of limited subjects distorted the popular understanding of adult life for many years. Children were always available for study because adults controlled them. But the only adults easily obtainable for monitoring were those still pinned down in school and those flat on their backs in institutions. So we were told more about adolescence than we cared to know and were left to assume that nothing much happened after that until we turned up in the death-and-dying books. Unless you came up with something interesting, like schizophrenia or frigidity, your life stage was ignored. Only very recently has the study of mid-life and middle age focused on healthy people and on the continuing and predictable possibilities for development in those years. But the same old disservice is still being done to the elderly.

Contrary to impressions received from many social scientists that old age is a time of depression, poor health, rejection by children, creeping impoverishment, loneliness, and loss, only 5 percent of all Americans over 65 are in institutions. The other 95 percent remain relatively independent in their own communities. What is more, 80 percent of older Americans have children nearby and see them weekly. And fully two-thirds live in their own, paid-for homes.[6]

One source of the misinformation might be the researchers' own ages. It may not be possible for people early in mid-life to interpret properly the experience of people well into middle or advanced age. I could not. When I was in my mid-thirties and interviewing people who were over 50 for *Passages*, much of their outlook on time, work, personal relationships, children, health, activity, loneliness, the meaning of life, was informed by a perspective to which I had no personal access. It was as though they all had been to Brazil and I had only read about it.

As we get older, for example, funerals become a more natural addition to our social rituals. But when younger analysts look at the prospect of losing friends to death and having to go to funerals, they perceive the change from *their* perspective: how depressing, how terrifying to be reminded so often that *it could happen to you!* The analyst himself may be right on the rim of mid-life and, like a soldier seeing combat for the first time, is faced with the indiscriminate finality of death. The person already past 50, or older, is more like a general who has seen many fall; there is regret, but not shock. He or she compares protective strategies for continued health with those of contemporaries. In the midst of mourning for a dear friend lost there is also an emotionally neutral sense of one's own survivorship: *I must be fighting a good fight* or *I must be a tough old bird.*

"My mother's transition to old age hit me much harder than it did her!" I was told by a 45-year-old radio commentator. "She was a dynamo for as far back as I can remember. Worked her tail off until she was seventy-two. My sister and I finally convinced her to let us bring her out here to California. Last fall, it became clear she needed a more structured life-style, so we were able to make that change for her—we found a lovely retirement community. Then six weeks ago she had a stroke. She's now paralyzed on one side, she's coping, she's determined to get up on a cane. But it's *unfair!*"

The person feeling betrayed in this instance is the middle-aged one. No matter what she did to outwit or elude it on behalf of her mother, and despite all the manic activity by which she denies it in her own life, death remains real.

Another misconception about middle age is that people naturally grow more conservative and closed-minded. "Hidebound" is the favorite cliché, evoking images of some uptight leather-bottomed old cuss who starts every sentence with "The trouble with young people today . . ."

Yet in my studies, the people of highest well-being said that they were becoming *more* spontaneous with age.

People who grow older successfully refuse to be defined by their losses and failures. Such a view is not acquired as part of the wisdom of old age, however. It is an outgrowth of the way pathfinders have learned to adapt to their adult lives.

This chapter, then, picks up where *Passages* left off in the life cycle and explores the stages that begin with true middle age and extend into the eighties. The possibilities for developing and extending ourselves in these stages are more various and liberating than at any earlier period. But although older is generally better for pathfinding, a given age does not automatically assist the process. We all know older people who are supercautious or arrogant, cranky, or stick-in-the-mud, and possessed of approximately the same capacity for loving as a boiled lobster. To make age a quality of pathfinding requires that we see the oases and identify the wastelands that pathfinders themselves have mapped out before us. The remainder of the chapter has been divided into two sections:

"The Freestyle Fifties" covers true middle age and describes some of the inner changes of perspective that come naturally with the territory, as well as the special potential that pathfinders often see for expansion in this stage.

Then we move from "The Selective Sixties" through "The Thoughtful Seventies" and end with "The Proud-to-Be Eighties." Again, common perspectives are discussed, along with some uncommon adaptations found by pathfinders.

THE FREESTYLE FIFTIES

> The first forty years of life furnish the text, while the remaining thirty supply the commentary; without the commentary we are unable to understand aright the true sense and coherence of the text, together with the moral it contains.
>
> —SCHOPENHAUER

By middle age we know pretty much what we can and cannot do, which roles are essential to maintaining our core identity and which roles we can outlive. But probably few of us are aware of the new potentials and special strengths released between 45 and 60 that are *exclusive* to middle age:

- relaxation of roles
- greater assertiveness in women
- greater expressiveness in men
- being free to say what you think
- being free to pick up and go, again
- more time and money for yourself
- more tolerance for others
- greater opportunities for companionship with your mate
- chance to meet your children again as friends
- possibility for contributing to your community, your history, your culture

Putting it in the simplest terms, by middle age you know better than at any prior stage in life who you are, what you need, and how to get it. The question is, Are you still willing to try? The rewards can be splendid, but the traps are dangerously seductive.

A few of the traps are easily recognizable. Self-protective in the short run, they amount to anti-risk strategies. But the real trap is to lose, over the long run, the master quality of the pathfinder—a willingness to risk and change. For the average person, that attribute, together with the capacity for loving, may come more spontaneously when he or she is young. But people over 45 who consciously recultivate such youthful propensities can be the *most* receptive to change. If anything, older pathfinders are more interested than anyone else in making a fresh start.

The following are some of the common obstacles in the way of pathfinding through the middle years.

The Walking Dead

"Most people, if they haven't made it by forty-five, begin to coast," the savvy New York advertising man told me. "They just want to get to the end without making any mistakes." He had observed that among his firm's many clients, it was those between 45 and 50 who most often seemed to have their engines turned off. And so, at 45, an executive vice-president of his agency and quite certain that he was no longer on the path to the presidency, he followed the same route.

"I gave up. Decided I'd coast along until fifty and take an early retirement. I resigned myself to the fact I'd lost. I was going to be number-two guy. I was not going to win."

Had he considered quitting and starting a new career? I asked.

"I was too lazy," the adman admitted. "I had too soft a job. I had nothing to do—just supervise other people. I was too well paid and had too many comforts to let it go."

That may sound like a practical solution. And, God knows, there is precedent all around for eluding disappointments with accelerated consumption and driven leisure. The difficulty lies in the deterioration of self-image.

Americans of every class define themselves first and foremost by their work. Even at the very top it is hard to find a playboy. David Rockefeller worked ten-hour days running the Chase Manhattan Bank right up to his retirement in 1980 at 65. And when the secrets came out about rich eccentrics like Howard Hughes, what were they doing in the lavish suites with access to all the drugs and showgirls and go-fers a creature could ever want? Making deals, that's what.

Work is the first line of defense during rough spots for most pathfinders. It provides a shelter within which people can sublimate their problems in activity that is rarely destructive, the product of which quite possibly will make them feel better about themselves. Although many Americans may be eager to spend fewer hours pushing a pencil and more hours playing with their boats and cars, it would be cruel punishment to take their work away from them altogether. What reason would they have to get up on Monday morning? From what vantage point would they try to make sense of the world? What else would they do while they were waiting for the divorce? How would their obituaries begin? For all these reasons, and many more, pathfinders consider very carefully before giving up that part of their identity that has its source in their work.

People who have been "passed over" usually feel cheated out of what is rightfully theirs. Angry, but afraid to express their anger, they often take a position of passive resignation. Repressing all reminders of the mental and emotional excitement and the sense of personal importance formerly attached to their work, however, cuts them off in other ways. Withdrawal from other activities is common ("It used to be fun, but I don't enjoy it much anymore"). So is retreat from new sources of love and companionship ("I don't want anyone to get to know me *now*").

A list of five "early retirees" among middle to top Ford management was scraped together for me by then-president Lee Iacocca—the only examples he knew of men who had found some renewal of purpose after being kicked upstairs or pensioned off. Harold MacDonald* had been at Ford since 1948. By 1966 he was the company's chief engineer. He had created the whole concept of the Lincoln Continental.

A soft-boiled egg of a man with pinkish skin, freckles, and white hanging hair, MacDonald had been able to salve the

* Real name.

indignities of being put out to pasture by finding an avocation as a born-again Baptist. It was a way, for him, of repackaging the work ethic and providing himself with a replaced purpose in life.

"There's no way to fight it," Iacocca had told me. Along about the mid-fifties the company's grim reaper taps you on the shoulder and asks if you have been thinking about retirement and begins making sure the booklets get into your hands. If a senior staff man fights it, he is declawed, neutered, pulled out of the heat of combat and stuffed into the cooler of World Headquarters where there is no brawling, no smoke of ideas, no deadlines, only the drone of climate control and the conference room with its deeply tanned glass doors through which the heads arranged in a circle look like the last somnambulists hanging around a half-lit nightclub. Never again will there be the thrill of putting your decisions up against a profit-and-loss sheet and turning out—by sudden death—to be a hero or a fool.

"You weren't suggesting they were going to *retire* me." MacDonald laughed nervously as we began our interview. He couldn't imagine why he was on Iacocca's list. "I was sixty-one in June," he said with exceeding discomfort, "so theoretically I have four more years."

"Nine more, under the new rules!" the public-relations man who was present added brightly.

"Mr. Iacocca told me you were deeply involved in religious work," I said, trying to undo some of the discomfort. "He was probably thinking of you as a good example of one who *anticipates* retirement." It didn't take long for the reality to surface.

"I topped out," MacDonald said, "as far as my limits within the corporation were concerned." He grew very quiet when he talked about being moved from the fast pace of being in charge of product development and "hooked to a conveyor belt"—meaning where cars are actually *made*—to an advisory position in the staff freezer where he seldom saw another soul and couldn't hear even the hum of automobiles on the highway.

"My real life now comes from the conversion experience I had with the Lord, and what that has led to."

Pathfinders who have been passed over but who later make comebacks describe this period of inner resignation as a time of moving around in a cloud of ether, with little taste for life, knowing their behavior is erratic. They report having felt a diffusion in their sense of time. That is because, with no faith in their future, they could not bear to anticipate it.

Professor Harry Levinson, an expert on the reciprocal effects of age and roles on the individual and the organization, has observed, "When people can no longer feel that they are working successfully at being good and becoming better, they will become frustrated, depressed, and feel . . . worthless, no matter what they have achieved up to that point."[7]

The spouses of such people are in a painful position. "Nothing I do helps to bring him back" was the plaint of several wives. They felt the hopelessness of trying to resurrect a person who had chosen to live out his days in dead time. The only question was, How much longer would they share the open coffin before they, too, gave up?

The Secondary Saboteur

This person, too, accepts being passed over, stays where he or she is, feels the days weighing stale and vapid, but keeps going by projecting his or her frustrations on others. The secondary saboteur may seize every opportunity to put down the company, play the petty tyrant with the people he supervises, or act as the bureaucratic commissar who stifles talent and individuality, thereby ensuring that no young person will succeed where he has failed. Dangerous enough to himself, he is also dangerous to the well-being of the pathfinder—a natural enemy.

The Single-Track Compulsive

Having fallen short of the recognition one feels one deserves, one may attempt this adaptation, which involves putting even more time and effort into the same single source of identity that has not yet paid off. Toiling more hours, heaping on more clients or patients or accounts is like putting all your money into one stock: not wise.

If the tension in the first half of life is between intensity and balance, the pull in the second half is between the opposite attractions of self-protectiveness and renewal. Renewal has always been possible for men and women who prepared themselves for a new life in the second half. The secret is not to withdraw all nourishment from our dormant aspects, but to keep them alive, if only on a subsistence level, in anticipation of their return in a future stage.

One of the worst mistakes in middle age is to confine oneself—and to continue to define oneself—by a single source of identity. Many of the unhappiest people in middle age are those who continue flogging that single source of self-esteem until they virtually beat it to death. The older woman who reminds her family continually of the long-suffering caregiver she has been eventually drives them away. The older man who desperately seeks "love" from his work is likely to be devastated when he retires and people stop returning his phone calls.

But even for those who did not plan ahead when they were younger, the opportunities for renewal are vastly greater today than in the past. America has become an age-fluid society. So relaxed have age and social limitations become that a 12-year-old can gain credibility as a religious guru and a 69-year-old can exert enough charisma to be elected President; a governor can be elected at 34 in California and a mayor at 28 in Cleveland. The sensational crime of passion at the start of the 1980's concerned a sex triangle composed of a 69-year-old doctor, a 56-year-old headmistress, and her 38-year-old rival.

An age-fluid society makes it possible for the pathfinder candidate to explore aspects of himself or herself that may have remained nascent until middle age. Simply putting those capacities to the test can be a source of exhilaration.

Having looked at several of the common obstacles, let us ride along now with several different pathfinders who have found less-traveled roads to new beginnings in middle age.

Last-Chance Leap

No one can put an actual number on it, but there is a moment somewhere between the mid-forties and the late fifties for the person who finds himself coasting and unhappy when the last-chance leap must be risked if there is going to be a second orbit. Beyond a certain point, too much momentum has been lost, one has coasted too long, and it is probably too late to pull up from the landing.

"Absolutely right," said Congressman Lloyd Meeds. He began to feel it when he was addressing a group of steelhead fishermen in his state of Washington. All at once Meeds heard another man talking through him, a frightened man, a demagogue, a phony. He looked in the mirror after that meeting and was chilled by what he saw: a man of 50, wanting so badly to keep his job that he was changing, almost imperceptibly, into an imposter.

"If you're fifty years old and you don't like yourself," he said to the image in the mirror, "nothing goes well." Uncertain about where to start building a hopeful future, Lloyd Meeds knew he had reached a psychological point of no return.

On the Friday I went to Washington to see another congressman, George Shipley, the sky was carelessly dabbed with creamy clouds and the fields grinned with buttercups as they fell away to the Annapolis basin. Congressman Shipley had left the Hill early—gone fishin'. I found him with his wife and a beer and what was left of his mostly grown family on the deck of a brand-new rubber-bumpered boat, rocking at its slip like a grown-up tub toy.

"One has to make the decision after twenty years in Congress," he said. "Either you stay until you're ninety or until you get defeated—or you get out while you still have enough juice to start something new."

Shipley was gambling that he still had enough juice at 51 to begin a second career as a commercial fisherman in the Florida Keys. "I slowed down a lot after forty-five," he admitted frankly. The moves of the Illinois congressman on his spotless boat were not those of a confident seaman. He was heading for hot, hard days that would call his body to work two hours before the sun was up. He would have to haul and scrape and heave fish guts ten hours a day if he was to make his nut of a thousand a month. But that was only part of the year. The rest of the time he could be a captain of the Keys and seas; the gleam in his eyes said the trip would be worth all the trouble.

Everyone who contemplates a late career change wonders what the actual transition would feel like. To shift from a high-demand job to relative formlessness can be a threatening experience at first. I talked to four people from different professional and managerial careers who were on the other side of such a move. They described a transitional depression that centered on their sudden anonymity.

"You think for a while, 'My God, why did I shoot myself in the foot?'" a city planner described it. "You believe it's the end of the world. You call people you used to work with and they don't call you back until the day after next, saying, 'Jack, damn, I'm sorry, I was in conference . . .' You hear your old self in their voices."

All agreed it took them about a year to come out of the depression period and rev up for a new project. But as one public-relations woman added pointedly, "I would have died on the vine if I hadn't stopped clinging to the company. Now I have a personal-services business with a few other refugees. I'm meeting new people. I like them. They like me. It's more intimate. Those ties aren't going to be cut just because I no longer work for an important firm."

The risk of starting one's own business in middle life is offset for many people by the promise that nobody will be able to tell them when—or if—to retire. "I see men in my club who reach sixty-five, and after a lifetime of going off daily to work, they are dropped out of the mainstream of life by retirement," I was told by an Arkansas man who had held his breath and plunged into his own small business at the age of 54. "This is where I think we, as individual businessmen, have it 'knocked.' We can retain people who carry the heavy load, but still help to build the business, guide it, and enjoy it. With good people on stream, we can also leave it for travel or relaxation. So when I say I am never going to 'retire,' I guess I should say I'm already living the best half of both worlds—work and retirement."

You may be as surprised as I was to learn that there are thirteen million small businesses in the United States and that they employ half the country's labor force and support 100 million people.[8] What differentiates those who try such a business from those who "wait" forever? Being able to conceive of themselves doing it is the decisive factor, according to a study at Ohio State University.[9] Usually people follow the example of a mentor or a parent who also was an entrepreneur.

Not Too Late to Transfer

The last-chance leap does not have to be to an entirely new life, despite the fact that an astonishing number of Americans are game enough to make a complete career change. It is much easier to shift one's emphasis within the same career path, and easier now than when one was in the family-rearing years.

"Cindy, please come out of the shower," the 49-year-old Texas department-store president coaxed his wife. He knew that she knew that something was up; otherwise, why was he back from the office at ten in the morning? Okay, maybe he was crazy to think about transferring to New York. He would be going in to bail out a branch in serious trouble. He didn't need it for promotion. And hadn't they just shipped the last boy off to college, bought a weekend hideaway, and moved back into the city of Dallas? Life-after-parenthood was shaping up nice and easy, but there was a disturbing complacency about it all.

A year and a half later they were thrilled with their new home. Every weekend and many weeknights they strolled the streets, people-watching and window-shopping, finally ducking into a romantic bistro for dinner. The best thing about it was that they could never find the same bistro again.

Passionate Sideline

It also is possible to find an avenue of renewal off the main drag of one's paid job. It might tap a long-neglected talent—in community theater or local politics—or turn a passing interest into a major crush—organic gardening, say, could lead to opening a farmers' market in the summers. Several Ivy League executives I met had found a pleasurable sense of purpose in joining a volunteer fire department, either in the exurban towns where they lived or in the remote villages where they had a second, weekend life. When there was nothing doing, it felt good to sit around and jaw with the locals, and when the siren went off, they had the good feeling of being caretakers of their sleeping community.

This pull toward engagement in community rather than

exclusive concern with individual advancement becomes particularly important for most middle-aged men. Some express it, after working as a wage slave for Big Brother all week, by volunteering as the big brother who takes kids to the circus or who coaches the local hockey team. One lonely free-lance writer turned his experience with keeping a journal into a periodic teaching stint at a fitness ranch. He became the conduit through which other people, mostly in their middle years too, could partake of "process meditation" (as psychologist Ira Progoff calls it in his books and workshops).[10] But the insights went both ways. The male writer was casually edified by conversations with women who were in a particularly candid mood because of their journal meditations. He suddenly understood what had gone wrong with many of his relationships. The experience lifted him out of isolated attention to the "terrors of the forties," as he called them. Oh, yes, the painless by-product: he dropped fifty pounds.

Women who have been accustomed to giving their time and talents as community volunteers all during their child-raising years naturally do not see anything particularly refreshing in the prospect of more unpaid work. Most middle-aged women need a salary. They want to know what they are worth. If they do assume leadership roles in community institutions, it may be their chance to upgrade them to paid positions.

Politics seems to be a natural magnet for women in the mid-forties through the Freestyle Fifties. The National Information Bank on Women in Public Office* reports that the average age at which contemporary American women enter their first political races is 44. And once women have a taste of public life—the power to do, the recognition for doing—they want more. Half the women mayors and a whopping 82 percent of female state senators around the country aspire to holding one or more *higher* offices in the future. When male and female officeholders at all levels are compared in selected states, the women turn out to be *more* politically ambitious than their male counterparts; more of them were determined to seek an additional term in their current office

---

* The National Information Bank is a section of the Center for the American Woman and Politics, Eagleton Institute of Politics, Rutgers University.

or to move on to other offices. The political arena accommodates superbly the strengths naturally ascendant in women's middle years, their newfound assertiveness and the excitement they enjoy in exerting power.

Teaming Up

One other form of renewal particularly well suited to the middle years is a husband and wife teaming up in a joint enterprise. The experience of one couple, recommended by a pivotal member of their community, illustrates how the potentials of middle age dovetailed to reinvolve delightfully a husband, wife, and grown son.

Bert Moeller* was lured away from his middle-management position with a big oil company by a brilliant dreamer whose computer business had grown too fast. "What we need is a professional sales manager" had been the decree from the computer company's board of directors, the usual floral centerpiece of lawyers. The president complied by putting Bert in charge of the sales force, and Bert had tried to fire up the men about having a forecast for the next year. The salesmen said, "Whaddya mean, forecast? We never had no forecasts. We never had no professional sales managers. Mr. President, who is this creep?"

Bert spent three years doing handsprings for his sales force, passing most of his weekends eating Paw 'n' Claw specials with them in Marriotts a thousand miles from home. And he always knew, when he landed in New York, that those clowns were back there doing it just the way they had always done it before.

One day Sam, the company accountant, told Bert that they were being set up to kill each other off in a power struggle. The president needed a sacrificial lamb to appease his board. Profits were down. Bert and Sam did not cooperate.

At 48 Bert came dangerously close to retreating into bitter sarcasm: he talked incessantly about being mousetrapped by corporate politics, skunked by inflation, and now, "You watch—the government is going to screw us out of Social Security," he prophesied.

* A pseudonym.

But when Sam and he realized "those bums are going to fire us," they decided that instead of playing the game, or becoming bitter old-young men, they would cast their lot together and bust out. The product he and his partner chose was not likely to go out of style: milk and its by-products. And they chose a blue-collar, beat-up secondhand-car community where price really counted.

"We decided, 'Let's open up our own dairy and do what the minority groups do—work!'" Bert explained. "All you need is a truck and cash. No board of directors, no lawyers. Just my partner and myself. We make milk. We sell bread and eggs cheaper than everybody else. And we work every day. It's a whole new concept!"

Bert gave up airplanes. He gave up ties. The idea was to build a dairy with a retail outlet adjoining it. They installed a computer to direct the entire process, from pasteurizing to bottling to moving the milk onto the selling floor. Then they made deals with local farmers to pick up their milk cans directly—all of which chopped about four middlemen from the distribution chain.

Imagine the little old ladies staggering out of the new dairy with their six half gallons, which is about sixty pounds of milk, lugging them home and—surprise!—it's cottage cheese. This was not something these philosopher-entrepreneurs had figured on. But to their amazement, the townsfolk kept coming back. They were intrigued by these two hotshots out of the world of high technology who had raised a million dollars to buy a computer to put out sour milk.

One weekend Bert gave them a hell of a show—for thirty-six hours straight he stood on the floor of his bottling room until he tamed the computer. Everyone cheered. But he need not have worried that pure milk would dampen the excitement. The electric eye on the door had a nervous breakdown and began crushing the customers on the way out. In his new role as hands-on maintenance man, Bert adjusted the eye. After that, it crushed only short children.

By the end of the first year, they had enlarged the retail adjunct to their dairy five times.

"Beating up the big companies is the best thing you can do," as Bert saw it. "The bigger the company, the more fun we have." The two guerrilla businessmen buy bread for their store, for instance, from ITT, whose Continental Baking Division makes Wonder bread. But Bert and his partner do not see their competition in terms of local, regional, or even divisional levels; they see themselves in direct combat with Harold Geneen! Once, a professor of Bert's had taken him to gaze upon Mr. Geneen's five-year plan. Seven thousand pages! Twenty years later, Bert's awe was gone. "The only problem with Mr. Geneen's plan is that he can't make bread cheaper. He doesn't eat it, he just plans it."

By working harder and caring more than many employees do in any large company, Bert Moeller and his partner have been able to "win" back some of the self-respect that was eroded by their earlier experience. In terms of self-image, they are able to "beat" the big guys at their own game—if only in one town, and only on the milk-and-bread run. "The best part," Bert told me, "is we're not afraid of fifty." Today he and Sam have two stores, open seven days a week until ten P.M. But now there are three of them. Mrs. Moeller has joined the fun.

"I'd been selling real estate for three years," Joanna Moeller told me as she slipped a coat over her grocer's uniform to meet her husband for lunch. Intending to make a smooth passage from deferred nurturer to "nice, refined real-estate lady," she had run into the reality that real estate is a recreational career and often a pseudo-job that cost her money despite sales of a couple of big houses a year.

"Jo was desperate." Her husband picked up the story at lunch. "All her friends were casualties of overblown expectations. We've seen no less than ten professional families in our neighborhood go through this. The women came into their middle age and were ready to make the step away from home to a working environment—but they all related to their past academic credentials as assurance of their worth. They either went back to school to polish up or headed right out to look for professional positions that suited their self-image, usually championed by their husbands. They all ended up with broken dreams and broken families—not one of them made it. My wife came up against the very same thing—good college background, kids running off, no paid track record. What the hell is she going to do? Jo had spent years giving her time free to community organizations. She goes out, convinced the world is going to reciprocate, right? Guess what? No takers!

"So she sold me on the idea of starting her as a checkout girl. She's now running our second store, lifting fifty-pound bags of onions, building displays, unloading trucks, dealing with irate customers. She wears a uniform. And guess what? She's happy as a clam."

One could not help assuming that a little nepotism had gone a long way toward making Jo Moeller a manager. The Moellers' partner, who surpervised that store, put me straight.

"Joanna is paid less than the man who preceded her," he said matter-of-factly, "because at the moment she hasn't got the seniority. But even at that, she had to run over the guy to get his job."

This brought forth muffled laughter from all three. "It's probably one of the toughest things a woman could do," Jo admitted. "The man was twenty-two. I worked harder until I outperformed him. He happened to be dating our daughter." One could imagine the scene at home: "I'd like to take you to the movies tonight, but your mother took my job."

But this Lady of Perpetual Help, who had walked in the raiments of respectable self-effacement to raise funds in town, had started to work with grubs half her age and at minimum wage. Today, six months later, when her neighbors come into the store, they look up and do a double-take at seeing Jo behind the counter. They cannot bear eye contact with her. The former president of the League of Women Voters running a cash register? So—proletarian. "Even the men who come in get upset because I'm piling cases of soda six feet high." Jo is five foot four. "They see me mopping the floor and they say, 'This is what they pay you for?' Americans have no concept of what a store manager does."

When I followed this middle-aged team around their respective stores, it became clear that the wife was cast in a role traditionally played by a son. By following the trail her husband had blazed, she endorsed him and his adjusted value system.

"Jo's learning a trade," he boasted.

Their handsome, smug son had come home from college over the holidays. It was his habit to take his mother's car without asking but to go to his father to ask for a job. "Hey, my store's scheduled out," Bert Moeller told his son. "See our manager at the other store." The son had to deal with his mother for pay and hours and performance reviews.

"You can't believe the difference in respect," said Bert Moeller. This couple was at the stage of becoming friends with their children and clearly delighted with it. From what Bert Moeller said, he anticipated that his wife would grow stronger and bring their son into the business. And when the time came, the "old man" would step out like a happy King Lear and enjoy the family continuity.

His Happiness, Her Happiness

One sees a great deal in the literature on middle age about the "empty nest." It conjures up an image of a couple of old ducks left in their bed of straw, pecking at each other.

Okay, Donald, now it's just me against you.

But there are pronounced differences between his definition of happiness in middle age and hers. We don't need studies to tell us that women, at every stage, are able to handle, indeed seem to thrive on, emotional complexity. Men are distressed by the ups and downs of emotional life and try to avoid them, reports one major study on human development.[11] This difference between the sexes only becomes more pronounced with age. In fact, among the men studied who were facing retirement, so overwhelming was their desire for a calm, uncritical climate at home that they preferred either wholly positive emotional experiences—or none at all! Those who had totally bland or distant relationships with others— what women might call an "empty" emotional life—were happier than those still in volatile situations.

But even middle age does not neatly tie up all the loose ends for couples.

For many who stay together and settle back into the "empty nest," middle life is when they come to understand each other best, feeling each mood like movements in a familiar symphony and delighting in each other's companionship. The transition to this state of seamless intimacy may take a year or two or three, but husbands and wives in the middle of middle age, who were still on their first marriage and whose children had left home—facing what is usually presumed to be the dreariest period of life—turned out to be the happiest pairs of all. This discovery was highlighted by the academic study by Marjorie Fiske Lowenthal, director of the Human Development Program, University of California, San Francisco, reported in *Four Stages of Life*. The people who perceived themselves as most satisfied, most nearly stress-free, and most positive about their future were "those men and women [in their late fifties] whose children are grown and who are themselves still married."

The average man has spent half his life building his career. Having pushed himself for twenty or thirty years along a narrow career track, he suddenly may look up and say, "Wait a minute, when is it my time to play?" His thoughts turn to travel, improving his golf game, maybe a sabbatical. Should he try early retirement? Why not?

The husband who shifts from active and ascendant stages to a playful or passive period in middle age often does so just as his wife is coming into her own. Released at last from daily responsibility for her children, she may well be looking for something in life besides another person to mother. If she plans to retool her skills with the aim of finding well-paid and satisfying work, she will not be free to be folded up like a leisure suit and taken along on pleasure trips whenever her husband has the time.

Occasionally, fate intervenes to cut women off at the pass. In one case reported by David Gutmann, a woman hospitalized for depression was diagnosed as suffering a "preemptive mourning" for her terminally ill husband. Then somebody happened to notice that the woman had been going to school. In fact, she was about to begin a postgraduate career. Those plans were aborted when her husband became bedridden. She was not to have a comeback, but would become a shut-in caretaker mirroring the slow death of her husband. When her test results cried out with images of imprisonment, claustrophobia, and rage, the doctors were baffled. Therapists had focused entirely on getting the woman to face her impending loss—which was like trying to get someone to read the letters of an old lover. Gutmann was able to discern that "the patient was not suffering the pain of loss, but the pain of guilt and self-reproach: she could not forgive herself for desiring the quick death—the death that would free her to an expanded life—of a beloved husband."[12]

The prospect of a wife revving up just when he is ready to enter a well-earned cooling-down period does not sit well with some men. Gutmann reports tentative diagnostic impressions of male patients from 45 to 60 who are reasonably established in love and work and have no prior psychiatric record, until they come into the hospital at Northwestern University with a psychiatric crisis. The crisis is usually precipitated by mid-life changes in their wives:

> She has become financially and/or emotionally independent . . . more assertive, and she has become less adoring. . . . [The wife's] newfound autonomy is experienced . . . as a personal rebuff, a distressing separation from the "maternal" figure. . . . He is confronted with his own ["womanly" aspect] and panic ensues, often taking the form of an agitated depression.[13]

"Any resolution which would free one of them might well threaten the marriage," comments Marjorie Fiske Lowenthal.[14] In groups she has studied, the women often seek a compromise solution: they stay at home and respond to their husbands' bids for nurturance by becoming "bossy," as many of their husbands put it. This rebirth as "battle-ax" usually extends to efforts to boss around adult children as well.

Even couples in which the wife has always worked are not entirely exempt from the personality shifts between the sexes common to the middle years. In fact, it can come as a greater surprise to a couple of workaholics, accustomed to snuggling up on either side of their weekly sales sheets, when the man begins making noises as if he is neglected just when the woman decides she wants to make a tender offer for Revlon.

Here is how that conflict hit a man and a woman accustomed to a working "marriage" as major executives in the same talent agency, once they decided to make the marriage official in their private lives. He was near 50, she near 40. It was some months after the wedding. One night, after they had made love and he had drifted off into a blissfully noisy aftersleep, she slipped out of bed. She had a hot property that required a reading before the auction deadline the next noon. When one is talking about a book being put on the auction block for between $1 and $2 million, one does not skim. An hour later she was curled up in a living-room chair under a reading lamp when her husband suddenly appeared in the doorway.

"I want a divorce," he said.

But the infantile outburst passed, and they stayed together. Like most professional couples, they had too much else to do to stew about feeling neglected.

Except for people who have invested themselves solely in the nurturing of children, the transition to an empty nest is generally not seen as one of terrible loss but as one of relief and intriguing opportunities. Men welcome becoming again the center of a wife's attention. And women (leaving aside those who dread having the reins of their destinies left in their own hands) build up as much eagerness as apprehension about testing themselves in new ways.

The Sexual Shell Game

For many couples, improved sex is another surprise gain on entering middle age—for couples who feel the flush of renewed challenge and self-esteem in other areas; for couples who notice inhibitions dropping away once the children have left and the fears of pregnancy are past; for people who rediscover in their fifties the playfulness they lost somewhere back in their thirties.

People who remarry in middle age or later generally say that they are looking for companionship more than anything else. What they usually get as a bonus is a splendid sexual resurgence.

The Freestyle Fifties may be the occasion to release one's secret sexual fantasies *into* the marriage relationship. Particularly if one's spouse is not one's natural sexual fantasy, the relationship can be wonderfully revived by "inviting" that fantasy to join the twosome's embrace. For people who are unattached, this can be a period for sowing wild oats never sown: full of surprises, unlikely encounters, and possibly sexual reassurance.

Sexual *tempo* does begin to change very gradually for both men and women as they get older. For people who remain healthy in body and outlook, and who maintain regular sexual relations once or twice a week, there is no decline in the quality of lovemaking. This finding, confirmed by my interviewees, was reported earlier by Masters and Johnson. There may be, however, a decline in frequency. Among married women over 55, whose partners were presumably older, the frequency of lovemaking in one study was two or three times a month—roughly half as often as the average woman in her twenties had sex.[15]

The only thing to fear about sex in middle age and beyond is fear itself. Nervous laughter at sex jokes, cruel and ignorant references to menopause—male or female—accumulate a deadly poison of apprehension.

"The fact is, female sex hormones do not have a direct influence on sexual desire, sexual performance, or sexual response," emphatically states Dr. Sherwin Kaufman,[16] a practicing gynecologist and faculty member at New York University medical school for many years. Desire, in men as well as women, is governed predominantly by psychological factors. Says Dr. Kaufman: "The real reasons for the commonly observed decline in sex drive with advancing years have to do with such factors as chronic illness, fatigue, disability, and plain loss of interest because of new areas of concern or stress in the lives of both partners. . . . When there is a remarriage of an older man or woman, [there is a] consequent resurgence of sexual drive that neither partner would have thought possible."*

The fact that a man's sexual tempo becomes less staccato than sostenuto is not a loss but a potential, if it is so used. It may take an older man longer to become erect; his erections may be less an automatic response to just any woman than a specific response to a certain woman or women; and his penis may sometimes be less than fully hard. The older man's capacity to sustain an erection, however, is superior. He can control and extend his own threshold of pleasure much long-

---

* Yet the notion that middle-aged impotence is predominantly psychological in origin may have been overstated. As many as one-third of sexually blocked men may have medically correctable hormonal abnormalities, according to Doctors Richard F. Spark and Robert A. White.[17] Recent discoveries involving the influence of hormones on the male sexual response have made it possible to restore to full potency some men who previously failed to respond to testosterone therapy or psychotherapy. The impotence of half the sexually impaired men studied was traceable to medications or to diseases such as diabetes.

er than a young man, giving him time to touch all the right chords that harmonize with his partner's mood and tempo.

The question in my surveys that drew the most varied answers was "At what age did you (or do you expect to) reach your sexual peak?" Both men and women gave ages that ranged from 20 to 80, further evidence that sex is a largely subjective territory. The one area of agreement was among older women, who consistently mentioned that their confidence in making love had improved with age (and with delayed admission to the sexual revolution). Evidently there is no age limit to sexual awakening.

The healthy man's worst enemy is overreacting to minor and gradual changes in his sexual functioning by becoming defensive, depressed, withdrawn, and ultimately, perhaps, driving his woman into having an affair just to prove to herself that *she* is still sexually alive and appealing—thereby compounding his sense of inadequacy. The terrible problem here is that most men hold to the line: "No problem." They commonly repress all conscious recognition of sex as a factor in their passage through the middle of life.

After two hundred interviews, Michael F. McGill, in his book on common crises in the male middle years,[18] reported that discussions with men who proclaimed their own sexual normalcy and lack of concern were consistently contradicted by the women who knew them. In order to preserve the facade of unfazed virility, many men seem willing to sacrifice the actual practice of manhood. They avoid reminders of age by avoiding sex altogether.

This comes as a total shock to a woman married to a man who always had a healthy sexual appetite and took every opportunity to pat her on the bottom or spring a surprise lovemaking session. Suddenly, in middle age, he seems to find every excuse to "fade out early" and go to bed first, to leave the house for breakfast meetings or a religious jogging hour, and to need to sleep "like a log" on weekend mornings. *He doesn't want me*, she thinks. Or, as bad, *It must be another woman*. It is probably neither.

Some men, of course, do react in the opposite fashion, flirting obsessively with young women, or seeking proof in conquering girls not unlike their daughters that they are still in sexual control, of themselves and of their partners.

Everybody needs reassurance that aging has not, or will

not, suddenly render them unfit or laughable as partners for love. One woman I interviewed described her profound feeling, at 38, that she had entered middle age. Having just returned to college after a divorce for recertification as a college administrator, she was overwhelmed both by how dewy the freshmen looked and by how shabby her intellectual skills seemed. "My mental picture of myself then boiled down to two words: *dopey* and *frumpy*," she recalled. "I didn't feel sexually alive either." She dragged through the school year but by summer trimmed down, bought a flattering swimsuit, took a holiday alone, and enjoyed an effortless dalliance with a young lover. By the time I met her, she was 48 and going strong, with several favorite friends and lovers in each of the cities she visited for college conferences. How did she make this comeback?

"I *outgrew* feeling middle-aged."

Vanity, virility, and femininity are the hypersensitive lightning rods we often use to gauge whether we are "aging well" in general. This assigns great power to the inner *imagery* by which we sense our outer selves—our bodies, posture, muscle tone, skin and hair, and especially our faces, on which the bargain we have struck with life becomes indelibly written.

It would be nice if everyone could say, at 50, "Who needs beauty or strength or grace any longer? I have wisdom instead." But as long as our imagery equates desirability exclusively with being young, we must acknowledge the power of inner imagery before we become cunningly defeated by it. In this we are beginning to receive some aid from society. The range of female desirability has expanded upward from the days when Hollywood stars like Garbo and Mary Pickford withdrew before they were even ripe to self-imposed exile in stuffy bedrooms. Jacqueline Kennedy Onassis is continually photographed as a beauty; Lauren Bacall pursued to do movies, theater, and television commercials; Chita Rivera to kick her legs to the rafters in Broadway musicals; and Angie Dickinson to do nude sex scenes—all beyond the age of 50.

Two rituals that affirm the extension of one's years of sexual appeal have surfaced recently. One is women giving themselves 40th- or 50th-birthday parties—announcing themselves as proud to be adults, rather than betraying themselves by lying about their age as women used to do. The other is the ritual escape by middle-aged couples to their version of a "desert island" (which could be the local motel). To a long weekend together each brings surprises of wine or sweets and gifts of the imagination; together they rediscover the delight of hours of lying with each other, not necessarily or continuously *making* love, but feeling happy and fortunate to *have* love together.

The kind of partner every woman probably would like to take away on such a tryst is a man who has memorized the poem "When You are Old" by William Butler Yeats:

> How many loved your moments of glad grace,
> And loved your beauty, with love false or true,
> But one man loved the pilgrim soul in you,
> And loved the sorrows of your changing face.

I Am Who I Am

Simply by virtue of age and experience, people find it easier to do and say things in their fifties that would have tied them up in knots ten years before. Exemplary is the vivacious woman of 52 who had had a mastectomy twenty-two years earlier. All her children were now independent. Her husband was dead. She had taken up many activities for the first time: counseling patients at the state hospital, traveling, even enjoying a younger lover. She found herself becoming more accepting of her own body. Why, not so long ago she rarely took off her jacket. One day, while planning a small party for close friends at her home, she felt a twinge of regret. She could not remember having been unashamed of her body at a party; it was always torture to enter a room. It should no longer be like that at her age, she reflected.

Artfully, she constructed a Grecian-style one-shouldered dress. The clinging fabric revealed the contour of her good breast, which was still lovely. On the other side she was flat as a boy, softened by many draped folds but obviously, for the first time, without a prosthesis.

Halfway through the party, her friends began taking her aside to say it thrilled them to see her looking so radiant. "In a funny way," one young man told her, "you've made it easier for me to accept myself. You've got a beautiful heart."

Middle age is the time to take a look at the things we do mostly because we feel we *should* do them. *Why am I keeping up this pretense? Is there a good reason to keep doing this?* There may indeed be a good reason, but since a major task of the fifties is to improve the alignment of our inner convictions with our outer presentation, it is a question worth asking. Accepting the errors and defeats of the past—as one woman accepted her "deformity"—leads the way toward an oasis of integrity, from which we would all hope in advanced age to survey our own history.

There is a considerable difference between cleaning out one's closet of outgrown "shoulds" and making others a captive audience to one's determination to "let it all hang out." Being able to say "I am who I am" does not mean acting out one's suddenly sprung inhibitions on other people's time and turf. But middle age is a time to be done with apologizing for the accidents of one's birth and background. At an Americans for Democratic Action dinner in the winter of 1979, a former mayor of New York City, John Lindsay, did just that.

Lindsay was stone cold sober and dangerously bored by the after-dinner speeches, thinking to himself, *This outfit is dead—a lot of self-congratulatory liberals with old ideas,* when a young woman took the platform and began a harangue about WASPs. Big John began to mutter under his breath. His table partners shifted in embarrassment. At that point the speaker narrowed her ridicule still further to what she called the "WASM"—white Anglo-Saxon males.

"That's it, I'm leaving!" John Lindsay sounded out.

"John!" Gasps all around. "You can't be serious."

"Serious? Where does this broad get off insulting a minority? Do you know how many WASPs there are in New York? Seven percent! She's going to dump all over my people and I'm supposed to sit here and take it smiling? I'm pissed! And I'm walking out!"

The only sounds around the stunned table were of jaws locking. Two women on either side of the politician tried to sandbag him while imploring him in whispers to stay. It was not clear whether Big John's table partners were scandalized by the fact that a former liberal mayor of the upper-middle class, having been turned out of office for giving away too much to the blacks, should now Mau Mau back at liberals, or floored by the betrayal of class he had shown in reacting with any sort of emotion at all.

How un-WASP-like.

Being able to say "I am who I am" also implies having the confidence to admit we do not always know the answer (but I'll find out and get back to you). At 25 most of us would kill ourselves before admitting ignorance, and one foul-up has us certain we will be fired. By the time we have another twenty-five years in the bank, we understand the relative unimportance of any single act. There simply are more data in the personal computers after 50. Having seen it with our own eyes, we have a better idea of how the world works.

Admitting the Unknowable

That does not mean we have all the answers by the time we reach the half-century mark. But for people who are both middle-aged and good at what they do, there is not the same need to market themselves as having all the right answers all the time. Now comes the press of a counter-urge: to permit doubts, to admit the unknowable, to allow for the misfitting of things, to be amused rather than frightened by the inconsistencies in oneself. In light of this more philosophical turn of mind, and the ebbing of raw competitiveness that characterized the climb toward command, there may be a desire to share the burdens.

"I am fifty-four, but it is only in the last five years that I have felt the permission to do things that I like to do," I was told by a German scientist who directed his own clinic. In the course of treating many important people, he made a discovery. "I had been feeling more flawed and weak than people are always thinking I am, but I saw that my patients had the same problem."

Having reached the height of his symbolic power in the social and family structure, the middle-aged man is called upon to assume paternal duties with regard to the "family" in his workplace, community, or the culture at large. He becomes more concerned than ever with fulfilling expectations and obligations to others, and with protecting his already established identity, a known if not entirely satisfactory commodity.

The German scientist found a path around the covert depression and anxiety this immobilized posture often inspires. He divested himself of the exclusive directorship of the clinic and placed the position on a rotating basis with several professional colleagues. Giving up his seat as a little god had a salutary effect on his ability to write—not in the tongues required for approval by the academic club, but in the flowing language of a man freed to express what he does not know as well as what he does.

As they move up the ladder, people often become keenly aware of contradictions between the position they hold and the ideals they once championed. Some, in their bid for full acceptance and personal comfort, forfeit the capacity to say, "No, this isn't right" or "It need not be this way." Others wear ideological blinders. Pathfinders, however, are most likely in the middle years to look at the world as it exists and to ask realistically, "What can I do, given my position in the world, to make things a little better?" There is hardly a more suitable time to be an activist than in middle age, when one has the power or friends or potential to make something happen.

It is not a coincidence that so many of the truly long-distance runners stop and take time out to write their memoirs. Henry Kissinger did it; so did Anwar Sadat, Moshe Dayan, and Jimmy Carter, to name a few. Late middle age cries out to be a period of reflection, a time to rework one's own history, to edit and incorporate it.

THE SELECTIVE SIXTIES

Curious, at first—I mean this business of men in their fifties boasting about being in better health with trimmer waistlines and smoother heart rates. Some have put more pivot in their spines since they started yogic postures. Others rate easier credit on their oxygen debt when they play squash. They laugh about that old lumpish, winded, phobic wreck they were at 40 or so, when they began to show a preference for sex in the side-stroke position. That, of course, was before they stopped eating meat, drinking hard liquor, inhaling Monte Cristos, and sitting at their desk all through lunch wondering who had put a grenade in their hamburger. That was before they took up walking and raw Japanese fish.

The improved health noted by many of the mid-fifties men in my studies was undoubtedly a result of their having begun to consider their own bodies as one might an irreplaceable antique car—definitely worth the money and effort to maintain in peak condition. But even so, in looking beyond these years, many contend with what Susan Sontag has called a "poignant apprehension of unremitting loss."[19]

It is difficult for many of us to look far down the road. One reason is that our need to deny death causes us to refer to the later years of life vaguely, if at all. Whether it is government statistics or sociological surveys, after measuring off every nine years down to decimal points, everything drops off after 55 on most charts into a vast, flat gray expanse: the parking lot at the end of active life, or at what is *assumed* to be the end before we get there.

Do You Sincerely Want to Be Eighty-five?

Aging, fortunately, is a commutable sentence. There is no fixed number at which we stop being middle-aged and are sentenced to being "old." Yet we are our own harshest judges. We tell ourselves at 40 that it will be all over at 50. But nearing 50, we revoke the sentence and impose something less severe—say, 55—and by the time we near that surrender date, we may be willing to grant ourselves another ten years. What is so treacherous about this otherwise comically human deception is that before each stay of sentence, we are likely to lop off arbitrarily some other activity we think we are "too old for now."

Having seen little distinction made between the early and late sixties, seldom hearing about the seventies if it can be helped, and blanching if someone brings up the eighties, most people assume that old people are pretty much alike. Nothing could be further from the truth. Older people's personalities are far more distinct from their contemporaries' than they were in their twenties or thirties.[20] The accumulated wisdom and differing experiences of the first two-thirds of life broaden the philosophies and sharpen the distinctions among those over 50.

No less distinct are the differences among those over 50 in longevity and health. An important task in middle age, then, is to adopt a stance in regard to death: *How long do I want to live?*

"If I could convince you that to be eighty-five is really an exciting opportunity and that you will be valuable to yourself and others, then you would give up smoking; you'd run three times a week; you'd lose weight; and you'd live longer." The challenge was put by Dr. Walter Bortz of Stanford's medical school.[21] The *physical* secrets of longer life are so simple and obvious; why do so few people regularly pursue them? Good nutrition, good exercise, and good rest, coupled with an aggressive program of preventive medicine, Dr. Bortz asserted, is a prescription that would add at least ten years to the average American life span. The barrier is not so much what we do not know but what we will not do. "Our idea of who we're going to be when we're 85 is just so grim," he acknowledged. "And if there is no value to it, then why seek it?"

The statistics keep shifting in our favor. In 1900 the average life expectancy was 37; today it is 70. By the end of this decade we may see fifteen or twenty years added because of advances in cardiovascular research. Americans born in 1990 may therefore *expect* to live to be 85. Even those of us today who have already reached 85 can expect *another* six or seven years. Indeed, it is the two million people now over 85 who have enjoyed the greatest reduction in mortality of any adult age group: a 25 percent drop over the course of thirty years.[22]

There is more to look forward to. Today, 12 percent of Americans over 65 have no health problems whatsoever.[23] But many of them are presumably people who work at it. A recent study of seventeen thousand Harvard alumni produced evidence that those who participated in strenuous physical activities at least three hours a week—jogging, swimming, tennis, mountain climbing, squash, and the like—had fewer heart attacks, even if they were overweight or already at risk because of high blood pressure.[24] Milder forms of activity, such as walking, biking, golf, baseball, bowling, and boating, left the men no better off than those who were completely sedentary. Nor were onetime varsity athletes protected against heart disease unless they continued a high level of physical activity.

Women seemed better prepared for the predictable infirmities of old age, Dr. Barbara Myerhoff, chairman of the department of anthropology at UCLA, reported.[25] "From childhood on, women find their bodies intruding on their plans. They learn to come to terms with physiological limits and demands. Thus, women have less difficulty acknowledging the ailments of old age infirmities for which the men, by contrast, seem almost wholly unprepared."

The currently popular strenuous physical activity is running, which supplies a regular dose of natural body opiates. "Running addiction" can be healthy or unhealthy. The "unhealthy" running addict lets this ritual eclipse all other social, professional, and personal activities, finally resenting their intrusion on his "perfect control of the running situation." The "healthy" addict uses the high he gets from running to return to his other activities feeling more eager and sound. With his blood oxygenated and his breathing apparatus cleared out, his brain and body should in fact perform more efficiently.

What Really Matters

"I've come to the stage beyond where *Passages* stopped," the party guest said, he being a prosperous independent film producer in his early sixties. "You know what? It's the best. Because by now you know you're *not* going to die tomorrow, the way you thought in your forties. Your business life has shaken down one way or another, and all those questions you lashed yourself with in the forties either have been settled or they don't matter anymore. The man-and-woman thing is all calmed down—you're more alike and there isn't much left to fight about; sex is still good but there's no more the question of who you're going to marry, or divorce, or remarry. Your bed is made.

"The best thing is, you don't care about saying the right thing anymore. You can say what you think. You don't even have to ask yourself the Peggy Lee question: 'Is that all there is?' It's a feeling of—of . . ." He groped for the word.

"Detachment?" I offered.

"Yes. Precisely the word to describe it."

The speaker was David Brown, a veteran of the wild and woolly film business who had married Helen Gurley Brown, editor of *Cosmopolitan*, and who had ridden the horse at Universal Pictures and been thrown off at one point, but who came back with his own company to produce *Jaws* and *The Sting* and *Jaws II*. He also has the distinction of being one of the best-loved people in his business.

On further thought, however, the word *detachment* seemed too remote to describe the experience of this stage. Pathfinders in their sixties were disengaged from certain concerns that were once primary for them, but definitely moved to action by others. As one of them put it: "I am more detached from a lot of things that I used to think were important. But I feel a greater intensity about the things that I do consider important."

Selective intensity—that was more like the potential particular to the sixties. For a motto appropriate to this stage, one might recast the Reinhold Niebuhr prayer that became the Alcoholics Anonymous creed:

"I still have the energy to pursue what is important to me, the selectivity to walk away from what is not, but now the wisdom to know the difference."

When social scientists write about "disengagement"[26] as characterizing people in their sixties, one wishes for more subtle distinctions. To be sure, there are those who say, "I've paid my dues; now I'm only interested in living well." Others, needing a morally based justification, point to the dismal discrepancies between man as he might be and man as he is, shrugging off any further engagement. But pathfinders in their sixties find themselves active in service, in intellectual endeavors, in whatever it is they feel really matters.

It is the quality, rather than the scope, of loves and friendships that becomes increasingly critical to pathfinding as one moves along the life cycle. My interviewees repeatedly expressed this. Several studies have reported that after age 60 the most rewarding aspects of married life are mutual love, companionship, and the ability to speak what one truly feels.[27] The greatest source of antagonism in older marriages seems to be having different values and philosophies of life.

Many studies have made the connection between higher satisfaction among older people and greater levels of activity.[28] There is also a good deal of empirical evidence that personal tempo—one of the three basic heritable personality traits—continues to play an important part in determining one's basic mood and level of vital energy. A great many people in their sixties are constantly active; they come home from work and run the mower up and down or have a game of catch with some kids. A great many more say, "What a day; I'm pooped," flop down, have a stiff drink, and go to sleep. One spectacularly healthy 60-year-old told me he felt terribly sorry for his neighbors who did that, because they were old men. Then he realized they were ten years younger than he.

When I called my own father on his 65th birthday, the tempo that moved his words along was familiar from as far back as I can remember.

"I wake up in the morning, sniff the air, and I can't wait to do whatever it is that I have to do," he said, "as compared to those who say, 'Oh, my God, I have to open my eyes again'—that attitude. It isn't something that I concocted. I felt that way when I was a kid and I still feel that way."

It may be, however, that the degree of enthusiasm and hopefulness one brings to an activity is at least as important as the energy one has available.

The sixties are drawn with bolder brush strokes in certain areas, more somber and sentimental undertones in others. Every study shows, for example, that people continue to have sexual urges even when they are very old, and that their happiness continues to depend in part on satisfying those desires. Yet the movies and television portray the elderly (when they portray them at all) as "inferior in many ways—less active sexually and socially, less effective, more eccentric and stubborn."[29]

Anticipation continues to be important as one seeks a satisfying path into the last part of life. If retirement is not planned, if no new goals are set or horizons sighted, the *Playboy* life-style many people envision as their reward soon becomes monotonous, leaving them with a beer in hand on the poop deck, bobbing like a cork in the bay. But when retirement is used as a channel to possibilities never attempted when there was no time, there is every reason for refreshment.

Structurelessness is what is newest to the post-retirement period, particularly for high achievers accustomed to living with structured tension.

"I used to bewail the fact that I had not enough free time;

there were so many things I wanted to do. Now I have all that time, but not the will to do anything," described an anonymous editorial-page writer after retiring as an assistant professor of English at a New York City university.[30]

Time must be structured if it is to have value. Otherwise it accumulates the implausible weight of fallen snow and moves with glacial slowness.

Who Goes the Distance?

What are the most promising post-retirement directions? Provocative answers emerge from a study conducted by the Institute of Human Development at the University of California, Berkeley.[31] Four combinations of personality and way of life appeared to exhibit the highest satisfaction in the sixties and seventies:

Dominant women whose lives extended beyond family and into clubs, church, politics, where they often performed in leadership roles, were in the best shape physically and mentally. Whatever employment had engaged them earlier was not now missed. It had been replaced with these community management functions and by diverse recreational interests, which they often pursued alone. Notably, none of these women looked to her family for her primary satisfaction, beyond giving her children advice. Their marriages tended to be distant, uncommunicative, and polite.

Married men who were involved with large social issues enjoyed the greatest satisfaction among men in their sixties and seventies. Many of them had taken up political volunteer work since retirement. Like the dominant women, they had little emotional involvement with their marriage partners, and relationships with their children were becoming increasingly remote with age. But they were vigorously involved in social networks and current issues. In dramatic contrast to family-centered or disengaged men, they were optimistic about "how the world is going today." And like the dominant women, they had noticed little change in their health since their forties.

Work-centered women who were divorced or widowed but still enthusiastically engaged in their careers suggested a third path to high well-being in the late sixties. Importantly, these women also had children and were seeing at least one of them more frequently now than they did in their forties. They generally saw a grandchild once a week as well. Their relish for life was not shared by the widows who did not work, many of whom had gradually withdrawn from their interests since their husbands had died.

Among the retired male blue-collar workers, the happiest were the "hobbyists" who had put major investments of effort, time, and money into an interest they could pursue on their own. They often had workshops away from home to which they went every day.

The single common denominator of all four successful combinations of personality and life-style—dominant women, socially active men, career mothers, and hobbyist fathers—was independence. All had prepared themselves beforehand to fill their days with meaning and varied activities that do not depend on anyone else. Moreover, *the aging life patterns of husbands and wives developed quite independently of each other.*

The most dangerous thing about retirement is that almost no one practices it before he or she tries it. A common compensation for a man unprepared for the loss of authority is to begin ordering around whichever members of his family are handy. Given a wife who may have dreaded "having him underfoot all day," the elements are present for years of border wars.

Rehearsals for retirement—refining a craft or service that can be self-operated or exploring a parallel avenue of authority—are useful. For a man to become a volunteer while he is still employed may help him to overcome the idea that volunteer positions are "women's work," inferior in status, and not worth his time. Many voluntary organizations have vast budgets and affect public policy. Whatever its scope, though, this alternate avenue for exercising authority can become a new tribe, a network to belong to, a source of friends and of friction, recognition and competition—of all the things that contribute to a continuing sense of engagement.

Anticipation also is the most important aid for wives approaching the transition to a husband's retirement. Unlike the negative wives who "don't think about the future much, just, you know, live a day at a time," those who look ahead are most likely to have a positive attitude.[32] Planning reduces apprehension and adds to one's sense of inner control, which in turn helps to improve the future.

Rehearsals of place can be important as well. Spending weekends or holidays where you fancy you might like to live later on can establish ties to a community converting one gradually from "outsider" status to acceptance as a perennial visitor. And if during your rehearsal years you become a contributing part of that community, using your skills for fund raising or rare bird sighting, you are not likely to be regarded, when the time comes, as one of my interviewees feared—"as just another fixed-income fart."

THE THOUGHTFUL SEVENTIES
AND
THE PROUD-TO-BE EIGHTIES

George Burns, the octogenarian comedian, gave us a motto for the seventies:

"The nicest thing about getting to be old is you don't have to worry about it anymore."

When achieving success no longer yields novelty, and discharging one's duty or wielding authority has become repetitious and stale, as time invariably dulls some of the acuteness of sex and the senses, one is freed to move on to the next stage: exploring the life of the mind, of memory, and thinking about the meaning of one's existence.

Not surprisingly, one of the things older people do particularly well is to turn abstract principles into realities. The efficiency of thought they have reached in their own lives can make shorthand of long and hard ideas. Speaking out as history's advocate to challenge the abbreviated vision of younger leaders through writing, teaching, continued engagement in community affairs—simply, doing what has to be done—can fill the days of those in advanced age with thought for others. At 71, Kant conceived of a peace-maintaining United Federation of Free Nations. It took younger people 130 years to catch up with his freshness of mind.

Many people in their seventies still maintain the illusion that they are middle-aged—the subterfuge never stops! But given the falling death rate among very old Americans, today's healthy 70-year-old is equivalent to yesterday's 60-year-old.

Older people are remarkably content to be by themselves. But when they do want to be with others, an exclusive quality of their age is that they generally find it easy to make connection with another person, quietly, honestly, and to go to the heart of matters quickly.[33]

Loneliness is mainly the problem of the young, as discovered by psychologists Phillip Shaver and Carin M. Rubenstein in their study on loneliness at New York University.[34] The surprise of their study was that not only do people over 60 have higher self-esteem than young lions under 25, but they also feel more "independent." Their elderly subjects even complained less than the young people about common physical and psychological aches and pains such as headaches, crying spells, feeling irritable or angry.

Age does in fact reduce some of the sharpness of the eyes, the ears, and often the recent memory. But scientists state emphatically that senility is not a normal part of old age. The vast majority of the elderly—even those in their eighties and nineties—remain untouched by it.

At the UCLA Gerontology Center, psychiatrist James E. Birren, 62, divides the elderly into three categories. At the top are the "elite aged," perhaps a quarter of the elderly whose lives and interests are still expanding—not because of how much money they have, Birren emphasizes, but because they have learned how to experiment—and now they are able to try more new things that they have always wanted to do. At the bottom are roughly 10 percent who are sick and dependent. The large range in between, he suggests, is made up of people whose lives change very little from year to year.[35]

To attain the age of 80, we are informed by Malcolm Cowley's lovely book,[36] is truly a *rite de passage*, a "belated bar mitzvah" celebrating the beginning of a new life. Again and again, the people I interviewed in advanced age spoke of the discrepancy between the way they *looked* or what their bodies permitted, and the way they felt inside: "same as always." On that subject Mr. Cowley was particularly moving: "The new octogenarian feels as strong as ever sitting back in a comfortable chair. . . . Then he creaks to his feet, bends forward to keep his balance, and realizes . . ." Along with many others of his age, Cowley believes that work is the best conditioner.

No shortage exists of models who have done profound work in their eighties. Consider Goethe, or Michelangelo, who worked on St. Peter's when he was only years away from 90. The names in *Time* of prominent people who had died in 1980 included several who had stretched their work into their eighties: William Douglas, 81; Alfred Hitchcock, 80; Alice Roosevelt Longworth, 96; George Meany, 85; Josip Broz Tito, 87.[37]

Cataracts did not inhibit the late water-garden pictures of Claude Monet; indeed, throughout the second half of his life his paintings translated limitations of space and optical breadth into the intense selectivity and more detached contemplation most natural to advancing age. He had anticipated the perfect place for contemplation, at the age of 55, when he saw the possibilities for the garden at Giverny in a piece of marshy meadowland across a railroad track. In his seventies and eighties, writes art historian Kirk Varnedoe, "Monet had reached a stage in his passion for sensation where borders between memory and immediate experience may have been less clearly fixed and less crucial."[38] Monet lived to the age of 86. In his last days, although he ceased to talk of painting, he remained selectively obsessed with his garden. It is a lesson to remember in imagining how to achieve harmony between the late-acquired perspectives of the mind and our own old age.

But many people cannot remain outside an institution to the end of their days. In such cases, the secret of retaining the spirit of a pathfinder may be a continuation of giving and resistance to the retreat into total self-absorption. Perhaps all one can give is an amusing remark to others. But hierarchical divisions occur within any group and probably remain right to the end. One can imagine those most vigorous in a home for the aged identifying for help those whom President Reagan would call "the truly needy."

After four years of studying and living with a group of elderly Jews who had been born in *shtetls* but who were ending their days in a senior citizens' center in Venice, California, Barbara Myerhoff sensitively described in *Number Our Days* the relative well-being of those who "see themselves as givers, not takers, and devote enormous effort toward supporting others more needy than they. . . ."[39] It does not occur to these people that old age diminishes their responsibility to others, but rather reassures them that they are still *menschen*—that is, good, decent human beings.[40]

It seems to me not only cruel but ignorant to make the clichéd equation between old people and little children. Old people spend a good deal of their most enjoyable time doing mental embroidery on their fondest memories and in trying to find the unifying threads in their personal or social history. Little children have no past and little capacity for remembering anything. Old people are remarkably content to be by themselves. Children demand constant attention. Old people are shrewd and efficient in their movements. Children founder about, not knowing where they want to go or what they want to do. Old people know. They just cannot always get there on their own.

As pathfinders come closer to death, they describe it more familiarly, not as a terror or a disaster but more as a matter for serious thought and preparation. Their well-measured moments in no way discourage the continued pursuit of learning or the appetite for growth. While Socrates awaited death in prison, he was learning to play the lyre.

11.
PURPOSE

At the age of 94, speaking before five hundred people, he did not need the microphone. Blue eyes flashing, forefinger waving in the air, he leaned passionately over the podium at the 1978 ACLU Convocation on Free Speech to say:

"I've been traveling hopefully for all these years, and I'm still traveling hopefully and so is the world. And someday, someday, though the road is hard, the goal is clear—we are beginning to approach an organized world of peace, order, and justice."

Roger Baldwin,* founder of the American Civil Liberties Union, has fought through the years for social rights that are now ingrained in the American way of life. What must it have been like to see the century from one end to the other, to go through all those passages, both private and public? What secret quality did the man have so that after ninety-four years he still saw the world hopefully?

A little research sketched in the most colorful of lives . . . Born to a comfortable family in Wellesley, Massachusetts, in 1884, he grew up on stories of their abolitionist activities. After Harvard, he was urged by the Baldwin's lawyer, eminent jurist Louis Brandeis, to escape the coils of family by moving to St. Louis, which he did. Flourishing, he taught sociology at the university, headed the juvenile court, and directed a civic reform league. He adopted two boys out of institutions. He explored revolutionary philosophies with Emma Goldman, the "Red Queen of Anarchy," as the newspapers called her. She first thought the young reformer something of

---

* Real name.

a dilettante but later wrote him an apology, and they kept up a correspondence throughout her life.

When World War I engulfed the United States, Roger Baldwin gave up his job in St. Louis to become an active pacifist and form an antiwar organization in New York. Organizing the precursor to the ACLU (of which he remained director until 1950) brought Baldwin into fellowship with a whole circle of liberals, including Clarence Darrow, Helen Keller, Jeanette Rankin, and Norman Thomas who became his "constant ally." As a conscientious objector he refused military service and was sent to prison on Armistice Day. He served nine months and found the prison experience "useful."

After the war, the bogeymen for the ACLU were the Russian Revolution and the rights of labor. It fell to Roger Baldwin to broaden his organization to defend labor organizers, liberals, aliens, radicals, novelists, and other exotic minorities. Still, in the middle of the 1920's the Union's membership stood at only about twenty-five hundred.

When Roger Baldwin read about the Tennessee legislature forbidding the teaching of Darwin's theory of evolution in the state's public schools, he advertised for a teacher who would make a test case. John Scopes volunteered to become a party in the most famous trial the Union ever had. Baldwin pressed Clarence Darrow into defending the case without fee, but he feared the theatrics of a clash between Darrow's unchurched humanism and William Jennings Bryan's backwoods fundamentalist position—that every word in the Bible was true, that it provided the only political guide the country needed. Darrow mocked Bryan mercilessly when Bryan took the witness stand. Did he really believe that Jonah lived several days inside a whale's belly? The Bible says that every living creature was drowned in the flood except those on Noah's Ark—where did all the fish go? Bryan died of exhaustion several weeks after the trial. And although, as Baldwin feared, the case proved nothing about freedom of teaching, the fundamentalists' position had been rendered so absurd that they dropped out of the political fray. Of course, in the late 1970's they came back, big.

Here was a man who had been alive through two world wars, five grand political swings, and heaven knows how many demographic aberrations in American life. Would it not be entirely appropriate for Roger Baldwin to say, "Why haven't we learned?"

It is natural for a wise older person to become exasperated at society's continuing refusal to learn from at least some of its mistakes. What is exceptional about Roger Baldwin is the sense of affection and humor he has maintained for this human experiment. Why, and how, had this been possible? Serendipitously, I was asked to interview Roger Baldwin.

Thumping down a narrow road into the woodlands of New Jersey on a sparkling September day, looking for the farmhouse built in 1840 where Roger Baldwin makes his home, it seemed doubtful that a house would be there at all. The land was uncleared. Bracken and bittersweet tumbled over liverwort down a mountain. A flush of crystal water spangled boulders in a stream bed, then stopped to fill a pond with mirror images, then slid into a beaded string and disappeared under a bridge and downstream to become part of a splendid canoeing river. "We're here!"

Abruptly, we were in a small clearing. All the symbols befitted the man: the innocence, the Walden-like simplicity of the place, the frugality suggested by curtains sagging on their strings across the windows of the old bungalow, the exposed hanging bulb in the kitchen, the old tin table on a listing back porch . . . and Roger Baldwin himself, interrupted in his tiny workroom by a phone call as we arrived, shouting an exuberant "Yes!"

He was lean and hard-beaked. The quick, deep eyes missed nothing. They bore no spectacles. The hands suffered no swelling, the legs needed no cane. He wore a white shirt billowed out over khaki pants, a touch of emphysema giving a slight bow to his chest. Delighted by the sunny day after a recent hurricane, he was eager to sit in the backyard and talk good talk.

"Over these ninety-five years, you have seen the birth of electricity, the telephone, the automobile, the aircraft industry, radio and television, the bomb—most everything," I began, probing for the source of his hopeful outlook.

"Yes, I began with the horse and buggy." Roger Baldwin's smile pulled his whole face into a crescent of mirth.

"Is there any invention during your lifetime that you would rather mankind be without?"

"No, I think most of them have been extraordinarily helpful in bringing people together. I took to each of them rather easily. I remember when we had electric lights put in—amazing! Of course, automobiles were very slow in coming—they had to make the roads. The most astounding and the most dangerous, both, was the atomic age. That, I wouldn't like to see evolve again."

"Do you think the peaceful uses of nuclear energy can ever outweigh the threat?"

"Not until we learn how to handle the waste," he said.

"What about the effect of television?"

"Television has made life brighter for so many more millions of people. It can become a weakening influence like anything else. But it is proved all over the globe that people are getting what they never did before in comprehension of the world around them."

His own habit has been to look at television news for an hour a night. Then he devours all the newspapers and current periodicals and dips into his favorite books. He retires at midnight and is up eight or nine hours later, utterly refreshed, always having slept well. He has never taken a nap. Often, he travels into New York to work. Still organizing, still making speeches, still religiously riding the subways ("until the steps got higher a couple of years ago; now I ride the buses"), Roger Baldwin is still, at 95, trying to make the world better.

"Do you see important leadership developing in the world today?" I asked.

"Well, Gandhi, Churchill, those fellows are not with us," he began, appearing unconcerned. "There are schools of thought that say to trust leaders is dangerous. One might take us the wrong way. Trust institutions. Trust yourself."

"But we are living in a period when Americans have little faith in their institutions, or themselves, do you agree?"

"Yes, there is a tendency to let the other fellow do it for you." Now, he did sound concerned. Self-reliance was rooted in Roger Baldwin as deeply as oak in the forest primeval. The grain shone through unvarnished of one of America's great philosophical traditions.

"I have no leader, no guru," Roger Baldwin was saying. "I help myself and hope I'm capable of it."

"Are you a religious man?"

"In a very wide sense of the word, yes, but I don't have

any God looking after me. I don't rely upon any supernatural authority to pray to or call upon for help. My religious beliefs are confined to the relations of man to man."

What was his guide to those relations?

"The ethics of Jesus, particularly the Sermon on the Mount, had a great influence on me. That sermon is a declaration of love. To love your enemies, to do good to people who do ill to you, this is a great doctrine, the basis of all future order. If people can do that, they can live together. So I have a humanitarian religion, not a supernatural one."

Had there been any polestars who guided him?

"Of course, I was influenced by my New England neighbors—Emerson and Thoreau were household names. Their very free attitude, free of dogma, influenced me a good deal."

But in traveling hopefully, Roger Baldwin kept in mind several points on the ethical compass that he sees as "religious" in aspect. "Justice, fair play, tolerance—these are qualities we try to keep inside ourselves as a guide to our conduct. I think the civil liberties business has the same spiritual character."

Not that Roger Baldwin escaped ambiguities that seemed at the time to have no satisfactory resolution. Like many liberals who believed they were supporting the only sound counterforce to fascism in the Thirties, he chose to travel in sympathy with Soviet Russia. In 1934 he confronted his dilemma in print: How could he be for civil liberties in the United States and support dictatorship in the Soviet Union? In 1937, still in the thrall of a Leninist-inspired movement that was now international and had real power, in contrast to the piddling status of socialism in the United States, Baldwin nevertheless helped Trotsky (Lenin's bitterest enemy) to find asylum in Mexico. He saw no contradiction.

"Even in the Thirties, Baldwin was a 'United Fronter' with a difference," wrote Dwight MacDonald in a *New Yorker* profile. The anecdote that tells it all has to do with Baldwin's application for a visa to visit Russia that same year.

"Do you really think my government will let you in when you have helped our worst enemy?" asked the amused Soviet ambassador.

"Why, that's just plain civil liberty," Baldwin replied, his

New England conscience poking out awkwardly through all the smooth "isms."

Although he never became a Communist, Baldwin told me that the greatest political shock of his lifetime was the Nazi-Soviet pact. I asked Roger Baldwin if he had gone into a depression during that difficult period.

"Oh, no, I never go into depression. I was just indignant—I'd been fooled." He was forced to put his principles on the line in a personally painful way. Deciding finally that it was impossible to have Communists loyal to Soviet policies in the same organization with civil libertarians, the Union's board expelled one of his dearest friends, Elizabeth Gurley Flynn. "It was really a sad occasion for me," he admitted. Vilified by certain segments of the Left, he took the attitude "Criticism is a temporary habit. We had a lot of resignations, but later more people joined than had left."

When I mentioned my interest in life stages, Roger Baldwin jumped in to say, "But so much of my life has been shaped by *accidents!* Marriages, divorces, deaths, especially the deaths."

His first marriage, at 35, was to Madeleine Z. Doty, whom he described to me as "a lawyer, a socialist, feminist, pacifist—all the good things—and very good-looking!" They did not clash ideologically. Just domestically.

She thought she was making too many sacrifices; he felt marriage obligations to be a burden. They had no time for children. So engrossed was each in outside activities that they had little time together. Four years after the marriage, Madeleine was called off to work in Geneva. Ten years later they were amicably divorced.

"It all sounds embarrassingly contemporary," I said. "Can you tell us what you learned?"

"You have to make compromises to create the continuity of a full marriage," he replied. The only time in five hours of indefatigable discussion that Roger Baldwin showed the weight of losses was when I asked if he were lonelier now than when he was younger. He had outlived three successor directors of the ACLU. He talked about losing his second wife, Evelyn Preston. And the previous spring, his only daughter had died.

"Sometimes," he mused, "I sit and think for a while about old friends, not daydreaming exactly. It's a way of conjuring them up and having their company again for a short while. It's a form of entertainment. But I don't dwell on it. I have many young friends."

His senses of smell and taste might be slightly diminished by age, he acknowledged, but emotions do not wear out. "Love and friendship and all the really human qualities stay with you." Many people lose those qualities because things that once had meaning for them no longer hold meaning as life nears the end. But to Roger Baldwin, no less than everything still holds meaning—the next canoe trip, the next conversation with his only remaining contemporary, the next time the ACLU will have to explain patiently, for the thousandth time, what he has been saying for fifty years, and what he said again in the mid-Seventies when 20 percent of his membership quit over the ACLU's defense in Skokie of the American Nazi Party's right to demonstrate:

"In a democratic society, if you let them all talk, that's the best way of guarding against any minority taking over the society. *Mein Kampf* did not result in a takeover of Germany. It took storm troopers and *Kristallnachts*, which were made possible by crushing civil liberties, by not permitting freedom of expression."

Later in the day he wanted to take a walk. We strolled rather briskly down to the pond he loves. I asked how it felt, being 95.

"I never thought longevity itself was worth much. I think that what you do with life, the way you enjoy it, is more important than how long you live." We watched a waterfall froth over rocks. "I feel just the same as when I was in my twenties," he added.

The circles of movement he maintained were no accident but seemed motivated by his strong and specific love of nature—to see it, to be in it. "Your physical activities do become bounded. I like to dance but I can't dance anymore. I like to climb mountains but that is over. I can still canoe. A year ago I tried horseback riding. It was all right—with a slow horse. But I am not aware that my pleasure in living has diminished."

His cue for handling old age and death he took from Gandhi's answer, which seemed about right. "I don't think about it," Gandhi said. "Every night I die and every morning I am reborn. That is enough."

Health was obviously crucial to Roger Baldwin's ability to transcend those losses by which old people usually allow themselves to be defined. He was quick to point out that it is an accident that one stays well, that one's hearing and eyesight remain good. I asked him if he believed certain qualities of mind helped along that accident.

"Yes. I think your attitude has a great deal to do with your body," he amended. "This idea of mind controlling matter, the old Christian Science idea, has a lot to be said for it. If you keep a healthy attitude, your body responds."

He had been through a period of darkness in his early twenties, more harrowing even than the usual pathfinder testing period. When he was in the hospital with pneumonia, the doctor gave up on him. "Theoretically, I died," he described. "I didn't want to see anyone or do anything—I lost all interest. I realized then what death was. I've never been bored with life since."

"If you had one secret to pass on to young people, what would it be?"

"Enjoy more things. Grow. Develop. Most of them get into a specialty, a rut of doing one thing well, and they don't live fully. Music, art, nature, reading, drama—all these things should have attention. Cover it all, as much as you can."

"What would you tell them about their duty to their fellow man?"

"Their duty?"

The rectitudinous word seemed to stick to the roof of his mouth. "I don't believe much in duty," he said. "I enjoy doing the kinds of things that help other people. But I do them to satisfy myself."

"But if everyone wanted only to satisfy himself or herself, and didn't find the same enjoyment in acting with and for others as you do, could the society's fabric hold together?"

"If you are social-minded and love your fellow man," he replied with conviction, "you want to associate with him and act collectively. Most everyone becomes part of something else. We don't do it from a motive of trying to help somebody, or duty."

"You believe then that love between people is the natural state?"

"Oh, I do think so. We are all dependent upon each other

and on the corporate social body. Nobody can successfully live for himself or herself."

"Aren't many people today trying?"

"They find themselves badly deprived. You have to have the closeness of other humans in order really to live."

When a picture was to be taken, Roger Baldwin deftly finger-combed the longest strands of his hair across a marginal bald spot. "Got to be sure my hair's on straight," he said. It took a second to register, with astonishment, that his hair was almost entirely brown, with no more than an inch of white fringe across the back of his neck. "It changes," he explained. "Sometimes more comes in white, then it grows out brown again."

Ever-renewing Roger Baldwin.

The preservation of vanity, commonly thought to be unseemly in old people, seemed on the contrary to be another prod to vitality. If you care how you look, you still care. Baldwin's energy level was formidably consistent, his mind was as quick and informed when he spoke of up-to-the-minute political events as when he recalled which liberal publication endorsed Woodrow Wilson in 1916 and which did not.

How did this country look to him sixty years later?

"I've never lost my faith in this country and its ability to correct its errors and solve its problems. I think we do better than most."

"Are times more precarious now than they were?"

"Oh, less, less."

Other guests joined us on the walk; a rousing debate started. Roger Baldwin was in his element. Everyone else spoke with millennial gloom about the problems all around us, but what did we know, we in our forties and fifties, mere pups? Roger Baldwin had twice as long a yardstick.

"We're much better off now," he said definitively. "There were people literally starving before. Nobody's getting killed today for political or racial activities in this country. And because communication is so immediate and direct, whenever something goes wrong anywhere in the world, everybody knows about it."

"How can mankind be better off with the possibility of nuclear warfare?"

"War itself is suicidal." Therefore, he said, the possibility of any broad-scale war was out. "You can't have war and gasoline too." The second possibility that's out today, he reminded us, is the control of much of humanity by a very small part of it. "The Western Europeans created their empires in Asia and Africa and made economic slaves of whole populations. In the last thirty years, all those nations are different, those people are free."

"But haven't we become subject to control by other means," I pressed, "by small groups of terrorists who can hold up whole countries?"

"There aren't many terrorists," he demurred. "We've created all these dangers, and I think we can overcome them."

"How can you be sure that your being so hopeful, as a way of life, is not blinding you to reality?" I asked.

"There are other realities," Roger Baldwin said, walking around his pond once more, delighting in the shimmer of late-afternoon sun on the lap of clear water. "The realities of our communication, the fact that salvation lies only in working together and the other way lies destruction. There is more cooperation every day, in trade, in credit. You can't put up a television station or get on an airplane without permission of an international authority."

He had been quoted as saying that it seems to him amazing that the late years of his life should be the most exciting and productive. He acquired a happy family for the first time after 50. Internationalism became his new cause, the building of networks of human rights and justice. What he was able to do was rather dazzling—establishing a Civil Liberties Union in Japan in 1947, the next year awakening the Germans to protect their rights. He has traveled around the world for the United Nations as a consultant on human rights. Ever since the issue of Puerto Rican self-government came before the United Nations, he has visited that island every winter to teach law and help with constitutional rights.

"It is now possible for the first time, by international cooperation, to create hundreds of networks between peoples of the world," he believes. "The world is growing closer together, that is the source of my hope."

"You have managed to keep your enthusiasm for life full and your optimism for the world undiminished—how is this done?"

Roger Baldwin's face flushed with curiosity, his juice. "I

think this process of looking ahead into tomorrow, not only to the distant future but to the next day, looking ahead hopefully—that is the essence of being happy."

As he spoke, I noticed behind him the burst of white star-flowers cascading down a clematis vine. He followed my gaze.

"It's a fall-blooming vine," he explained. It is also Roger Baldwin. Perennially innocent, hopeful, a stargazer, this man was blooming deep into his autumn as if he had not yet heard the spring was past. The afternoon had been good, because it had surprises, he said. "I didn't expect this kind of philosophy to emerge."

He kissed me good-bye. They were the cool lips of an old man, but the embrace was quick, warm, bold. Ever-renewing Roger Baldwin—a man of undiminished appeal.

The picture that remained indelible from that day with Roger Baldwin was of the pond he so loves. I had stumbled upon it while wandering down his wooded road alone in the early morning. The air, the mountain water, both were stunningly clear. The limbs painted on the pond's mirrored face were identical to the limbs flung out from its banks. It was an Impressionist painting—each leaf a single, square brush stroke; the trunks, the clouds, the sky, the entire slice of nature stroked in as precisely as if on graph paper. Should we say, then, that the Impressionists were not painting subjectively at all, that they were painting realistically? Could it be that Roger Baldwin's impression of his fellow man as naturally loving becomes "true" because it is self-fulfilling? The enterprise of his life has been to enable people to behave better toward one another, not out of noblesse oblige or a need to sacrifice, not because he thinks it is one's duty to tame the noble savage, but because it is most agreeable for him to live his belief that the natural state between people is one of love.

Although one might have guessed the other qualities vital to pathfinding, would any child of a century that has conceived of God as dead, man as a being in nothingness, and morality as relative to the situation have guessed that one of the chief requisites of a happy life is purpose?

Yet the one constant in the lives of people who enjoy high well-being—in every group I studied—was a devotion to some cause or purpose beyond themselves. To put it as simply as possible, my research offered impressive evidence that we feel better when we attempt to make our world better.

What do people derive from having a cause or a purpose?

People often say, "There's nothing that makes you feel so good as doing something nice for somebody else." We need to feel that we are good. Not everybody feels that way, and nobody feels that way all the time, but there is evidence that to believe we are good people, and becoming better, is one of the natural imperatives in our development. A sense of purpose also helps to satisfy the need to believe "I matter," that a single life might "make a difference." Further, to have a purpose beyond oneself lends to existence a meaning and direction—the most important characteristic of high well-being.

Work as Purpose

Few of us could, or would, embrace the quality of purpose as thoroughly as Roger Baldwin. But each of us has the capacity to partake, with some part of our lives, in the obvious joy that Roger Baldwin finds.

That sense of purpose may come from our work. There always will be those who, because of their talent or superior brain power or social skills, have work that is exciting, sometimes compelling, even potentially ennobling. Their work is not only their livelihood and pleasure but their purpose. As such people attain success, they become natural contributors to the social enterprise. The revolutions in communications and transportation have multiplied their impact, taking their political concepts and scientific discoveries, cultural innovations and entertainments, and flinging them like cosmic pollen all over the world.

Some work naturally has social benefit and translates easily into a sense of purpose: a dedicated teacher or a principal who turns around a deteriorating school; the "helping professions," of course. Even those whose work does not, on objective observation, appear to contribute to the greater social good surprisingly often convince themselves that what they are doing is worthwhile, and that therefore they must be good. Almost all the chief executives I interviewed, for example, said they believed their work makes a contribution to society.

But that self-deception more often does not work. In 1977 I met with seven hundred designers, members of the Aspen Design Conference, the majority of them professionals between the ages of 30 and 44. The relationship between work and personal values emerged as a critical question. Many of the designers were in advertising or were corporate art directors, yet the majority perceived themselves as primarily "artistic" rather than "business-oriented" and derived their greatest pleasure from the creative process. Despite registering a remarkably high degree of control over their lives (88 percent felt they had control half the time or more), uncommon enjoyment in their work (84 percent enjoy their work all or most of the time), and only rare instances of boredom (half of them never), many of these professionals felt they were designing products that did not mesh with their values. Although half saw themselves as not having sold out, and one-quarter (most of them under 30) had not thought about it, one-quarter of the group *did* perceive themselves as having sold out. And the majority of those designers were in turmoil.

The turmoil may be part of what motivates many people to seek greater independence in their work as they grow older, in order to bring their daily efforts into better alignment with their values. Among the designers between 46 and 55, independence became of critical importance—even more important than achievement. The other value on which increased emphasis was placed after the age of 46 was moral integrity.

For many people, the unease following from a lack of purpose in their work may have a deeper source than the friction with their values. Earlier in our history people offered their daily activities as a "thank you" to God, not only for the life and health to carry out those activities, but also because all enterprise was ultimately intended *for* God. That was, of course, the basis of the Judeo-Christian work ethic. The Protestant concept of "stewardship," by which one made an offering to the Lord from one's best efforts, elevated a person's work, no matter how mean, to the status of purpose.

In the last half-century, the omnipotence of God and His mysteries has been dwarfed for some by the miracles of humankind's spaceships and satellites and test-tube babies, and by the barbarities of near-genocide. At the same time, work-places have grown so huge and impersonal that the individ-ual becomes increasingly frustrated in an attempt to find meaning, even simple affirmation that he matters at all, in the unit of work he adds to the incomprehensible cybernetics of the post-industrial state.

By 1975 the three hundred largest American corporations were transnational operations.[1] The business-school-trained hit-and-run American manager is encouraged today to maxi-mize short-term profit, at the expense of long-term planning, and, when the picture is rosy, to leverage himself into an-other company for a higher salary. The leukemic effects on companies so managed stem from the unwillingness to make risky, long-term investments, and a commitment to creative accounting and market research that usually exceeds the commitment to improved production methods and techno-logical research and development.

At a symposium sponsored by Syracuse University addressed to the crises of the 1980's, Dr. Lester Thurow, pro-fessor of economics and management at MIT (and author of *The Zero-Sum Society*), observed that in recent years "none of the engineers graduating from MIT could be persuaded to work for General Motors. Not because the pay was too nig-gardly or Detroit too distant . . . but because GM had been doing nothing of interest in the way of technological innova-tions."[2] They could not bear living in lavishly paid boredom. Dr. Jacob Goldman, now vice-president for research at Xerox and a refugee from the automotive industry, added, "it was the failure of imagination that wrecked the automobile business, not the cost of labor, the interference of the federal government, or the arrival of Japanese imports."[3] Recall that the single highest goal among the blue-collar people in my surveys was to reach self-respect. Fundamental to the success of the Japanese management style is the intention to make the worker feel that both he and the work he is doing mat-ter, and the reassurance that his loyalty will be rewarded.

The inability of many Americans to find purpose in their work has helped to create the shift from a work ethic to a self-fulfillment ethic. Most people no longer want to work hard. They demand more leisure hours in which to seek some other purpose or pleasure—under the catchall contemporary concept of "self-development."

The "disease" of low productivity, as it is often seen from society's viewpoint, has now spread to almost all Western democracies, most recently and surprisingly to Germany, and even behind the Iron Curtain. One of the key issues for which the Polish workers of Solidarity were willing to risk a Russian invasion was a five-day work week.

This profound social change can produce individuals who are healthier physically, mentally, even spiritually, and who find in their independence from valueless or value-violating work the impetus to do something original or worthwhile. Many such people have already been created—call them the New Independents. If enough people end up on this side of the ledger, there might form a critical mass that can become the source of a new social ethic to motivate our society. But if the retreat from work becomes a withdrawal from the actual world of uncertainty and change—a mere bachelor's holiday for a whole society—then the hope for progressive improvement of the collective life is forfeited.

Children as Purpose

Many people, when pressed to define what finally forces them to get up on the most miserable of mornings, say it is their responsibility to their children. For some, that purpose can propel them out of the boxes that are their lives.

Consider those who are knocked off the ladder early in adult life, and who fall into the diminishing circles of movement known so well to young and poor jobless men and teenage mothers. They have nowhere to go, no function in society other than to be recipients of "entitlements"; their chances of making a leap out of this induced entropy are slim. One of the best hopes lies in the acquisition of a sense of purpose from the transfer of self-concern to another, even more helpless, human being.

A young welfare mother who was in the process of making such a leap—after "being down so far, I fell through concrete"—was referred to me by a community health center in a tough, working-class area of California's San Fernando Valley. I had been asking around the country for two years for a teen mother, one who was part of the epidemic of unplanned pregnancies among unmarried girls between 10 and 17, but who looked as if she might find her way to independence and self-respect. Most unmarried teen mothers, I discovered, make one of several poor adaptions. If they do not rush into a panic marriage, they are likely to abandon the child (often to their own mothers) or to abuse it—little babies, they discover, are not grateful. Iris Ruiz,* as I will call her, was not easy to find.

I met Iris on a windy street corner where she waited, the color high in her cheeks and a cap of breezy blunt-cut black hair blowing lightly. Immediately friendly, she jumped into the car and directed me to a McDonald's. As we relaxed into the reassuring aura of absolutely reproducible experience, Iris breathed, "I'm out. This appointment, then another one, then half a day's work—I planned it so I could be out the whole day today!"

She was 20 years old and had a two-year-old son at home. Her mother was watching him. This was a breather. Iris obviously enjoyed having an "interview" to dress up for; her pastel suit was freshly ironed, and it set off her pride—the straight black hair. She looked as soft as a sofa pillow.

Although no one had ever guided her, Iris knew she would not get very far without a high-school diploma, and so she got that, at least. Then came the family pressure to marry. The girls she knew in the neighborhood grew old and flabby and mean and sat with big white pocketbooks in their laps at church suppers and were finished at 25. Not for her. Next thing she knew, she was pregnant. Although her condition was still not absolutely certain, she entertained advanced ideas about terminating the pregnancy so that it would not close off her future, but the moment she found out the results, cues as old as her culture itself took over: he would marry her, she would have a baby to love her, and her mother would be ecstatic.

The downward spiral began after the wedding. Her husband became two people. The one she got came home from hours of drinking with the guys after work and slapped her around the house. There was always the excuse, "Well, he

* A pseudonym.

was drunk." After a year and a half she said, "Uh-uh, he knows what he's doing."

She was not going to fight with him for the next fifty years, a replica of her interminably scrapping parents.

"If living with it is making me a miserable person," she told her mother, "hey, don't tell me that divorce is something no nice girls should do." She did it.

That turned her into a welfare mother. It was nothing to be proud of, a mass-produced identity. She wanted to shake free, but how?

She began to spend time with a boy she had known affectionately all through childhood. How amazing, the tenderness between them. It made up for everything. She loved him. He loved her. Iris had all that she wanted. And then he was dead. Just like that. Darvon overdose. She had come into the room to drive him to work and leaned over to kiss him awake and his body was cold. Funny cold. Right there on that bed in that sweet boy's body every hope of joy and deliverance had slipped out of her arms. No tears came. Something else began, a boiling sensation she could not name. She decided not to go through the funeral all doped up with the Valium they wanted to give her. You had to deal with your blows sooner or later, she realized; might as well face it right away.

But the tears did not come. Not at the funeral, not for weeks afterward. One day this soft pillow of a girl punched her hand through a window. The blood streamed down the glass, but she was strangely separate from it, as if she were sitting on a bus in a thunderstorm and watching the rain streak along the window. Slipping down over the next six months into the rough embraces of unreliable men, her hands clutching as at the smoothness of a window, grasping for a hold of tenderness, she slid down and down a glass wall of pain into the numbness of promiscuity.

At times during that year, she would take out the bottle of sleeping pills she had been given and think about emptying it into her stomach. Once, the baby crawled into her room and knocked the pills across the floor and the cat started eating them, and the boiling sensation came up so evilly inside her that she began pounding the baby with her fists.

"I need help." She managed to get that message across to the local community health center.

It was almost unheard of in her circles to take one's troubles to a therapist. That was the second hole—the first having been the divorce—she punched through the invisible wall that hems in working-class women by customs of class, by religious proscriptions, by shaming and rigid role dictates. When the pressure built up, Iris would slip out to the mental-health center with her son and find someone to talk to.

"I'm no good. I can't take care of my baby. Welfare gives me fifty dollars a week and the whole world is jumping on me for money. I'm nobody." The therapist encouraged her to talk it through, providing a protected enclosure in which she could boil over without hurting herself.

But what finally pulled her up from depression was a sudden flash of foresight one day when she was bathing her son.

He's so beautiful now, what will he be when he's eight? When he's ten? Oh, yes—and I want to see him as a teenager. And a big man.

"I wanted to be around to see him grow," she told me emphatically.

Once that window on the future opened, everything began to change.

Iris applied to the local community college to begin nurse's training. The summer before she was to enter she found a switchboard job through CETA* and lined up a baby-sitter. "That really lifted my spirits." She was all set to start pulling forward in the fall of her 20th year when the baby-sitter disappeared. *What good were goals?* she was tempted to think. And what would the people who had accepted her at college think when she didn't show up?

"Just another dumb welfare mother." Her lips curled down with self-contempt as she remembered the feeling. "But I wasn't. So I went over to the college and told them, 'I really want this.'" The supervisor said it sounded as if Iris had the determination and willpower. They would keep a place open for her. She entered the program the next semester,

---

* The Comprehensive Employment and Training Act, a federal program, provided work experience to people at the poverty line, who in turn provided many community services, such as child care and shelters for women and children who were victims of domestic violence. In 1982 the entire program will be discontinued.

paying her new baby-sitter most of what she earned by working the switchboard job at night. It was an investment in her future.

"I thought I was nobody," Iris told me as we walked through a patchwork of repossessed bungalows and pastel stucco homes toward her own tiny house. "But I'm turning out to be a real person. I can make a living and pay the rent and take care of my son." Her voice trembled with the unimagined joy of it. "I can really take care of myself!"

Already this youngest pathfinder had lengthened her anticipation of the future to five years. "I'm not getting married again for at least that long," she had promised herself. "I need those five years to come back and grow into a whole person."

We walked past blocks of garden apartments with tiny kidney-shaped pools spilling over with small children and their listless welfare mothers.

"That's how I'll know I've made it back." The breezy cap of hair on Iris's head shook vehemently. "The day I get off welfare."

"Do you see that day in your future?"

"I live for it."

Commitment to a child can be a galvanizing purpose in extraordinary situations, but it probably was not what most people of high well-being had in mind when they described themselves on the questionnaire as having "a cause or purpose beyond myself." In any case, a little later there comes a time, painfully obvious, when children do not want to be fussed over and shown off like their parents' pet horses; children want their heads. Easily a third of a parent's life is left to be infused with newly created commitments to people or ideas. Finding a replaced sense of purpose is particularly imperative if parenthood, as it is for many, has not been entirely rewarding.

Finding Purpose at the Local Level

It is assumed that those of the upper-middle class have the time and inclination to devote themselves to good works. At no time in the recent past has faith in Lady Bountiful been so heavily invoked as now to justify budget cuts in social services.

Yet the evidence in my research was that more blue-collar people (61 percent) were devoted to a cause than those in the upper-middle class. Often that cause was union-related. Professionals and white-collar workers, when they did not have a cause, most often said that was because they had no time. But the working-class people made time—an average of an hour to two hours a day—to help other people, despite the other claims on their energy: eight hours of work, two hours of housework/household cleaning/repairing or maintaining, and five hours engaged in family life.

In fact, social action programs often benefit society best as a springboard for natural leaders from the community. As described by James MacGregor Burns in his scholarly work on *Leadership*, "The need for affection and belongingness . . . has long been considered a stimulus toward political participation and leadership . . . likely to attract many who are not necessarily seeking power or leadership but who crave a comradeship and acceptance that they have felt has been denied them."[4]

Close the doors through which the distressed or frustrated have passed into active social participation within their communities, and the very people with nascent pathfinder qualities who have nowhere to go except into the streets will emerge leading protest demonstrations or mobs. This phenomenon was recognized during the Sixties at the highest level of government. A presidential task force assigned by John F. Kennedy to address the problem of political violence developing among educated young people recommended that the best response to radicalism was to create a national youth corps. It came into being under President Johnson and is known as VISTA. In fact, many of the people behind the desks in government regulatory agencies and on congressional staffs through the 1970's were Sixties radicals just crossing into the second half of life themselves—our new vested revolutionaries.

Pathfinders with a purpose are not heroic statue material, looking down their holy noses at the grubs who are all the rest of us. Many are people who say: "This neighborhood (or city, school, church, country) is going to the dogs. It's my responsibility to make it better." Most commonly such people find a purpose—or respond when it finds them—at the local level, or take on leadership roles in small groups.

Their involvement may not be noisy or dramatic or even public, but it connects the individual to his or her neighborhood or culture at more than the level of "Dear Occupant." As much as does helping a friend in trouble or despair, purpose makes a person feel good. It is a friendship for the world. The mission of many members of the eighteen Federated Garden Clubs of Vermont, for instance, is to save the leafy overhangs on rural roads from state pruning machines and to replace the wild flowers destroyed by necessary saltings during winter snows. Adding in a small way to the joy of all who pass by provides a quiet purpose; there are many such examples. The "cause" does not have to be the center of a life. It may represent 10 percent of one's time and effort, although the increase in the sense of mattering may far exceed the actual weight of that investment. Some pathfinders find ways to add purpose as the rich shading on an otherwise full canvas.

Naturally, there is some desire for ego reward mixed into the motivation to pursue a cause. "Man's devotion to his community always means the expression of a transferred egoism as well as of altruism," stated theologian Reinhold Niebuhr in his philosophical classic *Moral Man and Immoral Society*.[5] Quite possibly some negative emotions are being sublimated. "Altruism" means regard for the interests and needs of others. Inventing an ingenious form of altruism, according to psychiatric theory, is one of the healthiest adaptations a person can make to conflict. Psychiatrist George Vaillant described one of the privileged men in the Harvard Grant Study who was both ashamed of and afraid for his bigoted father, and who sublimated that conflict by mediating between hard-hats and poor blacks in an urban ghetto in Detroit: his altruism allowed him to combat his father's prejudices while in a real sense also protecting his father from attack.

"Altruism is better than projection not because it is more moral," concluded Vaillant, "but because it is more effective."[6]

When one considers the passions and prejudices inflamed by the issue of forced busing over the past ten years, it is astonishing that no major race war broke out in any city. The credit can be given in part to the strong political force that matured during the 1970's from thousands of local activist organizations formed across the country to stabilize and renew neighborhoods. By the end of the decade this lobby had eclipsed some of the traditional institutions, which had lost their vigor and credibility.[7]

A Blue-Collar "General"—A New Battle of Bunker Hill

When one considers a man like the figure we shall call Bingo Doyle,* a public utility employee who has lived forty years in a tightly knit, almost all-white, Irish Catholic enclave of Boston, there is every reason to suspect he might be among those determined to firebomb the first bus that brought black children into his own children's school. But he had taken a different turn. Besides being a meter reader for the local utility and holding three other part-time jobs to make ends meet for his family of six, Doyle acted for three years as volunteer head of a local multiservice social agency. When crisis came to his community, he expanded from an angry and limited man into a leader.

To hear it from local professionals who suggested him as a pathfinder candidate, Bingo Doyle sounded like the very embodiment of Charlestown—its defensiveness, its spunk, its tattered pride.

One square mile of close, uniform, brick row houses hugged together against eternal damp like a forgotten cellar of the Industrial Revolution, Charlestown nonetheless has its dignity. The private homes are scrubbed and patched. The community, which has been exhaustively studied, is classified as "stable, isolated, working-class." It is all piled up on a hill and severed from the rest of Boston by the harbor and the railroad tracks. Charlestown puts up its dukes at the outskirts. Bumper stickers warn, "I'm a proud townie." A billboard announces, "I bank at Charlestown because it looks out for Number One!" Anyone who is not a resident is a "stranger" and not to be trusted. Strangers want only to exploit or cause trouble or shove some cockeyed liberal social

---

* A pseudonym.

welfare scheme down these proud throats. Like busing. Like the projects.

The second-largest public housing project in New England is sited there. That was one of those bright ideas of the social reformers. It is now official: the people shunted into it are guaranteed downward social mobility; therefore, they tend to be hostile. Crime is overwhelming; cops resist answering calls there at night; cabbies prefer to drive into solid black areas such as Roxbury or Dorchester. The projects were forced on the community. That blow by the heavy hand of government exaggerated the sense of isolation and powerlessness of the people who live in Charlestown to shape their own fate. By the time government struck the next blow—court-ordered busing—the community was surly, ready to fight back and draw blood and go down, this time, at least spitting teeth.

The smile hung over the bar like a hat with its brim cocked back, full of pride and swagger and prejudices. It sat on the handsome, much-clefted Irish face of Bingo Doyle while he waited for what he thought of as the jet-set, shrinky-dink writer from New York who had better not stand him up. She was half an hour late. He was into his second beer and counting.

Fortunately for this writer, Bingo had already received a boost that morning with an invitation to come down to the *Boston Globe* for an interview. He told them they ought to rename the paper the Eastern Globe or the World Globe, anything but the *Boston Globe*: "You never cover *us*, and Charlestown was here before Boston." The photographer drove back with him onto his turf, for the picture.

His milky blue eyes rolled up in mock injury when I came into the family tavern (from a weather-delayed shuttle), and he waited for me to approach him, salve his pride, apologize. He noted with approval that I ordered a domestic beer and not some effete foreign label. Immediately he let me know where *Passages* fell short.

"I don't know the people Gail Sheehy knows," he began. "What I know is housewives, ya' know, mothers, truck drivers, plumbers, firemen, policemen. I've read *Passages*, and I can understand the crises they went through are natural, but everything with us is geared around the neighborhood and family. I can speak with some authority about the second-generation white Irish working class, and we tend to go to work and come home. The social structure *is* the family. Our time is spent fixin' the house or takin' the kids here or there. The few social functions are neighborhood parties, a church social, a sports banquet. This is where we cannot relate in any way to this mobile, nomadic America the media keep tellin' us exists. It might be part of America, but we're part of America too, and we're the part that never gets reported."

Bingo established the ground rules. Seeking recognition for his turf, he asked that the proper name of Charlestown be used. But to demonstrate his contention that some people serve not for personal glory but out of love for their communities, he wished his own name to be withheld.

"But you don't confine yourself to being a parent to your own brood," I suggested. "Don't you have another role, as a town father?"

"Yeah." Still wary, he protected himself with sarcasm. "The flaw in my character is that I was brought up by four parents with ethics. Had even one of them trained me how to exploit things, I might be a wealthier man than I am today. But I was brought up that you do something for someone because it's the right thing to do, not to gain power over them. And you don't need everybody bowin' and scrapin' and sayin' what a wunnerful guy you are."

The few people Bingo knows who did not become municipal workers or public utility employees left Charlestown long ago. Most of the townies perform their jobs, but during working hours the bodies they occupy are essentially lifeless. Many hold a second or third job and turn mean on the other side of midlife because they see too much on TV that pretends that the free-spending, holiday-seeking life of the elite is the payoff for all Americans. It never was going to pay off for them, let alone what happened when double-digit inflation settled in. Bingo himself works seventy paid hours a week, distributed among four jobs. On an average day he spends three hours with his kids, two with his wife, and two more in volunteer work. His marriage was made for "continuity, as opposed to adventure."

"What is success? If you're going to measure it in money, I'm a failure. If you're going to measure it in growth, I'm a person who has influenced others far beyond what I ever set out to do. I haven't got paid fer it. So who's successful?"

His mid-life passage, as Bingo saw it, was stepping out on the busing issue. Elected leaders who should have come forward and rallied the town to face the crisis did not. He spoke up and his friends agreed with him. "So they did me the disservice of naming me chairman!"

Charlestown had been invaded twice before, first by the Puritans, then by the British. Now, two hundred years after the Brits, the constabulary and the media were about to come over the hill to make the town surrender on busing.

"There were threats from the outside, talk of bridges being blown up—it was like a war being planned. Either we were going to control our destiny, or let others destroy it. Schisms in families set brothers to hating each other, but nothing was strong enough to make us lie down for another onslaught of 'urban renewal.' We had to understand what we could do for ourselves—and that was tough. It was also dangerous."

Every night, like trunks of hardwood trees moving abreast, the mothers of Charlestown marched. School officials sweated in their palms, and community health and welfare professionals worried that wild elements—kids or the racist fringe—would blister through the raw surface of order. Bingo knew the professionals from his volunteer work. He could act as an interpreter between them and the locals. Every segment among the residents was opposed to busing, but a dangerous schism was developing between moderate community elements and extremists. Bingo's overriding concern was this: no matter how it came out, this issue should not be allowed to tear apart the connective tissue that had held the town together for at least two centuries.

Drawing upon his gift for the gab and the barb, and honing a late-discovered knack for gaining respect from many different kinds of people, he created a forum that brought school officials together with moderate residents and got them both talking to police and community professionals and Justice Department people. "Almost everyone who had a responsibility related to the deseg order was ambivalent," Bingo discovered. They welcomed the chance to show that they did not have stone hearts or pointed ears. Bingo brought them all together on a first-name basis—it was Captain Bill from the NDF and Joe from Justice—so that when officials and residents clashed under volatile circumstances, as was inevitable, it would not be "us" against "them."

Still, the night came when the town threatened to blow. Five hundred mothers, their phalanx formed in close deep ranks around baby strollers, were stopped as they marched past a school. A dispute broke out over whether this was on their permitted route. The Tactical Patrol Force was called in to back up the familiar police.

"This is shooting ants with an elephant gun," Bingo tried to persuade police officials, who finally agreed to allow the mothers to proceed, two by two, on the sidewalk. Nothing doing, replied the mothers after caucusing. They would continue to march eight abreast.

Husbands and sons stood on the sidelines, breathing hot. Bingo tried to pull his own wife out of the line of march. "If this thing blows, we can't both be in jail," he warned. "Listen," he remembers Mrs. Doyle's adamant words, "I love my town as much as you do."

At the intersection of Bunker Hill and High Street, two hundred uniformed men stood in a wall of linked arms, their riot batons between their knees. Their line was a model of restraint; their officers paced back and forth, proudly inspecting them. The awe of history filled Bingo Doyle. In his mind's eye he saw these men as British officers, reviewing their army moments before the Battle of Bunker Hill, exhorting them to hold the line, while the colonial mothers rallied their numbers to come out and fight. He was the only man this group of mothers had allowed to march with them. Suddenly, an elite projectile force of the TPF broke through the police line from the back and charged into the mothers' march. Bingo found himself holding up several reeling women and praying. Sons went in for their mothers; arrests began. Bingo recovered control of the situation, prevailing on the police officials he knew to get the menacing and unfamiliar riot police out of town. The battle cooled. Amazingly, no one was hurt.

As a direct result of keeping the lid on strong feelings and not allowing either the racists or the TPF to incense feelings, Bingo Doyle was able to fire up his people to the heritage of their square mile, at the same time containing the fires so that they did not destroy the town.

It is true that, today, the public schools of Boston are

desegregated. It is also true that no exodus took place from Charlestown.

"It's a Pyrrhic victory for the federal government," as Bingo sees it. "What they have now is a virtually white city with virtually all-black public schools. Charlestown kids all attend private, parochial, or special-exam schools. Our victory was this. They got the schools, but they didn't destroy our community."

Bingo's own turning point became a passage for his community: both reached a stage of development where contradictions can be accepted and the best made of them. But what made Bingo a pathfinder?

Bingo Doyle's personality was not shaped by middle-class parents vigilantly pointing out the fruits of knowledge and virtue to be plucked from the learning tree. His father worked for the city. But his father was politically active and had imprinted on the boy a fierce personal independence. He died when Bingo was 12—"probably why I wasn't the achiever my older brothers were. I knew I wasn't any brain to go on to college." But as a potential pathfinder, Bingo found what he needed. He adopted two "civic parents," as he calls them, both of whom nurtured the seed of social conscience.

Bingo met his civic mother when, in the act that marked coming of age in Charlestown, he joined the Knights of Columbus at 18. She was the wife of the secretary, but she was at the center of every issue in town and had been for all of her 60-odd years. His civic father was the first man Tip O'Neill went to see when he came to town. When Bingo was first married, he moved into an apartment in the older man's house and was immediately folded into the family of eleven. Bingo watched his heroes take positions that put the good of the town before their own fortunes and take fire for it.

"Fortunately, both of them lived long enough to be vindicated."

How far ahead did he anticipate?

"How far do I look? Into a vague beyond. I'd like to string it out with the company until the kids are grown and my retirement benefits are in. Then . . ."

Ordinarily, his perspective is still what it was when he started out—week to week. In his role as town father, however, he does have an extended concept of time, which allows him to risk standing up for what he believes in today, with the faith that the future will vindicate him as well.

Bingo does have a clear image of the broader man he could be if all his responsibilities could be reconciled with his values.

"I like to think I'm tryin' to pass on now to my children the kind of values my mother and father passed on to myself and my four brothers and sisters. The most important thing was not money. At least in the Irish Catholic workin' class, if you're not a caring person, it is secondary whether or not you've achieved worldly success. . . .

"Where does the responsibility to family, as opposed to the better good, cut in? That's why I'm fighting so hard for the public-affairs job at my company—I believe the large corporation should have a social awareness. Then someone like me could do it all."

The crossroads he faces now:

"Somehow, I have to make the passage, if you will, from being top of the heap as a volunteer—who *suggests* to the powers that be that there are ways to solve the social problems of the city. I want to pass into a role that has the influence and power to *implement* a change."

Bingo believed that this goal could best be met within the large utility corporation for which he has worked most of his life. The company was stalling, obviously preferring to keep this hot potato at arm's length and to take credit for him without any of the heat. When he considers where he would like to be ten years from now, at age 50, only one of the descriptions of himself changes, but that one is key. He would like to be middle-class. The change from working-class, he explains, from being perceived as a meter reader to being seen as director of community affairs for an important company, although representing little change in income, would decidedly boost him from working-class to community professional.

How long would he give the company to make its move? I asked.

"Forever. I've already made a judgment that it is not in my family's best interests for me to leave the company. So they have me over a barrel, they know I'm locked in."

His wife seldom leaves the house; only a few close friends come by. He has been loyal to her for twenty years, he says with that twinge of self-righteousness that acknowledges it will never be properly rewarded. As Bingo said soberly when we talked in 1979, in "our system, a woman can determine a man's career." Mrs. Doyle had not adjusted to the fact that her husband was on call to all kinds of others in the community, and she was less than impressed with his explanation that he had to talk to reporters because they were the vehicle for the working class to get their story across. "I've been takin' to this role like a duck to water. She's jealous at times, and she's right to be. So that's part of the problem."

A clear facet of Bingo's image of himself had become that of the town "facilitator." He still took a razzing from his friends for being able to speak urban professionalese as easily as he can talk to townies, but it was, of course, a backhanded compliment. To retreat from this broader identity would be a bitter sacrifice.

"All those years would have been wasted. I would be relegating myself for the rest of my workin' life to bein' a two-jobber. Consumed with just that. Never being able to bridge the gap between providing for my family and working for the greater social good. That's the crux of the problem."

The conflict between social conscience and economic reward set off little explosions of ambivalence in his conversation, as if gunpowder had been scattered along his train of thought. The contradictions between the egalitarianism America preaches and the elitism it usually practices kept setting him off.

"I wish one of my four parents had trained me how to make money. Another side of you wishes that, the side with six kids, ya know? And seein' a lot of fakers in positions you wish you were in, not so much for the money but because there's so much more good you could do."

For five months during 1980, when his company sent him out as an employee representative to coordinate its United Way campaign, Bingo was hopeful. Even a little giddy. "Imagine me, a Gentile, making speeches to Jewish philanthropy organizations on how to raise money." After raising more money for the fund than his company ever had, Bingo went back to the Boston office and—"They didn't know me. The wife and I almost came to divorce court." When I last spoke to Bingo in the spring of 1981, his social purpose was of necessity on the back burner. Survival—economic, marital, psychological—were at the forefront.

"With all the college tuitions coming up," he told me, "I'm driving a truck on the side."

One of the hopes Bingo holds out for his fifties and sixties is playing the role of mentor. That would offer him a sublime continuity with his surrogate parents, who are now both very old and, for him, forbiddingly close to the end.

"I like to think I am the beneficiary of two people who had the grief of the old days. The attitude they instilled in me about helping people and touching a lot of lives is one I should pass on. I'll be reaching out to groom people younger than me. Bingo Doyle is best forgotten. But there always has to be somebody that cares more than for their own narrow interests."

The Purpose of Purpose

There is evidence in both psychology and philosophy that the making of rules, setting of values, and seeking out of universal concepts of justice is a natural developmental need in man, one that is either stimulated or retarded by his environment. Piaget[8] limned that process in children, and the phenomenon is implicit in Lawrence Kohlberg's studies of our ascension throughout life along a hierarchy of moral values.[9] By the time a child reaches the autonomous stage, writes Piaget, he or she defines obligations in terms of mutual respect, reciprocity, and responsibility. "An essential product . . . is the sense of justice [wherein] justice prevails over obedience itself." Kohlberg refined the Piagetian model by postulating three levels of moral development. Beginning at the "preconventional" level during childhood, our values generally are organized around manipulating rewards from others and avoiding punishment. Most adults move on to one of two "conventional" levels, in which one's values are shaped largely by situation and expediency; the need for belonging, community respect, and social esteem; and the avoidance of criticism and of self-punishment. Some people reach the "post-conventional" stage, in which they are able to adopt "higher" values; such people make moral choices from a consideration of the needs of society and of universal principles of justice and human rights.

Regrettably, Kohlberg omitted from the research for his six stages of moral development data on women and cross-cultural data. His conclusions, however, are buttressed by the studies of Dr. June Louin Tapp, senior social psychologist for the American Bar Foundation and a coauthor of some of the Kohlberg work. Her model of legal development is based on a consideration of the interaction of psychology and the law. "In all, philosophically and psychologically, there is an advance from a dependent, hedonistic, and uncritical mode to an independent, altruistic, and rational manner," writes Dr. Tapp.[10]

The work of Piaget, Kohlberg, and Tapp suggests underpinnings for my own conclusion, that an excessive focus on interests that are strictly personal and a consequent disregard for social participation penalizes the individual. A person who is not connected to something larger than himself has no hope of continuity or breadth of vision; nothing in his world surmounts time or his own death. The other victim is the society that becomes host to this parasitic impulse.

So far we have discussed purpose largely in terms of "What's in it for me?" That is only part of the story. What makes purpose both so individually satisfying and so culturally necessary is what is in it for society.

We should not make the mistake of thinking that the state of the world begins and ends in the level of our own consciousness, that by overcoming our own psychic handicaps we can automatically turn inequality into equality, injustice into justice, condescension into respect. Obsessive preoccupation with the psychological can be misused as a way of excusing selfishness, of explaining away hesitation and failure, and of ignoring the structural inequities of any system.

If we become a random assortment of "selves," living off the fruits of our formerly productive and competitive interdependence, we will eventually divide between those who have drifted off into states of fantasy or addictive escape and are virtually unemployable, and those who struggle still to prop up a declining prosperity base. A crucial quality for both the individual and the society, then, is a sense of purpose.

12.

FAITH

As any bartender knows, politics and religion are two subjects that should never be discussed in public or a fight is sure to start. To declare myself up front, although I hold with many humanistic principles, I also believe in God. That never seemed to me a particularly exclusive or political stance, until I found myself interviewing a fundamentalist Christian leader who seethed when she described the enemy as those who hold "the one-world, humanist, feminist philosophy." Her political organization sends new applicants a loyalty oath of sorts that commits them to anti-feminist and anti-abortion positions, as well as to the belief that churches have the right to designate traditional roles for men and women. The oath is to be returned with a membership fee of up to $250, for which she will send the applicant one of her inspirational tapes.

This sort of prix-fixe, table d'hôte belief system is not what pathfinders describe when they talk about their faith. In return for their independence, they are left to pursue within their own souls the endless and unanswerable debate about first and last things.

In every group I surveyed, people of high well-being were more likely than the others to speak of having a faith. As we know, one of the ways such people most often meet a crisis is through prayer.

Pathfinders, however, although most of them were raised in a religious tradition, tend to become less concerned with formal church ties as they grow older. By midlife they often move away from dogmatic or formal professions of their religion and forge a more individual concept of the Divine.

Some have relied on a combination of logic and intuition to work out their own position within the formal religious construct in which they were raised. As Cate O'Neil, the pathfinding lawyer, said upon reaching her mid-forties: "Basically, I'm a Catholic—I just won't let them kick me out. But by now there are a lot of things I don't go along with. My personal relationship with God is much more important to me than any organization or church."

Others have picked up the trail to spiritual expression seemingly by accident, having walked away from religion when they were young adults and rebellious against anything that labeled them or left them feeling hypocritical. Upon reflection, the "accident" of rediscovering faith often occurred when a major passage—symbolized by becoming involved in an important cause—converged with the unexpressed, unmet, possibly unconscious need to feel part of a larger intention toward love and justice.

Other pathfinders have become committed to an ethical system that struggles in as vigorous a way as any religion with the meaning of life and death, but also takes on the specific paradoxes of our time.

Anything that stimulates honesty of mind, or that rare form of love that is unconditional, can be a conduit for spiritual expression. Some of the pathfinders found that membership in a church or temple was not as meaningful for them as literature, music, or climbing a mountain to seek that silence unadorned by illusion, where the presence of God may be felt.

Not uncommonly, a person is unaware of the absence of a spiritual dimension if the daily business of life is proceeding reasonably well. But when confronted with one of the conundrums of a complex adult life, the pathfinder may gravitate toward a renewed source of faith and clarity, drawing upon the environment as such people do for whatever form of sustenance is needed. A woman with a midwestern Protestant background, recommended by members of her adopted community as a possible pathfinder, came circuitously to her adult faith, in much the same manner I had found my own way back.

A Down-to-Earth Comeback to Faith

Having endured a religious upbringing that she now refers to as rice-pudding Protestantism (so soft, squishy, indistinct, that it nearly bored one to the distractions of evil), it would have been laughable to the woman whose pseudonym shall be Elizabeth Bain Loeb* to look for what she was missing in church. Besides, pulling out life in great bolts of yardage and enjoying many of its finest textures through romantic love with her husband, through family love with her three children, through many friends and ample demonstrations that she mattered and that she was good, she found that the hole in it all was no more noticeable than a moth's teeth in a quilt. And one simply turns that side to the wall.

A direct and sensible lady who did not deal in mystical concepts, Liz Loeb got the job done, whatever it was. She could talk to you about death matter-of-factly. One of her children had had a brush with it, and already she had buried one of her parents. She would not claim to have it all figured out and she would rather there were another alternative, but not for her any "hocus-pocus" about life in the hereafter. Yet, despite her resourcefulness, truth be told, there was something missing, something important with which she had not come to terms.

Her religious training had consisted primarily of the tenets "Eat your oatmeal and don't marry a Catholic." But upon bringing home a Jewish prospect, she discovered that not even prejudice is something one can count on to be consistent. "Oh, wonderful, dear," her mother said. "Jewish men are so good to their wives." It was on his side that she ran into a wall. Not in the least dissuaded from him by discovering that Jewish parents could be against a Protestant girl, on the contrary, she remembers, "That's when I got really interested."

After their marriage, she went through an agnostic phase, then converted to Judaism, then pretty much forgot about the whole thing. Or to be more precise, the strenuous inner debate about what she actually believed and in what style she preferred to worship went dormant, in the same way that

* A pseudonym.

her bachelor's degree and her master's in botany became irrelevant. She was teaching to help put her husband through medical school and specialty training, and having babies. That plus a fast inhale of the Sunday paper seemed all there was time for. They lived in a heavily debted postgraduate limbo for nearly ten years.

When Dr. Loeb was offered a teaching appointment in a city on one of the Great Lakes, he and Liz looked over the town and decided they might like to put down roots there. It was about time. She was 35 and he close to 40. She kidded her husband, "Do you think we're really ready to handle our own charge accounts?" They bought a house adjacent to Lake Park, one of the prime attractions the town held for Liz with her botanical background, and for two years they explored its many moods.

The third year, the trees billowed with parasols of pale green atop full sweeping umbrellas of foliage. The river that ran all through town, dividing the park into an east and west bank, looked refreshing. But the park, they discovered, had been mysteriously closed. After a week, it was littered, being vandalized. And nobody seemed to be doing anything about it.

Appalled, Liz looked into the situation and found one of those classical East Bank–West Bank standoffs that paralyze many cities in the modern world. Control of the two banks was divided between city and county. The city side had a swimming pool and abutted a black middle-class neighborhood. The county side presided over the golf course and acres of lush woods and lapped up to the lawns of a white upper-middle-class enclave. When contract negotiations broke down between park employees and the warring city-county politicos, the matter was referred to the Friends of Lake Park Society, a blue-ribbon board of old-timers, most of whom had been appointed by the city manager. And the park society had flatly refused to grant the fifty employees any raise.

"I wasn't looking for any great social purpose," Liz says, "but this impasse looked like it would keep the park closed down all summer. What would the inner-city kids do? Hack their frustrations into the poor trees? What about all the people who count on a park as their outdoor terrace, as their summer home? It was so cruel and pointless. I began writing letters to the editor."

She became involved with a group of citizens, mostly housewives, who rallied together to raise the money to meet the difference between the employees' modest wage demands and the line being held by the park society. Fund raising went well, but soon they were into July and the park was still closed. She began to suspect the park society had motives other than civic virtue. They did not seem to like ordinary citizens messing about in their business. They did not want to be rescued.

That was when Liz got really interested. She appeared at an open city council meeting and tried to put her point across with logic. Using the information her committee had unearthed, she spoke in her usual direct and sensible style. One man called her a liar. The spectators rustled with excitement. She failed. (It was not until two years later, while reexamining her failure, that she realized an open city meeting is not a logical body but an emotional one.)

One of the oldest Episcopal churches in the city contacted her with a bright idea. The church had sponsored the admission of fifty Cambodian refugees who were desperate to be productive but could find few jobs. Why not organize those interested into an all-volunteer force that would open and maintain the park? The Cambodians would be doing something worthwhile to ingratiate themselves into the resistant community, and the park could function while the fund-raising drive was coming to fruition.

Suddenly swept up in the euphoria of this good cause, and thrown together with people from the church who bore no resemblance to the social climbers and snobs she associated with her rice-pudding Protestant background, Liz was amazed to find herself attending a service that Sunday. Her stance, however, remained that of the objective observer.

That evening, two days after the Cambodian work crew had begun cleaning up the park, Liz and her husband walked down by the river to see how things were going. A strong fishy odor assaulted them. Could the river have gone stagnant? They found no such signs. As they walked north, the odor made their heads swim. They followed it to the road, and there, parked behind bushes, was a station wagon

from which a man and two boys were unloading one of
several bushel baskets.

"Fish heads!" Liz's husband gasped.

"What for?"

"It's just a guess, but it could be to make the Cambodians
look like savages."

They checked out the license plate through the
emergency-room police officer at Dr. Loeb's hospital. Owner:
a board member of the Friends of Lake Park Society. The
whole thing stank.

All hell broke loose the next day and continued through
the long, hot summer. Representatives of the park employees,
mostly black, sent up a huge outcry over the Cambodians'
weaseling in on their job territory. "Get the Fish Pickers
Out" was one of their less xenophobic slogans. A minor riot
broke out when three Vietnam veterans took on a bunch of
Cambodians and scarred up the putting green. Toward the
end of July, Liz and her committee called a press conference
to hand the park society the check that would end the impasse.

No one from the society came.

"I'm beginning to think it's not easy to do good to people,"
Liz quipped to her husband, but underneath her front she
felt as bad as she had in a long time.

"Everything I had done backfired. I felt as if I'd been run
over by a truck and my mother had just died. It didn't help
when people from the park society would say to me, 'Why
aren't you home taking care of your children?' "

Liz began calling herself names—naive, do-gooder, dilettante—and came dangerously close to seeing the whole mess
as her fault. But she never let her doubts show, continuing to
coordinate the efforts of her committee and the church,
working as always out of her home, juggling dishes, laundry,
cooking, and children at loose ends, with the phone growing
like a toadstool out of her ear. She longed for some peace
and quiet to piece it all together.

Her husband started meditation. "It's really very useful."
He encouraged her to take the training.

"If I feel the need, sweetheart, you can loan me your man-
tra." Nor could she sit still for the idea of going to a
psychiatrist—"It would seem to me a weakness." Someone

else suggested running. But the riverside flasher, who wintered elsewhere, was back for a return engagement.

Besides, her natural way of dealing with a problem was to work it almost all the way through in her own mind first, before discussing it with anyone. Her husband, possibly wishing to be more important in her life, tried to coax her to lean on him. Affectionate as she was physically, given to hugging and kissing at the drop of a hat, mentally there was a *No Trespassing* sign protecting the boundaries of her philosophy of life, despite its holes.

One Sunday morning, she rose before the world had awakened and padded out into the yard with a book of Walt Whitman poems. It felt wonderful. She began to realize how starved she was for a time to reach clarity, a place for complete honesty. Halfway through a thought that had a fighting chance of being profound, she saw a vaguely familiar woman at the kitchen door.

"I have a five-year-old, and I know you have a little one too," the neighbor woman enthused, "so I thought we might enjoy each other's company."

There went Sunday morning.

Fragments of Whitman's words stayed in her mind . . . something about being alone at sea where one could . . . ponder night, sleep, death, and stars . . . and another poem that asked, "Do I contradict myself? Very well, then I contradict myself. . . ." But she never had the time to find the same poems again and complete the thought. The next Sunday, to elude her neighbor, she actually went to church.

The first moments were blessedly quiet, and private, far less boring than she would have thought. In fact, she felt an upheaval. All that had happened, but that had not been felt, was felt. It was the beginning of a fertile upheaval. Her thoughts did not have to be restricted, her feelings edited. Then a command of Christ's called her out of herself:

Come unto me, all ye that travail and are heavy laden, and I will refresh you.

The act of coming to a source of truth and clarity, where the deceptions and false fronts of daily life could be dropped, where the defenses kept high all week could be relaxed, seemed all at once so necessary, obvious, natural. She felt deserving of refreshment. Christ's words passed a cool hand across her brow, and she wept.

Toward the end of the service, strangers and parishoners alike rose and turned to one another and clasped hands, saying, "God be with you"—as if they meant it.

"There was warmth and humor and goodwill moving through that church," Liz recalls. "What can I say? It felt like coming home to a spiritual bond that was real, that endures everything. Sometime in the middle of that service, I moved from the purely objective outsider to being a grateful participant. We were all included in a ritual of devotion and in a circle of friendship that went beyond that church, that denomination, and that took full notice of what was going on in our culture at the time. My hunch was that this kind of religious experience wouldn't be a running away or a denial of reality. I found myself going back many Sundays."

Things began to sort out. She realized that the board members of the Lake Park Society wanted the park to remain closed for the season. They were banking on a massive attrition of its employees, which ultimately would make their political benefactor, the city manager, look very good on revenue savings just before reelection time. It was all so obvious. Now she had to do something about it. Yes, she. The replenishment of her faith in God had begun to restore the confidence in herself that she was not even aware had been eroding.

"I suddenly realized that I probably had more strength than the people around me."

She studied the bylaws of the park society inside and out. At an open city council meeting in late August, Liz rose and first deftly poked fun at the man who had called her a liar at the last meeting. The spectators roared with pleasure. Then she made a little fun of herself. When everyone was softened up, she took on the president of the park society.

"Thirty percent of your board is sitting illegally."

In his fury the president—head of the leading department store—exposed the fact that he did not know what a proxy vote was. Discredited by embarrassment, he was overruled when nominations were made that would change the character of the board and throw out some of the city manager's cronies. At last, things began to move.

The sermons at her church became more meaty, sometimes even touching on this issue as a parable.

"We grappled with the contradictions between what the

Scriptures say and the way people actually behave with one another," Liz described. "Even harder, we tried to look at the ambiguities within ourselves. It became a place for me to be asolutely real, at least for an hour a week."

Why couldn't she feel that elsewhere? I asked.

"I brought no poses into that situation. There was no need for a mask or a demonstration of my abilities. I wasn't being measured or sized up. I was just another seeker."

She felt at church the exchange of an unconditional love. Logic yielded to intuition, and sometimes she did feel a spiritual presence. Coming out into the splash of sun or, later, into the prewinter fog, she found that weather did not change her frame of mind. Those moments of effervescence she had felt in that place would stay with her all week. It was as if she took home a little vial of strength inside. The rediscovered paradox, she realized, was an old truth: to have a sense of your self, you must feel part of something larger than yourself.

The park reopened on Labor Day. People were jubilant. The next thing Liz knew, she was being contacted by groups all over the city who asked her to get involved in this project or that; she was testifying at state committee hearings; her name was being mentioned for parks commissioner. But she wanted to wait until the smoke cleared before she put her head up for any public office, so that a hostile standoff did not harden between the forces of city and county.

"You have to learn to accept pieces of something as an accomplishment." This broader view, as it turned out, would apply to her renewed faith as well. Time passed and the church changed.

"The church at that point in history was a little utopia," she recalled the last time we spoke. Her eyes moistened. "Of course, utopias are by nature evanescent."

Eventually, her association with that particular church ended, but it had added a deeply important dimension, a quiet background of support and enrichment, to every other part of her life. It was in her. It would remain in her.

A Reanimation Through Religion

Faith is not a necessary quality of pathfinders, but like a sense of humor it is frequently associated with pathfinding.

For some, it becomes the source of a sense of purpose. For others, it is a secondary support that shores up the meaning and direction they feel in their lives.

For Liz Loeb, the addition of a spiritual dimension fortified her other pathfinder qualities. It helped her to put into perspective the inevitable confusions and contradictions faced by anyone who attempts to intervene on the side of the angels, so to speak, in human affairs.

Many people look to organized religion to provide some of the strengths Liz had already developed before renewing her faith. Among them, perhaps none is more universally desired than the confidence that one is a good person, that one matters, that one's existence makes a difference. Believing that you are a good person can go a long way toward releasing your best possibilities, and often that belief is endorsed by a person's acceptance of God or Christ into his life.

For the ordinary mortal, as T. S. Eliot observed, "nothing dies harder than the desire to think well of oneself." Consider Ned Parker,* a man who had tried all his life to emerge from the shadow of a successful father and who ultimately found in Christ what he called the perfect answer.

Ned was recommended as a person who enjoyed exceptional well-being both by his questionnaire and by his colleagues in the American Bar Association. Happy to be interviewed, he preferred the use of his real name. Ned was well liked and seemed to like himself. Nothing could have been further from the truth of the early years of his adult existence.

Doomed to mediocrity. That was the portent that haunted him as he grew up shy, not athletic, not social, and eclipsed by a potent father and successful older brother. "I felt I was totally incapable of excelling at anything. I came back from the service in '55 and went into my father's law firm. For a year, everything was just beautiful because I was being very dependent on my father."

Ned's father was not only successful but also dearly loved. The young man's beautiful dependency was brief, however. His father made him a mature if painful gift—he resigned from the firm and left the young man to pull his own weight.

"I immediately went into a very deep identity crisis," he

---

* Real name.

described. "I couldn't sleep at night. I was in the depths of despair, and a very ineffective person because of it."

The icing over Ned's "friendships" with other men in the firm quickly soured into honesty: they resented him for coming in without having earned his own way.

"The greatest thing that could have happened to me during that time, I thought, was for someone to put a gun to my head and pull the trigger."

The white spear of insomnia struck two hours after midnight, every night. In anguish because he knew he had to be in possession of his faculties to go to work in the morning, he forced himself to lie in bed until seven. He started a strenuous calisthenics program hoping at least to feel better about his body. Then he realized that tossing all night was destructive. He forced himself to get up at two and do something productive. Why not go into the office? It took some doing to rouse the janitor and persuade the man he was not suffering from delirium tremens. But once Ned began to make a habit of nocturnal workaholism, he even began to enjoy it.

If he could not excel by innate abilities, maybe he could beat the game simply by getting up before anyone else in the world.

"If I just kept up this frantic activity, I thought I would accomplish something," he recalled, "but much of the activity was fruitless." He tells people today how lethargic and indecisive he was as a young man. "They just can't believe it. I'm totally in contrast to that now—an idiot optimist!"

The man recounting this severe but short-lived depression—not uncommon to the mid-twenties—had no more than a superficial interest in religious faith until he was past 40. But as he stood before me, I saw an eager, expressive man, trying in every way he knew to be "caring"—his favorite word. He had a naturally thin-lipped mouth that might well have pulled taut and sour by the age of 49, but instead was gentle and determined and often rippled with smiles.

Twenty years before, having decided he could do better on his own, Ned had left his father's former law firm. He was married by then and a deacon in his church. A new minister spoke to the sophisticated and wealthy lay hierarchy. Within ten minutes, Ned observed, he had compelled the complete respect of many of the leaders of the city.

"I said, 'I've got to find out how on earth this guy has been so incredibly successful!' "

Ned Parker asked to meet with the new minister every Wednesday morning at six. The age of a guru, 68, but lonely, the minister agreed. They spent that hour together for the next three years. Ned's first father substitute taught him anticipation and attention to detail; the minister had beautiful files. With the shameless appetite of ambitious youth, Ned sat at the feet of his mentor almost cannibalizing him. When he thought he had taken in the secrets of excelling, he broke off the relationship. Ned remembers the old man's sadness. Ned himself felt no particular loss.

"By the time we broke up, I believed I had it made." Certain deficits in his first mentor became evident only in retrospect. The minister commanded respect, but no one could get close to him.

Still hungry and not a happy man, Ned Parker was now putting in 2,400 billable hours a year and arriving at the office at four A.M. He specialized in estate planning and probate, an area of the law that, some say, is dull enough to depress anyone. Typically manipulative teenage behavior by Ned's son caused major marital problems. And the worse things got, the more rigid Ned became.

Then he met a second mentor, a young layman involved full-time in Christian ministry. Like Ned's first mentor, this layman excelled in all that he touched. But unlike the first, he called forth love from everyone who met him.

"He had something I wanted very badly," Ned Parker admitted. "What my first mentor had was something material. What this man had was something spiritual." Moreover, in Ned's eyes, the young man surpassed even Ned's father.

"The lives I saw changing right before my eyes made me deeply believe that the Lord was working through this man," Ned explained. "I was immediately sold. It manifested so much of what I thought I should be."

This time, Ned hoped to learn the secret of having a glorious relationship with his Creator. "Although I wasn't able to state it that way before, I had read enough of the New Testament to know that it could free a person to have the joy-filled life I really, badly, wanted to have."

He was 43 before this "in-depth spiritual experience" took, but Ned assured me it had made him a changed man. His wife confirmed this convincingly. He became a part of a prayer breakfast fellowship, which was part of a worldwide network of Christian lay people who meet in small groups for prayer, Bible study, and camaraderie once a week. Several years later he joined a charismatic Presbyterian church. Not incidentally, Ned's breakfast fellowship includes several United States senators and representatives and other influential types. Among them is Chuck Colson, the former special counsel to President Nixon, who developed religious conviction after leaving the White House and serving a year in prison.

Ned Parker now has two missions in life.

"If I don't share my faith with two or three people every day, I don't feel I'm doing what the Lord would want me to do. That's my obligation."

Didn't he have clients and friends who told him to keep his faith to himself? I asked.

"I've got a very tough shell now," he said. "It's very difficult for people to bust me."

Describing his other mission, his voice rose to the vibrato of a trumpet. "I really want to *lead* my law firm to great things." He paused and added softly, "It worries me a little why that is so important to me." Then he added, "More important, I want to make sure we become a *caring* law firm." But his is not to reason why, when things are going so well. For the last few years Ned Parker worked fewer than a thousand billable hours and still his seven-lawyer firm did very well (he raised his fees). Ned finds in his new faith the most intimate spiritual companionship. "Jesus Christ is close to me as I move through my life," he said. "It's as if He's with me as I walk down the street."

If you do not believe you are good enough, faith like Ned Parker's can provide you with the possibility of exceeding what you believe are your limits. Ned looked to a religious mentor to lead him to confidence and a sense of abiding companionship. The closeness he feels to Christ also seems to elevate his success drive to the level of a mission—his will be the best law firm, for God. His religious association also offers him good social and business contacts. Undoubtedly, Ned Parker has been able to expand himself, has not unnecessarily hurt others in the course of his own passage, and is working toward a balance between developing himself and commitment to purposes beyond himself—the basic pathfinder criteria. He ascribes all this to his newfound faith. The only thing that bothers me about it is that his testimony makes religious commitment sound a bit like a personal convenience: the Gospel-as-custom-salvation.

Accepting God requires that one forfeit some control, but religion promises that in that act of humility, in the surrender of ego, one can transcend fear and failure and possibly even the mortal boundaries of time and death. In exchange for asking that the great unknowables be accepted on faith, the embrace of God gives many the reassurance that "everything happens for a purpose."

Belief that behind the rudeness of daily life and random malevolence is a divine organization may encourage people to seek meaning and direction in their own lives. One never knows what might have happened to a person trapped by social conditions if religious faith had not channeled his or her anger and frustration. Looking to God, trusting that He has some reason or ultimate design in mind, can lift people out of the squalid and into the ecstatic—if only for a few moments in a beautiful church. Religion is optimism taken to its highest power.

In a confusing world, the individual may also consult religious values as rules or guidelines, choosing to derive from them a certainty that might otherwise be impossible. Or the person may completely internalize the tenets and approach life with a cheerful fatalism (it is God's will). Those who surrender unconditionally to God may be directed by the most spiritual sort of passion. All religion represents to some degree a surrender of one's will. The word *Islam* itself means "submission." Through Exodus, Leviticus, Numbers, and Deuteronomy, God commanded Moses, and Moses dutifully submitted, finally dying "as Yahweh decreed" in sight of the Promised Land, never to cross over himself. And Christ on the cross uttered these words of ecstatic surrender: "It is finished! Father, into Thy hands I commend my Spirit."

But there is another kind of surrender of will that is not associated with passion, or with pathfinding. That is when a person feels too tired, weak, or frightened to struggle any longer with the hard questions.

One of the sobering aspects of getting older is realizing

that there is no construct that explains it all, into which all the loose ends fit. It is awesome to live with that awareness, tempting to adopt faith in some airtight moral and religious package that purports to explain it all. It is safe to say that for many people, particularly those for whom life does not afford many open doors, it is a relief to give up the attempt to sort out the grays and embrace a black-and-white system of belief.

Ma Belle, a Moving Church

Some pathfinders make of faith, creative acts. Although God is their polestar, they are more than God-receivers. Two people, as different as they can be in background and in the ways in which they choose to witness their faith, suggest the broad outlines of religion's function in the lives of pathfinders.

Whatever the mood of the culture, there are always a few people here and there who do not wait for a personal interview with God, but who transcend their own circumstances to bring love and comfort, on a one-on-one basis, to the broken wings around them. Such a woman was recommended to me as a possible pathfinder by an intern in an East Harlem community health center. Belle Cogdell* is her real name, her title "senior health coordinator and leader of the SRO outreach team." She never mentioned religion or, for that matter, having a purpose. But for many of her 250 patients, she was the only reason to get up in the morning and crawl out of their bins in the single-room-occupancy hotels. One day I made the rounds with her. She was a moving church.

When Belle walks the Upper West Side of Manhattan, the streets part. They wait for her, the swollen-footed diabetics and the fugitive teen mothers, the discards with rheumy eyes or a whiskey list. Word passes among the wobbly-minded ones emptied out of the state's huge mental institutions, those who have not yet crawled into a corner to rot. She looks for them and they look for her, the one they call Ma Belle.

"Hey, Ma Belle, put your bright and shining eyes on me," a man called from the steps of the Continental Hotel. The

* Real name.

man had been fished up that morning from his usual alcoholic swill. "I haven't seen you in a long time," he said.

"I've seen *you*," Ma Belle replied.

When she looks at them, those who have vacated their faces come back into their eyes and flicker there, for a few moments at least, like fluorescent lights trying to come on.

"Hello, remember me?" she will say to the new ones. "Where do you get your health care?" Every day for the last ten years Miss Belle has worked these same streets, keeping an eye on what they call the medically indigent. Out of their solitary hells she leads those whom the rest of society has condemned to invisibility. To stay alive for Belle has become *their* purpose.

It was not as though Belle had been blessed with enough harmony in her life to give some back. Her early childhood was touched by a gentle man, however. The grandfather who raised her, a brakeman on the railroad, was the kind of person who, if he just went across the street, would bring back a little twig and say, "Here, I brought you some flowers." But he changed after his stroke. He no longer recognized his wife. Belle had to come home from school and do everything for him.

"I thought it was fun—it made me feel grown-up," she explained, with a typical pathfinder attitude.

The dark time came when Belle was 13 and she stood by the bedside to watch her "daddy" pass. She still remembers the shock of her grandmother's words to her a year later.

"I'm not going to take care of you anymore," the widowed woman said. "You have to earn all your own money now." Belle made the age-old bargain of upward mobility on her older brother's behalf—"You go off to school. I'll stay and earn money and send it to you"—and she supported her brother until he entered the Army, whereupon he was killed.

Belle's life suddenly had no center at all. She longed to take flight and hoped to find, beyond the dirt-scratching farms of the rural South, another reason to live. She found a sleep-in job with a family who intended to travel all over the country. After seven years she settled in New York, married, started another job, and waited to have her own children. None came. Her body was not properly made to bear children, it turned out. Her dead brother's wife sent all his offspring. Friends sent others. Altogether, Belle raised eleven

foster children. They lived reasonably well in a building su-
perintended by her husband on the fringes of Harlem. But
child after child reached 17 and succumbed to the local
anesthetics of drugs or alcohol and turned sour on her, every
one. The last was the girl she called "my heart." The girl
turned her back on the road to college, paved over ten years
by the nickels and dimes that had come out of her mother's
vanished social life. She became rebelliously pregnant and
broke her mother's heart.

The walls began closing in on Belle Cogdell. She wept
constantly for over a year, for she felt she had lost everything
in the world that mattered. Then she "came on my menopause," as if upon a final degradation of her womanhood.

"I thought I might go down." It occurred to her that her
brother had lived out his fantasy of dying young, and she
had played out the part he had always had in mind for her.
"I was so stupid," she saw it in retrospect. "I thought that
was what I should do—I took my brother's children and they
took my youth." She would not do it again, but having done
it, she refused to allow herself self-pity.

One day Belle had a revelation: "I lived my life as an old
woman. I'm going to begin a new life, as a young woman,
before it's too late!"

No sooner did Belle glimpse this window than a new spirit
came over her. Something lifted. She felt young. Forgetting
about her shyness with strangers and the fact that she had
not finished high school, she applied for a job at the community health center. When she passed the test, she said to the
supervisor, "I can't do it, but I'll try."

The young people of the neighborhood stopped her one
night and asked her to join their social club. She had not
been out for years, her husband being a solitary drinker.
Belle began dancing and going to restaurants and let the
young people make her laugh again. The old people she
transported to clinics began to call her their "nurse." She did
not feel alone anymore. A decade later, Belle Cogdell could
not hit the corner of 96 Street and Broadway without a
trail of followers worthy of the Pied Piper.

On the strength of her will to turn the defeats of her
young years into a second life, she had forgiven her past and
folded all humanity into that act of forgiveness. It had given
her the gift of love that surpasses helplessness.

Into the Continental Hotel she walked, tall and straight, great joined watermelon of a breast riding high over half-bushel hips on a pair of legs so long that some of her followers call her "the lady on stilts."

"They're waiting for you, Miss Belle," announced the young social worker with a stick of burning incense behind his ear.

"You're going to burn someone's eye out with that thing," Miss Belle said.

"I gotta keep it in my ear for the smell," the social worker demurred. "You know that old lady who sleeps with all the cats, smells like she melted into that bed!"

Belle said no more. Of all the arbitrary factors bearing on whether or not her followers actually will get health care, probably none is more critical than smell. Whenever the doctors or nurses at the clinic run into a "hygiene problem"—meaning a patient sufficiently malodorous to be denied treatment—they send for Miss Belle. She walks the reject up the block, feeling her way along before she says, as if it would be her pleasure rather than the patient's shame, "Would you let me give you a bath sometime?"

Half her patients are "mental" and hospital castoffs. Most of her clients admit their lumps or sores or tubercular coughs to no one but Ma Belle.

"I hurt." The young man in her clinic with a colostomy bag for his collapsed colon bent in pain. Belle prepared him for the reality that he might have cancer. His thoughts became scattered out of fear of soiling himself. She leaned down close, letting her breath touch the face of the frightened man. "Don't let your bags run out," she whispered. "When you get down to five or six, go out for more."

She sends them all cards at Christmas so that they know they have a friend on the outside. They would not be in an SRO if they had family who wanted to hear from them. Many fear going into the menacing streets to fill their prescriptions. Belle goes for them, and gives them their flu shots, and goes over with them the instructions on their hospital appointment slips. Some, perhaps 10 percent, she can "bring over to my side," meaning they will osmose enough will to leave the comforting anarchy of the SRO and try to take hold in a world where people cook on a stove of their own. She gives some a little push, opening bank accounts for them and saving their money until there is enough for them to rent their own place. Most cannot be taken that far.

Most she helps simply by being there, every week, to see the broken wings for whom the best bargain to be struck with life is a gentle fall downward, with someone watching, seeing to it that they change the colostomy bag before hitting bottom.

"She found me," said Annie the blind woman, who had stopped going to clinics when hospital aides let her fall off an open van. "The people in these buildings love Ma Belle—they need to be guided or they'd go into their rooms and sit down and die." Annie said she wished she had planted a picture of Miss Belle in her mind right then, five years ago, when she could still see a little. What was her picture of Miss Belle now? I asked her. Annie the blind woman described a nice tall fat lady with a face like a dark moon and sad sweet eyes. She was dead accurate.

Perhaps nowhere is our existence more fully affirmed than when reflected in another human face. With an efficiency that would put most therapists to shame, Belle Cogdell animates her followers by looking into their souls and making them feel seen. To make reciprocal the needs of the culture and the individual's need for some form of transcendence, a stake must be offered in the society to women like Belle Cogdell. Of an age to be released from mothering their own children, of indigenous gifts but no formal credentials, the entrée to a purpose in the community is through jobs as paraprofessionals. Under the politics of austerity, such "exotic" services are being cut. Mental-health services must go. Many community health centers must go. Ma Belle must go.

Annie the blind woman articulated the feeling of Belle's flock. "All the bellyaching you hear on the TV about mental patients walking the streets, but when they got somethin' beautiful going like this, the government's got to close it up so things can get bad again so they can have a watchacallit—an investigation."

Annie pounded her cane on the clinic floor. "They should know that Ma Belle is a godsend."

New Territory for the Religious Caretaker

A more formally religious pathfinder was suggested to me by one of the pivotal Americans in a major western city. But this was a man who had dropped the formality in favor of putting his faith into active service to a broader segment of humanity.

For a young Catholic boy who faces a decision on entering the priesthood, it is strongly stressed that the correct attitude is not "Okay, let me try this out for a while." At the age of 18 then, the man we shall call Keith Buckley* entered wholeheartedly into the thirteen-year Jesuit training program. He had identified strongly with the young Jesuit trainees who were his teachers.

"They demonstrated a kind of altruism that appealed to me. It wasn't a very sophisticated altruism, and nothing like going to a leper colony—in fact, the Jesuits lived well and ministered mostly to the upper-middle class. But there was always the promise that you would be called upon to do something great," he described.

He enjoyed the companionship of intellectually compatible people. The regimentation must have appealed to him as well, for he followed it without difficulty. When the time came to take his final vows, he was 32. At that point the vow of celibacy did not trouble him.

"Everybody has one kind of trouble with celibacy—you don't have a disappearance of sexuality as such. It's how one handles it emotionally and psychologically that counts. You sublimate. And since you have a very strong motivation to sublimate, you don't put yourself in situations where you have close contact with women."

A more serious question came up later, when he was ten years older but still sailing through life insulated from criticism and practically immune to failure, owing to membership in the brotherhood of Jesuits. After a year of teaching at a fine Jesuit university, order began to break down there as it did on campuses everywhere—it was 1968. The president did not know how to deal with student revolutionaries.

* A pseudonym.

One day Keith Buckley received a call from the provincial of the Jesuits' western province.

"I'm appointing you president of the graduate university next year," he said.

"That's crazy." Father Buckley tried to persuade his superior that he had no experience with mediating in a polarized situation.

"Well, I'm ordering you to do it."

For three years, the worst years on campuses, Keith Buckley rode as if bareback the bucking horse of student dissent and faculty resentment, attempting at every turn to resist tergiversations. One never knew when a bomb might go off; he was painfully aware of being unable to protect his flock.

"I think I favored the revolutionaries much too much," he said in retrospect. "I found that leaders of the black students I'd been dealing with, in what I felt was a very positive way, were actually out to get me. That hurt a lot."

A trustee of another graduate theological school visited him one day and asked if Father Buckley would be interested in standing for the presidency of his institution. "I saw it as an escape," he described. "I went to the trustees at my university and told them I was being considered for the presidency of another institution, and that if they voted to approve me, I would accept. The trustees of my university called a closed meeting, and I offered my resignation. There was an argument between members of the board, who split down the middle for and against me. They went into closed session for six hours."

When they came out, Father Buckley's resignation had been accepted. For reasons that remain unknown but with a result that abraded the tenderest of his ties to the brotherhood, some of his Jesuit colleagues declined to vote for him. The next day the other theological school was to hold its vote. A storm of protest arose from students and faculty who, *sui generis* to the times, were hypersensitive about being consulted on every decision. At the risk of walking into another badly divided situation, Keith Buckley told the chairman of that board, before it voted, that he could not accept.

"The upshot was, I lost two presidencies in two days! I didn't feel I'd gone wrong, but that there were forces rejecting me over which I had no control. This was the first rejection I had ever experienced." Quite extraordinary, for a man of 42. "I pretended to a certain amount of insouciance about it all, but it really did hurt me. The rejection by the Jesuits bothered me greatly. That was the group I felt I had given my life to."

Only later, when the emotion had neutralized somewhat, was Father Buckley able to accept what his intellect told him: when one assumes any position of authority, it is irrational to expect not to make enemies. But at that time he was stung into numbness.

"I handled it the way I had all my great losses—the death of my father and my grandfather. I didn't acknowledge them. I denied them." His feelings about the two men, as a result, were both intense and exaggerated. He had turned away from his father as a man of no spiritual depth. "He was a person who lived on the surface of things, and I was always afraid that side of him would become evident in me. That if I stepped away from formal religious commitment and practice, I would become as uncommitted as my father was." His grandfather, by contrast, served as an ideal of wise and gentle equanimity, whose gift was for "bringing peace to troubled waters."

As it turned out, the fact that Keith Buckley had never mourned his grandfather or accepted that part in himself that was reflective of his father slowed his emancipation from crisis and into full adulthood for several more years.

He did take action, in the midst of his crisis of failure, to open up another avenue for work that would reestablish his self-respect. He called the former chancellor of the university's medical school and asked if he could lend himself to the new health policy program. The medical school was delighted to welcome him as a visiting professor for the following year.

That year marked the separation phase of his midlife passage. Although he continued to reside at the seminary, where some of the Jesuits who had rejected his presidency also lived, he seldom left the university before nine or ten at night. Physically separated from his religious brothers for the first time since he was 18, he also began to wear lay clothes for the first time as an adult. People began to address him as Dr. Buckley instead of Father Buckley. And while these tangible perforations from his former identity were in progress, the board of another fine Jesuit university across the country elected him its chairman. He would have the boost of flying coast to coast every month between two institutions where he was accepted and could be successful.

"The year passed very well. In the spring the dean of the med school announced he was opening a position for a professor of ethics, the first in the country within a department of medicine. He asked for me. So I became a regular, full faculty appointee. And even though I would turn it back to the order, they had to pay me. I was even more independent."

Like the woman who goes back to school in her forties and becomes capable of supporting herself for the first time, he knew now, even if unconsciously, that he *could* leave.

"By the end of that year, I felt very stable but with much less of a tie with my Jesuit brethren. The physical signs of my Jesuit identity were no longer present. I began to realize I didn't know them anymore."

Before assuming his assistant professorship, Dr. Buckley took what amounted to a six-month moratorium as a visiting scholar at a distant prep school. It served as a tonic in every way—including his first close relationship with a woman. In his office worked an administrative assistant who was strong, concerned about the same issues that engaged him, gently intelligent, and had the most beautifully deep blue eyes he had ever seen. Having worked around Jesuits for many years, Mary Dunne kept a friendly distance. One day, toward the end of their working association, Dr. Buckley asked her to an afternoon concert. It was the first time he had ever asked a woman out. (As for his sexual education, it amounted to having read *Ulysses*.) To his surprise, Miss Dunne agreed to go. At the end of a pleasant afternoon, she asked him home to join her and her parents for supper.

"In the course of the next few weeks," Keith Buckley remembers, "I reflected a lot on that day."

While one line of affection was weakening, another began to grow. It was during this six-month incubation period, Dr. Buckley later realized, that a complete change of his identity had taken place in a very quiet, easy way. "By the end of that six months, when I returned the following January, I felt almost no emotional association with the Jesuits anymore. But strangely enough, I hadn't said to myself, 'I am going to quit.'"

It was not until the following summer that the first consideration of actually leaving the order arose. By that time the law of the church had been changed to make that a realistic possibility; much of the discrimination against former priests had eased. Having decided that the time had come to think explicitly and seriously about risking this dramatic change of path, Keith Buckley flew to a Jesuit retreat house on the New England coast. He did not know the exact connection, but the time had also come, he sensed, to mourn his idealized grandfather and to reconsider his frivolous father.

"I set myself to meditate precisely on these things, to do as deep a self-analysis as I could do. I spent nine days in the retreat house alone. Absolutely alone. Talked to nobody. I'd have dinner with the others there, but in silence. Once a day I would talk to a counselor just to have somebody to bounce things off of. The Jesuits have a book called *The Exercises* of St. Ignatius Loyola, the founder, who devised the system of self-analysis when he himself underwent a change from soldier to monk. The exercises say there should always be a counselor to confer with daily—someone who shares your value system rather than the absolutely value-free psychiatrist.

"I made a rule that I would follow any line of thought that came to me. That led me along a lot of paths that I'd not entered before, some I didn't even know were there. One thing came up very, very clearly in my mind: I was not in the right place any longer. I wanted to leave."

The mourning for his grandfather became cathartic. He understood that in modeling himself after that gentle mediator, he was doomed to failure in a polarized situation such as the university presidency, where it had been impossible for him, for almost anyone at that time, to reconcile differences. But more important than forgiving himself for that failure was accepting the fun-loving part of his father in himself. These levels of discernment and acceptance were necessary before he could separate from his old life.

"What I could say when I came out at the end was: 'The decision that I'm making is a decision which will not turn me from being a good man into being a bad man.'"

When he came back from retreat, instead of housing his faith in organized religious associations, he opened it out into a secular application that reflected an even broader faith in humankind.

His new channel, medical ethics, provides a philosophical analysis of the moral problems arising in medicine. It thrilled him to be among the first generation of idea guides in a new field, one that is concerned with the oldest questions of life and death in face of the newest technological breakthroughs. Should month-old premature newborns, for instance, who are now able to be sustained by a respirator, be maintained indefinitely if their physical development does not progress? What if prolonged breathing by respirator exposes them to almost certain brain damage? Should Siamese twins, or any child with a severe deformity, be given basic nourishment, or should it be allowed to die, if that is the parents' wish? Dr. Buckley grappled with the matter of how to make legally binding a patient's written instructions to his doctor in the case of terminal illness. He helped to draft the legislation on that issue passed by his state and went on to counsel other citizens' groups. Shortly thereafter he was appointed to the President's Commission for the Study of Ethical Problems in Medicine, where his broadened scope enabled him to achieve national exposure for the idea of the "living will." His latest concentration has been a research project that examines the ethics of government-subsidized heart transplants for indigent patients.

Although he had been ill suited to sorting out the grays in a polarized political situation, Keith Buckley seems made for setting out the fine distinctions inherent today in living and dying.

He has entered uncharted territory in his private life as well. After writing a letter to the pope in which he asked to be released from the order, he called Mary Dunne. She was the first person he told. When he was free, he said, he would like to see her, if she felt the same way. She said yes. When his dispensation came through, just before Christmas in the first year of his appointment as an assistant professor, he was jubilant.

"The barriers were down. I was a free man. And there was nothing 'outlaw' about getting together with Mary." They honeymooned in Barbados.

"Was that your first sexual experience?" I asked Keith Buckley later.

"Yes."

"Were you nervous?"

"No."

Is Happiness Unlimited Narcissism?

The science of ethics is an adjunct, if not an alternative, to religion. It incorporates the study of values. The very fact that Keith Buckley had been engrossed for so many years both intellectually and emotionally in the mysteries of religion prepared him brilliantly for that new territory, one that is uncomfortably divvied up at present among several disciplines.

The adoption of "value-free" scientific methodology, however, has become the preferred model for almost all academic inquiry. Perhaps nowhere is this more noticeable than in the field of psychology.

Psychology was once a subdiscipline within the academic realm of philosophy. Eager to "scientize" their status, investigative psychologists began to insist that only those elements of behavior that can be counted, and therefore replicated in later experiments, offer worthwhile results. The human personality itself, of course, cannot be replicated from one day to the next. The mind with its craters of memory and the dark side of its unconscious, along with the imprint of daily events and human relations, makes minute adjustments in the settings of an individual's values all the time. Indeed, the whole counting game is practiced by people who are themselves weighted with their own values and cultural baggage, role assumptions, religious and ethical biases. It therefore troubled me to read psychological literature limited to such mechanical measurements as Optimal Adjustment and Coping Scores, *chi* squares, and Cramer's V.

Hard science would dwindle into the haphazard unless guided by a theory that determines what counts as relevant fact. Yet when investigators G. Gregg[1] and associates surveyed forty years of social science research, they unearthed the "simplistic, fragmented, and nontheoretical nature" of much of the enterprise. It was rare to find research, even on race relations or juvenile delinquency, that was guided by anything approaching a grand theory. Most of the investigations were limited to simple, single levels of analysis of data, with primary attention to technique. Gregg and his group predicted no change in the shape of social science in the next twenty years.

This emphasis is further exacerbated by the practice of psychiatry, which places far more weight on the benefits of concern with the self than on social participation. This is the opposite of the balance between inner and outer expansion that we see among pathfinders.

I took this observation to Geissen, Germany, to Dr. Horst Richter, pioneer in psychosomatic medicine, who surprised me with a summary of Freud's position on the matter. In *Civilization and Its Discontents* Freud portrayed the person with the best technique for living as one who adapts to what is, who does not attempt to change it. The man of action squanders his energies in a vain onslaught upon all-powerful reality, but "the more self-sufficient narcissistic type of individual will seek the major satisfactions in his inner spiritual experiences."[2]

Freud favored passive acceptance of the status quo; the primary rewards of life were to be derived from narcissistic pursuits and inner, psychic fulfillment. He argued that a state of transcendence—"oneness with the universe"—is derived from a return to the unity of early childhood. He called this a "restoration of limitless narcissism." Freud rejected as unhealthy and virtually hopeless any adaptation through challenging political reality, taking on a social purpose, or trying to change things. One might say that he paved the way for the rush to self-fulfillment. An exclusive concern with self runs directly counter to the evidence that emerged from my research: the consistent finding that the highest-satisfaction people were devoted to some cause or purpose beyond themselves.

If Freud had had his way, we might have benefited by few of the pathfinders in this book.

Where psychology and philosophy come together is precisely at this critical issue of finding "meaning and direction" in one's life. People who have reached well-being require a clear purpose beyond themselves in order to sustain that well-being. If this premise is accepted, it would seem imperative that we begin to construct a philosophy of adult development.

Part III

DARK HOURS

They were skiing in Sun Valley when out of the blue, April Johnson felt a numbness in her fingertips. The third diagnosis confirmed multiple sclerosis. "How could my body do this to me!" she railed. "I've always taken great care of myself."

"What do you think of the idea of boycotting the Olympics?"

Al Oerter, making a comeback at the age of 42 to go for a fifth Olympic gold medal, looked at the NBC sportscaster uncomprehendingly.

"Boycott?" Anger exploded in his gut. Disbelief. "No way! I'm going to throw."

At 28, right on schedule, Meredith married. Her strategic plan, for stepping off the treadmill to have children and hopping back on without losing her place in the race for top management slots in corporate America, was going fine. Six months later, Meredith's husband received a splendid offer in Australia. All Meredith's "systems" suddenly were on the blink.

By now it should be clear that pathfinders are not magically shielded from surprise bumps in the road. All the anticipation in the world cannot protect us from the accidents of life.

In the course of nine years of studying adult behavior, I have learned to distinguish between the predictable crises of life—those that initiate a new stage in the life cycle—and another kind of transition, which I have called a life accident. That is an event we are virtually powerless to predict or to prevent—the loss of someone we love to a premature death, a forced separation, sudden divorce, illness, abandonment, the house burning down, the economy falling out of bed. To paraphrase John Lennon, life's accidents are what happen to us while we are making other plans.

In observing over those nine years the ways in which many different people react to life accidents, I also have come to this conclusion: a terrible blow to the body or to the ego does not automatically make one "a better person." On the contrary, at first that blow usually drives us back into using more primitive defenses; we become less willing than ever to dream or to risk. But if enduring the dark hours does not break us or freeze us in place, it eventually may make us pathfinders.

13.

COPING
AND
MOURNING

Sometimes they are personal, and sometimes they are cultural, these unpredictable accidents of life. Bingo Doyle ran up against a Supreme Court order on forced busing that threatened to tear apart his neighborhood with violence. Al Oerter's comeback hopes were dashed by events half a world away in Afghanistan. When government policy favored fighting inflation with unemployment, people with jobs they believed were secure found layoff slips in their pay envelopes.

"Even though you've been working short shifts for months," one auto worker told me, "you never believe it when it happens to you."

When a parent or a spouse dies at an advanced age, when a couple finally calls a halt to a progressively deteriorating marriage, the loss is grave, but the event is at least anticipated. It lacks the shock felt by, say, a 33-year-old woman with four children who picks up the phone two days before Christmas and hears that her husband has been killed in a freak accident.

"I lost twenty pounds in the first six weeks and had no taste for anything," Julia Walsh recounted. "Everybody goes through that. Then I got my act together, and in three months I came back in full bloom." Julia was confident that her old techniques would work for her. They were the coping devices with which people of high well-being most commonly react to a rough passage or a period of uncertainty: work more, depend on friends, keep a sense of humor, pray.

Using each of the key pathfinder coping skills, Julia channeled her grief into work, boldly entering an all-male school. A friend rallied his associates to help her. As with many pathfinders, her own good-sport humor made her more attractive to those who did offer help. And being a strong Catholic, she found considerable comfort in prayer.

But all the skills in the pathfinders' armamentarium were not enough. Eighteen months after she lost her husband, Julia Walsh's "act"—as she accurately called it—fell apart. The physical drain of expending so much manic energy in a largely unconscious effort to avoid grieving ultimately caused her to collapse, exhausted.

When the ego is not strong enough to endure a loss or failure, defense mechanisms mobilize to protect it from disintegration.[1] These defense mechanisms are different from the protective strategies that healthy people use during times of "normal" stress, strategies identified by George Vaillant, professor of psychiatry at Harvard Medical School, as "mature." The five healthy strategies Vaillant describes are anticipation, altruism, suppression, sublimation, and humor.[2]

Protective Strategies

Anticipation we have already noted as one of the qualities that distinguish pathfinders. That is, they prepare themselves for future needs and anticipate future discomforts.

Altruism is also familiar as a quality of pathfinders, most of whom have a cause or purpose beyond themselves. As a coping device, altruism—being of service to others—not only takes one's mind off the problem but also shores up the ego by making one feel like a good person.

Suppression is postponement. When a person makes a conscious or semiconscious decision to put off acting on an impulse produced by conflict, he does recognize that the insult to his ego has occurred. And he does feel the emotions the event normally generates. But he suppresses action that might be inappropriate or self-destructive. He does not throw the punch, but the next day expresses his anger in a letter to the editor. She does not give up trying to succeed as a landscape designer because the old-time gardeners make fun of her; she suppresses the impulse to lash out, which would lose her what little cooperation she does get from her tormentors. She uses that energy to land a client the gardeners cannot afford to turn down.

Although the words are only a few letters apart, there is a crucial difference between suppression and repression. When a person cannot bear to face an emotion and *represses* it, a whole tract of mental landscape is submerged and may not come back to consciousness for weeks or months or years. When people face an emotion they do not know how to handle and *suppress* it—"I'll think about that tomorrow"—they *think* about it tomorrow.

Suppression is also the foundation for deferred gratification. It is a strategy that offers a grab bag of variations, one of the more common of which is sublimation.

Sublimation channels raw instincts, rather than damming them up or visiting them on a target in a way that will backfire. Sublimating by working harder is the pathfinder's first line of defense when facing problems that cannot be resolved immediately. Sublimation is also the fierce game of tennis or the furious concentration on a crossword puzzle—letting off steam or applying the mind to problems that *can* be solved. Sublimation is part of what draws people into the performing arts. As dancer Claudia Asbury described her motives to *New York Times* reporter Suzanne Daley, "The bank screwed up your account or a taxi almost ran over you. Well, you get to the theater and you have to put all that away. It's a different world because you're performing . . . it's almost a relief to get to the theater. I think that's probably why people perform even when they're sick or injured."[3] An act of creativity may represent the sublimation of powerful instincts or emotions into the shaping of art.

Humor, probably the most purely intellectual defense, has been extolled for centuries. Descartes made it an article of his philosophy: "Modest bantering . . . gives evidence of the gaiety of his temper and the tranquility of his soul." At a meeting of the first class of women to survive Harvard Law School, the alumnae generally agreed that their best defense continues to be "humor, with a fast exit—over and out." Humor, like hope, allows one to acknowledge and endure what is otherwise unendurable.

Each of these strategies permits a person to recognize the existence of an unpleasant reality and to accept it. But, as Vaillant warns, under increased stress these strategies may deteriorate into more desperate and self-destructive defenses. A life accident is just that sort of stress.

Even a combination of altruism, sublimation, and humor will not work for you if your child dies in an airplane crash, if you learn that your fifty-year-old father has had a stroke, if your mate announces he or she is leaving you. A shock considerably less severe also may prompt us to dip into the bag of potentially more dangerous defenses. When first reeling under a grave accidental blow, we have little control over which defense mechanism we use; our unconscious makes the choice. But we can exert some control over how long we use it.

Cinderella with a Second Act

The Susanna Cary* I met in 1976 was a public-relations lady. Where had I seen her before? She had a pair of saucer eyes and a slender silhouette that no one could forget. It came out that in her old life, as Susanna Page, movie actress, she had played a character who was part of American legend, in a television series. Here she was, turning up at the age of 45 as a real person, who had an entirely different career and who walked with a cane. She was always so busy giving out-of-towners pleasure by driving them up into Hollywood Hills to see the lights, or dragging around overweight male clients who probably would not have noticed if she fell off the Scenic Overlook, that one tended to forget she was crippled. Oh, every now and then she would crack a joke about "staggering around" while everyone else had to wait for her. But in practice, Susanna Cary was usually out in front of everyone else, not that anyone minded—Susanna's friends were more than willing to catch up with her.

We had been friends for three years before I asked her about her life accident.

"It was a creeping accident," she explained, "one I ignored for a long time. It began to manifest itself in a kind of genius

* A pseudonym.

I had for tripping over anything on the sidewalk—a pebble, a matchstick. . . ."

She had been hit with several bouts of flu that winter, and the third time, completely out of character, she took to her bed for a week. Susanna was then only 34. When she got up, she was aware of an almost imperceptible tingling in her limbs. One foot dragged just a little. It was as if the pin that started the whole process of muscles firing was a little off.

Her husband-to-be kidded her. "C'mon, Stumbles," he would say.

"Okay, okay, I'm coming." Having had a mild bout of polio as a child, she was used to coordination that could not always be relied upon. That made the funny feeling easy to ignore.

"After a couple of years, I got around to stumbling, clinging to strangers on the street, holding up buildings, and not feeling very secure," she recalled. "I knew I couldn't be an actress and not walk."

Without a word, she left the set of the last TV episode of that spring season, knowing she would never be back. That fall Susanna Page Cary became what she jokingly referred to as a "housewife's decorator." She let it be known among her friends. Soon she had lots of clients, and she was having fun.

"It was a tremendous bridge," she described. "I recognized very quickly that the client was the star. Putting oneself in the background and letting the other person talk was altogether different from being an actress. And it wasn't my taste that was important, it was theirs. I began to enjoy enormously thinking about how other people thought, what would please them."

Meanwhile, the "accident" crept along and her recognition of it crept along apace.

"There is obviously something very wrong," her husband said at last, after three years. He asked Susanna to let him take a home movie of her, had her put on a bathing suit and walk around the pool. Confronted with her strange gait in the film, Susanna said, "Okay, okay, I'll see a doctor."

But "it" had no name. Doctors believed she probably had contracted meningitis as a child along with the polio. The bout of viral flu in adulthood had moved in and attacked what was already damaged. The sheath covering her nerve endings was disintegrating. Whatever "it" was, it seemed to have run its course and reached a plateau.

She bought a cane, mainly, she told herself, as a prop —"so people wouldn't think I was some dipsomaniac reeling toward them." She never accepted help—"I'm fine, I can manage"—and with a fierce independence she focused those saucer eyes on a point in a restaurant, or a hassock at a party, and willed herself to walk alone. At other times she relied on her clownish facility. "I'd never thought of myself as a beauty. I've just always had 'good bones.' But I was tiny and scrawny and I talked a lot—so what's different now? Only that I look slightly demented when I walk across a room."

A year later, at 41, she had a "simple" mastectomy.

"You mention that as if it were a little hiccup on the side," I interrupted as Susanna talked.

"Endowed as I am in that department," she said, "it *was* like a hiccup. I suggested to the hospital they give me half-price."

"So you joked your way through that one."

"Yep. Came home exhausted from playing Carol Burnett for ten days."

The hospital did not get the joke, but her husband appreciated it. It was a tension breaker. "He's covered with so many wounds and scars from his life that I don't think this bothered him," Susanna said. He took great pains to reassure her right from the beginning. "Even before I went into the hospital, he gave me a beautiful nightgown and a peignoir to match, with very soft construction on top, so I could wear it before and after and not look any different."

Shortly after her operation, Susanna joined a public-relations firm, and a few years later she was running the public-relations department of a major television station. As head of press relations, she found herself tapped one day to read the on-camera editorial. She became a permanent fixture. It was a perfect slot for a brainy and beautiful lady who talks a lot but does not get around much anymore.

So, what was her secret?

"The secret, if there is one, is the Scarlett O'Hara technique—thinking about it tomorrow," she said. "To some degree, that's destructive. On the other hand, a lot of what Scarlett coped with, and accomplished, was a direct result of the ability so shove under the carpet what she didn't have the means to cope with. If you have a concept of what your tolerance is, you're making some kind of calculated decision about the art of the possible. And if you're dealing with the art of the possible, in most cases you'll be dealing constructively. If there's any kind of pattern, that's what it is."

She never mentioned the pain. When I asked her about it, she admitted it was still there every day. "It's tantamount to what happens when you break an ankle and while you're wearing the cast, you ache all over because your body is being used in a lopsided, awkward way." But she emphasized again that her life accident had been a cumulative one. "I had time to adjust to it, to 'rehearse' it, to incorporate it."

At the end of our talk, Susanna drove me to my hotel. As she slid into her sports car, her skirt hiked up to show an exceptionally pretty pair of knees. I kidded her about masquerading as a cripple when she had the best-looking legs around.

"It amuses me to see that I'm now wearing skirts again," she said. "It must mean I think of myself as a feminine person and not totally ugly."

There were other aspects of her accident that she still did not permit herself to think about too often or too deeply. Because "it" had begun almost simultaneously with her marriage, she realized it had been a life accident for her husband, too. "His lady is not someone who can go galloping up and down a beach with him. Life tricked us both. I used to have bad moments of thinking, 'I am not all the divine things that I was perfectly secure about being when I met him.'"

And she still has bad days. "This morning I overslept and had more things to do than I should have. I couldn't get my body to move as fast as I wanted it to, so I was in a snit and I spilled the cereal bowl—full—all over the floor. That's when I have to stand back and say, 'Susanna, you're absurd. Now, pull your socks up and let's get in the car,' and pretty soon, the mind will take over."

Her affliction was not aggravating, she said, unless she let it be. And sometimes she let it be. "But most of the time my focus is on something ahead of me—on a task, an idea, a person who needs help."

As Susanna Cary dropped me off, she said she could not imagine what I might find to write about from our talk. As far as she was concerned, she had come up with one good line in the whole four hours:

"It's very tough to play Hamlet when you keep seeing the joke."

Would You Know a Healthy Defense If You Saw One?

It is quite true that the more abruptly a life accident hits, the more ill prepared we are to handle it and the more likely we are to fall back on extreme defenses, at least temporarily. It also is evident that Susanna Cary had a particularly supportive husband, a comfortable home, a plan, a career, and an effortless sense of humor. With ready access to healthy protective strategies, she was able to retain considerable equilibrium by working more, depending on friends, and seeing the humor in the situation.

She also made the most of these "mature" defenses. Sublimation worked for her during the long period when she had no answers for her own physical problems. She took up other people's decorating puzzles instead, interesting problems that she *could* solve. Later, when doctors had no clear diagnosis for "it," Susanna turned her mind to figuring out the logistics and the theatrics of putting forward the best foot for her public-relations clients—an occupation that in a sprawling, promotion-soaked city like Los Angeles offers more vexatious entertainment than playing chess with a computer.

A warm circle of friends was something that Susanna had worked on building before her accident. But her efforts to expand that circle and to keep in close touch with distant friends increased noticeably after "it" began to restrict her movements. Lacking the legs to visit people often, Susanna began using her telephone wires like a giant pool sweep, making ripples all over the country.

Like most pathfinders, being more given to action than to introspection, Susanna Cary probably would never think of activities that came so naturally to her as "protective strategies," nor would she articulate their necessity to her well-being. It would scarcely occur to any of the people described in this book to say, "Gee, I've got a degenerative disease. I guess I'd better call Jane and Jim and Joanie and get my friendship network going strong again." Yet pathfinders, as we have discovered, do have a knack for drawing from the environment what they need. It probably is instinctive with them to replenish their friendships and try to replace those interrupted by circumstance. Continuing to be concerned with how one's friends' lives are going, even while going through dark hours oneself, represents another of those victories over self-preoccupation that we have come to associate with successful pathfinding.

But even with her sheath of healthy protective strategies, Susanna Cary reached during the first years of her "creeping" accident for more hazardous weapons to defend herself from facing the full reality. Outright denial—simply refusing to acknowledge what is readily perceptible to anyone else—worked for her for nearly three of those years. So devastating was the possibility that "it" might be progressive, totally paralyzing, even fatal, that her ego apparently willed these thoughts out of mind. She could walk away from her acting career without a word if it meant that she could postpone a little longer having to go to a doctor and hear the grim news.

Crossing far over the line from the protective strategies of suppression and sublimation, which allow one to accept the truth, she had helped herself to repressive defenses, which prompt one to deny reality. The simplest distinction would be:

Suppression (mature): "It bothers me like hell, but there's nothing I can do about it right now, so I'll try to take my mind off it and keep functioning in the meantime."

Repression (neurotic): "What gunshot wound? Things like that don't bother me at all."

In real life, however, the line between what is unhealthy, and what is possible for a person's mental survival under circumstances of severe stress, is not nearly so precise. Susanna Cary described reaching a middle ground. After her husband prodded her to face the truth, she was able to begin making calculated decisions about how many of the implications of her accident she could face and cope with constructively, and how many she had to continue to repress. I like her notion of relying on the "art of the possible," a form of personal diplomacy through which any of us might become more innovative in mediating between our conscious and unconscious mental processes.

The important thing to be aware of is what kind of defenses we are using, what they are doing for us, and how long we should allow ourselves to rely on them before we try, either by ourselves or with help, to wean ourselves. If Susanna Cary had denied the lump in her breast as assiduously as she denied her viral disease, or if the latter had been life-threatening without treatment, she would not be telling many jokes today.

Desperate Measures

Technically speaking, all defense mechanisms are neurotic. They are unconscious thought processes that redirect an emotion. Simply, the emotion that belongs to one event or idea is detached from its source and left to float (as in free-floating anxiety) or is reattached to some other idea or object, as when one lashes out at a family member after having suffered some humiliation at work. That concept of unconscious thought processes, introduced as revolutionary a hundred years ago, was perhaps the most original contribution of Sigmund Freud.[4] Since Freud's treatise, other theorists, including his daughter, Anna Freud, have elaborated greatly on the basic defense mechanisms and have conceptualized new ones.

Most theorists speak of denial, regression, projection, repression, and reaction formation. If those terms sound familiarly fuzzy, you would find the psychiatric literature even more confusing. The experts disagree on what are the major defense mechanisms, what they do, which are normal and which are neurotic, and when—to wit, the chart on the facing page.

In *repression*, the grandaddy of defenses, the conscious mind jettisons into the moonscape of the unconscious an instinct or an idea or an emotional response that is unacceptable. We have already met a form of repression—the happyface syndrome, a primary defense used by women and minorities. As a temporary measure when we find ourselves

MECHANISMS OF DEFENSE ACCEPTED BY MORE THAN ONE THEORIST

	A. Freud	E. Hinsie	O. Fenichel	N. Haan	G. Vaillant	R. Lazarus
REPRESSION	A. Freud	E. Hinsie	O. Fenichel	N. Haan	G. Vaillant	R. Lazarus
PROJECTION	A. Freud	E. Hinsie	O. Fenichel	N. Haan	G. Vaillant	R. Lazarus
REACTION FORMATION	A. Freud	E. Hinsie	O. Fenichel	N. Haan	G. Vaillant	R. Lazarus
DISPLACEMENT	A. Freud	E. Hinsie	O. Fenichel	N. Haan	G. Vaillant	R. Lazarus
ISOLATION	A. Freud	E. Hinsie	O. Fenichel	N. Haan	G. Vaillant	R. Lazarus
DENIAL		E. Hinsie	O. Fenichel	N. Haan	G. Vaillant	R. Lazarus
RATIONALIZATION	A. Freud	E. Hinsie	O. Fenichel	N. Haan		R. Lazarus
REGRESSION		E. Hinsie	O. Fenichel	N. Haan		R. Lazarus
IDENTIFICATION	A. Freud	E. Hinsie		N. Haan		R. Lazarus
INTELLECTUALIZING		E. Hinsie				R. Lazarus
SUBLIMATION (called normal)	A. Freud	E. Hinsie	O. Fenichel	N. Haan		R. Lazarus

MECHANISMS OF DEFENSE NAMED BY ONLY ONE THEORIST

	A. Freud	E. Hinsie	O. Fenichel	N. Haan	G. Vaillant	R. Lazarus
TURNING AGAINST THE SELF	A. Freud					
REVERSAL	A. Freud					
CONDENSATION		E. Hinsie				
TRANSFERENCE		E. Hinsie				
SYMBOLIZATION AND TRANSPOSITION		E. Hinsie				
CONVERSION		E. Hinsie				
FANTASY		E. Hinsie				
DAYDREAMING		E. Hinsie				
POSTPONEMENT OF AFFECTS			O. Fenichel			
AFFECT EQUIVALENTS			O. Fenichel			
CHANGE IN THE QUALITY OF AFFECTS			O. Fenichel			
DOUBT				N. Haan		
SCHIZOID FANTASIES					G. Vaillant	
HYPOCHONDRIASIS					G. Vaillant	
PASSIVE-AGGRESSIVE BEHAVIOR					G. Vaillant	
ACTING OUT					G. Vaillant	
DISSOCIATION					G. Vaillant	

There are many other theorists on defense mechanisms. This list represents the following: Anna Freud, *The Ego and the Mechanisms of Defense* (London: Hogarth, 1948); E. Hinsie, *Visual Outline of Psychiatry* (New York: Oxford University Press, 1940); O. Fenichel, *The Psychoanalytic Theory of Neurosis* (London: Hogarth, 1948); Norma Haan, *Coping and Defending: Processes of Self-Environment Organization* (New York: Academic Press, 1977); G. E. Vaillant, *Adaptation to Life* (Boston: Little Brown, 1977); Richard S. Lazarus and Alan Monat, *Personality* (Englewood Cliffs, N.J.: Prentice-Hall, 1979).

up against negative circumstances we cannot, or dare not, oppose, repression can be useful.

A man has been passed over for a promotion. He represses his anger and dismay so that he can function well enough to get a new job. But carried on for too long, repression numbs almost all sensation. The same man retreats into auto-hypnotic television watching, becomes obsessed with spectator sports or with his diet and digestion. He finally achieves a squidlike state: colorless and rubbery, hard to hurt or even to reach. What is happening? His ego is fearful it will not be able to defend itself in conflict, or is apprehensive about the potentially disastrous consequences of releasing even a fraction of his rage. So his mind represses the wound to his ego and in the bargain cauterizes most other raw ends of feeling he still has. So astringent is repression that it shuts off pathways to other emotions. And once that is done, he no longer even knows what he wants. It may be that the other defense mechanisms are used only to complete what repression has left undone, as Anna Freud has observed.

Intellectualization, a form of repression described by Jung, operates when a person tries to meet all the demands of living by using his rational mental skills, figuring out events, instead of responding with emotion to the feelings they engender.

Denial is an extreme form of repression and a protection almost all of us use at least briefly. "This can't be happening. I don't believe it." People who believe in a life after death can hardly be classified as neurotic, yet they do use denial to dismiss the possibility that death may indeed be final. In using denial as a defense against a life accident, the unconscious mind plays for time until the ego is ready to take over and deal with the new reality in a healthier way. Denial is psychotic when it becomes a continuing distortion of a demonstrated fact, such as telling the doctor it is impossible that you are pregnant because you have never had intercourse, or convincing yourself that your father is in Africa when actually he is dead.

Projection is a defense mechanism used to deal with unacceptable anger, either self-loathing or feelings of inferiority or rage felt toward someone else against whom anger may not be expressed safely. Instead, the anger is transferred to a relatively safe person or to an external situation. In its common forms, as earlier discussed, it is a favorite defense of men. In its extreme form, projection is paranoia; the paranoid makes everything and everybody but himself the problem.

Reaction formation is another of those desperate measures. In a pilot study of Right to Life members in the Cleveland area, a disproportionate number of the women were found to be childless, and in interviews by social psychologists many disclosed that they were unable to have children. Even those for whom this had meant losing their husbands to younger, fertile women seldom connected their politicization as Right to Life activists to their own tragic inability to create life. Connections so hurtful are usually repressed. The unconscious reaction formation is for the woman to defend against that unendurably painful reality by throwing herself obsessively into an activity that forces on others a duty that she herself is incapable of performing. A healthier adaptation for such a woman would be to admit the painful reality and then to throw her energies into caring in some way for the already born and neglected children of the world.

The danger with the defense mechanisms, short of ending in psychosis because they remove a person utterly from reality, is that their prolonged use stunts development. The mechanisms are not precise; they cannot isolate a single problem or painful event and numb awareness of that alone. So they restrict the spontaneous functioning of personality in a gross way. It would be something like freezing your entire mouth with Novocain against the chance that you might be served soup too hot.

We are not in control when we resort to defense mechanisms, but it is fairly well accepted today that reliance on them is reversible. A major objective of psychoanalysis is to lift harmful repressions and channel the underlying impulses into constructive or creative pursuits.

The distortions produced by using any such defense mechanism over a period of years, as Vaillant points out, become part of a person's view of the world. "Truth too awful to bear is unconsciously altered or postponed; the altered truth then becomes subjectively true."[5]

How, then, do people survive life accidents without thwarting their future growth?

The Mourning Process

Although people generally associate mourning with death, some psychologists now suggest that mourning is the basis of the healing process that should follow any blow or loss characterizable as a life accident.

In his classic monograph *The Rites of Passage*,[6] published in 1908, anthropologist Arnold Van Gennep described major transitions that occur throughout the life cycle of people in primitive societies. Childhood initiation rites, betrothal, marriage, pregnancy, childbirth, and going off to war all were such transitions. Each was treated as something of a death change, and each required a preparatory period of mourning during which the individual parted with his or her old self and was transformed and revived as a new being, with a new inner identity to fit his new outer social role. Wrote Van Gennep, "The transition from one state to another is literally equivalent to giving up the old life and 'turning over a new leaf.' "

From her work with the terminally ill, Dr. Elisabeth Kübler-Ross identified five different phases of the mourning process: denial, anger, bargaining, depression, and acceptance.[7] When reacting to any life accident, we are likely to pass through many of the same mental states. Because volumes have been written on each of these conditions, I will review them only briefly before adding several steps to the process of mourning. It is through completing this process that the living can be not only annealed, but rendered broader, stronger, and more emotionally eloquent as people.

"Not me—I don't believe it" is an almost universal first response to the blow of a life accident. In a temporary state of shock, we may feel the need to crawl into a hole and lick our wounds. Requiring most of our energy simply to compensate for eating and sleeping poorly, we cannot expect to do much that is actively healing until that initial reactive period has spent itself. Ideally, the need to deny should subside after several weeks or months, depending on the severity of the accident. The longer we pretend that something once thought to be firmly possessed has *not* been lost—whether the loss is of love, health, youth, money, or an important person—the longer our own defenses may restrict us. Although it is common to return to denying the painful reality from time to time, the task that awaits us is to feel the weight of the strong emotions that underlie even the best performance of "I'm holding up just fine, thanks."

Anger almost inevitably flares up over a life accident at some point. *Why me? Why now?* One feels betrayed by life.

When a life accident cuts down someone loved, the survivors struggle with their own anger at circumstance, at God, sometimes even with the dying relative. The inexpressible but almost unavoidable sentiment is: *How could you do this to me?* Because anger is perceived under such circumstances to be inappropriate, it is often denied or otherwise repressed. What cannot be spoken aloud to other sufferers can, and probably should, be expressed to a trusted friend. To feel anger does not mean one is a bad person but a normal human being in great pain. When anger is not expressed in some way, it can turn into bitterness or a wad of self-pity—two particularly corrosive reactions. Bill Johnston described an actual physical sensation of self-pity after he quit his job and found that his health problems would prevent him from being hired elsewhere: "It felt like a heavy wet ball I carried around in the well of my abdomen."

Bitterness can render a person unable to function. One woman went through an episode of acute bitterness when, after a year of battling over a divorce settlement, her lawyers made a mistake and set back still further the date when she might receive any money at all.

"For three weeks I felt the bitterness like an acid, like the bitter gall the poets write about. I couldn't do any work, which was disastrous, since I had to make money to support the children." Consciously intervening after those first three weeks, she told herself, "You must stop feeling this way; you have to be able to function." She expressed her fury by allowing herself to complain at unusual length to friends; she sublimated the anger she still could not express by becoming obsessive about her own work and money-making endeavors.

Keeping anger bottled up after a life accident may cause us to fail at the next endeavor because we are stuck at that point in the medley of mourning emotions. It is not easy to form a new attachment to anything or anybody so long as our mental batteries continue to be drained by a negative charge. And to follow an accidental loss with a self-made failure, when our ego is already shaky or our support system damaged, only compounds the problems of recovery.

It is not outside events that heal us or bring us back. It is doing the tough repair work from the inside. Consulting our past behavior in a similar situation for guidance on where we may have misused defenses can only be helpful. Gradually, too, we must form a new inner image of ourselves that reflects the new outer reality—not a grim image, but one that casts us in a role that appeals to us in new ways. Julia Walsh, the widow, began to see herself as an adventurous stockbroker. Susanna Cary recast herself as a decorator.

It is worthwhile, too, to make the effort to understand our own contradictions. Most of us have mixed emotions about any life accident, and some of us wish for dual outcomes that are incompatible. The man who was fired, for example, wishes that he could have his dignity restored by being offered his job back, but he also wants to keep the new flexibility he enjoys by working for himself. Life accidents turn up the lights and make possible startling illuminations of our own behavior. Those insights can be translated into action. We may leave the dark hours made of far stronger stuff.

Bargaining is an effort to postpone such action. Dying patients, although theirs is an extreme illustration, make all sorts of promises to God to gain more time "for good behavior." When remission occurs, these promises are almost never kept, according to Kübler-Ross. But don't we all bargain with God or with our own consciences when something terrible happens?

Around three in the morning: "I'll never tell my daughter again that her boyfriend is a schnook—if only he gets her home from that party alive." Like each of the other emotional states that normally follow in the wake of a life accident, bargaining is useful, if it is transient. "I'm just taking a day at a time" may be the best temporary adaptation for a person under acute stress, but living for too long without anticipation makes it impossible to accept the new reality fully and to compose new goals that reflect it. To bargain too long on a day-to-day basis becomes a forfeit of control.

Because women have been so long and systematically trained to hide aggressive impulses, they are particularly prone to the unconscious abuse of repression as a response to anger, and thus particularly likely to slide into depression. From his vantage point at the psychiatric clinic of Northwestern University Medical School, psychologist David Gutmann has observed that many women appear to need to endure their own anger, in the form of depression, before they can own it, enjoy it, and use it constructively. Women may go into a period of mourning over the fear, or the actuality, of losing a sexual identity in their middle years, a persona on which they may have relied heavily for the sense of worth in earlier years. Underneath, they are furious at the theft of youthful attractiveness.

In many cases, the hospitalized mid-life woman can be seen as suffering a kind of token death in depression, as a prelude to her "rebirth" in a more active stance. The period of hospitalization can be seen as a kind of "lying-in," during which the patient, through much pain, gives birth to a new self.[8]

Depression is an almost necessary stage of the mourning process, for anyone. Often it appears, subsides, and later reappears in the course of mourning. Martha Lear, whose book *Heartsounds* is a moving account of her husband when his heart was attacked by American middle age,[9] described to me two years after his death the persistence of this thing we call mourning:

"This process is so strange. You think you're stable again—it's all accepted. Then the hit comes—out of the blue—you never know what will do it. And you feel yourself falling into a pit. The freshness of the pain is extraordinary. The intensity doesn't change. What happens is, those times come less often, and they don't last as long."

The initial depression usually is associated with the shattering of plans, links, assumptions—the sudden loss of an important limb of one's security. That early and paralyzing form of depression should lift quite remarkably after a time, sometimes abruptly, as if one had awakened one day measurably lighter, more buoyant, able again to go into the world. The resulting form of intermittent depression is hardly distinguishable from grief. And to do the work of grieving is the crux of the mourning process.

I watched a friend wrestle with the fierce grief she felt

when informed, secondhand, of the sudden death of her lover. Not included in the rituals of mourning available to the man's wife and family, she might have become morose and isolated with her "illegitimate" grief. But she was far too creative for that. Her shock and grief bubbled to the surface and mingled with a suddenly effervescent surge of love. Night after night, unable to sleep, she made the rounds of her friends, of whom she had many, telling stories of the romantic and hilarious adventures she and her lover had enjoyed. She had never seemed so animated. Her face was beautiful when she narrated their life together. The humor she was able to see in his failings as well as her own made the storytelling an unexpected treat for her listeners. She drank too much, but that seemed only to color her already heightened emotions with reds and golds. Her *Walpurgisnacht* went on for several months. Having entered so deeply into the nightmare of grief, she was able then to begin a quieter, creative enterprise that helped her to put the dead relationship to rest. She spent the next months sorting, editing, and typing his love letters into what she thought might be a small book. It never materialized as a commercial endeavor, but that did not matter. By then she had lost interest in completing the project; she had recovered from the accident.

Acceptance is that point toward the end of the long dark hours when the new reality registers as clearly in our inner images as in our outer adjustment. It was a point Susanna Cary reached sometime after the day of our interview.

"The stage I finally got to was this," she told me two years later. "I stopped resisting letting people take my arm. Instead of a ridiculous pride that prevents you from getting the help you need, and letting others provide the help they feel better providing, instead of taking forever to get your footing and showing off at other people's expense, I've come to be able to let go a little." There was a resonance in a similar act of acceptance by her own mother. A dynamo all her life, after suffering a stroke in her eighties she had fought just as Susanna had. But at the last she seemed content to be not busy every minute, not intimidatingly independent, and able to allow others to feel good by doing some things *for* her.

The stage of acceptance may be curiously neutral in emotion. Not depressed, angry, or elated, the person primarily is relieved to be out of the darkness and feels more peaceful than he or she has in a long time.

If we are to replenish our enthusiasm for living and prepare ourselves for new emotional attachments of any depth, we must recover from our losses. If we do not grieve, time will heal the wound eventually. After five or ten years, the event becomes so distant that it seems often as though it belongs to another life. But if we wish to hasten that process, we must do the work of grieving, which requires the endurance of fresh pain. Julia Walsh probably never did do the work of grieving for her first husband. Rather, she sublimated some of her anger at his pointless death by developing a furious ambition and repressed the rest. "Anger is a very tiring experience," she had decided. The result was that for the next seven years only the most superficial acquaintanceships with men were possible. And a good deal of emotional flavor was withheld from all her relationships. Time had healed the wound by the time she was 40, but most people who lose a spouse do not have that kind of time; Julia was widowed, after all, at 33. Time does heal, but it takes precious expanses of life with it.

Grief is a necessary part of accepting the fact that vital bonds of affection have been broken. That is as true for those divorced or abandoned by the one they love as it is for those who are bereaved. So natural is the need to grieve that there is in the body an almost discernible well of sadness. Scientists have noted that chemical excretions from the bodies of people recently bereaved are different from those of people unaffected by a loss.[10] Rather than indicating weakness, being able to grieve openly is one sign of the human spirit's strength and spontaneity in restoring itself.

Pathfinder Steps to Full Recovery

After interviewing many pathfinders whose forward movement had been interrupted by a life accident, I observed several additional stages that seemed essential to full recovery. Because Kübler-Ross's stages are focused on the dying, it stands to reason that further refinements are necessary for people whose lives will continue. If fully completing the four phases of a normal passage—anticipation, separation, expansion, incorporation—is essential to successful pathfinding, it could be said that the person who is forged by a life accident into a pathfinder is one who probably has fully completed the mourning process. The critical tasks that I would suggest turn adversity into strength are these:

Making sound detachments: In the grip of the most acute pain, anger, fear, and confusion, making extraordinary efforts to separate from the person or situation with thought for the future.

Intervention: Consciously changing our inner image (initially negative) of what we will be like after the accident. Plunging into some constructive action during the recovery process.

Transcendence: Linking up the end of the mourning process with another beginning—a commitment to a new work, love, idea, or a purpose larger than oneself.

Making sound detachments is as important to sustaining a sense of well-being as forming intimate attachments. Consider how often we must separate ourselves from people or situations that have become dear, or at least comfortably familiar. When we switch schools as children, leave home as tryout adults—every time we move, change jobs, "break up" a romance, dissolve a business relationship, or lose someone to the hereafter—we have made a major detachment. And a major detachment is a small death. Yet in our concentration on the importance of forming attachments, little attention has been paid to preparing for healthy, possibly even growth-inciting, detachments. The psychological literature scarcely mentions the subject.

Since 1970 the number of single-parent families has increased by 79 percent, leaving one family in five with children under the age of 18 a detached unit.[11] In the midst of this staggering fragmentation of the family, imaginative variations on split parenting are emerging that may offer a child a healthier and happier environment than an embattled marriage. If a marriage bond is severed and the two sides learn nothing from it but how to vilify one another, the prognosis for sustaining other, nourishing human attachments in the future is poor. It is a matter deserving the most thoughtful consideration, in my opinion, because divorce seldom means a total schism. If two people share children, if their work brings them together, if some of their friends or favorite relatives remain in common, life will be infinitely smoother if they invest in their disengagement the same time and care they spent in becoming engaged.

A Personal Memoir of Detachment

As the beneficiary of at least one detachment successfully made, I felt it was important to try to remember what I learned when Maura's father and I pulled apart. I was thinking about the day Maura was to return from the month in the summer she spends at her father's house. I mentioned to a divorced father that I had to leave a gathering early because my daughter's father was bringing her back.

"Do you meet at the DMZ?" He was accustomed to exchanging the prisoner of his divorce in sour pantomime.

"No, it's not a war with us." Our ritual had come more nearly to resemble a wedding, the sort of occasion when any accident of feeling can easily rattle the participants, but everyone knows the ceremony will go off anyway. And everyone gains a little and loses a little. It was our daughter's favorite day of the year.

Probably it is one of my favorite days, too, the day that my daughter grafts back over the stumpy place she left a month before. The little amputations of separate parenting are familiar now. Anything close to real pain has been worked out of them and replaced with habits of fondness and trust. In fact, Maura's two families get together several times a year. We have a Christmas celebration, we form a united front on major decisions, we even coordinate certain delicate psychological maneuvers. Yet if I am honest, even now, in the middle of handling the exchange of our child smoothly and thinking how healed I am, there is a part of me that has never gotten over the death of that marriage. Mercifully, it has entered the pantheon of disappointments I had at eight, 16, 22, the kind that become part of the background of a life.

I recalled the moment of illumination Albert and I had shared years ago.

For the first several months after we separated, we thought we were doing the most humane thing. Three times a week "for the baby's sake" we would go through all the motions of a normal family dinner. Those evenings always ended with Albert at the door hugging the baby and then passing her back to me, all of us sobbing inconsolably.

One night, in the doorway of our walk-up, the two-and-a-half-year-old child clung to her father. She must have felt the sweat of guilt dampen his hairline because she knew, as certainly as a dog knows when to secrete itself on the floor of the family car, that this signaled another moment of abandonment. Suddenly, she drew back.

"Who's coming next time?" she demanded of the man holding her. "Daddy, or Albert?"

Stunned by her clarity out of sentimental pretense, we began to learn from our daughter that distinctions must be made. However painful the truth, it was preferable, to a child, to waiting for this shifty facsimile of a family to collapse altogether. She knew something about detaching that we did not. Dutifully moving through the pantomime of a phantom family life three nights a week was for her father and me a desiccating process; it drew off any emotional vigor we might have felt trickling back to help in the rough and lonely patches up ahead. Sooner or later one of us would have to make the separation real. If it were felt by the other as a brutality, the dialogue to follow would be that of punishment—the by-product of every divorce where pain is not allowed to be felt at the time and consequently acts up in every future conversation like a pinched nerve.

Should our child suffer the battered blood of a thousand rough exchanges between embittered parents? I would rather my hands were cut off; he felt the same. This child was an unflawed expression of our love. We would try to honor that.

We agreed to jump over the rupture, leave the gap and go on to something else, a distanced but sacred ground where we could meet each other only as parents, and in that partiality try to find the enthusiasm to clear a new path.

But first, we would have to become strangers.

For several months we did not see each other at all. And Maura did not see her father. But she did learn the difference between him and the undependable visitor called Albert. The separateness sank in. After that, there could be regular visits. She began to believe her father would always be part of her life. Soon there were two homes.

By now Maura was 14 and returning from a sojourn at her father's house for the tenth summer in a row. The two families met and touched lightly, each member bending for kisses from the other's children and mates, and then the dance began.

It is a slow, graceful dance, thoroughly considered, composed of short steps and respectful distances. Society offers no formal ceremony for exchange-of-child day. Yet we move through it as if we all hear the same music. No one attempts a solo performance. That is imperative. Once the cooperative effort is introduced by the ritual minuet, it begins to find its composition. Over the next hours it becomes rounded and almost satisfying. The children work harder than anyone.

One of Maura's half brothers runs to bring me a basket of hand-dated eggs from his chickens. The other boy tries bravely to get along without the puffer for his asthma. And Maura—except when fatigue reduces her to morbid ruminations on earthquakes, typhoons, children whose siblings commit suicide, and the manifold ills of the world—Maura is more knowing about what other people need than any adult.

The other mother stands behind her eight-year-old at the piano while he empties his emotions into an abrupt and mournful sarabande.

"Maura tells me you used to lose yourself at the piano when you came home from school as a kid—he does too," she says. "He would be a good son for you."

But we were spread too thin for a second child back then; that is one of the regrets. Albert came from a family of modest income and had years of medical training ahead. For the seven years of our marriage, he was on duty every other night and weekend. Coming home from work to our East Village walk-up over the Ukrainian grocery, I would always run the four flights, hoping to release the subsistence babysitter before she made the baby clean the roaches out of the cat's dish again. The sitter had a habit of sloshing the baby's breakfast cereal with Tropicana because it was too much trouble to walk down four flights for milk. When they tell you there is no difference between a mother and a mother-substitute, you know in your heart it's a party line.

When Maura's other family left at the end of that summer day, all the emotion had been strained out of me. But my sense of continuity was never stronger.

For Maura, for any child, the demands are vastly greater. They are the true refugees of divorce, perpetually in transit with the rags and bones of their love stuffed into backpacks. She cannot turn a corner or stick her hand into a cupboard for a glass without coming up against the sudden bruising strangeness of her own home. Here, the cups are up. There, the cups are down. She catches herself thinking she still lives in the other place, tripping on the rules and ways of here before she has sloughed off the habits of there. Each house has its own system, composed of hundreds of minute and unspoken subsystems.

"It's like going back and forth between two foreign countries," she says. "Every weekend."

She has an intricate web of half-kith and step-kin to keep straight. Her stepmother's half brother is her half step-uncle. She has two half brothers, two half uncles, a pair of half step-cousins, a step-grandmother, and one step-step-grandmother.

A child of modern times.

My suspicion is that these children of contemporary divorce will be much wiser in ways of the heart when they grow up—and perhaps more considerate of their marriages, having known the pain of loss.

This was vividly suggested to me when I took my daughter and her best friend to California for spring vacation. Maura was the one who found the fare bargains that added up to $500 to take two children and one mother to Los Angeles and back. That was not the problem. The problem was: Should Sally see her father? Her mother had decreed she should not.

The little girls touched me so. They were elaborately concerned with the ethics of Sally's contacting her estranged father, while concerned about protecting my position and protecting Sally's mother's feelings—saving fresh pain on all sides. They were so grave in their premature knowledge of the human condition, and yet so innocent in their own experimentations. A couple of cigarettes each, and they decided they would rather be able to do laps; lolling by the pool, they alternated between reading *Anna Karenina* and Archie comics. But between pool-lolling and comparing creative L.A. license plates—"2 TACKY" on a flamingo-pink custom convertible; "X CUSE ME" on a dime-a-dozen Mercedes—they discussed the serious business of how Sally should approach her father to spare *his* feelings.

The night Sally came back from seeing her father for the first time in two years stirred in Maura the held-back brine of hundreds of either-or-weekends, when she was with me and aching for her father, or with her father and longing for me. She climbed into the hotel bed with me, an outsized accommodation we had agreed was as big as the continental United States. For one whole night we held hands across from Maine to Alaska.

It is never easy, and some scars never heal. But given the alternatives, I think we have all reaped an ease and certain unanticipated joys from the painstaking work to build a bridge for Maura between her two families. That was made possible only because our child compelled us to stand still and feel the pain while it was happening.

Intervention in the postaccident disarray to take some action that instinctively feels right can be a liberating step. My friend whose lover died tried to shape her grief into coherence through compiling his letters. She was able to enjoy again all his endearments, excising the distress in between. It was possible to idealize the special quality of their alliance, and to recreate herself as one who had been well loved. She would be freer now to love a more suitable man; that act of intervention hastened the conclusion to her grieving work.

Transcendence is a realm beyond all the negative emotions of mourning, beyond even the neutral point of acceptance. When it happens that a life accident creates a pathfinder, the person is able to transcend his former self as well. A positive self-fulfilling prophecy is made as one comes out of the dark hours. And around a new work, idea, purpose, faith, or a love inspired by the accident, one's goals are realigned. Transcendence is an act of creativity. One creates a partial replacement for what has been lost. The light at the end of mourning is glimpsed, and it is cause for new joy.

14.

THE LIGHT
BEYOND
MOURNING

Rarely does creative endurance, or courage, much less leadership, become possible without the introduction of adversity. One can almost watch the painful emotions produced by a life accident—denial, anger, depression, fear—become catalyzed into a harder compound in certain people. Call it grit. It is upon developing that grit and daring to enter an unknown territory beyond negative emotions that the untested sometimes emerge as different people. They transcend themselves, and become pathfinders.

When Moorhead Kennedy, Jr.,* telephoned his wife, Louisa, on Labor Day weekend in 1979 to announce his decision to go to Teheran—a post where families were not permitted—anger ripped through her. Behind it was the whole rag bag of resentment accumulated in the course of Foreign Service life.

"The idea of your going off to this particular country at this dangerous moment," she fumed, "where we don't have any control on our side, where I don't think anybody should be—it makes me mad. It makes me so mad. It makes me wild!"

"Oh, for Christ's sake, 'Wee,' it's only three months," she

* Real names are used throughout this chapter.

remembers him saying. (Although, at six foot one, Louisa is a shade taller than he, Mike Kennedy's diminutive for his wife is the middle syllable of her name.)

"But I'm tired of separations," she said. "I'm fed up."

They had just come through a miserable year apart while Kennedy was assigned to the embassy in Beirut. This was his chance to go to Iran as the senior economic officer, number three in the mission. She could hear the excitement in his voice. He wanted the Teheran post, even though it meant leaving his wife and family behind.

On Friday, January 16, 1981, after more than fourteen months of enforced separation from her husband, Louisa Kennedy was in the State Department, in Washington. "My fingers are braided to the elbows," she murmured when word came that the negotiations were on the brink of an agreement. By that time, as one of the moving forces in FLAG (Family Liaison Action Group), Louisa Kennedy had become something of a moral bellwether for the nation. The following Tuesday, Inauguration Day, at ten o'clock, as the whole country trembled in anticipation and began spilling tears of joy, Louisa Kennedy said, "I don't lose my cool until that moment comes when we *know* they are free."

At 12:10 P.M., with the new President barely sworn in, CBS announced on television, "They're out! They're out!" But no one in State, or its Iran Working Group, could give Louisa Kennedy confirmation. "I want answers now!" she demanded. Flashing looks of scorn at the Reagan neophytes who had barely found their desks, "Wee" Louisa blew. The months of bottled-up emotions had reached boiling point.

And then came her first electronic glimpse of her husband, at the airport in Algiers. Mike Kennedy looked like the shaggy man of Oz, but he was smiling! The first phone call—he was euphoric. The second call—dazed. On the third—he suggested they collaborate on a book; the one he had written in captivity had been confiscated. Like the other wives, Louisa could hear the changes taking place hourly. It was as if their husbands were undergoing some profound molecular rearrangement.

The hostages and their families were unwilling emigrés to the little-charted territory of deprivation of security into which most of us are driven at some point in life. They endured a special kind of suffering, called waiting. Often, a life accident is not hit-and-run; it happens in slow motion. Will the next tests still be inconclusive, or show a tumor? Will a mate's fling wear off or destroy the marriage? Will a child discovered using dangerous drugs ever straighten out?

The seizure of Americans in the embassy in Teheran created two sets of victims: the hostages and their families. By what process were some able to transcend the experience and grow into stronger persons than before, becoming leaders, comforters, and catalysts for us all?

None of the hostages had been dragooned to go to Iran. Those who did go were aware that the American Embassy in Teheran had been stormed by revolutionaries the previous February, and two marines were wounded, after which the diplomatic staff had shrunk to five. The State Department began staffing up again in June '79. By the first week of November, when demonstrators were snaking around the embassy in long and vicious dances, there were more than seventy Americans working inside.

"*Everybody* was unhappy about their people going to Teheran, with the exception perhaps of the marines," observed one of the leaders of FLAG. "'Why did my husband take this assignment?' 'Even when I told him not to go, why did he go anyway?'"

One motive was career advancement. A senior officer who showed up well in a difficult assignment might have one last shot at an ambassadorship. But sometimes an unspoken motive also operated. "For some of the hostages," said a psychologist who worked with the State Department medical team, "their presence in Teheran during that dangerous period was a response to family disunity and pain in the first place."

At Wiesbaden, that first day after release, only his wonderment at being free surpassed Mike Kennedy's amazement at hearing about Louisa from one high government official after another, beginning with Jimmy Carter.

"Louisa," he teased over the phone, "you know *everybody* now, intimately!"

That amused him. Yet on the threshold of resuming their life together, Louisa realized that he had not yet truly grasped what had happened to her: "He's still thinking of me as his old 'Wee.'" It was all happening too fast for husbands and wives to assimilate the new people each had become.

For John and Bonnie Graves, too, the parting had not been altogether sweet. "Look, I'm perfectly willing to do anything I have to do," Bonnie had told her husband. "But I don't believe in separation. I thought we were in this career together." It was one thing to be left behind when she had small children, part of the price of Foreign Service life, but now the man to whose life and fortune she had bound herself was going to leave her behind again.

After a career spent becoming an expert on French-speaking Africa, John Graves, a former professor of English, was not entirely happy about going in cold as public-affairs officer to set up communications with the new Islamic revolutionary government of Iran. He did not know the language. But it was a challenge. It was far better than being a *petit* bureaucrat.

"It's difficult enough for a marriage to survive under any circumstances," Bonnie grumbled. "Putting those strains on it doesn't make it any easier."

When his wife protested, John Graves arranged for her to take consular training. Racing through classes from seven in the morning until eleven at night, Bonnie was hoping to finish in time to go to Teheran with John, as a temporary employee. She passed all the tests. She was ready. All at once, her husband suggested she delay her departure for at least a couple of weeks—to finish her shopping, he said. She could join him later.

As Bonnie Graves drove John to the airport from their home in Reston, Virginia, on October 22, 1979, he seemed to be trying to tell her something. He acknowledged that she had never been afraid in situations of danger. That had been a comfort to him. But this time it would be particularly difficult, he warned. They would need a lot of luck.

Driving home, Bonnie Graves heard on her car radio what her husband had been unable to tell her. The Shah of Iran had just been admitted to the United States. She would never make it to Teheran.

Ten days *after* the U.S. Embassy was seized, Bonnie Graves received a phone call from an agitated young woman at the State Department travel desk.

"Mrs. Graves, your flight to Teheran is in four days. You haven't picked up your tickets!"

On January 21, 1981, at three o'clock in the morning, Bonnie Graves picked up the telephone in her home:

"*C'est moi*," said the familiar voice.

"*Enfin*," she replied.

With those words John Graves let his wife know that it was indisputably he and that he had not lost his romantic nature. He, too, had written a book in captivity—the first time in French so that the terrorists could not read it, then a second time in English. The first was seized in prison, the second at the Teheran airport.

"The third time around it should come quickly," he quipped.

Bonnie Graves went back to bed but couldn't sleep. A whole stage of life had passed by since he had become a prisoner. The children had all moved on, and for her the role of "mother hen" was emphatically over. But, at 4:20 that morning, a second call came from her husband. It was true. He was coming back.

Dorothea Morefield and her husband, consul general Richard Morefield, were no strangers to life accidents. Five years before, their eldest son, not yet having reached his twenties, was murdered. Dottie Morefield had been to the kingdom of the damned and back. She had no more doubts about herself.

"As far as I'm concerned, the worst has been done to me and I survived it," she said at the second Christmas. "Both my husband and I know we can cope with anything. We allowed the children to see the grieving process take place, so they wouldn't be afraid of it either."

When her husband was taken hostage, Dottie knew she would go on. And the longer the ordeal lasted, the more aware she became that the discrete sequence of emotions triggered by both of the tragedies in her life was essentially the same: "I think I went through all the phases of the mourning process this time, even to the point of acceptance—not of permanent loss, but acceptance that this had happened. My husband was in captivity; we had to live with it.

"This was very much the same as dealing with a death—you think you've gotten to a point beyond anger, and suddenly rage comes over you," said Dorothea Morefield. At that same Christmas, while watching an Iranian TV film for a glimpse of Dick, weeping silently after she saw him, all at once she flew into a fury at his captors. "Here we're being grateful for this little crumb they're throwing us, and they've still got our people locked up—no, no, no!" As well defined as are the stages of the mourning process, Dottie would be the first to admit that there is always a bouncing back and forth between regions of emotion.

Put yourself in the position of Louisa Kennedy or Bonnie Graves or Dottie Morefield. Think of the web of interdependencies woven in any long marriage, the grooves of family traditions, the thousand unhealed cuts, the things left unsaid, the seasons of discontent, of giddy flings, the apprehensions that age may overtake passion, and—suddenly—the door is slammed on all of it. You are left with the ashes of yesterday's words burning on your tongue.

At some level, many of the wives felt this separation as something of an abandonment. For those who were most dependent on their husbands before the crisis, who had no source of self-esteem outside the home, dependence grew into a sense of betrayal: "He was supposed to take care of me!" "I can't even drive!" "Do I have to move back with my parents?"

"The angriest people were the wives who had no other arrows in their quiver, who did not believe they were cut out for anything like a career," one FLAG staffer observed. "As they lost self-confidence, they began to strike out, become belligerent. They found scapegoats everywhere to explain why they couldn't make it, because they really didn't think they could."

On the first day of the crisis, Louisa Kennedy stood amid the chaos at the State Department and thought, *Somebody ought to be calling the other families*. She collared volunteers and set up a family-support group on the spot. FLAG flourished throughout the crisis. But even as she continued to function that first week, she admitted feeling panic. It was impossible to take in the situation. At times, even she denied it.

Perhaps it was not surprising that Louisa Kennedy should have emerged as one of the strongest personalities, indefatigably chugging along, setting the pace and tone for others. Born in an aristocratic enclave of New York City, descendant of Robert R. Livingston, who helped draft the Declaration of Independence, and granddaughter of the illustrious architect Goodhue Livingston, she was groomed at the proper schools and waltzed around the Plaza by all the right boys before going to college at Sarah Lawrence and meeting her future husband. Louisa Kennedy has a will of iron. Unfailingly articulate, her low, napped voice and a light dusting of freckles keep her presence just this side of formidable.

Mike Kennedy was taking a CIA training course when they met in 1954, but rejected that route in favor of Harvard Law School. She dropped out of college to marry him. Throughout her twenties, Louisa said, "I never channeled myself; I wasted a lot of time."

After bearing four children, by the age of 30, she felt just about out of control of her life. Mike had joined the Foreign Service, however, and their first postings were exhilarating. At the age of 35, uprooted from Beirut—where she had flourished in the cosmopolitan capital of the Levant—she came back to relative anonymity in Washington, feeling cheated. Louisa Kennedy had no official status that carried over from one post to the next. She was a Foreign Service wife.

Moorhead Kennedy found the prospect of reaching 50 quite unsettling. Having returned with Louisa from an upsetting year in Chile, he elected to go back to Beirut in the fall of 1978. For the better part of the year *before* the takeover in Teheran, Mike and Louisa Kennedy had been apart.

The Kennedys' home in Washington was still let. Louisa faced a serious operation. She had to find temporary digs and concern herself with the patchwork education of their youngest child, Duncan, 15. Perhaps sensing that his mother needed a shoulder, Philip Kennedy, her second-eldest son, did not go back to college after Christmas vacation that year.

"It turned out to be a lovely year, a consolidation," Louisa told me wistfully. "By the time Mike came home from Beirut, in June 1979, we were prepared to move back into our own house and put this marriage back on the tracks. Our lives would no longer be organized around family and home—the children were ready to go off. I had a novel blocked out. It all sounded very exciting, once I'd gotten myself up for it."

Louisa Kennedy successfully revived a real-estate business and sold a half million dollars' worth of property over several weeks. She was raring to go. Perhaps Mike would start something entirely new. She looked forward to the phase beyond parenthood as possibly the closest and most creative in their lives.

"The rites of passage should have started right after Labor Day," Louisa Kennedy lamented. "He left for Teheran a week later."

In the first stun of a life accident, when doing almost anything seems impossible, living a day at a time is a self-protective adaptation. But as a prolonged solution, taking a day at a time makes it impossible to invest in the future. For the first three months of her husband's captivity, Louisa Kennedy, too, fiercely narrowed her field of vision to the immediate present. The first word from her husband, received in January 1980, changed everything.

"It was an electrifying letter," she recalled, "obviously written while they were still in a situation of violent upheaval and thought they might lose their lives any minute. He laid out the situation in a wonderfully controlled way, as only my husband can do.

"'Please be assured that I am capable of being very serene in accepting my fate. . . .' were his first words," she said thoughtfully. "He had a word for each of the children, about having no doubts they could carry on, particularly if he didn't come back. There was a small paragraph for me, about how he knew I was intelligent and could do well professionally in the real-estate business." Mike Kennedy had added the line of Samuel Johnson's: "When a man knows he is to be hanged . . . it concentrates his mind wonderfully."

All right, if Moorhead Kennedy had chosen to die a patriot, if things came to that, it was up to her to carve out another purpose for herself. The letter operated almost as a boomerang, propelling her beyond depression into a willed acceptance. For perhaps the first time in Louisa Kennedy's

45 years, both her mind and her goals became concentrated wonderfully.

"He had freed us. I took off at that moment."

The hardest decision Dottie Morefield had to make was whether to go public. "Nobody knows what diplomats do," she thought, "except to go to cocktail parties and ride around in chauffeur-driven cars—it's all a blur. If I talk to the press about Dick, let people see he's got kids and they're frightened, then people will have to *care* about him."

She read into one of her husband's early letters a cue that he wanted her to act as his proxy. From a nervous Nellie who could barely get through a talk to the PTA equivalent in Bogotá, Dottie Morefield became a public speaker, making an average of two public appearances a week. She tangled on a television show with Ali Agah, the Iranian chargé d'affaires in Washington: "If, as you say, these militants are such a compassionate and lovely bunch, why don't they let letters through?" She lashed herself afterward: "I'm a housewife and he's a professional. He can outtalk me any day."

What Dottie did not know until Dick came home was that his captors raved at him for two days about her interview. It tickled him that she had done what he, under the circumstances, dared not: she had made his captors furious. They were shamed into giving Dick the mail for his group. After his release, the Morefields discovered that their minds had often been mirrors.

Bonnie Graves took interventionist action into the mourning process right from the beginning, but her anger, now transferred by necessity from her husband, remained uncomfortably compelling. Strong individualists, she and her husband often had paid the price. Assigned to Vietnam as a provincial adviser, John Graves had written a formal memorandum in 1967 asserting that the war was a civil conflict and that the United States did not belong there. His foresight earned him years of slowed advancement in Foreign Service grades. This time his first letter home had suggested they were all hostages of Henry Kissinger, David Rockefeller, and Richard Helms.

Bonnie turned up at the first Christmas meeting of FLAG in plumed hat, black boots, and big gold earrings, a Don

Quixote come to demand that the families join in a public denunciation of U.S. policy in Iran.

"If you were a loyal American and a loving wife," intoned a hostage father, "you would go home and pray.".

For three months Bonnie Graves's nights were sleepless. She was wretched, presumably mired in the depression phase of the mourning process. By March she decided to break with the group on policy and make her own public declaration of dismay with American policy in Iran. It did not help.

Six months into the crisis she tamed down her style of dress and began to feel empathy for the pain other hostage relatives were suffering. She took time to do some things for them. She led area families around Capitol Hill to lobby through the Hostage Relief Act. And despite her qualms about FLAG's being too close to the official State Department line, she continued to function faithfully as its treasurer.

Bonnie Graves had reached the point of acceptance: that she would have been a greater burden to her husband in Teheran, that she belonged here to sustain her family. Indeed, having begun to think of herself as superfluous, she was touched to find herself needed again. At the final Christmas meeting, the hostage families seemed happy to see Bonnie, and some thanked her for having taken her courageous position.

As we know, depression is a necessary part of the mourning process. Among the hostage families, as the crisis dragged on past the unthinkable deadline of a year, some sank into a limbo of chronic depression and helplessness, while others completed the mourning process. They accepted.

Acceptance does not mean that it stops costing you something. The flares of temper, the middle-of-the-night nothingness, the splurges of hope and backslides into despair—these things leave their mark. Yet from such depths may come acts of courage, performed by ordinary people made extraordinary by events.

The last and most important part of dealing with a life accident, I believe, is to *transcend the point of acceptance*. People who seem to do best in surviving life accidents do not simply accept the deprivation and say, "I really don't mind having no left leg." Spurred on by the sharp emotions of crisis and often by painful exposures to hypocrisy, false priorities, or empty places in their lives, they reinvest their hopes in a new undertaking, love, idea, purpose, or faith. Transcendence is the link to the future.

"It gives you a feeling of some kind of control over your life again," Dorothea Morefield agreed. "Becoming very involved in FLAG and the fight not to let our government forget the hostages certainly helped me enormously."

When fevered exchanges between spokesmen for the Iranian *majlis* and spokesmen for President Carter began to heat up the November election campaigns, Louisa Kennedy thought long and hard about how to give the President a signal. The idea that our government might be negotiating with a terrorist government, on its timetable, to pay ransom for an unspeakable act—not to mention compromising U.S. neutrality in the Iran-Iraq war—gave her grave pause.

"A line came to me from a Frost poem that says it all," she confided. "'We have promises to keep.'"

In an op-ed page piece for the *Washington Post*, Mrs. Kennedy tried to take Americans back to one of our basic moral contracts. "I have realized that there *might* come a time when the national interest would conflict with . . . the safety of the hostages, and the hostages could be considered expendable. Giving one's life or sacrificing for the country . . . is an honor given to reasonably few people."

At the time she said in private, "If somehow all this emotionalism around election time pressures the country into giving in to a terrorist operation, we'd be letting the hostages down as well as our nation."

On television the only emotion her soft, flannelly voice might show was a touch of weariness, but of a worldly dimension. Nothing personal. Never anything personal about her husband.

She was walking a tightrope between the hope of influencing the administration's policy and the fear of upsetting other hostage families. And all the while she was wondering what her husband would think, what their marriage would be like, when and if he came home.

The dense web of emotions directing her actions at that time may never be sorted out with accuracy, but her husband's subsequent letters had made one thing clear to her. If the settlement of the hostage crisis would humiliate or dishonor his country, Mike Kennedy preferred to wait, perhaps even to die. To help keep that promise on her husband's part, Louisa Kennedy had to set aside her love and her anger, her protectiveness as a mother and her needs as a woman—she had to transcend the concerns to her own life.

The bittersweet irony was that even as she stood precariously on this position that covered so much pain, the world was paying her the attention of a celebrity. One day, she and Barbara Rosen were backed up against the *Pietà* in St. Patrick's Cathedral by reporters from three TV networks. They were filmed kissing Cardinal Cooke, being kissed by the vicar sent over from the Church of England, for a service dedicated to the hostages' well-being.

Aside, in a whisper, Louisa Kennedy said, "I can never tell my husband what a remarkable year this has been for me."

Imagine the magnitude of the transition facing the returning captives. From being isolated, reduced to the behavior of infants who had to raise their hands to go to the toilet, from spending months as enforced mutes suspended in time in windowless cells without clocks, they had to rejoin society as adults who could express emotions, assert their will, act on sexual urges, structure time, and make their own decisions.

Curiously, the hostages underwent a process similar to that experienced by their families, except that to survive their long Persian night, many hostages had to retreat beyond acceptance and into apathy. Apathy is the natural protective state for any prisoner of war or terrorism who cannot afford to show emotion to his captors. Psychologists have learned that recovery from apathy is typically marked by euphoria, followed by recriminations. On Freedom Night, Americans were cheered to watch on TV their missing fellows move from bland to bubbling in a matter of hours.

The wives' euphoria matched their husbands' in those first phone calls from the Air Force hospital in Germany. Louisa Kennedy thought her husband was coming out with—she groped for words for the first time—"greater compassion? I don't know! Maybe because I'm going through transformations too. I think we're both being propelled into some change of a scope we can't even tell yet, perhaps a new consolidation in the marriage. I suddenly feel convinced."

Some of the wives sounded full of equal parts of fear and confidence that their man was one of the people who had survived best. Bonnie Graves was delighted to hear how well her husband had used fantasy. "John's an excellent compartmentalizer. He would see snow out the window and engage in vignettes of our skiing in Iran. Every night before he went to sleep he played inner tennis. He was seriously thinking of joining the pro circuit. . . ." She erupted with laughter.

When such adaptations were made by prisoners of the Punic Wars, we did not have social scientists to scrutinize their behavior. By now, several studies exist of stress and repatriation in prisoners of war. When the eighty-two surviving crew members of the U.S.S. *Pueblo* were released in 1967 after eleven months as military hostages in North Korea, evaluations conducted at the U.S. Naval Hospital in San Diego were compared with those of POWs during World War II and the Korean conflict.[1] Striking echoes from those earlier situations emerged in the behavior noticed by the families of our exhostages in Iran and reported by the State Department medical team.

Fantasy, in fact, worked very well for the *Pueblo* survivors. Three personality types fared best, all capable of isolating the emotional impact of their captivity and withdrawing into another compartment of their minds to entertain themselves with fantasy. The most extreme of these personality types was the bright schizoid. Personalities tending toward the psychopathic also did well: protected by their moral and emotional shallowness, they were able effectively to manipulate other prisoners, as well as their captors, to get what they wanted. The third group of supercopers, exceptionally mature individuals, survived only by regressing to the temporary use of neurotic defense mechanisms, such as denial and repression. Anyone capable of emotional unresponsiveness was ahead of the game.

The survival pattern among the *Pueblo* men, as noted, paralleled that found in earlier studies of American prisoners of war. Surviving the experience relatively intact depended most heavily upon courage, emotional detachment, eternal hope, the belief in one's superiority over the enemy, the imagination to have fantasies, the ability to suppress awareness of the ever-present threat of death. And a sense of humor. Pure intelligence, if unrelated to the ability to get along with people, was less advantageous.

Shame and ostracism began to show among the Teheran exhostages, after several days of observation by State Department psychiatrists in a compound far better guarded than the American Embassy in Teheran. Hostages who had cooperated with Iranian propaganda films felt guilty about not having lived up to their personal ideals. The marine guard chosen to star in a film attesting to happy, apple-cheeked hostages sat in his hospital room, depressed, nervous, still isolated.

This is a normal reaction for a group of people exposed together to a life accident. As they compare experiences, an unspoken scale of behavior emerges against which each one measures "How did I do?" Ostracism of those perceived as having behaved the worst serves to set them apart so that they cannot contaminate the reputation of the group.

As reports of random Iranian brutalities trickled out, so did word of small acts of hostage defiance: refusal to play the charade of praising their jailers' exemplary behavior; Sergeant James Lopez's salute to the American flag, scrawled on his prison wall in Spanish, "*Viva la roja, blanca y azul!*" Resistance writ larger, in escape attempts and insults to their captors, was rewarded with more severe physical abuse. Although sometimes invisible as wounds, these punishments could now become emblematic of the endurance of the whole group. A group rationalization could begin developing to ease prisoners' guilt over their weaker moments. That was what helped to save the *Pueblo* crew from the overpowering guilt attached to "confessions" they all made for propaganda films. Pointing to the obscene finger gesture some had made in the films, undetected by their captors, they boasted, "We really screwed them over."

Having learned a sad lesson from pushing reentry of the *Pueblo* crew too fast, the State Department took counsel this time from more satisfactory repatriation processes, such as when 442 American POWs captured in the Korean conflict were deliberately returned on a slow boat from the Pacific. A reentry period was provided by four days in an Air Force hospital in Germany.

As the overlay of euphoria slipped away for the hostages

released from Iran, depression began to spread. A cashier at the hospital was quoted as saying the older hostages seemed the most depressed. In fact, studies have demonstrated that older people in such a situation tend to suffer fewer symptoms, although at first, with physical vigor to mask their inner trauma, the younger ones often appear to be better off. While the young marines were out on the balcony of the hospital flirting with nurses, some of the older hostages were already beginning to work through their natural depression, already beginning to confront the profound metaphysical experience of having, in effect, come back from the dead.

Certain themes emerged in interviews given by the returnees to describe their survival pattern. They said they were determined, almost to a man, to come out the winners. "The whole point was to beat them at their own game, and we feel we did," said Mike Kennedy, quickly resuming his professional air. "Had the United States intervened with violence, the Iranians would have become martyrs and we would have become the villains of the Third World. By our tremendous self-discipline, we became the moderates."

Other vital mechanisms for coping often mentioned were supportive camaraderie among roommates, a sense of the ridiculous, and the comfort of knowing that their families would cope too.

One important change for which few were prepared was learning to live *without* the structured tension of the year in captivity or the year of waiting.

The third morning after her husband's release, Louisa Kennedy said to me, "You know, I was just lying here in bed thinking and I noticed I was tense. Suddenly, I thought, 'You don't have to be tense anymore, because the horror and danger are finished.' "

"Did you miss the tension a little bit?"

Pause. Then, "In the sense that I was so used to it, yes. Just for a second you feel, 'There is nothing to do.' Strange."

Seldom does one have a purpose so absolute and so constant as survival from one day to the next, whether physical or emotional. It is a long way from that to having to set goals that are not immediately obvious, and to searching out meaning in the mundane affairs of middle-class life.

The alchemy of transmutation proceeded. If the pattern

following prolonged captivity in Vietnam was borne out, the released captives could expect to be dependent on their wives for two or three months, when a striking change usually occurs. The formerly cooperative returnee becomes increasingly irritable, even belligerent, and critical of just about everybody. Often, quite suddenly, the repatriate reclaims his dominant role. According to the new software industry of hostage specialists, that transition from apathy to hostility is essential to restoring mental health and normal family life. However, in the process by which the husband and father reasserts his dominant family role, the wife is most likely to suffer. When the husband is deaf to her predicament, the wife's sense of emotional isolation becomes the most severe family problem.

In this instance the hostages almost unanimously recognized the role their families played in the crisis. As William Daugherty plainly put it at the hostages' first press conference: "The real heroes of this event have been the families."

Asked what lay ahead, Dottie Morefield exclaimed, "Time to put all of this behind us, and go back to just what it was like before."

But these wives were now different people. If they did go back to the way it was before, it would be with a difference.

Shy Dorothea Morefield had become accustomed to picking up her phone at four in the morning to "call the Charlie show"—as she came to refer to Charles Kuralt on the CBS Morning News—and speaking her mind on affairs of the world. Shortly before the "rescue" raid, when tension reached a peak and she was beset with odd premonitions, Louisa Kennedy had flown to Europe, leading a FLAG delegation to talk to "Maggie" Thatcher and Giscard d'Estaing. She had found herself debating in French on television with the high-heeled hippie Marxist daughter of Iran's President Bani-Sadr—and comfortable in the role.

Only a few went this far. But many others who were caught up in the accident made developmental gains they never would have thought possible in the context of quiet lives.

Almost all the wives achieved at least minor victories. "Many had a struggle making that jump from what they thought their husbands would want them to do, to making decisions for themselves," observed FLAG president Katherine Keough. They bargained endlessly with a phantom partner over how much authority they should take over—"Should I choose a new carpet for the living room?" "Sign a letter to the President?" "What will my husband think if I buy a $400 coat?" "I don't know if Jim/Joe/Harry would want me to do that."

Again and again, Katherine Keough would say, "Jim's not here. It's *you*." Many outgrew the need to ask permission.

Parents, too, found the crisis a stretching experience. Some Marine parents had never been out of their hometowns or east of the Mississippi; some had never been on an airplane. To them, Washington was like a game with too many rules, rigged against the little fellow. Suddenly, these same parents were visiting the State Department ("Which branch of government is that?") and preparing to meet the President ("What do you wear?"). One older woman went out and bought a blue suit. She had heard everyone wore blue suits at the State Department, and she wanted to fit in. "She looked lovely," said Mrs. Keough.

The returning hostages, too, had undergone a profound experience that might have lasting, transformative effects. That certainly proved to be the case for Mike Kennedy. When I spoke with him in May 1981, he had left the Foreign Service and taken up an entirely new direction as head of the Cathedral Peace Institute, a new study center on "the role of religion in foreign policy." He said, "The hostage crisis acted as kind of a catalyst, did you notice?"

Yes, I said, it seemed to be a purification ritual.

The announcement that Moorhead C. Kennedy, Jr., would be cochairman, with former Secretary of State Cyrus R. Vance, of a fund-raising drive for the new peace institute seemed, therefore, predictable. He told me, "This grew out of my hostage experience, as a result of an Islamic revolution which was not all that well foreseen, although elements that went into it were perfectly well known. Everybody who practices abroad, not just government but media, banks, international law firms, needs to be more sensitive to this restless factor called religion which is surging around out there and sometimes can go critical on us." He went on to say that Americans, with the First Amendment, are conditioned to think of religion as a personal subject, not suitable for parlor conversation, and that is to our disadvantage. "It

certainly was in Teheran. Given the strains that modern-
ization is putting on large areas of the rest of the world, we
may find these strains surfacing in a religious reaction somewhere once again. In a nutshell," he said, "the Cathedral
Peace Institute is to raise the level of consciousness of Americans by every possible means about the force that religion
represents in international affairs."

> For this my son was dead, and is alive again; he was
> lost, and is found. And they began to be merry.
> —LUKE 15

Homecoming is a profound human experience. For those
who stay behind, it expresses a universal yearning to welcome back someone once deeply loved who was thought lost.
Yet we must ask ourselves: Why did Americans care about
the hostages with such constancy over fourteen months,
when we knew next to nothing about their harsh treatment?
Why did Americans identify with these *victims?*

Have we not all felt for some time now that we were victims, innocents, captives of international fortune, bystanders
at the spectacle of civilization threatened by terrorists around
the world and breaking down in our cities?

Our innocence, our pride, our sense of ourselves as good—
these were the gifts our hostages brought back. They gave us
our first moment of unambiguous self-acceptance in years.
And when we embraced them with joy and bathed them in
our tears and feted them for days and days, we felt ourselves
come back from alienation, not so homesick for what it
means to be an American, once again—however briefly—at
home.

The transforming events in any nation are those that reas-
sert a country's fundamental myths and codes. By the
strength of their endurance, these fifty-two Americans and
their families helped reanchor Americans to the ideals of our
past and renewed our strength to meet the future.

No people can rely solely on cultural life accidents, however, to support their shared identity and offer to them as
citizens something to believe in beyond themselves. Societies
go through cycles of development, too. The ebb and flow of
political and religious cycles in any society has a profound
effect on how people go about seeking well-being and what

they think it is when they get there. It is these changing values that determine whom we select to be our pathleaders.

What is the interactive effect between pathfinders and society?

Part IV

TRAVELING
THE
HIGH ROAD

Some of us have to travel a long way from our center in order to see it. The odyssey in search of pathfinders already had carried me up and down my own land as far as Alaska, then through Europe, now across the Arabian desert, and the question had become more fundamental. What qualities allow civilization to prosper? What does a society need to last? It was natural to take the question back to where civilization began.

"You must go to Upper Egypt," people kept urging me. "It has lasted for seven thousand years."

And so I booked passage on a twelve-hour train ride back to where time begins. To Luxor, site of the world's first city, Thebes, and before that, the place where the first god, Amon, is said to have separated the earth from the waters of the Nile and then to have sat and thought up the world.

To travel anywhere by train in Egypt is an act of faith. The prewar heap pulled in, human flies motionless all over the face of its head car and on its roof and pasted between every car. The train had barely slowed before they dropped off into the track bed, running, beckoning to waiting passengers to pull them out. People in front of me strained to help, then, having little time left for their own efforts, began hurling on their cloth packs and monster fans and cases of imported Pampers. Bodies surged up, doors banged open, shut. Suddenly, I was aware of a deadening in my thumb. I looked back. It was squashed in the door jamb.

"*Ryas!*" called a fellow passenger.

The steward came running. He washed the wound, and he and several other passengers hovered over me for the rest of the trip. This is Egypt. In the midst of rampant impoverishment and the apparent impossibility of performing the simplest acts of personal safety—the sweetness, always the sweetness. The social distance may be subzero, but that does not diminish regard for each human life. The primary natural resource of Egypt, I was to learn, is her people.

For every five kilometers traveled outside Cairo, another century of civilization falls away. A few hours south of Cairo even the modernity of irrigating by an Archimedes screw is replaced with a crude mud dipper swung by a human counterbalance. Out of the murderous dust swimming over the eastern desert life erupts abruptly—clean green ribbon quenched down the center by the Nile—until just as abruptly the hag's fingers of the western desert reach in to choke it off.

The train pulled into Luxor at night. The only thing I could see on the way to the hotel was a rare Egyptian graffito.

The words said in English: *Sadat is our hope.*

I thought of the leader I had come to Egypt to meet. Muhammad Anwar el-Sadat was one who would know some profound secrets, not only about the process of change but also about the art of endurance. Here was a man who had disappeared, from the age of 34 through 52, into the shadow of Nasser, giving every sign that his youthful fire had dissipated into a lukewarm middle-aged flunkydom. But when an accident of destiny thrust the presidency upon him, Sadat galvanized virtually overnight into a leader so bold that he dared to reverse the very national orientation he had helped to impose. He threw out the Soviets and turned to the West. The mystery was, how a man could withdraw into the wings and remain there deep into the middle of his life, then suddenly emerge—all his fire and commitment intact—as one of the most vital leaders on the world stage?

Sadat would eventually teach me about transcendence.* He knew how to withdraw into a spiritual state of relaxed awareness—or what might also be called creative endurance—for days, weeks, months, once even for the better part of

---

* The profile of Sadat appears in Chapter Seventeen.

eighteen years. And he knew how to come back, whereupon he was able to change utterly, to dispossess his former self, and originate a new self with renewed spiritual and physical energy for the task ahead.

Luxor rising. I was awakened by the clop of horse-drawn carts and a donkey smooching at grass beneath my shutters. I looked out at the sun, a great baked peach, lifting out of the sands of the Sinai to waken a people seven thousand years old. This was the same sun, their god, that inspired pharaohs to erect colossi of stone representing men and women as tall as mountains.

"Obviously, the stuff doesn't last," quipped the Pennsylvania man from a nation two hundred years old, as we stood gaping at the sight behind the pylons. The mud-brick scaffolding upon which workmen stood to build the Temple at Karnak more than four thousand years ago—the same mud bricks that provide shelter for most villagers today—stood intact.

They must know something about what sustains, I thought.

When it came time to visit the City of the Dead, I hoped to absorb something from the pharaonic approach to the ultimate change. Each pharaoh began at the start of his reign to have a tomb burrowed through rock in order to guarantee eternal seclusion. The primary concern of the pharaoh clearly was not with his death, which was inevitable, but with the smoothness of his passage into the hereafter. The journey to the underworld was made in stages, I read, represented by rock-hewn passages that were divided into twelve hours, or caverns. "The deceased sailed through them at night in the boat of the Sun God . . . surrounded by his retinue who are . . . temporarily bringing light to the places he traverses."[1]

It was satisfying to think of being guided through lighted passages on a journey of self-judgment. This might be similar to the enlightened life review described by people who have been pronounced technically dead but who come back.

Imagine the surprise, amid sixty pharaonic tombs, of finding the most impressive mortuary temple built to a woman— Hatshepsut, not only a queen, but a pharaoh. How had she survived in a game of kings? With a stroke of unforgettable creativity.

The lawful heir among the children of Thutmose I in the 1100s B.C., she was held back only by the accident of having been born a woman. To disarm resistance to her rule, Hatshepsut had a magnificent colonnade added to her mortuary temple, which depicted her birth as divine. What a tall story! On the walls the great god Amon hands the key of life to Hatshepsut's mother, who, dignified and radiant in her pregnancy, is borne toward the heavens by goddesses. The divine child presented to her after the birth is Hatshepsut, rendered as a boy. After the death of her half brother and coregent, Queen Hatshepsut, said to be beautiful, adopted the badges of kingship: the royal shirt and ceremonial beard. During her reign she refused to fight wars of expansion.

Another lesson in how to last: aspiring to one's highest possibility, and using one's imagination to create the cultural images needed to support it.

At dusk, back on the east bank, I looked across the Nile at the mesa of the City of the Dead, white as bleached and powdered bones but now hollowed with purple-shadowed depths. They were strangely inviting. I thought about some of the things that have lasted, and why. The casual miracle of sun-baked mud bricks and the simple blessing of a good diet, yes, but there was also a nonviolent society based on strong religious tenets stressing social sharing. It had sustained this people through countless advances and retreats of armies, other religions, political leaders, and cycles of nature. They absorbed it all. And always, they came back.

In those few moments of thought, the light over the Valley of Kings had turned pearlish, and the hills themselves seemed to lift off the land and float in the eye of the river. I was drawn to the very edge of the riverbank, where the light became yet more enchanted. As I looked toward the floating opalescence of the Necropolis, time itself began to float. I had a sudden sensation of weightlessness, of a kind I associate with soaring across a dance studio when the leap comes so easily one is suspended for a timeless second in ecstasy.

A strong impression came over me on that riverbank in Egypt: one might sail across on the boat of the sun god and circle through the underworld to come up on the other side joyously free, a hundred feet tall but buoyant as air. And there, set upon by all the incomplete truths like buzzards swirling about and biting each other's tails, one would have the chance to go mad, or to hike across the silvery spine of those hills, concentrating on the lastingness, to the place where time and death are suspended and the light of deity penetrates directly to the soul—and there, where all lines of human history meet, to enjoy a moment of transcendence that makes everything clear without being known.

15.

WITHDRAWAL AND COMEBACK

Nearing the end of my odyssey, I realized that the qualities that transform people into pathfinders are resonant in the qualities a society requires to progress, to reflect, and to renew itself.

A society must be willing to risk and change. The alternatives are stagnation and decline, or totalitarian management. The ordinary Soviet citizen, for instance, believes his government is there, "like the wind, like a wall, like the sky—something permanent, unchangeable," as a Russian dissident described it to political scientist James MacGregor Burns.[1] "So the individual acquiesces, does not dream of changing it—except a few, few people. . . ."

But changing only in reaction to events is not healthy; a society needs the wit and the will to anticipate. The penalty for not standing back, to formulate a life strategy in the case of the individual or a world strategy at the societal level, is the same. The person or the nation overtaken by events lurches reactively from one crisis to another and is unable to learn from failure or to admit mistakes.

Edward Heath, former prime minister of Great Britain, in retrospect saw the need for societal introspection vividly:

There comes a point in every crisis when political leaders involved should disengage from the immediate operations,

434

stand back and assess the whole situation afresh. This may require a superhuman effort but . . . in my 30 years in political life I have seen more catastrophes brought about by the failure to do this than in any other way.[2]

At the start of this decade, Mr. Heath saw no sign of such a grand design being created by the leadership in the West. "Until it is," he warned, "the West will continue to react to events in a vain attempt to catch up with them, rather than foreseeing developments and trying to control them."

In addition to the willingness to risk and the ability to anticipate, a society needs constantly to replenish the capacity for loving its people. Even in times of economic malaise, the United States is a country with a vast social conscience. But when a contracting economy touches off a natural retrenchment in the nation's generosity of spirit, and the government shrinks the blanket of security around its citizens, the capacity for loving is sorely tested. The full powers of a nation's creativity should be turned to keeping windows of opportunity open at the entry level, to introducing new incentives for productivity at the middle level, and to providing for the needs of the helpless and nearly hopeless at either end of the life cycle.

Friendship among its citizens is also vital to the cohesiveness of a society. The degree to which tolerance can be refreshed among its disparate groups, and reasonable relations worked out between the haves and have-nots and the heres and the just-came-overs, determines how much of a society's energies are spent on constructive association and how much misspent in destructive dissent. A strong society must not only set a tone for friendships within, but also must take the lead in fostering international friendships on our small, missile-shrunken planet.

Beyond risk, timing, love, and friendship, a society often benefits by the accumulated experience of a certain age. It also doubles its creativity and its potential productivity when both men and women are justly encouraged to incorporate the strengths of the opposite gender. And a country cries out, always, for a unifying national purpose.

It is the objective of this part of the book to examine how society is the beneficiary of pathfinding, and how at the same time society both defines the need for pathfinders to surpass themselves and provides genesis for the discovery by path-finders of their own highest purpose.

Cycles of Revitalization

In our individual life cycle, we go over old conflicts in a jagged, ascending spiral. As the result of weathering a passage or contending with a life accident our values may change. Societies also develop in this cyclical way: with thrusts of energy, innovation, and optimism, followed by periods of uncertainty, retrenchment, and denial of social problems that its citizens temporarily have lost the patience, prosperity, or political will to face.

We shall be concerned here with the effect that these cycles in society have on individual development, and with the more intriguing possibility that it is the pathfinders among us who affect the cycles of society.

Arthur Schlesinger, Sr.,[3] was first to use a cyclical perspective to explain American political life. Scrutinizing our history from 1765 through 1947, he found that swings from conservatism to liberalism occurred with startling regularity. A period of concern for the rights of the few was followed inevitably by a period of concern for wrongs done to the many. Each swing lasted an average of seventeen years. But beyond those clear empirical observations, Schlesinger could find no correlation to peaks and valleys in the economy, to periods of peace and war, not even to which political party was in power: that is, "A party in one climate of opinion may move to the right and in another shift to the left, yet proclaim to a forgetful electorate that it is still the same residuary of immortal truth." Schlesinger concluded in his influential essay that the motive force behind American politics was an interplay of subjective influences "springing from something basic in human nature." That basic human rhythm was an alternation between adventure and retreat. As he summed up: "A period of imaginative leadership, of experimentalism and democratic innovation, has been followed by one of sober reflection, of digestion of the gains and renewed vigilance for the rights of property."

Anthropologists and historians who study larger cultural swings generally observe that it takes twice as long—thirty to forty years—for a new spiritual awakening to work its way through a people's consciousness. These are the great sea changes that are too broad to be reflected in daily news reports and that contemporary intellectuals, often in rebellion against the religious constraints of their own childhoods, are emotionally prone to dismiss as "just more of that old God business."

Yet long-wave cycles of political decline and spiritual comeback are seen to occur in almost all cultures.

That set of shared beliefs and attitudes by which a culture hangs together is what people refer to in rearing their children, relating to neighbors, dealing with employers, reacting to authority, and perceiving their own place within the system of which they are a part, as well as its position relative to the world. In some periods those shared attitudes are as sharp as gemstones. They help people in cutting out their own paths and in recognizing the leaders among them. Inevitably, there are also periods of crisis in the cultural cycle, when events have scratched the innocence off old beliefs and the people feel their worth diminished, their confidence dulled; when they begin doubting the authority of their leaders and become disoriented in the world.

A model that breaks down each stage within a major cultural swing was provided by anthropologist Anthony F. C. Wallace in an essay in 1956 on "Revitalization Movements."[4] He adapted his theory to the modern world from a study of primitive societies. Remarkable in its applications, not to mention its reassuring effect, Wallace's construct has provided grist for subsequent analyses by historians of America's downswings and great awakenings—of which, depending on who is counting, there have been four or five.[5]

The first stage, as Wallace describes it, begins with a period of "individual stress." One by one people lose their bearings, exhibit mental and physical illnesses associated with stress, either lash out in violent acts against family, friends, and authorities or suffer loss of identity and withdraw into apathy, often destroying themselves with their society's equivalent of drugs and alcohol, or by suicide. The human institutions (marriage, family, schools in contemporary times, tribal groups in the past) as well as the "medicine men" of the culture (today, ministers and psychotherapists) stretch so far in the attempt to "readapt" these individuals, and the bulge of upset individuals becomes so great, that the bonds of society begin to snap. The religious or ethical compass by which people operated, sometimes even without putting their beliefs into words, no longer can be consulted for help. Husbands and wives quarrel, children are neglected or mistreated, families and kinship networks weaken.

In the second stage of one of these great cultural swings, people gradually come to the conclusion that it is not they but their institutions that are malfunctioning. In a primitive society this is reflected in loss of faith in the tribal organization, perhaps a fatal repudiation of the chief. In a more contemporary version, as people see it, their courts cannot mediate, their jails do not reform, their churches offer little relief, their leaders cannot be believed. As people lose confidence in their institutions, they begin to insulate themselves and become intent on finding their own accommodations with life. But even the sports and recreations that normally serve in any culture to siphon off people's frustrations are not enough. The search for techniques to reduce the pressure becomes in itself somewhat desperate; distortions in individual lives mirror profound cultural disorientation. The crucial web of generous-spiritedness toward strangers that allows a people to join in meeting culture-wide dangers from within or without becomes tattered. The people quarrel and divide.

At the third stage of the process leading toward revitalization, according to Wallace, the older generation almost always produces a reactionary movement. The call is taken up, especially by those with rigid personalities and those with the greatest stake in the previous order, for a return to the "old-time religion" and "respect for the flag" (or to other appropriate symbols or former totems of the old tribal order). Using the psychological technique of projection, these new leaders find scapegoats among the less popular groups in the culture and make them repositories of people's fears and frustrations. This traditionalist movement warns the people that it is their failure to hold strictly to the old set of beliefs and behaviors that has disrupted the civil system (or displeased the gods). "They mistake symptoms for causes," observes Wallace.

In the fourth stage, people's confidence begins to return. The catalyst is a prophet who appears with a reinterpretation of the people's covenant with God. This is a person who has personally undergone a traumatic religious experience that symbolizes the crisis of the culture to which he belongs. (As we shall see presently, historian Arnold Toynbee introduced this idea in 1947.) But although in preliterate cultures or in the rise of the great religions the prophet was usually one charismatic figure, historian William C. McLoughlin points out that America's great awakenings have never revolved around a single holy figure. Rather, the catalysts have been many figures who cross religious and political lines.

The figures who come to mind when one thinks of the wrenching, culture-wide American revitalizations are adventurers, reformers, poet-preachers (Emerson), do-gooders (abolitionists), philosophers, even psychologists, together with those visionary politicians who sense the readiness of the people to raise the level of their moral aspirations.

America was born with the Great Awakening of Puritanism (1730–1760). It was more than a religious creed; it was a philosophical system that organized a person's entire emotional and intellectual life. Puritanism gave emotional depth and resilience to the American in the Revolution and sustained the colonists while they attempted to forge out of the confusion and crisis a new nation.

The second great awakening (1800–1830 according to McLoughlin) put the prevailing world view of the Calvinists, who stressed man's depravity and insisted upon his predestination, into conflict with the new self-reliant optimists, who emphasized man's innate goodness and insisted he had free will. Calvinism was the voice of the fathers, the "law and order" of the day. Yet a new consensus formed among those who saw America as having a manifest destiny: their country had been chosen by God to perfect the world. The second great awakening inspired most and infused all of the social reforms of the era, an era that culminated in Jacksonian participatory democracy.

In the third awakening (1890–1920) there was a rejection of unregulated capitalistic exploitation and a beginning of the welfare state. Our foremost native philosopher, William James, began studying both ethics and religion—having published the principles of psychology in 1890—and became widely influential in espousing the basic American philosophy of pragmatism, personified by Theodore Roosevelt.

The ritual process by which a culture comes back from a

period of losing faith in its own legitimacy is usually religious in inspiration. Although the majority of the people may not undergo a "revival" in the old Protestant sense—being transported by Preacher Finney's pumping epiglottis as he pushes his parishioners to the point of audible groaning and indiscreet seizures—there does spring up some sort of revivalist wind that spreads the new word.

When the reinterpreted word is taken up by articulators and leaders who cross denominational and political lines, a culture enters what Wallace saw in primitive societies as the ultimate stage: the awakening. The younger and more flexible members of the society are the first to experiment with changes in their personal lives. The social landscape becomes freckled with fresh attempts at utopian social relationships. Churches cannot contain the idea of God in such a period. A spiritual excitement may be anywhere and everywhere. All things, both good and evil, become possible.

"Then logic yields to intuition . . . self-discipline yields to impulse, science to magic, formal worship to vision."[6]

During such revitalization movements a nation reshapes its identity, transforms its patterns of thought and action, and seeks a healthy realignment with social, environmental, and world change. McLoughlin adds an ominous reality: "It might be more accurately said that our periods of great awakening have produced wars rather than resulted from them."

Where Have We Been?

By now, you probably have the last twenty years of American history all figured out. There are some theorists who agree with you. The latest culture-wide swing, they say, began in 1960 and promises to leave our cultural landscape transformed by 1990—if it has not been wasted by war.

The end of the 1950s marked a period of remarkably strong national unity. Building on postwar prosperity, family "togetherness" ran high, and for the first time Americans came close to practicing the pluralism we had preached—at least to the extent of Protestants acknowledging that Catholics and Jews were full Americans too. We elected a Roman Catholic to our highest office. As the Sixties dawned, a new spirit, later announced as the Aquarian rebirth, built directly on the civil rights movement. That movement exerted a deep emotional pull on young Americans, who began reviving America's religious reverence for the individual. A confident young president also provided fresh moral initiative. John Kennedy's most famous political line—"Ask not what your country can do for you, but what you can do for your country"—was an official call to pathfinders to take up a social commitment.

It appeared a comeback was under way. The young were emboldened to experiment with changes in their personal lives. White and black rebels forged utopian bonds. With spiritual energy uncontained, all things both good and evil did seem possible. And the spirit of renewal was not exclusive to the young.

At times like the early 1960s, when the vision of what people want for their lives, their children, and their country is clearly visible, if somewhat naive, the led have little trouble uniting behind their leaders to ward off external dangers. When Kennedy blundered into the Bay of Pigs, there was scarcely a tremor in the national faith. (In a later and darker stage of the cycle, when Jimmy Carter bungled the Iranian hostage rescue raid, it was seen as just another in a series of betrayals: the war in Vietnam; the ideals of the Sixties; Watergate; the pardon.)

The Vietnam War dealt a mortal blow to the core belief of our culture: that Americans had been chosen by God to lead the world to perfection. Unable to reconcile our belief in ourselves with our devastation of Vietnam and Cambodia and our total failure to keep Southeast Asia "safe from communism," temporarily stymied by what it was we stood for, Americans simply shut off debate on such subjects for the last half of the 1970s. We buried Vietnam in our collective unconscious. And with it we buried alive the wretched veterans of that war, who were never permitted, psychologically, to come back.

Once again, as during each period of crisis in cultural legitimacy that initiates a new cultural swing, Americans became disillusioned with the ability of their government and its leaders to solve their basic problems. But this time the loss of faith was drastic. Historians have noted that since the beginning of the Republic, a vivid idiosyncrasy of Americans has been their abiding faith and trust in American institutions.[7] Now, government, the military, academia, the courts—all lost some of their magical powers. The human institutions of marriage and the family were infected with dissatisfaction. Assumptions upon which many people had based their major life choices were shaken. Alienation progressed to the point where people had little to believe in but themselves.

By the early 1970s, America had lapsed into a period of withdrawal.

People's personal anxiety and frustration turned into reaction against their institutions as the cause of all their problems. That is the natural response to systematic betrayal—taking matters into our own hands. People looked to themselves as the one form of transport through life that could be trusted. It therefore became imperative that one's physical plant was scrupulously maintained and monitored, not too much baggage was taken on (human or otherwise), and personal radar was not distracted by others' needs or appeals. Every American was a special interest, unto himself. The Seventies were a time when people invoked their own physical or economic survival over civil law. They turned their backs on court-ordered busing, armed themselves with guns, dismantled taxes.

It is instructive to follow along in our contemporary cultural cycle with Wallace and McLoughlin's construct as a guide. But two additional interpretations might be made:

The inward-turning phase of a society also can be seen as a necessary period of withdrawal. Times of withdrawal are essential for introspection and healing. For an individual going through a passage, we have called this the separation and incubation phase. A similar period of incubation may be necessary—even predictable—for a society in disequilibrium. Withdrawal into what Tom Wolfe so aptly named the Me Decade can be reconsidered in this light. It has been written off as purely selfish in motive. Although there is no doubt that Americans went to new lengths of self-indulgence, we may have needed that period to absorb the shocks that had challenged many of our youthful illusions. During such apparently self-indulgent periods things can be sorted out, values of lasting merit separated from spasms of overreaction, and the national spirit often reinvigorated to mount a comeback.

The liberal ideals on which our system was built had not crumbled. National surveys near the end of the Seventies indicated that Americans were just as concerned about ideals and egalitarian goals as they had been twenty or thirty years earlier.[8] It was not the goals but the apparent inability of big government to meet them that left people jaded and cynical, adding to the other causes for withdrawal into themselves or turning to religion. By the end of the 1970s one-third of Americans claimed to be "born again."

An additional phenomenon unaccounted for in classical long-swing theory is the occurrence of cultural life accidents. Major shifts in climate, for example, and the happy accidents of unexpected technological breakthroughs—these forces, too, produce great sea changes in history. Cultural life accidents may be altogether unpreventable. But they may also be brought on by a society's leaders' refusal to change paths voluntarily or by a nation that holds back on choosing sides in an international crisis and does business as usual while hoping to have it both ways. Refusal to anticipate and hesitation in taking the lead are invitations to traumatic cultural accidents visited by outside forces.

In the middle of America's present crisis in legitimacy we suffered an accident of hemispheric proportions. The oil embargo of 1973 initiated the greatest transregional transfer of wealth since the birth of this nation. Americans did not quite believe the pain until each one personally felt it. Financial writer Andrew Tobias used all his metaphoric skills to evoke the staggering payments the United States would have to make to OPEC, which he estimated (in 1979) at $65 billion a year.

> How much is $65 billion? At $400 an ounce, it is all the gold in Fort Knox ($58 billion) and then some—and that would just pay for 1979. . . . In 1981, they could have Wisconsin. In 1982, we could trade our entire steel industry for part of the oil we will be importing and give them Sears and A & P for the rest. (Oops—A & P is no longer ours to give; controlling interest belongs to the Germans.) In 1983, based on current market values, we could pay the bill by giving them IBM, RCA, and General Motors, plus the copyrights to all our motion pictures.[9]

Given that accident, there seemed no way to put the plug back in the hole of inflation, not so long as Americans maintained the government spending and energy consumption that we had gotten away with when the reservoir of GNP was growing at 3 or 4 percent a year. At zero productivity growth—but who was counting?—we were in a position similar to those who refused to believe New York City was about to sink into bankruptcy, described by Felix Rohatyn as sitting in a warm tub with their wrists slit.

As we have discovered, the result of a life accident can be no less than transformative for a pathfinder. And when a *cultural* life accident—war, civil strife, economic disaster, flood, famine, a brush with authoritarian takeover—coincides with a period of withdrawal, the tempo of comeback may be quickened.

By 1981, more swiftly than anyone might have imagined, there was an international oil glut. Continued price hikes by OPEC had forced Western nations to seek new energy sources, and decontrol of America's oil prices had made it attractive to develop better methods of retrieval for old oil. Increasing conservation combined with these efforts to bring prices down all over the world in 1981 and cool a crisis, at least temporarily, that had threatened to choke off the industrial life's blood of the West.

But we had begun in the process to sense acutely that our nation could go down the drain. Not only by thermonuclear means, but now simply by remaining hostage to appetites and entitlements we once took for granted, we could destroy ourselves. Just as in personal development, where the first glimpse of one's own mortality is most stunning, a shadow of the ultimate crisis hung over our land of plenty, lending a chiaroscuro to our national image that cannot be ignored. Life accidents do have a way of forcing the body politic to regain its will and to return to the hard work of growth.

Where Are We Going?

Where are we, then, in the present political and cultural cycles? Three points of analysis converge around the same forecast: a new dawn can be expected sometime in the 1980s.

Demographically: The year 1980 marked the peak of competitive strain on college and career entry for young Americans. They were at the tail end of the baby boom that can be traced back to the economic joyride, touched off by the end of the Second World War, that made it unnecessary for most women to work and fueled an uncommon optimism about the future that was reflected in a flourishing birthrate.

Those 64 million infants who were the bumper crops of the good times, between 1946 and 1961, are now of voting age—between 20 and 35 years old—and since they encompass one-third of the entire United States population, they represent a colossus of value-setting potential.

Having been raised with padded expectations in a period of incomparable prosperity, they walked into the job market at the start of the new Age of Scarcity and had doors slammed in their faces. Because they are twice as likely to be unemployed as their parents were during the 1950s, intense competition for promotions and top salaries will dog them throughout their working lives. The sobering bottom line: they may do well simply to hold to their parents' standard of living, never mind trying to upgrade.

As a result of these realities, the baby-boom generation has little commitment to the system. Their solutions tend toward the private—they will work for the big corporations or the government, but use the position solely for their own ends. Fierce competition will be justified by all means, including crime. Already the dollar is favored above the man.

But as they reach their middle and most productive years (30 to 45), the conditions for producing pathfinders among them should improve: their income level will near its peak, saving will be a little easier, and the impact of their tax revenues on the national economy should be salubrious. The spirit of adventure is likely to reawaken among the baby boomers in the next ten years. They should be ready for a period of expansion beginning in the mid- to late 1980s. And as the 1980s and 1990s progress, a dramatic shrinkage will be seen in the number of teenagers and young adults competing for schooling, jobs, and advancement.

The impact on an individual's life choices of—simply—how many other people were born in the same year is considerable. Lots of company means lots of competition, less optimism, and lowered enthusiasm for raising large families. Roughly twenty years later, a reverse swing usually takes effect, according to demographic interpreters.[10] As a result of the scarcity of young adults produced by their overcrowded parents, opportunities open up again and optimism rises. And young married couples once more dream of larger families.

Politically: "Sometime in the 1980s the dam will break, as it broke at the turn of the century, in the 1930s and in the 1960s," writes Arthur Schlesinger, Jr.[11] Pointing out that the cyclical perspective he inherited from his father has held up pretty well, he predicts, "There will be a breakthrough into a new political epoch, a new conviction of social possibility, a new hunger for dynamism, innovation, crusading, new efforts to redeem the promise of American life."

Culturally: The long-swing historian William McLoughlin observes that although the new evangelism is significant, there is too much of the old political conservatism of fundamentalist ideology and too much authoritarianism among its leaders to offer "new light" for the future. He predicts that an ideological reorientation will take place sometime in the 1980s. Its guiding deity will be defined less in terms of a punishing, judgmental Almighty Father in heaven and more as a supporting, easygoing, parental image embracing both fatherly and motherly qualities. Helping others will emerge as a more positive value than competitiveness. Institutions will be reorganized with more thought given to participation by workers and neighborhoods, and families will find forms other than the nuclear family.

McLoughlin's is a liberal utopian view, and I find utopian constructs of little use or credibility. More important to my way of thinking is to discern and define the roots of a reawakening. In my view the next great awakening, like those of the past, will gather force only when it finds a quintessential American form, calling up our common history and our core values and recombining them with new information and new world realities.

Youth, Health, Vigor!

"The spirit of self-help is the root of all genuine growth in the individual; and, exhibited in the lives of many, it constitutes the true course of national vigor and strength. . . . Hence the value of legislation as an agent in human advancement has always been greatly over-estimated."

The quote is from the roaring best-seller *Self Help*, by Samuel Smiles, translated into seventeen languages. All part of a fad cooked up by the publishing industry to prey on the Me Decade? Well, not exactly. *Self Help* was published in 1859.

In Europe the tradition is to look to the state for improvements in the human condition. When enough people become fed up with the rudeness or conformity or stagnation in their lives, they revolt against the state and rally around the next dissenting political ideologue who promises them a new doctrine that will write a new page of history.

Whereas a country like France is a nation of ideologues, the United States eschews ideologues for a strong, deep, if seldom articulated, consensual ideology, one that is based on self-help and individualism. For all that we have trusted our institutions, we have not looked to them or to their representatives as responsible for our personal fate. To the American mind, the promise and the uniqueness, the imagination and the vigor, lie with the individual, as does the fundamental responsibility for making good. (This is in large part the reason that Americans and Europeans have so much trouble understanding each other, even though it says on paper we all live in democracies. The basic platforms on which we build our attitudes and opinions are composed from very different fundamental propositions.)

There is, of course, a down side to a merit system built around the individual, and it profoundly affects the development of Americans born into limited circumstances. The exceptional individuals advance, but they tend to leave their class behind.

To read history is to realize that for two hundred years belief in the individual has been the single most distinguishing characteristic of Americans. As Tocqueville pointed out, voluntary association, cooperation, and institution building also have been uniquely American strengths. But backed against the wall, Americans have demonstrated again and again a readiness to rely on themselves. My own studies affirmed this: 90 percent of the professionals I surveyed indicated a belief that they were in control of their destiny. Professor Alex Inkeles, in a study at Stanford University, found that three-quarters of American blue-collar workers believe that "What happens to me is my own doing."[12]

Our tradition of self-reliance was inherent in the colonial breakaways and the Puritans, but it took Ralph Waldo Emerson to recombine Yankee self-reliance with his own plain pipe-rack religious vision. That vision emerged after a period of personal withdrawal between 1832 and 1836 when Emerson, beset by domestic sorrows, resigned as minister of the Second Church in Boston and went to Europe to think things out. Upon his comeback, he gave us the gift of his own transformation, between the covers of his book *Nature*.

"Transcendental optimism," as it became known, expressed Emerson's belief that man has a perpetual possibility of direct contact with the Deity, and that through such intuitions, each person can experience his soul as contained in and made one with all others. "All lines meet at infinity, so all individual affirmations fuse in God."[13] Emerson's concept of the Oversoul raised the individual to the highest spiritual power. Twenty years after his death, at the dawn of the 20th century, Emerson's attitude had been absorbed into the cultural blood.

"Emerson incarnated the moral optimism, the progress, and the energy of the American spirit," wrote his biographer Howard Mumford Jones. He was also a profound influence on the recognized leader of American philosophy, William James, who was led by the study of medicine into psychology and who himself helped to put an entirely American stamp on this worship of the individual.

In a famous series of lectures at Harvard at the turn of the century, the benign, humorous, and beloved James taught Americans how to use philosophy to analyze a variety of religious viewpoints. He was a heretical Protestant; his sympathies were obviously with what he called "the religion of healthy-mindedness." A new generation of preachers in Europe and America had already moved beyond the preoccupation with morbid fantasies of wayward toes being scorched by eternal hellfire.

The most important and intriguing idea to emerge from his new pragmatic approach to religion, James declared, was what he named in 1901 the "mind-cure movement."[14] This adoption of a deliberately optimistic scheme of life swept across the United States. People began jumping about as they dressed in the morning, repeating the motto "Youth, health, vigor!" Others took up the "Gospel of Relaxation" or the "Don't Worry Movement." Founders of different mind-cure sects exhorted followers to feel their continuity with the Infinite Power through exercises in meditation, passive relaxation, even hypnosis. All sickness, weakness, or depression was said to be caused by the human sense of separateness from that divine energy called God. By concentrating a beam of optimism on a darkened or diseased inner state, one could burn out the imperfection all by oneself.

James wanted the individual to be happy. But as the British philosopher Bertrand Russell pointed out in dismay, James's approach was that if belief in God made people happy, let them believe.[15] That line of thought might have stopped at benevolence if James had not made the next mental jump: if belief in God made people happy, then it was true that God exists. James actually wrote, "An idea is 'true' so long as to believe it is profitable to our lives." In other words, truth *happens* to an idea; it is *made* true by positive events. And with that jump, James gave the individual the power to concoct whatever notion of God might give him the most tonic effects.

James pronounced the mind-cure movement "the only decidedly original contribution of the American people to the systematic philosophy of life."

The pragmatism with which his countrymen approached even the sacred in their lives amused this philosopher of pragmatism. Americans wanted no blue-lipped blather about salvation in the hereafter—they would have wrinkles and gout and probably croquet elbow by then. What they wanted from a philosophy of life was concrete therapeutics. *Youth, health, vigor!*

Mind-cure satisfied that demand by making an unprecedented use of the unconscious. With such lofty powers to create one's own happiness already assigned to the self, no wonder our intellectuals snapped up Freudianism in the 1930s—even before the father of psychoanalysis had completely won the trust of his own bourgeois Viennese cronies. It must have seemed a natural extension of the native American mind-cure philosophy. But that marked the point at which classical philosophy parted company with psychology—the two disciplines pretending ever since, like two women at a party in the same dress, that the other is not there.

In the process, there was a small but crucial slippage, a mistranslation of Emersonian self-reliance into an illusory "self-help" maintained by various dependencies. Purveyors of modern mind-cures can easily exploit the weak, but also susceptible are those who think they can think their way to power.[16]

Pilgrims of the Sixties

If self-help has been the closest thing to American's native religion for the past 150 years, why isn't it working better today to help people transcend their obsessions with personal problems? Why can't we overcome our anxieties and conflicts by our inner powers alone, supplemented by vitamins and various therapeutic booster shots?

We have already met individuals in this book who have been able to transcend their personal problems without dependence on mind-cures or therapists. Many pathfinders might be said to have had a transcendent experience as children. Facing a dark period, they leaped over childish limitations and found themselves suddenly performing on a level of maturity well beyond their years. Transcendence is also the final and most important step in surviving a life accident. "My focus is on something ahead of me—on a task, an idea, a person who needs help." Or "I will not give in to my fears as a hostage wife—I'll try to raise the level of debate instead." The average person would do well simply to reach a point of full acceptance after such a blow, but the pathfinder who goes on to place hope in a new source of meaning for his or her life may transcend ordinary human limitations.

Transcendence also is the last and richest phase of the creative process. Aware of how one solved the last creative problem, but willing to let go of that solution, one opens oneself to fresh solutions, as well as to fresh possibilities for failure. The transcendent artist emerges from the destruction of his own certainties.

Transcendence also describes an experience—one that can be induced artificially by deep concentration, sleep deprivation, fasting, extreme exertion, chemicals—and that allows one to glimpse fleetingly the whole picture. The transcendent experience provides a moment of centering, carries one beyond the boundaries of time and death. Many natural activities can elevate us into the same temporary state of ecstasy—becoming "lost" in music, dance, battle, sexual love, childbirth, athletic effort, soaring flight, artistic or intellectual creation. These, as well as induced transcendent experiences, came under study by Marghanita Laski at Indiana University. She found they all produced the same four effects:

"An extraordinary sense of psychic unity [inner harmony]; intensity [deep feeling]; illumination [creative thought]; and insight [Now, I understand!]."[17]

But although such an experience can transport a person to regions of ecstasy or clarity unimagined, or to an ineffable harmony between pleasure and pain, and although it may lead to a creative act, a transcendent experience is by nature evanescent—at once as powerful and as temporal as orgasm. It cannot sustain an individual.

The qualities of a transcendent experience set forth by Dr. Laski describe what the young in the early Sixties sought: magic, not logic; sensibility, not responsibility; equality, spirituality, a kingdom of flowers on earth. The real world was rejected and remade in images, mostly borrowed from other cultures, that had no link to the psychic or social history of Americans. As a result, many of the potential pathfinders of that period came loose rather than becoming centered. How they went off the track from self-reliance to self-obsession has much to teach us about the purchase the "moral majority" has gained over our political process today.

The great awakening begun in the Sixties built at first on the cause of civil rights. That movement had deep native roots in our culture. The pull of our unfinished history—the fact of a black sharecropper who still could not vote, of any American who could not sit at certain lunch counters or go to certain colleges—stirred deep emotional chords and revived white guilt. It galvanized the young to revive and restate core cultural values and goals. That rare sort of unification of disparate groups did occur but was diverted. Further into the Sixties, a movement that had united black and white protesters around a clear domestic injustice became divided by antiwar passions.

"That provided the white student movement with something to do of its own," Mario Savio told journalist Alexander Cockburn in 1981,[18] drawing lessons from the fervor he helped to start with the Berkeley Free Speech Movement. "The bad effects of that . . . break between the black and white movement in the mid-'60s . . . have never really been overcome." When the war disappeared as an issue, Savio says, the white movement was cut off without an ongoing link to domestic evils. "It wasn't much of an event for the media and the great world, but in fact it was crucial in terms of the development of the United States."

Many of the young of the Sixties could not grow up. They were without a raison d'être. Their polestars had been shot down. There was a perversion of individualism into "What can the society do for me?" Whenever pilgrims (or artists) feel betrayed by reason, they fall back on a belief in instinct. The spirit of the Sixties turned anti-intellectual. It was easy to drift off into music and drugs and simply repeat the purely sensate experience of induced "transcendence" over and over—but that was rather like racing the motor of Ken Kesey's psychedelic bus in a locked garage.

Assuming for the moment, according to Jamesian optimism, that the *belief* by an individual that his or her acts *can* make a difference actually invests these acts with a transcending power—why didn't flower power work? When children of the late Sixties dropped out to form communes and lose their egos in Zen Buddhism and other Eastern religions, when they tried to practice the concentrated optimism of unbounded love, why were they not able to come back and transform their society in keeping with their personal experiences of transcendence?

The images they borrowed from other cultures called up no shared values, history, or suitable heroic models. And transcendent experiences, just as they cannot sustain an individual, are not strong enough to sustain a society unless anchored in its collective history, values, and images.

Much of the message of America's consensual ideology is conveyed nonverbally, through a continuous spring of cultural imagery: the lone silhouette of George Washington in a boat taking him to battle; the pioneer wife of the "big sky" movies, who draws a weary hand across her brow, straightens her apron, and tramps back through the flood-stricken fields determined to get the new seed in the ground; the lonesome cowboy after whom Kissinger patterned his shuttle diplomacy; the tight focus on two men in a space shuttle; right up to the hero's welcome given President Reagan by Congress a month after his stunning comeback from mortal attack. Our reverence is saved for victories of the indomitable individual over fate or circumstance, victories that are often beyond politics and religion. Mantras, prayer wheels, Tibetan death verse, martial arts, Muslim fervor, flowing Indian or African robes, and kids cavorting about Yankee fields draped in Siddartha loincloths—they are all remnants of value systems unconnected with the individualistic spirit that is in the American blood.

For American Indians who participated in peyote rituals, an important condition kept them grounded while their minds lifted off toward a transcendent faith that "a new road" could be found. They had "a reservoir of shared cultural imagery—usually religious," psychiatrist Robert Jay Lifton explains in *The Broken Connection*.[19] Transcendence almost inevitably requires imagery that concerns life, its ultimate meaning, and some symbol of immortality, Lifton reminds us. When the imagery anchors the person in his individual as well as his collective history, the moment of transcendence may offer the vision of a new road to "come home." That sort of content was explicitly missing for most Sixties pilgrims in search of a new consciousness under acid. Their rituals offered no promise of immortality, or at least none sufficiently invested with emotion by the culture or religious belief to hold up and become a springboard for rebirth.

Average people do not usually think of themselves as being "in search of the transcendent." They just feel a dull hunger for some meaning at the core of their lives—for a centering—and they cast about for something to make them feel better. Maybe it will be drugs, or self-hypnosis, or honing the body into a jackknife of physical fitness; perhaps it will be the rituals of submission and self-punishment in est, or "going through the wall" in marathon running.

Our young, searching in the Sixties for altered states of being in the ashrams of India, fished out of the curry pot those most concrete and therapeutic aspects of the otherwise ascetic Hindu religion, whereupon these were adapted to reducing the tensions of a fast-paced, otherwise indulgent American life. Yoga and transcendental meditation are now endorsed by the American Management Association and the Heart Association and recommended for getting through diets and past smoking and over broken love affairs. Biofeedback is a machine-monitored reissue of the Mary Baker Eddy principles of Christian Science. Our latest religion, Fitness, is one more method to achieve the results promised by all the old-time religions of healthy-mindedness, the new twist being: sound in body, sound in mind. Beyond the few hours or days of residual results, however, any one of the contemporary rituals of self-help can become ironically empty. I suspect that is because each is a valueless experience. No images of immortality deriving from cultural or religious belief exist in these rituals, which might challenge the unease of suspecting that our lives are meaningless.

Encapsulated in private rituals of self-help, one is shut off from what is shared—from community, from history, from the social forces that shape our lives. "The ecstatic or meditative experience then takes on the near-absolute irony of furthering the very focus on the technical and prosaic it was originally called forth to transcend," writes Lifton.

Music is the one artifact remaining from the counterculture's search for rebirth. But even their most sacred music dealt with the evanescent, when it was not obsessed with death. Their music did not set them free. Beyond the reverence for feeling, for tuning in and treating people more gently, there was no ethical system for sorting things out. Feeling is not enough. The young man who shot his impotent rage into John Lennon had strong feelings too; were they enough to give ethical justification to his act?

Because these groundings in shared cultural values were missing, and because there was no content that surpassed time and death, the moments of transcendence experienced by pilgrims of the Sixties did not add up to a great culture-wide awakening. Instead, they sent many potential pathfinders off into bad trips.

Back to the Old-Time Religion

With Aquarian spirituality having fizzled into privatism, it was no surprise that the old-time religions of pentecostal and charismatic Christian persuasion came back and spread across the nation in the late Seventies. Evangelical Christianity offered a strong alternative to the protean style. Evangelism substitutes an airtight construct for the burdens of forming and re-forming an individual identity to allow for continuing adult development and social change, and modifying values to fit circumstance. Inside it, all personal, social, and moral questions are answered. There need be no risk, no change, no mystery, no uncertainty. A further promise is the ultimate transcendence: to be freed of these mortal coils to come back, after death, in a rebirth through God.

If we assume that each great cultural awakening begins with a period of individual stress, who is looking out for the growing legions of people who have lost their bearings and who exhibit mental or physical illness? Where are the traditional churches when people need help to orient themselves during a period of disenchantment with their institutions? Many mainline Protestant churches rendered themselves irrelevant to both the Left and the Right by their ambiguous stand during the civil rights movement. The Catholic church and many of its contemporary communicants have become seriously at odds over the birth control issue (76.5 percent of American Catholics practice it) and more recently over abortion (77 percent favor it as a choice in all, or certain, circumstances).[20] On an individual level the local church often has failed to deliver what people really need during a personal passage or a time of national transition: a sense of intimacy with their spiritual guides, a community of shared values, and the reassurance that members of that community care about them.

Where do people turn, especially those who are old, frightened, not the winners in American life? Who reaches out for those weakened by illness, recovering from operations, shaken by one life accident or another, and often limited in their mobility or ordered to "stay at home and take it easy"? Who talks every day to those who have been consigned to invisibility for being retired, obsolete in skills, of the wrong color or accent?

The new televangelists,[21] that's who.

"One of the most striking characteristics of the new mass media," wrote Donald Horton and Richard Wohl in *Psychiatry* a quarter of a century ago, "is that they give the illusion of face-to-face relationship with the performer. . . . In time, the devotee—the 'fan'—comes to believe that he 'knows' the person more intimately and profoundly than others do; that he 'understands' his character and appreciates his values and motives. . . . The persona may be considered by his audience as a friend, counselor, comforter, and model."[22]

Thus is created, of a total stranger, a polestar. Through simulated intimacy, this stranger becomes a direct link to God. People feel as close to Jerry Falwell or Rex Humbard or James Robison as they did to Uncle Walter or Archie Bunker, or before television, to the mind's image of the Shadow. What is more, all these people are professional performers. They will not drop you to sing the Doxology while some dour Scotch Presbyterian processes up an aisle, leaving the altar altogether bare. No video preacher would ever leave his set empty. He has stirring music and bright lights and fabulous close-ups and fantasy sets—a crystal cathedral, for heaven's sake! Televangelists rarely break their cardinal covenant with the consciousness of viewers: "Thou shalt not bore!"

And when their eyes look directly into the living room, the viewer imagines, at last, *I am seen.*

People do become more involved in religion or religious questions as they grow older; that is evident not only in my data but by simple observation of any church congregation. And, in fact, the whopping majority of the audience who seek a polestar among the televangelists are over 50 years of age. Two-thirds to three-quarters was the figure released by the Arbitron research firm to Jeffrey K. Hadden, a sociologist, and Charles E. Swann, an ordained Presbyterian minister, who wrote *Prime Time Preachers.* It should come as no surprise that, as the authors point out, the elderly are more likely to embrace evangelical as opposed to liberal or mainstream beliefs. Those who have already lived more than half their lives, and are not happy with the results, are naturally more likely to seek a "born-again" experience. It is more common to hear the elderly represent the Bible as the literal word of God and to "witness" their faith to others.

But born-again fever is not confined just to little old ladies in tennis shoes. It has swept through the professional sports world. Strapping young athletes get down on their knees in locker rooms these days, not to swill a little bourbon or pop some "ludes," but to join the pregame prayer meeting.

Thank you, Jesus, for giving us your blessing to go out there and skin 'em alive!

Besides comforting the weak, evangelism can also be used to justify any form of opportunism.

It is not quite fair to take the New Evangelical Right to task for promising a heaven on earth. Each past wave of religious optimism has envisioned remaking the world in the image of heaven, whether it was the hotbed of Christian Socialists at Union Theological in the early 1900s who dreamed of peasant revolt in the streets of Hell's Kitchen (where one rarely saw a plow) or the children of the Sixties who put flowers in gun barrels while chanting, "No more war!" The Marxists' dream, the pacifists' dream, and the evangelists' dream are kept alive only by ignoring all historical attempts to achieve them. But when the leaders of the "moral majority" fire up their flock to demand politically the same certainty they have embraced theologically, there is this problem: to succeed would spell the end of our pluralistic society.

If they had their way, they would coerce others into practicing their own beliefs by passing laws that make any deviation punishable. They would "protect" the Republic from "demoralizing" ideas by banning the books and suspending from the schools and taking away the television licenses of anyone who does not have the "right" set of beliefs—that is, theirs. All this would be done in the name of a higher morality. No one is ever sure what "morality" means, except that it is usually the last word spoken before someone is burned at the stake.

Whether there is life after death; whether there is viable, birth-supporting life before the third trimester; whether any one person can sentence another to death and not be guilty of murder—these are the subjects of philosophical and ethical debate, not of legal fiat. There are no incontrovertible facts. There never have been. These are the questions that try, and train, the human conscience.

Return with a Difference

Given these recent examples of larger cultural swings, let us consider now the symbiosis between exceptional individuals and the periods of a cycle, and the effect of this symbiosis on history.

One theme is repeated through both the political and the cyclical swing theories—the theme of Withdrawal and Comeback. The same dynamic is seen among armies when they retreat to gather forces, in music with recapitulation of a modified theme followed by the flourish of a coda, in the systole and diastole of the human heart, and in the cycles of nature's withdrawal in winter and comeback in spring. It is of course the apotheosis of Christian religions: the theme of crucifixion and resurrection. The entire New Testament is woven around a single theme: Christ came back, and so can you.

We see the same phenomenon in the lives of many world figures, suggesting an important interplay between culture and individual pathfinders. Historian Arnold Toynbee devoted one book of his nine-volume study of civilizations to the theme of withdrawal and return.[28] He saw as the catalyst for a culture's return the individual who moves through his or her own momentous passage.

"It is through the inward development of personality that individual human beings are able to perform those creative acts, in the outward field of action, that cause growths of human societies," he wrote. This state of being is reached by creative personalities, inspired leaders, geniuses, and mystics, through a process of withdrawal that provides opportunity for a personal transfiguration. Following the personal withdrawal into solitude there is a return to transformational leadership, as Toynbee pointed out in the lives of Buddha, Jesus, Muhammad, Dante, and Machiavelli.

"The essence of the whole movement, as well as its final cause . . . is the return of the transfigured personality into a social milieu out of which he had originally come."

Anwar Sadat exemplifies this dynamic, which applies to other towering 20th-century world leaders as well—Mahatma Gandhi, Churchill, Stalin, Nehru, de Gaulle, Boumédienne. But although the ebb and flow of withdrawal and comeback can be seen in oceanic proportions in such lives, it is not in the least limited to them.

It is possible—through engaging in the struggle of life beyond the importance of self—to reach a point of self-knowledge and self-acceptance where, as Hegel described it, we can "come home" to ourselves, where alienation is overcome. It was in that fragment of a moment on the riverbank across from the City of the Dead that I had what I think of now as a transcendent glimpse: the possibility of comeback for a society in an evolutionary sense. Although I did not yet know the phrases for it, the impulse had already been spelled out as a "return with a difference," in Hegel's words, and in Toynbee as the "return that is the essence."

What brings a culture back from withdrawal and loss of faith in its institutions and leaders is a redefinition of its core beliefs and values. Those values must be realigned around the changed realities of our social contract and changes in the world order. This process has enabled us to emerge from each period of great cultural crisis with our self-confidence as a people refreshed and renewed, and with an effervescence of ideas and energy for facing our problems, not in fear or atomization, but together, once more, in a spirit of adventure.

The great awakenings are not only moral or religious but also scientific and technological. The biochemical revolution upon us, for instance, will create new microorganisms and assign them the task of regenerating resources of which we are running out, perhaps turning us into a microregenerative society. An immediately previous explosion of technologic innovation—microcircuitry and the semiconductors—already has made it possible to regenerate dead hearts and replace other organs, to computerize almost everything, and to "get small" in many dimensions in an otherwise shrinking and overpopulated world. Biotechnology will play a critical role in the comeback for the West from the new Age of Scarcity. But to look exclusively to science for sources of renewal would be as shortsighted as our earlier romance with technology, which produced the mixed blessing of nuclear fission.

A return with a difference means to me the necessity for *recombining*—coming back to old conflicts and solving or resolving them at a higher level. In *The Third Wave*[24] Alvin Toffler reminds us that formerly agricultural societies, and many today, "see time as a circle, not a straight line. From the Mayas to the Buddhists and the Hindus, time was circular and repetitive . . . lives perhaps reliving themselves through reincarnation." This meant coming back only by repetition (within one's karma, in the Eastern concept) and cast the possibility of self-improvement and cultural progress as mere illusions. The seasons, repeating themselves year after year, would have fortified this concept in agricultural societies. The concept had to be changed to accommodate industrialization.

A linear or linelike concept "fostered by the mercantile class and the rise of a money economy" eventually dominated all industrial societies. In the 1970s—for the first time in the history of the modern world, according to historian and social theorist Robert Nisbet[25]—a society discarded belief in the idea of unlimited progress: the United States seemed about to embrace a philosophy of no growth. We were up against a setback of unlimited progress that had been based on natural resources formerly taken for granted—cheap oil, clean air and water, space. At last we recognized these resources as finite. But upon entering the 1980s, the dawn of another revolution in technology—the biochemical revolution—promised ways of regenerating even the finite. *Recombinant* is the operative word. This kind of recombining means the formation of new combinations of linked genes in organisms capable of undreamed-of tasks and even new heritable characteristics for human beings.

This breakthrough is one of many evidences of a different model of cultural development in advanced societies, one that would have pleased the late American anthropologist Gregory Bateson. The linear model of causal progression, Bateson believed, failed to account for what he called "stochastic" processes, which make it possible for events to evolve by leaps and bounds.

The Role of Transcendent Pathfinders

Who among us is likely to take up the work of redefining and revitalizing our core values? Who is ready to take up a cause or purpose beyond his own advancement or security? Who is given to leaps of development?

I speak, of course, of pathfinders.

The jagged, zigzag course taken by transcendent pathfinders who are able to ascend, beyond problems of personal development, to leave a mark of improvement on their society, is a course paralleled by societies in comeback. As I see it, this course is neither circular nor linear, but a spiral. Each great awakening makes a startling leap—of thought or technology, or both—and jumps us ahead to a higher curve in the road up the mountain. This interaction between the individual visionary pathfinder and the proper social and political climate permits a course of development that might be seen as a transformative spiral.

Beyond the enriched well-being of the people we have met so far, then, is yet another level: the mountain that transcendent pathfinders attempt to climb toward their highest social or spiritual or creative purpose. The dictionary definition of *transcendence* that comes closest to what we are getting at is "extending or being beyond the limits of ordinary experience."

That level of transcendence may turn a pathfinder into a pathleader—one who has the power or position to influence many people and who makes a transformative ethical, political, or moral impact on the times. Martin Luther and Mahatma Gandhi, as their lives have been analyzed by Erik Erickson,[26] both expressed their personal salvation as a political act. That personal transformation may occur in the course of a passage of Withdrawal and Comeback.

When the two most important women in Theodore Roosevelt's life died on the same day, he folded up his life as a conventional lawyer in the East and lit out to become a cowboy. He bought a ranch and killed about twelve hundred animals before his mourning was done. He had plunged into the heart of the American myth—into hunting and bloodshed in the Wild West. When a blizzard wiped him out, he failed as a rancher. But from that withdrawal, Roosevelt emerged a transformative leader.

J. P. Morgan, the financier, had several early mental breakdowns, the first when his young wife died; at other times he succumbed to the weight of a dominating father. Morgan's withdrawal was periodic, and into Eastern culture: he escaped to Egypt each year. His strongest comeback occurred in the middle of his fifties, after his father's death. From that time on, J. P. Morgan became a one-man engine of economic acceleration for his society.

The idea of such a pathleader may seem larger than life. More plentiful and possible to emulate are transcendent pathfinders. They are not people who are likely to be walking around composing a rough draft of the Declaration of Independence or planning how to defeat the forces of darkness. For the most part transcendent pathfinders look just like you and me. They probably were like you and me at an earlier point, but something prompted them to make a sacrifice or to take a great risk—something that to an outsider's eyes would not have appeared sensible, yet to them had a compelling logic. For a time, they were seized by a goal that transcended self-interest.

If someone suggested that you take off for Africa and save lepers because it would make you feel wonderful, you would probably sit in your straw hut feeling miserable and slapping at flies. But if you were compelled by something within you, an entirely different set of values would surface; an altogether different wellspring of pleasure would be tapped. Transcendent pathfinders who appear to be models of self-sacrifice often are not. Normal material values have lessened in weight for them, at least temporarily.

One transcendent pathfinder we have already met is the former Jesuit, Keith Buckley. Fearful that if he stepped outside formal religious commitment he would become as superficial as his father had been, he did make an early sacrifice and found the regimentation and denial of Jesuit life compatible for the first half of his life. But after a period of withdrawal in his 41st year, he came back strong, separated himself from the order, and affirmed that the decision he was making would not change him from a good man into a bad one. Dr. Buckley transcended his personal history and went on to become one of the earliest watchers over our medical technological revolution. He is uniquely suited to be a sentinel. Supported by his timeless religious values, elevated in the watchtower of academia in a department he himself created, he can be free enough from the *process* to recognize what is ephemeral, to act as witness to careless crimes of technology.

If we wish to focus on those people who have refreshed their society after a period of individual withdrawal and comeback, where do we begin looking? Among politicians there does develop the occasional transcendent pathfinder, but most politicians carry out their transactions with society primarily in the interest of their own reelection. If we wait for our political leaders to commit acts of courage or to produce original ideas, we may be cubes under the next polar ice cap before America comes back.

It is to others that we should look—to the artist who imagines new possibilities, to the articulator who gives voice to what many sense, to the observer who sees, the sentinel who warns, the witness who testifies. These are the often unlikely and sometimes even quiet, but transcendent, pathfinders who offer the fresh blood of their own rebirths to transfuse their society.

16.
AN ACT
OF
COURAGE

One snow-muffled morning in February of 1976, I awoke to the radio news of three nuclear engineers who were quitting their industry to launch a national debate on the safety of nuclear power. They were on their way to Washington to appear at a special joint congressional committee hearing. Something instinctively told me that the bold path these people had chosen might help us to pick up the examination of our core values where it had been dropped, from exhaustion, with the ending of the Vietnam War. I caught a plane to meet them that day.

They had been members of the nuclear brotherhood from the very beginning. And what a beginning! For three engineers from the American Midwest, even the starch of conservatism in their marrow was no match for the goading of hubris in their hearts, not with mentors like the first chairman of the Atomic Energy Commission, who fired up young men by prophesying, "We can travel at the speed of enlightenment. . . ." What was to check them from flying straight up to the sun, half blinded by the dream of replacing the very source of energy with a bigger-than-man machine system, the nuclear reactor, and taming that savage beast into giving us benign BTUs to pop our toast and power our industrial complex? How much closer could one come to engineers' paradise? Up until 1976, these three men—Dale Bridenbaugh, Greg Minor, and Dick Hubbard*—had been part of a dynamic corps building an industry that bordered on the incredible.

They belonged to a generation brought up on the religion of technology. Total belief in man-machine systems was commonly taught in the small, single-focus midwestern technical colleges out of which came many of those who now command our aerospace industries, our airlines, our giant utilities and nuclear hardware manufacturers. The dogma said the machine was perfect. Any flaw had to be the fault of its one inferior component—man. Men describe the attraction of their machines in the military back in the 1950s as not unlike that of a lover wooing an ice maiden, yearning to be accepted, suspending judgment as they surrendered themselves to the cold brilliance of that closed system, even at the price of death!

"That kind of closed-system thinking is very seductive," recalls Dr. Isaiah Zimmerman from his years of heading the mental-health unit at Lackland Air Force Base. "When we asked pilots if they ever checked out their planes other than by relying on instruments—ever *looked* at rear cargo doors or kicked the tires—never."

Each of the engineers together with his wife had taken a safe, socially approved, and well-marked path. And coming up on their late thirties and early forties, all three couples found they had more or less "made it" in material terms. What, then, could have prompted these middle-level technocrats to turn off the well-traveled path at the juncture to middle life?

They would have to let go of some very important attachments. They were naturally quite tied to a certain job status, income level, and social acceptance, but found themselves a little muddy about what it all meant. The engineers were coming through the Deadline Decade, all of them being between the ages of 35 and 45. Each couple—unknown to the others—had initiated a search for greater meaning in the personal sphere. What began as an effort to shore up their marital commitments soon took them well beyond the personal realm, until each one was immersed in an astringent stock-taking of his values and faith.

* Real names.

Most people would assume that the engineers' decision on the nuclear question was the great turning point in their lives. It became clear during our first talk, however, that leaving their jobs was the outcome of a passage that had begun some years before. The general public having forfeited its watchdog responsibility for this newest offspring of technology, they were quite alone when they began.

In bread-and-butter terms, the question for the men and their families was: Can members of the command generation meet the challenge of middle age choosing to live by what they now believe? What states of mind would they pass through as they navigated this tricky course? How would their marriages and friendships be affected? How would they defend their weaknesses, nourish their strengths? Where would they be several years down the road?

Would it turn out to be worthwhile for them or for their society to take the less-traveled path?

Private Courage, Public Courage

A larger question must be asked before we can place the human drama of the engineers and their families in perspective: Is everyone presented with the opportunity to become a transcendent pathfinder?

Taking the risk of leaving a marriage, changing a job, escaping a trap, may be hard and even for a while harrowing, but, assuming it works, things will become better for the risker. The incentive is clear. Therefore, the usual willingness pathfinders show in taking risks draws upon a different sort of courage from that demanded of the transcendent pathfinder.

Also different is the risk of taking up a purpose beyond one's own advancement as an adjunct to one's daily work and pleasure. The risk is only of giving up some time and convenience, and as people repeatedly explained, the certain reward is "it makes you feel good." The nuclear engineers did not have to draw fire. They might have said, "Sure, we'll sign a petition," or written a thoughtful article for *Atomic Industrial Forum*. Transcendent pathfinding generally demands that one make a sacrifice.

We are talking about a relatively special group here, but

not so special as you might think. If you have any influence in your field or your community, it may occur to you at some point to make a decision that involves sacrificing your comfort for the good of strangers.

There is no certainty of return. This is a long shot, a personal and often a moral gamble. People who engage in social or political resistance, for instance, may not even be utterly certain at first that they are on the right side. Consider people who joined the French Resistance, whose moral probity can be seen clearly today. At the time it could only have been murky. With French police deporting 100,000 Jews while the nation made not the slightest gesture of support for those victims, the very meaning of history, of normalcy, seemed to the majority to reside in collaboration.[1]

Most of us are not called upon to perform public acts of courage, as in such harrowing periods of history, or in combat, or in political life. But once to every line worker or manager or professional probably does come the chance to live his or her ethics and values in the face of practical pressures to do otherwise.

The usual choice is to compromise with the system and to rationalize that compromise.

"There are trade-offs in everything," says the executive.

"I'm doing the best I can in my area of responsibility," says the specialist.

"It's beyond my control," says the hourly worker.

"This is my bread and butter," says just about anyone.

Even those who do speak up for concerns larger than self can be easily ignored. Several different people within the nuclear industry, for instance, wrote separate memos pointing to deficiencies that were later exposed by the accident at Three Mile Island. Each memo died on the desk of the next person in the pecking order. To make a real change in people's thinking demands that one go still further.

My God, am I going to jeopardize my career, my family, my whole financial future? would be the normal response. It is this entirely rational self-interest that is transcended. An affirmative answer comes only from those whose conviction is so strong that others may call it "crazy." To them it is the only sane alternative.

Most people, as theologian Reinhold Niebuhr reasoned, "lack the intellectual penetration to form independent judgments and therefore [they] accept the moral opinions of their society. Even when they do form their own judgments there is no certainty that their sense of obligation toward moral values, defined by their own mind, will . . . overcome the fear of social disapproval . . . and the pressure of society upon an individual."[2]

Sitting on an Accident Waiting to Happen

Dale Bridenbaugh was one of a handful of field engineers chosen in 1958 to supervise construction of General Electric's first nuclear installation, Dresden I in Illinois. His value system at that stage followed the usual lines of a middle-class American in his Trying Twenties—although he did have glimpses of something more to come.

"You go to work as a young graduate, you work hard to prove you can do a good job—I'm sure I did things I didn't believe in—and all because you want that approval," he came to understand. "It's not until later in life that you begin doing what you think is right. And if it works out, eventually you can get social approval for being independent."

For Dale Bridenbaugh, there was a particularly painful conflict between the hunger for independence and the desire for social acceptance and security. He had been a young teenager when his mother died. His father, forced to sell the family farm, set off for the western expanse to seek a solid second chance. Virtually orphaned, Dale endured his adolescence with two elderly aunts in the stark mesas of South Dakota. He sat in the hills, listening to the wind croon through the brakes, and imagined how it would be to live just like other boys. Someday he would build for himself a solid, stable life with close friends and family and a place to belong.

By 1970, when Dale reached his late thirties, he had a son and a daughter and a wife with a ripe and healthy face who kept their conformist suburban home reassuringly unchanged year after year behind an *allée* of walnut trees in a smug northern California valley. They belonged to a big corporate family, to a traditional Protestant church, and to the unexamined political background of their parents. Dale was offered the job in California as managing supervisor of all field engineers, which meant he could not remain one himself. Because that was the door to management, it never occurred to the Bridenbaughs to ask, *But is this right for a man who's never happier than when he's sent out to clamber around steam turbines in a strange plant?* Time with his family was precious but scant. At 40, Dale found himself relatively successful in a narrow field, feeling utterly trapped.

That would help to explain why he had jumped so hard on his wife, Char, in '68 when she made the first attempt to open the seams on their strict Republican uniform. She wanted to vote for Humphrey over Nixon. Certainly not! Not if *he* was going to stay in the straitjacket. Char's father, too, was scandalized—that a daughter could be so ungrateful, so misguided.

Char had always kept peace by knuckling under, but she knew her weakness for what it was. She vowed this time, silently, to grow strong enough so that she would not have to bend her beliefs to please the men.

Suppose the issue of nuclear safety had never come up. Would Dale have felt too constrained to remain in the structured corporate life anyway? He believes he probably would have stayed but changed his focus. Even in 1972, when he began having doubts about reactor designs, he never dreamed he would end up leaving the industry. He still thought of the Nuclear Regulatory Commission as the traffic cop who pulls you over for no good reason. So thoroughly had he digested corporate values that he took the approach, "We know what's good for the country, if only the government would get out of the way and let us design the future properly."

Ripples of change began when Dale and Char realized their churchgoing had become rote and meaningless. They stopped going but soon found themselves miserable as atheists. Friends in the environmental movement introduced them to a quasi-religious foundation centered around the proposition that a mature philosophy and psychology could serve the same purpose as organized religion. The foundation emphasized reconnecting couples who were drifting apart because they had lost track of a clear line of values.

To welcome in the New Year of 1973, the Bridenbaughs got together with several couples and piles of kids to rent a house in the High Sierras, the idea being to take a long

look at their future commitments while in the company of
friends. Dale and Char found themselves under the glory sky
of the year's first morning singing a hymn:

> Once to every man and nation comes the moment to
> decide . . . for some great cause. . . . And the choice goes
> by forever 'twixt that darkness and that light.

"It left a powerful impression on both of us," Char recalls.
It would take considerable time for the powerful impression
evoked by that hymn to shape itself into an idea from which
the Bridenbaughs would choose their own path at the intersection of middle life. But the first phase of a major
passage—the anticipation phase—had been set in motion.

Disturbing tests alerted Dale that an older generation of
reactors had a defective containment design. He formed a
safety review committee to work with utility owners and the
NRC, but after a year of effort, nothing. All nineteen of the
utilities involved refused to shut down for refitting. The NRC
looked the other way.

By the summer of 1975, Dale Bridenbaugh was 43 and
naturally feeling his own mortality acutely. At the same time
he was sitting on a nuclear accident waiting to happen. He
could not look at the kids in his boy scout troop any longer
without thinking about the fact that he worked for an industry that was producing radioactive waste by the metric
ton—one teaspoonful of which, borne on a brisk wind, could
sow thousands of cancers—and there was no feasible plan for
safely disposing of it. He caught Char staring at their son,
the one who looked at people sideways through the murk of
cataracts. Was Char thinking the same thing he was? Dale
had been exposed to low-level radiation on the job for years,
and congenital cataracts have been linked to radiation exposure. But such things were too threatening for Dale and
Char to speak of, yet.

Gradually, individually, they understood that life is what
one does every day. Dale did everything he knew how to fix
it, make it better, bring the industry around from the inside.
At a certain point he had to accept defeat and compromise
his beliefs to protect his comforts—or cut his ties and walk
away. Without consciously acknowledging it, the Briden-

baughs had been approaching this crossroads for the past five years.

Mr. Bridenbaugh Goes to Washington

It was an unremarkable summer day when Char Bridenbaugh, bending over the ironing board to press some silly shirt, felt the rip inside. She knew her husband felt alone and trapped with his own doubts about his job. But other GE wives said there was nothing to worry about. People were pulling her apart.

"If I do what I sense Dale wants to do, I could be sending him down the tube, throwing away my marriage, my kids, everything." She remembers the course of her thoughts vividly. "If I listen to GE, I could be throwing away the whole country."

Digging at the shirt with the iron, she longed for some mooring, a checkpoint between the competing moralities. A wave of fatigue came over her and beckoned her toward the cave of sleep.

She drifted toward the bedroom. Something flickered inside her, like a burner refiring, and a roar of energy pressed up against her inner walls. "No!" she cried out. "I'm scared to death to do this thing, but I'm not going to roll over and play dead. My God, I don't want to be dead inside a body that goes on walking around!"

What came to her then was her vow of seven years before: to learn to listen to herself. That was the only mooring.

"As strong as were the pulls of security," she told me later, "I knew I would be selling my soul. There was no choice."

That night Char told Dale that she had concluded independently that nuclear power was not right.

"I also know you have to support us, and I in no way claim to understand the pressure a husband feels," she said quietly. "But I want you to know that if you ever come to feel as I do, I will go out and scrub toilets. I don't care, we'll get along."

So began the separation phase of their passage—a series of detachments laid side by side over the next nine months like razor cuts. But once Dale had decided to coordinate his resignation with those of the two other GE engineers, and they had all talked it over with their families, a new support network was formed: six people who would be crucial to one another's survival.

A great deal of publicity attended their departure from General Electric.

"You couldn't have done more damage to the organization if you'd fired a cannon in the hallway and blown everyone to kingdom come," a colleague at GE told one of the men much later. "Everything ground to a halt. All anybody could do was sit around and talk about what you guys did. Until management said, 'This is war.' "

Because of the media coverage, the engineers were invited to appear in the nation's capital to give definitive testimony before a congressional committee, called together in a crisis atmosphere. They had four days to prepare. Working around the clock, they gathered no fewer than seventy pages of hard-packed testimony. Just enough to bomb. Like Mr. Smith in the old movie, the men went to Washington utterly unguarded and simply goodwilled, eager to alert the guardians of the public weal to the perils of becoming dependent on commercial nuclear power.

The hearing room of the Joint Committee on Atomic Energy on that morning of February 17 was SRO. The committee members did not appear at all pleased with the three men who had brought the blaze of television lights into their hearing room. The engineers had thrown down a moral gauntlet to anyone deriving financial gain from any arm of the nuclear industry.

As if anticipating the mood of his colleagues, Chairman John Pastore admonished, "There will be no harassment of any witness."

Greg Minor went first. He testified to the excitement the men had felt when they first joined the infant atomic power industry and their gradual disenchantment. The committee sat tight, mostly scowling. Dick Hubbard followed, describing in a meticulous monotone reports of indirect deaths due to radiation. He lost them.

It took Dale Bridenbaugh, then 44, to win the audience back. Retaining the detachment of a mountain man, he seldom speaks more than he has to, but when he does there is a big-sky sprawl to his speech, a natural sincerity.

"We are not here to argue whether or not deaths have occurred in the past," he began. "What I am here to present are my deep personal concerns about the technological flaws that I see developing in the program and the vast potential this has for future deaths and consequences to the total public."

Pastore shot back: "Are these defects you speak of correctable?"

"Many are correctable, yes, sir," Bridenbaugh said politely.

Pastore pressed: "Are they correctable to the point of being safe?"

"In my opinion, they are not."

The crowd bristled with excitement. This was not going to be any quick kill.

"Why?" Pastore demanded.

"Because I think we have no way of minimizing, or getting to a reasonably low enough level, the human error, the oversights, and the generic problems that are inherent in the program," Bridenbaugh replied.

"In other words," Pastore prompted, "you are saying we never should have started in the first place?"

"At least," Bridenbaugh said reasonably, "we are going too fast." He began summarizing from their prepared testimony.

"Is this a lecture?" one of the senators grumbled.

The scene turned nasty. When the engineers talked nuts and bolts, one of the committee members would draw them out into larger, peripheral concerns. Once there, another committee member would box their ears for straying from their area of expertise. Bridenbaugh tried to explain that this was the crux of the problem: no one in the nuclear industry was putting all the pieces of the picture together.

Back came a contemptuous blast from Congressman Mike McCormack, a nuclear champion for his state of Washington. Outraged that *his* baby and the committee's exclusive bailiwick had been invaded by mere dime-a-dozen engineers, he charged the trio with a "calculated program to achieve the maximum political effect" (as if no politician had ever tried that). But then McCormack swung hard and low. He hit them with their religious affiliation.

"I have here statements written by . . . employees of General Electric, also members of [the religious foundation Dale and Char had joined]." Brandishing papers in true Joe McCarthy tradition, McCormack began reading about a meeting of the group at which one of the leaders had allegedly said, "God did not create plutonium and therefore it is evil." "Do you agree with this statement?" he demanded of the engineers.

Weird, Dale Bridenbaugh thought. Two of the "colleagues" who had signed the condemnatory statements claimed to be very close friends—he scarcely knew them. Another name belonged to an engineer who himself was wracked over whether or not to sacrifice his job to state his concerns. *Does everyone, sooner or later, succumb to the thought police?* Dale wondered. He thought he had anticipated what it would be like when he handed in his resignation. He didn't know the half of it.

"To leave his friends of twenty-two years?" his wife had explained. "It was unspeakable agony, like going into exile. He had to do it—you can't ignore a moral situation that is becoming intolerable—but as a human being you do have all these *attachments*. Dale was among the most highly respected men in the company for his integrity. He didn't have any ax to grind, he was always so good with people—when anybody had a personal problem at GE, it was most often Dale they came to. That's why his resignation shocked them so much."

Now it was Dale's turn to be shocked. Congressman McCormack raised questions about the engineers' mental weight. Could be, he seemed to imply, they were just part of the general flakiness blowing out of California: people poaching their brains in hot tubs and doing "fango therapy"; people taking such pains to keep young and fit and thin, calibrating each ounce put on and taken off with such devotion to minutiae that it seemed entirely possible they scooped out their own giblets every morning and weighed them one by one before settling on that day's course of spot reduction. Who knew, listening to the congressman, if the engineers were not pursuing a path of integrity into middle life after all but merely looking, like many others in the golden land, for one of those intimate little sects where sanctification would be as bracingly pleasurable as, say, a loofah scrub?

"You gentlemen have been pressured into these resignations by this religious group," McCormack charged. Dale stated for the record that he had received no pressure whatsoever to resign from his job.

The truth of it was that the religious foundation had been useful as a way station for Dale and Char: it had drawn them out of the gray area, forced them to make distinctions, focused them around a core of values they not only believed in but were willing to live by. They had already outgrown it.

"I don't think we should get into religion and what group they belong to." Chairman Pastore cut into McCormack's attempt to discredit the men. "What difference does it make?"

But Dale Bridenbaugh knew the difference already had been made. The engineers had poleaxed their careers to get the word out, and the politicians had strung them up like fools.

"We were still naive enough to think they were all trying to get at the truth, too," Dale ruminated later. In the coming months the men would learn a great deal about treacheries awaiting those who stray from the predictable route. GE management mobilized its own team, using the Vince Lombardi technique: *Are you gonna let these guys run around loose saying this stuff? We've gotta be out there chasing their tails.* Once the built-in corporate mechanism for ejecting contaminants went into effect, these formerly well-liked members of the brotherhood were reduced to the dimension of gnats, jiggers, pissants—small pests to be brushed off with bored disgust.

Bumping into his old college roommate, who still worked for GE's nuclear division, Dale inquired, "Uh, how is it on your side?"

"Great! Just like back in college—everybody pulled together like a fraternity."

Dale looked again at him, at the newborn son the man had clasped to his chest. "Bill, what did *you* do?"

"I went around door to door explaining that radiation is no problem."

Another GE man told him later, "I felt you had betrayed me personally."

Notwithstanding, the first four months after resignation were possibly the most intense in the Bridenbaughs' lives. They were united with the other two families around a single goal: campaigning for Proposition 15 in California, the first state referendum to seek a moratorium on nuclear power until waste disposal and other safety problems were solved.

I watched euphoria take hold of them, as if they were a

team of climbers tied together to ascend a virgin mountain. They pulsed with vitality. Their perceptions were sharp. They spoke of being focused, energized. So this is what it's like to move out of stagnant passivity and have the senses spring full and keen again. They would never forget the feeling. In those first months they knew how it feels, just once, to be lined up plumb with one's conscience.

Then they failed. The referendum was defeated. The less-followed route was going to take longer than they had thought.

"It's bloody, it's dark, it's unknown, it's thrilling," Char Bridenbaugh described to me. "It's tough and lonely and un-marked and exhilarating. Sometimes you stumble into a pit, you can't find the top, you're falling back . . . just then, there comes a sign, totally out of the black, a sign that you are not really alone."

Congressman McCormack made a very different and ominous prophecy:

"In two years they'll be totally forgotten by the public, frozen out of the industry, and of no further use to the people who exploited them. They'll be dead."

Separating, Reconnecting

Most people modify what they believe to make it fit under the umbrella of majority opinion, so fearful are we all of isolation from the group. Dale and Char Bridenbaugh did not modify. The day after the California referendum was defeated, Dale and the other two engineers decided to stick together, keep their homes in San Jose—the heart of an industry now hostile to them—and return to the trail again the following fall to campaign for nuclear referenda in four other states. They hit on the idea of forming an energy consulting business. If they could conduct studies and give expert testimony for various groups considering energy alternatives, they could continue to articulate their deepest concerns about the future of society and still support their families. It was worth a try.

Their future commitments made, each family felt the same urgency. It was the summer of America's Bicentennial. People all over the country were performing rituals of afiliation, but having so freshly severed all their professional and most of their personal connections, these six Americans were floating and felt a little lost. The Bridenbaughs needed to go back to Aunt Bea and Grandma Jean and the chums of high school to cultivate a support network from out of the old blood and friendship lines.

"It was as if we had an unconscious compulsion to reestablish every important relationship in our lives," Char related. They fitted out a Volkswagen bus. To be in a cozy capsule with their children would be important too, a shoring up. Sensing that Dale needed time to withdraw into silence, "to know his own thoughts," Char appointed herself driver and general organizer of the summer.

"We're proud of you!" That's what everybody they visited said. No one asked questions. Kinfolk and friends did not want any facts: they might have to disagree. Each couple in its own milieu was received with the kind of exaggerated heartiness accorded wounded soldiers.

Char's intuitions were right. Dale had needed that time in reverie to prepare for the struggle ahead. Autumn would plunge him into nonstop conflict between his old need for social belonging and his maturing need for autonomy. Char's transition would have to be postponed.

Got to get home, get going . . . all the nobility of the Grand Canyon at sunrise could not keep the Bridenbaughs, after two months of deliberately losing themselves in the past, from driving straight through to San Jose. A teller in their bank was thunderstruck to see them back in town. "We heard you were living in a commune." Gone to rack and ruin.

The minute the Minors and Hubbards also returned, the men got together to chart the goals of their new consulting business. They agreed to stake their savings and to try to live on about two-thirds of the $30,000 to $40,000 incomes they had earned before.

The Bridenbaughs were invited by Friends of the Earth to tour Australia. The nuclear issue was flaming hot there. Dale seemed to be in five or six places at once—there were that many speaking engagements each day, that much excitement. He was becoming quite good.

Char held back at first. After all, she had never spoken authoritatively to a soul outside her own home. But as they traveled, she began to seek out small groups to talk to. Once Dale had to travel to Perth while Char stayed in Adelaide. What was expected to be a small rally where she would "say a few words" turned out to be five thousand people, and the speakers were poor. Wrapped in the mantle of the cause, rather than self, Char trooped to the platform and turned to face the crowd. It was something like looking out on the Great Wall of China. She closed her eyes and reached for the words. She spoke out passionately. She touched people.

"If you really believe in something, you're not afraid," Char discovered. "It's when you don't know what you think that you have trouble with what to say." It was a revelation.

After that, Dale said, she was fearless. They became a team. The laces loosened on some of the stereotyped sex roles they had felt constrained to perform, and both of them began expanding into more complex people. They were well into the Expansion Phase of their passage, which would engage them for a year and a half in active efforts toward change, and accelerate their personal tempo dramatically.

Failure continued to plague the engineers that fall. Every one of the state nuclear initiatives went down to defeat. They held out until Christmas, whereupon they landed their first assignment as fully fee-paid experts. Over the next year various state energy commissions and several foreign governments hired them as professional "intervenors." The Nuclear Regulatory Commission itself became a client! When the NRC found the men did not arrive with bare feet and love beads, the comment came back, "These are really good ideas—you guys aren't so radical after all!"

Although they felt jubilantly free underneath, they became on the surface more correct than the most clichéd corporate stiff. The men thought twice before going into a hardware store on Saturday wearing Levis. Their wives wore pumps to the grocery store. It was a reflex action to prove they were still respectable people, not freaks.

To their surprise, peace offerings began to trickle in, the most touching from those colleagues who were formerly most condemnatory. The man who had felt personally betrayed by Bridenbaugh came forward with an explanation in the third person: "Hell, when you guys left, a lot of people were forced to look at what they really thought about the work they were doing. Some of them needed to get angry at you instead of looking."

Hostility continued, of course. Sometimes it was expressed in a nullifying silence when the men spoke before other technocrats. Sometimes the lid would blow off in the middle of a rally—*riot call*—and police cars would scream up to the platform and fold the men like card tables and take them away.

Eighteen months after their resignations, in the spring of 1978, when I saw them again, they were happy survivors: a little amazed they had come through intact, nobody wounded too badly, their marriages not only holding up but noticeably stronger. The men had all grown mustaches; that was the most obvious change. It appeared to be a statement of confidence in their choice of path. But the jury was still out, and although there was hardly anyone to whom they could admit it, they felt something of a letdown.

The state of euphoria that often follows upon completion of a painful separation and that lightens the step during those first, pure explorations of a new life path cannot, of course, last forever. Greg Minor explained how they really felt now:

"That first year after resigning was so intense. We absorbed so many joyful experiences and so much abuse, but with no time to process it. We discovered that one person can make a difference. But by the end of that year we had said everything we had to say once. We're now beginning to repeat ourselves. We can see a long gray road ahead where only repetition and patience will counteract the inertia of the public and the self-interest of the opposition."

By the next year when I saw them, all traces of facial hair were gone. The mustaches had served their purpose as talismans of individuality to bolster them during a disorienting period of change. Now they were more relaxed, more concerned with improving the quality of their work and making tricky policy distinctions. No matter how great the cause, purity must be sacrificed eventually if one is going to continue being active in an imperfect world. There were temptations to play demagogic hero to the passionate young siblings of Sixties antiwar activists, who were now into no-nuke protests and pressing the engineers to make a case for their "right" to go over the fence and occupy plant sites. The men would have to proclaim, in effect, *This plant represents such a clear and present danger that everyone living around it ought to get out, or else.* Dale told the kids, "I can't say that. I don't believe it. The risk is long-term."

Playing the Part of "Techno-Twits"

Still, wherever they went, they felt the cold shoulder from the industry. "Social acceptance—over and over again it came back to that issue," said Dick Hubbard.

A case in point:

Two brand-new reactors were built on the California coast in the 1970s—right over the Hosgri Fault Zone. Would they withstand an earthquake? No one in government or industry thought to press the question *before* the nuclear facility was finished and the taxpayers were picking up the bill. Mothers for Peace became the official intervenors. A public-interest law firm hired the engineers' company to evaluate the data presented by the utility, Westinghouse. The utility would not permit Hubbard within shouting distance of its plants. So it was that the NRC insisted: "Either Dick Hubbard comes to the audit, or we don't either."

Westinghouse brought all its records to a motel. The company took a suite so that "their people" could sit around it and nosh with the NRC's people. Hubbard sat alone at the motel's lunch counter. Nobody spoke to him. "You go back into a room with ninety people and eighty-nine are saying, 'Everything's okay,'" he remembered. "You want so badly to be one of the guys."

All they were asking was that he suspend his concern, for the prize of belonging. That is to say (although, of course, no one would actually have put it this way), to demoralize himself—for just a few hours! Then it would be over and they could all relax around the suite together and have some great booze sent up and a catered feast . . . *Hell, we're all decent people here, we make a good living for our families, we take our kids on trips, and when you think about it, more people kill themselves in car accidents than . . .*

In the course of following up on the engineers, I was allowed into the inner sanctum of the very reactor at the "Devil's Canyon" to which Dick Hubbard had been denied access. It was important, I thought, to try to understand the subliminal symbols that were evoking a fervor of religious intensity, not only here but in advanced countries around the world.

The reactor was a bull in a cave. A minotaur twelve feet high and twenty feet in girth, its core was sunk below ground level with an eighty-ton hatch cover plugging the hole to the outside. Steel rope spiraled all around it. Finally, a three-foot movable concrete wall was rolled over the entrance. What might be called the beast's nervous system was controlled by silver and cadmium staves that were driven into the core rather like a picador's *banderillas* to slow the ferocious energy of the fission process. In case of emergency, they could be driven deep into the beast to shut down its vital functions altogether—unless pressure or water were lost. If enough water were lost to uncover the core, the products of fission would continue to decay, that heat would begin to melt the fuel pellets with their deadly filling of plutonium, then the metal tubes, and then, if not stopped, the concrete cage housing it. It would take quite some time for a complete meltdown to occur. It takes very little time, however, at any point where the fission process is not perfectly controlled and cooled, for nuclear debris to escape. The main line of defense, industry-wide, is the Emergency Core Cooling System. It has never been tested on a full-sized reactor, anywhere.

These are very deep and powerful symbols. Devils. Earthquakes. Mothers for Peace. A beast that can work up enough heat in its belly to send out the energy equivalent to 24 million barrels of oil annually, a beast with breath more lethal than nerve gas, caged in a brute structure and tied up with steel cords, a stone bigger than Ali Baba could have imagined rolled across the entrance to its cave. The fission process may be one of the most sophisticated inspirations of mankind. But the feelings it evokes in people are primitive. No wonder the debate was growing daily less technical and more irrationally evangelical—on all sides.

Again, questions about these men were left hanging. Were they religious zealots? Passing victims of mid-life crisis who needed a break from routine? Merely nay-sayers? Exactly the sorts of questions the men were asking themselves by the autumn of 1978.

"We're going through a transition in our own thinking about where we fit in society," Greg Minor told me.

They were accustomed to being builders of things. All their training and experience had revolved around the same closed circuit, beautiful in its self-containment. Find a problem—solve it; find a new problem—solve it; until eventually someone would say, "Okay, let's build the damn thing." It was foreign to them to be in the position of tearing down, undermining confidence, raising problems with no clearly deducible answers and perhaps no answers at all.

Jump now to the Christmas season of 1978. The engineers have been brought together for a screening of the rough cut of *The China Syndrome* before the film's release. The house "techno-twits," as the movie people sometimes called them, are supposed to be men with computers in their pockets who do not carry around the usual emotional flab. That is why they were hired as technical consultants. It is assumed they will reserve character and value judgments. Each one has a Cross mechanical pencil. Their lined pads are already tessellated with notations.

They watch the supervisor of the fictional nuclear plant's control room as he discovers a cover-up of welding defects that could be deadly. The engineers are completely involved with his thinking. The supervisor, Godell, as played by Jack Lemmon, is a calm and seasoned veteran of the brotherhood, a man who believes with all the breath in his body in backup systems and "defense in depth"—a man very much like them. Now Godell insists the plant be closed before there is a rupture that could expose the radioactive core. Management ignores him. Suddenly Godell snatches a gun from the guard and takes over the control room. He orders everyone out except for the television newswoman, played by Jane Fonda. He says he wants to go on television—live—to tell the public what has happened.

All at once the engineers stop writing. It begins boiling up, everything they have not let themselves feel over the last few emotionally battered years. The three men stiffen in the darkened screening room, hopelessly expectant that the hero of the film will be made of less expendable stuff than they.

"I—uh—I'm Jack Godell," the film's hero talks into a TV camera. "I want you to know that I'm not going to hurt anybody and I'm not going to destroy all of southern California. I mean, I'm a *trained nuclear engineer.*"

The engineers' breath comes in lumps as they feel Godell's frustration, the garble of technical jargon he attempts to spell out. The words Godell is trying to say are exactly the kind of thing the engineers have wanted to get across for so long.

"The water pressure was still above four hundred psi . . ." Godell is trying to explain to the TV audience. "I'm not making much sense, I know, but—" Poor techno-twit. He can't wedge into five minutes of hijacked air time, on a medium through which viewers expect the ether of light entertainment, what all his years of speechless intimacy with the instrumentation of a nuclear reactor tell him is perilous about bringing this plant back to full power.

A cry breaks in Dale Bridenbaugh's throat. The other two engineers shift uncomfortably, sensing a breached seal on their years of impacted feelings. Now another one starts to give. *Oh, God, will we never find the right words to reach people?*

Clip! Off their shirt pockets come the mechanical pencils again. This is no way for grown engineers to behave. Back they go to making notes. . . . *pump support problem involves possibility of lamellar tearing.* . . . but the truth is that the film has become for them an epiphany. It seems to be soaking up the pain of the first half of their passage. Possibly it will leave them lighter, clearer, lined up again with the present.

The last scenes of the film turn the emotional ratchet inside Dale Bridenbaugh to a point almost beyond bearing. A klaxon begins to bray on Godell's generator console: management has forced the plant to a SCRAM condition under full power.

"Oh, no—" Godell yells. Then the door on his control room blasts off and a police team drills a bullet into his body. There is an ominous rumble of immense water pumps set on huge tripods that are beginning to buckle. Employees look for Godell to set the emergency right. Godell is dead.

Later, employees are interviewed about this fellow, Godell, whom the utility is trying to paint as a loony. Everyone is passing the buck. "Wait a minute!" one older man interrupts management. "I don't like it that Jack Godell is going to be marked down as some kind of nut case. As a matter of fact, he was the sanest guy I ever met."

The engineers in the screening room, remembering their humiliation before the congressional committee, choke up at the idea that even one fellow worker would stand up and say what he thought.

Lights come up in the screening room. "Well?" The director twists around in his chair. "What did you think of it?" Two of the men have their chins spiked to their chests.

"It was so real, we can't stop crying right now."

Half blind with unbottled emotions, they hit the wintry night air with relief and walked all the way home, and the next day they made an important policy decision. They would cut back on their adversary activities. They would try to get more work promoting energy alternatives—a positive approach. The best-laid plans, however, are no match for life's accidents. In early March the movie was released. Three weeks later, on March 28, 1979, an early-morning phone call from a reporter in Harrisburg, Pennsylvania, awoke the Bridenbaughs.

"Is Three Mile Island going to be another 'China syndrome'?"

The war had changed overnight. Just as they had been ready to leave the battleground to others, a new front had opened up. Their callers over the next ten days mounted into the hundreds. Public officials as well as the media demanded to know, *Is there going to be a meltdown?*

"We just don't know," the engineers had to say. "We consciously chose not to take the accident in the film as far as a meltdown. Unfortunately, we can't make that decision for Three Mile Island."

Personally, the engineers felt ambivalent. The event was vindicating them, but who cared about that if it became a national catastrophe? The accident was of a kind never considered by the plant designers—a basic flaw pointed out by the engineers in their hearing on Capitol Hill. The NRC had come up with a classification system for possible nuclear accidents from one to nine, class eight being the "maximum credible" accident a plant design had to take into account. Class nine was the catchall for events said to be "incredible," such as two different failures occurring simultaneously. The commercial nuclear power industry was not expected to address itself to that level at all. Thus, as the men had testified, nobody was taking responsibility for whether the *overall system* was designed for safety.

Later, a special investigating committee determined that the Three Mile Island reactor had come within thirty to sixty minutes of a meltdown.[3] The engineers attended another hearing in Washington. This time the NRC was in the witness box and they were in the audience. And the debate was not about "What if?" but "Why was this allowed to happen?"

It happened because, as any housewife knows, not only can two things go wrong at the same time—they usually do. The nuclear industry had officially grown up and entered the realm of the "incredible."

Deciding for the Promethean Path

I visited the three engineers' families again in midsummer 1979. Long hours of taping for a book had helped the men enormously in doing the work of the Incorporation Phase. It was probably the equivalent of several years of good therapy. Only in retrospect had it become apparent to them all that they had initiated the momentous passage they were about to complete a full *seven years* before the actual break with GE!

Greg Minor sat back on his heels in his garden and reflected, "I had the distinct sense that I had completed a whole life, as I understood the life cycle. But I was only forty-two. I wasn't ready to die!"

He had begun lingering around the house to have breakfast with his family and coming home early from the office to lose himself in digging out weeds. "This may sound silly, but I feel drawn toward a monkish period," Greg described it. "We're all more contemplative now—it feels as if we're in a dormant phase."

I went on to visit the Bridenbaughs. Dale had just come down from his beloved Sierras. Seeking silence and closeness with his last child, he had taken his 14-year-old son deep into wilderness; they had not seen half a dozen other souls in a week. I sensed in Dale a new acceptance tinged with cynicism about how much could be done. Was it all worth it? I asked.

Dale answered with his usual candor. "The slowness of reform is frustrating. Although I know the three of us have probably had as much impact as anybody on the whole scheme of things."

Forty-seven by now, Dale was only a few years away from another milestone in the life cycle: the Half-Century Reckoning. He was wrestling with new questions. Should he spend the rest of his days making minute incremental gains? Or had he done his best work in this field? Did continued growth demand he move on again? I said I thought he should be proud to have come so far.

"What I was thinking about up in the mountains rather than 'How far have I gotten?' is 'What do I need to do now?' "

When his son left home, Dale said, he would be ready to do something else. "You and I have talked a lot about independence versus social acceptance," he added. "What I've learned is that you can't have it on both sides of the line. You've got to know what you believe, decide what you think is right, and stay with that."

When the other Bridenbaugh came out from the same suburban house in San Jose to greet Dale and me, I was startled. "I didn't recognize Char; I thought you'd turned her in for a new model."

Deadpan, Dale said, "I didn't have to."

In Char's demeanor was a reissue of what she must have been as a girl—a new slimness, an ebullience, a snap of mischief in the eye, a voltage about her movements. Once Dale was "out of the woods," Char had faced the question "Do I want to continue coattailing, or should I strike out and try to find my own place in the world?" There had been a hysterectomy. The finality of lost procreative powers seemed to have redirected her creativity. Shortly after recovering, she had entered graduate school and was now beginning independent research into learning disabilities. She would express her concern for the next generation as an educator.

Just in time. Her daughter, now 17, had barely returned from her own first solo flight, a summer in Switzerland. She passed around a box of Swiss chocolates, stood on one bare leg and then the other in front of her luggage, and said, "I've only been home an hour and I'm bored."

Char gave the sigh that marks the slipping of a childhood out of a parent's heart. "I suddenly realized," she confided later, "the old mother-daughter thing wasn't going to work anymore."

Neither would the old couple contract. With the work of parenthood nearing an end, this man and woman could both become more than their gender roles. At the moment, Dale could not help being a little envious of Char. Here she was trying out her wings, starting a brand-new season, while he was having symptoms common to the end of a strenuous passage—emotional depletion, a simultaneous feeling of dormancy and restlessness, a need to reflect on what might have been—before wrapping it up to go on. Char, too, could not help letting a little unswallowed bitterness spill out as she tried to digest all that had happened.

"The men are heroes to a certain element. It's all just wonderful to be a hero, but we've got three kids to put through college. The guy down the street brags about driving his Seville to pick up his unemployment check. Most of the world is out there operating like this fink, and you try to do something—you wonder sometimes, are we crazy?"

The outburst passed. Then she dipped into a little nostalgia for the values of her parents' generation. Why should her daughter have had to earn most of the money for her trip abroad? "You feel that in order to progress from where you were as a kid, you want to be able to tie it all up with a ribbon and give her this splendid gift of The World."

She heard the ridiculousness of what she had just said. All kinds of kids float around in a stupor for lack of something to work toward and parents to respect. This family had pulled together to keep a world for this child.

While Char talked, we were stuffing our summer-fat feet into jogging shoes. It was 6:30 in the morning. She said we should run before it became unbearably hot. Bobbing through the monotonous streets, Char mused, "What we've learned is that there's pain in any accomplishment. Whether it's jogging or writing a book or being able to give your kids everything, it still hurts—and the human side of us wants to avoid that. I guess we're talking about the duality in the nature of man. The will decides which of the two natures will prevail."

She was huffing by now. She did not stop running. But she wanted to.

"Since I've grown up over the last ten years, my will has decided for the Promethean path." Every now and then, she said, she would catch a fleeting glimpse of the Divine. "I wouldn't try to describe what it is," she hastened to add. "I can only describe how it is felt."

What she was describing, of course, was something close to transcendence.

When the Personal Path Sets a National Direction

Initially, each of these three couples interpreted the first twinges of mid-life crisis as a signal that something was not right in their marriage. They had stumbled upon the asynchrony between the development of men and women that reaches an extreme in the middle years—but that was not all. They were coming up on the Deadline Decade during which they would each, as individuals, face any number of predictable inner changes: seeing the dark side; needing to disassemble the idealized identities of their youth; glimpsing their own truths; groping toward authenticity; each one gathering up his or her suspended and expanded parts and eventually achieving a renewal. In the process, they were led to commit an act of decency.

The crisis for a transcendent pathfinder may begin on a personal level. The transcendent aspect of it is that the path on which one embarks becomes guided, after a time, *primarily* by interests beyond the self.

All through their ordeal, the engineers had to keep convincing themselves there was worth in trying to bring about a change in values in society. They were uncomfortable with the idea of shifting to a role of intellectual leadership—these were no elitist eggheads!

They could never have done it alone, they all agreed.

The engineers were not the only people standing up to ask questions about commercial nuclear power in 1976. They were part of a grass-roots movement in California that was the first to achieve expression of their concerns in a state-wide referendum. What made the engineers' act special was the congruence of their age, stage, temperaments, and the position of high respect they had attained in their professional family, together with a cause that needed sponsors, and their willingness to gamble that they would never work in their industry again. Char, too, was struck by that congruence.

"How all these forces came to be present at the same time in the same corner of the universe, I don't pretend to know," she commented, "but you feel really lucky that you were presented with such an opportunity. Otherwise, Dale might just have said, 'Oh, well, I guess I'll just change jobs.'"

One could as easily see it the other way around. Perhaps the cause found them because they were at the point where they needed to slough off their private capsules of development and go beyond. They were ready for a suspension of pragmatic routine and allegiances—a withdrawal to the "watchtower," in effect, where it is possible to commit oneself to observing truth, to deciding between things, to judging, and then to attempting to act on behalf of the family of man. They did not transcend prosaic cares forever. I have yet to meet a transcendent pathfinder who did. After the time out on another plane, they came back to laboring under the burden of what we are on earth. But not only did they personally "come back with a difference," they had helped to guide their society through a complete reorientation of thinking on commercial nuclear power.

By 1981 experts were already looking toward the end of the decade with confidence that our energy crisis might be resolved, without either extreme being pursued where nuclear power is concerned: without shutting down the industry until the impossible task of making it risk-free is accomplished, but also without crash programming on new nuclear plants and breeder technology in a climate of induced amnesia about the perils of waste, safety, and sabotage. Neither true believers nor your average rationalizers, the engineers and their wives took a lead in the dialectical process by which core values are realigned around new realities.

The story of the engineers again raises the question whether philosophy can be broken off from personal development. It is not as if decisions about right and wrong or on the ultimate reason for getting up in the morning were merely the decorative shutters on our inner domain. Such philosophical questions are more like large, gelatinous, don't-have-to-think-about-them-today thought masses that shift around behind our snap judgments. It takes a long time for our decisions on them—our end values—to set. Before then, they may change form more than once or dramatically. As we have learned, it is precisely those people who dare to allow changes in their personal values and goals who are most likely to be rewarded with a sense of well-being.

Once the fling of youthful idealism is past, most people, like Dale Bridenbaugh, are not particularly concerned in their twenties and thirties with "the broader social contract." Proving competence and conforming to gain social approval usually are the paramount values in those stages. The forties and fifties seem to be the natural time of life for the duel between acting on painfully sorted-out convictions or preserving hard-won comforts.

A "comfortable life" had slid to the bottom of Dale's values by the time he filled in the Life History Questionnaire at the age of 44. The values on which he now places the highest importance are "independence and free choice." And the personal quality he most cherishes is "courage—standing up for your beliefs." (It was rare to find the last among the primary personal values.)

Until her forties, Char Bridenbaugh's primary value was "inner harmony," in which yearning she is joined by all the conventional women I studied. But once having struck out on the less-traveled path, Char was conscious of waiving that wish. One might say that inner harmony is the psychic counterpart to the physical state of having a "comfortable life." Important personal change or growth is inhibited if those consistently remain a couple's highest values. One who is bent on "making a lasting contribution" and reaching "a mature understanding of life" must expect periodic turmoil.

It is not unusual to sense an increased drive for social contribution during the middle years. Indeed, it may be that a natural progression for a developing pathfinder is one of detaching roughly every twenty years from another outgrown family: moving from the parental family, to the occupational and personal family, to efforts on behalf of the family of man.

The risks taken by people who stand up as individuals against powerful industrial, military, or congressional interests are especially grave. But to achieve the ends of society they do not necessarily have to win. If they merely raise the level of discourse, they make us all more confident in our ability to know what is right.

17.

VIEW FROM
THE TOP OF
THE MOUNTAIN

Come with me for a moment up to the top of the mountain. Not because that is where you and I expect to arrive someday, but because some of the most inspired examples of successful pathfinding, as well as some of the most instructive mistakes, are to be found in the histories of figures such as Gandhi, Churchill, de Gaulle, Golda Meir, and Anwar Sadat—among the pathfinders of our century.

Writ large, the qualities of a pathfinder are among the highest qualifications for leadership. We can think of them as an index in reviewing those who appeal to us to permit them to carry the public trust. Leaders are people we as followers want to regard with awe as the fullest flowering of our own possibilities. We present some of them with the mandate to be our world-class pathleaders: persons of surpassing vision to whom we look for hope that a path can be found to prosperity, stability, honor, and peace.

Pathleaders as Failures

Although it is difficult to believe, great men and women often feel helpless and afraid, confused or infantile, or so historians later record. It is the rare leader who at some point in life does not become convinced that he or she has failed.

Lord Randolph Churchill once described Disraeli's career

as "failure, failure, failure, partial success, renewed failure, ultimate and complete triumph."

At 55, Winston Churchill, son of Lord Randolph, was junked. From then until he was 65 he held no public office, and his career seemed to have ended in total failure. Political biographer Robert Rhodes James comments: "Throughout his period of exclusion and isolation Churchill had maintained his public poise. Only those who knew him best appreciated the depths of depression into which he descended on occasion. . . . By 1937, Churchill was in his sixty-third year, and it was eight years—a political eternity—since he had held public office."[1]

Golda Meir was a flop as a wife and a mother, some might say. Her own early childhood was spent in unrelieved fear and frustration over the accident of having been born poor and Jewish in Czarist Russia. At 17, after an adolescence in Milwaukee, she fell in love with Morris, a man older and, it seemed to her, steadier than she. She told him of her dream that the Jews must have a land of their own and that she must help to build it. He reluctantly agreed to go to Palestine, and together they left in 1921, man and wife.

Morris hated kibbutz life. He wanted his wife all for himself and refused to have children unless she left the kibbutz. Eventually, his wife acquiesced.

Six months after the birth of her son, Golda Meir felt like a prisoner. Cooped up in a tiny apartment in Jerusalem, she was terrified that her child would go hungry unless she could find some sort of work to supplement Morris's meager wages. But she could not leave the baby alone. After a second child reached nursery-school age, she arranged to do the school laundry in exchange for their fees. Scrubbing for hours, Golda Meir chafed with a bitter resentment.

The cruelest deprivation, to her mind, was being prevented from doing the work for which she had come to Palestine. After many attempts to make it right with Morris, and now approaching the age of 30, Golda Meir silently accepted the defeat of her marriage and went back to work in the movement. Her mother chastised her. Even her sister, the flaming revolutionary who had ignited Golda with Zionism as a child, accused her of turning into "a public person, not a homebody." In an article written at the age of 32, trying to justify the agonizing failure to fit together the jagged pieces of her various purposes, Golda Meir stated a common dilemma:

> There are mothers who work only when they are forced to. . . . But there is a type of woman who cannot remain home for other reasons. In spite of the place which her children and her family take up in her life, her nature and being demands something more; she cannot divorce herself from a larger social life. She cannot let her children narrow her horizon. And for such a woman, there is no rest . . . this eternal inner division, this double pull, this alternating feeling of unfulfilled duty—today toward her family, the next day toward her work—this is the burden of the working mother.[2]

Golda Meir ultimately became the mother of modern Israel. Providing social guidance for a nation, she could assuage some of the guilt that taunted her to the end for not having been a model mother.

Charles de Gaulle, who also had youthful dreams of saving his people, was a late bloomer. Still repeating his lectures at the Sorbonne in his late thirties, nearly devoured by unfulfilled ambitions, he was past 40 before his destiny began to take shape.

His father died the year that de Gaulle defied Marshal Pétain, the mentor who had replaced his father as a model. In the same personally cataclysmic year, de Gaulle watched the national government of France thrown out by an unexpected union of the Left. Only then, at 42, finding himself on the precipice of mid-life with painful evidences of death and the ephemeral nature of politics all around him, did he commit himself unequivocally to one road.

De Gaulle determined to go it alone, and in time he would take his country down the isolationist path with him. He came to personify France.

"I began my adventure at forty-nine," he wrote in his memoirs. Although he dedicated himself to France alone and fought for her freedom from German occupation, real political power eluded him until he was 55. At last he was elected president. Even in the thrall of that success he was seized by fears of failure, reports his psychohistorian.[3] Two years later, apparently unable to shake his demons, de Gaulle shocked his supporters by announcing his resignation. Not only did he withdraw from politics in 1946 at the age of 57; he retreated from the world, and in all areas of growth save the cerebral he appears to have gone into an involution.

Withdrawing into the "wilderness," as he called it, to his forest-bound estate two hundred miles from Paris, de Gaulle waited to be recalled. No calls came. He dug into an isolation that would last until he was 68, for eleven long years. He began to refer to himself in the third person and surrender to bouts of melancholia.

"How many hours slipped by," he later wrote, "where reading, writing, or dreaming, no illusion could soften my bitter serenity."

Eventually de Gaulle retreated even from his devoted wife, into a tower he had constructed on the estate, and there focused his frustrated energies on writing a thousand pages of *Mémoires*.

Consider the relative merits of de Gaulle's adaptation to rejection, and Lyndon Johnson's.

In the winter of 1968, academic James MacGregor Burns was invited to a White House covered like a shroud with hatred for a war that President Johnson could see in no other terms but a final victory. Burns learned that Johnson was having a recurring dream of impotence.

He dreamed that he was lying in bed in the Red Room of the White House, paralyzed from the neck down, listening to his aides in the next room quarreling over the division of power. He could hear them but could not speak to them. Waking from his sleep after such a dream, the President would make his way through the empty corridors of the White House to the place where Woodrow Wilson's portrait hung. It soothed him to touch Wilson's portrait, for Wilson had been paralyzed and now was dead but Johnson was still alive and active. In the morning the fears would return—of paralysis of the body, paralysis of his presidency. And soon he would quit.[4]

The psychological pressure on Lyndon Johnson appears to have decided his personal course and therefore the next turn of his country. Obsessed with potency—apparently equating it with keeping up the fight and proving that he was right—and rather than admit he might have been wrong about widening the war in Vietnam, Johnson preferred to step down from power and die, both of which he did within the next five years.

Historian Barbara Tuchman suggests a troubling hypothesis: policy founded upon error only multiplies the mistake, she points out, which is self-evident to anyone thinking reasonably. Why, then, should otherwise reasonable men, once they are in positions of power, find it so difficult to admit error? "Somehow," observed Tuchman, "men equate being wrong with being impotent."[5]

Being wrong also implies failure. In American life, failure is a disease. And disease is failure. That is why associates commonly ostracize the powerful figure who has just suffered a sudden loss of status as if it were a contaminating illness, and why strong people such as pathfinders when struck by serious illness often find it easier to hold on to the company of their friends if they deny the failure of their bodies. When a charismatic figure had to drop out of public life to battle uterine cancer, for instance, she tried telling a few of her closest friends. They could not handle the idea of being in the same room with someone whom they had idealized and who looked as sound as they on the outside, but whose insides were prey to a cellular derangement that could strike them, anyone, anytime. Only by denying the cancer was she able to keep her support system intact.

People who are willing to risk, who try to change and reform society, must become philosophical about failure. Consider the example of Norman Thomas. After studying at Union Theological Seminary to become a Presbyterian minister, he spent seven years in an East Harlem church where many of his parishioners were locked by the economic system into a lifetime of poverty. His view of capitalist values changed profoundly. He became a Christian socialist and for many years was the voice and the leader of the American Socialist Party. Like many reformers whose beliefs shock their contemporaries, he lived a personally stable and conventional life. He never won an election. His party failed to gain anything like the official strength of the two major parties. Yet, being unconcerned by personal defeat, Norman Thomas endured as a leader of ideas. Far ahead of his time, he laid the groundwork for the New Deal, Social Security, collective bargaining, and protection of civil liberties.

Thomas's biographer called him "the most successful failure" of any political figure in the United States.[6]

Pathleaders in Withdrawal and Comeback

A striking similarity exists among world figures. Most did not run at full tilt all the way, nor did they necessarily even stay in the race right along. At some point, usually during or soon after mid-life, they withdrew into a period of retreat. And then they made a comeback.

Among the earliest records of this phenomenon is the Bible, a collection of accounts of the withdrawal and comeback of spiritual leaders. In the Old Testament, Moses went up to Mount Sinai and disappeared into clouds of confusion and apparent danger, then came back with revelation and the means for self-control and social regulation. Jesus, in the New Testament, withdrew to fast in the wilderness, where he was tempted by the devil for forty days. Both men returned reinforced in their faith and eager to convey their insights to their followers.

Winston Churchill was called back from a withdrawal of ten years by a world accident, World War II, which gave him the opportunity to become "the living incarnation of the resistance to Nazi aggression . . . and to direct the strategy of the vast conflict."[7]

Charles de Gaulle, as I have just noted, withdrew into retirement between the ages of 57 and 68. He did not believe he would be called upon again to save France. But after the revolt by the settlers and the army in Algeria, he was finally summoned. The nation accepted his condition, that France finally become a constitutional democracy, and de Gaulle came back to become the first president of the Fifth Republic in January 1958.[8]

Comebacks can, of course, be manipulated and false. The American people knew from having lived through the 1960 presidential campaign that Richard Nixon was severely flawed of character. But in 1968, led by a silent majority wanting redress against all the upstart troublemaking groups, voters conspired in an amnesia of convenience. We conferred the ultimate power over our land on a man riddled with inferiority and persecution complexes, pretending to believe he had come back a "new" Nixon.

Jimmy Carter withdrew for a year, his 42nd, into the backwoods of Massachusetts and Pennsylvania on a "pioneer mission." He immersed himself as a Baptist lay preacher in missionary work with complete strangers. Carter came back renewed as a Christian and reaffirmed as a person, as he described the experience to psychohistorians Bruce Mazlish and Edwin Diamond.[9] Having tied his earlier identity to his intellectual involvement with nuclear power, he was now able to release an emotional generosity that allowed him to speak on an intimate level with other people, even strangers, and to give them the sense that he cared.

In addition to the obvious practical advantage such a change affords a politician, it also awakened hope in many Americans that Jimmy Carter might pass on to them the benefits of his own personal transformation. Carter entered our public consciousness in the aftermath of Vietnam and Watergate, a time when feelings of national shame and inferiority ran high. Reassured by a pioneer mission of his own essential goodness, Jimmy Carter was able to return to us and tap our desire to believe that we, too, were basically good, that as a nation, we, too, could make a comeback.

It was not some cynical trick. Jimmy Carter was exactly the man he told us he was. He qualified on all counts as a pathfinder—in the personal realm. And he worked hard at setting a principled tone both in foreign and domestic policy—but he failed as a pathleader. That competence is as important as character for a leader was an afterthought—even, it seemed, to Carter. Rare among leaders, he was not afraid to admit his mistakes. In fact, he could not seem to *stop* confessing them. That made Americans nervous. The man they had elected, hoping he had a direct line to God, was not in control after all. When he withdrew to the mountains of Camp David to ponder the "national malaise," he was not up there alone, talking to Yahweh. He was flying in big shots and ordinary citizens—grasping for advice even from *people we knew.*

Many pathleaders transmit a special confidence that comes from accepting who they are and knowing what they believe. They are in alignment, comfortable in their own skins. Others sense this. Particularly during a period of confusion and cultural doubt, people are drawn to one who seems in control. If such a person also embodies the values or behavioral style that touches in the populace a chord seeking expression, he or she is likely to become charismatic.

At one point Jimmy Carter could not seem to lose a primary—although people scarcely knew his name. His confident smile melted doubts; his gentle simplicity and personal conviction revived a little of the old pietistic belief in ourselves as God's chosen people. Needing so badly something or someone to believe in, Americans conferred upon Jimmy Carter the shimmer that is called charisma.

Not long after taking office, the same man was being called "wishy-washy." Carter was, in fact, a passive person, and he made a passive president. His personality came to symbolize the vacillation of our economy and the impotence of our foreign policy. Toward the end of his term, Jimmy Carter had become for Americans emblematic of our status as passive victims—in our homes, in our city streets, in the world. We routed him out of power and turned our backs. Overnight, Jimmy Carter became a non-person. The first time he spoke again for publication was four months after being parted from the charisma of presidential office. The *New York Times* buried the interview on page 10 of Section B.[10]

The post-Carter charisma came from western elegance, Hollywood glamour, and a man who projected the confidence of thirty years in full control of the camera. As every producer knows, the director of a movie, the writers, the cameraman can be fired—but you can never replace the star. Ronald Reagan not only was comfortable in his own skin, said what he believed, and stuck to it, but he also had the most valuable of all qualities for a leader in the electronic age: camera charisma. He played the role of President as if John Wayne had come back from the last roundup. Simple language, easy humor, and a laid-back work pattern: the style was exactly right to calm the times. Reagan's style took the curse of rigidity off his ideology. What is more, he was giving us back what had already been. Even as Americans registered in polls serious doubts about Reagan's political medicine, they were prepared to take it—along with a dose of old-time religion—from a man who passed on to them his own seemingly effortless self-confidence.

* * *

There is a pronounced interaction between leaders themselves becoming transformative and societies being ready to be transformed. As James MacGregor Burns defines transforming leadership, it "ultimately becomes *moral* in that it raises the level of human conduct and ethical aspiration of both leader and led, and thus it has a transforming effect on both."[11] What is the impetus for this form of pathleadership?

The Great Refusal

Many of those who have become pathleaders faced a severe test or personal trial during their childhoods. Grappling with it, they resisted accepting an injustice. And in adult life they determined to benefit other people who face similar obstacles.

An echo of this form of transcendence is heard in those who overcome life accidents by saying, "No! I refuse to be defined by my losses," and who commit to an idea or goal that surmounts their own self-interest. Another echo of this strength through resistance has been noted among those who age best—the dominant women and politically active men who refuse to take a backseat in community or family affairs well into late life.

Pathleaders take their personal refusal another step, one that is central to the extending process by which they become pathleaders. They transmute their personal refusal into a more global "no"—*I cannot tolerate it, not only for me, it's the general injustice*. In so saying, they galvanize many others to speak up: *Yes, that's right, we shouldn't take it anymore*. The act of personal transcendence then takes on a force of its own, becoming the spontaneous combustion behind social change.

This transformed personal refusal is most likely to be found among minorities and out groups. In searching for pathleaders among women, I discovered relatively few. But in comparing half a dozen women pathleaders of the 19th century with an equal number of those who might qualify in contemporary American life, I found they shared one factor without exception: they all had said no.

At some point, each of these women resisted an accepted

dogma. In private, and later in public, each staged what Jane Addams called "the great refusal."

Stand-up Women of the 19th Century

Elizabeth Cady Stanton was born in 1815 and planted the seed of the women's movement. Like most 19th-century feminists, she enjoyed an extraordinarily long life in which to persevere. From her autobiography, *Eighty Years and More*, comes this description of early precipitating events:

> When I was eleven years old two events occurred which changed the current of my life. My only brother came home to die. I still recall my father seated by his side . . . he thinking of the wreck of all his hopes in the loss of a dear son. . . . He took no notice of me.
>
> Then and there I resolved that I would study and strive to be at the head of all my classes and thus delight my father's heart. . . . Two prizes were offered in Greek. I strove for one, and took the second. "Now," said I, "my father will be satisfied with me." . . . He kissed me on the forehead and exclaimed, with a sigh, "Ah, you should have been a boy!"
>
> My joy was turned to ashes.

Like many childhoods of the 19th century, Stanton's was haunted by dolorous theological dogma. It also was shaped by the common experience of watching her mother grow weary with the cares of a large family and seeing five of ten children die, while her lawyer father was "fully occupied with the duties of his profession, which often called him from home."

At 13, Elizabeth Cady Stanton said "no" in secret rebellion. Poring over the odious laws she found in her father's books, laws that made widows unhappy dependents on the bounty of their eldest sons, she marked them with a pencil. Suddenly, she saw her father as one who did nothing to relieve the sufferings of these women. Convinced "of the necessity of taking some active measures against these unjust provisions, I resolved to seek the first opportunity, when alone in the office, to cut every one of them out of the books."

As a wife herself, home with a brood of small children

while her husband was frequently away on business, she became immersed in the slavery issue. But when she and other prominent female abolitionists were barred from the debates of the World Anti-Slavery Convention, the 25-year-old Elizabeth realized that women were manacled themselves. She and other contemporary female abolitionists almost were forced by conscience into becoming advocates of women's rights.

Eight years later (1848) she and Lucretia Mott organized the Seneca Falls Convention and drafted a Declaration of Principles that attempted to write equal protection for women into the Constitution. She planted the seed of the suffragette movement that continued through the Civil War and on through the First World War, and that finally, after seventy years, gained women the right to vote in 1920. Her work remains incomplete today in the unratified Equal Rights Amendment.

Margaret Sanger, born in 1879, was the sixth of eleven children. Her father, a "philosopher with a rich Irish brogue, often failed in his role of breadwinner," she wrote.

Her mother was the one whose feet stayed on the ground, who made do, who took over as the practical guardian of the family welfare. Workworn, she died young of consumption. Young Margaret "had to take mother's place—manage the finances, order the meals, pay the debts. Father suddenly metamorphosed from a loving, gentle, benevolent parent into a tyrant: nobody in any fairy tale I had ever read was quite so cruel. I did not know this monster. Between us a deep silence had fallen."

Her father lived to be 80. Her mother had died at half his age. The contrast was inescapable. Filled with the conviction that her mother and many other mothers might have been saved if they had been more knowledgeable about and responsible for their own bodies, Margaret Sanger determined to study medicine. She devoted her life to helping women to control their anatomy through birth control.

Not all historical pathleaders were without praise or assistance from their fathers. Susan B. Anthony's father installed her at the age of 15 (in 1835) as a teacher in a summer school. He was much criticized, but he was far enough in advance of his time to believe that every girl should be trained to take care of herself.

The historical evidence, however, leans strongly toward fathers who were remote, if not formidable. Onto every word of their scant and careless praise these girls clung breathlessly, idealizing their fathers as the whole world, as reality. If they passed the test with their fathers, they passed reality.

Two heartbreaking lines of poetry found by Jane Addams in the work of Elizabeth Browning conveyed the unfulfilled yearning in all of Jane's childhood conversations with her father:

> He wrapt me in his large
> Man's doublet, careless did it fit or no.

Jane Addams became known the world over as a propagandist for peace and founder of Hull House, where she threw her own doublet over the teeming chaos of Chicago's immigrant populations. At the age of 71, she was honored with the Nobel Peace Prize.

One can imagine a link of impulses from the youthful determination to make things better in their own homes to the later impulse for allying themselves with others who have suffered—to show them the way out. While empathizing with the victim, each of these women refused to become one.

After saying no, they took a risk or went out from the shelter of their lives to expose themselves to the world. And from that risk or exposure came a life-shaping conviction. On the family level, as later on the public level, none was afraid to challenge injustice.

The impetus to pathleadership through the great refusal may be in part, then, the wish to undo the private guilt of having been unable to prevent pain in one's own family, and in part the will to ease the collective guilt of an abundant society implicated in the injustice or unfairness. Of their suffering no less than their strengths, we are the beneficiaries.

Where Women Pathleaders Go Wrong, and Right

Further instructive examples and inspired mistakes can be found among women of our own era.

Eleanor Roosevelt cast the mold for women leaders in this century. Finding herself in a position of great affiliative power, she resisted the temptation to exercise it by cloaking herself in the offices of her husband. She managed in large measure to separate her purposes and channels of influence from his, and to speak from the outside, becoming a powerful humanitarian leader in her own right.

This is a lesson of critical importance for women who have the inclination—or the unexpected opportunity—to become pathleaders. Exercising power only through one's mate (although it might temporarily calm the fears of those easily threatened by able women) almost inevitably backfires. The public cannot argue with a phantom who exercises power through pillow talk, or who uses the cloak of power but hides behind her mate. And sooner or later, when things go wrong, the public will turn on her.

As they did on Rosalynn Carter. She had in fact studied Eleanor Roosevelt and adopted her as a heroine. But the transmogrification was imprecise. On election eve, when the Carters were swept into power, I asked one of the shrewdest politicians in the country if he had met Rosalynn Carter. He said he had.

"I take that back," he amended. "I met two Jimmy Carters."

Rosalynn Carter was dedicated both to helping her man and to making the world better. She had come a long way on sheer will. Thirteen when her father died, she gave up her adolescence to raise the young ones at home while her mother worked. She married a dashing young naval officer who emancipated her from the red-dirt dreariness of Plains and put her on the white-sugar beaches of Hawaii, in the green-rolling hills of the Northeast, and with no one around to tell her what to do. In love with being the naval wife, she had been certain Jimmy Carter would move straight up through the nuclear Navy to the admiralty, and she was enjoying the ride enormously. Suddenly, Jimmy Carter insisted upon going home to Plains to fill his late father's shoes. Back to Plains. Back to being a little girl again, she feared. Back to a formidable mother-in-law who had opposed the marriage.

No! she told her husband. She lost that battle, but not the war. Back on the peanut farm she made herself into an indispensable half of the mama-and-papa store. Jimmy was laborer and inventor; Rosalynn was front office. Come the hot, dry harvest months, she would work from six in the morning until midnight, or until her head dropped over her calculator onto the breakfast table. Lord knows, some mornings she would look up through the haze of peanut dust and pray for rain, although rain wasn't good for the farmers, just to give herself a day to catch up.

Rosalynn worked even when Miz Lillian criticized her for neglecting her children. She would never be caught, like her mother, by the unexpected death or departure of a husband and consigned to the discard pile of the unskilled. Years later, the redoubtable Miz Lillian would acknowledge to this reporter, wistfully, "Everything Jimmy has ever owned, she was copartner. My husband owned the business and I was just his wife."

When Jimmy Carter fell into despondency after losing his first gubernatorial race, Rosalynn set aside her reluctance to have more children. The birth of a perfect daughter to a beaten Jimmy Carter was cause for great rejoicing. "Amy made me young again," he said. During his second run for governor, he asked Rosalynn to campaign for him. There was no precedent for refusing Jimmy Carter when he asked any member of his clan to rise to an occasion. The nausea would begin along about halfway to a rally. Sometimes she had to stop the car and get out. Just the anticipation of standing up before an audience to make a formal speech in Jimmy Carter's place made her physically ill.

"But I did it," Rosalynn Carter said. Jimmy Carter had no idea of the giant step this represented to Rosalynn. She told me, "It was the hardest thing I'd ever had to do in my life."

The real leap for Sister Rosalynn was from farm wife to first lady of Georgia. Jimmy Carter took on the role of her political mentor, advising and praising her until she surmounted her speech-making terrors and they discovered, underneath it all, that Rosalynn Carter had astute political instincts.

By 1973, when half a dozen of his closest friends sat down with Jimmy Carter to write the book of strategy for his preposterous dream of becoming President of the United States in three years, it was Rosalynn who pressed him to run in *all* the primaries. It turned out to be, of course, a crucial part of the winning strategy.

Jimmy Carter made it official while campaigning for the presidency. "Rosalynn is an almost equal extension of me."

The first impression most of the electorate had, however, was that Mrs. Carter was wholly dependent on her "Jimmeh." It drove reporters crazy that she never made any of the juicy mistakes that he did on the campaign trail. In her familiar refrain—"I wukked. We really scrimped and saved"—many people thought they heard another Pat Nixon. What they did not see for a while was that Sister Rosalynn was the essence of the pioneer wife. Earnest and good, she was dedicated to teaching people to be more compassionate. Having shared the load all along, she and Jimmy Carter were going to turn the White House into the first Mom-and-Pop Presidency.

Watching her wind up the campaign in 1976, I had a hunch that instead of being the First Lady, Rosalynn Carter would become, as I described her then, "the Second President."[12] She did set out at the start of the Carter administration with an almost grim determination to do good to people. But from the beginning, her Methodist going-on-to-perfectionism began to backfire. When the President sent her on a state visit to see Latin American leaders in the opening months of his term, the wails of wounded machismo were heard around the diplomatic world. Rosalynn was put in the political closet for the next six months. Two years later, determined to get it right, Rosalynn made another Latin American tour. She wasted no more than ten minutes with each head of state before making it clear she was there to talk substantive issues.

"Now," she would say, opening her folder ("I'd have a two-page summary of Jimmy's policy for Latin America"), and she would run down the list. Then on to her own missionary message, as she described it to me:

"You know, I'd talk to them all and say, 'Why don't you do like Costa Rica and not buy so many arms and then you could feed your children?' "

But while Rosalynn Carter seemed to feel free to speak her

own mind on foreign soil, White House reporters could not remember hearing her utter a public word distinguishable from Jimmy Carter's, not ever.

The elasticity of egos they had cultivated between them allowed Jimmy Carter to stay home in the Rose Garden marshalling key congressional votes and demonstrating hands-on management of world crises, while Rosalynn Carter went out and did the political dirty work. In 1979 she made more than fifty political appearances for the President. They divided the work just as they always had on the farm. In their Washington partnership, Jimmy Carter took Congress, mayors, the military, and small-town folks. Rosalynn Carter took women, blacks, the mentally disturbed, and old folks. He took the northern half of the hemisphere; she took the southern. He took the Middle East; she took Cambodia. With the Carters, we got two presidents for the price of one.

Many people did not see this as a bargain. The voters had not elected a Second President. The idea of *anyone* playing musical chairs with the most awesome seat of power on the planet made people nervous.

My second interview with Mrs. Carter was three weeks after the seizure of American embassy personnel in Iran. Often confusing the pronouns *I* and *we*, Rosalynn Carter openly described how closely she and the President shared the hard decisions.

"He can talk things out with me," she said. "Like we were talking about in Iran, if we do this, what will Iran do, and if we do that, what will be their next step, and how far can we go?"

I asked if there was any area of leadership in which she felt she did not belong.

"Oh, my." She laughed. "A lot of them. But the position that I am in gives you an opportunity to do things and to take a leadership role when otherwise you would not."

"How do you keep your political disagreements with the President from spilling into your private life with Jimmy Carter?" I asked.

"Oh, we talk about politics all the time—I don't know there's a dividing line. Sometimes I really get mean." She took the curse off it with a titter.

"Did you agree or advise the President on his decision to admit the Shah?" I inquired.

"We talked about it. You see, Jimmy had some pressure to bring him in. When the Shah got sick, they had some pretty good discussions about it here for a few days. Then we went to Camp David on the weekend. Sunday we got a message . . . 'What is your decision?' Jimmy said for humanitarian reasons he felt that he couldn't turn him down"—her voice became abruptly louder and brittle—"and I agreed with that. This is America! We can't keep somebody out that really needs help to save a life."

I asked if it had been an agonizing decision for the President.

"He always has it on his mind—but he's at ease with himself," she purred. "I guess maybe it just comes with knowing that you're the ones [*sic*] that make the decision and the one that has the best knowledge and information about it."

To my mind, the more serious question than how much information the Carters shared was where they got it, and how naive—or politically cynical—they might be as a leadership dyad. And so I asked the Second President if it were possible that Henry Kissinger and David Rockefeller had exaggerated the Shah's condition.

She said she did not know, and then added with a nervous laugh, "I don't know that the information about the Shah came directly from David Rockefeller."

I mentioned that it was a Rockefeller-connected doctor who had examined the Shah in Mexico.

"I just know that we got a report on his health [again, *we*], a confidential thing."

"Did you wrestle with the moral question of which was the surpassing obligation, to American personnel in Teheran or to asylum for a deposed tyrant under whose regime there were killings and torture?"

"We let everybody into our country," she replied.

"Yes, but—"

At this point in the interview, instead of sitting with her hands folded in dutiful Sunday-school-teacher style, Rosalynn Carter began stabbing the air with her ball-point pen, defensive about her decision on the Iranian situation.

"We made arrangements with the Iranian government that our embassy would be secure and nothing would happen to our people. In the meantime, we had gotten almost all of them out. You can't retreat from the world. We're a strong country, and that would really look bad, in the eyes of the world."

If she had a free hand in the hostage situation, I asked Rosalynn Carter, how would she handle it? She took a great breath.

"I would like to think that I could go over there and talk to Khomeini and tell him to let all our hostages go." An evangelical tremble began to build in her voice. "I *know* if we could just go and *talk* to him, he would understand." For an instant her voice broke into a self-deprecating giggle, then snapped back to solemnity. "Just yesterday I was saying about Cambodia, 'If I could just go into Phnom Penh and talk to Heng Samrin—' "

Our conversation was taking place in the East Wing, where Mrs. Carter ran her half of the Mom-and-Pop Presidency. It was a Friday afternoon. Any moment she expected a call from the Oval Office, whereupon she would tear off to meet the President in the backyard. After hopping into the helicopter, she with a folder marked "RC," he with a folder marked "JC," they would fly to Camp David as they did almost every Friday afternoon to spend the next forty-eight hours together, alone, deciding what to do about the world.

"Is war unthinkable to you, in any event?" I inquired of the Second President, knowing she was the hard-liner of the two.

"Oh, I can imagine war—and I think Jimmy has always known ever since he's been president that there are times that you *have* to go to war to defend the honor of your country."

A few moments later Mrs. Carter turned abruptly giggly and whispered, "I really shouldn't be talking about this."

Sitting there in her office, which had the size and ambience of a converted bedroom, felt all at once like two little girls being caught talking about grown-up things—war and politics and international intrigue—men's things. It was the moment of truth. For only when a woman who exercises awesome affiliative power is able to speak of adult things with a straight face can she be taken seriously as a leader.

It was a year and a half later, in May 1981—five months after the hostage crisis was over—that Mrs. Carter's account of the motives behind the Shah's admission were refuted by reporting in the *New York Times:*

> It is now evident that [Mr. Carter's] decision was not the spontaneous, humanitarian act it was described at the time. It was a calculated political gamble taken after months of argument among Administration officials, and it was influenced by an intensive lobbying campaign on behalf of the Shah by an "old boy network" that included some of the nation's most influential citizens, including Henry A. Kissinger, David Rockefeller and John J. McCloy.[13]

One week before that last interview with Rosalynn Carter, in fact, Mr. Carter had come close to ordering military action against Iran, including a blockade, mining of its harbors, seizure of a huge oil depot, and an air strike against the vast refineries at Abadan.

The forgotten lesson was painfully relearned: purely affiliative power is always suspect. In the latter part of Jimmy Carter's term, it became apparent to the whole country that his wife wielded great but unaccountable influence over presidential decisions. When her husband's popularity in the polls sank to a Nixonian low, Rosalynn Carter lost patience. Staff and Cabinet had to curry favor with her if they hoped to play on the team at all. Mrs. Carter wanted a second term badly. But her failure to stake out distinct purposes and separate channels of power only added to the public's perception of Jimmy Carter as a weak President.

When the Carters were defeated and went home to a listless welcome in Plains, it was the Second President who looked bitter. The curse of leading from behind is that when one's surrogate falls, one has no defense. The First Lady of a rejected president, along with him, is buried alive.

In comparison, consider Gloria Steinem. Everybody who lived through the last decade's earthquake in gender knows the name—a buzzword for the women's movement all over the world. But the more I coaxed, the more deftly she tried to duck an interview: "Just say that my form of leadership is to put forward other women who are not as well known."

That is Gloria Steinem inside and out.

On the outside, functioning as the stage manager, she recognizes that if the movement is to have a long run, women must be represented not by a few stars but by a full cast. Despite the fact that her style is not imitable (one can stand in the dressing room for hours trying to be Gloria Steinem and come out looking like just another aviator needing a haircut), she is tireless in her attempts to transfer her own star power to other women.

"I'm old news," Gloria Steinem said. "Why don't you write about leaders like Carolyn Reed and Koryne Horbal?"

"Who?"

That was just the point, of course.

But her reluctance to be interviewed was also a clue to the inner Steinem. The champion of equal standing for women is, by her own admission, "very afraid of conflict."

How could that be, when leadership demands that one deal with conflict, embody it, mediate and shape it? "I've never been prepared to take it on the chin," she insisted. "I'm still not."

Her very demeanor—she sat folded in, the curtains of hair characteristically drawn halfway across the sides of an otherwise strong jawline—together with the hesitant "I means" and "I don't knows" with which she prefaced otherwise cogent answers throughout our interview, lent credibility to her self-criticism.

The handicap that deterred Gloria Steinem from developing a fighter's instincts was imposed by her girlhood and appears to be with her for life. How she compensates for that handicap, without being ruled by anger or bitterness, is a source of hope profound in its implication for other potential women pathleaders.

One careless caravan between Florida and California with a jolly, free-spirited father who never held a job, never wore a hat, never sent her to school, but always let her share his dreams, delicious pipe dreams of inventing the jackpot orange drink or getting back a giant check for sending off ad slogans—this was Gloria Steinem's childhood until the age of 11, painting out the tragic shadow of her mother. A near-invalid who sank often into depression, Gloria's mother had become very early Gloria's child.

"I never felt angry," she said, at pains today as then to put herself in her father's shoes, to blunt the fact of his abandonment when she was 12.

"He was really trying but he just—" She swallowed hard.

"Because of the way he lived, I mean, he was unconventional and wonderful and"—she laughed—"like a child."

Alone with the scratch of rats in the walls of a ramshackle house where water froze in the glass before morning because the furnace was always being condemned, shunned by the Polish and Hungarian working people who looked upon hers as the only family in the neighborhood on its way down—that was Gloria Steinem's adolescence. That and "a blind emphasis on getting out," she said, "whether it happened through becoming 'Miss Capehart TV' or joining the Radio City kick line or going to college."

She could not confront her father—he was the child who ran away—or her mother, for whom she bore total responsibility. And so Gloria Steinem learned how to empathize and forgive.

She never actually said no to the programming followed by all the other girls—marriage and pregnancy right out of high school. "I just kept putting it off: 'I will definitely do that. But not right now.'"

College did not fit, but remarkably, her mother sold the house and sent Gloria to Smith, where, close to graduation, she became engaged.

"I didn't know how not to get married, so I went to India."

The two years in India were catalytic. Burning with the refusal to accept the poverty and inequity she had discovered in the world, she returned convinced that no one else knew. ("I must have been a terrible pain in the ass.") Over the twenty years since, she has journeyed prolifically from writer-investigator-explorer to activist to pathleader, one who reaches into the existing value structure and excites men and women to support the higher values of justice, equality, individual dignity. But Gloria Steinem also had to sail enough worlds away from her personal disappointments to render them global and, rather than sinking into self-absorption, to dissolve them in the cries of all the powerless and impoverished.

Still, she fears face-to-face confrontations.

"What gives you confidence," she said, "is the sense there is a clear injustice. Trying to change that gives you a shared purpose with other people."

"Do you mind being a buzzword?" I asked at the end of

our talk. She paused, thought, smiled, and came back strong: "Being a buzzword for half the human race is pretty diverse."

Though imperfect and often unsuccessful, the men and women so far presented have escaped the boundaries of personal experience and exercised their wits and will in the world. These pathleaders are the spirit of humanity correcting itself.

The Saga of Sadat

For good reason, the world reserves its highest honors for the pathfinder to peace. Rare, and sometimes emergent from unexpected quarters or unlikely personalities, these are people who cause whole nations to transcend themselves.

Anwar el-Sadat's journey to Jerusalem was the most innovative act of peace in recent history. The man was somehow ready for it. The development of his personality intersected with history at a moment when he could find the opening and move through it to initiate enormous structural change.

"His political courage is astonishing," United Nations diplomats say today. "Only Sadat could have achieved a Middle East peace. He made all the unthinkable decisions."

Where did this inner strength come from?

In November 1978, a month after the Camp David summit meeting, I went to Egypt, hoping to meet and come to know Sadat. Like de Gaulle and Bismarck and other heroic leaders of the last hundred years, he had made a comeback after the age of 50 and burst into late bloom.

While waiting in a Cairo hotel for an audience, I scanned recent press clippings. Sadat was a visual shock. His picture had not appeared in the Egyptian paper for days, and when it did, suddenly, he was someone other than the warm, voluptuous personality who had reached out to Americans so often through the television screen with an almost palpable magnetism.

Each day, in his photographs, he seemed to shrink. He had been home a month from the Camp David summit meeting. In the latest news photos he looked cadaverous, like a prisoner of war. Or was he, I mused, a prisoner of peace?

It was only upon meeting him face to face that the meaning of the man began to take flesh.

"Good morning!"

He did not enter the room; he materialized from nowhere, unannounced and unguarded, as if a puff of smoke had taken form before me. Not a tall man. Dark, smoky, ascetic. He was all in black, gaunt, not an inch of excess flesh to be seen. Even as other of his dimensions engaged me—his charm, freshness, theatricality—I was puzzled by the sense that the man's energy was totally concentrated in some inner space that was becoming more centered even as we talked.

The first clue to his inner strength dropped accidentally. I asked him conversationally if he had been fasting. Yes, for four months, since August. It had begun during the Muslim holy month of Ramadan, but it had not stopped there. He had kept up the fast throughout the Camp David summit meetings in the hills of Maryland. Then he had come home to Egypt to start a social revolution by first consuming himself.

By withdrawing to his favorite sanctum, the Barrages rest house north of Cairo, Sadat was literally reconstituting himself in preparation for the next great initiative. For the first thirty days after Camp David, he had touched not a morsel of food or a drop of water, not even a pipe of tobacco, until after sundown. He had returned almost to the body weight of his revolutionary youth. The fasting, he told me, also helped his mental discipline. And he was not finished yet.

"Mr. President, you have proved Egypt to the world, yourself to the world, and you no longer have to be quite so careful," I began my formal interview. "It is important for people to know you in your depth. No one is without some frailties, some imperfections. Will you join with me in the objective of following your passages—by that I mean the transitions between stages of adult life when we have the chance to grow or to go backward? You emerged from the shadow of Nasser after twenty years and made a tremendous passage to become a national leader, a world leader, a pioneer of peace. How did you accomplish this?"

He said he found my approach very interesting. "For me it is quite simply like this: since my childhood, even when I was very poor but proud, I was asking to be a different guy from the others."

As he spun his tale it became obvious that the man had many sides. They form a geometry as pure in its logic as the Great Pyramid. Sitting before him, just as when standing at the bottom of a pyramid, one can never quite distinguish between the side one is looking at and the side one has just seen. So I tried to take a point of view from the apex of the pyramid, looking down into Sadat, from that high point of his ability to conserve and reconstitute himself, down the sides to those foundations that shaped him: as a peasant, terrorist-patriot, prisoner, and "poodle" to Nasser.

Dim, soft light. Mud-enclosed cool. A gleam of copper bowl on the dirt floor. A woman bends over a mud-brick oven and draws out a soft cap of *baladi* bread. The boy sleeping on top of the oven stirs. He sleeps in the village where Anwar Sadat slept in a similar mud house as a small boy, devouring stories of Egyptian patriots hanged or poisoned by the British.

Even today, in the buzz of afternoon, the air of his village of Mit Abul-Kum was filled only with the song of swallows and the flutter of children's laughter as school let out; the girls in long flowered dresses, the shy boys inventing pull toys of tin cans and tamarind branches. They pitched in to help one another flatten dung patties, clambering up the hand-tied ladders to stack the patties for fuel. They had time for foolishness, for rocking the ladder, for standing on the roof and spinning dreams.

Childhood in this delta village was for Sadat an "inexhaustible source of happiness." But his appetite for self-improvement surpassed that of any ordinary villager's son.

"Whenever I see a good quality in someone else that is not in me," Sadat explained, "I always try to take it and put it in myself." He does not stop to fault himself for being without the quality or to envy its possessor. He simply adopts it.

This is an important facility. As we have learned, part of what marks pathfinders is the ability to identify with figures of strength from whom to draw sustenance that will help pull them across a difficult passage.

The first blow to the serenity of Sadat's childhood came when his father suddenly moved the family of thirteen children to Cairo. Sadat suffered the same twist of regret felt by many of the *fellahin* who today migrate into Egypt's cities. City life was harsh, human contact hollow by comparison. His inchoate revolutionary zeal as a boy was intensified by the first exposure to a rich city pasha. To be sponsored by a pasha was the only hope Sadat had to join the military academy. The description, in his autobiography, *In Search of Identity*, shows a revealing discrepancy between Sadat and the average Egyptian.

> The pasha looked at my father and said very haughtily: "Oh, yes. You're the senior clerk of the Health Department, and that's your son who . . . I see . . . all right, all right!"
> It was an experience that has remained with me all my life. I don't think I shall ever forget it.[14]

Virtually every Egyptian boy not born to wealth during Farouk's reign went through a similar scene of supplication if he wanted to better himself, but in Sadat it evoked a sense of humiliation so exaggerated as to provide him with enough fuel for years of revolutionary activism.

"He was a high-spirited boy," I was told by the mayor of Sadat's village, a man long in the tooth who had known the patriot as a youngster. "He was always thinking to topple the figure of King Farouk."

Living the heightened reality of the young patriot to the full, Sadat spent his twenties on the run: plotting, collaborating, waiting for revolutionary armies that never showed up, suffering arrests. It was in prison that Sadat first learned how to vacate his empirical reality in order to reside variously in religious, meditative, or self-teaching states of mind.

> One of the things Cell 54 taught me was to value that inner success which alone maintains one's inward equilibrium and helps a man to be true to himself. No man can be honest with others unless he is true to himself. . . .
> •   •   •
> Once released from the narrow confines of the "self," . . . a man will have stepped into a new, undiscovered world which is vaster and richer. . . .
> This is why I regard my last eight months in prison as the happiest period in my life. . . . Now that I had discovered and actually begun to live in that "new world," things began to change. My narrow self ceased to exist and the

only recognizable entity was the totality of existence, which aspired to a higher, transcendental reality. It was genuinely a conquest, for in that world I came to experience friendship with God—the only friend who never lets you down or abandons you.

In this state Sadat formed the lifelong conviction that the source of permanent power is inner success. To be dependent upon outward success is to be always susceptible to circumstances eluding one's control.

Most people are fascinated by outward success. . . . If their external image is, for any reason, shaken, they are inevitably shaken and may even collapse. . . .

• • •

Outward success alienates a man from himself. Self-alienation, another name for self-ignorance, is the worst that can befall a man inasmuch as it leads to the loss of inner light and, inevitably, the loss of his vision altogether. A person's inability to see his way ahead makes him a prisoner within himself; it isolates him from everything outside the narrow entity of the "self" and, therefore, annuls his belonging in humanity.

The rest of his young manhood spent on the run, shunted from one detention center to another, Sadat was sustained by the dream of every revolutionary who believes the culmination of life will come with the overthrow of the old. And when the birth of the revolution did come in 1952, a jubilant Sadat asked himself, "What else could I want?"

The end of the old culminated, of course, in the shattering of his youthful dream. Sadat and the rest of the dozen soldiers who took over the country with Gamal Abdel Nasser had no idea what to do with the revolution once they had won it. Heaping upon the West all the blame for the failure of a previous revolution, they turned from European influence to Islam. Sadat and the new leadership cadre were eager to be subsumed in a greater Arab national character—so eager that they blotted out nearly all traces of Egyptian cultural heritage, including, from 1958 to 1971, the very name of Egypt. They called it then the United Arab Republic. And with the rest of their frustration, the others fell to struggling for power among themselves.

Sadat's devotion to Nasser was complete. He urged his leader to be done with distracting power struggles by eschewing democracy for a dictatorship. In return, his beloved leader turned on Sadat with a volcanic attack.

Why me, Sadat cried to himself, *the only one who has never been competitive with him?*

But the greater the devotion he showed, the crueler the ridicule he earned. To examine undercurrents of the betrayal, while that close, was impossible. Only when Sadat confronted the pain again years later, while writing about himself, was he able to permit the realization that Nasser did not trust him, indeed, that Nasser's envy caused him to hold against Sadat the very heroic exploits by which the young revolutionary sought to prove his selflessness.

In his pain and bewilderment, Sadat withdrew and took up an extreme form of self-defense:

> From that moment on I withdrew, taking up the position of a detached observer. . . .
>
> •   •   •
>
> . . . I felt there was nothing that deserved bothering too much about. They repeatedly tried to find out why I adopted that stand, putting it down to weakness, inexperience, or indifference. They could not have been further from the truth.

The truth was that Sadat had taken up the ancient posture of the cunning *fellah:* when up against the insurmountable, withdraw. He went into hibernation. Not only did he avoid falling like a comet, as did eventually all the other members of the revolutionary council; Sadat also created a metaphysical state in which he could endure indefinitely without being self-destructive.

Consider it a prolonged version of the state of being he had found preservative while imprisoned.

> I have, since then, realized that my real self is a greater entity than any possible post or title. Why be surprised, then, to see me shun such human conflicts?

One of the greatest assets for a pathfinder is a sense of timing for the push and pull of life. To know how to anticipate the times to push and how to resist during times that pull—this is a skill worth every effort to cultivate. Sadat's eighteen-year adaptation to a reality he could not change—without going to sleep or doing something self-destructive and without allowing his confidence to deteriorate—is an inspiring model for all of us.

Sadat remained those years in the background of government, but he had no real vocation. His disagreements with Nasser could never be aired publicly or his head, too, would have rolled. And so he learned from his superior: "Gamal was much more able than myself, so I spent eighteen years beside him studying him." Meanwhile, Sadat shed the family of his first marriage, arranged in childhood, and started another by marrying a strong-minded half-English woman who became the love of his life.

Sadat was 52 when Nasser died. He claims never to have harbored even the hope of succeeding his leader, being both older himself and already the victim of a heart attack. There must be truth in this, because while he was speaker of the assembly, and hoping to build his father a better house, Sadat tore down the mud hut of his childhood—an act of ill prophecy he could kick himself for today. Abe Lincoln is his great American hero; if Sadat had felt he would become Egypt's president, that house would have stood as Honest Anwar's mud hut.

The idea that Sadat would emerge at all could not have been further from what the Nasserists expected. They saw him as a juiceless leftover—and let him be named interim president until they were ready to chew him up.

A wise former aide of Sadat's gave this telling description: "He is an actor, a ham who also has depth. One should not detract from the other." And so, while the people were distracted by his first tragic performance as a Hamlet beset by enemies, Sadat swooped down upon his opponents and threw them all in jail. So swiftly did it happen that the Nasserists missed the fact that they were part of a "corrective revolution." The Russians are still scratching their heads over how Sadat's palace guard could have purged a conspiracy without firing a single shot.

Not many people after two decades of passivity could reshape themselves and emerge, every fiber of stifled intuition intact, ready to take risks at an age when most people are allergic to risk, able to become not only a politically cunning national leader but to elevate the role of leader to pathleading statesman.

Sadat's confidence had, however, slipped somewhat during the withdrawal period. In the first few years of his presidency, as observed by a senior American diplomat in Egypt, "signs of uncertainty showed in vacillations of policy: two steps forward, one step back." The diplomat dated the first surge in President Sadat's confidence to the reception he received when he appeared before the U.S. Congress in 1975. "Since then, he's been much more confident that he's not going to be deterred by other Arab states or critics." The second turning point, of course, came with the risk of going to Jerusalem.

One of the ways Sadat went about fortifying his confidence was to zero in on the most powerful transitional figures he could find to help him. He would lure them into the tent and then use them to the full.

He started with Henry Kissinger.

In 1970 Western leaders considered Sadat a joke. The CIA gave his presidency four to six weeks. "A buffoon, an operatic figure," Kissinger admitted was his own opinion for the first two years. In 1972 Sadat tried to impress Kissinger by booting Soviet military advisers out of Egypt. Kissinger ignored him.

And so a year later, Sadat came back with a thunderbolt a hundred times more electrifying. He led his thrice-whipped army into a Suez Canal that every major intelligence agency said he could never cross. Why did he do it?

The remains of the revolution he had helped to foment at home were necrotic. The nation's treasury was empty, her institutions tottering, her equipment vintage 1938; the population was multiplying perilously while public services were collapsing; the decomposition of Cairo had begun. On top of it all, Egypt was suffering the humiliation of seeing her territory under foreign rule. And it would stay that way as long as the legend of Israeli invincibility remained unchallenged.

Sadat could look across the Canal from his rest house in Ismailia and see it all in the Israeli soldier, sitting with his rifle slung over a camp chair, a sandal dangling off his toes.

Sadat did not want a war. He wanted to shock America into taking him seriously, and it was as much for that reason as it was to redress Arab humiliation that he initiated the Six-Day War on Israel.

Even then, it was not until 1974, when Sadat astonished Kissinger one more time by asking if the American President would help him dredge out and reopen the Canal, that Kissinger admitted, "For the first time, I began to take the man seriously."

Next, Sadat went to work on the American Congress. Then, on Jimmy Carter. Then, on world opinion. The time for resistance was over. His confidence restored, Anwar Sadat sprang into action, showing a gift for anticipation—that is, a long-range vision of the future.

From then on, consistently, Sadat has been ten minutes ahead of world history.

I asked President Sadat about his willingness to risk. "To take such bold gambles—expelling the Soviets, crossing the Canal, going to Jerusalem—you have to be willing to lose. No one wins all the time—"

He chuckled. "Not even me."

"But how do you reconcile that possibility with your decision to move boldly?"

The man's booming voice came down to a hush. "Let me tell you," he said. "I'm a true believer. I believe that every human being has got a mission to fulfill, and a time to live. I start with what we call in the military 'the appreciation of situation.' *What's my duty now?* I ask myself. Then I make a plan. And then, once I take my decision, I am putting my destiny in the hands of God. Whatever happens, I am happy. Succeed or die, I have done my best."

It would be difficult to exaggerate the advantage a Muslim leader enjoys during times of uncertainty and decision. While the Christian or Jew heaps guilt upon himself for every decision that goes wrong, the belief in predestination relieves the Muslim in advance of any retrospective guilt. Our culture limits us in this regard. The Judeo-Christian tradition does emphasize that making the right decision in terms of moral choice is enough to please God. The fatalism taught by Islam is, however, a powerful cultural component.

No modern American president has approached events quite like Sadat, with the possible exception of Truman, who within the boundaries of an Occidental decision maker was a fatalist. Truman split off the act of making the decision from the outcome of the decision and was said to go to sleep at night with ease (as does Sadat, reading Gothic mysteries). It is rare to be able to separate the act of deciding from the reaction to consequences of one's decision. But, oh my! Could it help us all to practice it!

"Some philosophers say there is only one subject worth discussing seriously," I had said to President Sadat. "What is your personal attitude toward death?"

"I don't fear it at all," he replied. "The Koran tells us it is but God who has fixed this hour, and He has fixed it already for you. This may answer for you why I could make my October War when every computer in the world said, 'Sadat will be buried in the Canal.' I knew that neither the Israelis nor the U.S., that no one from this earth will rob me of one hour of my life. God has put it. So I am at ease. Great ease."

Robert Kennedy had some of this. The arithmetic of life and death in his family seemed inevitable. Ethel Kennedy probably knew it and kept her faith. Robert Kennedy knew it and kept his fatalism. He also shared with Sadat something of that same capacity for vacating an upsetting reality.

"I remove myself," Kennedy once told me. "My mind is somewhere else a lot of the time."

During the last week of his campaign for the presidency, he was being chased around the west coast with a vengeance by his opponent, Eugene McCarthy. I shall never forget Kennedy in his campaign plane going over a briefing sheet on Roseburg, Oregon, where we were about to land. I happened to be sitting beside him. A DC-3 came straight at us. It ducked under our plane's wing as close as two gulls mating. The reporters on the plane gasped and flinched, and I did too. The man beside me did not move a muscle.

"I knew Gene McCarthy was desperate," he quipped, "but did you hear that pilot yell 'Banzai' as he passed?"

The next day newspapers said America had almost lost a presidential candidate in an air disaster. They were a week early and had the wrong weapon.

Beyond the fervor of the true believer, beyond his willingness to risk, Sadat has demonstrated a pragmatic grasp of the *Realpolitik*. This combination is his uniqueness. And in large measure, his practical political abilities stem from qualities usually associated with females.

He is intuitive. He avoids conflict. Having been for so long the underdog, he knows more about the overlords than they know about themselves—such is the case with all the formerly powerless. He has a gift for empathy. And he knows how to endure creatively.

It is this last, according to a senior American official in Egypt, that is the key to Sadat's sense of timing.

When asked if he could have taken his historic journey to Jerusalem, say, two years before, the president retorted, "No. Never! It could not have been done even a few months before."

When I pressed on how he knew that moment was the right one, Sadat sat forward and described with passion how he had led up to—and engineered—the meeting at Camp David.

"Since the first day Henry Kissinger visited me here, in Egypt, yes, yes, I was calculating everything. It was a week or two after the October War of '73. No one believed that the time will come when the United States can take a position that's not one hundred percent with the Israelis. But I felt it. When we started the peace process together, I *felt* it."

When describing such intuitions, Sadat virtually reenacts the release it gave him, an intense and visceral connection between body and mind.

The decision to go to Israel was not a vision that sprang full-blown from his brow in a process that cannot be copied by ordinary mortals. It was a breathtaking act of creativity, to be sure, but we can all absorb something from it.

Ten months before inviting himself to the Knesset, let us not forget, Sadat made the grand declaration, "As long as there is an Israeli soldier on my land, I am not ready to shake the hand of anyone in Israel at all." But Sadat's instincts had told him he might find an opening to move ahead through Jimmy Carter. And so he had gone to see the American President for the first time in April 1977. "Carter told me that all the Israelis want is direct negotiations, full normal relations, and in the future, an exchange of embassies and economic cooperation," Sadat described it to me. "The next five months the man did his best."

Carter sent a personal letter to Sadat five months later, expressing some frustration. "In my answer to President

Carter," Sadat described, "I wrote, 'My dear friend, some bold action should be risked.' But what were the dimensions of this bold action? Two months before my initiative there was nothing in my head."

Convinced that he now had his best shot out of the three American presidents he had dealt with, Sadat moved swiftly to take the measure of his enemy. Discovering that his friend Nicolae Ceausescu, president of Rumania, had recently received Menachem Begin, Sadat invited himself to Rumania and came right to the point: "I want you to answer me two questions," he said to Ceausescu. "First, is Menachem Begin sincere for peace? And is the man strong enough to work in this project?"

After six hours of counsel, Ceausescu gave him the measure of Begin: yes, on both counts.

Passing over Turkey en route from Rumania to Iran, Sadat told me, he was tortured with "How am I going to make this bold act that I promised Carter?" He began preparing himself for a state of creativity, letting go of old fears and suspicions, worn-out ideas and methods, even historical facts that carried the weight of certainties. In Sadat's book I later found this explanation of how he was able to vacate the emotional set that had made Israel taboo for his whole generation:

> It was then that I drew, almost unconsciously, on the inner strength I had developed in Cell 54 of Cairo Central Prison—a strength, call it a talent or capacity, for change. . . . My contemplation of life and human nature in that secluded place had taught me that he who *cannot change the very fabric of his thought* [emphasis added] will never be able to change reality, and will never, therefore, make any progress. The fact that change is a prerequisite of progress may be axiomatic; but the fact that change should take place first *at a deeper and perhaps subtler level than the conscious level* [emphasis added] was one I had established as a basis of action ever since I discovered my real self in Cell 54.

The self-knowledge indicated by that statement is remarkable.

In midair over Turkey, Sadat told his foreign minister his idea. The official thought he was raving mad. When the foreign minister advised his deputies about the plan for Sadat to go to Jerusalem, one said, "You cannot be serious, knowing the facts!"

"I know the facts," the minister said. "But I also know the man."

Transmitting Personal Powers of Rebirth

No time to rest on his laurels. A month after the Camp David accord Sadat was on the threshold of another staggering task. He must pick up his dirt-poor, noncompetitive society and somehow turn it into a society where the cities work, foreign aid can be absorbed, and Egypt's productivity rate can enter the 20th century.

"I have already started the social revolution in Egypt," boomed Sadat. It being the first private interview he had granted in two months, he was in great form.

"But, Mr. President, under Nasser the people were taught that it was the government's responsibility to do everything for them," I said. "How do you plan to mobilize a national incentive?"

"Terrible, terrible. Without the human effort, nothing can be done." A moment later he was off on an existential leap of flying proportions, looking inward at that utterly original compass of his, visions caroming off his mind from the American westerns he watches on a home projector night after night. "Those shacks all over the West only fifty or sixty years ago," he narrated his vision. "No one can believe that this has turned in two hundred years to be the most powerful, richest country in the world." As if compelled by his movie-struck version of the American prosperity formula, Sadat came to the edge of his chair, eyes bright as planets, and he delivered his next great epic poem:

"I am asking my people to start like you started, the drive to the West. Everyone can achieve his ambitions! But leave this old valley, go out and find it in the western desert! Go west, young man! And fight like fighters! Like America."

Coming away from our meeting, exhilarated by Sadat's vision, I was plunged unceremoniously back into the streets of Cairo . . . dear, demented Cairo, half blind and mostly deaf, the once classical French face fallen to ruin; it leaks everywhere and its communication organs are feeble and its buses and trains are laden all over with humanity so that it has just about lost all motor abilities. This is Sadat's reality. Every wayfarer through life has one, whether it is a retarded child or an alcoholic mate or a period of financial peril. How, I puzzled, can even a gifted pathleader keep people calm in a city built for a million and a half where ten million now huddle and where nothing works? On hope, I supposed.

Sadat, of course, not only runs his country on hope but rules with a certain measure of benign dictatorship. The press is controlled. A state of emergency gives the president power to veto a court decision in the case of a political trial. And after food riots erupted in 1977, he saw to it that a referendum was passed that makes rioting punishable by life imprisonment. Although the young students, intellectuals, and politicians who do not agree with Sadat's policies are limited in the channels available for their opposition, no torture or even widespread imprisonment of political enemies is reported in Egypt.

But with a national population of forty million, increasing by one million a year, the economic outlook would appear to be hopeless. There would seem no way that the Egyptian government can meet the expectations of prosperity raised by the Camp David agreements without a resumption of the money flow from Saudi Arabia. That looks impossible without a comprehensive Middle East peace. And a comprehensive Arab-Egyptian-Israeli peace is something many forces in the world have vested interests in preventing.

The arrogance of anyone who dares to lead others in working toward transformational change, anyone who dares creative work, anyone who has the drive to overcome obstacles of class or race or money or the absence of supportive parents, must require a tilt toward the euphoric—what might be called *a concentration of optimism.*

Roger Baldwin certainly showed it when I interviewed him. In fact, every one of the pathleaders I have attempted to describe would seem to have at least this facet in common. It is the only quality that Sadat consciously recultivates in himself at each turning point and insists upon in his people:

. . . he who cannot change the very fabric of his thought will never be able to change reality, and will never, therefore, make any progress . . . but the fact that change should take place first at a deeper and perhaps subtler level than the conscious level was one I had established as a basis of action . . .

In the myth of Pandora's Box, each of the gods gave the first woman some power to bring about the ruin of man. When Pandora's husband opened the box, all the evils flew forth. One only remained safe inside: Hope.

The last bulwark between mankind and ruin, then, may be optimism—and the pathleaders who still feel it.

Afterword

Much has been made in this book of the benefits of risk and change, but change is not always or exclusively the best response when one is enduring a personal crucible. The same may be said of society. One further strength that a society requires is people who have the ability to distinguish between that which passes and that which must last. In our enthusiasm for personal transformation and cultural reawakenings, we would do well to consider the importance of maintaining, recombining, and enduring.

Maintaining is the reverse side of innovation. By definition, innovation replaces the old and familiar with the disconcertingly new. Innovation is necessary. But newness should not be permitted to shatter and discard all that existed in the prelude to its emergence.

To gauge how much effort a society usefully might put into maintenance, consider the ratio in your own life between the time you spend trying out new things and the time you need to maintain what exists—if your family is to be kept happy, if your friendships are not to lapse, if your desk is not to drown you in paper, or your car to fall apart, your pipes to burst, your walls to crack, your grass to go to seed, if your mind is to remain acute and your body to be other than a lump—when you add it all up, maintenance work may be three-quarters of life.

Something is wrong when a society cannot count on its helicopters to rescue hostages, or command its computers to send up space ships on time, or make its cars and appliances and war planes work reliably. A society that thinks all it need do is market well and manipulate accounting methods is losing sight—and possibly grasp—of the future. Moreover, if we choose the path of blind faith in technology and more and more elaborate war machines, we flirt with the possibility of becoming a country of passing greatness. And when government officials talk casually, on the record, about "winnable" nuclear wars, we have come perilously close to the end of that which lasts.

Some pathfinders act as ensurers of continuity. They transcend themselves through a commitment to cultural symbols that are beyond time and individual death—such as their nation's laws or literature, its language or traditions. By exhibiting their own conviction, they may be able to return luster to tarnished institutions. Although Americans approached a Constitutional crisis during the Nixon debacle, for example, elderly judges such as John Sirica came forward to rescue us. Not a pathfinder, Nixon perceived only a personal emergency—he was in danger of being driven from office. By setting himself above the courts and our constitutional form of government, he contemned both the system that had conferred upon him its highest powers and the distinctions between right and wrong in which that system is grounded. Judge John J. Sirica's behavior stood in contrast:

"Here I was, an obscure judge, facing the President of the United States. . . . It made me extremely nervous," he later wrote. " 'Suppose I'm wrong in my decision,' I would think. . . . I felt like hell." But as he took his place on the bench when the Watergate trial began, the stone figures of Moses, Hammurabi, Justinian, and Solon dwarfing him from the wall behind his chair, Sirica was made larger by the cultural tradition he was committed to uphold:

"I had the deep feeling that something I had spent my life serving—the rule of law—was in terrible danger."

Sirica transcended a sense of inferiority and extended his working life for five more years, to the age of 73, in order to reinfuse the Constitution with meaning, and then to leave a record, in the form of a book,[1] so that history would be less likely to be perverted by political revisionism.

Other pathfinders will become guardians of our society's ethics in a new era of scientific breakthrough, perhaps in a manner like that of the former Jesuit earlier described. They transcend themselves on our behalf by remaining concerned with the maintenance of standards and practices that will protect future generations. Society is also the beneficiary of pathfinders who raise us above the level of ethical chic, a task already being undertaken by certain new corporate philosophers.

Only the poets remind us that political and economic institutions are but the fancy skyscrapers built on top of any culture's foundation—which is its spiritual base. When those great deposits of bedrock begin to rumble and shift, it is a warning that no less than everything else may be changed. At the moment, the evangelical right has taken on as its mission the "salvation" of America which, if successful, would mean political and economic control as well as religious leadership. It scarcely requires statement that this runs explicitly counter to the tradition of individualism and tolerance that is America's heart. That must be maintained.

Equally necessary to our collective well-being are those pathfinders who are able to perform feats of recombining. In truth, we innovate faster than we can integrate. Insecticides, X rays, birth control pills—almost every major scientific or technological breakthrough has carried with it an unsuspected peril and required reconsideration and reform before it has been integrated satisfactorily. People capable of recombining old and new information offer an antidote to either-or thinking about how to make use of technological advances. The same phenomenon operates in the personal realm. Consider the many women who did decide in the last decade to stop trying so hard to please. That innovation of personality released buried deposits of anger; the air around many of those women filled with hostility; they drove people away. It is necessary now for women and men to recombine. They should be ready to come back from the combat zone to which so many withdrew over the last fifteen years, and to join in an embrace where the self is merged and at the same time strengthened. This coming together "with a difference" would be the essence of highest sexual union, a forging of power and compassion that transcends anger and destructiveness.

An understanding of the symbiosis between industrialized and developing nations also will be vital to the future. Properly used, the minds of the pathfinders in our midst and of pathleaders, like Sadat, from other cultures can lead us out of withdrawal and rigid self-interest to where the transcendent correspondences between people's yearnings—wherever they are on the planet—can be clearly appreciated.

Pathfinders are those most capable of merging contemporary contradictions into clearer truths that can be understood by many. When enough people accept both the insights and inconsistencies of new truths, they will press their institutions to accommodate them and to evolve more equitable rules. Inevitably, the cultural memory of any new generation will be hit or miss. The values of a society, therefore, need continuous debate, reform, and public restatement—if the spiral of development is to continue. From the thesis and antithesis of the comeback generation, a new synthesis should emerge. But the old contradictions never quite die, and the victories are never permanent.

Out of the fog of melancholia that settles wherever there is conviction that the West is in an inexorable decline, there are voices that shout, *No! We refuse to go backward!*

These are people who were dealt much the same mixed pack of flaws and strengths that we all receive. They leave childhood with no fewer scratches on the soul. They choose from the same two or three life paths on which we all set out in the vanity that we are unique. Many of us contemplate fording the difficult passages that we meet, or consider taking the less-traveled path, but we do not dare because we have no idea what is on the other side. Some of us wrestle all our lives with the possible but never do it.

The difference is, pathfinders do it.

Innovative, excited about being on the brink of evolutionary change, while actively skeptical about the West's will to survive; seasoned with humor, love, compassion, and plain orneriness, these people have the dual capacity for pragmatism and for transcendence. In their normal workaday identities—as teachers, technicians, housewives, scientists, municipal employees, volunteers, artists, writers, whatever—they work hard and enjoy as well as radiate well-being. But they also can shift to a transcendent frame of mind—to reframe a problem, reach for a creative solution, rise above individual pain or stress or ostracism or even imprisonment. Many of them know what it is to surmount a life accident. They possess an overview of where they, and their society, fit in the larger scheme. Whether that view is one of concentrated optimism or philosophical pessimism, they care about binding the wandering shepherd to his flock. It is through them that we may find our way home.

The remainder of this century probably will see continued attempts to reach for certainty through a revival of religious commitment, whether to new cults or to old fundamentalist faiths. But the path to America's return will become clear, in my view, only when we again become united around a transcending moral issue. If the climate is not ready, the transcendent pathfinders among us will not be spotted, their ideas not repeated by one person to another. Such people can only come out of a society that is ready to risk a new path. It is their patience in explaining new realities with which they have wrestled in private periods of withdrawal, and their passion for breathing new life into our oldest, shared beliefs and values, that permits them to help a confused society find its way back to a clarity of purpose. Let us hope we shall continue to know them when we see them.

—And this alone awaits you, when you dare
To that sheer verge where horror hangs, and tremble
Against the falling rock; and, looking down,
Search the dark kingdom. It is to self you come,—
And that is God. It is the seed of seeds:
Seed for disastrous and immortal worlds.

It is the answer that no question asked.

—CONRAD AIKEN, "Preludes for Memnon or Preludes to
   Attitude"

Acknowledgments

Although I write for myself and for strangers, I do not work alone. There are people who, in the course of the writing of this book, made the difference between a tedious and lonely labor and a spirit of camaraderie and shared adventure that kept my attention on the same field of ideas for four and a half years. They grew the garden with me.

It began in a most civilized manner. There was a delightful new editor to get to know, Hillel Black, Editor-in-Chief at William Morrow and Company. He flew out to the country to spend a day with me discussing the book that would follow *Passages*. In between the beach, cold lobster and beer, beach again, we even managed to have a little chat about this thing I planned to call *Pathfinders*.

Since it was going to take considerable effort even to devise a plan for research, much less to escape being desiccated by it, I decided to try to make working on this book a more genteel process than the usual—enough of those hysterical deadlines and dreary working conditions. Hill, along with Sherry Arden, Associate Publisher of Morrow, encouraged me in my illusions. They invited me to play tennis at night on the company court, taking me out afterward for pasta and wine. They treated me so well, I made it a policy to take my own staff (of two) out for a long lunch every Friday to indulge in a bottle of wine and frivolous chatter.

I began to think, yes, at last, maybe it is possible to become one of those wonderfully organized writers who types a thousand words from six to noon, takes a three-hour Continental lunch, and then comes home to write letters for

P.E.N. championing the cause of writers held political prisoner elsewhere in the world.

That supremely civilized schedule lasted about three months. By then, the basic research instrument, the Life History Questionnaire, was ready for a pilot study.

Enter Milton Glaser, one of my dearest friends from the old *New York* magazine days, who was enthusiastic about using the questionnaire at the Aspen Design Conference as the basis of the first major survey of designers' attitudes toward their work and their lives. Being Milton Glaser, he planned a *tour de force:* to turn the survey around within the five days of the conference and to publish a newspaper—called *Life Times*—reporting all the results, illustrated with self-portraits by the conferees.

There was only one catch. We would not know, until we arrived in the Rockies with our 2,000 questionnaires in cartons, whether or not computer facilities would be available to tabulate them. They weren't.

"Never mind," Milton said. "We'll put together an all-volunteer team and count by hand."

It was a primitive start to the research, but we did put out the newspaper. And the enthusiasm of the all-volunteer effort was infectious—it gave me hope. Nevertheless, it was clear that I would have to find more formal research assistance.

For the statistical part of the explorations my colleagues became Phillip Shaver, then Associate Professor and coordinator of the doctoral research program in Social Psychology at New York University, and Carin Rubenstein, a gifted doctoral candidate in psychology. The three of us further developed and refined the scale that measures well-being and tested it on new groups. Both Phil and Carin were well-grounded in social science methodology but not in bondage to it. They were refreshingly sensible and imaginative in their approach to codifying, distributing, tabulating, and helping to interpret the raw data.

Peggy Barber joined the team as administrative assistant. I knew I was blessed when Peggy told me, "Don't worry—when I believe in what I'm doing, I stick like a mother-in-law." She stuck for the next year and a half of what is loosely referred to as "field work." That means going out to interview among the natives—congressmen, corporate chiefs, women brokers and bankers, homemakers, automotive workers, professional athletes, lawyers, municipal employees—the whole gamut. Peggy was always there when I came back from a trip, with acres of freshly transcribed tapes and a good Irish laugh and a hug. Also there to contribute at critical moments were Emily Greenspan and Sean Gresh, both writers themselves, and Muriel Bedrick, whose gifts of poetry across the back fence obscured a while longer the gathering frenzy.

In January 1980 the writing began. Civilities quickly dropped away. With the few people I saw, communication was reduced to grunts and non sequiturs. I was sealed off in a small, cold glass box, my feet in Eskimo mukluks, nobody to talk to—perfect conditions either for writing a book or for going stark raving mad. Once again, I was rescued, this time by Gladd Patterson.

People had been telling me, the way everyone tells writers these days, "You really ought to get a word processor." Well, I have one—with a memory for retrieval that would make IBM whimper. But much more—Gladd, who worked with me on *Passages*, is a word processor with a heart and a soul. She cares. She thinks. She asks all the right questions. She never bruises the delicate writer's ego. And she always, I mean always, shows up.

Once it came time to rake over the field work, Hill Black evolved into a jovial gamekeeper. With wit and unfailing good nature, he helped in staking out the territory, in preventing me from going out of bounds, in driving away the wilder ideas and distractions—not to mention keeping the wolf from my door. In the process, he grew into a friend who will last. Further encouragement came from Rollene Saal, whose elegant mind was then in the employ of Bantam Books as their Editor-in-Chief.

After the first six months of writing, I had an intriguing tangle of half-grown ideas. They cried out for cultivation, transplantation, cross-fertilization. What I needed—what any writer dreams of—is a gardener of the mind. But who does one dare send in with a rake and hoe? Only one who has earned pure trust. I was fortunate to have found such a person in the final weeks of editing *Passages*. Carol Eisen Rinzler has as precise and clear a mind as minds come. But she also appreciates the uses of disorder. She is that rare editor with a cool eye but a soft touch. We engaged in wonderful days that I think of as the Country Lane Dialogues, debating and digging out the better ideas. Part of the trust was I knew I could always count on Carol, in the end, to weed out the purple and provoke me to reach further.

The final months, the home stretch, tried the band of faithful to its human limits. They trooped in on Sundays, showed up at six in the morning, dragging their pinched nerves and floating collarbones and irritable intestines. The place began to look like Tobacco Road. For a last marathon of copy editing, Morrow sent me a lovely pair of eyes, those of Barbara Wood.

The inner circle drew up in their wagons. Ella Council, the manager and heartbeat of my household, kept us watered down with iced coffee. She nourishes us all. I hardly know what to say about Clay Felker. Days went by, months, years, and he always said the same thing to friends who asked where I was. "Oh, she's home writing." He helped me in a hundred ways, supporting and cajoling, telling me when my writing had gone flabby and suggesting how I might get back in training; but most of all, wondrously, he waited. My daughter, Maura, having brought to the book the withering honesty of adolescence—"Mom, I fell asleep on page fifteen of that chapter. Could I finish it in the morning?"—began assuring me that all her friends were really going to love the book, when they're old.

But in truth, when my spirits flagged and my disposition deteriorated, when doubt invaded, it was Maura's belief in me and in this book that sustained.

What the process of writing this book lacked in gentility, I can vouchsafe was made up for in humility. I believe I can speak for the others in saying that we all felt animated by knowing the people in this book. They prompted us to identify our own victories and to approach future paths more boldly. I hope that readers will inspect their own hearts, for, if I have served my purpose, this book is about you and me as well.

I am also deeply grateful to the scholars who corresponded with me: Steven G. Vandenberg (now on sabbatical from the University of Colorado at the University of Amsterdam) for his guidance on studies of hereditary factors in personality; David L. Gutmann, Professor and Chief of Division of

Psychology, Northwestern University Medical School, for discussing his theories and enlightening papers on development in middle and later life; Robert May, director of the mental health clinic at Amherst College, for his keen observations on male and female fantasies and myths; Professor June Louin Tapp, senior social psychologist for the American Bar Foundation, who efficiently condensed for me the essence of ten years' research and writing on the interaction between psychology and the law; Paul C. Glick, senior demographer at the Population Division of the Bureau of the Census, whose expert knowledge on the American family has been invaluable; Arthur Schlesinger, Jr., Albert Schweitzer Professor of the Humanities at City University of New York, who aided me in my research into cyclical theories of history and did me the kindness of reading and commenting upon the chapter in which those theories are presented; John Murrin, Professor of History at Princeton University, whose pithy and particular comments on the last section of the book were most welcome; and John Guarnaschelli, Associate Professor of History at City University of New York, who provided a provocative critique of my view. Questions 29 and 30 in the Life History Questionnaire were adapted from Dr. Milton Rokeach's "Value Survey" and used with his permission. The copyrighted "Value Survey" is available from Halgren Tests, 873 Persimmon Avenue, Sunnyvale, California 94087, and is described in *The Nature of Human Values* (Free Press, 1973).

Cooperative research efforts were mounted with twelve large organizations, the goal being to provide a broad background against which the biographies of selected individuals could later be highlighted. The organizations that graciously cooperated were the American Bar Association, the Proprietary Association, the Financial Women's Association of New York, District 37 Municipal Trades Council, Harvard Business School, Washington University Continuing Education for Women (St. Louis), The Mental Health Association of Johnson County (Overland Park, Kansas), National Council on Labor Union Women, International Women's Year (national convention), Bunker Hill Community College (Boston), Interface Ecumenical Center (Houston), New School for Social Research (New York), Harvard Law Women, and the national Aspen Design Conference.

Over two hundred Americans, whose names I have listed in Appendix IV and who hold pivotal positions in their communities, suggested candidates for interviews. The enthusiasm and discretion with which they participated added an incalculable diversity to this book.

Most important of all, I want to thank the sixty thousand people who took the time to complete and return the Life History Questionnaire. I am especially grateful to those hundreds of people who were interviewed by telephone and in person. The pathfinders I found among them have become true friends and models, not only for me, but I hope for all the readers of this book.

Appendix I
Life History Questionnaire

The questions that follow made up the basic questionnaire for this book. After recording your own answers, you may want to score yourself on the Well-being Scale that follows in Appendix II.

1. What is your age? _____ years old

2. What is your sex (Circle answer)

   1. Male
   2. Female

3. What is your current marital status? (Please circle only one.)

   1. Single
   2. Living with a lover
   3. Married, for the first time
   4. Remarried, once
   5. Remarried, more than once
   6. Separated
   7. Divorced
   8. Widowed

4. Have you ever been separated, divorced, or widowed? (Circle as many as apply.)

   1. Separated
   2. Divorced
   3. Widowed
   4. None of the above

5. If you have ever been married, how old were you when you first got married? _____ years old

540

6. How many children do you have? _____ children

7. How old were you when your first child was born? (If you don't have any children, skip to the next question.) _____ years old

8. How do you feel about the number of children you have?

    1. Content with the number of children I have
    2. Content that I have no children
    3. Feel that I have too many children
    4. Feel that I have too few children, but don't expect to have more
    5. Feel that I have too few children, and expect to have more
    6. Sorry that I have no children, but don't expect to have any
    7. Sorry that I have no children, and expect to have one or more
    8. Uncertain

9. Circle the number of the statement that <u>best</u> characterizes you.

    1. I postponed (or am postponing) marriage until my career was (is) well established.
    2. I postponed (or am postponing) having children until my career was (is) well established.
    3. I postponed (or am postponing) having children until my marriage was (is) well established.
    4. I postponed (or am postponing) active pursuit of a career until my family was (is) well established.
    5. I am married and pursuing a career and plan never to have children.
    6. I am married and have child(ren) and plan never to pursue a career.
    7. I am pursuing a career, have never married, and plan never to marry or have children.
    8. I didn't postpone marriage, parenthood, or career—I started on all three in my twenties.

9. I am a single parent (divorced, separated, never married) and am pursuing a career.
10. Other: _____

10. Below, briefly list three benefits and three costs of the life pattern you have described in question 9.

Benefits	Costs
a. _____	a. _____
b. _____	b. _____
c. _____	c. _____

11. How often do you feel bored?

1. Almost never
2. Rarely
3. Occasionally
4. Fairly often
5. Most of the time
6. Almost all the time

12. Have you ever failed at a major personal or professional endeavor?

1. Yes, and I found the experience useful. I am better off for it.
2. Yes, and it was a destructive experience. I am worst off for it.
3. No.
4. Not applicable.

In questions 13 to 15, "work" refers to your main work activity, whether inside the home or outside.

13. How often do you enjoy the work that you do?

1. Almost all the time
2. Most of the time
3. Fairly often
4. Occasionally
5. Rarely
6. Almost never

14. Do you feel that your major work activity makes a contribution to society?

1. Definitely yes
2. Most of the time
3. Some of the time
4. Almost none of the time
5. Definitely no
6. Not applicable

15. If you would like to make a major change in the kind of work you do but feel you can't at this time, what are the reasons? (Circle as many as apply.)

1. Loss of income
2. Loss of prestige
3. Risk of failure
4. Spouse and/or family wouldn't approve
5. Friends and/or colleagues wouldn't approve
6. No decent opportunity at my age
7. Lack of training or skills
8. Just feel scared
9. Would damage children
10. I don't want to make a career change at this time
11. Other: _____

Questions 16 to 18 refer to work outside the home. If you are not employed outside the home, please circle "not applicable" or "no."

16. Do you have a paying job outside the home?

1. No
2. Yes, part-time
3. Yes, full-time

17. Which of the following would you be willing to do in order to attain professional success? (Circle as many as apply.)

1. Work a few extra nights per week
2. Work on weekends
3. Work during vacations
4. Spend several nights away from home each month
5. Move to another part of the country
6. Allow marriage or major love affair to break up
7. If you are divorced and have children, move away from the children
8. Not applicable

18. True or false? I prefer the security and comfort of working within a large corporation (or other institution—government, university, hospital) to the high risk and longer hours usually involved in self-employment or a small business.

    1. Very true
    2. Moderately true
    3. Slightly true
    4. False
    5. Not applicable

19. Looking back at the goals, aspirations, or "dreams" you had as you entered adulthood, how do you feel at this point in your life?

    1. I am just beginning to shape my dream.
    2. I am on my way to achieving my dream.
    3. I have achieved my original dream and have generated a new one.
    4. I have achieved a great deal but it's quite different from my original dream.
    5. I have never had a clear dream or aspiration.
    6. I am not sure whether I am on my way to achieving my dream.
    7. I will probably never achieve my original dream.
    8. I have achieved my original dream and haven't generated a new one.

20. What was your original "dream" as you entered adulthood? (Please write your answer in the space provided below.)

21. Using the numbers below (1 to 8), indicate in the answer column at right how you have been feeling about each of the following aspects of your life during the past several months.

1. Delighted
2. Pleased
3. Mostly satisfied
4. Mixed (about equally satisfied and dissatisfied)
5. Mostly dissatisfied
6. Unhappy
7. Terrible
8. Not applicable; no feelings on this aspect of life, etc.

a. My work or primary activity _____
b. My love relationship or marriage _____
c. Children and being a parent _____
d. Degree of recognition, success _____
e. My financial situation _____
f. My health _____
g. Personal growth and development _____
h. Exercise and physical recreation _____
i. Religion, spiritual life _____
j. My sex life _____
k. The way my spouse or lover's life is going _____
l. Friends and social life _____
m. My physical attractiveness _____
n. The degree to which I make a contribution to others _____
o. Balance of time between work, family, leisure, home responsibilities, etc. _____
p. My life as a whole _____

22. Which of the following have been true of you in the last year? (Circle as many as apply.)

1. Frequent headaches
2. Digestive problems
3. High blood pressure
4. Insomnia
5. Constant worry and anxiety
6. Tiring easily
7. Often feeling guilty
8. Feeling that I just can't cope
9. Crying spells
10. Often feeling lonely
11. Feeling fat, gaining weight
12. Lack of interest or pleasure in sex
13. Feelings of worthlessness
14. Often feeling irritable or angry
15. Feeling sad or depressed

23. In general, how has your health changed over the last five years?

1. It has gotten much better
2. It has gotten some-what better
3. It has stayed about the same

4. It has gotten somewhat worse
5. It has gotten much worse

24. On the happiness graph below is a list of age periods followed by a seven-point scale. For each period you've lived through, circle a number indicating how happy or unhappy (satisfied-dissatisfied, content-discontent) you were during that period. Then do the same for the periods you haven't yet lived through—circle a number indicating how happy (satisfied, content) you expect to be during each of those periods. Of course, no one knows for sure what the future will be like. Just make the best guess you can.

Age	Very Unhappy			Equally Happy & Unhappy			Very Happy
0–9	−3	−2	−1	0	+1	+2	+3
10–15	−3	−2	−1	0	+1	+2	+3
16–21	−3	−2	−1	0	+1	+2	+3
22–27	−3	−2	−1	0	+1	+2	+3
28–33	−3	−2	−1	0	+1	+2	+3
34–39	−3	−2	−1	0	+1	+2	+3
40–45	−3	−2	−1	0	+1	+2	+3
46–51	−3	−2	−1	0	+1	+2	+3
52–57	−3	−2	−1	0	+1	+2	+3

58–63	−3	−2	−1	0	+1	+2	+3
64–69	−3	−2	−1	0	+1	+2	+3
70 +	−3	−2	−1	0	+1	+2	+3

25. In general, how would you describe your life?

1. It's a very unusual life.

2. It's a fairly unusual life.

3. It's a fairly ordinary life.

4. It's a very ordinary life.

26. Using the numbers below (1 to 6), indicate in the answer column at right the most appropriate response to statements *a* to *z*.

1. Strongly agree
2. Moderately agree
3. Slightly agree
4. Slightly disagree
5. Moderately disagree
6. Strongly disagree

a. I am a genuinely dependable and responsible person. ___

b. I am "thin-skinned" and sensitive to criticism. ___

c. I engage in a wide range of activities outside of my job (e.g., artistic, physical, political, familial, etc.). ___

d. I am generous and considerate toward others. ___

e. I am uncomfortable with uncertainty and complexity. ___

f. I am introspective; I often examine my thoughts and feelings. ___

g. Humor is an important part of my personality. ___

h. I find it difficult to request or accept help or support from others. ___

i. I am an unusually energetic person. ___

j. I am highly controlled and find it difficult to "let go" or relax. ___

k. I am productive; I get things done. ___

l. I find it difficult to be assertive. ___

m. I can usually influence people to get them to do what I want. _____

n. Most people find it easy to like me. _____

o. I find it difficult to make important decisions. _____

p. I am often turned to for advice or reassurance. _____

q. I feel that my life has meaning and direction. _____

r. I often have creative or unusual ideas. _____

s. I try hard to live according to my ethical and moral standards. _____

t. I'm a survivor; I know how to look out for myself. _____

u. I am highly intelligent. _____

v. I have set a high level of aspiration for myself. _____

w. I often feel cheated or disappointed by life. _____

x. I am a cheerful person. _____

y. I am a person who plans carefully for the future. _____

z. I am flexible and resilient; I have successfully weathered some of life's harsh storms. _____

27. How much control do you have over the important events in your life?

1. Almost total control
2. Mostly under my control
3. About half the time I can control the important events
4. Mostly not under my control
5. Almost no control

28. Looking back over your adult life, how responsible do you feel for the way it has turned out?

1. Totally responsible   4. Slightly responsible
2. Very responsible   5. Not at all responsible
3. Somewhat responsible

29. Below is a list of 16 long-range values or goals which at least some people say are important. Please choose the three that are most important to you and place their numbers in the spaces provided below labeled "most important." Then go back and choose the three that are

least important to you and put their numbers in the blanks labeled "least important." Finally, circle the number of each value or goal that you feel you have already attained.

1. A comfortable life (prosperous life)
2. A sense of accomplishment (a lasting contribution)
3. Equality (social justice, equal opportunity for all)
4. Family security (taking care of loved ones)
5. Freedom (independence, free choice)
6. Inner harmony (freedom from inner conflicts)
7. Mature love (sexual and personal intimacy)
8. Power (the ability to influence events and make things happen)
9. Spiritual development (salvation)
10. Self-respect (self-esteem)
11. True friendship (close companionship)
12. Wisdom (a mature understanding of life)
13. Recognition (fame)
14. Personal growth (self-development)
15. An exciting life (a stimulating, active life)
16. A life full of sensual pleasure

Most Important to Me

a. _____
b. _____
c. _____

Least Important to Me

a. _____
b. _____
c. _____

30. Below is a list of 16 personal qualities or ways of behaving which people may value in varying degrees. Please

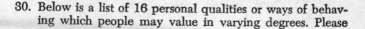

choose the three that are most important to you and write their numbers in the appropriate blanks below marked "most important." Then choose the three that are least important to you and write their numbers in the appropriate blanks ("least important"). Finally, circle the number of each quality or way of behaving that you feel already describes you.

1. Ambitious (hardworking, aspiring)
2. Capable (competent)
3. Courageous (standing up for your beliefs)
4. Forgiving (willing to pardon others)
5. Helpful (working for the welfare of others)
6. Honest (sincere, truthful)
7. Imaginative (daring, creative)
8. Independent (self-reliant, self-sufficient)
9. Knowledgeable (intelligent, reflective)
10. Loving (affectionate, tender)
11. Responsible (dependable, reliable)
12. Self-controlled (restrained, self-disciplined)
13. Open to new experiences
14. Able to lead effectively
15. Physically fit
16. Playful, humorous

Most Important to Me
a. _____
b. _____
c. _____

Least Important to Me
a. _____
b. _____
c. _____

31. On the average, how many hours each 24-hour work day do you spend in the following activities? (Indicate number of hours for each activity in the answer column at right. These time allotments do not necessarily have to add to 24.)

1. Work   ————
2. Work-related travel (commuting, business trips, etc.)
3. Housework   ————
4. Time with my children   ————
5. Time with my spouse or lover   ————
6. Time to myself (reading, thinking, walking, etc.)
7. Time volunteered to help others   ————
8. Sleeping   ————

32. If you could allocate your time ideally, how many hours would you spend in each of the activities listed below in an average 24-hour work day? (Again, indicate number of hours for each activity in the answer column at right. Remember that these allotments need not add to 24.)

1. Work   ————
2. Work-related travel (commuting, business trips, etc.)
3. Housework   ————
4. Time with my children   ————
5. Time with my spouse or lover   ————
6. Time to myself (reading, thinking, walking, etc.)
7. Time volunteered to help others   ————
8. Sleeping   ————

33. How many female friends and how many male friends do you have on whom you could rely in times of crisis or emergency? (Please do not include your spouse or lover. Write your answers in the blanks.)

—————— male friends   —————— female friends

34. If you had personal problems, were in trouble, or had to make a difficult decision, on whom could you rely for understanding and support? (Circle as many as apply.)

1. Spouse
2. Lover
3. My children
4. My mother
5. My father
6. One or more of my brothers and sisters
7. Other relatives
8. My close friends
9. Other: _____

35. Below is a chart that allows you to record whether you have had certain feelings or experiences and, if so, at what age(s). Below is also a list of 14 feelings or experiences that some people have reported. For each period you have lived through, place the numbers of the one or two most important feelings, changes, or experiences that occurred during that period. You may use each number as many times as you like. Then consider each of the periods you have yet to live through. For each future period, place the numbers of the one or two most important feelings, changes, or experiences that you think are likely to occur during each of those periods.

1. Felt a firm sense of my own identity
2. Felt secure enough to stop running or struggling, to relax and open myself to new feelings
3. Felt a new tolerance and companionship with my mate
4. Felt my life was pretty well set
5. Had a feeling of being refreshed and renewed
6. Stopped trying so hard to please others and began to validate myself
7. Became aware of monitoring my health
8. Found pleasure in helping others and/or giving to worthwhile causes
9. Found a new sense of purpose
10. Spiritual matters became more important to me
11. Felt comfortably independent of my parent(s)
12. Found myself loving someone in a much more mature way
13. Experienced a new level of sexual pleasure and satisfaction
14. Felt I finally "had it all together"

Age Periods

Experience Numbers	18–28	29–35	36–45	46–55	56–65	66 +
	□ □	□ □	□ □	□ □	□ □	□ □

36. Below is another chart, similar to the one you have just completed. Complete this one in the same manner. For each age period you have lived through, place the number(s) of the <u>one</u> or <u>two</u> <u>most</u> important feelings, changes, or experiences in the appropriate boxes. (This time the list includes 15 items.) You may use each number as many times as you like. Then consider each of the periods you have <u>yet</u> to <u>live</u> <u>through</u>. For each future period, place the number(s) of the <u>one</u> or <u>two</u> most important feelings, changes, or experiences that you think are <u>likely</u> to occur during each of those periods.

1. Felt that time was running out
2. Felt this was my last chance to "pull away from the pack"
3. Felt confused or conflicted about choice of career or career direction
4. Seriously questioned my parents' beliefs and values
5. Felt stagnant in my work
6. Felt stagnant in my home life
7. Felt truly middle-aged
8. Felt I had probably reached my peak earning years
9. Asked myself, "Is anything worthwhile? Does anything matter?"
10. Felt "no longer young"
11. Suddenly noticed my friends were looking old
12. Had serious marital difficulties
13. Felt confused or conflicted about proper sexual standards for myself
14. Began to think seriously about my own mortality
15. Became seriously depressed or discontent

Age Periods

Experience Numbers	18–28	29–35	36–45	46–55	56–65	66 +
	□ □	□ □	□ □	□ □	□ □	□ □

37. If you have undergone one or more important transitions (major changes in your outlook, values, or career) during your adult years, was it:

1. Similar to transitions experienced by others and handled in similar ways?
2. Similar to transitions experienced by others but handled in an unusual, personal, or creative way?
3. An unusual transition, one that called for an innovative solution?
4. Not applicable

38. At this stage in your life, what are your major fears? (Circle as many as apply.)

1. Others will find out I'm not as good as they think
2. I will find out I'm not as good as I thought I was
3. Lack of recognition
4. Not advancing fast enough
5. Time running out
6. No longer being physically attractive
7. Loneliness
8. Messing up my personal life
9. Being "locked in," unable to freely change my way of life
10. Being surpassed by younger people in my field
11. Not having enough money
12. Being abandoned by spouse or lover
13. Declining physical capabilities, illness
14. I have no major fear
15. Other: _____

39. Do you feel a sense of obligation to live near your parent(s)?

1. Yes, I do live near them.
2. Yes, but I don't live near them.
3. No, but I may in the future.
4. No.
5. My parents are both dead.

40. At this point in your life, how emotionally dependent are you on your parent(s) or on parental approval?

    1. Not at all dependent
    2. Slightly dependent
    3. Moderately dependent
    4. Very dependent

41. How easy is it for you to reveal your intimate thoughts and feelings to your friends and relatives?

    1. Very easy
    2. Fairly easy
    3. Fairly difficult
    4. Very difficult
    5. Not applicable

42. Are you currently in love?

    1. Yes, for the first time.
    2. Yes, but not for the first time.
    3. No, but I have been.
    4. I have never been in love.

43. In many relationships, one person loves more than the other. Who now loves more in your love relationship?

    1. My love is not returned.
    2. I love more than my partner.
    3. We love equally.
    4. My partner loves more.
    5. I don't return my partner's love.
    6. Not applicable.

44. Please indicate by circling the appropriate letters which (if any) persons close to you have died. Give your age when each of these people died. (If more than one person in a category has died, list your age for each one.)

Your Age

    a. Mother   _____

    b. Father   _____

    c. Brother or sister   _____

    d. Spouse or lover   _____

    e. Close friend   _____

45. Which of the following best describes your feelings about death?

    1. I am afraid of death.

    2. It troubles me, but I wouldn't say I fear it.

    3. I haven't given it much thought.

    4. I've decided not to think or worry about it.

    5. I'm working toward accepting it.

    6. I've thought about it a great deal and come to accept it.

    7. I am looking forward to it.

    8. Other: _____

46. Are you devoted to some purpose or cause outside yourself and larger than yourself?

    1. No

    2. Yes (specify): _____

47. If you are not devoted to a cause or purpose outside yourself, what is the reason?

    1. I haven't found a cause that engages me.

    2. I am too busy at this point in my life.

    3. I have been frustrated or disappointed by causes to which I was once devoted.

    4. I have no interest in causes.

    5. Not applicable; I am devoted to a cause.

    6. Other: _____

48. Is there one person, about five or ten years older than you, who serves as a model for you of the way you would like to be at that age?

1. No
2. No, but there are a few people of that age whose combined good qualities serve as my model
3. Yes

49. Did you have (or do you have) a mentor—an older, non-parental person who has helped to guide, encourage, and inspire you over a period of years (after age 18)?

    1. No
    2. Yes
    3. Yes, more than one

50. Besides coping and direct problem solving, how do you typically react to rough spots, serious problems, or periods of great uncertainty in your life? (Circle as many as apply.)

    1. Devote more time and energy to work
    2. Devote more time and energy to recreation
    3. Develop physical symptoms (headaches, ulcers, diarrhea, insomnia, etc.)
    4. Do more drinking, eating, taking drugs, etc.
    5. Seek new romantic and/or sexual involvements
    6. Pretend publicly that the problem doesn't exist
    7. Depend on friends and associates for help
    8. See a counselor or therapist
    9. Mostly wait until the problem solves itself
    10. Try to see the humorous side of the situation
    11. Escape into fantasy
    12. Pray, seek help from God
    13. Other: _____

51. When you were growing up, was your family:

    1. Lower-class?   4. Upper-middle-class?
    2. Lower-middle class?   5. Upper-class?
    3. Middle-class?

52. What is the highest level of education you have completed?

1. Grade school or less
2. Some high school
3. Graduated from high school
4. Some college
5. Graduated from college
6. Some graduate or professional school
7. Received a graduate or professional degree

53. If you returned to school during adulthood, after a gap of some years, what was the <u>main</u> reason?

1. Intrinsic pleasure in learning
2. To complete degree requirements
3. To relieve boredom
4. To meet new people
5. To explore new options, to decide where to go from here
6. To gain access to the professional middle class
7. To train for a specific profession I had decided, in advance, to pursue
8. To learn a trade
9. Not applicable
10. Other: _____

54. How old were you when you first had sexual intercourse? _____ years old

55. At what age did you, or do you think you will, reach your highest level of sexual satisfaction? _____ years old

56. What size city do you live in?

1. Metropolis (with a population of at least a million)
2. Large city (with a population of at least 500,000)
3. Medium-sized city (with a population of at least 100,000)
4. Small city (with a population of at least 25,000)
5. Suburb
6. Small town (with a population of at least 10,000)
7. Rural area (with a population less than 10,000)

57. What state do you live in? (If not in the United States, what country?)_____

58. What is your race? _____

59. What is your religion?

    1. Catholic
    2. Protestant
    3. Jewish
    4. Agnostic/Atheist
    5. Other: _____

60. Would you describe yourself as:

    1. Very religious?
    2. Moderately religious?
    3. Slightly religious?
    4. Not at all religious?
    5. Antireligious?

61. Which of the following statements describes you best?
    1. I have never been very religious.
    2. I was religious at an earlier point in my life but am not religious now.
    3. I was not very religious earlier in my life but am religious now.
    4. I have always been fairly religious.

62. What is your annual income?

    1. Less than $5,000
    2. $5,000 to $9,999
    3. $10,000 to $14,999
    4. $15,000 to $19,999
    5. $20,000 to $24,999
    6. $25,000 to $29,999
    7. $30,000 to $39,999
    8. $40,000 to $49,999
    9. $50,000 to $99,999
    10. $100,000 or above

63. What is the total annual income of your family?

    1. Less than $5,000
    2. $5,000 to $9,999
    3. $10,000 to $14,999
    4. $15,000 to $19,999
    5. $20,000 to $24,999
    6. $25,000 to $29,999
    7. $30,000 to $39,999
    8. $40,000 to $49,999
    9. $50,000 to $99,999
    10. $100,000 or above

64. Which of the following best describes your occupation?

    1. Artist, writer, craftsperson
    2. Farming, agriculture
    3. Homemaker
    4. Managerial, administrative

5. Professional with advanced degree (e.g., doctor, lawyer)
6. Semiskilled or unskilled worker
7. Student
8. Teacher, counselor, nurse, social worker
9. Technician, skilled worker
10. White-collar (secretarial, sales, clerical)
11. Retired
12. Other: _____

65. If you are self-employed, how would you classify the work that you do?

1. Own a private business with fewer than 25 employees
2. Own a private business with 25 to 100 employees
3. Own a private business with over 100 employees
4. Free-lance
5. Consultant
6. Contract work
7. Not applicable
8. Other: _____

66. If you work for a company, organization, or institution, about how many people does it employ? (Include all offices or branches and all types of workers.)

1. Fewer than 50
2. 50 to 99
3. 100 to 499
4. 500 to 999
5. 1,000 to 1,999
6. 2,000 to 4,999
7. 5,000 to 10,000
8. Over 10,000
9. Not applicable

67. If you hold a managerial position in a company, organization, or institution, how would you characterize the level of this position?

1. President or chairman of the board
2. Vice-president or equivalent
3. Upper middle management, division manager
4. Lower middle management, department manager
5. Lower management, first and second level
6. Not applicable

68. When we are getting to know
    another person both of us
    usually reveal, bit by bit, the
    characteristics that define us—
    for example, "I am married,
    a former state champion
    diver, an ambitious young
    executive, a very controlled
    person, a person who loves
    camping, not a very good
    father." Another example:
    "I am an accountant, mother
    of two children, a widow, a
    person who likes privacy,   a. _____
    confused about proper sexual   b. _____
    standards." At right are ten lines c. _____
    on which you may describe   d. _____
    yourself in your own words.   e. _____
    Write a different self-descrip-   f. _____
    tive phrase on each line.   g. _____
    Answer the question "Who   h. _____
    am I?" as accurately as you   i. _____
    can with ten phrases.   j. _____

69. At right are ten more
    lines on which you may de-   a. _____
    scribe yourself as you would   b. _____
    like to be ten years from   c. _____
    now. This should be a real-   d. _____
    istic picture, not a wild fan-   e. _____
    tasy. Consider what you will   f. _____
    be like in ten years—how you   g. _____
    will describe yourself then—   h. _____
    if everything goes well for you   i. _____
    between now and then.   j. _____

70. If you would like to do so, please write a brief descrip-
    tion of the most recent major change or transition in
    your life. Include your age at the time, a description of
    the change, the cause of the transition, and how you felt
    during and after the transition period.

Appendix II
The Well-being Scale

If you would like to know approximately where you stand in the sense of overall well-being, compared with the 60,000 people surveyed for this book, go back and complete the Life History Questionnaire that appears on the preceding pages. You can score yourself by noting your answers to questions 11, 13, 14, 19, 21a to 21p, 25, 27, 28, and 42, which are reproduced below. There are twenty-four questions in all.

Now look back at your answer for each question. Check to see whether your answer falls above or below the arrow shown here. If your answer is above the arrow, you fall above average for that item on the well-being scale. If your answer is below the arrow, you fall below the average.

Follow this procedure with each of the questions. Then count how many of your twenty-four answers were above average.

If you scored above average on eleven or twelve of the questions, you probably are of medium well-being. If you answered more than seventeen of the questions in the above-average range, you are likely to be enjoying especially high well-being.

11. How often do you feel bored?
    1. Almost never
    2. Rarely

Average →

3. Occasionally
4. Fairly often
5. Most of the time
6. Almost all the time

13. How often do you enjoy the work that you do?
    1. Almost all the time

Average →

2. Most of the time
3. Fairly often
4. Occasionally
5. Rarely
6. Almost never

14. Do you feel that your major work activity makes a contribution to society?
    1. Definitely yes

Average →

2. Most of the time
3. Some of the time
4. Almost none of the time
5. Definitely no
6. Not applicable

19. Looking back at the goals, aspirations, or "dreams" you had as you entered adulthood, how do you feel at this point in your life?
    1. I am just beginning to shape my dream.
    2. I am on my way to achieving my dream.
    3. I have achieved my original dream and have generated a new one.
    4. I have achieved a great deal but it's quite different from my original dream.

Average →

5. I have never had a clear dream or aspiration.
6. I am not sure whether I am on my way to achieving my dream.
7. I will probably never achieve my original dream.
8. I have achieved my original dream and haven't generated a new one.

21. How have you been feeling about:
a. My work or primary activity
     1. Delighted
     2. Pleased
Average →
     3. Mostly satisfied
     4. Mixed (about equally satisfied and dissatisfied)
     5. Mostly dissatisfied
     6. Unhappy
     7. Terrible
     8. Not applicable

21b. My love relationship or marriage
     1. Delighted
     2. Pleased
Average →
     3. Mostly satisfied
     4. Mixed (about equally satisfied and dissatisfied)
     5. Mostly dissatisfied
     6. Unhappy
     7. Terrible
     8. Not applicable

21c. Children and being a parent
     1. Delighted
     2. Pleased
Average →
     3. Mostly satisfied
     4. Mixed (about equally satisfied and dissatisfied)
     5. Mostly dissatisfied
     6. Unhappy
     7. Terrible
     8. Not applicable

21d. Degree of recognition, success
     1. Delighted
     2. Pleased
Average →
     3. Mostly satisfied
     4. Mixed (about equally satisfied and dissatisfied)
     5. Mostly dissatisfied

6. Unhappy
7. Terrible
8. Not applicable

21e. My financial situation
1. Delighted
2. Pleased
3. Mostly satisfied

Average →

4. Mixed (about equally satisfied and dissatisfied)
5. Mostly dissatisfied
6. Unhappy
7. Terrible
8. Not applicable

21f. My health
1. Delighted
2. Pleased

Average →

3. Mostly satisfied
4. Mixed (about equally satisfied and dissatisfied)
5. Mostly dissatisfied
6. Unhappy
7. Terrible
8. Not applicable

21g. Personal growth and development
1. Delighted
2. Pleased

Average →

3. Mostly satisfied
4. Mixed (about equally satisfied and dissatisfied)
5. Mostly dissatisfied
6. Unhappy
7. Terrible
8. Not applicable

21h. Exercise and physical recreation
1. Delighted
2. Pleased
3. Mostly satisfied

Average →
    4. Mixed (about equally satisfied or dissatisfied)
    5. Mostly dissatisfied
    6. Unhappy
    7. Terrible
    8. Not applicable

21i. Religion, spiritual life
    1. Delighted
    2. Pleased
    3. Mostly satisfied
Average →
    4. Mixed (about equally satisfied and dissatisfied)
    5. Mostly dissatisfied
    6. Unhappy
    7. Terrible
    8. Not applicable

21j. My sex life
    1. Delighted
    2. Pleased
    3. Mostly satisfied
Average →
    4. Mixed (about equally satisfied and dissatisfied)
    5. Mostly dissatisfied
    6. Unhappy
    7. Terrible
    8. Not applicable

21k. The way my spouse or lover's life is going
    1. Delighted
    2. Pleased
Average →
    3. Mostly satisfied
    4. Mixed (about equally satisfied and dissatisfied)
    5. Mostly dissatisfied
    6. Unhappy
    7. Terrible
    8. Not applicable

21l. Friends and social life
    1. Delighted

2. Pleased

Average →

3. Mostly satisfied
4. Mixed (about equally satisfied and dissatisfied)
5. Mostly dissatisfied
6. Unhappy
7. Terrible
8. Not applicable

21m. My physical attractiveness
1. Delighted
2. Pleased
3. Mostly satisfied

Average →

4. Mixed (about equally satisfied and dissatisfied)
5. Mostly dissatisfied
6. Unhappy
7. Terrible
8. Not applicable

21n. The degree to which I make a contribution to others
1. Delighted
2. Pleased

Average →

3. Mostly satisfied
4. Mixed (about equally satisfied and dissatisfied)
5. Mostly dissatisfied
6. Unhappy
7. Terrible
8. Not applicable

21o. Balance of time between work, family, leisure, home responsibilities, etc.
1. Delighted
2. Pleased
3. Mostly satisfied

Average →

4. Mixed (about equally satisfied and dissatisfied)
5. Mostly dissatisfied
6. Unhappy

7. Terrible
8. Not applicable

21p. My life as a whole
1. Delighted
2. Pleased
Average →
3. Mostly satisfied
4. Mixed (about equally satisfied and dissatisfied)
5. Mostly dissatisfied
6. Unhappy
7. Terrible
8. Not applicable

25. In general, how would you describe your life?
1. It's a very unusual life.
2. It's a fairly unusual life.
Average →
3. It's a fairly ordinary life.
4. It's a very ordinary life.

27. How much control do you have over the important events in your life?
1. Almost total control
2. Mostly under my control
Average →
3. About half the time I can control the important events
4. Mostly not under my control
5. Almost no control

28. Looking back over your adult life, how responsible do you feel for the way it has turned out?
1. Totally responsible
2. Very responsible
Average →
3. Somewhat responsible
4. Slightly responsible
5. Not at all responsible

42. Are you currently in love?
1. Yes, for the first time.

2. Yes, but not for the first time.

Average →

3. No, but I have been.
4. I have never been in love.

Appendix III

Statistical Analysis of Life Line Chart

($X^2 = 33.93$, $p < 0.001$)
The following table shows the frequencies for highest lines on the 99 completed charts:

	Affiliation	Achievement	Life Satisfaction
Highest Line	18	65	16

($X^2 = 11.79$, $p < 0.01$)
The following table shows the frequencies for line closest to the life satisfaction line on 101 completed charts:

	Affiliation	Achievement
Line closest to life satisfaction	68	33

Appendix IV

People Who Suggested Pathfinder Candidates

PIVOTAL AMERICANS FROM UNIVERSITIES, SCHOOLS, AND LIBRARIES

Emily Stier Adler, Rhode Island College

Richard F. Andrus, Brookdale Community College, Lincroft, N.J.

Carol Bardon, University of Houston, Clear Lake City, Texas

Elizabeth R. Beall, Georgetown University

Stephanie M. Bennett, Westhampton College, Richmond, Va.

Ruth Berger, Lehman College, Bronx, N.Y.

Judith Bernstein, White Plains Public Library, N.Y.

Frank L. Borelli, William Rainey Harper College, Palatine, Ill.

Keith L. Broman, Mira Costa College, Oceanside, Calif.

Anne Burns, Southampton College, N.Y.

Martha Caldwell, The University of Vermont

A. Brian Calhoun, Gateway Technical Institute, Racine, Wis.

Paul Chaffee, University of Southern California, Los Angeles

Sharon Childs, University of Kentucky

Carol Colligan, Webster College, St. Louis, Mo.

Faith B. Collins, University of Victoria, Canada

Sandra L. Cook, University of Texas at San Antonio

George S. Craft, California State University, Sacramento

Mary Dalton, Archdiocese of Chicago Schools

Fran Danowski, University of Rhode Island

Kay H. DeMooy, University of California, Santa Cruz

Susan Dolin, Cleveland State University

Enid Edwards, Fanshawe College, London, Canada
Janet Epp, College of Marin, Kentfield, Calif.
Charlotte Epstein, Union College, Cranford, N.J.
Richard H. Erickson, University of Missouri
Richard B. Fischer, University of Delaware
Rosalie Flynn, College of Mount Saint Vincent, Riverdale, N.Y.
Virginia D. Franklin, University of Alabama in Birmingham
John Geisler, Western Michigan University
Carole Getzoff, WPLJ Radio, New York, N.Y.
Sherry B. Gill, Johns Hopkins University
Ronald H. Gorsegner, Eau Claire Public Library
Kathryn F. Green, Oberlin College, Ohio
Emily S. Harkins, Norfolk Forum, Va.
Doe Hentschel, University of Illinois, Chicago
Mary Lou Hess, The Plaza Frontenac, St. Louis, Mo.
John C. Hoy, University of California, Irvine
Nancy Jo Hoy, Saddleback Community College, Mission Viejo, Calif.
Satoru Izutsu, University of Hawaii at Manoa
Judy Johnson, Mamaroneck High School, N.Y.
Jack A. Jordon, University of Wisconsin, La Crosse
Barbara Kallir, Edgemont High School, Scarsdale, N.Y.
Lynne Kaufman, University of California, San Francisco
Patricia Kenny, Peoria Forum, Ill.
Louis L. Klitzke, University of Wisconsin-Stout, Menomonie
Ellie Kurtz, University of Dayton
Sharon Mayer Libera, Mount Holyoke College, South Hadley, Mass.
Jeannette F. Lieberman, South Orange-Maplewood Adult School, N.J.
Frances Litman, Wheelock College, Boston, Mass.
Barbara Lovenheim, Barnard/Columbia Alumni, New York, N.Y.
Janine MacLean, St. Andrew Church, Portland, Oreg.
B. Mags, Long Beach City College, Calif.
Evelyn Mandel, Institute for Creative Aging, Malibu, Calif.
Sue Mathews, Eastern Montana College, Billings
Carol L. McCulloch, Villa Julie College, Stevenson, Md.
Eva B. Messro, Marycrest College, Davenport, Iowa
Harold A. Miller, University of Minnesota
Wilma Miller, Michigan State University

Ann Molison, Iowa State University

Joan Quigley Monnig, Villanova University, Pa.

Susan Morgan, Georgia State University, Atlanta

Gail S. Nagel, Greenville Technical College, S.C.

Janet L. Niles, Atlanta, Ga.

Henry Obermeyer, The Hartford Graduate Center, Conn.

Nancy O'Connor, University of Arizona

Ray Olitt, University of California, Riverside

Sigrid Olson, University of Missouri, Kansas City

R. Oostingh, Sweet Briar College, Va.

Mon O'Shea, Bunker Hill Community College, Charleston, Mass.

Frieda Porat, West Valley Community College, Saratoga, Calif.

Agnes A. Reinders, Marquette University, Milwaukee, Wis.

Alice Rhynhart, Northern Kentucky University, Highland Heights

Dorothy Rupert, Fairview High School, Boulder, Colo.

Dolores Sapienza, Delaware Technical and Community College, Dover

Hazel Sprandel, Washington University, St. Louis, Mo.

Jo Ann Stolley, Tredyffrin Public Library, Strafford-Wayne, Pa.

Edward N. Strait, Macalester College, Saint Paul, Minn.

Arlene M. Straughn, Huntington Public Library, N.Y.

Edward M. Szynaka, Grace A. Dow Memorial Library, Midland, Mich.

Ginnie Thorp, Edgemont High School, Scarsdale, N.Y.

Kit Tucker, Westhampton College, Richmond, Va.

Janice Wood Wetzel, University of Texas at Austin

PIVOTAL AMERICANS FROM WOMEN'S GROUPS

Maryann Abrahams, Greensboro Hadassah, N.C.

Elaine Adler, Brandeis University National Women's Committee

Marie R. Badaracco, New Jersey Medical Women's Association, Union

Peg Bandy, Cultural Resources Council, Onondaga County Civic Center, Syracuse, N.Y.

Doris Basmajian, North Hollywood, Calif.

Bob Blaich, Women's Resource Center, Zeeland, Mich.

Patricia Brennan, Ohio Child Conservation League

Judith Bryan, Women's Day/Illinois Alumni Association, Champaign

Wynne Delmhorst, Junior League of Greenwich, Conn.

K. Ann Dempsey, Committee for the Humanities Resource Center, St. Louis

Margaret H. Denton, Women's Center, Brookings, S.Dak.

Ginny Ford, Birmingham, Mich.

Patricia Gentry, Junior League of Colorado Springs

Naomi Globerman, Y. M. H. A., Winnipeg, Canada

Joan Grady, Newcomers Club, Darien, Conn.

Judy Gwartz, United Jewish Appeal, Toronto, Canada

Hannelore Hahn, International Women's Writing Guild, New York, N.Y.

Mrs. William Hallenbeck, Albert Einstein College of Medicine, New York, N.Y.

Candy Heinrich, Worlds for Women, Denver, Colo.

Sandra Holdsworth, Committee on Women's Issues, Cumberland Center, Maine

Betty S. Hornstein, National Council of Jewish Women, Baltimore, Md.

Carolyn H. Jones, Junior League of Norfolk-Virginia Beach, Va.

Beth Kaplan, Sisterhood of Wilshire Boulevard Temple, Los Angeles

Dorothy Kates, Women's City Club, Cleveland, Ohio

JoAnn Kelly, Bambergers, Whitehall, Pa.

Kate Kelsall, Calgary Status of Women Action Committee, Alta.

Judith Kinney, Junior League of Canton, Ohio

B. Kurtzman, Community Woman's Center, Birmingham, Mich.

Claire Laufman, Hadassah, East Northport, N.Y.

Barbara Leslie, National Council of Jewish Women, Woodmere, N.Y.

Nancy Mahaney, Temple Beth Zion Sisterhood, Clarence, N.Y.

Joyce Margulis, Jewish Hospital Auxiliary, St. Louis, Mo.

Mrs. James I. Marsh, Jr., Junior League of Greater Utica, N.Y.

Catherine B. Martin, Junior League of Charleston, W.Va.

Janice McElroy, Florida Association for Health and Social Services, Tallahassee

Laura Meadows, Harvard Law Women, Mass.

Patricia S. Meyers, Women's National Democratic Club, Washington, D.C.

Phryne Osborne, Junior League of Palo Alto, Calif.

Nancy Popkin, New England Dairy and Food Council, Boston, Mass.

Marcia J. Posner, Manhasset Hills, N.Y.

Marian Reich, Women's Institute for Self Enrichment, Cherry Hill, N.J.

Dorothy M. Reynolds, Columbus Metropolitan Club, Ohio

Eleanor Schelling, San Francisco, Calif.

Paula Sharf, Temple Emanuel of Great Neck, N.Y.

Mary Sherman, American Association of University Women, Purcell, Okla.

Marilyn Siriebrick, National Council of Jewish Women, Teaneck, N.J.

Sandra Thompson, Federation of Women Teachers' Association, Toronto, Canada

Mrs. Milton Tolmach, Great Neck, N.Y.

Elizabeth Wells, AAHE Women's Caucus, Washington, D.C.

Mrs. John S. Wheeler, Sherborn, Mass.

Claudine Wilder, Belmont, Mass.

Patricia Bogin Wisch, Institute of Awareness, Philadelphia, Pa.

Constance D. Wry, Pima County Medical Society Auxiliary, Tucson, Ariz.

PIVOTAL AMERICANS FROM CORPORATE GROUPS

Atherton Flager, San Francisco, Calif.

Gilbert E. Johnson, Young Presidents' Organization, Colorado Springs, Colo.

Marty Kleindienst, American Telephone & Telegraph, N.J.

Arthur McDermott, Advanced Management Research, New York, N.Y.

E. L. McNeely, The Wickes Corporation, San Diego, Calif.

Nancy Nelson, Matterhorn Sports Club, New York, N.Y.

Wilma Nelson, Center for the Family, Washington, D.C.

Anne Perzeszty, New York State Home Economics Association, Valley Stream, N.Y.

Nancy Mitchell Petersen, National Solid Wastes Management Association, Washington, D.C.

Thomas L. Reese, Universal Tank & Iron Works, Indianapolis, Ind.

Eriberto Scocimara, Young Presidents' Organization, New York, N.Y.

Eleanor Shelling, Resource Center for Women, Palo Alto, Calif.

Jerry Sloane, The Ford Motor Co., Detroit, Mich.

Fran Russell Sprouse, Sprouse Reitz Stores, Portland, Oreg.

Mort Weisinger, American Society of Journalists and Authors, Inc., New York, N.Y.

PIVOTAL AMERICANS FROM RELIGIOUS AND ARTS GROUPS

Barbara Bakst, The Unitarian Church of Montclair, N.J.

Lynn Bokman, YWCA of Minneapolis, Minn.

Judith Jolie Branson, Commission on the Ministry, Episcopal Diocese, Farmington, Conn.

Harriet Epstein, *Long Island Magazine*, N.Y.

Larry K. Hayes, Church of the Servant, Oklahoma City, Okla.

Al Herzog, Hartford Unitarian Church, Conn.

Edith Hull, The Universalist Church of New York City, N.Y.

Marjorie Jenkins, Interface, Houston, Tex.

Arnold Kupetz, Temple Judea, Hidden Hills, Calif.

Sandra Kutik, Womantime & Co., KQED, San Francisco, Calif.

Vilma Lennox, First Unitarian Church of Pittsburgh, Pa.

Glennis Lundberg, First Congregational Church, Evanston, Ill.

Eugenia S. Marks, The Mediator Fellowship, Providence, R.I.

Armistead Maupin, San Francisco, Calif.

Leah Nepom, Jewish Community Center, Portland, Oreg.

Mark Rubin, YM-YWHA of Metropolitan New Jersey, East Orange

Judith Stairman, Temple Israel, Swampscott, Mass.

Harriet Weintraub, The Poetry Center, YM-YWHA, New York, N.Y.

PIVOTAL AMERICANS FROM HEALTH CARE GROUPS

Kenneth L. Barun, Cenikor Foundation, Houston, Tex.

Joey Benson, Carroll County Council of Social Agencies, Westminster, Md.

Donald A. Bloch, Ackerman Institute for Family Therapy, New York, N.Y.

W. D. Brymer, North Vancouver Dental Group, B.C.

Bernard J. Carey, Jr., Massachusetts Association for Mental Health, Boston

Ted Chapman, George Washington University Medical Center, Washington, D.C.

Joan Deeter, Mental Health Association in Wabash County, North Manchester, Ind.

William M. Dirrig, Portage Path Community Mental Health Center, Akron, Ohio

Theresa Eldridge, University of Colorado Medical Center, Denver

Barbara Feig, The Institute for Psychoanalysis, Chicago, Ill.

Faye First, Jewish Centers of Greater Philadelphia, Pa.

Suzanne B. Fornaro, Mobile Mental Health Center, Ala.

Keith Froehlich, VA Hospital, Brentwood, Calif.

Kathleen Gamblin, Community Mental Health Seminar, Colorado Springs, Colo.

Ruth Gollubier, University of Arizona, Tucson

Marty Grasley, Larc, Inc., Bethlehem, Pa.

Myra M. Hart, Northwood Institute, Midland, Mich.

James T. Harvey, Colorado Juvenile Council, Lakewood

Lucie Jamison, Kangaroo, San Francisco, Calif.

David B. Kaminsky, Pan-American Association of Diagnostic Cytology, Rockville, Md.

Steve Kearney, Winnebago Mental Health Institute, Wis.

Ward Kromer, Massachusetts General Hospital, Boston

Marian C. Leavitt, Family Service, Norfolk, Va.

Miriam Lubow, Wainwright House, Rye, N.Y.

Margaret E. Marshall, Conciliation Court, Phoenix, Ariz.

Jo Ann B. McCraw, IWY Taskforce, Portland, Oreg.

Ellen McGrath, Convalescent Hospital for Children, Rochester, N.Y.

Edwin R. Miles, Jr., Children and Family Service Association, Wheeling, W.Va.

Gertha Moyd, Greenville County Mental Health Association, S.C.

Helen E. Nash, St. Louis Children's Hospital, Mo.

Bedford Pace, Bell and Stanton, Inc., New York, N.Y.

James W. Parker, Parker Chiropractic Research Foundation, Fort Worth, Tex.

Peg Patrick, Bethesda Hospital & Community Mental Health Center, Denver, Colo.

Barbara L. Pearson, Association for Clinical and Research Studies, Ypsilanti, Mich.

Clarence E. Pearson, International Health Resource Consortium, Washington, D.C.

Martha Scott Perkins, Stow, Mass.

Peg Raines, Columbus Area Community Mental Health Center, Ohio

Robert J. Resnik, Virginia Academy Clinical Psychologists, Richmond

L. D. Richman, Adolph Richman Family Foundation, Chicago, Ill.

JoAnne Ritter, Cleveland Clinic Foundation, Ohio

Ruth Rootberg, Mental Health Association of Evanston, Ill.

Eleanor Rosenblum, Massachusetts Psychological Association, Boston

Malwina Rottenberg, New Jersey Association for Mental Health, Montclair

Si Shaltz, CF Foundation, Philadelphia, Pa.

Larry Slayen, Kangaroo, San Francisco, Calif.

Jackie Soliz, Colorado Rehabilitation Counseling Association, Denver

Sandra Sroka, Mental Health Association of Hillsborough County, Tampa, Fla.

Morton R. Startz, Jewish Family Service, Cincinnati, Ohio

Davis A. Suskind, San Diego Psychiatric Society, Calif.

Jayne Talmage, Media Collaborative, Boston, Mass.

Linda V. Urda, Mental Health Association of Johnson County, Overland Park, Kans.

Anna J. Ward, Southern California Medical Record Association, Los Angeles

Nancy Whitacre, Ohio League for Nursing, Columbus
Linda Williams, Human Growth & Training Associates, Wilmington, N.C.
Rebecca B. Wilson, W Workshops, Montgomery, Ala.

Notes and Sources

Chapter 1:
HUNTING THE SECRETS OF WELL-BEING

1. Gail Sheehy, *Passages: Predictable Crises of Adult Life* (New York: Dutton, 1976). In this, as in other notes, because sources were reviewed as a whole, individual page numbers are not indicated.

2. Among those longitudinal studies are the Human Development Program, University of California, San Francisco; the Grant Study of Adult Development at Harvard University; the Oakland Growth Study; and the Kansas City Studies of Adult Life, described in notes that follow.

In 1928 two longitudinal studies were begun at the Institute of Human Development, University of California at Berkeley: (1) the Guidance Study of personality development and (2) the Berkeley Growth Study of physical, mental, and motor development, and parent-infant relationships. Two follow-up studies were conducted, the first in 1958, when the "children" were 30, the second in the late 1960s. In the latter study, the surviving parents were also studied. Because of the difficulty in locating parents from the Guidance roster, they were drawn from the Berkeley Growth Study, where the emphasis had been on physical rather than personality development, and longitudinal comparisons were difficult. About fifty of the original seventy-five infants, now in their fifties, continue to be assessed. Numerous satellite studies on adult development have evolved from this early effort. Among the early researchers was Erik Erikson; later investigators at Berkeley included Norma Haan, Jack Block, Henry Maas, Bernice L. Neugarten, and Marjorie Lowenthal.

3. Sigmund Freud, "Civilization and Its Discontents" (1929), in *The Major Works of Sigmund Freud*, trans. Joan Riviere (Chicago: Encyclopaedia Britannica, 1952).

4. Gail Sheehy, "What Makes You Happy?" *Esquire*, July 4, 1978; "The Truth About Today's Young Men," *Esquire*, October

1979; "What Will Make You Happy?" *Redbook*, July 1978; "Happiness Report, Part One, Part Two," *Redbook*, July–August 1979.

5. Phillip Shaver and Jonathan L. Freedman, "Your Pursuit of Happiness," *Psychology Today*, August 1976. This article reported results from 52,000 questionnaires about happiness completed by *Psychology Today* readers. The survey, and a similar one in *Good Housekeeping*, became the basis for Freedman's book *Happy People: What Happiness Is, Who Has It, and Why* (New York: Harcourt Brace Jovanovich, 1978).

6. Ibid.

Angus Campbell, *The Sense of Well-being in America: Recent Patterns and Trends* (New York: McGraw-Hill, 1980). Campbell's book reports statistical studies conducted by the Institute for Social Research at the University of Michigan between 1957 and 1978, in which 2,164 women and men were surveyed. The study was based on a probability sample of all persons 18 years and older living in private households in the forty-eight continental states and measured satisfaction with fifteen aspects of life.

Marjorie Fiske Lowenthal, Majda Thurnher, David Chiriboga, and associates, *Four Stages of Life: A Comparative Study of Women and Men Facing Transitions* (San Francisco: Jossey-Bass, 1976). In this study by the Human Development Program, University of California, San Francisco, 216 adults were interviewed at four life stages: as high school seniors (before they set out in the work world), as newlyweds (before their first children), as middle-aged parents (as their "nest" emptied), and as an older group (about to retire). Emphasis was on middle and lower-middle classes, roughly half blue-collar and half white-collar (policemen, firemen, nurses, teachers, small businessmen, and minor executives). No reports have been published yet on the longitudinal phase of the study, begun in 1975, which follows the subjects through and after their passages. Young parents, therefore, have not yet been reported on, and there will be no attempt to compare professionals with blue-collar people.

7. Richard Polenberg, "A U.S. Unhomogenized," *New York Times*, March 12, 1980.

8. Campbell, *Sense of Well-being;* Lowenthal et al., *Four Stages*.

9. Susan L. Farber, *Identical Twins Reared Apart: A Reanalysis* (New York: Basic Books, 1981).

10. A team at the University of Minnesota, under Gloria Leon, compared the scores on the Minnesota Multiphasic Personality Inventory (MMPI) of seventy-one men tested when they were 50, in 1947, and when they were 80, in 1977. The highest correlation over this thirty-year span was in "Social Introversion."

Paul T. Costa, Jr., and Robert R. McCrae, "Still Stable After All These Years: Personality as a Key to Some Issues in Adulthood and Old Age," in *Life-span Development and Behavior*, vol. 3, ed. P. B. Baltes and O. G. Grim (New York: Academic Press, 1980). See also, "Influence of Extraversion and Neuroticism on Subjective Well-being: Happy and Unhappy People," *Journal of Personality and Social Psychology* 38, no. 4 (1980). The authors found the highest degree of stability to be in measures of introversion and extraversion: gregariousness, warmth, assertiveness. Arnold Buss and Robert Plomin, *Temperament Theory of Personality* (New York: Wiley, 1975). This earlier study concludes that activity level, emotionality, and sociability all are inherited personality traits.

Jack Block, "Some Enduring and Consequential Structures of Personality," *Further Explorations in Personality*, ed. A. I. Rabin (New York: Wiley, 1981). Researchers at Berkeley's Institute of Human Development followed students from their late teens to their mid-thirties, and again in their mid-forties. They, too, found stability in basic moods.

11. K. Gottschaldt, "Das Problem der Phanogenetik der Personalichkeit," *Personalichkeitsforschung und Personlichkeitstheorie, Handbuch der Psychologie*, vol. 4, ed. Lersch and Thomae (Gottingen: Hogrefe, 1960). Gottschaldt is cited by Steven G. Vandenberg, "Hereditary Factors in Normal Personality Traits (as Measured by Inventories)," in *Recent Advances in Biological Psychiatry*, vol. 9 (New York: Plenum Press, 1967). Gottschaldt called the basic mood and energy level of an individual "personal tempo" and found that heredity plays an important part in determining it. The studies of twins concur.

Orville G. Brim, Jr., and Jerome Kagan, eds., *Constancy and Change in Human Development* (Cambridge, Mass.: Harvard University Press, 1980). Brim, president of the Foundation for Child Development, agrees that aspects of social and emotional style—such as introversion-extraversion, depression, and anxiety—have been shown to be relatively stable.

12. Lionel Tiger, *Optimism: The Biology of Hope* (New York: Simon & Schuster, 1979).

Chapter 2:
EARLY CANDIDATES

1. Frank Allen, "Chief Executives Say Job Requires Many Family and Personal Sacrifices," *Wall Street Journal*, August 20,

1980; a report on a *WSJ*/Gallup survey of chief executives about their work attitudes, the kinds of personal sacrifices they have made to advance, and the ways they cope with job pressures.

Chapter 4:
ANATOMY OF A PASSAGE

1. Stanley D. Rosenberg and Michael P. Farrell, "Identity and Crisis in Middle Aged Men," *International Journal of Aging and Human Development 7*, no. 2 (1976).

Chapter 5:
WILLINGNESS TO RISK

1. Erik H. Erikson, "Identity and the Life Cycle," *Psychological Issues* 1 (1959); Daniel J. Levinson, with Charlotte N. Darrow, E. B. Klein, M. H. Levinson, and B. McKee, *The Seasons of a Man's Life* (New York: Knopf, 1978); Gail Sheehy, *Passages: Predictable Crises of Adult Life* (New York: Dutton, 1976).

2. René Descartes, *The Philosophical Works of Descartes,* trans. Elizabeth S. Haldane and G. R. T. Ross (Cambridge: Cambridge University Press, 1978).

3. Marjorie Fiske Lowenthal, "Changing Hierarchies of Commitment in Adulthood," in *Themes of Work and Love in Adulthood,* ed. Neil J. Smelser and Erik H. Erikson (Cambridge, Mass.: Harvard University Press, 1980).

4. Marilyn Wellemeyer, "The Class the Dollars Fell On," *Fortune,* May 1974.

5. I. H. Frieze, "Women's Expectations for and Casual Attributions of Success and Failure," in *Women and Achievement: Social and Motivational Analysis,* ed. M. S. Mednick, S. S. Tangri, and L. W. Hoffman (New York: Wiley, 1975).

6. The work on depression of Martin E. P. Seligman, professor of psychology, and Aaron T. Beck, director of the Center for Cognitive Therapy, both at the University of Pennsylvania, was discussed in "New Theories of Depression Hold Promise of Simpler Remedy" by Marilyn Machlowitz, *New York Times,* Section C, June 2, 1981.

7. Christoper Jencks, *Who Gets Ahead? The Determinants of Economic Success in America* (New York: Basic Books, 1979).

8. Marjorie Fiske Lowenthal, Majda Thurnher, David Chiriboga,

and associates, *Four Stages of Life: A Comparative Study of Women and Men Facing Transitions* (San Francisco: Jossey-Bass, 1976).

9. Lillian Hellman, *Maybe* (Boston: Little, Brown, 1980).

10. George Gallup, *American Families—1980: A Summary of Findings* (Princeton, N.J.: The Gallup Organization, 1980).

11. Lynne Sharon Schwartz, "Fragile Places," *New York Times Book Review*, November 9, 1980.

12. Daniel Bell, *The Winding Passage: Essays and Sociological Journeys 1960–1980* (Cambridge, Mass.: ABT Books, 1980).

13. U.S. Department of Labor, Bureau of Labor Statistics, "Autumn 1979 Urban Family Budgets and Comparative Indexes for Selected Urban Areas," Washington, D.C. 20212; released April 30, 1980. The subsequent report, for 1980, still reads: "The family consists of an employed husband, age 38, a wife not employed outside the home, an 8-year-old girl, and a 13-year-old boy."

14. Paul C. Glick, senior demographer, Population Division, U.S. Bureau of the Census, April 28, 1981. The report of the National Commission on the Observance of International Women's Year, *The Spirit of Houston* (1978), stated that in 1976 only 6 percent of married couples lived in the idealized "nuclear" family. Dr. Glick checked the latest figures and said that in 1979 the figure was 6.5 percent. He cautioned, however, that this figure represents only one point in time. Some of the women had not yet had children; some of the women would go to work; some of them would leave work to stay at home.

15. Rosemarie Tauris, "Spiritual Hunger: An Interview with William Sloane Coffin, Jr.," *Self*, September 1979.

16. Abraham H. Maslow, *The Farther Reaches of Human Nature* (New York: Penguin, 1976).

17. Mike Samuels and Nancy Samuels, *Seeing with the Mind's Eye* (New York: Random House, 1975); and C. Patrick, *What Is Creative Thinking?* (New York: Philosophical Library, 1955).

18. *New York Times*, May 8, 1981.

19. Edward Hoagland, "Natural Man: The Tree," *New York Times Book Review*, March 30, 1980.

Chapter 6:
THE RIGHT TIMING

1. Daniel J. Levinson, with Charlotte N. Darrow, E. B. Klein, M. H. Levinson, and B. McKee, *The Seasons of a Man's Life* (New York: Knopf, 1978).

2. George Vecsey, "The Real Challenge Begins When the Games Are Over," *New York Times*, October 27, 1980.

3. Gerard J. Heymans, *Introduction to Differential Psychology* (Haarlem, The Netherlands: Bohn, 1948).

4. Steven G. Vandenberg and Allen R. Kuse, "Temperaments in Twins," *Twin Research: Psychology and Methodology* (New York: Liss, 1978).

5. "The Baby Boomers Come of Age," *Newsweek*, March 30, 1981. A study for the Joint Center for Urban Studies of the Massachusetts Institute of Technology and Harvard University (George Masnick and Mary Jo Bane, *The Nation's Families: 1960–1990*) also predicts that as many as half the women born during the mid-1950s will have passed through their prime childbearing years by 1990 childless or with only one child.

6. Paul C. Glick, "Updating the Life Cycle of the Family," *Journal of Marriage and the Family*, February 1977.

7. Gail Sheehy, "The Truth About Today's Young Men," *Esquire*, October 1979.

8. Erik H. Erikson, address before the 31st Congress of the International Psycho-Analytical Association, New York, August 1979.

9. Mildred George Goertzel, Victor Goertzel, and Ted George Goertzel, *Three Hundred Eminent Personalities* (San Francisco: Jossey-Bass, 1978).

10. Jane Adams, *Women on Top: Success Patterns and Personal Fulfillment* (New York: Dutton, 1979).

11. The 1980 survey conducted by the University of California at Los Angeles and the American Council on Education was based on questionnaires completed by 291,491 freshmen entering 540 two- and four-year colleges and universities. The results were adjusted statistically to represent the nation's approximately 1.7 million full-time freshmen.

12. Ursula Goodenough was a member of the faculty at Harvard Alumnae College's course "Critical Stages in the Psychology of the Human Life Cycle," held July 10–15, 1977, under director George W. Goethals. The other faculty members were Robert Coles, Erik Erikson, Carol Gilligan, Douglas Powell, Gail Sheehy, and George Vaillant.

13. Jack Rosenthal, *Harvard 25th Reunion Report* (Cambridge, Mass.: Harvard University Press, 1981).

14. Carl Jung, *The Portable Jung*, ed. Joseph Campbell (New York: Viking, 1971).

Chapter 7:
CAPACITY FOR LOVING

1. David L. Gutmann, "Transformations of Narcissism Across the Life Cycle," undated paper from author, received 1980.

Chapter 8:
FRIENDSHIP, KINSHIP, SUPPORT NETWORKS

1. Elaine Donelson and Jeanne E. Gullahorn, *Women: A Psychological Perspective* (New York: Wiley, 1978).

2. Harry Levinson, "On Being a Middle-aged Manager," *Harvard Business Review*, July–August 1969.

3. Larry H. Long and Cecilia G. Boertlein, "The Geographical Mobility of Americans: An International Comparison," *Current Population Reports*, Special Studies series P-23, no. 64 (Washington, D.C.: U.S. Bureau of the Census, 1976).

4. "Apartment Rents Force Compromises" (coverage of U.S. Census Bureau report), *New York Times*, January 22, 1980.

5. Isabel V. Sawhill, "Women and Children on Their Own," *Challenge*, September–October 1976.

6. Horst-Eberhard Richter, "The Relationship of Psychoanalysis to the Inner World and to Social Reality," translation of unpublished paper given by Dr. Richter to author in Geissen, Germany, 1978.

7. Angus Campbell, *The Sense of Well-being in America: Recent Patterns and Trends* (New York: McGraw-Hill, 1980).

8. George E. Vaillant, *Adaptation to Life* (Boston: Little, Brown, 1977). The Grant Study of Adult Development at Harvard University vies with the Oakland Growth Study for the distinction of being the longest prospective study of adult development. Begun in 1938 when the average subject was 18, the Grant Study continued until the average subject passed his 50th birthday. Two hundred sixty-eight men were selected on the basis of their good health and favored position in society. Areas studied emphasized family, career, and value systems. The study, which illustrates how the male life cycle progresses under favorable circumstances, is limited to a single culture and a single point in history.

9. Cynthia S. Pincus, Assistant Clinical Professor, Department of

NOTES AND SOURCES 587

Psychiatry in Social Work, Yale University, letter to the editor, *New York Times Magazine*, August 10, 1981.

10. Psychiatrists for ERA (25 West 68th Street, New York, N.Y. 10023), news release, February 1, 1980.

11. Clair Blank, *The Beverly Gray College Mystery Series* (New York: Grosset & Dunlap, 1934–1939).

Chapter 9:
BEST OF MALE AND FEMALE STRENGTHS

1. See also, by David L. Gutmann, "A Key to the Comparative Psychology of the Life Cycle," in *Life Span Developmental Psychology: Normative Life Crises*, ed. Nancy Datan and Leon H. Ginsberg (New York: Academic Press, 1975); "The Cross-Cultural Perspective: Notes Toward a Comparative Psychology of Aging," in *Handbook of the Psychology of Aging*, ed. James E. Birren and K. Warner Schaie (New York: Van Nostrand Reinhold, 1977); "Observations on Culture and Mental Health in Later Life," in *Handbook of Mental Health and Aging*, ed. James E. Birren and R. Bruce Sloane (Englewood Cliffs, N.J.: Prentice-Hall, 1980); "The Post-Parental Years: Clinical Problems and Developmental Possibilities," in *Mid-life: Developmental and Clinical Issues*, ed. William H. Norman and Thomas J. Scaramella (New York: Brunner/Mazel, 1980).

2. David L. Gutmann, "Psychoanalysis and Aging: A Developmental View," Northwestern University Medical School, Chicago, Ill., undated paper from author, received 1980.

3. Anna Quindlen, *New York Times*, May 13, 1980.

4. John Nobel Wilford, "Father and Son Achieve Their Goal: First Balloon Trip Across Continent," *New York Times*, May 13, 1980.

5. Tom Wolfe, *The Right Stuff* (New York: Farrar, Straus and Giroux, 1979).

6. Daniel Bell, *The Winding Passage: Essays and Sociological Journeys 1960–1980*(Cambridge, Mass.: ABT Books, 1980).

7. *New Larousse Encyclopedia of Mythology* (London: Hamlyn, 1968).

8. Robert May, *Sex and Fantasy: Patterns of Male and Female Development* (New York: Norton, 1980).

9. *New Larousse Encyclopedia.*

10. Georgia Sassen, "Success Anxiety in Women: A Constructivist Interpretation of Its Source and Its Significance," *Harvard Education Review* 50, no. 1 (February 1980).

11. The Bureau of the Census reports 700,000 women 35 years and over in college in 1976, up from 418,000 in 1972:

"School Enrollment—Social and Economic Characteristics of Students: October 1976," *Current Population Reports*, series P. 20, no. 309 (Washington, D.C.: U.S. Government Printing Office, July 1977). The American Association of Community and Junior Colleges counts more than one million women over 21, their average age 30, enrolled in two-year community and junior colleges in 1976. Undergraduate enrollment of women increased by two-thirds in two-year colleges and by one-third in four-year colleges between 1970 and 1975 (AACJC, Washington, D.C., "Fact Sheet on Two-Year Colleges," May 1977).

Chapter 10:
A CERTAIN AGE

1. Bernice L. Neugarten, "Adaptation and the Life Cycle," *Journal of Geriatric Psychiatry* 4 (1970).

2. Rosalind C. Barnett and Grace K. Baruch, "Women in the Middle Years: A Critique of Research and Theory," *Psychology of Women Quarterly* 3, no. 2 (Winter 1978). The authors' latest findings were summarized in "A New Start for Women at Midlife," *New York Times Magazine*, December 7, 1970.

3. Florine B. Livson, "Patterns of Personality Development in Middle-aged Women: A Longitudinal Study," *International Journal of Aging and Human Development* 7, no. 2 (1976). The 200 participants in the Oakland Growth Study, a satellite of the Berkeley Growth Study, which began in 1931 and 1932, were observed as high school students and were interviewed again intensively in the late 1950s and 1960s. When Dr. Livson conducted her study, forty-two women remained. At age 50, they were predominantly middle-class housewives, their average educational level slightly beyond high school. All but one were married and had children, the average two to three. Half the women held jobs; a few worked full-time. One-third had been divorced, but most were remarried. The forty-two women were predominantly Protestant, urban, and upper middle-class. All of the original subjects were white.

4. Three books summarize these studies. Marjorie Fiske Lowenthal, Majda Thurnher, David Chiriboga, and associates, *Four Stages of Life: A Comparative Study of Women and Men Facing Transitions* (San Francisco: Jossey-Bass, 1976); Angus Campbell, *The Sense of Well-being in America: Recent Patterns and Trends* (New York: McGraw-Hill, 1980); Jonathan L. Freedman, *Happy People: What Happiness Is, Who Has It, and Why* (New York: Harcourt Brace Jovanovich, 1978).

5. The Srole/Fischer Midtown Manhattan Longitudinal Study

is discussed in David Sobel, "Urbanites Improve in Mental Fitness," *New York Times*, March 18, 1980.

6. Alvin Rabushka and Bruce Jacobs, "Are Old Folks Really Poor? Herewith a Look at Some Common Views," *New York Times*, February 15, 1980. Rabushka, senior fellow at the Hoover Institution at Stanford University, and Jacobs, assistant professor of political science at the University of Rochester, are authors of the book *Old Folks at Home*.

7. Harry Levinson, "Easing the Pain of Personal Loss," *Harvard Business Review*, September–October 1972.

8. Hugh Sidey, "The Presidency: Majesty in a Democracy," *Time*, December 1, 1980.

9. Albert Shapero, "Have You Got What It Takes to Start Your Own Business?" *Savvy*, April 1980.

10. Robert Blair Kaiser, "The Way of the Journal," *Psychology Today*, March 1981.

11. Marjorie Fiske Lowenthal, Majda Thurnher, David Chiriboga, and associates, *Four Stages of Life: A Comparative Study of Women and Men Facing Transitions* (San Francisco: Jossey-Bass, 1976).

12. David Gutmann, "Psychoanalysis and Aging: A Developmental View," paper from author, received 1980.

13. David L. Gutmann, "The Post-Parental Years: Clinical Problems and Developmental Possibilities," in *Mid-life: Developmental and Clinical Issues*, ed. William H. Norman and Thomas J. Scaramella (New York: Brunner/Mazel, 1980).

14. Marjorie Fiske Lowenthal, "Changing Hierarchies of Commitment in Adulthood," in *Themes of Work and Love in Adulthood*, ed. Neil J. Smelser and Erik H. Erikson (Cambridge, Mass.: Harvard University Press, 1980).

15. Jonathan L. Freedman, *Happy People: What Happiness Is, Who Has It, and Why* (New York: Harcourt Brace Jovanovich, 1978).

16. Sherwin A. Kaufman, "Menopause and Sex," *Sexual Behavior*, May 1971.

17. Richard F. Spark and Robert A. White, "Impotence Is Not Always Psychogenic," *Journal of the American Medical Association*, February 22–29, 1980.

18. Michael E. McGill, *The Common Crises of the Male Middle Years: A Survival Guide for Men—and for Women* (New York: Simon & Schuster, 1980).

19. Susan Sontag, "The Double Standard of Aging" (1972), reprinted in *Cosmopolitan*, March 1973.

20. Robert J. Havighurst, as reported by Derek Gill, in *Modern Maturity*, October–November 1979. The longitudinal studies on aging conducted by Professor Havighurst and the Committee

on Human Development, University of Chicago, are known as the Kansas City Studies of Adult Life. The studies were begun in 1958 and have produced forty-seven books and several hundred papers. Although the one thousand subjects all were between the ages of 40 and 90, this is one of the few studies of a large representative sample over a long period of time.

21. Robert Locke, "Fear of Age Kills Early: Human Life Should Last 120 Years," *The Oregonian*, December 11, 1978.

22. Ira Rosenwaike, Nurit Yaffe, and Philip C. Sagi, "The Recent Decline in Mortality of the Extreme Aged: An Analysis of Statistical Data," *American Journal of Public Health* 70, no. 10 (October 1980).

23. Deborah Newquist and Joseph DiMento, "Ask Not How Old the Candidate Is," *New York Times*, February 25, 1980.

24. Ralph S. Paffenbarger, Jr., Stanford University School of Medicine, report to American Heart Association meeting, Miami Beach, Fla., November 28, 1977.

25. Barbara Myerhoff, *Number Our Days* (New York: Dutton, 1979).

26. Elaine Cumming and W. E. Henry, *Growing Old: The Process of Disengagement* (New York: Basic Books, 1961) is one of many recent works on "discouragement theory." For a discussion of the controversy whether or not disengagement benefits the older person, see Bernice L. Neugarten, "Personality Change in Late Life: A Developmental Perspective," in *The Psychology of Adult Development and Aging*, ed. C. Eisdorfer and M. P. Lawton (Washington, D.C.: American Psychological Association, 1973).

27. N. Stinnett, Janet Collins, and J. E. Montgomery, "Marital Need and Satisfaction of Older Husbands and Wives," *Journal of Marriage and the Family* 32, no. 3 (1970); N. Stinnett, Linda M. Carter, and J. E. Montgomery, "Older Persons' Perceptions of Their Marriages," *Journal of Marriage and the Family* 34, no. 4 (November 1972); W. C. McCain, *Retirement Marriage* (Storrs, Conn.: University of Connecticut Press, 1969).

28. Robert J. Havighurst, B. L. Neugarten, and S. S. Tobin, "Disengagement and Patterns of Aging," *Middle Age and Aging*, ed. Bernice L. Neugarten (Chicago: University of Chicago Press, 1968); V. L. Bengtson, D. A. Chiriboga, and A. C. Keller, "Occupational Differences in Retirement: Patterns of Role Activity and Life-Outlook Among Chicago Retired Teachers and Steelworkers," *Adjustment to Retirement: A Cross-National Study*, ed. Robert J. Havighurst et al. (Assen, The Netherlands: Van Gorkum, 1979); N. M. Bradburn, *The Structure of Psychological Well-being* (Chicago: Aldine, 1969).

29. Dr. George Gerbner, "Elderly Found Portrayed as Stereo-

types on TV," *New York Times*, September 23, 1979 (report on two-year study conducted at Annenberg School of Communications, University of Pennsylvania).

30. "How Old Is Old?" *New York Times*, August 8, 1977.

31. Henry S. Maas and Joseph A. Kuypers, *From Thirty to Seventy: A Forty-Year Longitudinal Study of Adult Life Styles and Personality* (San Francisco: Jossey-Bass, 1974). A total of 142 people—the women an average age of 69 and the men 71—were interviewed during the mid-1970's, providing a rare view of forty-seven long-term married couples and forty-eight divorced or widowed women. Most of the men had retired from occupations as small-business owners, executives of large corporations, or professionals; more than half were college graduates. One-quarter of the women had not completed high school, but even among those no longer married, about half had above-average incomes.

32. Marjorie Fiske Lowenthal, Majda Thurnher, David Chiriboga, and associates, *Four Stages of Life: A Comparative Study of Women and Men Facing Transitions* (San Francisco: Jossey-Bass, 1976).

33. David L. Gutmann, "The Post-Parental Years: Clinical Problems and Developmental Possibilities," *Mid-life: Developmental and Clinical Issues*, eds. William H. Norman and Thomas J. Scaramella (New York: Brunner/Mazel, 1980).

34. Carin M. Rubenstein and Phillip Shaver, "Loneliness in Two Northeastern Cities," *The Anatomy of Loneliness*, ed. J. Hartog, J. R. Audy, and Y. A. Cohen (New York: International Universities Press, 1980).

35. James E. Birren, interviewed by Robert Locke, "Senility, the Dread of Old Age, Often Yields to Medical Treatment," *Los Angeles Times*, January 4, 1981.

36. Malcolm Cowley, *The View from 80* (New York: Viking, 1980).

37. *Time*, January 5, 1981.

38. Kirk Varnedoe, "Monet and His Gardens," *New York Times Magazine*, April 2, 1978.

39. Myerhoff, *Number Our Days*.

40. Charles E. Silberman, "A Proper Way to Live: Number Our Days," *New York Times Book Review*, April 1, 1979.

Chapter 11:
PURPOSE

1. R. Buckminster Fuller, *Critical Path* (New York: St. Martin's Press, 1981).

2. Lewis H. Lapham, "The Easy Chair: The Glass Bead Game, a Shrinking Future," *Harper's*, May 1981.

3. Ibid.

4. James MacGregor Burns, *Leadership* (New York: Harper & Row, 1978).

5. Reinhold Niebuhr, *Moral Man and Immoral Society* (New York: Scribners, 1932; reprinted 1960).

6. G. E. Vaillant, *Adaptation to Life* (Boston: Little, Brown, 1977).

7. John Herbers, "Activist Neighborhood Groups Are Becoming a New Political Force," *New York Times*, June 15, 1979.

8. Jean Piaget, *The Moral Judgment of the Child* (New York: Kegan Paul, Trench, Trubner, 1932).

9. Lawrence Kohlberg, "Development of Children's Orientations Toward a Moral Order: I. Sequence in the Development of Moral Thought," *Vita Humana* 6 (Winter/Spring 1963); "Development of Moral Character and Moral Ideology," in *Review of Child Development Research*, ed. Martin L. Hoffman and Lois Wladis Hoffman (New York: Russell Sage Foundation, 1964); "Stage and Sequence: The Cognitive Development Approach to Socialization," in *Handbook of Socialization Theory and Research*, ed. D. Goslin (Chicago: Rand McNally, 1969).

10. June Louin Tapp and Lawrence Kohlberg, "Developing Senses of Law and Legal Justice," *Journal of Social Issues* 27, no. 2 (1971); Felice J. Levine and June Louin Tapp, "The Dialectic of Legal Socialization in Community and School," in *Law, Justice, and the Individual in Society: Psychological and Legal Issues*, ed. J. L. Tapp and F. J. Levine (New York: Holt, Rinehart and Winston, 1977); June Louin Tapp, "Psychological and Policy Perspectives on the Law: Reflections on a Decade," *Journal of Social Issues* 36, no. 2 (1980).

Chapter 12:
FAITH

1. G. Gregg, T. Preston, A. Geist, and N. Caplan, "The Caravan Rolls On: Forty Years of Social Problem Research," *Knowledge: Creation, Diffusion, Utilization* 1 (1979).

2. Horst-Eberhard Richter, "The Relationship of Psychoanalysis to the Inner World and to Social Reality," trans. of unpublished paper given by Dr. Richter to author in Geissen, Germany, 1978.

3. Sigmund Freud, "Civilization and Its Discontents" (1929),

in *The Major Works of Sigmund Freud*, trans. Joan Riviere (Chicago: Encyclopaedia Britannica, 1952).

Chapter 13:
COPING AND MOURNING

1. Helen Deutsch, "Absence of Grief," *Psychoanalytic Quarterly* 6 (1937). This pioneering report on mourning and the defenses used is cited in George H. Pollock, "Process and Affect: Mourning and Grief," *International Journal of Psychoanalysis* (in press, 1981).

2. George E. Vaillant, *Adaptation to Life* (Boston: Little, Brown, 1977).

3. Suzanne Daley, "The Very Model of a Modern 'Chorus Girl,'" *New York Times*, May 17, 1981.

4. Sigmund Freud, "The Neuro-Psychoses of Defense" (1894), *The Complete Psychological Works of Sigmund Freud* (London: Hogarth, 1964).

5. George E. Vaillant, *Adaptation to Life* (Boston: Little, Brown, 1977).

6. Arnold Van Gennep, *The Rites of Passage* (1908), trans. Monika B. Vizedon and Gabrielle Kaffee (Chicago: University of Chicago Press, 1960).

7. Elisabeth Kübler-Ross, *On Death and Dying* (New York: Macmillan, 1970).

8. David L. Gutmann, "The Post-Parental Years: Clinical Problems and Developmental Possibilities," in *Mid-life: Developmental and Clinical Issues*, ed. William H. Norman and Thomas J. Scaramella (New York: Brunner/Mazel, 1980).

9. Martha Weinman Lear, *Heartsounds* (New York: Simon & Schuster, 1980).

10. Lionel Tiger, *Optimism: The Biology of Hope* (New York: Simon & Schuster, 1979); Myron A. Hofer, "A Psychoendocrine Study of Bereavement, Part I," *Psychosomatic Medicine* 34, no. 6 (November–December 1972).

11. Glen Collins, "Schools Stereotype Children with One Parent," *New York Times*, February 2, 1981.

Chapter 14:
THE LIGHT BEYOND MOURNING

1. Raymond C. Spalding and Charles V. Ford, "The *Pueblo* Incident: Psychological Reactions to the Stresses of Imprisonment and Repatriation," *American Journal of Psychiatry* 129, no. 1

(July 1972); Richard C. W. Hall and Patrick T. Malone, "Psychiatric Effects of Prolonged Asian Captivity: A Two-Year Follow-up," *American Journal of Psychiatry* 133, no. 7 (July 1976).

Part IV:
TRAVELING THE HIGH ROAD

1. Jill Kamil, *Luxor: A Guide to Ancient Thebes*, 2d ed. (London: Longman, 1976).

Chapter 15:
WITHDRAWAL AND COMEBACK

1. James MacGregor Burns, *Leadership* (New York: Harper & Row, 1978).
2. Edward Heath, "Foreign Affairs: 10 Precepts for a Strategy," *New York Times*, March 19, 1980.
3. Arthur M. Schlesinger, Sr., "The Tides of National Politics," *Paths to the Present* (Boston: Houghton-Mifflin, Sentry Edition, 1964). Professor Schlesinger's controversial essay evolved from a lecture delivered by him in the late 1920s and was first published in 1939 in the *Yale Review*.
4. Anthony F. C. Wallace, "Revitalization Movements," *American Anthropology* 58 (1956).
5. A stimulating op-ed page piece in the *New York Times* by William G. McLoughlin ("Wakening Again," August 5, 1978) led me to his book on the subject: *Revivals, Awakenings, and Reform: An Essay of Religion and Social Change in America, 1607-1977* (Chicago: University of Chicago Press, 1978).
6. Ibid. paraphrasing Wallace, "Revitalization Movements."
7. Alex Inkeles, "What Makes Americans Different? Study Lists 10 Significant—And Lasting—Traits," *International Herald-Tribune*, October 3, 1977. Stanford University social psychologist Alex Inkeles compared American characteristics as recorded for two hundred years with contemporary public opinion data and psychological tests. He found that seven out of our ten most salient American characteristics have shown remarkable persistence. Openness to new experience continues to rank high among Americans, as do anti-authoritarianism, restless energy, pragmatism, and a sense that one's worth is the same as anyone else's.
8. Barry Sussman, "Extreme Dissatisfaction with Washington Cited—[*Washington Post*] Poll Finds Conservative Mood No Move

to Right in U.S.," *International Herald-Tribune*, March 14, 1978.

9. Andrew Tobias, *Getting By on $100,000 a Year (and Other Sad Tales)* (New York: Simon & Schuster, 1980).

10. Richard A. Easterlin, "What Will 1984 Be Like? Socio-economic Implications of Recent Twists in Age Structure," *Demography*, November 1978.

11. Arthur Schlesinger, Jr., "Is Liberalism Dead?" *New York Times Magazine*, March 30, 1980.

12. Inkeles, "What Makes Americans Different? Study Lists 10 Significant—And Lasting—Traits," *International Herald-Tribune*, October 3, 1977.

13. Howard Mumford Jones, "Ralph Waldo Emerson," *Atlantic Brief Lives: A Biographical Companion to the Arts*, ed. Louis Kronenberger (Boston: Little, Brown, 1965).

14. William James, *The Varieties of Religious Experience* (1902; reprint ed., New York: Collier, 1961).

15. Bertrand Russell, *A History of Western Philosophy* (New York: Simon & Schuster, 1945).

16. Professor John Murrin, Department of History, Princeton University, drew my attention to Donald Meyer's *The Positive Thinkers: Religion as Pop Psychology from Mary Baker Eddy to Oral Roberts* (New York: Pantheon, reissue, 1980). Meyer views mind-cure as a religion of the powerless.

17. Marghanita Laski, *Ecstasy: A Study of Some Secular and Religious Experiences* (Bloomington, Ind.: Indiana University Press, 1961).

18. Alexander Cockburn and James Ridgeway, "Revolt in Reagan's Backyard: Dispelling the Myth of a Reactionary Age," *Village Voice*, April 22–28, 1981.

19. Robert Jay Lifton, *The Broken Connection: On Death and the Continuity of Life* (New York: Simon & Schuster, 1979).

20. Catholics for Free Choice in Washington, D.C., verified these percentages in June 1981 from recent polls conducted by Andrew J. Greeley and The Gallup Organization.

21. Jeffrey K. Hadden and Charles E. Swann, *Prime Time Preachers: The Rising Power of Televangelism* (Reading, Mass.: Addison-Wesley, 1981).

22. Cited ibid.

23. Arnold J. Toynbee, *A Study of History* (New York: Oxford University Press, 1946).

24. Alvin Toffler, *The Third Wave* (New York: Morrow, 1980).

25. Robert Nisbet, *History of the Idea of Progress* (New York: Basic Books, 1980).

26. Erik Erikson's analyses are in *Young Martin Luther* (New

York: Norton, 1958) and *Gandhi's Truth* (New York: Norton, 1969).

Chapter 16:
AN ACT OF COURAGE

1. Bernard-Henri Lévy, *The Testament of God* (New York: Harper & Row, 1980). *Nouvelle* philosopher Lévy points out: "The seven thousand exiles of Free France could justify themselves only by a pure moral wager, posited in the absolute, 'against all opposition,' as one of them said, hovering over a world from which the obvious itself had disappeared.

2. Reinhold Niebuhr, *Moral Man and Immoral Society* (New York: Scribners, 1932; reprinted 1960).

3. Mitchell Rogovin, director, and George T. Frampton, Jr., deputy director, Nuclear Regulatory Commission Special Inquiry Group, *Three Mile Island: A Report to the Commissioners and to the Public*, presented to the commissioners on January 24, 1980. The report states: "If that block valve had remained open, our projections show that within 30 to 60 minutes a substantial amount of the reactor fuel would have begun to melt down—requiring at least a precautionary evacuation of thousands of people living near the plant, and potentially serious public health and safety consequences for the immediate area."

Chapter 17:
VIEW FROM THE TOP OF THE MOUNTAIN

1. Robert Rhodes James, *Churchill: A Study in Failure* (New York: World, 1970).

2. Golda Meir, *My Life* (New York: Putnam's, 1975).

3. Jacques de Launay, *De Gaulle and His France: A Psychopolitical and Historical Portrait of Charles de Gaulle* (New York: Julian Press, 1968).

4. James MacGregor Burns, *Leadership* (New York: Harper & Row, 1978).

5. Barbara W. Tuchman, "An Inquiry into the Persistence of Unwisdom in Government," *Esquire*, May 1980.

6. Mildred George Goertzel, Victor Goertzel, and Ted George Goertzel, *Three Hundred Eminent Personalities* (San Francisco: Jossey-Bass, 1978).

7. Malcolm Thomson, "Winston S. Churchill," in *100 Great Modern Lives*, ed. John Canning (London: Souvenir, 1972).

8. Jacques de Launay, *De Gaulle and His France: A Psy-*

chopolitical and Historical Portrait of Charles de Gaulle (New York: Julian Press, 1968).

9. Bruce Mazlish and Edwin Diamond, *Jimmy Carter: An Interpretive Biography* (New York: Simon & Schuster, 1979).

10. "Carter Is Troubled at Scuttling of Programs," *New York Times*, March 16, 1981.

11. James MacGregor Burns, *Leadership* (New York: Harper & Row, 1978).

12. Gail Sheehy, "Ladies and Gentlemen, the Second President—Sister Rosalynn," *New York*, November 22, 1976.

13. "Shah's Admission to U.S. Is Linked to Misinformation on His Sickness," *New York Times*, May 13, 1981.

14. Anwar el-Sadat, *In Search of Identity: An Autobiography* (New York: Harper & Row, 1978). The quotations in this chapter that follow are from the same source.

AFTERWORD

1. John J. Sirica, *To Set the Record Straight: The Break-in, the Tapes, the Conspirators, the Pardon* (New York: Norton, 1979).

Bibliography

ADAMS, JANE. *Women on Top: Success Patterns and Personal Fulfillment*. New York: Dutton, 1979.

The Alan Guttmacher Institute. *Teenage Pregnancy: The Problem That Hasn't Gone Away*. New York: The Alan Guttmacher Institute, 1981.

ALEXANDER, F. *Psychosomatic Medicine, Its Principles and Applications*. New York: Norton, 1950.

BALTES, P.B., AND SCHAIE, K. W., eds. *Life-Span Developmental Psychology: Personality and Socialization*. New York: Academic Press, 1973.

BARNET, RICHARD J. *The Lean Years: Politics in the Age of Scarcity*. New York: Simon & Schuster, 1980.

BARNETT, ROSALIND C., AND BARUCH, GRACE K. "Women in the Middle Years: A Critique of Research and Theory." *Psychology of Women Quarterly* 3, No. 2 (Winter 1978).

BELL, DANIEL. *The Winding Passage: Essays and Sociological Journeys 1960–1980*. Cambridge, Mass.: ABT Books, 1980.

BEREZIN, MARTIN A., AND CATH, STANLEY H. *Geriatric Psychiatry: Grief, Loss and Emotional Disorders in the Aging Process*. New York: International Universities Press, 1965.

BIRREN, JAMES E., AND SCHAIE, K. WARNER, eds. *Handbook of the Psychology of Aging*. New York: Van Nostrand Reinhold, 1977.

BIRREN, JAMES E., AND SLOANE, R. BRUCE, eds. *Handbook of Mental Health and Aging*. Englewood Cliffs, N.J.: Prentice-Hall, 1980.

BLAU, ZENA SMITH. "Structural Constraints on Friendships in Old Age." *American Sociological Review* 26, No. 3 (1961).

BRADBURN, N. W. *The Structure of Psychological Well-being*. Chicago: Aldine, 1969.

BRAY, DOUGLAS W.; CAMPBELL, RICHARD J.; AND GRANT, DONALD L. *Formative Years in Business*. New York: Wiley, 1974.

BRIM, ORVILLE G., JR., AND KAGAN, JEROME, eds. *Constancy and Change in Human Development*. Cambridge, Mass.: Harvard University Press, 1980.

598

BRODER, DAVID S. *Changing of the Guard: Power and Leadership in America.* New York: Simon & Schuster, 1980.

BURNS, JAMES MACGREGOR. *Leadership.* New York: Harper & Row, 1978.

BUSS, ARNOLD, AND PLOMIN, ROBERT. *Temperament Theory of Personality.* New York: Wiley, 1975.

CAMPBELL, ANGUS. *The Sense of Well-being in America: Recent Patterns and Trends.* New York: McGraw-Hill, 1980.

CANNING, JOHN, ed. *100 Great Modern Lives.* London: Souvenir, 1972.

CANTRIL, HADLEY. *The Pattern of Human Concerns.* New Brunswick, N.J.: Rutgers University Press, 1965.

CLARK, KENNETH (SIR). *The Artist Grows Old.* Cambridge: Cambridge University Press, 1972.

CLARK, KENNETH B. *Dark Ghetto: Dilemmas of Social Power.* New York: Harper & Row, 1965.

COHEN, JOAN Z.; COBURN, KAREN LEVIN; AND PEARLMAN, JOAN CRYSTAL. *Hitting Our Stride: Good News About Women in Their Middle Years.* New York: Delacorte, 1980.

COLEMAN, J. C. *Abnormal Psychology and Modern Life,* 5th ed. Glenview, Ill.: Scott, Foresman, 1976.

COSTA, PAUL T., JR., AND MCCRAE, ROBERT R. "Influence of Extraversion and Neuroticism on Subjective Well-being: Happy and Unhappy People." *Journal of Personality and Social Psychology* 38, No. 4 (1980).

COWLEY, MALCOLM. *The View from 80.* New York: Viking, 1980.

CUMMING, ELAINE, AND HENRY, W. E. *Growing Old: The Process of Disengagement.* New York: Basic Books, 1961.

DATAN, NANCY, AND GINSBERG, LEON H., eds. *Life-Span Developmental Psychology: Normative Life Crises.* New York: Academic Press, 1975.

DELONE, RICHARD. *Small Futures: Children, Inequality, and the Limits of Liberal Reform.* New York: Harcourt Brace Jovanovich, 1979.

DESCARTES, RENÉ. *The Philosophical Works of Descartes,* translated by Elizabeth S. Haldane and G. R. T. Ross. Cambridge: Cambridge University Press, 1978.

DEUTSCH, HELEN. "Absence of Grief." *Psychoanalytic Quarterly* 6 (1937).

DEUTSCHER, IRWIN. "The Quality of Postparental Life." *Journal of Marriage and the Family,* February, 1964.

DONELSON, ELAINE, AND GULLAHORN, JEANNE E. *Women: A Psychological Perspective.* New York: Wiley, 1978.

EASTERLIN, RICHARD A. "What Will 1984 Be Like? Socioeconomic Implications of Recent Twists in Age Structure." *Demography,* November, 1978.

EISDORFER, C., AND LAWTON, M. P., eds. *The Psychology of Adult Development and Aging.* Washington, D.C.: American Psychological Association, 1973.

ERIKSON, ERIK H. *Childhood and Society,* 2d ed. New York: Norton, 1963.

——. *Gandhi's Truth.* New York: Norton, 1969.

——. *Identity: Youth and Crisis.* New York: Norton, 1968.

——. "Identity and the Life Cycle." *Psychological Issues* 1 (1959).

——. *Young Man Luther.* New York: Norton, 1958.

FARBER, SUSAN I. *Identical Twins Reared Apart: A Reanalysis.* New York: Basic Books, 1981.

FERGUSON, MARILYN. *The Aquarian Conspiracy: Personal and Social Transformation in the 1980s.* Los Angeles: Tarcher, 1980.

FREEDMAN, JONATHAN L. *Happy People: What Happiness Is, Who Has It, and Why.* New York: Harcourt Brace Jovanovich, 1978.

FREUD, ANNA. *The Ego and the Mechanisms of Defense,* rev. ed. New York: International Universities Press, 1966.

FREUD, SIGMUND. *The Complete Psychological Works of Sigmund Freud.* London: Hogarth, 1964.

——. *The Major Works of Sigmund Freud.* Chicago: Encyclopaedia Britannica, 1952.

FULLER, R. BUCKMINSTER. *Critical Path.* New York: St. Martin's Press, 1981.

GALLUP, GEORGE. *American Families—1980: A Summary of Findings.* Princeton, N.J.: The Gallup Organization, 1980.

GLICK, PAUL C. "Updating the Life Cycle of the Family." *Journal of Marriage and the Family,* February, 1977.

GLICK, PAUL C., AND SPANIER, GRAHAM B. "Married and Unmarried Cohabitation in the United States." *Journal of Marriage and the Family,* February, 1980.

GOERTZEL, MILDRED GEORGE; GOERTZEL, VICTOR; AND GOERTZEL, TED GEORGE. *Three Hundred Eminent Personalities.* San Francisco: Jossey-Bass, 1978.

GOSLIN, D. A., ed. *Handbook of Socialization Theory and Research.* New York: Rand McNally, 1969.

GREGG, G.; PRESTON, T.; GEIST, A.; AND CAPLAN, N. "The Caravan Rolls On: Forty Years of Social Problem Research." *Knowledge: Creation, Diffusion, Utilization* 1 (1979).

HAAN, NORMA. *Coping and Defending: Processes of Self-Environment Organization.* New York: Academic Press, 1977.

HADDEN, JEFFREY K., AND SWANN, CHARLES E. *Prime Time Preachers: The Rising Power of Televangelism.* Reading, Mass.: Addison-Wesley, 1981.

HARRINGTON, MICHAEL. *The Other America,* rev. ed. New York: Macmillan, 1971.

HAVIGHURST, ROBERT J., et al., eds. *Adjustment to Retirement: A Cross-National Study.* Assen, The Netherlands: Van Gorkum, 1969.

HEYMANS, GERARD J. *Introduction to Differential Psychology.* Haarlem, The Netherlands: Bohn, 1948.

HOFSTADTER, RICHARD. *The American Political Tradition and the Men Who Made It.* New York: Vintage, 1974.

HUBER, JOAN, ed. *Changing Women in a Changing Society.* Chicago: University of Chicago Press, 1973.

HUME, DAVID. *A Treatise of Human Nature* [1739], edited by Paul S. Ardal. Great Britain: Collins, 1972.

JAHODA, MARIE. *Current Concepts of Positive Mental Health.* New York: Basic Books, 1959.

JAMES, ROBERT RHODES. *Churchill: A Study in Failure.* New York: World, 1970.

JAMES, WILLIAM. *The Varieties of Religious Experience* [1902]. New York: Collier, 1961.

JENCKS, CHRISTOPHER. *Who Gets Ahead? The Determinants of Economic Success in America.* New York: Basic Books, 1979.

JUNG, CARL G. *Modern Man in Search of a Soul.* New York: Harcourt, Brace, 1933.

———. *The Portable Jung,* edited by Joseph Campbell. New York: Viking, 1971.

KAGAN, JEROME, AND MOSS, HOWARD A. *Birth to Maturity: A Study in Psychological Development.* New York: Wiley, 1962.

KOHLBERG, LAWRENCE. "Development of Children's Orientations Toward a Moral Order: I. Sequence in the Development of Moral Thought." *Vita Humana* 6 (Winter/Spring 1963).

———. "Development of Moral Character and Moral Ideology." In *Review of Child Development Research,* edited by Martin L. Hoffman and Lois Wladis Hoffman. New York: Russell Sage Foundation, 1964.

KÜBLER-ROSS, ELISABETH. *On Death and Dying.* New York: Macmillan, 1970.

LASKI, MARGHANITA. *Ecstasy: A Study of Some Secular and Religious Experiences.* Bloomington, Ind.: Indiana University Press, 1961.

LAUNAY, JACQUES DE. *De Gaulle and His France: A Psychopolitical and Historical Portrait of Charles de Gaulle.* New York: Julian Press, 1968.

LAZARUS, RICHARD S., AND MONAT, ALAN. *Personality,* 3d ed. Englewood Cliffs, N.J.: Prentice-Hall, 1979.

LEMASTERS, E. E. *Blue-Collar Aristocrats: Life-styles at a Working-Class Tavern.* Madison: University of Wisconsin Press, 1975.

LEVINE, FELICE J., AND TAPP, JUNE LOUIN, eds. *Law, Justice, and the Individual in Society: Psychological and Legal Issues.* New York: Holt, Rinehart and Winston, 1977.

LEVINSON, DANIEL J., et al. *The Seasons of a Man's Life.* New York: Knopf, 1978.

LÉVY, BERNARD-HENRI. *The Testament of God.* New York: Harper & Row, 1980.

LIFTON, ROBERT JAY. *The Broken Connection: On Death and the Continuity of Life.* New York: Simon & Schuster, 1979.

———. *The Life of the Self.* New York: Simon & Schuster, 1976.

LIVSON, FLORINE B. "Patterns of Personality Development in Middle-aged Women: A Longitudinal Study." *International Journal of Aging and Human Development* 7, No. 2 (1976).

LOEHLIN, JOHN C., AND NICHOLAS, ROBERT C. *Heredity, Environment, and Personality: A Study of 850 Sets of Twins.* Austin: University of Texas Press, 1976.

LOWENTHAL, MARJORIE FISKE, AND ROBINSON, BETSY. "Social Networks and Isolation." In *Handbook of Aging and the Social Sciences,* edited by Robert H. Binstock and Ethel Shanas. New York: Van Nostrand Reinhold, 1976.

LOWENTHAL, MARJORIE FISKE; BERKMAN, P. L.; and associates. *Aging and Mental Disorder in San Francisco.* San Francisco: Jossey-Bass, 1967.

LOWENTHAL, MARJORIE FISKE; THURNHER, MAJDA; CHIRIBOGA, DAVID; and associates. *Four Stages of Life: A Comparative Study of Women and Men Facing Transitions.* San Francisco: Jossey-Bass, 1976.

MAAS, HENRY S., AND KUYPERS, JOSEPH A. *From Thirty to Seventy: A Forty-Year Longitudinal Study of Adult Life Styles and Personality.* San Francisco: Jossey-Bass, 1974.

MCCAIN, W. C. *Retirement Marriage.* Storrs, Conn.: University of Connecticut Press, 1969.

MCGILL, MICHAEL E. *The Common Crises of the Male Middle Years: A Survival Guide for Men—and for Women.* New York: Simon & Schuster, 1980.

MCLOUGHLIN, WILLIAM G. *Revivals, Awakenings, and Reform: An Essay of Religion and Social Change in America, 1607–1977.* Chicago: University of Chicago Press, 1978.

MASLOW, ABRAHAM H. *The Farther Reaches of Human Nature.* New York: Penguin, 1976.

MASNICK, GEORGE, AND BANE, MARY JO. *The Nation's Families 1960–1990: An Outlook Report of the Joint Center for Urban Studies of MIT and Harvard University.* Cambridge, Mass.: Harvard University Press, 1980.

MAY, ROBERT. *Sex and Fantasy: Patterns of Male and Female Development.* New York: Norton, 1980.

MAZLISH, BRUCE, AND DIAMOND, EDWIN. *Jimmy Carter: An Interpretive Biography.* New York: Simon & Schuster, 1979.

MEDNICK, M.; TANGRI, S.; AND HOFFMAN, L., eds. *Women and Achievement: Social and Motivational Analysis.* New York: Wiley, 1975.

MEIR, GOLDA. *My Life.* New York: Putnam's, 1975.

MEYER, DONALD. *The Positive Thinkers: Religion as Pop Psychology from Mary Baker Eddy to Oral Roberts.* New York: Pantheon, 1980.

MYERHOFF, BARBARA. *Number Our Days.* New York: Dutton, 1979.

NEUGARTEN, BERNICE L. "Adaptation and the Life Cycle." *Journal of Geriatric Psychiatry* 4 (1970).

———, ed. *Personality in Middle and Late Life.* New York: Atherton, 1964.

———, ed. *Middle Age and Aging.* Chicago: University of Chicago Press, 1968.

NIEBUHR, REINHOLD. *Moral Man and Immoral Society.* New York: Scribners, 1932.

NISBET, ROBERT. *History of the Idea of Progress.* New York: Basic Books, 1980.

NORMAN, WILLIAM H., AND SCARAMELLA, THOMAS J., eds. *Mid-life: Developmental and Clinical Issues.* New York: Brunner/Mazel, 1980.

NORTON, ARTHUR J., AND GLICK, PAUL C. "Marital Instability: Past, Present and Future." *Journal of Social Issues* 32, No. 1 (1976).

NORTON, DAVID L. *Personal Destinies: A Philosophy of Ethical Individualism.* Princeton, N.J.: Princeton University Press, 1976.

PATRICK, C. *What Is Creative Thinking?* New York: Philosophical Library, 1955.

PIAGET, JEAN. "Intellectual Evolution from Adolescence to Adulthood." *Human Development* 15 (1972).

———. *The Moral Judgment of the Child.* New York: Kegan Paul, Trench, Trubner, 1932.

———. *Structuralism.* New York: Basic Books, 1970.

PLOMIN, ROBERT; DEFRIES, J. C.; AND MCCLEARN, G. E. *Behavioral Genetics.* San Francisco: Freeman, 1980.

POGREBIN, LETTY COTTIN. *Growing Up Free: Raising Your Child in the 80's.* New York: McGraw-Hill, 1980.

PRESSY, SIDNEY L., AND KUHLEN, RAYMOND G. *Psychological Development Through the Life Span.* New York: Harper & Brothers, 1957.

RABIN, A. I., ed. *Further Explorations in Personality.* New York: Wiley-Interscience, 1981.

ROSENBERG, STANLEY D., AND FARRELL, MICHAEL P. "Identity and Crisis in Middle Aged Men." *International Journal of Aging and Human Development* 7, No. 2 (1976).

ROSENWAIKE, IRA; YAFFE, NURIT; AND SAGI, PHILIP C. "The Recent Decline in Mortality of the Extreme Aged: An Analysis of Statistical Data." *American Journal of Public Health* 70, No. 10 (October, 1980).

RUBENSTEIN, CARIN M., AND SHAVER, PHILLIP. "Loneliness in Two Northeastern Cities." In *The Anatomy of Loneliness*, edited by J. Hartog, J. R. Audy, and Y. A. Cohen. New York: International Universities Press, 1980.

RUSSELL, BERTRAND. *A History of Western Philosophy*. New York: Simon & Schuster, 1945.

SADAT, ANWAR EL-. *In Search of Identity: An Autobiography*. New York: Harper & Row, 1978.

SAMUELS, MIKE, AND SAMUELS, NANCY. *Seeing with the Mind's Eye*. New York: Random House Bookworks, 1975.

SCHLESINGER, ARTHUR M. *Paths to the Present*. Boston: Houghton-Mifflin, Sentry Edition, 1964.

SEARS, PAULE S., AND BARBEE, ANN H. "Career and Life Satisfaction Among Terman's Gifted Women." *The Gifted and the Creative: A Fifty Year Perspective*, edited by William C. George and Cecilia H. Solano. Baltimore: Johns Hopkins University Press, 1977.

SENNETT, RICHARD. *The Uses of Disorder: Personal Identity and City Life*. New York: Vintage, 1970.

SHEEHY, GAIL. *Passages: Predictable Crises of Adult Life*. New York: Dutton, 1976.

SIRICA, JOHN J. *To Set the Record Straight: The Break-in, the Tapes, the Conspirators, the Pardon*. New York: Norton, 1979.

SMELSER, NEIL J., AND ERIKSON, ERIK H., eds. *Themes of Work and Love in Adulthood*. Cambridge, Mass.: Harvard University Press, 1980.

SPARK, RICHARD F., AND WHITE, ROBERT A. "Impotence Is Not Always Psychogenic." *Journal of the American Medical Association*, February 22–29, 1980.

The Spirit of Houston: Report of the National Commission on the Observance of International Women's Year. Washington, D.C.: Superintendent of Documents, U.S. Government Printing Office, March, 1978.

STENT, GUNTHER. *The Coming of the Golden Age: A View of the End of Progress*. Garden City, N.Y.: Natural History Press, 1969.

STINNETT, N.; COLLINS, JANET; AND MONTGOMERY, J. E. "Marital Need Satisfaction of Older Husbands and Wives." *Journal of Marriage and the Family* 32, No. 3 (1970).

STINNETT, N.; CARTER, LINDA MITTELSTET; AND MONTGOMERY, I. E. "Older Persons' Perceptions of Their Marriages." *Journal of Marriage and the Family* 34, no. 4 (1972).

TAPP, JUNE LOUIN. "Psychological and Policy Perspectives on the Law: Reflections on a Decade." *Journal of Social Issues* 36, No. 2 (1980).

TAPP, JUNE LOUIN, AND KOHLBERG, LAWRENCE. "Developing Senses of Law and Legal Justice." *Journal of Social Issues* 27, No. 2 (1971).

THURNHER, MAJDA. "Midlife Marriage: Sex Differences in Evaluation and Perspectives." *International Journal of Aging and Human Development* 7, No. 2 (1976).

TIGER, LIONEL. *Optimism: The Biology of Hope.* New York: Simon & Schuster, 1979.

TOBIAS, ANDREW. *Getting By on $100,000 a Year (and Other Sad Tales).* New York: Simon & Schuster, 1980.

TOFFLER, ALVIN. *The Third Wave.* New York: Morrow, 1980.

TOYNBEE, ARNOLD J. *A Study of History.* New York: Oxford University Press, 1946.

VAILLANT, GEORGE E. *Adaptation to Life.* Boston: Little, Brown, 1977.

VANDENBERG, STEVEN G. "Hereditary Factors in Normal Personality Traits (as Measured by Inventories)." In *Recent Advances in Biological Psychiatry.* Vol. 9. New York: Plenum Press, 1967.

———. "The Nature and Nurture of Intelligence." In *Genetics,* edited by David C. Glass. New York: Russell Sage Foundation, 1968.

VANDENBERG, STEVEN G., AND KUSE, ALLAN R. "Temperaments in Twins." In *Twin Research: Psychology and Methodology.* New York: Liss, 1978.

VAN GENNEP, ARNOLD. *The Rites of Passage* [1908]. Chicago: University of Chicago Press, 1960.

VEROFF, J., AND FELD, SHEILA. *Marriage and Work in America.* New York: Van Nostrand Reinhold, 1970.

WALLACE, ANTHONY F. C. "Revitalization Movements." *American Anthropology* 58 (1956).

WILLIAMS, RICHARD, AND WIRTHS, CLAUDINE. *Live Through the Years: Styles of Life and Successful Aging.* New York: Atherton, 1965.

WILSON, EDWARD O. *On Human Nature.* Cambridge, Mass.: Harvard University Press, 1978.

WOOD, GORDON. *The Creation of the American Republic.* Chapel Hill: University of North Carolina Press, 1969.

INDEX

A

abortion, 90, 356, 455
Abourezk, Charlie, 142
Abourezk, Jim, 141, 142, 144
acceptance, in mourning process, 398, 402–403, 418, 419
accomplishment, sense of, 18, 149
in Comeback Decade, 63–64, 280
Addams, Jane, 501, 503
adolescence, 2, 53, 83, 111, 287
Deadline Decade compared to, 63
dreams in, 115
friendships in, 209–210
identity crisis in, 109
unhappiness in, 23, 61, 371, 372
adoption, 152
adult development:
pattern of, 95
reality of, 2
see also passage, phases of; passages; specific passages
Afghanistan, Soviet invasion of, 246, 385
Agee, William, 156, 158
age 50, see Half-Century Reckoning passage
age-fluid society, U.S. as, 294
age 40, 142–143, 276
for corporation men, 45–46, 74–76
for independents, 280–281
Age of Entitlement, 53–57
Age of Scarcity, 53–54, 122–123, 145–146, 443–445, 459, 460
age range, of interviewees, 13
aging:
as factor in well-being, 18, 22–23, 278–279, 283–284
as loss, 286–287
myths about, 278–279, 286–289
sexual balance and, 19, 63, 88–89, 234, 237, 286, 290, 305, 523
aggressiveness:
in men, 9, 70, 88, 91
in women, 9, 64, 250
Aiken, Conrad, 533
Alaska, kinship network in, 214–223

Albee, Edward, 126
alcohol, 60, 340–341
as coping mechanism, 73, 80, 82, 112, 250, 272–273
alienation, 121, 166, 246–247
Allin, Kay, 269
alternating of extremes pattern, 162
altruism, 375
as coping mechanism, 345, 386
defined, 345
altruistic surrender, by wives, 42–43, 46
ambition:
in men, 53–54, 160, 236, 237–238, 239, 251, 285, 298, 367
in women, 18, 43, 236, 266, 269, 298
America, Americans, 439–458
great awakenings in, 439, 451–452, 455
mobility in, 213
pragmatism of, 3, 439, 449
Seventies in, 442–444
Sixties in, 122, 441–442, 450–455
American Bar Association, Life History Questionnaire and, 283–286, 365
American Civil Liberties Union (ACLU), 325, 326, 330, 331
American Indians, peyote rituals of, 453
American Management Association, 454
Anderson, Maxie, 237
anger, 252, 266, 322
in mourning process, 398, 399–401, 414–415, 418
repression of, 38, 44, 104–105, 202–203, 260, 281, 286, 291, 341
Annual Marriage Revival Weekend, 88, 91–92
Anthony, Susan B., 502–503
anticipation, 12, 16, 41–42, 264, 266, 276, 411
as coping mechanism, 386
as measure of social class, 131

of retirement, 292, 318, 320–321, 351
by society, 434, 435, 443
timing and, *see* timing
anticipation phase, *see* passage, phases of
anxiety, 4, 61, 251, 442
competition and, 270n
of professional women, 139, 169
in separation and incubation phase, 83, 85
apathy, as protective state, 421
Arden, Elizabeth, 153
Asbury, Claudia, 387
Aspen Design Conference, 336–337
assertiveness, 10, 86, 281, 289
athletes, 240–249
future planning by, 131–134
heart disease in, 315
Australia, mobility in, 213

B

baby givebacks, 152
Bacall, Lauren, 309
Baldwin, Roger, 325–335, 336, 526
Ball, George, 155
Barber, Peggy, 265–266
bargaining, in mourning process, 398, 400
"Barnes, Delia," 3–12, 16, 17, 19, 21, 123–124, 253–254
basic mood, 25–27, 59–60, 317–318
Bateson, Gregory, 460
Begin, Menachem, 524
behaviorists, 121
Bendix Corporation, 156
Bergman, Ingmar, 124
Bergson, Henri, 95
Berlin Olympics (1936), 247
Beverly Gray Mysteries, 232
Bible, 120–121, 196, 326, 497
biotechnology, 459, 460
Birren, James E., 322
black Americans:
busing and, 345–347, 349–351
childbearing by, 152
civil rights of, 441, 451–452, 455
as housekeepers, 179
income levels of, 23n
self-validation for, 110
blue-collar workers, 271–276

family income of, 23n
love as viewed by, 19–20
purpose and, 343–344, 346
retirement of, 319–320, 351
self-respect as viewed by, 19–20, 25, 352–353
well-being levels for, 22–23, 24–25
working wife and, 268, 272–276
Boos, John, 244
boredom, 116–117, 279, 332, 337, 338
Bortz, Walter, 315
Boumédienne, Houari, 459
Brandeis, Louis, 325–326
Bridenbaugh, Char, 468–470, 486–488, 489, 490
Bridenbaugh, Dale, 465–466, 468–480, 482–485, 488–489, 490
Broken Connection, The (Lifton), 453
Brown, David, 316–317
Brown, Helen Gurley, 316–317
Browning, Elizabeth, 503
Bryan, William Jennings, 326
"Buckley, Keith," 375–381, 462–463
Burns, George, 321
Burns, James MacGregor, 344, 434

C

California, University of, Human Development Program at, 97–98, 319–320
Calvinism, 439
Campbell, Angus, 286
Canada, mobility in, 213
cancer, denial of, 496
careers:
changes of, 84–85, 101–102, 247–248, 290, 295–296, 299
dreams of, 47, 75, 101, 102, 154–155, 230, 231–232, 286
interrupting of, 161, 162, 280
as reflection of male life cycle, 153–154
success and, 18, 30–46, 101, 102–103, 257–267, 412
transfers and, 297
Carpenter, Diane and Bob, 216–223
Carter, Jimmy, 100, 313, 412, 420, 441, 498–499, 504–506, 522–524

Carter, Lillian, 505
Carter, Rosalynn, 504–510
"Cary, Susanna," 388–394, 400,
    402
"Cashian, Herb," 30–32, 35–46
"Cashian, Judith," 31–32, 35–46,
    104
Castle, Lucy, 269
Catalyst, 38n
Catch-30 passage:
    characteristics of, 36–37, 63
    men in, 36–38, 39, 73, 182–184,
        185–186, 217–218, 240–243,
        272–273, 375–376
    tasks of, 36–37, 63
    women in, 4–6, 37–39, 42–43,
        63, 158–159, 167–170, 182–
        186, 190–191, 217–219, 279–
        280, 416–417, 493–494
Cathedral Peace Institute, 426–
    427
causal progression, 460
cause, *see* purpose
Ceausescu, Nicolae, 524
celibacy, 375
Census Bureau, U.S., 146, 277n–
    278n
change, 528
    continuity vs., 122
    loss and, 83, 84, 111, 200–201
    preemptive, 100
    pros and cons of, 16–17
    see also life accidents; passages;
        risk-taking
cheerfulness, high well-being char-
    acterized by, 21, 59–60
child abuse, 108, 340, 341
child-care facilities, 230
children, childhood:
    divorce and, 405–409
    effects of relocation on, 40, 42,
        43
    illegitimate, 49–51, 52
    loss of love of, 200–201
    moral development in, 354
    mourning and, 414, 416–417
    old people compared to, 323–
        324
    parents' friendships with, 223–
        226, 289
    of pathleaders, 501–505, 511–
        512
    polestars for, 61, 70, 80, 230–
        232, 352
    postponement of, 33, 145–146,
        151–152, 167, 170, 175, 182–
        183, 184
    as purpose, 339–343, 371
    reciprocal passages and, 223–
        226
    responsibility of, 201
    success vs., 147–154
    timing of bearing of, 139–140,
        145–159, 166, 170, 175
    unhappy, 60–61, 167, 450–451,
        511–512, 516
China Syndrome, The, 482, 484
Churchill, Lord Randolph, 492
Churchill, Winston, 328, 459, 492,
    493, 497
Civilization and Its Discontents
    (Freud), 382
civil rights movement, 441, 451–
    452, 455
class, *see* social class
Cockburn, Alexander, 452
Coffin, William Sloane, Jr., 123
Cogdell, Belle, 370–374
Colson, Chuck, 368
Comeback Decade passage:
    fears in, 22, 279
    men in, 48–53, 64, 88–92, 116–
        120, 249, 283–284, 285, 519
    money and, 277–279
    tasks of, 63–64
    women in, 16, 64, 192, 200–205,
        263–265, 279–283
comebacks, 434–463
    defined, 63–64
    to faith, 358–364, 379–380
    by men, 244–249, 276, 379, 383,
        430, 497, 498, 512, 519
    in middle age, 292, 294, 303–
        305, 309–310, 379, 383, 430
    by pathleaders, 497, 498, 512–
        513, 519
    societal, 437, 439–441, 458–460
    by women, 11, 200, 253, 304–
        305, 309
Commerce Department, U.S., in-
    come statistics by, 23n
company ghettos, 36
competition, 8, 217, 445–446
    anxiety due to, 270n
    in Comeback Decade, 64
    men and, 88, 242, 275
    women and, 192, 242
Comprehensive Employment and
    Training Act (CETA), 342n
compromise, 254
    advantages of ability to, 254
    well-being and, 16

by women, 5, 11–12, 200, 251–252, 254, 265–268, 363

conflicts of maturation:
dependency vs. autonomy, 36–37, 45–46, 70, 83, 86, 99, 217–219, 220, 249–250, 322, 332–333, 362, 365–366, 415
intensity vs. balance, 163–166, 293
personal status vs. social responsibility, 55, 86, 246–247, 348, 352, 385
pleasing vs. self-validation, 3–4, 5–6, 8–10, 64, 74, 86, 109–110, 186, 190, 201, 209, 269, 282
risk vs. security, see risk-taking
self-protection vs. renewal, 42–43, 293–294, 323, 417

conformity, 3, 49, 52, 192
children and, 263
in corporate life, 33–35, 467–469
religious, 22, 266, 375, 386

Congress, U.S., 246, 278, 520
absentee fatherhood and, 141–145
retirement from, 295

"Conti, James, Jr.," 223–226

"Conti, James, Sr.," 223–226

cookie-cutter life pattern, of businessmen, 33

coping mechanisms, 169, 308, 385–397
altruism as, 345–346, 386
anticipation as, 386
in Comeback Decade, 64, 280
defined, 394
denial as, 39, 45, 250, 377, 393, 394, 395, 422
escapism as, 73–74, 80, 82, 112, 249, 273, 340–341, 422
faith as, 112, 356, 385–386
friendship as, 112, 208, 385–386, 392
of high vs. low well-being people, 112
humor as, 112, 203, 386, 387, 390, 423
projection as, 100, 106, 293, 345, 394, 395, 438
reaction formation as, 394, 395
repression as, 38, 44, 72, 76, 104–105, 108, 191, 192, 197, 200, 202–203, 250, 260, 285, 291, 341, 387, 393, 394–396,

400, 422
risk-taking and, 112
sublimation as, 375, 387, 392, 393, 403
suppression as, 386–387, 390, 393
transference as, 248
work as, 112, 259–260, 290–291, 386

corporate divorce, 79, 84

corporate incest, 32, 155

corporate life, 30–46
benefits of, 34, 40–41
conformity in, 33–35, 468–469
costs of, 33–35, 46
diplomat stage in, 34–35
doer stage in, 34, 38
friendship in, 35, 36, 157, 158
learner stage in, 34, 36
pivotal Americans from, 575–576
professional women and, see professional women
terms for accelerated success in, 30

corporation men, 30–46, 73–85
in career changes, 84–85, 101–102, 291, 299
early retirement of, 291–292
generational assumptions and, 33–34, 70
in middle management, 24, 33, 34, 143–144, 299
secretary's "monogamous" relationship with, 155, 158
in senior management, 24, 33–34, 35, 101, 144, 459

corporation wives, 31–32, 35–46, 74, 76, 85, 89, 103–105, 154–155, 157–158
in doer stage, 37–38
in learner stage, 36
professional women vs., 154–155, 157–158

Council, Ella, 228

counterculture, 54, 121–122, 451–454

couples:
alternating as breadwinners by, 161, 162
competition by, 153
in Freestyle Fifties, 298–310
New Conventional, 268–276
responsibility and, 88, 193, 196
supportiveness in, 181, 186
two-carrer, 38n
see also marriage

courage, 16, 18, 67, 123, 410
  in women, 12, 18, 187, 236,
    254–265, 266, 281–283
Cousin, Cousine, 213
Cowley, Malcolm, 322
creative endurance, 97, 190–191,
  200, 251, 253, 410, 430, 523
creative process, phases of, 124,
  127
creativity, 27, 56, 124–126, 523
  capacity for loving as, 180
  heredity and, 25
  introspection and, 17
  at national level, 435
  pivotal Americans and, 576–577
  in solutions to passages, 16
criticism, 74, 115, 186, 210, 262,
  354
  high well-being and, 22, 113
cultural cycles, 436–440
cultural ties, 12
Cunningham, Mary, 156–159

D

Dajani, Virginia, 265
Daley, Suzanne, 387
Darrow, Clarence, 326
Darwin, Charles, 326
Daugherty, William, 425
"David," 54–55, 58
Dayan, Moshe, 313
Deadline Decade passage:
  love in, 188–205, 249
  men in, 32, 38, 39, 45, 47–48,
    73–88, 141–145, 219–220, 273–
    276, 377–381, 465–466, 469–
    470, 494–497
  tasks of, 63, 488
  women in, 6, 37–40, 42–43, 46,
    218–220, 260–264
decision making:
  as male strength, 238–239
  postponement of, 145–147
  well-being affected by, 24
defense mechanisms, *see* coping
  mechanisms
deferred achievement, 191, 280
deferred gratification, 135, 387
deferred nurturer, 151n, 301
deferred rewards, 131
De Gaulle, Charles, 459, 492, 494–
  495, 497
Demoiselles d'Avignon, Les, 188
denial:
  as coping mechanism, 39, 45,

  250, 377, 393, 394, 395, 422
  defined, 396
  in mourning process, 398–399
dependence, 36, 87, 99, 361, 365–
  366, 415
  in female myth, 249–250
  institutional, 46, 69, 83, 98
  intimacy and, 220
  in old age, 322
  social, 218, 220, 332–333, 334
depression, 4, 16, 26, 287, 293
  in men, 73, 82, 237, 296, 308,
    330, 366, 493
  in mourning process, 398, 401,
    417, 419, 424
  optimism-negativism dial and,
    26–27
  in separation and incubation
    phase, 83, 84
  in women, 3–4, 5, 7, 10, 17, 21,
    36, 104, 106, 108, 219, 242,
    279, 286, 341, 401, 417, 511
Descartes, René, 97, 387
designers, work as viewed by, 337
detachment:
  author's memoir of, 405–409
  defined, 403
  in old age, 323
  in recovery from mourning, 403,
    404
  in Selective Sixties, 65, 316–317
determination, 7, 9, 113, 174, 191,
  342–343, 500–503
diabetes, sexual impairment and,
  307n
Diamond, Edwin, 498
Dickinson, Angie, 309
DiMaggio, Joe, 132
Disraeli, Benjamin, 492
divorce, 122, 213
  corporate, 79–80, 84–85
  integrator pattern and, 168, 169
  men and, 51, 211, 242–243, 330
  parenting and, 404–409
  well-being and, 24, 188
  women and, 20, 24, 165, 168–
    169, 199, 341–343
domestic violence, 108, 193, 341
dominant group:
  insensitivity of, 213
  mimicking of, 150
dominant women, in Selective Sixties, 319–320
"Donna," 206–210, 214
Doty, Madeleine Z., 330
Douglas, William, 323

"Doyle, Bingo," 346–354, 385
"Doyle, Mrs." 350, 353
dreams:
    as anticipation, 131
    career, 47, 75, 101, 102, 154, 231, 285
    expansion phase and, 87
    of idealized self, 115
    of men, 47, 48, 53, 75, 101, 102, 161, 163, 285, 404
    mentor's influence on, 231
    original vs. new, 131
    parents as source of, 5, 9–10
    of women, 5, 6, 12, 231, 255, 493
drugs, as coping mechanism, 112, 250, 341
"Dunne, Mary," 378, 380

E

economics, U.S., 54, 145, 435, 443–445, 460
education:
    advantages of, 135
    forced busing and, 346–347, 349, 351
    illusions about, 167, 168
    pivotal Americans from, 571–573
ego, 99, 101, 118, 251, 253
    purpose and, 345
    surrender of, 369
ego ideal, 115, 193
Egypt, 429–433, 513–527
Eighties (1980s), 444–446
Eighty Years and More (Stanton), 501
Eliot, T. S., 365
Emerson, Ralph Waldo, 178, 329, 439, 448, 450
empathy, 199, 213, 236, 523
empty nest, 187, 243, 248, 303–306, 372, 414
endorphins, 21
endurance, importance of, 528, 531
energy levels, 190, 200, 260, 331, 333, 435
    in expansion phase, 86
    heredity and, 25, 27–28, 60
    repression and, 107
    in Selective Sixties, 318
entrepreneurism, 160
environment, 242, 279
    heredity vs., 25–28

men's enjoyment of, 64, 236, 285
    moral development affected by, 354
    pathfinders' reliance on, 61
    personality and, 25
Equal Rights Amendment, 502
Erickson, Erik, 109, 152, 461
Esquire, 14, 53
est, 55, 86, 454
Every Man for Himself, 149
exercise, 108, 366, 454
    benefits of, 27–28, 315
Exercises, The (St. Ignatius Loyola), 379
exhibition heart attack, 97, 100
expansion phase, see passage, phases of

F

Fader, Daniel, 134
failure, 45, 115–116, 242, 245, 360, 376–377, 379
    constructive vs. destructive, 16–17, 102, 112–113
    early, 113, 115
    finding fault within and, 106
    of pathleaders, 492–497
    resiliency in vs. immunity to, 112
faith, 20, 55, 356–382
    comebacks to, 358–364, 379
    conformity and, 22, 261, 266, 375
    as coping mechanism, 112, 356, 386
    cultural revival and, 438, 439–440, 446, 454–455
    foreign policy and, 426
    personal relationship to, 22, 90, 204, 329, 356–357, 469
    pivotal Americans and, 576–577
    as purpose, 6–12, 293, 364–365, 367–369, 521
    reanimation through, 179–180, 363, 364–370, 372
    risk-taking and, 9, 112, 124
    surrender of will and, 369–370
    work made purposeful by, 287, 368
fallback, 37, 271–272, 275
family:
    child-care arrangements with members of, 229, 257–258, 261–262, 267

effects of corporate life on, 33–44
extended, 11
incest in, 155
nuclear, 123
security of, 18, 20, 76, 85, 107
single-parent, 20, 122, 223, 404
therapy, 230
two-income, 23n, 122, 147, 268, 272
see also children, childhood; fathers; mothers; parents, parenting
family patterns, 5, 271, 341
fantasy, 231, 306
as coping mechanism, 112, 250, 422
see also myths
fantasy patterns, studies of, 250–251
Farouk, king of Egypt, 516
fast trackers, in corporate life, 30, 42
fathers:
absentee, 139–141, 159
of female pathleaders, 501, 502, 504, 511
as heroes, 48, 49
integrator pattern for, 167
military model for, 75
reciprocal passages and, 223–226
second, 49
unemployed, 123
Father's Footsteps Disease, 101
fears, 23, 132
in Comeback Decade, 22, 280
in Deadline Decade, 63
in Freestyle Fifties, 307, 308–309
of high vs. low well-being people, 22
about money, 55, 147
of risk-taking, 98, 109, 110
Federated Garden Clubs of Vermont, 345
feminists:
fantasy patterns of, 250–251
see also women's movement
fertility, age and, 151–152, 198
Fischer, Anita Kassen, 286
FLAG (Family Liaison Action Group), 411, 412, 415, 419
"Florio, John," 46–52
"Florio, Mrs.," 47, 49
Flynn, Elizabeth Gurley, 330

Fonda, Jane, 482
Ford Motor Company management, 291–292
Four Stages of Life (Lowenthal), 304
fragmentation, 167, 188, 404
France, kinship in, 213
Frantic Forties:
extramarital affairs in, 187
time perspective distorted in, 145
women in, 279
Freedman, Jonathan L., 286
Freestyle Fifties stage, 289–313
admitting the unknowable in, 312–313
career transfers in, 297
husband-wife joint enterprises in, 299–303
"I am who I am" in, 310–312
last-chance leap in, 145, 294–296
men in, 64, 283–285, 286, 289–293, 294–296, 297, 299–304, 305, 306–310, 493, 494–495
noncareer outlets in, 297–299
secondary saboteur in, 293
sex in, 306–310
tasks of, 64
walking dead in, 290–293
women in, 64, 283, 298, 301–302, 303–305, 306–308
Freud, Anna, 394, 396
Freud, Sigmund, 13, 121, 382, 394, 450
"Fried, Rebecca," 166–172, 175
friends, friendship, 18, 84, 206–213, 260, 267
child-care arrangements with, 230
as coping mechanism, 112, 208–210, 385–386, 393
in corporate life, 35, 36–37, 43, 158
defined, 20
in expansion phase, 89–90
female-female, 21, 89, 206–207, 212–213
with former loves, 188
high well-being characterized by, 21, 279
as kinship relation, 214–226
male-female, 11, 18–19, 91, 187, 210, 211, 263
male-male, 21, 90, 210–211
"mature" people and, 208

in old age, 261
parent-child, 223–226, 289
in social cohesion, 435
value of, 208–209
Frost, Robert, 1, 130, 420
frustration, 85–86, 438, 442
expression vs. transcendence of, 227
in middle age, 293
fundamentalist Christians, 123, 326, 356, 443, 455–457, 530
funerals, age and attitudes toward, 287
future, *see* time perceptions; timing

G

Gallup Organization, corporate survey by, 34
Gandhi, Indira, 153, 253
Gandhi, Mahatma, 328, 331, 459, 461, 492
Garbo, Greta, 309
generational differences:
in social contact, 55, 69–70
in views on old age, 287–288
generativity, defined, 91
"Ginny," 182
Giscard d'Estaing, Valéry, 425
Glaser, Milton, 126
Glick, Paul C., 146
Godard, Jean-Luc, 188
Goethe, Johann Wolfgang von, 323
Goldman, Emma, 325
Goldman, Jacob, 338
Goodenough, Ursula, 154
gratification, delayed, 135, 387
Graves, Bonnie, 413–414, 418–419, 422
Graves, John, 413–414, 418–419, 422
Great Depression, 69, 113
great refusal, 500–503
Gregg, G., 381
group therapy, 227
Gutmann, David L., 18, 235–236, 304, 401

H

Hadden, Jeffrey K., 456
Hailey, Arthur, 196
Half-Century Reckoning passage, 99

men in, 88, 283, 294–295, 334, 352, 416, 486
women in, 264–265
happiness, defined, 13
happyface syndrome, women and, 104–109, 187, 193, 251, 253, 281, 394
Hart, Philip A., 141
Harvard Business School, study on graduates of, 100–103
Harvard Grant Study, 345
Hatshepsut, queen of Egypt, 431
health, 22, 27–28, 77–78, 86, 91, 110, 332, 373
in Comeback Decade, 64
low well-being and, 81, 82, 103
mental, 97, 194, 196, 286
mind-cure movement and, 449
pivotal Americans and, 577–579
in Selective Sixties, 313–316
heart attacks, 315, 401, 519
exhibition, 97, 100
Heartsounds (Lear), 401
Heath, Edward, 434–435
Hegel, Georg W. F., 121, 459
Heike, Connie, 270
Hellman, Lillian, 107
Helms, Richard, 418
heredity, well-being and, 21, 25–26, 27–28, 59–60
heroes, heroines, 48, 49, 87, 439
high blood pressure, 77, 82, 85, 91, 315
Hitchcock, Alfred, 323
Hitler, Adolf, 246
Hoagland, Edward, 126
honesty, 201
in Selective Sixties, 317
value placed on, 18
Horbal, Koryne, 511
Horner, Matina, 270n
Horton, Donald, 456
Hostage Relief Act, 419
household workers, as support system, 228–230, 257–258, 261–262
Hubbard, Dick, 465, 472, 477, 480, 482–485
hubris, defined, 237
Hughes, Howard, 291
Hume, David, 121
humor, 18, 187, 327
as coping mechanism, 112, 203, 385–386, 387, 390, 423
husbands:
corporation men as, 33–34, 37,

73
long-term, 20
hysterectomy, 486

I

Iacocca, Lee, 254, 291, 292
idealism, 57
identity, 12, 115, 378
  expectations of others as foundation of, 5, 9, 19, 372
  loving and, 180–182
  multiple sources of, 45, 123–124, 185
  self-blame as basis of, 105
  single-track compulsive and, 293–294
  in Trying Twenties, 36, 62
  of women, 4–6, 9–10, 12, 19, 105, 109–110, 186, 279, 341, 415, 416
identity crisis, in adolescence, 109
imagination, 65, 67, 220–221, 231
  theories of, 125
imaging:
  cultural, 453
  by men, 276
  mourning and, 400, 404
  by women, 37, 309, 400
impotence, 77–78, 82, 286, 308, 495
improvement, 60–61
incest, 26, 155
income, 277n–288n
  of household workers, 229–230
  self-respect vs., 75
  well-being and, 22, 25
  of women, 20n, 23n, 147–149, 168, 204, 229–230, 278n
incubation phase, see passage, phases of
independents, in Comeback Decade, 281
individualism, 418, 447–448, 452–453
infidelity, 48–51, 89, 181, 187
Inkeles, Alex, 448
inner harmony, 107, 270, 490
innovation, 41, 244, 327–328, 435, 528
In Search of Identity (Sadat), 516, 524
institutions:
  continuity vs. change and, 122
  dependence on, 45, 69, 82–83, 99

malfunctioning of, 437–438, 443
  see also specific institutions
integrator pattern:
  men and, 167, 172
  new, 166–172
  old definition of, 166
  women and, 151n, 166–172, 187
intellectualization, as repression, 396
intensity:
  balance vs., 163–166, 293
  selective, 65, 317, 323
intervention:
  defined, 404
  in recovery from life accident, 404, 409, 418
interviewees, profile of, 13, 14–15
intimacy, 21, 220
  in corporate life, 36
  in Freestyle Fifties, 304
  men and, 18, 21, 163, 187, 211, 237, 242, 249
  in Trying Twenties, 36, 62
introspection, 197, 259, 392
  in old age, 66, 321, 323, 330–331
  societal, 434–435
  well-being and, 17
introversion-extroversion, hereditary factors in, 26
intuition, 84, 124, 150, 185, 357, 364, 440, 523
Iranian hostages, 105, 410–428, 441, 509
  mourning process for families of, 414–415, 417–421
  repatriation of, 421–422, 423–427
  survival patterns of, 421–424
isolation, 9, 226, 495
  see also ostracism

J

James, Robert Rhodes, 493
James, William, 439, 448–449
Japanese management style, 338
Jencks, Christopher, 106
Jesus, 203, 329, 369, 458, 497
"Jhana," 48–51
Johnson, Lyndon B., 344, 495
Johnson, Samuel, 417
Johnson, Virginia, 307
"Johnston, April," 72–76, 80, 81, 85–92

"Johnston, Bill," 70–92, 97, 110, 399
Jones, Howard Mumford, 448
Jones, Phil, 141
Jung, Carl, 164, 396
"just world" theory, 70, 98

K

Kant, Immanuel, 321
Kaufman, Sherwin, 307
Keller, Helen, 326
Kennedy, Duncan, 416
Kennedy, Ethel, 522
Kennedy, John F., 344, 441
Kennedy, Louisa, 410–412, 415–417, 420, 421, 424, 425
Kennedy, Moorhead, Jr., 410–412, 416–417, 421, 424, 426
Kennedy, Philip, 416
Kennedy, Robert, 522
Keough, Katherine, 426
Khomeini, Ayatollah Ruhollah, 100, 509
kinship, 142–144, 213–226
   friendships with quality of, 214–223
   reciprocal passages and, 223–226
Kissinger, Henry, 313, 418, 453, 508, 520, 523
Kohlberg, Lawrence, 354–355
"Kristol, Janice," 114, 116, 117–120
"Kristol, Stan," 113–120
Kübler-Ross, Elisabeth, 398, 400–403
Kuralt, Charles, 425

L

Labor Department, U.S. Bureau of Labor Statistics of, 122
laid-back men, 54, 58, 159–163, 172, 251
Larsen, Don, 132
Laski, Marghanita, 451
last-chance leap, in Freestyle Fifties, 145, 294–296
leadership, 19, 53, 160, 286, 328
   blue-collar, 346–354
   of old vs. young, 321
   social action programs in generating of, 344–345
   transforming, 500
   see also pathleaders

Leadership (Burns), 344
Lear, Martha, 401
learned helplessness, 108
legal development, 355
leisure, 41, 53, 290, 338–339
Lemmon, Jack, 482
Lenin, Vladimir I., 329
Lennon, John, 384, 454
"Leo," 206, 207, 209
Levinson, Harry, 211, 293
life accidents, 59, 61, 89, 138, 193, 200, 256, 330, 351, 371, 383–428, 505
   coping mechanisms and, 112, 208, 385–388
   cultural, 410–427, 443–444
   defined, 66, 383–384
   see also mourning
life expectancy, 315, 321–322
Life History Questionnaire, 13–15, 57, 109, 159, 174, 179, 540–560
   happyface syndrome and, 107
   methodology used for, 14–15
   sample used for, 14–15, 29
   well-being measured by, 12–14
Life Line Charts, 148–149, 450
life satisfaction, see well-being
Lifton, Robert Jay, 453
Lincoln, Abraham, 519
Lindsay, John, 311
Livingston, Goodhue, 416
Livingston, Robert R., 416
Livson, Florine B., 281
Locke, John, 121
"locked in" feeling, 4, 22, 55, 75, 146, 188–189, 268, 352
"Loeb, Elizabeth Bain," 358–364
loneliness, 22, 163, 281, 322
longitudinal studies, 3, 26, 281, 286
Longworth, Alice Roosevelt, 323
Lopez, James, 423
loss, 367, 377
   aging as, 286
   change and, 83, 84, 111, 200
   in Comeback Decade, 280–281
   in female myths, 250, 252–253
   mourning and, 247, 252–253, 257, 260, 304
love, loving, 18, 53, 178–205, 289
   class differences in, 19
   high well-being characterized by, 18–19
   identity and, 180–182
   laid-back men and, 160, 162

mature, 18, 20, 169, 188–205, 279
mutual, 19, 179–187, 195–196, 199, 202–205, 221, 317
New Young Tigresses and, 157–159
nonmutual, 187–188, 192
in old age, 331
pleasing vs., 186
by society, 435
timing and, 182–187
tolerance as requirement for, 179–180, 182, 188
unconditional, 357, 364
Lowenthal, Marjorie Fiske, 98, 286, 304, 305
lower class, 25
sense of purpose and, 339–343
time perceptions of, 130–131
Loyola, Saint Ignatius, 379
Luther, Martin, 461

M

McCarthy, Eugene, 522
McCormack, Mike, 473–474, 475, 476
MacDonald, Dwight, 329
MacDonald, Harold, 291–292
McGill, Michael F., 308
McLoughlin, William C., 439, 440, 442, 446
magicthink, men and, 42, 98–100, 274
maintaining, importance of, 528–531
male-female relationships:
a-synchrony in development and, 182, 202, 488
egalitarian, 6, 11
friendship, 11, 19, 91, 187, 210, 211, 262
manic-depressives, 26
"Maria Teresa," 180
"Maria Teresa's husband," 180
"Mark," 160–162
marriage, 330
bad, 187–188, 189–190, 191–193, 195, 340–341, 493
early, 33, 70, 72, 340–341
friendship in, 210, 262
postponement of, 33, 145, 173, 213–214
of professional women, 136, 139, 176, 261–262, 265–268, 383

revival weekends for, 88, 91
second, 211, 261–262, 266–268, 306–307, 330
well-being and, 23, 24
see also divorce; husbands; wives
Maslow, Abraham, 124, 208
mastectomy, 310, 390
Masters, William H., 307
May, Robert, 250–251
Maybe (Hellman), 107
Mazlish, Bruce, 498
Mazzilli, Lee, 134
Mead, Margaret, 212, 248
Meany, George, 323
medicine:
ethics and, 380
preventive, 315
meditation, 27, 76, 78, 82, 125, 361, 454, 516
"process," 298
Meeds, Lloyd, 295
Meir, Golda, 153, 253, 492, 493–494
me-ism, 3, 54–55, 56, 57
alternative to, 173–175
happiness as, 381–382
lack of purpose in work as contributor to, 338–339
in Sixties, 450–455
as withdrawal, 442
Mémoires (de Gaulle), 495
men:
aggressiveness in, 9, 70, 88, 91
ambition in, 53, 160, 236, 237, 239, 251, 286, 298, 367
average incomes of, 23n, 277n–278n
comebacks by, 244–249, 276, 379–380, 383, 430–431, 498, 513, 519
corporation, see corporation men
depression in, 73, 82, 237, 296, 308, 330, 366, 493
divorced, 51, 211, 242, 330
dreams of, 47, 48, 53, 75, 101, 102, 162, 285, 517
emotional response in, 64, 99, 238, 243, 249, 303–304
erection capacity, 307–308
female side of, 19, 64, 88, 234–236, 286, 523
friendships among, 21, 90, 211
integrator pattern and, 166, 172
intimacy and, 18, 21, 163, 187,

211, 237, 243, 249
laid-back, 53–55, 58, 159–163, 172, 251
magicthink and, 42, 98–100, 274
mentors for, 21, 211, 367, 369
myths about, 48, 50–51, 70, 237–240, 250–251
never-married, 24
nurturant, 240–243
Old Boys' Network for, 227
as pathleaders, 493, 494–499, 513–527
personal growth of, 34, 53, 56, 69–70, 159–160, 161, 163, 182
pleasing by, 74, 110
power and, 34, 35, 237, 269
protean, 54, 123
"strong" image for 69–70
as survivor guides, 91, 118, 354
see also fathers; husbands; specific passages
menopause, 64, 197, 223, 248, 279, 281, 307, 372
mental health:
  change vs. continuity and, 97
  of urban vs. rural dwellers, 286
  wife as responsible for, 193, 196
mentors, 21, 58, 194, 211, 231, 296, 351, 354
  in corporate life, 34, 158, 260
  defined, 230
  religious, 367, 368
"Meredith," 136–140, 150, 153, 176, 383
methodology:
  for Life History Questionnaire, 14–15
  value-free, 381
Michelangelo, 323
middle age, 277–313
  comebacks in, 292, 294, 304, 309, 379, 383, 430
  myths about, 286–289
  new challenges sought in, 48
  old age vs., 65, 314, 321
  renewal in, 293–313
  strengths exclusive to, 289
  see also Comeback Decade passage; Deadline Decade passage; Freestyle Fifties passage
middle class:
  black Americans in, 110
  dreams of, 131
  see also upper-middle class
midlife crisis, use of term, 63
Midtown Manhattan Longitudinal Study, 286
Miles, Carlotta, 152
mind-cure movement, 449
Minor, Greg, 465, 472, 479, 481, 482–484
"Moeller, Bert," 299–303
"Moeller, Joanna," 301–302
Mohammad Reza Shah Pahlavi, 43, 508, 510
Monet, Claude, 323
money, 5, 34, 55, 147, 210, 322
  in Comeback Decade vs. Entry Decade, 277–278
  as measure of success, 348, 352
  in middle age, 277–278, 289
  women and, 37–38, 216, 264
  see also income
Moneychangers, The (Hailey), 196
moral awakening, rejection of purposeless work as basis for, 339
moral development, Kohlberg's theory of, 354–355
Moral Man and Immoral Society (Niebuhr), 345
moral problems, 380
  cowardice and, 123
  responsibility vs. rights and, 270n
moral values, 337, 354–355
Morefield, Dorothea, 414–415, 418, 420, 425
Morefield, Richard, 414–415, 418
Morgan, J. P., 462
Morgan, Lila, 103
mortality, awareness of, 63, 64, 200, 287–288, 324, 470
Moscow Olympics (1980), 245–246
mothers:
  bonds between, 212
  early, 191
  of female pathleaders, 502, 504, 511
  as protector, 75
  stepmothers, 262–263
  surrogate, 61, 228–230
  unwed, 134, 340
  welfare, 134, 339, 341–343
Mott, Lucretia, 502
mourning, 193, 377, 379, 385–428, 461
  copnig mechanisms and, 385–397
  loss and, 248, 252, 256, 260, 304

preemptive, 304
process of, 398–403, 414, 417–421
recovery from, 403–409, 419–420
music, of counterculture, 454
Myerhoff, Barbara, 316, 323
Myers, Elaine, 143
Myers, Gary, 142–144
Myers, Michele, 143
mystics, 27
myths, 237–239, 240
    of Demeter, 252–253
    female, 249–251, 252–254
    male, 48, 51, 70, 237–240, 250, 251
    about middle age, 286–289
    of Pandora's Box, 527
    of Persephone, 252
    of Phaeton, 239, 250
    about youth, 278

N

narcissism, see me-ism
Nasser, Gamal Abdel, 430, 514, 517–518, 519, 525
National Committee on Household Employment, 229–230
National Information Bank on Women in Public Office, 298
National Science Foundation, 279n
National Women's Political Caucus, 20n
Nature (Emerson), 448
nature vs. nurture, 25–28
Nehru, Jawaharlal, 459
Nelson, George, 125
nervous system, delayed response and, 135
New Conventionals, 107, 268–276
New Girls' Network, 227
New Independents, work attitudes of, 339
New York Times, 499, 510
New Young Tigresses, 135–141, 147–159, 176–177
Niebuhr, Reinhold, 317, 345, 467
Nisbet, Robert, 460
Nixon, Pat, 506
Nixon, Richard, 368, 497, 529
"Novak, Irene and Joe," 271–276
nuclear energy, 328, 333, 464–491
Nuclear Regulatory Commission (NRC), 469, 470, 478, 480
Number Our Days (Myerhoff), 323

nurturers:
    deferred, 151n, 301
    men as, 240–243
    women as, 19, 151n, 234, 239, 301
nutrition, 315

O

Oakland Growth Study, 281
objectification, 7, 10, 115
occupations, as factor in well-being, 23–24
Oerter, Al, 240–249, 254, 268, 383, 385
Oerter, Mrs., 241–242
Ohio State University, business study by, 296
old age, 287–289, 321–324, 325–355
    middle age vs., 65, 314, 321
    myths about, 287
    uniqueness in, 314
    see also Proud-to-Be Eighties stage; Selective Sixties stage; Thoughtful Seventies stage
old age homes, 323
Old Boys' Network, 126, 227
Onassis, Jacqueline Kennedy, 309
"O'Neil, Cate," 188–205, 232, 357
optimism, 61, 326–327, 334–335, 436, 446, 452
    high well-being characterized by, 21–22
    transcendental, 448
optimism-negativism dial, 26–27
organization man, 122, 159
Organization of Petroleum Exporting Countries (OPEC), 443, 444
ostracism, 6, 7, 9, 201, 423
    in separation and incubation phase, 79, 84
over-preparation, by women, 6, 8

P

Parent, Bernie, 132
parents, parenting:
    absent, 60, 61, 139, 140, 141–142, 159, 230–231
    children filling roles of, 60
    post-parenting zest, 248
    product vs. process in, 152
    reciprocal passages and, 223–226

single, 20, 122, 223, 404
split, 404–409
see also fathers; mothers
Parker, Ned, 365–368
passage, phases of, 78–93
   anticipation, 78–83, 92, 127, 185, 194, 197, 470
   creative process compared to, 124, 127
   expansion, 86–90, 93, 127, 197–200, 478–485
   incorporation, 90–92, 93, 127, 200–205, 485
   moratoria and, 185
   separation and incubation, 79, 83–86, 93, 127, 185, 197, 246–247, 377–379, 471–479
passages, 62–66
   high vs. low well-being and attitudes toward, 17, 278
   incomplete, 37–41, 42–43, 45
   reciprocal, 223–226
   refusing experience of, 39, 42–43, 45
   use of term, 2
   see also specific passages
Passages (Sheehy), 2, 62, 63, 181, 234, 272, 287, 288, 316, 347
Pastore, John, 472–473, 475
Pathfinders:
   concept of, 67
   emphasis on process for, 67, 95
   high-well-being people vs., 59–60
   qualities of, 95–382
   transcendent, 461–491
pathleaders, 461, 492–527
   comebacks by, 497, 498, 513, 519
   as failures, 492–497
   great refusal by, 500–503
   men as, 493, 494–500, 513–527
   withdrawals by, 493, 495, 497–498, 514, 518–519
   women as, 493–494, 502–513
"Paul," 56, 58
Pavlova, Anna, 231
personal growth and development:
   corporate life cycle vs., 33–34
   in expansion phase, 86
   high well-being and, 18
   of men, 33–34, 53, 56, 70, 159–160, 161–162, 163, 182
   as purpose, 53, 54, 56–57
   social concern balanced with, 58
personality:

in Freudian theory, 121
   hereditary factors in, 21, 25–28
personal tempo, *see* energy levels
pessimism, 21, 26, 60
Pétain, Henri Philippe, 494
"Petershouse, R. W.," 33, 35, 43, 45
philosophy, *see* psychology/philosophy
Piaget, Jean, 354, 355
Picasso, Pablo, 188
Pickford, Mary, 309
pleasing:
   friendship and, 209–210
   by men, 74, 110
   by women, 3, 4–6, 7–9, 64, 109–110, 186, 189, 201, 270, 282
point women, 166, 167–168
polestars, 61, 71, 80, 329, 351, 370, 452, 456
   of author, 231–232
   defined, 230
politics:
   in corporate life, 34, 44
   for Freestyle Fifties women, 298
postponing generation, 145–147
   see also children, childhood; marriage
power, 123, 268, 317
   corporation men and, 33, 35
   in male myth, 237
   women's use of, 44, 159, 298
Prater, Alan, 173–175
pregnancy, unplanned, 130, 134, 340
presidents, of corporations, 33, 35, 100, 290
President's Commission for the Study of Ethical Problems in Medicine, 380
Preston, Evelyn, 330
preventive medicine, 315
Prime Time Preachers (Hadden and Swann), 456
professionals, well-being levels for, 23, 24
professional women, 254–268
   anxiety of, 139, 169
   corporate wives vs., 155, 158
   Life Line Chart of, 149–150
   male thinking copied by, 150
   marriages of, 136, 139, 176, 261–262, 266–267, 383
   professional men compared to, 136, 150–151, 155

sex lives of, 20
timing and, 135–141, 147–159, 169–172, 175–177
Progoff, Ira, 298
projection, as copying mechanism, 100, 107, 293, 345, 394, 395, 438
protean men, 53, 123
protective strategies, *see* coping mechanisms
Proud-to-Be Eighties stage, 321–324
tasks of, 66
Psychiatry (Horton and Wohl), 456
psychology/philosophy:
group as viewed in, 226–227
moral development as viewed in, 354–355
quantitative methods in, 381–382
self as viewed in, 120, 382
psychopathic personality, survival and, 422
"psychosocial crisis," 2
Pueblo hostages, 422–423
Pulling Up Roots passage:
delayed experiencing of, 5
tasks of, 62
Puritanism, 20, 439
purpose, 8, 54, 325–355, 371
benefits of, 335–336, 354–355
children as, 339–343, 371
in Deadline Decade, 63
high well-being characterized by, 15–17, 57, 335–336
personal growth as, 53, 55, 57–58
religion as, 5–12, 292, 364–365, 368–369, 521
social concern as, 15, 58, 118, 204, 246, 248, 332–333, 343–354, 360–361, 380, 493–494
work as, 15, 35, 41, 91, 336–339

R

Rankin, Jeanette, 326
reaction formation, as coping mechanism, 383, 395
Reagan, Ronald, 323, 453, 499
reciprocal passages, 223–226
reciprocity, 20, 230, 257–258, 261–262, 266
recognition, New Conventionals and, 269–270

recombining, importance of, 528, 530
Redbook, 14, 107
Red Shoes, The, 232
Reed, Carolyn, 229–230
religion, *see* faith
relocation, 117–118
corporate life and, 34, 36–41, 73, 76, 144
kinship and, 213
passages compared to, 44
of two-career couples, 38n–39n
repression, *see* coping mechanisms
responsibility:
of children, 201
men and, 88, 195, 196
self-blame and, 9, 74, 105, 115–116, 191–192
value placed on, 18
women and, 105–106, 191–192, 195, 196, 198, 261, 270n
retirement, 261–262, 318–321
anticipation of, 292, 318, 319, 320, 351
early, 290–292, 304
emotional life and, 303
mandatory, 33
of professional athletes, 131–132
structurelessness and, 318
reverie, 83–84, 125
"Revitalization Movements" (Wallace), 437–438
Richter, Horst, 382
Right to Life group, reaction formation and, 397
risk-allergic thinking, 116
in men, 99, 102, 271–272, 274–275
in women, 37, 242, 270
risk-taking, 8, 16, 37, 86, 95, 96–129, 183–184, 194, 257–258, 265, 471, 519–522
anticipation and, 106
creativity compared to, 124
faith and, 9, 112, 123
future risk-taking encouraged by, 116–120, 123
inner change as foundation for, 128
last-chance leap and, 294–296
loss of children's love and, 200–201
in male myth, 237
as master quality for pathfinding, 120–124, 190, 290

penalties of refusing to engage in, 5, 97–102
physical, 47–48, 49, 52, 117, 237, 271–272, 276
protection during, 112–113
in Proud-to-Be Eighties, 66
by society, 434, 435
timing of, 126–129, 275
of transcendent pathfinders, 466–468
Rites of Passage, The (Van Gennep), 398
Rivera, Chita, 309
Rockefeller, David, 291, 418, 508
Rogers, Carl, 208
Rohaytn, Felix, 444
role models:
  women and, 149, 156, 158, 168, 231, 260, 263
  see also heroes, heroines; mentors; polestars; survivor guides
role relaxation, 19, 63, 88–89, 200, 234–236, 285, 289, 305
Roosevelt, Eleanor, 504
Roosevelt, Theodore, 439, 461
Rooting and Extending passage, 62
  men in, 73, 141, 329–330
  women in, 37–38, 169–172, 258, 265–266, 274, 358–359, 416–417
Rosen, Barbara, 421
Rosenthal, Jack, 164
"Ross, Kenneth," 194, 198–199, 202, 204
Rubenstein, Carin M., 14, 322
Rubinstein, Helena, 153
"Ruiz, Iris," 340–343
running addiction, 316
Russell, Bertrand, 449
Russian Revolution, 326

S

Saarni, Carolyn, 251
Sadat, Anwar el-, 313, 430, 459, 492, 513–527
Salk, Jonas, 27
"Sam," 299–300
Sanger, Margaret, 502
Sassen, Georgia, 270n
satisfaction, *see* well-being
Savio, Mario, 452
scapegoating, 17, 99–100, 116, 415, 438
schizoid personality, survival and, 422

Schlesinger, Arthur, Jr., 446
Schlesinger, Arthur, Sr., 436
Schopenhauer, Arthur, 289
Schopes, John, 326
secondary saboteur, in Freestyle Fifties, 293
Selective Sixties stage, 313–321
  health in, 313–316
  men in, 283–284, 317, 319
  personal tempo in, 317
  retirement in, 318–321
  selective intensity in, 317
  sex in, 316, 318
  tasks of, 65
  women in, 283, 319, 320
self:
  changing vs. eternal, 121
  criticism and sense of, 22
  idealized, 115, 193
  social participation vs., 382
self-acceptance, 121, 246, 459
self-blame, 74
  by women, 8–9, 105, 193
self-consciousness, coining of term, 121
self-employment, 24, 160, 176
self-fulfillment, *see* me-ism
self-help, 447–455
Self Help (Smiles), 447
self-knowledge, 121, 133, 459, 524
self-love, 197–201
self-reliance, 328, 448, 449
self-respect, 75
  blue collar workers and, 20, 24, 352
Seneca Falls Convention (1848), 502
senility, 322
senses, in old age, 321, 323, 331
separation phase, *see* passage, phases of
Seventies (1970s), cultural withdrawal in, 441–444
Sex and Fantasy (May), 250–251
sexism, religion and, 5, 6, 7, 8
Sexual Diamond, 19, 63–64, 88, 234–240
  defined, 234–236
sexual drive, heredity and, 25
sexual intercourse, age and frequency of, 306–307
sexuality:
  in Comeback Decade, 19, 279
  in Deadline Decade, 6
  in Freestyle Fifties, 19, 306–310

in Selective Sixties, 317, 318
well-being levels and, 20, 187
sexual myths, *see* myths
sexual roles:
in Comeback Decade, 280–281
relaxation of, 19, 64, 88, 234–236, 285, 289, 305
Shah of Iran, 413, 508, 510
Shaver, Phillip, 14, 286, 322
Shiner, Mary Ann, 134
Shipley, George, 295
"shoulds," 36, 83, 86
single households, 214
single-track compulsive, 293–296
Sirica, John, 529
Sixties (1960s):
comeback in, 441
social revolutions of, 122, 440–441
transcendent experience sought in, 450–454
sleep, 328
"held arousal" during, 107
importance of, 125–126, 315
Smiles, Samuel, 447
Smith, Gretchen, 269
Smith, Red, 246
social class:
level of well-being and, 25
love and, 19
time perceptions and, 130–131, 134, 351
see also lower class; middle class; upper-middle class
social contract:
generational differences in, 54, 69–70
"just-world" theory and, 70, 98
social participation, self vs., 382
social style, hereditary factors in, 25, 59–60
society, 434–532
age-fluid, 294
as purpose, 15, 57–58, 119, 204, 246, 247–248, 332, 343–354, 360–361, 380, 493–494
revitalization cycles in, 436–440
timing of, 154–159
well-being of, 57–58
Socrates, 324
somatization, 22, 112, 286
defined, 97
Soviet Union, 245–246, 247, 326, 329–330, 385, 434
Spark, Richard F., 307n

spontaneity, age and, 288, 290
Srole, Leo, 286
Stalin, Joseph, 459
Stanton, Elizabeth Cady, 501–502
Steinem, Gloria, 510–513
stepmothers, 262–263
stewardship, concept of, 338
"stochastic" processes, 460
stress management, *see* coping mechanisms
student movement, 452
sublimation, as coping mechanism, 375, 387, 392, 393, 403
success:
career, 18, 30–46, 100, 102, 257–268, 413
children vs., 147–154
growth as measure of, 348–349
high vs. low well-being and, 17
inner vs. outer, 516–517
internal vs. external control of, 106, 242
success ethic, laid-back men and, 163
success shyness:
anxiety vs., 270n
in women, 37, 242, 269, 270, 272–273, 274
super-copers, survival of, 422
Superwoman, 165, 230, 251, 268
supportiveness, 181, 186, 251
in friendship, 208–209, 210
in marriage, 7, 10, 37, 43–44, 89–90, 210, 390, 392
support system, 157, 168, 226–233
co-workers as, 7, 11, 171
household workers in, 226–230, 257–258, 261–262
networking concept in, 227
therapy as, 227
see also mentors; polestars; survivor guides
suppression, as coping mechanism, 386–387, 390, 393
survival patterns, of hostages, 421–424
survivor guides, 58
defined, 232
men as, 91, 118, 353
women as, 8, 89, 204, 232, 264
Swann, Charles E., 456
Swider, Nancy, 164

T

Tapp, June Louin, 355
tax deductions, for household workers, 230
technology, 214, 463
    great awakenings and, 459–460
    nuclear, 328, 333, 459, 464–491
    pros and cons of, 328
    work life affected by, 337–338
tenure track:
    competition in, 168
    male life cycle reflected in, 154
testimonial woman, 48–51
testosterone therapy, 307n
Thatcher, Margaret, 253, 425
therapists, as mentors, 231
therapy, 11, 20, 55, 56–57, 196, 342
    family, 40
    group, 227
    impotence and, 307n
Third Wave, The (Toffler), 460
Thomas, Norman, 326, 496–497
Thoreau, Henry David, 69, 329
Thoughtful Seventies stage, 321–324
    tasks of, 65
Three Hundred Eminent Personalities, 152–153
Three Mile Island, nuclear accident at, 467, 484
Thurow, Lester, 338
time perceptions:
    in expansion phase, 86
    in Frantic Forties, 145
    of future, 16, 17, 61, 78–79, 130, 131–135, 141–147, 280, 283–284, 342
    high vs. low well-being and, 16, 22
    of past, 11, 16, 61, 133
    in separation and incubation phase, 83
    social class and, 130–131, 134, 351
timing, 130–177
    anticipating future needs and, 130, 131–135, 141–147, 153, 171, 175–177, 190, 191, 276, 285, 293, 343, 351, 518–519
    goal setting and, 131, 133, 134, 135–141, 147–149, 175
    intensity vs. balance in, 163–166

    of introspection, 17
    laid-back men and, 159–163
    love and, 182–187
    new integrators and, 166–172
    Old-Boy, 154, 155, 159
    professional women and, 135–141, 147–159, 170–171, 175–177
    of risk-taking, 126–129, 276
    of society, 154–159
Tito, Josip Broz, 323
Tobias, Andrew, 443
Tocqueville, Alexis de, 447
Toffler, Alvin, 460
Torre, Frank, 133–134
Toynbee, Arnold, 439, 458
transcendence, 410, 430, 433
    defined, 382, 404, 461
    great refusal as, 500–501
    in recovery from mourning, 404, 409, 420
    in Sixties, 450–455
transcendental optimism, 448
transcendent pathfinders, 461–491
transforming leadership, defined, 500
Trappists, virtuosity of, 55
Trotsky, Leon, 329
Truman, Harry, 521
Trying Twenties passage:
    in corporate life, 33, 35–36
    depression in, 21, 366
    fears in, 22
    men in, 36, 173–175, 217, 224, 240, 326, 332, 366, 517
    postponement of decisions in, 145
    tasks of, 35–36, 62
    women in, 36, 135–141, 151, 154, 166–168, 176–177, 184, 217, 255, 383, 416
Tuchman, Barbara, 496
twin studies, 25

U

UCLA Education Association's Joint Study of 1981, 153
unconscious, 84, 87, 125, 126, 394–397, 441
unions, 24, 344
upper-middle class, 23n, 25, 375
    adoption and, 152
    purpose and, 343–344
    time perceptions of, 131

V

Vaillant, George, 231, 345, 386, 388, 397
values:
  cultural, 452–455
  moral, 339, 354–355
  religious, 369, 379–380, 426
  untainted, 217, 222
  work and, 337
Vance, Cyrus R., 426
Van Gennep, Arnold, 398
Varnedoe, Kirk, 323
vice-presidents, of corporations, 33, 100
Vietnam War, 74–75, 425, 441, 495, 498
violence:
  domestic, 108, 193, 341
  political, 333, 344
volunteerism, 10–11, 37, 272
  blue-collar, 344, 346–350, 352
  in middle age, 297–299
  in retirement, 319–321

W

walking dead, 4, 276, 471
  in corporate life, 35
  in Freestyle Fifties, 290–293
Wallace, Anthony F. C., 437, 442
Wall Street Journal, corporate survey by, 34
Walsh, Julia, 255, 385–386, 400, 403
Washington Post, 420
Watergate, 441, 498, 529
weight changes, risk-taking and, 97
well-being, 2–29
  criteria for selecting models of, 44–58
  defined, 13, 15–22
  demographic factors in, 22–25
  happiness vs., 13
  hereditary factors in, 21, 25–28, 59–60
well-being, high:
  change vs. continuity and, 16–17, 98
  characteristics of, 15–22
  men of, 101, 102, 285
  pathfinders vs. people of, 59–60
  personal characteristics of people with, 18–19
  in retirement, 319–320

women of, 103–104, 165, 188
well-being, low:
  failure and, 16–17
  men of, 24, 102, 110, 182, 285
  self-reinforcing cycle of, 21
  time perceptions of people with, 16–17, 21
  women of, 24, 104, 105, 165
well-being scale, 13, 15, 562–569
Wells, H. G., 68
"When You Are Old" (Yeats), 310
White, Robert A., 307n
Whitman, Walt, 362
Who Gets Ahead? (Jencks), 106
widows, 211, 212, 257–261
withdrawals, 434–463
  by men, 241, 275, 291, 379, 430, 462, 493, 495, 497–498, 514, 518–519
  in middle age, 291, 294, 379, 430
  by pathleaders, 493, 495, 497–498, 514, 518–519
  societal, 436, 439–444, 458–460
  by women, 11, 76, 253
wives:
  abused, 108, 193, 340, 342n
  blue-collar, 268, 272–276
  corporation, *see* corporation wives
  full-time, 20
  of walking dead, 294
Wohl, Richard, 456
Wolfe, Tom, 237, 442
women:
  aggressiveness in, 9, 64, 250
  ambition in, 18, 236, 266, 268, 298
  assertiveness in, 9–10, 87, 281, 289
  behaving like men, 41, 44, 46, 150, 165, 169
  black, 152, 228–229
  comebacks by, 11, 200, 253, 304–305, 309
  compromise by, 5, 11–12, 200, 251, 254, 265–268, 364
  courage in, 12, 18, 187, 236, 254–265, 266, 281–282
  depression in, 3–4, 5, 7, 10, 17, 21, 36, 104, 106, 108, 219, 242, 280, 286, 341–342, 401–402, 417, 511
  divorced, 20, 24, 165, 168, 198–199, 341–343
  double life of, 168, 190–192, 195

dreams of, 5, 6–7, 12, 231, 255–256, 493

friendships among, 21, 89, 206–207, 210–211

happyface syndrome and, 104–109, 187, 193, 250, 253, 281, 394

of high well-being, 103–104, 165, 188

identity formation in, 5–6, 9-10, 13, 19, 105, 109–110, 187, 279, 341, 415, 416

incomes of, 20n, 23n, 147, 168, 204, 230, 278n

integrator pattern for, 151n, 166, 187

male side of, 19, 64, 89, 234–236, 305

never-married, 146, 151n

New Girls' Network for, 227

as nurturers, 19, 151n, 234, 239, 301

as pathleaders, 493–494, 501–513

pleasing by, 3, 4–6, 9, 64, 109–110, 186, 189, 201, 269–270, 282

point, 166, 168

power of, 44, 159, 298

professional, see professional women

responsibility and, 105–106, 193, 195, 196, 199, 270n

retirement and, 319, 320

as survivor guides, 9, 89, 204, 232, 265

testimonial, 48–51

see also mothers; wives; specific passages

women's movement, 154, 166, 212, 242, 268, 501–502

pivotal Americans from, 573–575

Worby, Gary and Trisha, 182–186, 217

work:

as coping mechanism, 112, 259–260, 290–291, 385–386

independence in, 337

in old age, 323

as purpose, 15, 34–35, 42, 90–91, 336–339

see also careers; corporate life; corporation men; professional women

workaholics, 161, 179, 366

work-centered women, in Selective Sixties, 319–320

work ethic, religious basis of, 337

work hours, of men vs. women, 136

World Anti-Slavery Convention, 502

wunderkind pattern, 30, 162

Y

Yeats, William Butler, 310

Z

Zimmerman, Isaiah, 465

ABOUT THE AUTHOR

GAIL SHEEHY is the author of six books: *Lovesounds,* a novel; *Panthermania,* a study of the clash between the middle class and radical blacks in New Haven; *Speed Is of the Essence,* a collection of articles; *Hustling,* a psychological and journalistic study of prostitution that also became a major ABC-TV documentary-drama; *Passages,* published in 1976, which firmly established that adult life proceeds by developmental stages; *Pathfinders;* and most recently, *Spirit of Survival.*

Ms. Sheehy graduated from the University of Vermont in 1958 and in 1970 received a fellowship to study at Columbia University under her mentor, Margaret Mead. In 1974 she was awarded a grant from the Alicia Patterson Foundation to continue her studies of adult development. Ms. Sheehy's honors include the National Magazine Award and the Penney-Missouri Journalism Award; she was twice the winner of the Newswomen's Club of New York Front Page Award. She lives in New York City.

Bantam
On Psychology

Special Offer
Buy a Bantam Book
for only 50¢.

Now you can have Bantam's catalog filled with hundreds of titles plus take advantage of our unique and exciting bonus book offer. A special offer which gives you the opportunity to purchase a Bantam book for only 50¢. Here's how!

By ordering any five books at the regular price per order, you can also choose any other single book listed (up to a $4.95 value) for just 50¢. Some restrictions do apply, but for further details why not send for Bantam's catalog of titles today!

Just send us your name and address and we will send you a catalog!